THE CACAO CHRONICLES

A DEEP JOURNEY INTO THE WORLDS, CULTURES, AND SECRETS OF CACAO AND CHOCOLATE

JOSH LEE

SAND HILL PUBLISHING GROUP

First published by Sand Hill Publishing Group 2025

First edition

ISBN (paperback): 979-8-9941034-0-1
ISBN (hardcover): 979-8-9941034-2-5
ISBN (ebook): 979-8-9941034-1-8

For Tyler and Katie

CONTENTS

PART III

Flavor, Sensory Science, and the Psychology of Taste

PART IV

Art, Culture, and the Aesthetics of Desire

PART V

Power, Scandal, Economics, and the Underground World

PART VI
Innovation, Technology, and the Future of Chocolate

APPENDIX

THE CHRONOLOGY OF CACAO

- **3500 BCE** The Mayo-Chinchipe culture in present-day Ecuador consumes cacao, likely as a fermented beverage—the earliest known use of chocolate, pre-dating the Olmecs by 1,500 years.
- **1900–1500 BCE** The Olmec civilization in Mexico cultivates cacao (*kakaw*) as a domesticated crop, establishing it as a ceremonial food.
- **250–900 CE** The Classic Maya period. Cacao becomes a currency and a ritual sacrament. The "Dresden Codex" depicts gods holding cacao pods, confirming its divine status.
- **1325–1521** The Aztec Empire imposes cacao tributes. Cacao seeds are used as legal tender; a rabbit costs 10 beans, a slave costs 100.
- **1502** Christopher Columbus intercepts a Mayan trading canoe carrying "almonds" (cacao) but dismisses them, missing the chance to introduce chocolate to Europe.
- **1528** Hernán Cortés presents cacao beans to King Charles V of Spain. The Spanish add sugar and cinnamon, keeping the drink a state secret for nearly a century.

- **1615** The secret is out. Anne of Austria, a Spanish princess, marries Louis XIII of France and introduces chocolate to the French court, sparking a craze among European nobility.
- **1670** The First Cacao in Asia. Spanish galleons carry cacao trees from Mexico to the Philippines, planting the seeds of the chocolate industry in Asia.
- **1753** The Naming. Swedish botanist Carl Linnaeus classifies the tree as *Theobroma cacao*—"Food of the Gods"— permanently encoding its mythic status into science.
- **1828** The Industrial Turning Point. Dutch chemist Coenraad Van Houten patents the hydraulic cocoa press, separating cocoa butter from solids. This creates "cocoa powder" and makes chocolate cheap and mass-producible.
- **1847** J.S. Fry & Sons in England mixes cocoa powder with sugar and melted cocoa butter to create the world's first solid chocolate bar.
- **1875** Daniel Peter and Henri Nestlé in Switzerland invent milk chocolate by adding condensed milk powder to the mix, creating the creamy texture we know today.
- **1879** Africa's Rise. Tetteh Quarshie successfully plants cacao pods in the Gold Coast (modern Ghana), shifting the center of gravity of the cocoa world from South America to West Africa. (Simultaneously, Rodolphe Lindt invents the conching machine).
- **1916** The Fall of Ecuador. Witches' Broom disease devastates the "Nacional" cacao plantations in Ecuador, ending its reign as the world's top producer and nearly driving the variety to extinction.
- **1937** The War Ration. The Hershey Company produces the Field Ration D bar for the U.S. Army. Designed to not melt and to taste "just a little better than a boiled potato," it introduces chocolate to millions of GIs.
- **1980s** The "Cacao Crisis": Global prices crash, causing economic devastation in West Africa and reshaping the geopolitical map of cocoa.

- **1996** Scharffen Berger is founded in San Francisco, sparking the modern American "Bean-to-Bar" craft chocolate revolution.
- **2001** The Ethical Reckoning. The Harkin-Engel Protocol is signed, an international agreement aiming to end the worst forms of child labor in the cocoa sector, bringing the "Dark Side" of chocolate into public consciousness.
- **2010** The cacao genome is fully sequenced by rival teams (Mars/USDA and Hershey/Penn State), revealing the genetic pathways behind flavor, disease resistance, and heritage, and giving breeders their first precise toolkit for protecting heirloom cacao and strengthening future crops.
- **2017** The Fourth Chocolate. Barry Callebaut unveils "Ruby Chocolate," naturally pink chocolate derived from specific cocoa beans, the first new major category since white chocolate in the 1930s.
- **2020s** The rise of "Chocolate 2.0"—lab-grown cocoa and fermentation alternatives emerge to combat climate change and deforestation.

INTRODUCTION

Deep in the emerald hush of a tropical forest, a ripe cacao pod splits open under gentle pressure. Its thick golden hull cracks to reveal a pale, sticky pulp studded with dozens of almond-sized seeds. The air fills with a perfume of damp earth and honeyed fruit as nectar drips from the split husk. From these bitter kernels, humanity would eventually coax one of its most enduring obsessions—a substance that would travel the world, reshape economies, inspire empires, and settle into millions of daily rituals.

For thousands of years, people have been drawn to the paradox of the cacao bean. It is bitter yet beguiling, requiring transformation to unleash its promise. The ancients of Mesoamerica were among the first to unlock its secrets. In the temples of the Maya, chocolate took the form of a sacred drink: cacao beans fermented, ground, and whipped into a frothy elixir with water, chili, and spices.

In a jungle clearing centuries ago, nobles raised clay cups of dark, fragrant cacao, not as refreshment but as an act of communion—each sip a gesture binding them to ancestors, gods, and one another. To these early chocolate makers, the drink was more than sustenance; it was a gift from the gods, an embodiment of vitality and mystique.

The Aztecs would later revere it as a source of wisdom and vigor, calling their spiced drink *cacahuatl*. The Aztec emperor Moctezuma II reportedly fortified himself with golden goblets of the beverage before addressing his council—seeking strength and inspiration in its bitter depths.

In those ancient societies, chocolate was woven into the fabric of ritual and power. It was offered in sacrifice to deities, included in wedding ceremonies, and even used as currency – a treasure literally minted from the soil of the earth. A few hundred cacao beans, it was said, could purchase a turkey or pay a laborer's wages. Thus, from the very beginning, chocolate was more than a food: it was a symbol of wealth, devotion, and the alchemy of human ingenuity.

The journey of chocolate spans worlds and ages. From the New World tropics it crossed oceans, carried on Spanish galleons that ferried both conquest and curiosity. In the sixteenth century, European explorers, awed by the strange spiced cacao of the Aztecs, brought beans and recipes back to royal courts. In Spain and beyond, the bitter drink was soon tempered with cane sugar and vanilla, mellowing into a sumptuous confection for the aristocracy.

For a time, chocolate lingered behind monastery walls and palace gates—a coveted drink whose reputation traveled faster than the recipe itself. But knowledge and desire cannot be contained indefinitely. As the taste for chocolate spread through Baroque Europe, it ignited new industries and trade routes that spanned the globe. Cacao plantations took root in equatorial colonies; sugar mills thrummed in the Caribbean; merchants and sailors wove a web of commerce linking tropical forests with European capitals.

By the eighteenth century, chocolate had become an engine of enterprise and empire, its production entwined with the fates of nations. In elegant Parisian salons and London's bustling chocolate houses, porcelain cups brimmed with the once-exotic drink. What was reserved for ancient gods and kings had become a staple of mercantile society, savored by poets, philosophers, and merchants in convivial exchange. The story of chocolate is, in many ways, the story of globalization's dawn: a tale of exploration and exchange, of wealth and exploitation, of disparate lives connected by a simple craving for sweetness.

If the early history of chocolate is a saga of ceremony and conquest, its modern evolution is one of invention and transformation. In the workshops of industrializing Europe, chocolate makers sought to tame this costly luxury and make it available to the masses. Through innovation, they changed not only chocolate's form but its very meaning in society. Chemists learned to press cacao, separating the silky cocoa butter from the bitter cocoa solids, an invention that refined texture and tempered bitterness. Visionaries found ways to solidify the drink into bars – portable, sturdy confections that could be unwrapped and carried in a pocket.

In the nineteenth century, the alchemy of chocolate entered the age of steam and steel: engineers built machines to grind the beans finer than any mortar and pestle, and great mixing conches to stir the potion until it turned velvety smooth. Each breakthrough – the cocoa press, the first molded bars, the marriage of milk with dark cacao – reinvented chocolate and expanded its reach. What had once been laboriously ground by hand met the precision of science and industry.

Chocolate became at once more accessible and more personal: a treat not only for nobles in gilded halls, but for children gazing wide-eyed into shop windows, for soldiers carrying a taste of home in their rucksacks, for families sharing simple gifts of sweetness during holidays. This convergence of discovery and democratization was itself a reflection of human progress. In the melting of a cocoa bean into something sublime, one can see an emblem of human creativity – the urge to experiment, to improve, to delight.

Yet even as chocolate grew commonplace, it never lost its aura of wonder. There is a precise, almost orchestral science behind every bite— a choreography of chemistry, heat, crystal structure, and volatile aromatics hidden beneath its effortless pleasure. A piece of chocolate is a capsule of complex chemistry, holding hundreds of distinct compounds that enchant the senses and quietly interact with the human body. The moment a square of chocolate begins to soften on the tongue, it releases a symphony of aromas and flavors – notes of vanilla and toasted nuts, of jasmine and jungle earth – all conjured by the careful roasting and blending of beans. Almost imperceptibly, soothing molecules of theobromine and caffeine enliven the pulse; anandamide and phenylethylamine whisper to the brain's receptors, kindling a gentle euphoria.

Little wonder that across cultures, chocolate has long been treasured as a comfort and even a kind of medicine for the heart. Modern science, with all its measurements, only confirms what ancient wisdom sensed: in moderation, chocolate can soothe stress, lift the mood, even offer healthful benefits. But beyond biochemistry, there is art in how chocolate beguiles.

Consider the lustrous sheen on a tempered chocolate truffle and the satisfying snap when it breaks – these are the hallmarks of precision and craft. A chocolatier, part artisan and part scientist, must coax the cacao's temperamental cocoa butter into a crystalline alignment, heating and cooling the molten chocolate in a delicate dance to produce that glossy finish and velvety melt. This exacting process is a reminder that behind the pleasure lies patience and knowledge, an interplay of invention and tradition quietly present in each creamy bite.

Culturally, scientifically, economically, emotionally – chocolate engages people at every level. It is at once a simple, familiar comfort and a global industry; an ancient ritual and a modern obsession. Across the world, it punctuates life's moments both great and small. Friends might break a chocolate bar to share as a gesture of companionship. Lovers and well-wishers exchange pralines and truffles as tokens of affection, apology, or celebration when words fall short.

Families retreat to the kitchen on rainy afternoons to bake rich chocolate cakes for birthdays, weaving the sweet scent into their happiest traditions. A steaming mug of cocoa on a cold night can summon the innocence of childhood or offer solace after a day's trials. Even in times of hardship, those forced to ration life's pleasures will save a bit of chocolate – tucking it away like an amulet against despair, a reminder that sweetness can still be found when the world turns bitter. In so many forms and occasions, chocolate has endured as a small beacon of solace and joy.

If chocolate stirs such emotion, it is because it serves as a mirror of humanity. In its story appear reflections of the human experience: the instinct for transformation, turning bitter into sweet; the pursuit of pleasure and meaning in the everyday; the spark of invention that propels progress; the connections forged across cultures and time; and the resilience by which people endure adversity.

It is astonishing that within the glossy wrapper of a single chocolate bar lies this entire tableau – a history of conquest and cooperation, a convergence of nature and knowledge, a testament to both cruelty and compassion, and an enduring promise of delight. The story of chocolate holds up a mirror to humanity's thirst for transformation, for pleasure, for invention, for connection, for resilience. The reflection, much like the taste of chocolate itself, is bittersweet and endlessly fascinating—an invitation to savor every moment of the journey.

PART I

ORIGINS, RITUAL, AND THE
HUMAN STORY OF CACAO

1

FROM SACRED DRINK
TO GLOBAL OBSESSION:
THE 4,000-YEAR JOURNEY

A t daybreak in the Petén lowlands more than a thousand years ago, a Maya scribe crouched beside a stone hearth as the first threads of sunlight filtered through the trees. He lifted a smooth metate onto his knees and began to grind roasted cacao beans into a warm, fragrant paste. The rhythmic scrape of stone against cacao mixed with the rising hum of the forest. Soon the paste would be blended with water, spices, and flowers, then whipped into a froth and poured into a painted cup reserved for ceremony. This was chocolate in its earliest form—part offering, part stimulant, part social glue. To understand the story of chocolate, we must begin not with sweetness or nostalgia, but with this ancient morning ritual, where a single drink shaped belief, hierarchy, trade, and identity across an entire civilization.

A Gift from the Gods

For generations scholars credited the Olmecs with discovering cacao around 1750 BCE, but the story reaches far deeper into time. Recent excavations in the upper Amazon have overturned the long-held timeline, revealing pottery stained with traces of cacao dating to 3500 BCE—evidence of an older, quieter civilization already experimenting with fermentation and ritual drink. What this discovery makes clear is that chocolate's origins lie in a vast rainforest world where human ingenuity, ecology, and spiritual imagination were inseparable. The journey from jungle pod to sacred drink began not in Mesoamerican courts, but in the deep river valleys of ancient Ecuador. At the Santa Ana-La Florida site in Ecuador, traces of cacao were found on pottery dating back to 3500 BCE —proving the Mayo-Chinchipe culture was consuming chocolate more than 1,500 years before the Olmecs.

They learned that fermenting, roasting, and grinding the seeds inside the cacao pod unlocked an entirely new class of flavor and energy —an alchemy at once agricultural and spiritual. The Maya refined this early discovery into a full cultural institution, where cacao was cultivated with intention, celebrated in ceremony, and woven into mythic and social identity. In Mayan society, chocolate was central to life—not an everyday candy, but a sacred and social centerpiece. They often blended the bitter cacao with spices like chili pepper, allspice, or a touch of honey to soften its bite, and shared it during important ceremonies, marriages, and rites of passage.

Dawn in the Petén lowlands: A Maya scribe grinds roasted cacao into a paste, the first step in creating the sacred frothy drink of the gods.

The Aztecs later embraced this sacred bean with equal fervor, believing the feathered serpent god Quetzalcoatl had journeyed from paradise to deliver cacao to humankind. The Latin name given to the cacao tree—*Theobroma cacao*—reflects these ancient reverences, though the scientific classification would not arrive for another three thousand years.

Cacao beans were not only consumed as a drink but treasured as currency—so prized that counterfeiters even forged fake cacao beans out of clay. For these ancient peoples, chocolate was food, drink, money, medicine, and myth all at once.

==

THE CHOCOLATE PANTHEON: A WHO'S WHO
Before it was a candy, it was a religion. Meet the gods of the pod.

Quetzalcoatl (The Giver): The Aztec "Feathered Serpent" who stole the cacao tree from paradise to give to humans. He was banished for his generosity.

Ek Chuah (The Merchant): The Mayan patron of trade and cacao. He is often depicted carrying a pack of cacao beans on his back.

IxCacao (The Nurturer): The Mayan fertility goddess. Often called the "Queen of Chocolate," she ensured the earth remained abundant for the farmers.

==

CONQUEST AND DISCOVERY
When Spanish conquistadors arrived in the early 1500s, they encountered this strange, dark drink in the court of Moctezuma II. Some found it bitter and unpalatable at first, but they noted how the Aztecs esteemed it. Hernán Cortés himself observed that this "divine drink... builds up resistance and fights fatigue." After the conquest of the Aztec Empire in 1521, the Spanish realized that, beyond gold and silver, they had stumbled upon another treasure in cacao.

By the 1540s, cacao beans and recipes for making chocolate had begun making their way back to Spain. The conquistadors learned to prepare the drink but quickly adapted it to suit European tastes—serving it hot rather than cold, sweetening it with cane sugar, and adding comforting Old World spices like cinnamon and vanilla. At first, Spain kept chocolate a secret indulgence, a delightful court luxury guarded closely. But secrets never last forever.

THE CONQUEST of Europe

By the early 1600s, chocolate began spreading across Europe, riding on the currents of trade and royal marriages. Spanish princesses brought their love of chocolate to the French court at Versailles. Italian merchants caught wind of the fashionable new drink and brought cacao home. Chocolate houses—elegant establishments where the well-heeled could sip hot chocolate and socialize—began appearing in London, Paris, and beyond. These became chic gathering spots where political schemers, poets, and dandies conducted lively debates with steaming cups of chocolate at hand.

Chocolate's rise was not without controversy. Some conservative voices initially scorned it as sinful or decadent—after all, it came from "pagan" lands and was consumed with near-addictive zeal. There were whispers that chocolate might inflame passions. Monks debated whether drinking chocolate broke religious fasts. But such resistance was fleeting. In most places, the delight of chocolate won out over moral qualms. By the late 1600s, chocolate had conquered the aristocratic palates of Europe, though it remained a luxury beyond the reach of common people.

THE INDUSTRIAL REVOLUTION

For centuries, chocolate was primarily consumed as a drink—a costly elixir associated with power, wealth, and ceremony. That began to change in the 19th century. The era of steam engines and innovation did not pass chocolate by; in fact, it utterly transformed it. A series of break-throughs in the Netherlands, England, and Switzerland—involving hydraulic presses, new mixing techniques, and revolutionary machines for refining chocolate's texture—made it possible to create solid chocolate bars for the first time. These same innovations eventually gave rise to milk chocolate, that smooth and creamy confection that would become the world's favorite.

Theobroma cacao, the "Food of the Gods." Its unique cauliflorous growth sees pods sprout directly from the trunk, a biological quirk that fascinated early botanists.

The late 19th century also saw the rise of chocolate dynasties—family-founded companies that still dominate the chocolate world today. Cadbury in England, Hershey and Mars in America, Nestlé and Lindt in Switzerland, Ferrero in Italy—all have their roots in this transformative era. These companies harnessed industrial processes to produce chocolate on a scale previously unimaginable. By the turn of the 20th century, chocolate had been democratized. No longer a rare luxury, it was being produced en masse, wrapped in bright papers, and sold for a few pennies.

A GLOBAL OBSESSION

As the 20th century unfurled, chocolate became not just a treat, but a global cultural icon. Its influence is everywhere—in our holidays, our language, our cravings, our memories. Heart-shaped chocolates on Valentine's Day, foil-wrapped eggs and bunnies at Easter, a steaming cup of hot cocoa on a winter's night. By mid-century, a world without chocolate was unimaginable. It had conquered every continent, every society, from the sweet shops of Paris to the stalls of Mumbai.

By the numbers, our modern appetite for chocolate is astounding. The world now consumes millions of tons of cocoa beans each year. Global chocolate sales reach tens of billions of dollars annually. This bean, once brewed by Maya priests for sacred rituals, is now the foundation of a vast global industry.

Yet even as chocolate pervades daily life, in some ways it is circling back to its roots. In recent years, there's been a growing appreciation for chocolate's heritage and craft. Just as wine lovers trace vintages, chocolate lovers now seek out single-origin chocolates, reveling in the distinct notes a cacao from Madagascar might have versus one from Ghana. Small "bean-to-bar" artisans have sprung up, devoted to sourcing high-quality beans directly from farmers and crafting chocolate in small batches. Some modern enthusiasts even participate in cacao ceremonies, harking back to the drink's spiritual beginnings, consuming bitter hot cacao in meditative group rituals intended to foster mindfulness and connection—a direct nod to chocolate's mystical past.

The "High Pour": Ancient Mesoamericans prized the foam, or spirit of the drink, created by pouring the liquid from a height.

The Journey Ahead

The story of chocolate is also a story of people—the farmers who tend the fragile cacao trees, the scientists who unlock its chemistry, the entrepreneurs who build empires, the artisans who treat it as high art, and the billions of us who simply enjoy it. It's a story that touches on questions of equity and sustainability: the late 20th and early 21st centuries have seen consumers and activists push for fair trade cocoa, seeking to ensure that the farmers who cultivate this beloved crop are paid fairly and work in humane conditions.

In the chapters that follow, we'll explore chocolate from every angle. We'll delve into the sacred rituals of ancient Mesoamerica, where cacao was currency and communion with the gods. We'll follow chocolate's journey through royal courts and revolutionary factories. We'll examine the science of flavor, the art of craft chocolate, and the complex economics of the cocoa trade. We'll meet the remarkable people—often women—who have shaped chocolate's history. And we'll travel the world to discover how different cultures have made chocolate their own.

After 4,000 years, chocolate still holds a dual identity. It is a modern mass-produced commodity, found in common vending machines and the grandest boutique windows. It is also a substance on the brink of a sci-fi revolution, where cacao grown in steel bioreactors may soon sit alongside beans grown in soil. It is at once cheap and ubiquitous, yet also capable of being refined into a luxury experience. And yet, peel back the foil, close your eyes as a piece of chocolate melts in your mouth, and you just might sense a flicker of its ancient soul—an echo of that first cacao brew sipped in a sacred grove long ago.

From sacred drink to global obsession, chocolate's journey is extraordinary not just for its length, but for how deeply it has touched humanity at every step. A simple bean, once worshipped and fought over, has become a source of simple pleasure for billions. In each creamy, sweet, dark, or spicy taste, chocolate carries with it a rich legacy—the prayers of priests, the ambitions of conquerors, the dreams of inventors, and the delights of everyday people. As we savor our next bite, we partake in this epic story, a small square of the world's history dissolving on the tongue, connecting us through time with all the other chocolate lovers who came before.

==

TASTE HISTORY: THE AZTEC "CACAHUATL" BREW

Stop reading and start tasting. To understand why this drink was sacred, you must experience the spice and grit that modern chocolate removes.

Ingredients:

- 3 tbsp pure cacao nibs (ground to a coarse paste)
- 1 cup water (room temperature or cool)
- 1 pinch dried chili flakes (start small!)
- 1 tsp honey or agave (optional, for the modern palate)
- 1 pinch cornmeal (masa) to thicken

Instructions:

- Mix ingredients in a jar.
- The Froth: The most important step. Pour the mixture back and forth between two cups from a height of 12 inches until a thick foam forms.
- Sip slowly. Note the absence of dairy and the heat of the chili. This is the flavor of 1500 CE.

==

2

COCOA CURRENCY: WHEN CHOCOLATE WAS MONEY

Picture a bustling Aztec marketplace in the 1400s. Shoppers weave between stalls piled with avocados, chili peppers, woven textiles, and jade trinkets. But instead of clinking coins or shells, the shoppers' purses rustle with cacao beans. A farmer counts out a dozen of these dark brown beans to buy a turkey egg. A noblewoman pays twenty beans to a porter for carrying her goods. A few children even toss beans in a game of chance, gambling their chocolate money. It might sound like a scene from Willy Wonka, but it's drawn from real history – a time when chocolate literally served as currency. For the Aztecs, the Maya, and other Mesoamerican peoples, cacao beans were cold, hard cash. More than just the source of a treasured drink, cacao beans became the lifeblood of commerce, tribute, and even myth. This is the rich story of how chocolate went from divine delicacy to economic cornerstone – and what that legacy means for how we value chocolate today.

MONEY THAT GREW on Trees

The transformation of cacao from sacred drink to circulating currency was not sudden but emerged from centuries of ritual, trade, and practical necessity. As cacao cultivation expanded and demand grew among elites and commoners alike, the bean's value solidified into something measurable, countable, and exchangeable. What began as a revered substance gradually evolved into one of the most trusted economic instruments in Mesoamerica. The Maya had transformed cacao from luxury into legal tender by around the 7th century CE, and the Aztecs embraced this system enthusiastically when they rose to power.

How did an ordinary bean become as good as gold? The answer lies in perfect economic conditions: limited supply (cacao only grows in tropical lowlands), universal demand (everyone craved chocolate), and cultural prestige.

By the seventh century CE, cacao had moved far beyond simple barter. Beans were counted, taxed, stored, and spent—treated with the same seriousness as coinage in other parts of the world. Maya vendors trusted them; rulers accepted them; traders carried them in woven sacks as they trekked between city-states. Once a ritual drink, cacao had become a fully functioning commodity currency whose value was understood from palace to marketplace.

The Aztecs, rising to power later (ca. 14th–16th century), adopted this cocoa currency enthusiastically. To them, cacao beans were a tangible form of wealth: portable, countable, and deeply desirable. The fact that beans could also be made into a prized chocolate drink only enhanced their status. Some Spanish chroniclers wrote that the Aztecs valued cacao beans more than gold – after all, you can't drink gold or make a spicy cocoa out of it! One poet of the time even mused that "the glory of the new king is measured in cacao". In economic terms, cacao beans functioned as a commodity currency with intrinsic value (people genuinely wanted them for consumption) and exchange value (they were used to buy things). It was one of history's most delicious forms of money.

It's worth noting that power followed the cacao supply. Control over fertile cacao-growing regions could make a city rich. For example, in the 600s CE, several Maya city-states fought a war for dominance of the cacao-producing region of Tabasco. When the dust settled, the victorious kingdom of Calakmul gained access to the coveted groves – and with them a stream of cocoa wealth. This "money that grew on trees" fueled Calakmul's prosperity. Similar stories played out later in Aztec conquests: lands that grew cacao were especially prized prizes. In this way, chocolate not only greased the wheels of commerce – it could literally spark conflicts and empire-building, just like control of oil or gold has in more recent times.

THE MARKETPLACE: Buying Goods with Chocolate Beans

Once cacao beans became currency, they transformed everyday economics. In the markets of Maya cities and Aztec capitals alike, cacao beans jingled in the pockets of commoners and nobles. They were the small change of the day, used to buy everything from food to services. Spanish observers who first witnessed this were amazed: an entire economy humming along on little brown seeds! One friar in the 1500s noted with astonishment that in the Aztec market, *"with five cacao beans one can buy something, with thirty beans another thing, and with a hundred beans yet another – and no haggling needed."* In other words, prices were understood in cacao units, and buyers and sellers had a shared trust in this chocolate money.

===

THE AZTEC PRICE LIST: SHOPPING IN 1500 AD

If you walked into the market at Tenochtitlán with a pocketful of beans, here is what you could buy.

- 1 Bean: A large tomato or a tamale.
- 3 Beans: A turkey egg or a fresh avocado.
- 10 Beans: A rabbit for dinner.
- 20 Beans: A trip to the next town (porter service).
- 100 Beans: A whole turkey hen (A feast).

===

What could you get for a cacao bean? Surprisingly much, as it turns out. Historical sources and Spanish accounts give us an enchanting price list of goods in cacao currency. The *Florentine Codex*, compiled by

Friar Bernardino de Sahagún between 1545 and 1590, provides one of the most detailed records. In an Aztec market, a large tomato or a tamale cost one cacao bean; a turkey egg or a bunch of fresh chili peppers cost three beans; and ten beans might be a fair price for a rabbit for dinner.

On the higher end of the scale, skilled labor or entertainment had its price. A porter might charge 20 beans for a journey—essentially the daily wage for common labor paid in chocolate. Historical records suggest a skilled, mesmerizing dancer could command 40 beans for a performance, a literal exchange of energy for art.

A basket of fine corn or a handmade cotton loincloth might cost 30 to 40 beans. On the higher end of the scale, 100 cacao beans could buy a turkey hen, a substantial purchase for a feast. Indeed, one colonial record from Tlaxcala around 1545 lists 100 cacao beans for a turkey as a going rate. Considering 100 beans was literally a sackful in your hand, you can imagine the gravity of such a transaction.

It's delightful to picture: an Aztec shopper counting out beans into the vendor's hand to pay for produce, much as we would count coins. The beans themselves varied in quality and size, and this was acknowledged in their value. Big, plump cacao beans – which made the richest chocolate – were *especially* esteemed. Ironically, that meant people tended to spend the best beans as currency (since everyone accepted them readily) and reserve the smaller or broken beans for making their own cup of chocolate at home. In a real sense, your money was too precious to drink!

Market transactions using cacao were so common that the language reflected it. The Aztecs had *quantitative terms* specific to cacao counts: a bunch of 20 beans (called a *zantli*) was a basic unit, and 8,000 beans (a *xiquipilli*) was a standard "sack" or load used for big trades. Professional merchants, known as pochteca, traveled great distances to trade cacao beans and other commodities, and they kept strict count of every bean.

In the famous market of Tlatelolco (the largest in the Aztec world), cacao beans flowed through the stalls like an edible currency exchange. There, one Spanish conquistador observed, *"they sold everything by count of cacao, no other money was seen."* Whether you were buying clay pots, clothing, pets, or food, everyone understood the worth of a cacao bean.

Money that grew on trees: In the Aztec economy, a turkey hen cost
100 cacao beans, while a fresh avocado could be bought for three.

The ubiquity of cacao as money also reshaped social relationships. A day's labor could be measured in beans; a feast could be financed with a handful of handfuls; an entire province might be judged prosperous based on the cacao tribute it sent to its rulers. In markets like Tlatelolco, cacao created a shared economic language that unified diverse peoples —an edible currency whose value was respected from village stalls to imperial courts.

Cacao currency also found its way into more leisurely pursuits. Gambling with cacao beans was a popular pastime – essentially betting chocolate money on games. Aztec nobles played games of patolli (a bit like dice or board games) where piles of cacao beans were wagered on the outcome. A tense round of gambling might see heaps of beans change ownership – fortunes won or lost in chocolate. You can imagine the mix of thrill and agony: winning a mound of tasty currency, or losing your pocket's worth of tomorrow's meals in one toss. In any case, cacao made the stakes tangible. (At least if you lost all your money, you could console yourself by drinking chocolate, if you saved a bit of it!)

TRIBUTE AND TAXES Paid in Chocolate

Money isn't just used to trade – it's also collected by rulers. And in Mesoamerica, chocolate was on the tax list. The Aztec and Maya

economies were agrarian but had formal systems of tribute (taxes)
imposed by kings on their subjects or conquered towns. Because cacao
beans were so valuable and widely accepted, they became a crucial part
of tribute payments. Subjects literally paid their taxes in chocolate
beans.

Aztec records (many recorded in pictographic codices) give us a
detailed look at this chocolate taxation. The Codex Mendoza, a post-
conquest manuscript recording Aztec life and tribute, includes pages
illustrating the yearly tribute from various provinces of the Aztec
Empire. One such province was Xoconochco (Soconusco), a hot coastal
region legendary for its prime cacao orchards. According to the Codex
Mendoza, Soconusco was obliged to send an eye-popping 200 loads of
cacao beans to the imperial treasury *every year*. Aztec artists depicted
this with bundles of beans tied in sacks, each marked with the Aztec
symbol for 20 (a flag icon) repeated in sets – essentially a graphic
accounting ledger in cacao. In total, the artwork shows two enormous
heaps of cacao beans with five little flags above each (five times twenty =
100 bundles per heap, two heaps = 200 bundles). It's a vivid image of just
how much chocolate wealth flowed from the provinces to Tenochtitlan,
the Aztec capital.

Tribute in cacao was not limited to Soconusco. Many other regions
paid the Aztec Empire in chocolate currency as part of their annual
dues, often thousands upon thousands of beans at a time. The king of
Texcoco, an allied city-state of the Aztecs, was said to receive over 11
million cacao beans in tribute each year from subordinate towns! This
astonishing amount was partially used to supply the royal court's chocoholics – Texcoco's ruler consumed nearly 2 million beans worth of
chocolate for his own household's drinks and festivities – and the
remaining 9 million beans went into state storage to be spent on other
needs of the kingdom. In effect, chocolate beans filled the royal trea-
suries much as gold and silver coins filled the coffers of European
monarchs.

How did rulers store and manage this chocolate treasure? They kept
cacao beans in large sacks or bins, carefully protected from moisture and
pests, often in secure storehouses within the palace complex. One
Spanish account describes great towers of cacao beans in Aztec store-

houses, guarded zealously. The beans were counted in standardized quantities; for instance, 8,000 beans (a xiquipil) were tied up as one sack or bundle. To make accounting easier, beans might be strung together in bunches or sealed in jars once counted. We even have records of tribute lists where, say, *"12,000 cacao beans"* are listed alongside so many cloth blankets and so many bushels of maize as a town's yearly obligation. Cacao beans were currency, tax revenue, and strategic reserve all at once.

Spanish conquerors, upon toppling the Aztec Empire in 1521, quickly realized the value of this unusual money. In the early colonial decades, Spaniards themselves used cacao beans to pay indigenous laborers and to buy local products, essentially plugging into the existing money system. For a while, "chocolate coins" remained legal tender in parts of New Spain. A traveler in the 1540s might have observed Spanish settlers at a market in Guatemala buying chickens or corn with handfuls of cacao alongside native people – coin minting was still in its infancy there, so the beans persisted in everyday use. In fact, as late as the 1600s, cacao beans were used as small change in some parts of Spanish America because official currency was scarce. Chocolate money had truly endured the test of time.

Of course, relying on edible money had its challenges – which the Aztecs and others were well aware of. Cacao beans can decay or get eaten (by insects or rodents) if stored too long. This meant cacao currency had a built-in *expiration date*. Typically, a dried cacao bean might last a year or a bit more before going bad. If you were an ancient accountant managing a royal cacao vault, you had to practice FIFO (first in, first out) inventory management: use the old beans to pay for goods before they spoil, and keep the new harvest stored for later. This perishability sometimes caused economic trouble. In drought years, for example, the cacao harvest might fail, suddenly shrinking the money supply and driving up prices for beans – a bit like currency inflation. On the other hand, because beans couldn't be hoarded forever, they encouraged a lively circulation. Stale beans weren't worth anyone's trouble, so people spent their "money" rather than let it rot. (Imagine if our cash could expire after a year – we'd be sure to use it!)

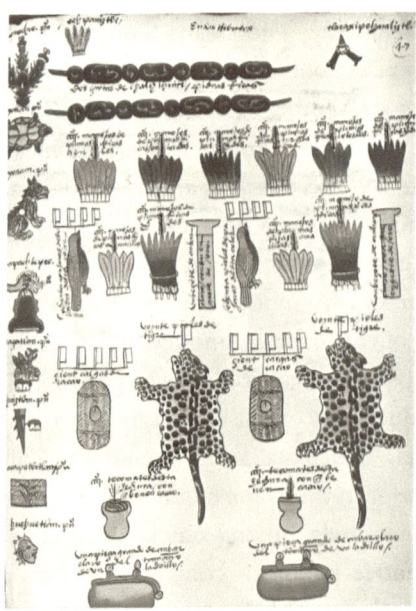

A page from the Codex Mendoza illustrating the massive tributes of cacao paid by conquered provinces to the Aztec Emperor.

Another issue was counterfeiting – yes, even chocolate had counterfeiters! Unscrupulous individuals found ingenious ways to forge cacao beans. One common scam involved hollowing out cacao husks and carefully filling them with mud, clay, or amaranth dough, then sealing the hole with wax to simulate the weight of a genuine bean.

These fake beans would be mixed into sacks of real cacao so the deception was hard to spot at a glance. Others crafted dummy beans out of hardened *amaranth dough* (a grain paste), painted to look like the real thing. In the marketplace, a vendor might slip in a few counterfeit beans as change, hoping the customer wouldn't notice until later. The problem became significant enough that Aztec officials had to impose penalties for cocoa counterfeiters – essentially early anti-fake-money laws. Archaeologists have even unearthed remains of clay-filled cacao beans from colonial-era sites, confirming that this chocolate forgery was indeed practiced. It's a testament to how valuable cacao currency was: if something is considered money, people will find a way to fake it!

Interestingly, towards the end of the Aztec era, there were signs of a transition to more conventional currency due to these practical issues.

The Aztecs began to cast small copper coins in the shape of mini axe blades, sometimes called "hoe money" or axe-monies. These copper tokens, worth a hefty amount of cacao each, were an attempt to create a more durable currency for large transactions (one copper axe coin might equal 8,000 beans or more). However, this experiment was still limited – right up to the Spanish conquest, cacao beans remained the dominant currency for everyday trade. The allure of chocolate was simply too strong to give up.

Food, Status, and Symbol: The Cultural Power of Cacao

Beyond its monetary and practical use, cacao had huge cultural and symbolic importance in Mesoamerican societies. It wasn't just money in the bank; it was food for the soul, a drink of the gods, and a mark of prestige. Understanding this deeper meaning helps explain why cacao was trusted as currency – it was revered in almost every aspect of life.

For one, cacao in the form of chocolate (the drink) was the beverage of the elite. Among the Aztec and Maya nobility, drinking chocolate was a grand luxury and a daily pleasure of kings. The thick, foamy cacao drink – often flavored with spices like chili, vanilla, or flor de cacao – was served in beautifully decorated cups. The Aztec emperor Moctezuma II famously would be served 50 golden goblets of chocolate each day—a display of immense wealth in an economy where money literally grew on trees. To consume such vast quantities of currency was the ultimate projection of imperial power. To be able to drink your cacao rather than spend it was the height of wealth. Common folk might only rarely taste chocolate, maybe at festivals or if it was offered by a patron, because it was literally like drinking money. This association of chocolate with status and wealth reinforced everyone's willingness to accept the beans as money – they knew *someone* would always desire cacao, either to sip or to save.

Cacao also played central roles in religious rituals and social ceremonies. The Maya, for example, used cacao in marriage negotiations and wedding ceremonies. There was a tradition in some regions of the bride and groom exchanging five cacao beans with each other during the wedding vows, or a father of the bride demanding a dowry partly in cacao from the groom's family. In the Mixtec culture (of Oaxaca), a codex illustration shows a bride and groom sharing a chalice of chocolate as part of their marriage bond. Here, chocolate symbolized prosperity, fertility, and the bittersweet richness of life – quite appropriate for a union.

In religious offerings, cacao was a common feature as well. Priests and devotees offered cacao beans to the gods by scattering them on temple altars or adding them to sacrificial rituals, almost as sacred currency for divine favor. Some ceremonies included chocolate drinks mixed with sacrificial blood or other potent ingredients, to be consumed by priests in communion with the gods. The Maya Popol Vuh (the book of creation) even describes the gods crafting human beings from a dough that included ground corn and *cacao*, among other ingredients – literally making mankind partly out of chocolate.

In Aztec myth, cacao was a divine gift to humanity. Such stories show cacao as a heaven-sent substance, a bridge between mortals and the divine.

Another fascinating symbol was the profound metaphysical connection between cacao and the human life force. To the Aztec worldview, this was not merely poetic, but physical: the cacao pod itself—specifically the native varieties which are tapered and furrowed—bears a striking resemblance to the human heart.

Because the plant's flowers and pods grow directly from the trunk of the tree, much like the heart resides within the human chest, the Aztecs viewed the cacao tree as a botanical mirror of the human body. In Nahuatl metaphors, chocolate was often equated with yollotl (heart) and eztli (blood).

This symbolism dictated how it was prepared and consumed. The drink was frequently dyed a deep, visceral crimson using achiote (annatto) or chili to mimic the appearance of blood—the 'sacred water' (chalchiuhatl) required to sustain the sun. In some ceremonies, the chocolate was used to wash the obsidian blades of sacrificial knives, creating a literal mixture of chocolate and blood. By drinking this 'heart blood,' the nobility weren't just enjoying a beverage; they were consuming the vital energy of the universe."

===

HISTORY ALIVE: THE 5-BEAN WEDDING VOW

Before diamond rings, there were cocoa beans. Recreate the Mayan engagement.

- **The Ritual:** In traditional Maya marriage negotiations, the groom didn't give a ring; he gave a wooden box containing five cacao beans.
- **The Meaning:** The beans represented the five elements of a prosperous life:
  - Wisdom
  - Strength
  - Abundance
  - Fertility
  - Spirit
- **Modern Twist:** Today, some couples exchange five high-quality beans or truffles during their vows to symbolize the "bittersweet" promise of marriage—mostly sweet, but requiring work to grow.

===

All these cultural layers – the mythology, ritual use, social prestige – meant that cacao beans carried a psychological value beyond their practical worth. People saw them as gifts of the gods and symbols of status, which bolstered their use as a trusted currency. In essence, chocolate was valuable not only because you could eat or drink it, but because it meant something profound in the cultural imagination. Imagine being paid in something that is both your favorite treat and imbued with sacred significance – you'd probably value those payments very highly! That's exactly how the peoples of Mesoamerica felt about cacao.

Chocolate's Worth in the Modern World

Today, we no longer pay our rent or taxes in bags of cacao beans. The "chocolate standard" gave way long ago to metal coins, paper bills, and digital money. Yet, the legacy of cacao currency is still felt in how we perceive the value of chocolate. Simply put, we continue to treat chocolate as something special – a symbol of luxury, love, and reward – echoing its exalted status of old.

Think about when we gift chocolate. A box of fine chocolates on Valentine's Day, a bar of silky dark chocolate as a thank-you, or a cup of rich hot cocoa on a chilly night – these carry a sense of indulgence and care. We instinctively know chocolate is a little treasure (for the tongue and the heart), perhaps not realizing that for centuries it was literally treasured as money.

Phrases like *"worth its weight in chocolate"* aren't common – but we do say *"worth its weight in gold,"* and in Mesoamerica gold and chocolate were nearly equivalent in worth. In fact, the Spanish who first encountered cacao beans being used as coins had to adjust their European mindset; they eventually wrote that a sack of cacao could buy a horse or that a single bean could buy a meal. That astonishment has faded, but the sense of chocolate as a precious commodity remains.

In a way, every time you enjoy a piece of chocolate, you're holding a fragment of that history. The addictive delight you feel has deep roots. This was a flavor and substance so esteemed that it powered trade networks and formed the backbone of kingdoms. Knowing that chocolate was once money might make you savor it even more – it's like nibbling on something that was literally priceless to our ancestors.

There's even a playful truth to the joke, *"money grows on trees"*, when it comes to chocolate. The cacao tree really did grow money on its branches in the form of those cocoa pods. Perhaps that's why we find something magical about strolling through a chocolate shop or a cacao plantation – subconsciously, we're tapping into an ancient dream of plucking riches from a tree.

In an economic sense, cacao is still a huge global commodity (a multi-billion dollar industry), and some farmers call the crop "brown gold." We no longer carry jute bags of cacao to the bank, but the global trade of chocolate is a serious business built on people's enduring love for this product.

The story of cocoa currency also offers a lesson: money is ultimately about shared belief in value. The Aztecs and Maya proved that anything can be money – even something as perishable and enjoyable as chocolate – if everyone agrees on its worth. In modern times we've seen similar things, like cigarettes used as currency in prisons or certain virtual game tokens taking on real monetary value. Cacao beans were an early example of alternative currency that worked surprisingly well in its context. It reminds us that behind our abstract currencies today lies a shared cultural story of value, not unlike the story that made chocolate into money.

Lastly, consider how we often talk about chocolate in language fit for riches: "rich chocolate cake," "decadent truffles," "luxurious cocoa butter". We don't describe broccoli or bread with such exalted terms. That linguistic flourish is, in a sense, the cultural memory of cacao's exalted place. Chocolate = luxury in our minds, just as it did for the Aztec nobility and Maya kings. When we splurge on gourmet chocolate, we become part of a long tradition of chocolate as a status symbol and cherished treasure.

So the next time you unwrap a chocolate bar, take a moment to appreciate that you're enjoying something that once functioned as coins in a marketplace and tribute to emperors. Those Mesoamerican chocoholics would surely smile to see their beloved cacao now circling the globe, still adored and still indulgent – even if we've moved on to credit cards and cryptocurrencies. In a world of changing currencies, chocolate's value remains a constant: measured not in beans anymore, but in the delight it brings. And in that sense, the spirit of the cocoa currency lives on, whenever chocolate lovers trade a bit of their wealth for a taste of heaven.

3

CHOCOLATE FOR THE DEAD: TOMBS, RITUALS, AND THE AFTERLIFE

D*eep beneath the jungle floor, in the sealed chamber of a Maya tomb, an earthen jar rests beside the bones of a long-dead noble. Its painted surface has faded, but chemical traces inside still whisper its purpose: it once held chocolate, prepared for a journey into the next world. In the ancient imagination of Mesoamerica, cacao was more than nourishment— it was a companion for the dead, a source of strength in the perilous passage to the afterlife. Across the Maya and Aztec realms, chocolate became one of the most intimate offerings placed with the deceased, a final gesture of care that bridged the worlds of the living and the departed. This chapter explores how cacao became entwined with funerary ritual, and why a drink we treat as comfort today once carried the weight of a soul's safe passage.*

Cacao and the Realm of the Dead

While previous chapters explore cacao's worldly roles, its most profound meaning emerged in rituals of departure and remembrance— where chocolate became not nourishment for the living, but provision for the dead. The cacao tree's life cycle resonated powerfully with concepts of regeneration: its cauliflorous nature—pods emerging directly from the trunk and major branches—evoked new life springing from what appeared dead, while the tree's ability to thrive in deep shade suggested that vitality could flourish even in darkness. In cultures where death marked a passage rather than a conclusion, cacao was regarded as indispensable for the soul's travel—sustenance, currency, and spiritual companion all at once.

Cacao as a Farewell Offering in Maya Tombs

For the Maya, cacao's role in funerary ritual was unmistakable. Death marked the beginning of a dangerous journey through Xibalba, the shadowy underworld whose trials required strength and protection. Just as a traveler in life needed provisions, a soul in the afterlife required nourishment—and no substance carried more symbolic or practical power than cacao. It was the drink of kings, the essence of vitality, and the offering most capable of sustaining a spirit on the road beyond death.

The confirmation of this ancient practice required a breakthrough in modern forensic chemistry. For decades, archaeologists found empty pots in tombs and could only guess at their contents based on glyphs. The physical proof had evaporated centuries ago. That changed in the 1980s when chemist W. Jeffrey Hurst at the Hershey Foods Technical Center applied High-Performance Liquid Chromatography (HPLC) to the dry, dusty scrapings from the inside of a Maya pot found at Río Azul.

Hurst was hunting for a specific chemical fingerprint: theobromine. Unlike caffeine, which is found in many plants, theobromine is unique to cacao in the Mesoamerican landscape. When Hurst's machine spit out the results, the spike in the graph was undeniable. It was the first chemical proof of ancient chocolate consumption, turning a dusty artifact into a certified chocolate mug. This "Cacao CSI" work proved that the vessel wasn't just decorative; it was a functional canteen for the afterlife, loaded with the stimulants needed for the soul's journey.

These findings are not isolated—they represent a pattern. At many Maya sites – Palenque in Mexico, Copán in Honduras, Tikal in Guatemala, and others – royal tombs have yielded cacao traces and even whole cacao beans left as offerings.

The Río Azul vessel, found in a royal tomb, was sealed with a twist-
top lid to prevent the evaporation of the precious chocolate drink
meant to sustain the soul in the afterlife.

In some cases, tiny clay pots shaped like cacao pods themselves were
found, a simulacrum of the treasured fruit for the departed. The consistent presence of cacao in tombs tells us that the Maya envisioned the
afterlife as a continuation of life's needs and pleasures. Just as a Maya
noble savored chocolate in life, so would his or her spirit require the
same treat in the afterworld. Cacao was a source of strength and a token
of honor to the ancestors.

Beyond its practical role as sustenance, cacao had powerful symbolic
resonance in Maya afterlife beliefs. The Maya conceived of the cosmos as
a great World Tree connecting the underworld, earth, and heavens. One
variety of this World Tree was envisioned as a cacao tree: its roots
reaching into Xibalba, its branches supporting the sky. In art and
inscriptions, cacao imagery was often associated with concepts of rebirth
and immortality. A stunning example comes from a tomb in Palenque,
where a carved relief depicts the dead queen mother of the dynasty
sprouting as a cacao tree. Her arms and fingers transform into elegant
branches laden with ripe cacao pods. This remarkable image conveyed
that through death, she was not gone but rather transformed – literally

becoming a source of life and fertility for her descendants. In essence, the cacao tree symbolized that the deceased royal, like a seed, had been planted in the earth and would bloom again in spirit. For the Maya, who prized cyclical patterns in nature, cacao perfectly embodied the cycle of life, death, and rebirth.

Maya funerary cacao was likely prepared much as it was in daily life: ground cacao beans mixed with water and often spices like chili pepper, maize, or honey to make a rich drink. The difference is that these special batches were lovingly sealed in tomb vessels and sometimes augmented with ritual substances. Some scholars speculate that chocolate drinks for the dead might have been made extra potent or pure, to fortify the soul. And these were no ordinary cups – the vessels were art pieces carrying messages. Hieroglyphic texts on tomb ceramics often named the owner and the intended contents. One painted vase might read "the drinking cup of so-and-so for cacao," essentially serving as a heavenly passport identifying both the rightful owner and the chocolate elixir inside meant for their journey.

To the Maya, the Cacao tree was a manifestation of the World Tree, bridging the gap between the living earth and Xibalba, the underworld.

By equipping their dead with chocolate, the Maya demonstrated a touching mix of practicality and deep spirituality. They took a sensory joy of earthly existence – the bittersweet, invigorating taste of chocolate – and turned it into a spiritual viaticum, a provision for crossing into eternity. It speaks volumes about how the Maya imagined the afterlife: not a stark void, but a place where ancestors could enjoy refined pleasures and continue to need the care of their living kin. Cacao in the tomb was an act of love, a final gift to sustain the beloved dead and perhaps to appease the gods of death with a precious offering.

Aztec Beliefs: Nourishing the Journey to Mictlan

Further north in central Mexico, the Aztec Empire in the 14th–16th centuries inherited many of the same traditions regarding cacao. Though separated from the Classic Maya by time and distance, the Aztecs – or more broadly the Nahua peoples – revered cacao just as deeply. They called chocolate xocoatl and valued cacao beans so highly that taxes and tributes to the emperor were often paid in cacao. For the Aztecs too, chocolate was a drink of the elite and a sacred substance used in ritual contexts. When it came to matters of death, the Aztecs had their own unique worldview, but cacao found a place there as well.

In Aztec cosmology, souls of the dead embarked on an arduous journey to reach their final resting place. Common folk who died of natural causes were believed to travel to Mictlan, the land of the dead ruled by the god Mictlantecuhtli. This journey took four years and was fraught with obstacles – raging rivers, mountains that clashed together, and winds of obsidian knives, to name a few.

The Aztecs prepared their dead for this voyage by ritually equipping them with what they might need. They often cremated the bodies and buried the ashes with offerings: food, water, tools, precious objects, and perhaps most importantly, a small dog to guide the soul through the underworld. Among these provisions, there is evidence that cacao beans and chocolate sometimes figured as part of the send-off. Just as the living needed nourishment, the dead would too, and what better energy source than cacao?

It's recorded that Aztec families would ritually offer food and drink during funerals and subsequent memorial ceremonies. Chocolate, being both valued and fortifying, made frequent appearances. Some accounts describe mourners sprinkling cacao or preparing chocolate drinks as offerings at the graveside.

==

MYTHOLOGY: THE CACAO WORLD TREE

For the Maya, the cacao tree was not just food; it was the cosmos.

- **The Canopy/Branches**
  - The Heavens: Home to the sun, moon, and supreme deities.
- **The Trunk/Surface**
  - The Middle Earth: The realm of human life, where the cacao pods ripen (symbolizing life springing from the trunk).
- **The Roots**
  - Xibalba (The Underworld): The destination of the soul after death, where the roots reach (symbolizing rebirth and the eternal cycle).

==

IN ONE TRADITIONAL Nahua practice (which persisted in some regions even after the Spanish conquest), relatives of the deceased offered cacao beans, tamales, and water while saying prayers to help the soul on its journey. The cacao beans, in addition to providing spiritual energy, may have been symbolically akin to currency for the afterlife – a way to pay tribute or secure safe passage among the gods of death. After all, if cacao greased the wheels of commerce on earth, why not also in the realm of the dead?

Aztec mythology contains hints of why cacao would be crucial in life and death alike. One legend tells that the god Quetzalcoatl, the benevolent Feathered Serpent deity, stole cacao from the celestial realm and gave it to humans as a gift. This act imbued cacao with divine favor. Drinking chocolate was in a sense drinking the wisdom and vigor of the gods. The Aztecs also associated cacao's reddish-brown hue with the vital fluid of life – blood. In some sacred rituals, chocolate was mixed with the blood from human sacrifices and shared among participants, as a powerful communion of life essence. Warriors who were to be sacrificed were sometimes feted with a gourd of chocolate tinged red (either with achiote spice or actual blood) to dignify their impending death. This "blooded" chocolate was a potent symbol: the merging of cacao (the food of gods) with human life-force, offered back to the gods in sacrificial ceremonies. It is chilling yet profound – chocolate here became a literal vessel of the soul.

Such rituals underscore how deeply cacao was interwoven with death in Aztec culture. Even beyond the grave, the Aztecs imagined chocolate as a solace and a companion. One fascinating account from colonial records describes how a departing Aztec king distributed his wealth of cacao among his retainers and also had some buried with him to enjoy in the afterlife. To the Aztecs, a life without chocolate would be as unthinkable as a life without the sun – why should death be any different?

If the Maya underworld was a dark labyrinth, the Aztec Mictlan was a long pilgrimage, and chocolate was a trusty ration for the soul along the way. At the same time, providing cacao in funerary rites also displayed the esteem in which the living held the departed. Burying someone with cacao beans or a fine chocolate cup was a mark of honor and love, ensuring the deceased would not lack luxury or comfort in the next world. It was both a spiritual act and a social one, reinforcing that this person mattered greatly – enough that their family would part with one of the most precious commodities on earth to enrich their tomb.

CHOCOLATE IN TOMBS: What Archaeology Reveals

For a long time, the sacred role of chocolate in funerals was known only through sparse Spanish chronicles and indigenous myths. But modern archaeology has painted a vivid picture by literally unearthing the chocolate of the dead. Scientific analysis of residues in pottery has become a key tool in understanding ancient diets and rituals. In the case of cacao, its chemical markers (theobromine and caffeine) are distinctive, allowing researchers to identify chocolate even after millennia.

One of the breakthrough moments in chocolate archaeology was the investigation of vessels from the Maya site of Río Azul (mentioned earlier). When Hershey Company scientists in the 1980s confirmed that those tomb vessels contained real chocolate remnants, it opened our eyes to how common this practice was. Subsequent digs found whole cacao beans carefully placed in elite burials at sites like Uaxactún and Kaminaljuyú in Guatemala. In Honduras, at Copán, dozens of Early Classic period tombs yielded cacao offerings: everything from large lidded jars that once held foaming drinks to tiny deer-shaped bowls likely containing powdered cacao. These discoveries suggest a standardized ritual – the dead were to receive cacao in some form, whether as a drink, paste, or raw beans.

Interestingly, archaeologists have also learned how these cacao offerings were prepared and stored. Many tomb vessels designed for chocolate have special features: some are tall with narrow necks (to keep the precious liquid from spilling or evaporating), others have built-in compartments or even locks. In one case, a Maya tomb contained several small stoppered bottles believed to hold different flavorings for cacao, such as chili or vanilla, implying that the dead might even enjoy a spiced chocolate cocktail in the afterlife! The care taken in sealing these containers – sometimes with cloth, clay, or lids – meant the contents were meant to last a long journey. Indeed, the Maya might have imagined their ancestor sipping slowly as they navigated the underworld, the chocolate sustaining them until they reached paradise.

Beyond the contents themselves, the art on funerary cacao vessels often depicts scenes of feasting or gods consuming cacao, reinforcing the theme that chocolate was the food of gods and nobles. Some show the maize god or rain god holding cacao pods, linking chocolate to agricultural fertility and thereby to the idea of resurrection (crops die and return each year). Even the shape of certain burial jars, like those shaped as gourds or cacao fruits, indicates they were symbolic of life's renewal. Thus, the archaeological evidence doesn't just tell us that cacao was present, but also helps us understand why – it was part of a broader symbolic language of death and rebirth.

In recent years, researchers have extended these studies beyond the Maya heartland. Traces of cacao have been found in much earlier contexts, such as pottery of the Mokaya people (~1900 BCE) and even the South American Mayo-Chinchipe culture (as far back as 3500 BCE) in what is now Ecuador. While those instances may not be explicitly funerary, they demonstrate that ritual cacao use has extremely deep roots. It's possible that as the custom of cacao drinking spread, so too did the practice of accompanying the dead with cacao. By the time of the Aztecs, any important burial might include cacao beans scattered among the grave goods or a chocolate-filled cup at the deceased's side. Although organic beverages seldom survive, the few that do – and the Spanish written accounts – confirm that the practice was widespread.

Cacao Ritual: Detail from a Late Classic Maya vessel showing the preparation of cacao. Its role in courtly life established its use as a prized offering for the dead in both elite and community burials.

One extraordinary finding comes not from a tomb but from a cave: a mortuary cave in Belize contained cacao seeds and vessels left as offerings to the dead who were interred there, dating to the Early Classic Maya era. The cave, viewed as a portal to the underworld, was essentially a communal tomb where cacao was a primary offering. This highlights that cacao was not only a privilege of kings; it was also used in broader community rites for the dead, whenever possible. Naturally, the most lavish examples come from the elite burials, because ordinary folks couldn't always spare precious cacao for the grave. But whenever a family could afford to, they did – showing even common people embraced the belief in chocolate's power to comfort and energize souls beyond death.

Modern Echoes of Ancient Traditions

Though the great pre-Columbian civilizations fell centuries ago, many of their customs surrounding death and cacao echo through time. Perhaps the most famous is Mexico's Día de los Muertos, the Day of the

Dead, celebrated each year in early November. This festival, with roots in both indigenous Aztec practices and Spanish Catholic observances, centers on honoring deceased loved ones. Families build altars (ofrendas) decorated with candles, marigold flowers, photos, and offerings of the departed's favorite foods and drinks. In many homes, you will find chocolate in one form or another on these altars – cups of hot chocolate or champurrado (a chocolatey maize drink), plates of mole sauce (a rich chocolate-based stew), or even candy in the shape of cacao pods. Just as the Maya and Aztecs did long ago, people today are offering chocolate to the spirits, believing that on these sacred nights, the souls of the dead return to taste the essence of the foods they enjoyed in life. The simple act of preparing grandma's special hot cocoa for her altar is a poignant modern continuation of a belief that love and nourishment transcend the grave.

===

CULTURAL RITUAL: BUILDING A CHOCOLATE OFRENDA

On Día de los Muertos (Nov 1-2), chocolate guides the spirits home. Here is how to set a traditional table.

- The Drink: Place a mug of hot Mexican Chocolate or Champurrado (thickened with corn masa) on the altar. The steam carries the aroma to the spirit world.
- The Food: Offer Mole Negro. This savory chocolate sauce, served over turkey or chicken, is a feast for the ancestors.
- The Skull: Include a Calavera (Sugar Skull) or a molded chocolate skull. It mocks death and celebrates the sweetness of life.

===

In the highlands of Guatemala, where Maya culture persists vibrantly, similar traditions continue. In some towns around Lake Atitlán, for example, relatives pour out chocolate drinks on the ground or leave cacao sweets on graves during All Saints' Day, symbolically sharing with their ancestors. It's a gesture of remembering and giving back. In one community, people even string cacao pods as decorations during certain religious holidays, reflecting the enduring status of cacao as a sacred plant. Moreover, a beautiful practice has been observed in Santiago Atitlán: villagers plant fruit trees on the graves of their family members, and notably, cacao trees are among the favored choices. Just as ancient carvings portrayed royal mothers becoming cacao trees in death, modern Maya literally cultivate cacao on burial sites, creating an "ancestor orchard" that keeps the memory of loved ones growing and bearing fruit.

One of the most startling modern echoes of pre-Hispanic custom survived in remote parts of the Yucatán Peninsula up until the 20th century. Indigenous Maya families there practiced a funerary ritual known as *P'ok'eb* – the cleansing of the corpse – with a special twist. After a person died, their body would be gently washed with water by relatives or ritual specialists. Instead of discarding that water, the family would use it as the base for making chocolate.

They would mix in ground cacao, cornmeal, and spices to create a chocolate drink which was then shared among all the close relatives and community members present at the wake. As macabre as this might sound to outside ears, the intent was deeply affectionate and spiritual. By drinking this chocolate infused with the essence of the deceased (via the bath water), the mourners believed they were literally ingesting the qualities and life-force of their loved one, thus keeping a part of them alive within themselves.

It was a final communion between the living and dead through the medium of cacao. Those who partook would symbolically carry the virtues, memories, and spirit of the departed onward. This tradition, often called *"chocolate of the dead,"* persisted quietly in villages until authorities and modern health sensibilities discouraged it. Today it is rarely, if ever, practiced – surviving mostly in the stories of elders – but its existence reveals the powerful ritual role chocolate once held. To these Maya, chocolate was not only a gift to the dead, but also a way for the living to absorb the spirit of the departed. It was, in essence, the drink of immortality.

Beyond indigenous communities, the idea of chocolate as a

comforting drink in times of death found its way into other cultures too. During the colonial era, Spaniards in the New World adopted the local love of chocolate and often served hot chocolate at funerals and wakes as a fortifying refreshment for mourners. In 18th-century Europe, drinking chocolate became popular at social gatherings – including post-funeral receptions – though by then the spiritual symbolism had faded, and it was more about hospitality. Still, one might poetically say that even when Europeans sipped chocolate to soothe their grief, they were unknowingly echoing a much older tradition: using the warmth of cacao to ward off the chill of death.

Pure Cacao, Pure Connection: The modern spiritual revival of cacao as a heart-opening and connecting force, reinforcing its profound, ancient sacred aura.

In recent decades, chocolate has re-entered spiritual practice in new forms. The rise of "cacao ceremonies" around the world – guided meditations or communal gatherings where participants drink pure cacao for emotional healing – is directly inspired by indigenous usage of cacao as a heart-opening, connecting force. People in these modern ceremonies often speak of connecting with ancestral wisdom or the spirit of cacao. Unwittingly or not, they are tapping into the ancient legacy of cacao as a sacred bridge between the earthly and the divine. While these contemporary practices are not funerary, they reinforce the notion that cacao carries an aura of profundity, a capacity to link hearts and perhaps even realms.

∼

THE IMMORTAL ALLURE of Chocolate

From the depths of prehistoric caves to the brightly adorned altars of today's festivals, chocolate has accompanied humans in confronting one of life's greatest mysteries – death. Its role in funerary rituals and tomb offerings reveals a touching continuity of thought across cultures and ages: the belief that love and care do not end with a last breath. For the Olmec, Maya, and Aztec, giving chocolate to the dead was a final act of devotion and hope. It was a way to ensure that those who passed on would carry a piece of home with them, a source of strength and delight as they ventured into the unknown. Chocolate's richness would nourish their souls; its very presence signified that the living remembered and honored them.

It is extraordinary to realize that a simple cup of cocoa could be laden with such significance – that a drink we might enjoy casually on a cold evening was once prepared with solemn ritual to serve kings in their eternal slumber. The next time you taste chocolate, consider the layers of meaning it has carried. For ancient peoples, chocolate was life, death, and rebirth distilled into a bittersweet brew. It was at once a real offering – calories and comfort to sustain a soul – and a metaphysical one, a prayer in physical form. In their funerary customs, chocolate became a metaphor for the afterlife itself: at the end of life's feast, the cup of chocolate sent with you meant that the story was not over. There were more journeys to undertake, more experiences to savor, in worlds beyond sight.

Even in modern times, when we raise a mug of hot chocolate in memory of someone or share a piece of chocolate at a remembrance, we are unknowingly partaking in this ancient narrative. We are saying, like the Maya and Aztecs before us, that the bond of love is stronger than death and that something as ordinary as a seed from the cacao tree can carry our sweetest sentiments across the divide between worlds. Chocolate for the dead may sound like a paradox, but it speaks to a universal human truth: in honoring our dead with the things that gave them joy in life, we keep their spirit alive. And so, in the cherished rituals of yesterday and today, the divine and comforting power of chocolate endures – a truly immortal treat.

4

CHOCOLATE BY CANDLELIGHT: MONKS AND THE PRESERVATION OF TRADITION

O
ne evening in the early 16th century, a warm glow flickered in the kitchen of a Spanish monastery. A Cistercian monk in coarse robes bent over a heavy clay pot, stirring a dark, fragrant liquid by candlelight. The rich aroma of roasted cacao wafted through the stone-walled kitchen, mingling with hints of cinnamon and vanilla. Moments later, he poured the steaming concoction into earthenware cups for his brethren. In this quiet corner of Aragon, within the Monasterio de Piedra's ancient walls, Europe was about to taste hot chocolate for the very first time. The monks sipped in wonder: the drink was exotic and invigorating, a gift from distant lands. Little did they know, their midnight experiment was a milestone in a journey that had begun centuries earlier in tropical groves across the ocean. It was the start of a chocolate tradition that these monastic orders would safeguard and refine for generations.

THUS UNFOLDS the remarkable saga of chocolate by candlelight – the tale of how devoted monks and friars helped carry cacao from the temples of the New World to the monasteries of the Old. Spanning continents and centuries, this history weaves through jungle missions and Baroque abbeys, binding together the sacred and the culinary. Monastic orders such as the Franciscans, Jesuits, Benedictines, and many others played unlikely but pivotal roles in preserving cacao's ancient legacy, even as they transformed it. In their cloisters, chocolate found new purposes: as spiritual sustenance, medicinal remedy, economic lifeline, and subtle indulgence. Through engaging storytelling and historical fact, let us journey alongside these robed guardians of cacao traditions, whose quiet zeal kept the flame of chocolate burning through the darkest of ages.

FROM AZTEC ALTARS to Spanish Abbeys

In 1521, the Aztec capital Tenochtitlán fell to Hernán Cortés, and with its collapse, the Spanish gained not only an empire but also an introduction to chocolate. Cortés and his men had seen firsthand the reverence with which the Aztec court treated cacao. They observed Emperor Moctezuma II's court rituals and tasted the strange spiced cocoa that was served in ornate cups.

While some Spaniards recoiled at its bitterness, others developed a curious taste for the brew – especially after learning to temper it with sugar or honey. Stories spread of chocolate's fortifying properties. As the Spanish established themselves in Mexico (Nueva España), a few enterprising souls began experimenting: what if this bitter potion could be made sweeter, more suited to European palates? Colonists' wives and local nuns in Mexico City's convents started blending chocolate with Old World ingredients like cane sugar, cinnamon, and almonds. A new, hybrid form of chocolate was quietly taking shape in the New World, even as its fame began to trickle across the ocean.

While the historical mechanisms by which friars and early colonists transmitted cacao knowledge to Europe are vast, the focus here shifts to how those exchanges shaped later cultural reinterpretations of chocolate.

Legend holds that not long after the conquest, around 1544, a delegation of Kekchi Mayan nobles traveled from Guatemala to Spain, escorted by Dominican friars, and presented the Spanish court with jars of foaming chocolate. The exotic drink caused a sensation among the Spanish nobility, who found it intriguing if not immediately delicious.

Whether or not that particular event is true, we do know that by the 1540s and 1550s, cacao beans and recipes were making their way to Europe, often in the hands of traveling monks or colonial officials. One pivotal figure was Friar Jerónimo de Aguilar – a Spaniard who had lived among the Maya as a castaway before aiding Cortés. Aguilar, having acquired a taste for chocolate in the New World, is said to have brought cacao beans and an authentic recipe back to Spain in the early 1530s.

Those precious beans found a receptive home in the Monasterio de Piedra, a secluded Cistercian abbey in northern Spain. There, in 1534, the Cistercian abbot Antonio de Álvaro and his monks conducted a culinary experiment that would change history: using Aguilar's Aztec recipe as a base, they prepared what many historians consider among the first cups of hot chocolate ever made on European soil—though the exact timing and location of Europe's first taste of cacao remains a subject of scholarly debate.

One can imagine their initial brew, faithfully following the New World style – ground cocoa mixed with hot water. The result was a dark, bitter tonic, rich in caffeine and theobromine, unlike any European drink of the time. The monks, determined to adapt this "sacred drink" to European tastes, soon began to tinker. They had on hand the fruits of Spain's burgeoning global trade: cane sugar from the Caribbean, cinnamon and vanilla from the Indies. Stirring these sweeteners and spices into the cacao, the monks transformed the austere Aztec beverage into something new: silky, sweet hot chocolate – at once a medicine, a delicacy, and a source of wonder.

Word of the monks' chocolate spread quickly through ecclesiastical and aristocratic circles. Spain's elite were enthralled. By the late 1500s, shipments of cacao beans became a regular part of galleon cargoes from Vera Cruz to Seville. But for a time, the secret of preparing chocolate remained largely confined to Spain – and often specifically to monastic kitchens and apothecaries. Spanish monks, by virtue of their literacy and cross-ocean connections, became early transmitters of cacao knowledge. A monastery might receive a crate of dried cacao beans sent by a brother stationed in Guatemala or Peru, along with instructions on roasting and brewing.

==

DIY RECIPE: THE "OLD WORLD" SPICE BLEND

Want to taste chocolate like a 17th-century Spanish monk? Pre-mix this spice jar.

- **The Mix:**
    - 2 tablespoons Cinnamon (The dominant note)
    - 1 tablespoon Vanilla Bean Powder (or scraped seeds)
    - 1 teaspoon Anise Seed (ground)
    - 1/2 teaspoon Nutmeg
    - 1/4 teaspoon Black Pepper (A nod to the Aztec chili roots)
- **The Use:** Whisk 1 teaspoon of this blend into any cup of hot chocolate to instantly transport it back to the Baroque era.

==

These monks would then introduce the drink to visiting dignitaries or fellow clergymen. In an age when monasteries were hubs of learning and hospitality, a new recipe could travel far along monastic networks. Through the 1570s and 1580s, delegates to church councils, traveling priests, and envoys carried tales of a marvelous chocolate drink from Spain to Italy, to France, and beyond.

While royal marriages would later glamorize chocolate in the courts of France (as we will explore later in the book), the initial spread of cacao across Europe was a quieter affair, conducted through the veins of the Church. It was not princesses, but traveling abbots and delegates to ecclesiastical councils who carried the first samples of chocolate from Spain to Italy, France, and Germany. In an age when monasteries served as the hotels, hospitals, and universities of Europe, a recipe could travel thousands of miles along this sacred network. Through the late 1500s, it was the Cistercian and Jesuit brothers who acted as the first transnational distributors of chocolate, gifting beans to fellow clergymen and teaching them the secrets of the whisk. This monastic innovation had a monumental effect: it turned chocolate from an acquired indigenous taste into a seductive European treat, preparing the palate of the continent one cloister at a time.

The Monastic Chocolate Revolution

As chocolate took root in Europe, it was the monasteries and convents that often nurtured its growth. The drink's rise in popularity during the 17th century owed much to the Church's enclaves, where innovation met tradition. Monks and nuns were among the first Europeans to consume chocolate routinely, and in doing so they spurred a revolution in taste and practice. Inside monastery refectories (dining halls), one might find the unusual sight of robed ascetics enjoying a steaming cup of rich cocoa alongside their morning prayers.

What made this permissible? For one, chocolate was seen as a form of medicine and nourishment – and importantly, it was liquid. According to the prevailing interpretations of religious fasting rules, liquids did not break the fast. This technicality made chocolate especially attractive in monasteries, where many days were set aside for fasting or abstinence. A cup of cacao offered both comfort and calories on those austere days when solid food was limited. One observer wryly noted that in certain Spanish cloisters, monks would practically live on "chocolate and bread" during Lent, considering the former not only allowable but divinely fortifying.

The practical benefits of chocolate did not go unnoticed. Replacing a meal with a hot, frothy cacao drink gave weary monks the energy to carry on long chants and manual labor without "technically" violating any rules. It was, as the Cistercians of Piedra put it, "the perfect monastic drink" – sustaining yet allowed. Naturally, this practice raised eyebrows and soon sparked debate within the Church. What started as a quiet monastic custom was about to become a full-fledged chocolate controversy. By the early 1600s, questions swirled through theological halls: Was drinking chocolate during fasting days a loophole or a lie? Did adding sugar or milk turn it into a food, thus breaking the fast? Different orders took different stances, and the issue became surprisingly heated.

Behind monastery walls, Spanish monks transformed the bitter
Aztec drink by adding sugar, cinnamon, and heat, keeping the
recipe a secret for nearly a century.

In Spain and its colonies, opinions split sharply among religious
orders. The Jesuits, ever pragmatic and worldly, generally approved of
chocolate's use. Jesuit missionaries had spent time in the Americas and
knew the value of cacao; many of them enjoyed chocolate and encouraged its moderate consumption. They argued that as long as one did not
add meat, egg, or too much milk to it, chocolate remained a drink –
essentially an energizing "tea" or "broth" – and thus posed no violation
of fasting. On the other hand, the Dominicans – known for their stricter
outlook – voiced strong objections.

Some Dominican friars thundered from the pulpit that chocolate
was an indulgence, a luxury that had no place in the refectory on fast
days (or perhaps any day, for truly ascetic souls). They warned that
chocolate's rich taste could tempt one into gluttony or distract from
pious focus. In their eyes, sipping sweet chocolate was a slippery slope
towards worldly excess.

It did not help matters that the Jesuits had a clear economic interest
in chocolate. By the 17th century, the Jesuit order had acquired or developed cacao plantations in parts of South America (notably in Amazonia
and coastal Brazil). Their missions oversaw the cultivation of tens of
thousands of cacao trees, yielding beans that filled the coffers of Jesuit
schools and churches.

Critics – including some Dominicans – whispered that the Jesuits defended chocolate's pious status mainly because it lined their pockets. The Jesuits retorted that cacao was a gift of God's creation and that they managed it responsibly for the good of their communities. This war of words played out in sermons, letters, and even academic tracts dedicated entirely to the morality of chocolate.

By the 1630s, the debate had grown so intense that learned men felt compelled to weigh in with formal treatises. In Seville, a scholarly cleric published a 238-page dissertation in 1636 pointedly titled *"A Question of Morality: Does Drinking Chocolate Break the Fast?"* After much reasoning, he concluded that drinking chocolate was acceptable, albeit with a caveat: it should be taken only once a day when fasting, not to become a feast unto itself. Yet not everyone was convinced.

A few years earlier, in 1591, a physician (aligned with more conservative churchmen) had argued the opposite – that chocolate, being made from a bean (a foodstuff), certainly broke the fast and even posed health risks if abused. Meanwhile, another voice – a former cocoa planter turned historian in 1609 – extolled chocolate's health benefits and suggested it was too useful to ban. The arguments ping-ponged through ecclesiastical courts and social circles alike.

Church services themselves became a stage for the chocolate drama. In the colony of New Spain (Mexico), attending Mass could be an hours-long affair, and wealthy parishioners were accustomed to bring along refreshments. It became fashionable for ladies in church to sip hot chocolate during the sermon – ostensibly to prevent fainting in the stifling heat. The conflict between piety and pleasure famously reached a boiling point in the 1640s with the Bishop of Chiapas. As explored in Chapter 7, the Bishop's attempt to ban the consumption of chocolate during Mass led to a standoff with the noblewomen of the region—a conflict that escalated into a legendary cautionary tale involving a deadly cup of cacao. The phrase "Beware the chocolate of Chiapas" entered folklore, a grim reminder of how dearly the congregation clung to their morning draught.

Shocking anecdotes aside, the question of chocolate and fasting ultimately reached the highest authority in Christendom. In 1662, Pope Alexander VII settled the matter with the pronouncement: *'Liquidum non frangit jejunum'*—Liquids do not break the fast. With this subtle ruling, a cup of plain chocolate (made with water) was officially deemed permissible, much to the relief of hungry monks across Christendom.

==

THEOLOGY CLASS: THE HOLY LOOPHOLE
How the Church decided chocolate was a drink, not a food.

- **The Problem:** In the 1600s, Catholics fasted until noon. Chocolate was rich and filling. Did it count as eating?
- **The Argument:**
    - The Dominicans (Against): It is too nutritious. It inflames passion. It breaks the fast.
    - The Jesuits (For): It is a liquid tonic (medicine). It aids the weak. It is allowed.
- **The Verdict (1662):**
    - Pope Alexander VII ruled: "Liquidum non frangit jejunum." (Liquids do not break the fast).
    - The Catch: You could drink it, but you couldn't eat the "dregs" (solids) at the bottom of the cup.

==

With this subtle ruling, a cup of plain chocolate (made with water, not with fat or meat) was officially deemed permissible on fasting days. Alexander VII's pronouncement (echoing a common saying of the time) finally gave the monastic chocoholics the Church's blessing. Of course, there were qualifiers: if one added things like milk, egg yolk, or bread to the chocolate – common enrichments by the 17th century – that crossed the line into nourishment and would break the fast. But a straightforward hot cocoa-water drink was allowed, much to the relief of monks and nuns across Europe and the Americas.

Not all discipline was relaxed, however. Even after the Pope's decision, individual orders maintained their own rules. For example, the reformed Carmelite monks, inspired by St. Teresa of Ávila's ascetic ideals, initially allowed their nuns to take chocolate as a consolation. Carmelite nuns in Spain were known to enjoy a cup to stave off the rigors of their penances. But conservative members of the order grew uneasy with the practice. In one Madrid convent, the monks in charge imposed a ban on chocolate for the nuns, considering it a frivolous pleasure. The dismayed nuns actually petitioned the Spanish queen, Margarita of Austria, in hopes of reversing the ban. The Queen – herself a chocolate lover at court – sympathized and attempted to intercede on their behalf. Yet even royal favor could not overturn the ruling of the Carmelite superiors. The Pope (likely hearing one more chocolate-related request with exasperation) upheld the monks' decision. The nuns would have to relinquish their cherished cups in obedience. Such episodes show how contentious chocolate had become within holy walls – straddling the line between necessity and luxury, between piety and indulgence.

By the late 17th century, the dust had settled: chocolate was here to stay in Christendom, not only as a secular delicacy but as a common part of monastic life. In Spain, Italy, France, and beyond, one could find devout monks and nuns quietly whisking their morning chocolate or offering a cup to visitors in the parlor. Far from eroding discipline, many argued, chocolate had helped monks persevere in their devotions. As one cardinal in Rome openly wrote, chocolate could be a "food" if taken thick with additives, but in its pure liquid form it was a "drink for fasts and feasts alike." This tacit acceptance allowed the traditions around cacao to flourish further. The controversy had, in a sense, legitimized chocolate, sparking even more interest in obtaining the best beans and perfecting recipes. And that, in turn, meant cultivation and supply had to increase – a mission field where monastic orders would again play a starring role.

∼

Missions, Plantations, and the Cacao Economy

Even as debates raged in European chapels, across the seas in the tropical Americas a more practical task was underway: growing the cacao itself. Demand for chocolate was exploding among Europe's elite and within monastic communities, and the supply of wild or cultivated cacao in Mesoamerica could barely keep up. So, throughout the 1600s and 1700s, Catholic monastic orders became deeply involved in the cacao economy – as planters, producers, and exporters of the precious beans. This involvement is a complex chapter, blending uplift and exploitation, but one thing is clear: without the organizational skills and global reach of these orders, cacao might never have spread as widely as it did.

The Jesuits, in particular, distinguished themselves as pioneers of cacao cultivation outside the traditional growing areas. In the Amazon basin and parts of coastal South America, Jesuit missionaries established large missions that were both spiritual communities and agricultural enterprises.

Along the great rivers of the Amazon and Orinoco, they encountered wild cacao growing in abundance. Seeing an opportunity, the Jesuits began to domesticate those wild cacao trees, setting up plantations on mission lands. By the 1690s, reports from Jesuit superiors noted tens of thousands of cacao trees flourishing under their care, tended by indigenous workers who had been converted and, in theory, protected within the mission system.

In the shade of the Amazon, Jesuit missionaries turned wild cacao
into thriving plantations, blending faith with agriculture.

The fertile soils of the Amazon and the Jesuits' rigorous approach to agriculture yielded cacao of fine quality. These beans were harvested, fermented, and packed into sacks emblazoned perhaps with the IHS emblem (the seal of the Society of Jesus), then sent downriver to coastal ports. From there, merchant ships carried the cacao to Spain, or sometimes overland to Lima and on to other colonies. Profits from these ventures helped fund Jesuit schools, churches, and charitable works across the Americas. In essence, the Jesuits became major cacao exporters, their networks spanning from the jungle mission stations to the trading houses of Cádiz.

Their involvement was not purely mercantile; it also had the effect of transplanting cacao to new regions. Jesuit botanists studied the plant closely and shared knowledge about its cultivation. They experimented with planting cacao in regions like the Philippines – another Spanish colony where Jesuits and other orders had a presence. By the late 17th century, cacao trees were growing in Asia's soils as well, introduced via the Spanish Manila galleons. It was often missionaries or friars who carried a few seedlings or sacks of beans to plant in the Philippines, hoping to provide local Christian communities with a source of income and a taste of a drink that reminded them of home. Thus, chocolate's realm quietly expanded to the islands of the Pacific, again with monks at the helm.

Other orders took part in the cacao boon too. The Franciscans, who had been early evangelists in Central America, encouraged cacao planting among indigenous villagers in Guatemala and Nicaragua, teaching cultivation methods to ensure a stable local supply. In parts of colonial Mexico, Franciscan and Dominican friars acted as intermediaries in the cacao trade, helping native growers get fair prices for their crops (at least in the ideal telling) and ensuring the church received its tithes in cacao beans, which could be traded onward.

Even cloistered nunneries in Mexico City became small-scale entrepreneurs: some convents were famous for the chocolate confections their sisters made and sold to support their charitable works. For example, the convent of Santa Clara produced such renowned spiced cocoa tablets and cookies that "Clarissa chocolate" became a byword for quality in New Spain.

Yet the Jesuits remained the most globally influential cacao custodians. Not without reason did some skeptics jest that "Jesuits would argue

chocolate's sanctity even if it were poison – for they grow rich on it."
Setting aside the cynicism, it's true the Society of Jesus leveraged its far-
flung network to turn cacao into a global commodity. They negotiated
with Spanish governors and Portuguese colonists alike to acquire lands
ideal for cacao trees (shaded beneath banana and cedar canopies).

In what is today Venezuela, Jesuits helped manage plantations that
supplied the lion's share of cacao consumed in Spain by 1700. When the
order was abruptly expelled from Spanish territories in 1767 (due to
political conflicts with the Crown), their estates – including thriving
cacao farms – were taken over by local authorities or private landowners.
But by then, the cacao industry was robust enough to continue without
them, a testament to the groundwork they had laid.

Meanwhile, back in Europe, some monastic communities found a
role at the other end of the supply chain: processing and refining the
cacao beans that arrived in ships' cargoes. Monasteries historically were
self-supporting economic units; many brewed beer, pressed wine, or
manufactured goods. In the 18th century, a few monasteries in Spain,
France, and Italy added chocolate-making to their artisanal output.

They would receive sacks of beans, roast them in large pans over
monastery fires, and grind them with sugar on heated slabs. The
resulting chocolate paste was formed into small bricks or tablets, sometimes flavored with anise, cinnamon, or other herbs from monastic
gardens. These chocolates could be sold to local gentry or traded for
other necessities. In some regions, the very first "chocolate shops" were
simply apothecary counters or monks' stalls offering these handmade
cocoa tablets which customers would then dissolve in hot water or milk
at home.

By the 1700s, chocolate had become a significant economic resource
in many Catholic colonies, and the Church – via its missions and
monastic holdings – stood among the beneficiaries. Cacao beans were
even used as currency in parts of Spanish America for everyday transactions (a practice inherited from pre-Columbian times). Imagine a
mission priest in rural Guatemala, collecting cacao beans in lieu of
coins from his parishioners during Sunday offertory; those beans
might later be used by the monastery cook or sent to market to buy
building materials for the church. In this way, cacao underpinned the

mission economy, blurring the line between the sacred and the mundane.

Yet, with all this growth, the monastic orders also acted as stewards of quality and tradition. They ensured that cacao cultivation techniques were passed on and improved. They taught generations of local farmers how to graft better cacao trees, how to ferment and dry the beans properly (critical steps to develop chocolate's flavor), and how to prepare the drink in the time-honored way.

If not for the stability and relative continuity of mission settlements, some of that delicate knowledge might have been lost in the upheavals of colonization. In effect, monks kept cacao traditions alive on the production side just as much as on the consumption side. Through droughts, wars, and political shifts, the mission orchards of cacao endured – silent orchards tended by determined hands in simple habits, dreaming perhaps of a heavenly reward but content meanwhile with a cup of earthly chocolate.

Elixirs and Apothecaries: Chocolate as Medicine

Why were monks and nuns so taken with chocolate in the first place? Part of the answer lies in its reputation as a medicinal elixir. From the start, Europeans learned about cacao's health benefits from indigenous sources. The Aztecs and Maya had long used cacao in healing: to reduce fever, ease stomach troubles, combat fatigue, and even as a remedy for anemia or heart palpitations. These uses were recorded in early colonial codices and reports. European doctors in the 16th century eagerly took note. In 1552, for example, a Spanish physician in Mexico City co-authored the Badianus Manuscript (an herbal guide) which listed cacao-based brews for ailments ranging from angina to diarrhea. Such findings dovetailed with the Renaissance European approach of seeking new world cures for old world maladies.

Monastic infirmaries and apothecaries became natural early homes for chocolate. In Catholic Europe, many monasteries ran their own pharmacies, formulating remedies for monks and the public. The learned friars who staffed these apothecaries often read the latest scientific and medical texts. By the early 17th century, treatises on the "virtues of chocolate" were circulating, and monks would have been among the literate elite privy to them.

One famous treatise, by a Spanish doctor named Antonio Colmenero de Ledesma in 1631, extolled chocolate's therapeutic qualities and even provided recipes (including one monastic-friendly version with achiote for coloring and spice). Monks tested these claims firsthand. After a dusty day in the fields or a long evening copying manuscripts by candle-light, a brother might take a dose of chocolate – sometimes mixed with cinnamon or orange blossom – and find his weariness relieved. It seemed to lift the mood and stimulate the body gently, much like the "nerve tonics" that herbalist monks were already concocting from ginseng or sage.

In many monasteries, chocolate began as a remedy and evolved into a daily tonic. A chronically ill abbot might be prescribed a cup of hot chocolate each morning to settle his digestion; an elderly nun might take a bit of cocoa with milk at night to help her sleep (hot chocolate has a calming, almost sedative effect on some). These were real treatments in an era when humoral medicine saw food and drink as key to balancing the body.

The fact that chocolate was delicious certainly encouraged compli-ance with these "prescriptions"! Across baroque Europe, the use of chocolate as medicine became so accepted that one could purchase chocolate tablets in pharmacies, pre-mixed with sugar and spices, ready to dissolve in water as a healing draught. And who made these tablets? Often it was monastic apothecaries or enterprising lay pharmacists using monastic recipes.

One renowned example of monastic pharmaceutical tradition is the Officina Profumo-Farmaceutica di Santa Maria Novella in Florence, run by Dominican friars since the 17th century. Famous for its herbal liquors and remedies, this apothecary almost certainly dealt in cacao. Historical records from similar institutions show that they stocked cocoa powder and even concocted chocolate-based syrups and liqueurs for health. If you walked into such a shop in the 1750s with complaints of low energy or melancholy, the friar dispensing medicines might recommend a daily cup of chocolate to "enliven the spirits and nourish the blood." Unlike many quack cures of the time, chocolate actually often did make patients feel better, thanks to its gentle stimulants and rich nutrients.

The medicinal reputation of chocolate helped it gain acceptance among even the initially skeptical. Many Church authorities who frowned on idle luxuries could be persuaded by the argument that chocolate was essentially a kind of drinkable medicine. After all, wine had long been considered a healthful tonic in moderation, even a symbol of sacred blood in the Eucharist. Chocolate, some argued, was not so different – a natural creation of God intended for our well-being if used rightly.

Monks wrote of chocolate's ability to "close the stomach" (meaning to cure hunger pangs), to alleviate coughing, and to strengthen one's capacity for study and prayer by banishing drowsiness. In monasteries dedicated to learning, like those of the Jesuits and Benedictines, a cup of cocoa could fuel late-night scholarship as effectively as coffee would in later centuries. It became the monastic equivalent of a strong cup of tea – a source of clarity and vigor.

Beyond the monasteries, this healing image carried chocolate into general society, but often it was monks and nuns who served as the messengers. Consider the midwife-nuns who ran hospitals, the kindly friars who tended to the sick poor – many of them incorporated chocolate into their caregiving. In Mexico, the *Hermanas de la Caridad* (Sisters of Charity) famously gave cups of cinnamon-laced hot chocolate to patients in convalescence, believing it would speed recovery.

In France, certain Carmelite sisters specialized in crafting chocolate pastilles mixed with ground lemon balm and other herbs, sold as calming sweets to soothe anxiety. Even in distant missions in the Philippines or Africa, where Western medicine was scarce, missionaries sometimes distributed cocoa as a restorative to those weakened by illness or hunger. In essence, chocolate functioned as both food and pharmacy, and the monastic orders embraced that duality.

Of course, not all uses were strictly clinical. We must admit the monks enjoyed the taste and comfort of chocolate as much as anyone. The line between taking medicine and indulging in a treat can be delightfully blurred when it comes to something like a warm chocolate drink. Chocolate's mood-lifting effects – thanks to compounds that stim- ulate pleasure receptors – did not go unnoticed.

A 18th-century Benedictine abbess once wryly commented that her nuns were far more cheerful on chocolate days, singing their psalms with added sweetness. Whether by design or happy side effect, the medical adoption of chocolate ensured it a lasting place in monastic life and European culture. By the eighteenth century, the idea of chocolate as a rare sacred beverage had expanded: it was now a beloved everyday potion, equally at home in a monk's cup, an apothecary's jar, or a noble's drawing-room. What remained constant was the aura of goodness surrounding it – a sense that chocolate was not only delicious, but somehow *beneficial* and even virtuous.

～

Legacy of a Sacred Brew

From the sacred groves of the Maya to the candlelit cells of Trappist monks, the journey of chocolate is a tapestry of devotion, innovation, and cross-cultural exchange. It's astonishing to think that a simple cacao bean, once used by priests in pre-Christian temples, found a second life nurtured in Christian monasteries. Monastic orders kept cacao tradi- tions alive during critical chapters of history, when tastes and technolo- gies were changing rapidly. They were the intermediaries between the indigenous wisdom of the Americas and the eager appetite of Europe, ensuring that the essence of chocolate survived even as it was transformed.

By the 19th century, chocolate had left the cloister and entered the factory; industrial processes made it cheaper and more widely available to the masses. One might assume the monks then faded from chocolate history – but that's not the case. In fact, some religious communities adapted and became chocolatiers themselves in the modern age.

In Rome, for instance, a group of Trappist monks famously began producing their own line of chocolate bars and liqueurs in the 1880s. Using cacao beans imported from distant mission lands and following a secret recipe, these Trappists of the Tre Fontane Abbey created confec- tions so beloved that "Trappist chocolate" became a celebrated local brand. They won prizes at international fairs, and to this day visitors to the Abbey can purchase chocolate made according to the monks' guarded methods – a sweet reminder that the monastic touch still lends magic to cacao.

Likewise, in far-flung places, new monastic chocolate traditions have sprung up. In Central Europe, Benedictine and Trappistine nuns now make exquisite chocolate truffles to support their convents. In the United States, the Brigittine monks of Oregon have earned renown for their handmade fudge and rich truffles, crafted in the peaceful silence of their monastery workshop. It seems that wherever monasteries exist, the affinity for chocolate is never far behind – a continuation of centuries of practice. The modern monk working over a tempering machine or stirring a copper pot of ganache is not so different from that 16th-century brother stirring his clay pot over coals. In both scenarios, chocolate by candlelight symbolizes comfort, creativity, and a labor of love.

Beyond the literal making of chocolate, the monastic legacy lives on in our very approach to this food. The idea of sipping hot chocolate for solace, of gifting a box of fine chocolates for well-being, of taking a small piece of dark chocolate each day "for your health" – all echo the themes championed by monks long ago. We treasure chocolate as something almost transcendent, a little luxury with almost mystical power to soothe and cheer. It's easy to forget that we owe much of this to those unsung brothers and sisters who bridged the gap between an ancient Aztec rite and a global habit. They experimented with recipes by midnight lamp, debated morality over cups of cocoa, and planted orchards in untamed lands – all so that the chain of tradition would remain unbroken.

Today, chocolate is enjoyed in countless forms by people of every creed and nation. It is thoroughly secularized and commercial, found in supermarket aisles and vending machines. Yet, if we peel back the layers of time, we find a rich spiritual heritage infused in every chocolate bar. The meticulous craft of the chocolatier has roots in the monastery; the concept of chocolate as solace harks back to the cloister; even the very spices we associate with good chocolate (vanilla, cinnamon) were first combined with cacao in those monastic kitchens experimenting with New World flavors. In a sense, every cup of hot cocoa or square of truffle we savor is a tiny heirloom handed down by monastic hands.

As evening falls and one perhaps lights a candle on a cold night, consider making a cup of old-fashioned hot chocolate – dark and spiced, whipped to a froth in the style the monks learned from the Aztecs. Wrap your hands around the warm cup and breathe in the aroma. In that simple pleasure, you partake in a ritual that spans centuries and continents. You may hear, in the quiet of your mind, the echo of Gregorian chant from a distant refectory, or the rustle of cacao leaves in a mission orchard, or the whispers of Aztec priests invoking their gods.

Chocolate by candlelight invites us to taste history. It is the story of how something as small as a bean can inspire devotion, how knowledge can be preserved through turmoil, and how the love of a good drink can unite very different worlds. The next time chocolate delights your senses, remember those watchful guardians in their monasteries – the Jesuits, the Franciscans, the Benedictines, the Carmelites – who kept the faith in cacao alive. Their legacy lives on in every luscious sip, a quiet toast across time to the monks in the cloisters, stirring their pots, keeping the light of cacao tradition aglow against the darkness.

5

THE CHOCOLATE HEALERS: SACRED MEDICINE AND MINDFUL WELLNESS

O*n a damp morning centuries ago in the Guatemalan lowlands, a healer knelt beside a stone metate and began to grind roasted cacao beans into a dark, fragrant paste. She added sapote seeds, maize, chili, and water, working the mixture until it frothed. The resulting drink was not dessert. It was medicine, sacrament, and strength in a cup—offered to the sick to banish fever, to warriors to staunch blood, and to mothers to ease the pangs of childbirth.*

HALF A WORLD and many centuries later, a volunteer in a modern clinic swallows a capsule filled with concentrated cocoa flavanols before lying back in an MRI scanner. Doctors are not praying to cacao gods; they are measuring blood flow, memory scores, and biochemical markers. Yet the question is startlingly familiar: can chocolate help us heal?

This chapter follows that enduring question from jungle shrines to hospital wards, from the four humors of Galen to the antioxidants of today. It is a story of how a bitter bean became a universal panacea, fell from grace as a "guilty pleasure," and is now being rehabilitated by science.

. . .

Ancient Tonics: Cacao in the Hands of Healers

Among the Maya and Aztec, cacao was never just a treat. It sat at the intersection of ritual, medicine, and diet. The Badianus Manuscript, an Aztec herbal text from 1552, lists cacao flowers as a cure for fatigue and the beans as a remedy for heart conditions.

Healers used cacao as a carrier for other medicines—much like a modern syrup—because its rich fat (cocoa butter) coated the stomach and made harsh herbs palatable. Aztec physicians prescribed cacao mixed with liquid rubber for dysentery, or blended with ground bones to set fractures.

But the most profound use was for the spirit. Cacao was believed to open the heart and fortify the blood. Warriors were given distinct recipes of "red" chocolate (dyed with achiote) to steel their nerves before battle. It was a substance of vitality, linked to the blood of the earth itself.

The Humoral Conflict: Is Chocolate Hot or Cold?

When chocolate arrived in Europe in the 16th century, it collided with the prevailing medical philosophy of the time: Humoral Theory. Derived from the ancient Greeks, this system believed health depended on balancing four bodily fluids (humors): blood, phlegm, yellow bile, and black bile. All foods were classified as "Hot," "Cold," "Wet," or "Dry" to treat imbalances.

Chocolate threw the European medical establishment into chaos. Was this strange new bean "Hot" or "Cold"?

It was a fierce debate. Spanish physicians initially classified cacao as "Cold and Dry" because it was bitter and astringent. Therefore, it was prescribed for "Hot" ailments like fevers or liver inflammation. But they noticed that when mixed with spices like chili or cinnamon (as the Aztecs did), it became "Hot."

This flexibility made chocolate a medical superstar. By the 1600s, doctors were prescribing it for everything. The French physician Henry Stubbe wrote in 1662 that chocolate could cure "Hypochondriacal Melancholy" and "wind in the guts." It was the ultimate restorative for the wasted and the weak. Cardinal Richelieu's brother famously used chocolate to treat his spleen (and reportedly his temperament).

. . .

THE APOTHECARY'S CABINET: **Chocolate as a Drug**

By the 17th and 18th centuries, chocolate had moved out of the monastery and into the pharmacy. In London and Paris, apothecaries sold chocolate alongside laudanum and quinine. It was not sold in candy shops; it was sold in drugstores.

Before it was a candy, chocolate was a drug. 17th-century
apothecaries sold cacao paste mixed with ambergris and brick dust
to cure everything from anemia to heartbreak.

This era saw the birth of "medical chocolate" recipes that would horrify a modern palate. Doctors prescribed mixing cocoa paste with ambergris (a waxy secretion from whale intestines), musk, brick dust, or even steel filings to treat anemia. The fat content of the cocoa butter was prized as a carrier for these harsh medicines, coating the stomach and allowing the "drugs" to be digested.

Sir Hans Sloane, the physician to British royalty, famously created a recipe for "Milk Chocolate" not as a confection, but as a health tonic. He found the Jamaican water-based cocoa too bitter and nauseating, so he emulsified it with milk to make it more digestible for invalids. His recipe was sold by apothecaries for over a century before the Cadbury brothers bought it and turned it into a candy.

For nearly two hundred years, before it was a treat, chocolate was a prescription—a bitter, thick suspension designed to shock the body back into health.

INSIDE THE BEAN: Modern Science Meets Old Beliefs

In the 20th century, as sugar was added and mass production took over, chocolate lost its medical halo. It became "junk food," blamed for cavities and acne. But in the last few decades, modern science has swung the pendulum back.

==

SAFETY WARNING: CHOCOLATE AND PETS

Theobromine is medicine for humans but poison for dogs. Know the danger zones.

- **The Toxicity Scale (for a 20lb Dog):**
    - White Chocolate: Non-toxic (negligible theobromine). Risk is mostly upset stomach from sugar/fat.
    - Milk Chocolate: Dangerous at 4-5 oz. (A large bar).
    - Dark Chocolate (70%): Dangerous at 1.5 oz. (Less than half a bar).
    - Baking Chocolate/Nibs: CRITICAL at 0.5 oz. (A single square).
- **Symptom Watch:** Vomiting, rapid heart rate, tremors. If ingested, go to the vet immediately.

==

Researchers began analyzing the chemical structure of the cacao bean and found a pharmacy hidden inside. Cacao is one of the most concentrated sources of flavanols (specifically epicatechin and catechin) in the plant kingdom.

In carefully controlled studies, high-flavanol cocoa has been shown to boost the production of nitric oxide in the blood vessels. A landmark study of the Kuna people off the coast of Panama found that they had virtually no age-related hypertension. Their secret? They drank five cups of unrefined, flavanol-rich cocoa every day. When they moved to the city and switched to processed soda, their blood pressure rose.

The brain appears to benefit, too. Trials involving older adults have shown that cocoa flavanols can increase blood flow to the hippocampus, the region involved in memory. It's not a cure for Alzheimer's, but it echoes the ancient Aztec belief that cacao "invigorates the mind."

However, there is a catch. Most of these studies use potent cocoa extracts, not candy bars. The "Dark Chocolate is Healthy" headlines often ignore the sugar and fat that come along for the ride. To get the medical dosage of flavanols used in clinical trials, you might have to eat 500 calories of dark chocolate—a trade-off that nutritionists view with caution.

===

THE HEALTH AUDIT: HOW TO BUY FOR YOUR BRAIN

Not all dark chocolate is superfood. Processing kills the medicine. Look for these clues.

- **1. Avoid "Dutched" or "Alkalized"**
  - The Sign: Label says "Cocoa processed with alkali."
  - The Reality: This process reduces bitterness but destroys up to 90% of the flavanols
- **2. The 85% Rule**
  - The Sign: Look at the percentage.
  - The Reality: To get a clinical dose of flavanols without spiking your blood sugar, you need 85% cacao or higher. 70% is still mostly candy.
- **3. Check the Order**
  - The Sign: Sugar is the first ingredient.
  - The Reality: In a healthy bar, Cocoa Mass or Cocoa Liquor must be first. Sugar should be last.

===

. . .

CRAVINGS, CHEMISTRY, AND THE "LOVE DRUG" Myth

If chocolate is medicine, it is also a spell. Why do we crave it so intensely? Science offers a few clues, though perhaps fewer than the tabloids suggest.

Chocolate contains phenylethylamine (PEA), a chemical released by the brain when people fall in love. This led to the popular myth that chocolate is a powerful aphrodisiac and antidepressant. While romantic, the science is shaky; most PEA in chocolate is broken down by the stomach before it reaches the brain.

More likely, the "high" comes from a synergy of other compounds: theobromine (a gentle stimulant), small amounts of caffeine, and anandamide, a lipid known as the "bliss molecule" because it binds to the same brain receptors as cannabis (though you'd have to eat pounds of chocolate to get a buzz).

===

MYTH-BUSTER: THE CAFFEINE COUNT

Will chocolate keep you awake? Probably not. Compare the numbers.

- White Chocolate (1.5 oz): 0 mg caffeine
- Milk Chocolate (1.5 oz): 9 mg caffeine (Less than decaf coffee)
- Dark Chocolate (1.5 oz): 30–40 mg caffeine
- Cup of Coffee (8 oz): 95–200 mg caffeine

Verdict: You would need to eat four entire bars of dark chocolate to get the buzz of one small coffee. The energy you feel is likely from Theobromine, which widens blood vessels rather than stressing the nervous system.

===

THE REAL DRUG, however, might just be the "orosensory" experience. The perfect melting point of cocoa butter (just below body temperature), combined with the sugar-fat ratio, lights up the brain's reward centers like a pinball machine. It is the ultimate comfort food, chemically engineered by nature to soothe.

MINDFUL INDULGENCE: **Chocolate in the Wellness Movement**

In the 21st century, chocolate has found its way back into rituals that would look strangely familiar to a Maya healer. The rise of "Cacao Ceremonies" in yoga studios and wellness retreats involves drinking thick, ceremonial-grade (unprocessed) paste to facilitate meditation and "heart opening."

While some claims in the wellness sphere border on pseudoscience, the underlying shift is positive. We are learning to treat chocolate as a functional food again. Consumers are reaching for 85% or 90% cacao bars, trading sugar for intensity. They are using raw cacao nibs in smoothies for energy.

Theobromine: The primary alkaloid in cacao. Unlike caffeine, it provides a gentle, widening effect on blood vessels, leading to chocolate's reputation as a heart-opener.

THE MODERN VERDICT parses the old healers' confidence into nuance: cacao is indeed a potent plant with real cardiovascular and cognitive benefits, provided it isn't buried under a mountain of sugar.

However, a word of caution is necessary regarding the "Health Halo." Since the early 2000s, manufacturers have aggressively funded studies to promote dark chocolate as a "superfood," often exaggerating the results to sell candy. While the flavanols in cacao are beneficial, one must be realistic about the delivery mechanism. A standard dark chocolate bar still contains significant calories and saturated fat. To ingest the amount of flavanols used in many successful clinical trials, one would often have to eat enough chocolate to consume over 700 calories. The "medicine" of the future may likely be cocoa extracts or supplements, rather than a justification for eating three dessert bars a day

==

THEN VS. NOW: THE MEDICINE CABINET

We have always used chocolate as a drug. We just changed the prescription.

- **1680 Prescription:**
  - The Cure: Hot Chocolate with Ambergris and Chili.
  - The Ailment: "Hypochondriacal Melancholy" and weak lungs.
  - The Logic: The heat and fat were thought to "grease" the body's humors.
- **2024 Prescription:**
  - The Cure: 85% High-Flavanol Dark Chocolate (20g).
  - The Ailment: High Blood Pressure and Cognitive Decline.
  - The Logic: Epicatechin (a flavanol) stimulates the production of Nitric Oxide, which dilates blood vessels and improves oxygen flow to the brain.

==

The cup that heals is shaped as much by context—lifestyle, diet, stress, and connection—as by the molecules swirling in the liquid.

The next time you feel a chocolate craving stir, you might pause and ask: What am I really seeking? Comfort? Energy? Connection? Then, rather than fighting the craving, you can turn it into a small act of healing. Choose a piece worthy of the moment. Sit down. Breathe. Let the chocolate melt slowly instead of disappearing. In that simple, deliberate act, you are participating in a very old tradition—one that links Maya healers, monastic infirmaries, and modern laboratories in a single, bittersweet thread.

6

THE GOLDEN AGE: SALONS OF SEDUCTION, DEBATE, AND DECADENCE

B y the mid-17th century, the secret of the Spanish court had thoroughly escaped. What began as a modified Aztec tonic—sweetened with cane sugar and perfumed with vanilla by Spanish monks—had transformed into the ultimate symbol of European luxury. Having crossed the Pyrenees and the English Channel, chocolate shed its austere origins to become the darling of the Baroque aristocracy. It was no longer just a drink; it was an event.

Soon, sipping chocolate became de rigueur at the French court as well. Across Europe, chocolate's reputation grew as something rare, refined, and faintly mysterious – part medicine, part aphrodisiac, and wholly status-defining. Only the wealthy could afford the costly beans and the elaborate process needed to grind, cook, and whip them into a proper drink. In royal palaces and aristocratic mansions, chocolate was not merely a treat; it was theater. The preparation and serving of a steaming cup of chocolate was an event – a fragrant ceremony that delighted the senses and signaled privilege.

THE DRINK of Kings and Courtiers

Chocolate had firmly established itself as the drink of kings, cardinals, and connoisseurs. Nowhere was this more evident than in Spain and France. In Madrid, the Spanish capital, chocolate was embraced with an almost fanatical fervor. As one contemporary remarked, by late 1600s there was scarcely a street in Madrid where one couldn't buy a cup of chocolate. The Spanish aristocracy adored it, developing myriad recipes – enriched with spices or even beaten egg yolks – and silver servingware to match their obsession. Spanish nobles would take chocolate at breakfast and again in the afternoon, often accompanied by small cakes or flaky *bizcochos* for dunking. According to colorful anecdotes of the era, fashionably late grand ladies even smuggled chocolate past their attendants to sip during long church sermons. This habit became so widespread that bishops in Spain eventually banned chocolate drinks from church – a prohibition that speaks volumes about both chocolate's addictive charm and its pervasiveness among the elite.

In France, chocolate's rise was equally tied to royalty. The Spanish princess María Teresa, upon marrying Louis XIV, helped establish chocolate's place at the French court (her story is told in detail later in the book). Thanks to such royal patronage, chocolate was firmly entrenched at Versailles by the late 1600s. Louis XIV granted a monopoly to his own chocolate-maker, authorizing in 1659 the first chocolate shop in Paris. This boutique on rue de l'Arbre Sec catered to the Parisian nobility, offering exotic chocolate beverages and pastilles. Soon other chocolatiers followed, and by the 1700s, Paris had a handful of exclusive chocolate shops serving the aristocracy and wealthy bourgeoisie. Still, chocolate remained an expensive habit. It was said that a skilled chocolatier's Paris shop could be "more profitable than a barony," as it satisfied the extravagant cravings of dukes, duchesses, and diplomats. Indeed, Louis XV himself was an avid chocolate lover who famously concocted his own chocolate recipe in his private kitchen at Versailles – a velvety mix of cocoa, sugar, and vanilla thickened with egg yolk.

Not to be outdone, Vienna's imperial court also acquired a taste for the cocoa bean. When the Habsburg Emperor Charles VI relocated his court from Spain to Austria in 1711, he brought with him Spanish chefs and the cherished custom of hot chocolate. The Austrian Habsburgs quickly became chocolate devotees. Empress Maria Theresa (daughter of Charles VI) employed her own personal chocolatier and owned an extravagant solid silver chocolate service, complete with ornate pots, cups, and bowls solely for her morning chocolate. At the Viennese court, chocolate was typically served at breakfast, fragranced with vanilla or cinnamon, accompanied by fresh bread and a glass of water on the side. In those Baroque halls, to present a dignitary with a steaming cup of spiced chocolate was the ultimate sign of imperial favor and hospitality.

Paris: Salons of Chocolate and Society

By the Enlightenment era of the 18th century, Paris was famed not just for its cafés and coffeehouses, but also for its salons – intimate gatherings hosted in aristocratic homes where literature, philosophy, and arts were discussed under the guidance of a witty hostess. In these glittering salons, presided over by figures like Madame de Pompadour or Madame Geoffrin, hot chocolate often made as grand an entrance as the intellectuals themselves. Unlike the rowdy public coffeehouses where pamphleteers argued politics over cheap coffee, the chocolate salon was a more rarefied affair.

This distinction was immortalized by the writers of the era. While coffeehouses were places of business, chocolate houses were targets of satire, often depicted as dens of gossip and vanity. In his mock-epic *The Rape of the Lock* (1712), Alexander Pope used chocolate as a symbol of aristocratic idleness, describing nymphs who "prepare their chocolate" not for sustenance, but as a ritual of the leisurely elite. Playwrights like William Congreve set scenes in chocolate houses to mock the frivolous intrigues of high society, cementing the drink's reputation as the fuel of the wealthy and somewhat scandalous.

Picture a high-ceilinged rococo drawing room on the Faubourg Saint-Germain: gilded mirrors reflecting candlelight across damask-covered chairs, a fire crackling, and on a side table an exquisite porcelain chocolatière pot kept warm for the guests. A footman in livery might enter bearing a tray of delicate Sevres china cups filled with a rich, mahogany-brown chocolate beverage. The air would be redolent of cocoa, vanilla, and sugar – an aroma that mingled with ladies' perfumes and the beeswax of candles.

In such salons, etiquette demanded grace and leisure. One sipped chocolate slowly, pausing to nibble a vanilla-scented biscuit or a tender macaron. It was a beverage to be savored in conversation, not merely consumed for thirst. Hosts prided themselves on their chocolate recipes and presentation. Some fashionable ladies insisted on chocolate "à l' espagnole" (in the Spanish style, dark and spiced with cinnamon), while others preferred it "à la française" (lightened with milk). Marie Antoinette, the last Queen of France, even appointed her own personal chocolatier, Sulpice Debauve (who would later found the famed house of Debauve & Gallais). She adored her chocolate à la Viennoise – served with a cap of whipped cream – often pairing her morning cup with delicate pastries. So enamored was Marie Antoinette of chocolate that she popularized new flavor combinations at court, blending her cocoa with sweet almond milk or orange blossom to soothe her nerves. Parisian society followed suit, experimenting with floral and nutty infusions to enrich their chocolate.

The cultural imprint of chocolate on Paris was evident in art and literature of the time. The Marquise de Sévigné, a famed letter-writer of the 17th century, both praised and teased the chocolate habit in her correspondence, at one moment urging her daughter to *"take chocolate, so that even the most unpleasant company seems agreeable to you,"* and at another warning that too much chocolate might inflame one's health or passions. Meanwhile, painters like François Boucher captured scenes of aristocratic life featuring the cherished drink – a mother tenderly pouring chocolate for her family at breakfast, servants attending with silver pots, and the entire tableau exuding comfort and luxury. Such images reinforced chocolate's status as a symbol of refined taste and domestic happiness in France. By the late 1700s, one could say that chocolate had woven itself into the fabric of Parisian high society – as much a part of the salon culture as witty conversation or the latest fashion from the court.

∼

===

TASTE HISTORY: CHOCOLAT À LA REINE (THE QUEEN'S STYLE)

Marie Antoinette preferred her chocolate thick and restorative. This recipe uses an egg yolk for a silkiness modern hot cocoa lacks.

Ingredients:

- 2 oz Dark Chocolate (70% or higher), chopped
- 1 cup Whole Milk (or Almond Milk, as the Queen preferred)
- 1 Egg Yolk, beaten
- 1 tsp Orange Blossom Water (optional)
- 1 tbsp Sugar

Instructions:

- Melt chocolate and milk in a saucepan over low heat.
- Temper the Egg: Whisk a spoonful of the hot liquid into the egg yolk (so it doesn't scramble), then pour the yolk mixture back into the pot.
- Whisk constantly for 2 minutes until thick and glossy. Add the orange blossom water and serve in your finest porcelain.

===

MADRID: The Chocolate Capital of Spain

While Paris swooned over chocolate in elite salons, Madrid lived and breathed chocolate on a broader scale. Spain had been the first European country to embrace chocolate, and by the eighteenth century Madrileños of all classes were devoted to their beloved *chocolate a la taza* – a thick, pudding-like hot chocolate often enjoyed with crispy churros or toasted bread. In the grand households of Madrid's aristocracy, chocolate was a fixture of daily life.

The day might begin with a steaming cup served upon waking, and no elegant afternoon gathering was complete without the *chocolatada*, a chocolate service accompanied by an array of sweets. Hosts in Madrid prided themselves on providing chocolate in sumptuous style: porcelain cups set into filigreed silver holders, matching sugar bowls and spoons, and perhaps a *mancerina* – a specially designed saucer with a clipped holder to steady the cup and catch any drips, an invention credited to a Spanish marquis to protect ladies' expensive gowns from spills.

Step into a Madrid chocolate house or *chocolatería* of the 1700s and you would find an atmosphere both vibrant and convivial. Unlike the hushed aristocratic salon of Paris, the Spanish chocolatería welcomed a mix of patrons. By this time, chocolate had trickled down from royal courts to well-to-do merchants and intellectuals. Men and women might gather in the back room of a confectioner's shop or a shaded garden patio, gossiping about court intrigues or debating the latest edict from the King, all while balancing small porcelain *jícaras* (handle-less cups) of chocolate in their hands.

These establishments were often decorated in a simple, comfortable fashion – polished wooden tables, ceramic tiles to keep the room cool, perhaps a painting of the Virgin Mary or a tapestry on the wall – but the focus was firmly on the chocolate. A skilled *chocolatero* (chocolate-maker) would be stationed in the kitchen, grinding roasted cacao beans on a heated stone metate, mixing in sugar and cinnamon, and vigorously whisking the brew with a carved wooden frother called a *molinillo* until it developed a generous cap of foam. He would then pour the liquid gold into cups and send them out to the eagerly awaiting guests. Contemporary accounts noted that some aficionados in Spain could drink chocolate cup after cup, sometimes six or more in a row, so delightful and fortifying was this beverage.

Chocolate in Spain also took on important cultural roles. The Spanish had a tradition of social gatherings known as *tertulias* – informal intellectual salons, not unlike the French Enlightenment gatherings, but often held in private homes or clubs. In the late 18th century, many tertulias centered around the ritual of sharing chocolate. Writers, poets, and thinkers in Madrid would convene to discuss art or politics over an evening chocolate service.

The richness of the drink seemed to lubricate conversation and spark creativity. It was said that some of the most lively debates in Bourbon Spain were fueled by theobromine and sugar. At the same time, chocolate's sensuous reputation continued to intrigue. The Jesuit chroniclers of the era noted both its popularity and the Church's ambivalence: on one hand, monks and nuns in Spanish monasteries enjoyed chocolate regularly as a source of energy during fasts; on the other hand, some moralists warned that chocolate's pleasures might lead to sin or excess. Despite occasional finger-wagging, the people of Madrid remained enamored.

By the 19th century, the city was truly a chocolate capital, home to both cherished old-style chocolaterías (one of which, San Ginés, would open in 1894 and become a Madrid institution) and new chocolate factories churning out bars and confections for a mass market. But during the golden age, it was the custom of gathering in person, cup in hand, that defined Madrid's love affair with chocolate.

VIENNA: Coffeehouse Meets Chocolate Salon

Vienna in the eighteenth and nineteenth centuries was a city where two caffeinated worlds mingled: the lively coffeehouse culture and the rarified chocolate traditions of the court. Famous for its grand cafés where composers and poets lingered over coffee and newspapers, Vienna gradually extended equal affection to chocolate as well. In the early 1700s, chocolate remained a privilege of the nobility here, as in Spain and France.

The Habsburg emperors and empresses treated chocolate as a treasure from their Spanish kin. Noble families in Vienna arranged for shipments of cacao and employed their own *Chocolademacher*. These chocolate-makers were often Italian or Spanish specialists invited to the city, and they guarded their recipes closely. At first, strict guild laws in Vienna actually forbade coffeehouse proprietors from serving chocolate beverages; chocolate could only be sold by licensed chocolate-makers and typically in solid or paste form to be prepared at home. Thus, for much of the 18th century, enjoying a cup of chocolate in Vienna meant being in a private salon or palace drawing room rather than a public café.

Nevertheless, the culture of the Viennese *coffeehouse* helped democratize chocolate by the turn of the 19th century. As regulations eased and public demand grew, coffeehouses – those smoke-filled parlors humming with violin music, chess games, and political gossip – began to offer hot chocolate alongside their famous brews. Imagine an elegant coffeehouse in Vienna, circa 1850: high vaulted ceilings, marble-topped tables, Thonet bentwood chairs, and large windows looking out onto the Ringstrasse.

At one table, a trio of businessmen huddle over the newspaper; at another, a young musician scribbles notes on a score. In a corner, a well-dressed couple in late-morning repose sip something other than coffee: they are each cradling a cup of *Wiener Schokolade*. This Viennese-style hot chocolate, inspired by recipes from the old imperial court, is a silky smooth blend of dark chocolate, hot milk, and sugar, topped with a flourish of whipped cream. The cream is unsweetened and fresh, a cool cloud floating atop the hot liquid. The effect is a delightful contrast in temperatures and textures with each sip. Viennese cafés quickly became renowned for this style of chocolate drink, turning it into a classic alongside the city's mélange coffee and Sachertorte.

Speaking of Sachertorte – the famous Viennese chocolate cake – its creation in 1832 by Franz Sacher for a prince's soirée underscores chocolate's evolving role in Vienna. What began as a drink exclusively has, by the 19th century, also become an edible art. The court confectioners of Vienna, such as the esteemed Demel bakery (established in 1786), took chocolate in new directions, creating pralines, cakes, and ices.

Yet the hot chocolate tradition remained strong. Empress Sisi (Elizabeth of Austria) in the late 1800s was known to enjoy a rich cup of cocoa on her visits to Demel, preserving the imperial link to the beverage. Thus, in Vienna, the golden age of chocolate houses is intertwined with the golden age of coffeehouses. The city offered both experiences: one could savor chocolate amid the private luxury of aristocratic salons **and** in the public intellectual arena of the café. This dual life gave Vienna's chocolate culture a special flavor – both intimate and convivial, traditional and modern.

⮐

THE SALON EXPERIENCE: **Rituals and Elegance**

What was it actually like to partake in chocolate during this golden age? It was nothing short of a sensory ceremony. Preparing and serving chocolate in the 17th and 18th centuries required specialized tools, refined skills, and a touch of drama. In aristocratic homes, servants might begin at dawn by roasting cocoa beans over a low fire, then laboriously grinding them on a heated slab until a paste formed. This paste – often mixed with sugar and fragrant spices – would be stored in tablets or cakes. When it was time to serve chocolate, the cook shaved off a portion of the cacao paste into a pot of hot water or milk. Using a long wooden whisk (the Spanish *molinillo*), they would beat the mixture vigorously until it frothed, all the while keeping the pot warm over coals.

The serving vessels themselves were artworks. A typical chocolate pot (or *chocolatière*) was made of gleaming silver or fine ceramic and featured a tight lid with a hole in the center, through which the wooden whisk could protrude for last-minute frothing. Once the chocolate was adequately whipped and steaming, it was poured into small cups. In Spain and France, chocolate cups often had no handles (to feel the warmth in one's hands) and sat in saucers specifically designed to avoid mess.

The Spanish mancerina saucer, for instance, had an indented holder to grip the cup, an ingenious guard against spills in a jostling salon. In Italy and France, some sets included deep saucers that could double as bowls in case one wanted to cool the chocolate by pouring it back and forth. In any case, serving chocolate required a steady hand and a keen eye for presentation. A frothy cap on each cup was highly desirable – the foam was thought to lighten the drink and improve its texture.

Guests would each receive their cup on a tray, often alongside accoutrements: perhaps a crystal glass of water (to cleanse the palate or dilute the richness), and a plate of accompaniments. *Petit fours*, lightly sweet biscuits, or brioche were common, and in Spain, long fried dough fritters known as churros became a traditional pairing with the thick chocolate by the 19th century. The etiquette of chocolate drinking in polite society dictated that one drink in small sips (to avoid unattractive chocolate mustaches or spills on silk garments) and that one could refresh one's cup as often as offered. It was not uncommon for chocolate enthusiasts to indulge in multiple cups, especially if conversation stretched on and the pot was kept warm by the hearth.

===

ETIQUETTE CLASS: HOW TO DRINK LIKE AN ARISTOCRAT

If you were in a 17th-century salon, gulping was forbidden. Here are the rules.

- **The Tool:** The Mancerina - Do not hold the cup directly. Use the mancerina—a specialized saucer with a built-in ring to hold the cup steady, designed to prevent spills on expensive silk clothing.
- **The Dip:** The Bizcocho - Do not drink on an empty stomach. Dip a crisp sponge finger or bizcocho into the foam.
- **The Sip:** Small and Slow - Chocolate was a dense, fatty emulsion. It was sipped in tiny quantities to savor the spices (ambergris, musk, or chili) without overwhelming the palate.

===

There were also seasonal and regional variations in the ritual. On cold winter mornings, nothing was more comforting than a steaming, almost pudding-thick chocolate by the fireside. But in summer, some hosts served *chocolate glacé* – cold, even iced chocolate – long before iced coffee was a thing. The Duchess of Alba in Spain was said to serve chocolate chilled with crushed ice during her garden parties, a refreshing twist that still kept the luxurious aura. Another variant was "Chocolate with egg" popular in 18th-century France: a raw egg yolk was beaten into the hot chocolate to create a custard-like richness (a precursor to today's chocolate mousse). No matter the recipe, the emphasis was on lavish flavor and texture. The chocolate of this era was a far cry from the thin cocoa one might find today; it was more akin to a melted truffle – dense, creamy, and intensely aromatic.

And yet, even with all this decadence, chocolate had an air of refinement rather than gluttony. It was served in demure portions and sipped with decorum. Gentlemen might stand in groups discussing the latest news from abroad, each cradling a porcelain cup, while ladies reclined on settees, delicately bringing the rim to their lips. To be invited to share chocolate was to be welcomed into intimacy. In many languages, the word for a casual social call – a *chocolateada* in Spanish, or taking a chocolate in French – became synonymous with friendly gathering. The ritual bound people together, providing both a stimulant for the mind and a balm for the spirit.

Coffeehouses vs. Chocolate Houses: A Tale of Two Cultures

Throughout this golden age, Europe saw the rise of two parallel social institutions – the coffeehouse and the chocolate house (or salon) – each with its own atmosphere and admirers. Comparing them offers a fascinating glimpse into the social fabric of the time.

The coffeehouse, born in cities like London, Vienna, and Istanbul, was a bustling hub of commerce, news, and public debate. In a typical 18th-century coffeehouse, one would find long wooden tables, newspapers and gazettes tacked to the walls, pipe smoke hanging in the air, and a cross-section of society from scholars to merchants to clergymen.

Coffeehouses were egalitarian (at least for men); for the price of a penny cup of coffee, any respectable gentleman could enter and join the conversation. Topics ranged from politics and science to gossip and literature. In London, coffeehouses earned nicknames like "penny universities" for the education one could get in spirited debate there. They served coffee primarily, of course, but also tea, chocolate, and sometimes stronger libations – anything to keep customers coming and talking. The vibe was energetic, sometimes rowdy, and fundamentally public.

In contrast, the European chocolate house or salon was more often a semi-private enclave of the elite. While a few commercial chocolate houses did exist – especially in London, where White's Chocolate House and Cocoa Tree were famous haunts of the aristocracy – they quickly evolved into exclusive gentlemen's clubs or high-society rendezvous spots rather than open-to-all cafés. The clientele at a chocolate house tended to be wealthier, more homogeneous, and often looking for pleasures beyond intellectual discourse.

London's chocolate houses were hotbeds of sedition and gambling, where the elite gathered to sip the expensive brew and plot the future of the Empire.

Indeed, by the late 1700s, London's chocolate houses had a scandalous reputation: they were the playgrounds of rakes and fashionables, associated with high-stakes gambling, political plotting, and amorous adventures. One satirist of the time wryly observed that coffeehouses were for sober discussion of news and philosophy, whereas chocolate houses were for *"idleness, luxury, and vice"*. The rich sweetness of the drink itself was thought to encourage a languid, indulgent mood as opposed to coffee's sharp stimulant effect that fueled debate.

On the continent, the difference was less morally charged but still distinct. In Paris, many coffeehouses (like the renowned Café Procope) became gathering spots for revolutionaries and Enlightenment thinkers, buzzing with seditious ideas and pamphlets. The chocolate salons, however, remained refuges of the nobility and haute bourgeoisie, where the talk was more likely of art, music, or courtly intrigue than of democratic fervor. One might have discussed Rousseau's latest treatise over coffee at a public café, but it was over chocolate in a noblewoman's drawing room that one complimented the texture of the hostess's satin gown or planned an evening at the opera. Even in Vienna, as we saw, coffeehouses were the democratic meeting grounds of all walks of life (including musicians like Mozart and Beethoven), while chocolate was originally confined to courtly circles and only gradually entered the public sphere.

There was also a religious and geographic pattern noted by contemporaries: chocolate drinking was often deemed a "Catholic and southern" habit, while coffee was seen as "Protestant and northern." This stereotype arose because Catholic monarchies like Spain, France, and Austria embraced chocolate early (even getting papal dispensation that drinking chocolate did not break the Lenten fast), whereas in Protestant England, the Netherlands, and much of Germany, coffee reigned as the more common brew. Of course, eventually both beverages crossed all borders and faiths, but the association held some truth in the 17th and early 18th centuries. It meant that chocolate houses, where they existed publicly, often thrived in Catholic capitals, and the culture around them was tinged with aristocratic excess; coffeehouses had a more workman-like, bourgeois reputation.

In summary, coffeehouses were the bright coffee-scented daylight of Europe's emerging public sphere, whereas chocolate salons were the candlelit chocolate-scented parlors of its old-world elite. Each had its golden moment and its legacy, but during the height of the chocolate house era, the latter offered an experience more intimate, luxurious, and exclusive. Both, in their own ways, contributed to the social and political ferment of the times – one through noisy debate, the other through quieter networking and alliance-building over a graceful cup of chocolate.

Fashion, Art, and Courtly Taste-Makers

The influence of chocolate salons extended well beyond the beverage itself; they left their mark on fashion, art, and the very aesthetics of European high society. In the 18th century, to be a chocolate enthusiast was to be en vogue. Consider the fashion elements first: serving chocolate became an opportunity to showcase one's finest porcelain from China or the latest silverware from a Parisian silversmith.

Wealthy families commissioned entire chocolate services from artisans – ornate trays, gleaming pots engraved with family crests, delicate cups painted with pastoral scenes or trimmed in gold leaf. Possessing a beautiful chocolate set and displaying it during a reception signaled taste and sophistication. It wasn't just tableware; even clothing felt the impact.

Voluminous silk gowns in shades of rich brown (the color newly dubbed "chocolate" in fashion palettes) became popular for ladies, a subtle homage to the drink's hue. Men's waistcoats and breeches likewise saw deep cocoa-brown tones become fashionable, perhaps because the color both hid any errant drips and evoked the luxurious commodity everyone was talking about.

Artistic depictions of chocolate capture the era's infatuation. Aside from domestic genre paintings showing families taking chocolate, there were also sensual and humorous takes. Chocolate's repute as an aphrodisiac – something that could arouse passions – made it a titillating subject.

In French rococo art, one finds flirtatious scenes: a suitor presenting a lady with a cup of chocolate as if it were a bouquet of roses, or a maid secretly preparing chocolate for her mistress and a lover to share. Writers, too, used chocolate as a literary device. Enlightenment wits penned verses about it; one poet in Valencia wrote an ode comparing the making of chocolate to a sacred rite ("*oh, divine chocolate, they grind thee kneeling...*"), blending humor with genuine reverence.

Meanwhile, the ever-quotable Madame de Sévigné in France turned chocolate into a conversational topic across her letters – at one point gossiping that a Marquise's overindulgence in chocolate to charm a lover had led to her untimely death, a story both scandalous and likely apocryphal, but eagerly repeated in society circles.

At the highest levels of court, the ritual of chocolate even influenced diplomatic and social protocols. In the 18th century, a visiting dignitary might be welcomed to a royal palace with a formal *chocolate audience* instead of tea. This was a gesture of great honor. The flavorings chosen could be tailored to impress – an infusion of jasmine from the King's own orangery, or a pinch of costly ambergris (a whale-derived essence) to add an exotic muskiness. Marie Antoinette's personal chocolatier famously created concoctions to boost her mood or health, blending cocoa with orange blossom for calm or with sweet almonds to aid digestion. These recipes became the talk of Paris and were emulated by confectioners all over Europe, demonstrating how a royal whim could turn into a continental trend.

Marie Antoinette employed a personal "Chocolate Maker to the Queen" to prepare her morning cup, often whipped with orange blossom and almond milk.

Chocolate also left its legacy in the rise of European porcelain manufacturing. The desire to have domestic sources for fine china was partly driven by the demand for tea and chocolate services. King Louis XV established the Sèvres porcelain manufactory in France, and among its earliest and most prized creations were elegant chocolate cups and pots adorned with painted bouquets and gilding. The same happened in other nations: Meissen in Saxony and Capodimonte in Naples produced lavish chocolate sets that today grace museum collections. In essence, the culture of chocolate propelled advancements in decorative arts as each court vied to have the most resplendent tableware for their beloved drink.

And of course, the influence went both ways – as much as chocolate influenced art and fashion, the salons themselves became artistic spaces. Many a salonnière (female salon host) took pride in curating the experience in her salon much like an artwork: the furnishings, the music played in the background (harpsichord or string quartet soft in the next room), the assortment of chocolate and confections laid out on a mirrored tray, even the mix of guests invited to spark just the right chemistry of conversation.

All these details were orchestrated to create a certain ambiance, a fleeting work of art in social form. The golden age of chocolate houses thus contributed to what we might call the "art of living." It elevated a mere drink into an occasion for style, conversation, and sensory delight – a total work of art that blended flavor, design, and sociability.

Twilight of an Era and Enduring Legacy

As the 19th century drew to a close, the golden age of the European chocolate house began to wane. The world was changing: industrialization, revolution, and new technologies were transforming how people lived and what they consumed. Chocolate was no longer so rare or exclusive. In 1828, Dutch chemist Coenraad Johannes van Houten patented his revolutionary cocoa press, which separated cocoa butter from the ground beans, producing a fine powder that could be easily mixed with water or milk.

Soon after, innovators in France, England, and Switzerland figured out how to make solid eating chocolate in bars and bonbons. What had once been an elite beverage tied to ceremonial salons became an everyday pleasure available to the middle class in many forms. By the mid-1800s, a respectable English family might have cocoa with breakfast, a Swiss child could enjoy a milk chocolate candy, and a Parisian bourgeois could buy a packet of chocolate pastilles at the corner confiserie. The democratization of chocolate had truly begun.

With chocolate's diffusion, the old chocolate houses either adapted or faded. In London, the legendary chocolate clubs like White's and Brooks's evolved into gentlemens' clubs focused more on dining and politics (they had long since ceased to be about the chocolate drink itself).

In Paris, many of the early chocolatiers closed during the disruptions of the Revolution and Napoleonic wars, though a few, like Debauve & Gallais (founded 1800 by a former royal chemist), carried on the heritage,

selling "health chocolates" and confections to a new generation. Public
cafés continued to serve chocolat chaud, but increasingly it was just one
menu item among many in the thriving café culture that defined 19th-
century Paris. Meanwhile, in Spain, the cherished ritual of thick hot
chocolate did persist as a popular custom – in fact, it became more
deeply ingrained as a comfort of everyday life rather than a privilege of
aristocrats. By late 19th century, Madrid's chocolaterías were frequented
by all strata of society, especially for the tradition of late-night *chocolate y
churros* after theater performances or as a warming treat in winter.

Vienna perhaps best preserved the feel of the old chocolate salon
within its grand coffeehouses. Even as powdered cocoa made the
beverage easier to prepare, the Viennese kept a sense of ceremony: a
Wiener Schokolade would still arrive on a silver tray with a glass of water
and a little cookie, maintaining the gracious habits of earlier times.
Confectionery dynasties like Demel and later Hotel Sacher ensured that
the mystique of royal chocolate consumption – whether as a drink or a
cake – survived well into the 20th century in Vienna, as an attraction for
tourists and a nostalgic indulgence for locals.

Though the true golden age had passed, its legacy lived on in various
ways. For one, Europe's renowned café and tea-room culture around
1900 often harkened back to the elegance of the chocolate salons. In
Paris, for example, the Angelina Tea Room opened in 1903 with Belle
Époque splendor, serving its signature *African* hot chocolate – almost as
thick as pudding – to a new generation of chocolate lovers including
Coco Chanel and Marcel Proust. Such establishments consciously
evoked the refinement of an earlier era, complete with marble-topped
tables, mirrored walls, and impeccably dressed waiters pouring rich
chocolate from porcelain pitchers. In Madrid, Chocolatería San Ginés
became famous for its no-frills 19th-century charm, with green wooden
paneling and marble counters, where one can still stand and sip chocolate that's virtually the same recipe enjoyed centuries ago.

Moreover, the idea of the chocolate house has seen a modest revival
in modern times. Specialty chocolate cafés and "chocolate bars" (playfully so-called) in cities around the world now attempt to create intimate
spaces for savoring high-quality drinking chocolate, often referencing
history in their decor and menus. A 21st-century visitor to such a café

might sample an *ancien régime*-style hot chocolate spiced with cinnamon and chili, or a Viennese chocolate with whipped cream, served in an elegant demitasse cup – small gestures that pay homage to the golden age.

Perhaps the most profound legacy is the way we still regard chocolate as something a bit magical, a treat that can transform an ordinary day into something special. We may no longer think of it as medicinal or exclusively aristocratic, but a hint of its romantic past remains each time we curl our fingers around a warm mug on a cold day or gift a box of fine chocolates to a loved one. The European chocolate houses of the 17th, 18th, and 19th centuries turned chocolate into more than a drink; they made it a cultural experience, a status symbol, a spur to creativity and conviviality. That golden age set the stage for the global love affair with chocolate that continues to this day.

In a modern world of mass production and quick consumption, it's comforting to recall that once upon a time people slowed down to sip their chocolate from porcelain cups, in gilded rooms filled with music and conversation. The golden age of European chocolate houses may have been ephemeral – a few shining centuries – but it left behind an enduring ideal of chocolate as something to be savored, shared, and celebrated. And in that sense, whenever we enjoy a particularly rich hot cocoa or delight in the perfect chocolate dessert, we are, in a small way, keeping the spirit of those elegant salons and buzzing chocolaterías alive. The romance, luxury, and camaraderie of the chocolate houses live on in each velvety sip.

7

THE WOMEN BEHIND THE CHOCOLATE: UNSUNG HEROINES OF HISTORY

C*hocolate has enchanted humanity for millennia – from ancient ceremonial cacao drinks to modern candy bars. When we think of chocolate's history, names like Hershey, Lindt, or Cadbury might spring to mind. But behind the famous brands and innovations, there lies a rich tapestry of unsung heroines. Around the world, women have nurtured the cacao tree, innovated beloved recipes, preserved time-honored techniques, and carried chocolate culture forward. This is the story of those women – indigenous cultivators, visionary entrepreneurs, artisanal chocolatiers, and everyone in between – whose quiet contributions helped make chocolate the global treasure it is today.*

ANCIENT ROOTS: **Goddesses and Indigenous Guardians of Cacao**

Long before chocolate was a commodity, it was a sacred substance in Mesoamerica. According to Mayan legend, the goddess IxCacao – whose name means "Cacao Woman" – was a deity of fertility and abundance. In myth, IxCacao introduced agriculture (including the planting of cacao trees) and ensured her people never went hungry. As an earth goddess in a matriarchal farming society, she embodied the nurturing, sustaining role of women in food cultivation. While largely mythic, her story highlights how deeply women were entwined with cacao from the very beginning.

In real life too, women were the first custodians of chocolate. While the previous chapters explored cacao's ritual significance in Mesoamerican civilization, what often goes unmentioned is who did the work. The answer: women. Archaeological evidence—Maya pottery, Aztec codices —consistently depicts women at the metate, grinding cacao into paste, frothing the sacred drink. This was hard physical work requiring skill and patience.

Mothers taught daughters the art of toasting and grinding cacao, ensuring the knowledge passed generation to generation. In some Mayan marriage rituals, a prospective bride even had to prove her cacao prowess – demonstrating she could make a perfect chocolate drink – as part of the wedding arrangements. Such traditions underlined that women were guardians of cacao recipes and techniques that held community together.

Beyond the hearth, women also used cacao in healing and even subtle forms of power. Indigenous midwives gave cacao to women before childbirth for strength, and warrior women (yes, there were some) might drink it for courage in battle. On the other hand, Spanish records from the 16th–17th centuries reveal that some colonial officials feared the influence women could wield through chocolate.

In colonial Mexico, a few women were accused of witchcraft, charged with brewing cacao concoctions laced with herbs or even blood to cast love spells or to poison unkind husbands. Many of these were likely just *curanderas* (healers) or ordinary women using chocolate in home remedies, but the fact they were targeted shows how *women's intimate knowledge of cacao* sometimes threatened those in power. Despite these challenges, the everyday labor and expertise of indigenous women kept the culture of chocolate alive from the Aztec and Maya eras right into the colonial period.

~

From Convent Kitchens to European Courts: Chocolate's Ladies of Influence

When Europeans encountered chocolate in the 1500s, they initially found it strange and bitter. Here again, women played a pivotal role – this time in transforming chocolate to suit new tastes. Around 1550 in New Spain (colonial Mexico), the nuns of a convent in Chiapas undertook a little culinary experiment that changed history. They took the traditional Aztec chocolate (ground cacao mixed in water) and added cane sugar and vanilla to sweeten it.

Legend has it they might have also tried cinnamon and milk. The result was a velvety, sweeter chocolate drink that was much more appealing to European palates. This sweet innovation spread from convent kitchens to high society, igniting a craze for chocolate in Spain. Soon, drinking chocolate wasn't just an indigenous custom or a monks' pick-me-up – it became *the* fashionable indulgence of the Spanish aristocracy, thanks in large part to these creative nuns.

Women of the Spanish colonies and the motherland continued to be chocolate's champions, often fiercely so. As detailed in the earlier chronicles of the church, it was the noblewomen of Chiapas who famously defied the Bishop's ban on drinking chocolate during Mass—a defiance that legend says ended in poison. Whether protecting their morning ritual or innovating new recipes in the convent kitchens, women consistently defended their chocolate traditions against patriarchal control.

The 'Chocolate Girls': Women on the Industrial Line

While queens and aristocrats sipped chocolate in salons, a different class of women became the backbone of the industry in the 19th century. As chocolate moved from the apothecary to the factory, it was women who staffed the production lines.

In the public imagination of the 19th century, the woman making chocolate was often romanticized. She was the "Chocolate Girl," an idealized figure of domestic grace frequently depicted in European art— a maid in a crisp apron serving cocoa on a silver platter. But inside the Victorian factories, the reality was far less picturesque. Thousands of women worked long hours in the enrobing rooms of industrial giants like Cadbury and Hershey, their labor defined not by silver platters but by the relentless rhythm of the conveyor belt.

These women were prized for their dexterity. Before automation, dipping chocolates and wrapping foil were tasks that required delicate hand-eye coordination. They were the "finishers" of the industry. It was often their hands that gave the chocolate its final glossy look and its precise pleats of foil. In an era when industrial labor was grueling, the chocolate factory was often seen as a respectable, "clean" place for young women to work, creating a unique matriarchal culture within the factory walls that persisted until the rise of heavy automation.

Women in the Cacao Fields

While society ladies were sipping chocolate in salons, countless anonymous women toiled in the cacao groves to make those luxuries possible. Cacao farming has historically been a family affair, and across the tropics women have been the unseen backbone of cacao cultivation.

On small farms in the lush rainforests of Latin America, Africa, and Asia, it's often women who do the painstaking work of tending cacao trees: planting seedlings, weeding under the tropical sun, pruning branches, and harvesting the ripe pods. They balance baskets of heavy cacao pods, split them open with machetes, scoop out the sticky beans, and carry them to ferment and dry – tasks done while also caring for children, cooking, and managing the household. This labor is vital to the very first step of the chocolate supply chain, yet for generations it went largely unrecognized.

In the indigenous cacao-growing communities of Central America and South America, women have traditionally been keepers of the grove. For example, among some Mayan groups, women inherited the knowledge of which wild cacao varieties made the best drinking chocolate or had medicinal properties.

They would oversee fermenting the cacao seeds in banana leaves and drying them, ensuring quality beans to trade at market. Their expertise meant the difference between ordinary cacao and the highly prized "fine flavor" cacao that merchants and chocolate makers coveted. Even today, in parts of southern Mexico or the Amazon, one can find matriarchs who are respected for their cacao wisdom – able to tell when a pod is ready by its color or sound, knowing the exact fermentation time by smell. These women quietly preserve biodiversity and cacao heritage on their small plots.

Halfway across the world in West Africa – which today produces the majority of the world's cocoa – women similarly form the backbone of the industry. In countries like Ghana and Côte d'Ivoire, cocoa farming is typically done by families in villages. Men often hold the title to the land, but it's frequently the wives who carry out or supervise much of the farm work day-to-day.

A Ghanaian woman on a cocoa farm might rise before dawn to fetch water, help her husband in the field cutting pods, ferment the beans in plantain leaves, dry them on mats under the sun – all while also running a small side business or tending food crops. Despite their huge contribution, these women have historically had less access to training, land ownership, or financing to improve their cocoa ventures. They are truly unsung heroines of chocolate, working behind each chocolate bar we enjoy.

Encouragingly, in recent years these women farmers are gaining recognition and support. One inspiring example is Christiana Ohene-Agyare of Ghana, who in 2010 became the first woman elected as president of the Kuapa Kokoo cocoa cooperative. (This co-op happens to co-own the famous Divine Chocolate brand in Europe.) Christiana started as a smallholder farmer herself and rose as a leader, proving that women can helm even large farmer organizations in a male-dominated field. Under her leadership, the cooperative invested in programs to support female cocoa farmers – from literacy classes to giving women a voice in decision-making.

Another modern heroine is Leticia Yankey, who leads a 600-member women's farming cooperative in Ghana, helping women farmers earn better incomes and become business savvy. Thanks to pioneers like these, tens of thousands of West African women are now receiving agricultural training, assuming leadership roles, and being celebrated for their vital work. The cocoa-growing world is slowly waking up to the fact that when you empower the women, you uplift entire communities and secure the future of sustainable chocolate.

Even on a smaller scale, we find remarkable stories of women devoted to cacao. In the foothills of Cuba's Baracoa region, an older woman affectionately nicknamed *"La Reina del Cacao"* (The Cacao Queen) carries on a lifetime of cacao farming. Daisy, a grandmother with weathered hands and a warm smile, has spent decades planting and grafting cacao trees on her family farm.

She expertly pares away shoot tips to encourage stronger branches and teaches younger villagers how to ferment beans just right. Locals call her the Cacao Queen because her harvested beans are consistently the best quality – coveted by buyers. People like Daisy rarely make headlines, but their dedication and know-how form the bedrock of chocolate culture. They *literally* bring cacao from seed to sack, one pod at a time.

INNOVATORS, Inventors, and Entrepreneurs in Chocolate

Beyond the plantations and royal courts, women have also been innovators and entrepreneurs, shaping chocolate in forms we adore today. Some of these contributions came in surprising ways. Consider the classic chocolate chip cookie: an invention not of corporate labs, but of a resourceful New England innkeeper named Ruth Wakefield. In the 1930s, Ruth ran the Toll House Inn in Massachusetts. One day, low on baker's chocolate for her cookies, she chopped up a Nestlé semisweet chocolate bar and stirred the chunks into the dough, expecting them to melt. They didn't – instead, they softened into gooey morsels. Her accidental creation, the Toll House chocolate chip cookie, became an American sensation. Ruth's recipe was published in newspapers and on radio; eventually she sold it to Nestlé (the company even began selling "chocolate chips" thanks to her). To this day, every time we bite into a warm chocolate chip cookie, we're enjoying Ruth Wakefield's innovation – a woman's delicious improvisation that changed dessert history.

Earlier in the 20th century, another woman's home recipes launched a chocolate empire on the U.S. West Coast. Mary See, a Canadian-born widow, moved to California with her son in the 1910s. Mary was a superb candy maker; her hand-rolled chocolates, caramels, and toffees – made from fresh ingredients in her own kitchen – were popular with friends and family.

==

BAKING PHYSICS: CHIPS VS. CHUNKS

Why did Ruth's chunks melt, but modern chips stay pointed? It is all in the fat.

- **Chocolate Chips:** Engineered to resist melting. They have less cocoa butter and more lecithin (a stabilizer). They keep their shape at 350°F.
- **Chopped Bars (Chunks):** High in cocoa butter. They melt into puddles, creating layers of chocolate in the dough (laminating it).
- **The Verdict:** Use Chips for texture/crunch. Use Chunks for gooey, flat, bakery-style cookies.

==

In 1921 her son Charles insisted they open a chocolate shop in Los Angeles to sell Mary's treats.

They called it *See's Candies* and used Mary's image as the company logo (the smiling kindly woman on every box is Mary See herself). Mary, dressed in her trademark white apron, supervised the early production and taught the staff her techniques for quality candy. As the business grew into a household name across California, Mary See remained its beloved figurehead. She passed away in 1939, but her legacy lives on whenever someone in America unwraps a famous See's chocolate. It's a reminder that a woman's tradition of homemade excellence was the heart of one of the country's most iconic chocolate brands.

Across the Atlantic, one of the great chocolate entrepreneurs of Europe was Luisa Spagnoli – a true visionary of confections. In 1907, in the medieval town of Perugia, Italy, Luisa co-founded a small chocolate and confectionery company called *Perugina*. At a time when business leadership was almost exclusively male, Luisa proved herself an extraordinary talent. She started by inventing new candies (like a type of nougatine). Then, in 1922, as Perugina expanded, Luisa created a chocolate that would become an Italian icon: the "Bacio".

Legend has it that she wanted to use up leftover bits of hazelnuts from the factory floor, so she mixed them into a paste with chocolate and sugar, shaped it into a bite-size dome, and topped it with a whole hazelnut before enrobing it in dark chocolate. Locally they joked the lumpy candy looked like a knuckle and even called it *Cazzotto* (punch), but Luisa's business partner (and secret sweetheart) Giovanni Buitoni wisely renamed it "Bacio" – meaning *kiss*. Thus was born Perugina's Baci Kiss, complete with a romantic note tucked in each wrapper (said to be inspired by Luisa and Giovanni's own covert love letters). The Bacio was a hit – it became one of Europe's most famous chocolates, and it's still made the same way a century later.

Luisa Spagnoli didn't stop at chocolate: ever the entrepreneur, she later launched a successful fashion knitwear company (today a global brand under her name). But in Italy she is fondly remembered as the "Queen of Chocolate" for her role in elevating Perugina and gifting the world those chocolate kisses. Perhaps even more impressive, Luisa was a progressive employer – she set up daycare for her factory workers' children and advocated for women in her workforce to have opportunities. In Mussolini's era, that was quietly revolutionary. Luisa Spagnoli's life reads like a novel, but it underscores how a determined woman turned a passion for chocolate into a transformative business.

Women's inventiveness in chocolate took other forms as well. In the 19th century, as chocolate manufacturing industrialized, women were often the ones working on factory floors, hand-dipping confections or wrapping bonbons. Their skilled labor made mass production possible, even if their names didn't make it onto company letterheads. Sometimes, though, a woman's influence peeked through in unexpected places. For instance, the Baker's Chocolate Company (America's first chocolate mill, established 1765) adopted a young serving girl as its emblem – the image was actually from a painting by Swiss artist Jean-Étienne Liotard called *"La Belle Chocolatière" (The Chocolate Girl)*, depicting a maid serving a cup of chocolate. The company began using her image in 1862, and for over a century, that demure chocolate-serving maiden (a symbol of quality and care) was printed on every box of Baker's Cocoa. It became one of the earliest brand logos in America – a woman, front and center, representing the product. It's poetic that, even symbolically, a woman's face became the trusted emblem for chocolate in so many kitchens.

===

ICONIC BRANDING: THE BAKER'S CHOCOLATE GIRL

One of the oldest trademarks in American history is a painting, not a logo.

- **The Muse:** La Belle Chocolatière by Jean-Étienne Liotard (c. 1744).
- **The Model:** Thought to be a Viennese chambermaid named Anna Baltauf.
- **The Legacy:** The Walter Baker Company adopted her image in the 1860s to symbolize purity and domestic quality. It remained on the box for over 150 years, proving that a woman's image could sell millions of pounds of cocoa.

===

CRAFT AND COMMUNITY: Modern Heroines of Chocolate Culture

In recent decades, as chocolate making has shifted toward artisan and ethical production, women have surged to the forefront as craft chocolatiers, educators, and community leaders. They are combining passion for chocolate with social conscience, often drawing on traditions of the past to create a sweeter future.

Take Chantal Coady in the United Kingdom. In 1983, as a young woman barely out of art college, Chantal dared to open an unconventional chocolate shop in London called *Rococo*. At that time, British chocolate was dominated by mass-market candy; high-quality artisan chocolate was nearly unheard of there. Chantal, however, had a vision of chocolate as an art form.

She painted her boutique in whimsical colors, stocked it with exquisite handmade chocolates and single-origin bars, and educated customers on cocoa origins and flavor nuances. People thought she was dreaming – but she succeeded, essentially pioneering Britain's bean-to-bar and fine chocolate movement. Over the next few decades, Chantal Coady wrote influential books on chocolate, won awards (including an OBE from the Queen for her contribution to chocolate!), and mentored other chocolatiers.

Jean-Étienne Liotard's *La Belle Chocolatière* (The Chocolate Girl). In 1862, the Baker's Chocolate Company adopted this image as its emblem, turning the demure serving maid into one of the earliest and most trusted brand logos in American history.

After Rococo, she launched The Chocolate Detective, focusing on ethically sourced cocoa. Her influence is evident every time you see an upscale chocolate tasting or a origin-focused chocolate bar in a UK shop – that trail was blazed by a woman with creativity and tenacity.

In the United States, Katrina Markoff charted a similar innovative path. In 1998, Katrina founded *Vosges Haut-Chocolat* with a daring idea: infuse fine chocolate with exotic, global flavors – Thai lemongrass,

Indian curry, Hungarian paprika, bacon(!) – and make chocolate a vehicle for storytelling. Many skeptics scoffed at things like chili-spiked truffles or cheese-and-chocolate pairings, but her sensibility struck a chord.

Katrina's collections (often inspired by her world travels) won over chocolate lovers and won multiple awards. She is frequently cited as one of the world's top chocolatiers, and she paved the way for other women artisan chocolatiers who think outside the box. By marrying culinary art with chocolate, she demonstrated that *innovation has no limits* – a very empowering message for young women entering what used to be a very old-school industry.

Back in the cacao-growing world, a modern heroine, María Fernanda Di Giacobbe of Venezuela, has proven that chocolate can be a force for women's empowerment. A chef-turned-chocolate ambassador, María Fernanda saw both the incredible quality of Venezuelan cacao and the struggles of women in cacao communities suffering economic hardship. She founded programs to train local women in the skills of chocolate making – from roasting and grinding cacao beans to crafting beautiful confections.

By doing so, she created new livelihoods for these women, turning them into entrepreneurs who sell gourmet chocolates from locally grown cacao. Her initiative, "Bean to Bar Chocolates Venezuela", and her school, Kakao, have trained hundreds of women to become chocolatiers. In 2016, María Fernanda Di Giacobbe won the inaugural Basque Culinary World Prize (a prestigious international award) for using gastronomy to improve lives – recognition of how her chocolate revolution uplifted women and preserved Venezuela's rich cacao heritage.

Her protégées, often mothers and farmers' wives who had never imagined running a business, now produce award-winning chocolates and proudly call themselves "cacao artisans." It's a powerful example of how one woman's vision can transform an entire community through chocolate.

Even large-scale chocolate is benefitting from women's leadership. Remember the Ghanaian farmers' cooperative that co-owns Divine Chocolate? When Divine launched in the late 1990s as the first farmer-owned fair-trade chocolate company, it had a dynamic woman at the helm in Europe – Sophi Tranchell, the CEO – and strong women like Christiana Ohene-Agyare among its farmer-shareholders.

This partnership across continents was built on shared values of gender equity and ethical trade. Under Sophi's leadership, Divine Chocolate marketed itself by sharing the faces and stories of Ghanaian women cocoa farmers on its wrappers – a radical departure from faceless commodity cocoa. They also developed recipes to suit local tastes and pushed for social programs benefiting women, such as wells (so women wouldn't walk miles for water) and scholarships for girls. Divine's success in the competitive chocolate market proved that doing good and making good chocolate can go hand in hand. It also proved that when women are decision-makers in the chocolate supply chain, the benefits ripple widely – families have better income, children go to school, communities thrive.

While history focuses on kings and industrialists, the labor of harvesting and fermenting cacao has largely been sustained by women across the global Cocoa Belt.

Meanwhile, countless other contemporary women continue to blend chocolate with artistry and activism. There are chocolate sommeliers and educators like Dr. Maricel Presilla, a Cuban-American who is a leading scholar on Latin American cacao varietals and a James Beard Award-winning author sharing chocolate's history and flavors.

There are taste-makers like Chloé Doutre-Roussel, a French chocolate connoisseur who has advised cacao cooperatives in Bolivia and introduced high-end chocolate to luxury retailers. There are grassroots advocates like those in Guatemala's highlands, where indigenous Maya women run cooperatives that produce organic cacao and sell handmade chocolate bars, preserving ancient techniques to share with the world.

In virtually every corner of the chocolate map, women are making a difference: whether by improving farming practices, developing new delights, or ensuring that chocolate production becomes more ethical and sustainable for future generations.

Continuing the Legacy

From the divine *Cacao Woman* of Mayan myth to the pioneering entrepreneurs of today, women have always been the heart and soul of chocolate. Often their contributions went uncredited – hidden behind the label of a big company or the shadow of a king – but their impact is woven into every stage of chocolate's journey. They are the nurturers who tended the first cacao orchards and ground the first cocoa beans; they are the workers bending under the sun in cacao fields and the creative minds concocting new delights in pastry kitchens. Chocolate as we know it owes a debt to their labor, love, and ingenuity.

Today, when you savor a piece of chocolate, you might taste raspberries or sea salt, or sense the silky melt on your tongue – but perhaps also, in that moment, reflect on the *human stories* that made it possible. Think of the grandmother in the village coaxing cacao pods from the tree, the visionary woman who imagined a novel flavor, the mentor teaching a younger generation the art of tempering chocolate. These are the women behind the chocolate. Their stories – full of resilience, creativity, and passion – continue to unfold with each chocolate season. By recognizing and celebrating them, we not only honor unsung heroines of the past and present, but we inspire the next generation of women and girls to carry cacao history forward.

8

A WORLD OF CHOCOLATE: GLOBAL CULTURES AND CELEBRATIONS

B eneath the jungle canopy, a farmer splits open a ripe cacao pod to reveal sticky white pulp encasing purple beans. These seeds, once fermented, dried, and roasted, become the basis for chocolate in all its forms. Yet the journey from bitter bean to beloved indulgence is anything but humble—it's a saga of ritual and innovation, of trade and transformation. As we travel from the temples of Mesoamerica to the ateliers of Europe, from African villages to Asian megacities, we'll see, smell, and taste chocolate anew through the eyes of the cultures that cherish it.

CHOCOLATE IS FAR MORE than a delicious treat—it's a rich cultural tapestry woven across continents and centuries. From its ancient origins as a sacred brew to its modern incarnations as luxury confections and holiday traditions, cacao has been adopted and reimagined by people around the world. In the process, every culture has transformed this tropical seed into something singular: a food, a flavor, even a symbol that reflects their own history and tastes. What unites all these stories is a passion for chocolate's deep, complex pleasures and the way it captures our imagination.

. . .

LATIN AMERICA: Where Chocolate Began and Lives On

While much of the world treats chocolate as a sweet indulgence, the peoples of Latin America—the very birthplace of cacao—have maintained their ancestral chocolate traditions while developing new ones of their own. In villages and cities from Mexico to the Andes, chocolate remains a cherished part of daily life and cultural identity, not just a commodity for export. Here, chocolate's soul stays closer to its original form: as warming drinks, hearty foods, and even healing remedies, often prepared in ways that echo pre-Columbian roots.

The *Molinillo*: An intricate wooden whisk used in Mexico to whip air into hot chocolate. The foam was considered the "spirit" of the drink by the ancients.

Nowhere is this heritage more alive than in Mexico, where a cup of hot chocolate is more than a beverage—it's a connection to the past. Early each morning in Oaxaca's marketplaces, you might find vendors hand-grinding cacao on stone metates just as their Zapotec or Mixtec great-grandmothers did. They blend it with cinnamon, sugar, and sometimes ground almonds to make tabletas (solid tablets of rustic chocolate). These tablets are dissolved in hot water or milk and whisked vigorously with a carved wooden molinillo, producing a fragrant foam. The result is a spiced, foamy chocolate drink that is central to Mexican comfort and hospitality.

Mexico also gave the world mole poblano, the celebrated sauce that marries savory and sweet, with a hint of chocolate at its core. In this Baroque symphony of a dish, ground cacao is combined with chilies, nuts, spices, and fruits to create a thick sauce that's deep mahogany in color and layered in flavor. When ladled over turkey or chicken, mole becomes a feast that embodies Mexico's history—mixing indigenous ingredients (chili, cacao) and Old World spices (cinnamon, anise, cloves) introduced by the Spanish. To taste mole is to taste a marriage of cultures.

THE KUNA PEOPLE: The Archipelago of Cacao

Off the coast of Panama, in the San Blas islands, the Kuna people have maintained a relationship with chocolate that is unique in the modern world. For the Kuna, cacao is not a dessert; it is water.

Traditional Kuna families consume an average of five cups of cocoa per day. Unlike the sugary, processed hot cocoa of the West, their drink is prepared from lightly roasted beans, ground fresh, and mixed with water and often bananas or plantains for sweetness. It is a staple of every meal, consumed by toddlers and elders alike.

This massive consumption has made the Kuna famous in medical and anthropological circles. Researchers discovered that the island-dwelling Kuna have astonishingly low rates of hypertension and heart disease compared to their mainland peers. The secret appears to be their "chocolate bloodstream"—a life sustained by the flavonoid-rich, unprocessed cocoa that flows through their daily rituals. For the Kuna, chocolate is not a special occasion; it is the rhythm of life itself.

Travel further south, and each country reveals its own cherished chocolate traditions. In Guatemala and Belize, descendants of the Maya still drink cacao atol—a warm, thick beverage of ground corn and cacao, sweetened lightly, consumed as a nourishing breakfast or an evening comfort. In Colombia, a charming custom surprises many outsiders: locals often drop a chunk of mild white cheese into their cup of hot chocolate. They let it soften and then fish out the melty, sweet-salty treasure with a spoon—a delightful textural contrast and a breakfast staple in the Andean region.

==

TRY THIS: A GLOBAL HOT CHOCOLATE FLIGHT

Chocolate is a shapeshifter. Try these three distinct drinking styles to taste the culture.

- The Colombian (Chocolate Santafereño)
  - The Twist: Savory Cheese.
  - The Method: Prepare a cup of hot chocolate using water (not milk). Drop in two cubes of mild, white cheese (like mozzarella or queso fresco). Let them soften for a minute. Spoon out the melty cheese while sipping the sweet broth.
- The Viennese (Wiener Schokolade)
  - The Twist: Egg Yolk & Cream.
  - The Method: Whisk an egg yolk into your hot milk/chocolate mixture (do not boil!) to create a rich custard texture. Top with a mountain of unsweetened whipped cream.
- The Mexican (Champurrado)
  - The Twist: Corn & Spice.
  - The Method: Dissolve a tablespoon of masa harina (corn flour) into water to create a thick, porridge-like base. Whisk in chocolate discs, cinnamon, and anise. It eats like a meal.

==

In Venezuela and Ecuador, countries famous for their exquisite cacao varieties, local chocolatiers now craft fine bars celebrating regional flavors, and a new generation of bean-to-bar makers is turning their inherited cacao heritage into world-class chocolate.

EUROPE: Where Chocolate Became Confection

When chocolate entered Europe in the 16th and 17th centuries, it arrived as an exotic treasure—part potion, part status-laden luxury. At first, only Spanish aristocrats and clergy had access to the "brown gold" from across the ocean. In Spain's elegant mansions and monasteries, the bitter Aztec drink slowly evolved into a richer, sweeter confection better suited to European tastes. By the 1600s, the habit of drinking chocolate had spread from Iberia to Italy, France, and beyond, becoming all the rage among European nobility—an indulgence, a fashion, even a symbol of wealth and refinement.

Each European nation put its own twist on chocolate, reflecting local palate and pride. Spain cherished its thick hot chocolate, often served with fried churros for breakfast—a tradition that lives on in Madrid's old chocolaterías. Italy invented gianduja during the Napoleonic era, a blend of chocolate with finely ground Piedmont hazelnuts (born of cocoa shortages, but so delicious it endured; think of today's Nutella, its famous descendant). In the city of Turin, they crafted the bicerin, a layered hot drink of espresso, chocolate, and cream that remains a cozy Italian treat.

===

DEFINITIONS: HOT COCOA VS. DRINKING CHOCOLATE

They are not synonyms. One is a comfort drink; the other is a meal.

- Hot Cocoa:
  - Base: Cocoa Powder (The fat has been removed).
  - Texture: Thin, milky, sweet.
  - Purpose: Quick warmth and sugar.
- Drinking Chocolate:
  - Base: Solid Chocolate (Contains all the cocoa butter).
  - Texture: Thick, rich, velvety, coats the tongue.
  - Purpose: Savoring the flavor nuances of the bean.

===

France became renowned for its haute chocolaterie—elegant bonbons infused with perfumes of jasmine, bergamot, or Armagnac brandy, elevating chocolate-making to an art akin to perfumery and patisserie. Switzerland's milk chocolate and truffles gained a reputation for exceptional creaminess and quality, turning brands like Lindt and Nestlé into global icons. Meanwhile, Britain embraced chocolate as an everyday pleasure, pioneering the first chocolate Easter eggs and popular bars, weaving chocolate into holiday traditions and the fabric of childhood memories.

Easter in Europe: From Eggs to Chocolate Bunnies. Easter, the Christian celebration of resurrection and new life, has long featured the egg as a symbol of rebirth. Centuries ago, people decorated real eggs in vibrant colors to celebrate the end of winter. In the 19th century, European chocolatiers in France and Germany hit upon a brilliant idea: why not make those eggs out of chocolate? The first chocolate Easter eggs were small and solid, but technology soon allowed for beautiful hollow eggs wrapped in foil.

Today, Easter and chocolate are nearly inseparable in many parts of the world. In Europe and North America, children wake up on Easter morning to hunt for chocolate eggs hidden in gardens and homes. The Easter Bunny often leaves baskets filled with chocolate rabbits, eggs, and chicks. Beyond the playful aspect, there's symbolism in these goodies: breaking open a chocolate egg evokes the emergence of new life, aligning perfectly with Easter's themes of spring renewal and hope. In countries like Italy and France, some Easter eggs are giant, elaborately decorated confections shared by the whole family—truly communal chocolate feasts.

During the winter holidays, chocolate brings warmth and cheer to countless celebrations. In Europe, the legacy of Saint Nicholas giving coins to children lives on as gold-foil chocolate coins tucked into Christmas stockings. Many families count down to Christmas with advent calendars that reveal a tiny piece of chocolate each day—a daily dose of joy in December. There's also the beloved Bûche de Noël, or Yule log cake, a rolled chocolate cake decorated like a log, symbolizing the warm hearth of old winter traditions. From a cup of spiced hot cocoa shared by the fire to foil-wrapped chocolate Santas on the tree, chocolate has become a classic part of Christmas around the globe, embodying generosity, comfort, and togetherness.

==

KITCHEN CRAFT: HOW TO MAKE HOLLOW FIGURES

Want to make an Easter Egg or a Chocolate Santa? You don't need a heavy solid block. You need centrifugal force.

The Method:

- Clean: Polish your mold cavities with a cotton ball. Any dust will show on the final chocolate.
- Fill: Pour tempered chocolate into the mold until full. Tap the side firmly to release air bubbles.
- Dump: Immediately flip the mold upside down over your bowl. Let the excess drip out.
- Rotate: Flip it upright. Run a spatula over the top to clean the edges. Place it face down on parchment paper.
- Cool: As it cools, the thin shell clings to the walls. Once hard, it will pop right out.

==

Asia: The New Chocolate Frontier

When chocolate first journeyed to Asia, it arrived as part of the wave of Western influence and colonialism. But in true Asian fashion, it has since been transformed, localized, and even elevated in unexpected ways. Across the vast continent, from the tea houses of Tokyo to the spice bazaars of Mumbai, chocolate has been blended with tea and tofu, spices and fruits, rituals and pop culture, resulting in a kaleidoscope of flavors and traditions.

In Japan, a country known for refining and reinventing foreign imports into something uniquely Japanese, chocolate found fertile ground. Perhaps nowhere else in the world is there such a proliferation of inventive chocolate flavors. Walk into a trendy sweets shop in Tokyo or Kyoto, and you might be greeted by rows of exquisite bonbons: matcha green tea truffles in white chocolate shells, capturing the essence of a Zen tea ceremony in one bite; yuzu citrus crème-filled chocolates that burst with bright tartness; sakura (cherry blossom) chocolates available in spring, faintly floral and pink.

Japanese KitKat bars have become the stuff of legend among chocolate aficionados—elevated to a cult item with limited-edition regional flavors like wasabi (a surprisingly pleasant mix of sweet and gently warm), purple sweet potato, soy sauce (yes, it exists, offering a salty caramel note), and Hokkaido melon. There's even a sake-infused KitKat, blending chocolate with the heady aroma of rice wine.

In Japan, chocolate is often reinvented with local flavors like Matcha and Yuzu, emphasizing texture and aesthetic perfection.

Valentine's Day, Japanese Style. Beyond flavors, Japan has folded chocolate into its social customs in unique complex ways. Consider Valentine's Day: unlike in the West, it's women who give chocolates to men on February 14th. This tradition is strictly codified into two categories: *giri-choco* ("obligation chocolate"), cheap bars given to bosses and male coworkers to maintain social harmony, and *honmei-choco* ("true feeling chocolate"), high-end or homemade truffles given to a romantic partner.

However, culture is shifting. In recent years, a backlash against the pressure of *giri-choco* has emerged. In a famous 2018 ad campaign, Godiva Japan urged women to stop giving obligation chocolate, sparking a national conversation about gendered labor. Today, many Japanese women are pivoting toward *tomo-choco* (friend chocolate) or *jibun-choco* (chocolate for oneself), reclaiming the holiday as a moment of personal indulgence rather than corporate duty.

Women often make elaborate homemade chocolates to express their feelings. In return, men reciprocate a month later on "White Day" with their own gifts (often chocolates or other sweets). This yearly dance has made Japan one of the largest consumers of fancy chocolates in Asia, with department stores setting up elaborate chocolate fairs every February, showcasing high-end brands from all over the world alongside native artisan chocolatiers.

Elsewhere in Asia, chocolate has mingled with local tastes in equally intriguing ways. In India, a land of spices and sweets, chocolate had to elbow its way into a very rich dessert tradition. Now it's firmly taken root. Indian bakeries and home cooks merrily fuse chocolate with subcontinental favorites: there's chocolate burfi (a twist on a fudgy milk-based sweet, now cocoa-infused), chocolate gulab jamuns (the syrup-soaked doughnuts turned cocoa-dark), and even spiced chocolate chai drinks on cafe menus. One might find a chic Mumbai chocolatier offering cardamom-and-chai-spiced chocolate truffles, or bonbons filled with mango-passion fruit gelée as a nod to India's revered mangoes.

In China, chocolate's rise is a more recent phenomenon—traditionally, Chinese cuisine doesn't have chocolate or similar flavors. But as the country opened up, chocolate became a symbol of status and modernity for the burgeoning middle class.

Imported European chocolates in elaborate gift boxes became hugely popular during Lunar New Year or Mid-Autumn Festival as sophisticated gifts. You might see chocolates filled with lychee ganache or jasmine tea essence, aligning with familiar fragrance profiles. Even the pungent durian fruit of Southeast Asia—infamous for its strong odor but beloved for its custardy taste—finds its way into some adventurous chocolate confections in Malaysia and Singapore.

Further north, China represents the final frontier for the chocolate industry. Historically, chocolate was virtually unknown in China, often dismissed as too sweet or exotic for the local palate. However, the last two decades have seen an explosion of interest, driven not by the candy bar, but by the gift box. In China, chocolate has been adopted as a luxury token of modern romance and prestige, heavily exchanged during weddings and the Qixi Festival (Chinese Valentine's Day). Unlike the West, where chocolate is a daily snack, here it is often reserved for high-end gifting, leading major brands to develop less-sweet, darker recipes specifically tailored to Chinese taste preferences.

One surprising chapter in Asia's chocolate saga is that some Asian countries have themselves become producers of high-quality cacao. Vietnam in particular has dazzled the chocolate world: farmers in the Mekong Delta grow cacao intercropped with coconut and fruit, and companies like Marou now produce award-winning single-province chocolate bars.

In the Philippines, where cacao first arrived via Spanish galleons in the 1600s, a resurgence of interest in local cacao has brought back the old tradition of tablea—pure cacao tablets used for making hot chocolate. Filipino chocolatiers are not only exporting their rich cacao tableas but also crafting beautiful chocolates with local cashew nuts, dried mango, and even barako coffee beans for a true Filipino flavor.

WEST AFRICA: The Cacao Heartland Reclaims Its Legacy

For over a century, West Africa has been the heartland of cacao cultivation, supplying the lion's share of the world's cocoa beans. In countries like Ghana, Côte d'Ivoire, Nigeria, and Cameroon, cacao orchards stretch as far as the eye can see, and millions of families' livelihoods are tied to the rhythm of the cocoa harvest. And yet, for much of that time, chocolate—the finished product—was a rarity in local markets.

The cacao beans would be packed into jute sacks and shipped off to Europe or America, disappearing from the farms only to return as imported chocolate bars few could afford. Today, however, a quiet revolution is underway: West African nations are beginning to reclaim their legacy and develop a culture of chocolate that is uniquely their own.

In Ghana, small-scale producers and bigger brands alike have started crafting made-in-Ghana chocolate bars and confections. Stroll through Accra today and you might come across boutique shops selling proudly Ghanaian chocolate truffles, bars, and powdered cocoa drink mixes.

Ghana's government even declared a "National Chocolate Day" on Valentine's Day—a clever initiative to promote domestic chocolate consumption and celebrate the nation's cocoa heritage. Schoolchildren are taught to take pride in cocoa not just as an export, but as something to savor with national pride.

One pioneer, Selassie Atadika, left a career in international aid to found Midunu Chocolates in Ghana. Her mission: to elevate Ghanaian cocoa and honor African flavors through chocolate. The result is a dazzling array of truffles infused with indigenous ingredients. Imagine biting into a silky chocolate truffle and tasting the zing of spiced hibiscus (a nod to the popular West African hibiscus tea called bissap), or the warmth of Nigerian ginger and lemongrass, or the aromatic spice blend of Ethiopian coffee with cardamom, even a hint of Guinean smoked chili in a dark chocolate ganache. Each piece is like a tiny map of Africa, telling a story of trade routes and local harvests. Midunu and others have proven that West African chocolate can be world-class and uniquely African in identity.

In Côte d'Ivoire, the world's largest cacao producer, similar shifts are happening. A new generation of Ivorian chocolatiers are experimenting with recipes to suit local tastes—which often means sweeter, milkier chocolates. Some incorporate ground peanuts into chocolate bars, akin to a West African version of peanut-studded chocolate clusters. Others flavor chocolate with local vanilla or cashew nuts. Meanwhile, Ivorians are discovering the joys of chocolate pastries and desserts; Abidjan's cafes now sell French-style chocolate croissants and éclairs made with Ivorian cocoa, a delightful full-circle narrative of influence.

THE MIDDLE EAST: Spice and Silk

Follow the ancient caravan routes and trade winds, and chocolate eventually found its way to the Middle East—a region already renowned for its sweet tooth and lavish hospitality. Though not a part of Middle Eastern cuisine historically (the Ottomans and Arabs of old had sugar, coffee, and confectionery aplenty, but no cacao until it was imported), chocolate was quickly embraced and blended with local tastes once it arrived. Today, from Istanbul to Dubai, chocolate has been woven into the fabric of Middle Eastern indulgence, often with a distinctive flair for spices, nuts, and luxurious presentation.

Turkey, straddling East and West, developed a chocolate culture that fuses European techniques with Ottoman-inspired flavors. A classic Turkish chocolate bar might be studded generously with Anatolian pistachios, those bright green nuts that Turks treasure like emeralds. Being one of the world's top hazelnut producers, Turks habitually pack their chocolate bars with whole roasted hazelnuts, resulting in a delightfully crunchy, nut-dense bite. Some Turkish chocolates hide a core of chewy Turkish delight or nougat inside, combining the old-world candy with the new.

In the Arab countries of the Gulf and Levant, chocolate has become an integral part of hospitality, especially in lavish gift-giving. It's common in places like Lebanon, Saudi Arabia, or the UAE to present guests with ornately wrapped chocolate pralines at weddings, engagements, or religious holidays like Eid.

But these aren't ordinary chocolates—they often incorporate Middle Eastern aromatics. Imagine a dark chocolate truffle infused with cardamom, that queen of spices which also flavors Arabic coffee, imparting a camphorous warmth to the ganache. Or picture a white chocolate bonbon delicately scented with orange blossom or rosewater, reminiscent of the syrups used in baklava and ma'amoul cookies.

There are milk chocolates sprinkled with toasted sesame or filled with date puree (a nod to the region's ancient date palm heritage, blending the caramel-y sweetness of dates with cocoa). One luxurious trend started in the Gulf is the use of camel's milk in chocolate—a chocolate with a subtle, unique maltiness and a whole lot of local character.

Eid and Diwali: Chocolate's Place in Festival Gift-Giving. Even festivals that have long traditions of other sweets are embracing chocolate in modern times. During Eid al-Fitr, which marks the end of Ramadan in Muslim communities, families typically visit each other and share sweet dishes. In addition to classic treats like dates and baklava, it's now common to offer chocolates to guests or give children fancy chocolate treats as Eid gifts.

Similarly, Diwali, the Hindu "festival of lights" celebrated in India and across the Indian diaspora, is a time to exchange gifts and confections in the joy of good triumphing over evil. Alongside traditional Indian mithai sweets, boxes of chocolates have become popular gifts during Diwali—a contemporary twist that appeals to the young and old alike. The universal appeal of chocolate fits naturally with the celebratory feasting and goodwill of these holidays, adding an international flavor to local traditions.

Modern Celebrations: **Chocolate Everywhere**

As chocolate has become a global delight, it features in an array of modern festivals and holidays on every continent. Beyond the historically rooted traditions, new customs continue to emerge, proving that any celebration can be a little sweeter with cocoa.

Valentine's Day Around the World. Come mid-February, shop windows around the world blossom with heart-shaped boxes and confections. Valentine's Day, celebrated in many countries on February 14, has become nearly synonymous with chocolate. While Victorian entrepreneurs (discussed in our packaging chronicles) popularized the fancy box, the modern holiday has morphed into a global economic force.

In the U.S. alone, consumers purchase 58 million pounds of chocolate during the week of Valentine's Day. The richness and indulgence of chocolate had long been rumored to stir passion—it was even used as a love potion in some older cultures—so it felt natural as a gift for one's sweetheart. Today, billions of dollars' worth of chocolate are exchanged every Valentine's season. In Ghana, one of the world's leading cocoa producers, February 14 has been declared National Chocolate Day. On this day, Ghanaians honor their country's rich cocoa heritage by sharing locally made chocolates, promoting both romance and national pride.

Halloween. October's spooky celebration has turned into a chocolate lover's dream, especially in the United States and growing globally. Halloween tradition dictates that costumed children go door-to-door trick-or-treating for candies.

More often than not, their bags fill up with chocolate bars, foil-wrapped bites, and cocoa-based candies of every kind. Neighbors delight in giving out treats, and kids trade their chocolate haul late into the night. The simple act of sharing chocolate treats on Halloween night brings communities together (with maybe a playful scare or two), proving that even ghosts and goblins have a sweet tooth.

Lunar New Year. Across China and other East Asian countries, the Lunar New Year is the biggest celebration of the year, full of symbolism for prosperity and good fortune. While red envelopes of money are the primary gift, modern festivities often include gold-wrapped chocolates shaped like coins or ingots as tokens of luck. Shiny chocolate coins in candy dishes or chocolate assortments in celebratory red packaging have become popular, blending in with the fireworks, lion dances, and family reunions.

Chocolate Festivals. In some places, chocolate has inspired festivals of its very own. Countries proud of their cocoa heritage or artisan chocolate culture hold events to honor the treat that brings so much joy. In Ivory Coast—the world's top cocoa producer—an annual National Cocoa and Chocolate Day in late September celebrates the economic and cultural significance of the cacao crop, featuring exhibits, tastings, and community activities. Similarly, chocolate fairs and festivals from Perugia's Eurochocolate in Italy to small-town chocolate days in the United States draw chocolate enthusiasts together. These gatherings are like carnivals for chocoholics, complete with chocolate sculptures, workshops, and endless samples.

ONE WORLD, **Many Chocolates**

From the sacred groves of the Maya to the chic boutiques of Paris, from West African villages to neon-lit Tokyo department stores, we have seen chocolate shape-shift and adapt, taking on the colors of each culture it touches. Yet, through all these transformations, there is a common thread: chocolate evokes passion. It tantalizes the senses—the aroma of roasting cacao that has drifted over jungles and factory towns alike, the velvety melt that people everywhere find so irresistible, the deep flavors that can be nurturing or stimulating, comforting or inspiring. Because of this, chocolate has been a connector across time and space.

Consider how one simple plant, the cacao tree, has given rise to so many expressions. To the ancients of Mesoamerica, it was a bridge to the divine; to a Belgian chocolatier, it's the medium for artistry and delight; to a Ghanaian farmer, it's both livelihood and now a newfound source of pride as they taste their own chocolate creations. In each place, people have poured their creativity, values, and local flavors into chocolate. In doing so, they haven't just adopted cacao—they've made it something singular, something that reflects them.

The result is a world of chocolates: spiced, floral, milky, bitter, nutty, fruity, raw or refined, hot or cold, solid or liquid. Each version tells a story of geography and tradition. Mexican chocolate speaks of cinnamon and chile and communal warmth; Swiss chocolate sings of cream and precision and mountain air; Middle Eastern chocolate whispers of roses and hospitality; Asian chocolate surprises with tea and seaweed and unbridled imagination. And yet, for all these differences, chocolate also unites us. A chocolate lover from California or London can travel to a market in Oaxaca or a café in Beirut or a department store in Shanghai, and find kinship in the shared joy of tasting chocolate—even if the form is new and unexpected.

As you savor your next chocolate—be it a cardamom-laced Arabic coffee truffle or a candy bar—remember that you are part of this grand story that spans millennia and continents. Each bite carries echoes of rainforest rains, sacred ceremonies, bustling bazaars, and inventive kitchens. It carries the imprint of countless hands: the farmer, the roaster, the chocolatier, maybe even a shaman or a monk from centuries past. It's remarkable that something so small and delicious can hold so much history and heart.

One world, many chocolates—each one a testament that food, like love, knows no borders. Chocolate has traveled and changed, yet remains universally beloved. And as cultures continue to mingle in our modern age, who knows what new chocolate traditions will emerge? The story is still being written, with every new recipe and every new enthusiast adding a line. One thing is certain: as long as the cacao tree grows and humans dream of flavor, the world of chocolate will never cease to amaze and delight us. Enjoy your journey, wherever chocolate may take you.

PART II

BOTANY, ECOLOGY, AND
THE SCIENCE OF THE BEAN

9

THE SECRET LIFE OF COCOA BEANS: FROM TROPICAL FRUIT TO GOURMET BAR

I n the lush, humid tropics, the journey of chocolate begins as a secret within a thick-skinned fruit. Amid broad-leaved cacao trees dappled with shade, vibrant pods ripen from green to sunset hues of orange, yellow, and red. Crack one open and you'll find a treasure of ivory-colored seeds embedded in sweet, sticky pulp. It's hard to imagine that these bitter seeds – cacao beans – will one day transform into silky, gourmet chocolate. Yet the journey from tropical fruit to a wrapped chocolate bar is a long, labor-intensive odyssey, one that marries traditional hands-on techniques with modern artisan craft. It's a story of nature and nurture: of farmers, fermenters, roasters, and chocolatiers each contributing to the alchemy that creates the treats beloved by chocolate lovers around the world. The path is rich and winding, full of sensory wonders at every stage. Let's peel back the curtain and follow the cocoa bean's voyage from rainforest to your palate.

Cultivation & Harvest: The Tropical Origins of Cacao

Chocolate's story begins with the cacao tree (*Theobroma cacao*), a finicky tropical plant that thrives in the warm, shaded understory of rainforests near the equator. Cacao trees grow delicate white and pink flowers on their trunks, which, once pollinated by tiny midges, swell into oval pods over the course of 5-6 months. Each mature pod, roughly the size of a papaya, hides 20 to 50 almond-shaped beans cushioned in fruity white pulp. Throughout the year – but especially during peak harvest seasons – farmers venture into the groves with machetes or long-handled knives. With careful, practiced cuts (to avoid harming the bark of the tree), they harvest the ripe pods that will yield the next batch of cacao.

Cacao flowers grow directly from the trunk, a phenomenon known as cauliflory. Only a fraction of these thousands of blossoms will be pollinated to become pods.

On the forest floor, a harvested pod is split open with a swift crack. Immediately, a rush of exotic aroma fills the air – a blend of tropical fruitiness and floral sweetness. Workers scoop out the wet cluster of beans and pulp swiftly, as each precious minute off the tree matters. The translucent pulp clinging to the beans tastes like a tangy sweet lemonade, a refreshing treat for those doing the harvest. But its true purpose is yet to come: this pulp will fuel the first crucial step in flavor development. The raw beans themselves are initially purple or pale and intensely bitter, nothing like chocolate. Yet the potential for greatness lies locked inside, dependent on a series of transformations about to unfold. With baskets full of wet seeds, the farmers move quickly to the next step before the jungle heat can dry or germinate them.

FERMENTATION: The Critical Transformation

The journey from bean to bar truly begins with fermentation—a stage so essential that without it, chocolate simply would not exist. Once extracted from the pods, the wet beans are heaped into wooden boxes or wrapped in banana leaves on the forest floor.

Over the next five to seven days, a natural reaction generates intense heat, raising the temperature of the pile to nearly 50°C (122°F). To the farmer, this is a period of vigilance; the pile must be turned regularly to ensure even heat distribution. Visually, the transformation is striking. The beans change from a vibrant purple or slate grey to a rich, deep brown, while the sticky white pulp liquefies and drains away. This heat kills the bean's germ, preventing germination, which is the biological trigger that forces the bean to release the enzymes responsible for reducing bitterness.

For the farmer, this is a period of vigilance; the pile must be turned regularly to ensure the heat doesn't rise too high or stay too low. Visually, the transformation is striking. The beans change from a vibrant purple to a deep brown, while the sticky white pulp liquefies and drains away. Once the heat kills the germ and the aroma shifts from fruity to vinegar-like, the farmer knows the batch is ready for the next crucial step: drying.

The Cut Test: The standard method for judging fermentation. A "slaty" grey bean is unfermented and bitter; a rich brown bean with fissures indicates perfect flavor development.

DRYING: **Under the Sun – Nature's Slow Roast**

After fermentation, cocoa beans are plump, acidic, and still loaded with moisture. To prepare them for travel and further transformation, they must be carefully dried. Farmers spread the fermented beans in a single layer across large bamboo mats, wooden trays, or concrete patios under the tropical sun. In some villages, you might see acres of shiny brown beans glistening in sunlight, being raked gently with wooden paddles.

==

QUALITY CONTROL: THE "CUT TEST"

How do buyers know if beans were fermented properly? They slice them open. Here is the color code.

- **The Slaty (Grey/Black):**
  - Verdict: Unfermented.
  - Taste: Astringent, bitter, rubbery. Zero chocolate flavor.
- **The Purple (Violet):**
  - Verdict: Under-fermented.
  - Taste: Harsh, grassy, and acidic. Needs more time.
- **The Brown (Deep Mahogany):**
  - Verdict: Perfect.
  - Taste: The cell walls have broken down, allowing enzymes to create the "cocoa" flavor precursors.
- **The Mold (White/Green Fuzz):**
  - Verdict: Rejected.
  - Taste: Musty. The entire sack is usually condemned.

==

The warm sun coaxes out moisture over several days, gradually bringing the beans from about 60% water content down to roughly 7%. This stage requires patience and watchfulness. If the beans are dried too quickly (say, under a scorching sun or forced hot air), residual acids can get trapped inside, leading to sharp or sour notes in the final chocolate.

Dry them too slowly or let them stay damp, and mold or off-flavors may develop, ruining an entire crop.

Daily rhythms on a cacao farm often revolve around the drying tables: beans are spread out at morning's first light and gathered under cover when afternoon rains sweep through. The farmers constantly rake and turn the beans, ensuring even exposure to sun and air. As they dry, the beans darken further and their aroma deepens from vinegary to softly cocoa-like, with hints of earth and fruit lingering from fermentation.

There is a quiet poetry to this process – a dance between tropical sun and farmer's hand, between nature and human care. In some regions with unpredictable weather (parts of West Africa or the Amazon, for example), traditional sun-drying may be supplemented by modern methods: solar dryers, greenhouse-like structures, or even mechanical dryers that gently finish off the process when rain threatens.

Artisanal producers favor sun-drying whenever possible, believing it best preserves nuanced flavors. After about a week, the beans are fully dried: you can hear a slight rattle if you shake one (the nib inside has shrunk away from the shell).

They are now stable, meaning they won't spoil easily, and are ready for the next leg of their adventure. Farmers bag the dried cocoa beans into burlap or jute sacks – each often 60 to 70 kilograms (a hefty load of future chocolate) – and the once-local harvest is now a globally traded product.

FROM FARM TO FACTORY: **The Long Journey**

Dried cacao beans typically must travel far from the tropical farms where they grow to the factories or workshops where chocolate is made. This stage of the journey is less romantic perhaps, but no less important. In village cooperatives, stacks of burlap sacks are loaded onto trucks, sometimes hauled by hand or donkey cart from remote farms to collection points. From there, the beans might head to a port, destined to cross oceans.

The global journey of cocoa is an epic in itself: West African beans sail toward Europe and North America; Latin American beans might journey north or across the Pacific; Southeast Asian beans travel to chocolate hubs in Asia or Australia. The export process is carefully managed to protect quality – beans must be kept dry and safe from pests. In the port warehouses, one can catch a faint whiff of cocoa amid the sea of cargo: a reminder of the riches inside these plain brown sacks.

===

DO THE MATH: WHAT DOES IT TAKE TO MAKE ONE BAR?
Chocolate is concentrated energy. Here is the cost of nature.

- 1 Pod = approx. 40 wet beans.
- 40 Wet Beans = approx. 1 oz (28g) of dried cocoa.

The Verdict: It takes roughly one entire cacao pod to make a single standard-sized dark chocolate bar.

The Tree: A typical tree produces only 20-30 pods a year. That means one tree supports only enough chocolate for a month of moderate snacking.

===

For craft chocolate makers – often located in cities far from any cacao grove – this stage is where they source their treasured ingredients. Many small-batch makers partner with specialty importers or directly trade with farmers, ensuring not only high quality but also ethical practices and traceability.

Some adventurous artisans even visit cacao farms personally, forging relationships and sometimes hand-carrying a suitcase or two of rare cacao back home! Whether by container ship, freight plane, or even canoe (in some remote Amazon cases), the beans eventually reach their destination. Each mode of transport has its traditions: shipping cocoa by sea in humid tropical ports goes back centuries (requiring well-dried beans and waterproof lining in sacks to prevent mold at sea), whereas air freight is a modern luxury used for small, precious lots that a chocolate maker might need quickly or in pristine condition.

Upon arrival at the chocolate workshop or factory, the cocoa beans often have one more rest period. Large chocolate manufacturers may store beans in climate-controlled silos for months or even years, blending origins to maintain consistency.

Artisan makers, on the other hand, typically work in smaller batches and often roast fresh beans soon after arrival to capture their peak flavor. No matter the scale, each incoming sack is a trove of possibility: inside are beans that carry the fingerprints of a distant soil, weather, and the hands of farmers who fermented and dried them to perfection. Now it's the chocolate maker's turn to carry the torch.

ROASTING: **Awakening the Aromas**

The roaster fills with a sound like gentle rain as beans tumble against the drum, and the air grows heavy with an aroma somewhere between fresh coffee and toasted bread. Stepping into a chocolate factory during roasting is a heavenly experience for any chocolate lover. This is the moment the quiet, dusty beans reveal their true potential.

The maker's goal in roasting is to develop the beans' flavor – much like coffee roasting – by applying heat carefully and evenly. After a quick inspection and cleaning (to remove any last bits of dried pulp, twigs, or the occasional stray pebble that might have hitched a ride from the farm), the beans enter the roaster.

In traditional chocolate-making, this might have been a simple clay pot or drum turning over an open fire, perfuming a whole village with the scent of cacao. Today, modern craft chocolatiers often use electric drum roasters, modified coffee roasters, or convection ovens for small batches, allowing precise control over temperature and time.

As the roasting begins, the beans make a gentle rattling sound, not unlike coffee beans cracking. Thin papery shells start to loosen and flake as the beans dry further and expand. The air fills with an intoxicating aroma: imagine the smell of brownies baking, mixed with toasted nuts and a hint of fruit. It's the same chemical reactions from fermentation now coming to fulfillment – the heat causes Maillard reactions and caramelization that bring out notes of chocolate, caramel, leather, berries, or smokiness, depending on the bean.

A lightly roasted Madagascar cacao, for instance, might give off whiffs of cherry and citrus, whereas a longer-roasted West African bean might develop deep classic cocoa and roasted nut aromas. Big industrial chocolate factories typically roast beans at high temperatures to a fairly dark degree, aiming for a uniform "chocolatey" flavor that will be consistent batch after batch. This often produces the familiar bold, one-note chocolate base we know from mass-market candy bars.

In contrast, artisan chocolate makers tend to roast more gently and tailor each roast to the specific origin and bean type. They treat roasting as a dialogue with the bean: a delicate dance of heat and time to tease out the bean's inherent flavor nuances. Some experiments might involve multiple small roasts of the same origin at different profiles – light, medium, dark – to decide which brings the best flavor balance.

Roasting typically lasts anywhere from 10 minutes to half an hour or more, at temperatures roughly between 120°C and 150°C (250–300°F), though every maker has their secret recipe. The endpoint is determined by aroma, color, even the sound of the beans – many artisans trust their senses over any automated timer.

When done, the beans have transformed: they're now brittle, dark brown throughout, and they truly smell like chocolate. But as tempting as they are right out of the roaster, you still couldn't make a smooth chocolate bar from a whole roasted bean. First, those papery shells must go, and the nib inside must be refined. It's time for the next step.

Cracking & Winnowing: Unlocking the Nibs

Fresh from roasting and cooled to handling temperature, the beans face a physical transformation. Each cocoa bean is composed of a rich inner kernel – the cocoa nib – enclosed in a thin, woody shell. That shell has done its duty protecting the bean through fermentation, drying, and roasting, but now it's an obstacle to fine chocolate.

The process of removing shells from roasted beans is called winnowing, an age-old agricultural practice (borrowed from grain processing) adapted for cacao. In small ateliers, one might crack the beans by hand or with a simple grinder, then shake and toss them in a bowl or basket, letting the lighter husks blow away in the breeze or with a fan. In larger operations, winnowing is accomplished by machines: the roasted beans go through a cracker that splits them into pieces, then a vacuum or blower system sucks away the lighter bits of shell, separating them from the heavier nibs.

What remains are the coveted cocoa nibs – essentially pure chocolate in its most rudimentary form. Nibs are crunchy and intensely flavored: you could nibble a few and taste the essence of the bean, albeit with a gritty texture. Some describe nibs as nutty, bitter, and slightly reminiscent of roasted coffee beans. They're a sought-after ingredient on their own (sprinkled in gourmet recipes or chocolate-covered as a snack), but for our purposes, the nibs are the intermediate step before we get something recognizably "chocolatey."

It's noteworthy that at this stage, all the careful work on the farm and in roasting really shines – if you smell a handful of freshly winnowed nibs, you can detect the primal notes of what that chocolate will become: maybe red fruit and oak, or maybe just a straightforward deep cocoa aroma, depending on origin.

The discarded shells don't go entirely to waste: many cocoa farms and makers compost them or even sell them as garden mulch or for making a light cocoa shell tea. But the spotlight now is on those broken bits of nib, which must somehow be turned from dry, coarse fragments into a smooth, flowing chocolate. The key? Grind them down until they reveal their hidden liquidity.

Grinding & Refining: From Gritty Nibs to Velvety Liquor

If you were to take those roasted cocoa nibs and crush them, you'd discover something magical: they are about half cocoa butter (a natural fat), so with enough pressure and friction, the nibs don't stay dry like a ground spice – they turn into a paste. In fact, traditional communities in Central America have done exactly this for centuries: grinding cacao nibs on a heated stone slab called a metate, they produced a thick, gritty cocoa paste that could be mixed with water and spices for the original chocolate drinks.

Today's many chocolate makers use machines to do the heavy grinding, but the principle remains the same. The nibs are poured into a grinder which crushes and grinds them into ever-finer particles. Initially, it might be two stone wheels turning within a stone bowl (a design that modern melangers still use, mirroring those ancient techniques). As the nibs break down, the fat (cocoa butter) melts from frictional heat and coats the tiny cocoa solids, creating a flowing substance known as cocoa liquor or cocoa mass. Don't be misled by the term "liquor" – there's no alcohol here. It's pure ground cocoa, the very essence of chocolate in fluid form.

In modern industrial production, grinding (particle reduction) is often a separate, rapid step performed by steel rollers. However, in small-batch craft production using stone melangers, grinding and conching occur simultaneously. These machines might churn anywhere from 24 to 72 hours, slowly pulverizing particles while aerating the mixture to develop flavor.

Early on, if you were to rub a drop of the grinding cocoa between your fingers, it would feel gritty; by the end, those particles are so small (often under 20 microns) that the human tongue can no longer discern them individually. This smoothness is a hallmark of quality chocolate – no one wants a sandy mouthfeel in a finished bar (unless it's intentionally rustic).

Modern refiners may use stainless steel ball mills or roller refiners to speed up this process for large volumes, achieving the same fine texture through different technology. Modern artisan makers often cleverly combine grinding with the next step, conching, in the same machine. As the melanger's stones grind, they simultaneously aerate and heat the chocolate, meaning the line between "grinding" and conching can blur in small-scale operations.

At this stage, chocolate makers also add other ingredients into the mix. For dark chocolate, it's usually just sugar (and sometimes a touch of additional cocoa butter for extra smoothness and easier melting). For milk chocolate, powdered milk joins the party; white chocolate, of course, contains no cocoa solids at all, just cocoa butter, sugar, and milk.

Some makers may introduce a bit of vanilla or a dash of lecithin (an emulsifier) to fine-tune flavor and texture. An interesting fork in the road appears here: traditional mass-market chocolate often incorporates a higher proportion of sugar and sometimes cheaper vegetable fats instead of some cocoa butter – creating what's technically known as "compound" chocolate – because it's easier to process and costs less. But these shortcuts come at the expense of flavor and that luxurious melt-in-your-mouth feel. In contrast, gourmet bean-to-bar makers eschew such substitutes, insisting that the only fat in real chocolate should be pure cocoa butter. They might also use less sugar, showcasing the cacao's natural flavor notes even if it means a more intense, less candy-sweet product. The grinding and refining stage is thus not only about texture, but also about flavor balance and purity. The choices made here – how fine to grind, how long to grind, and what (if anything) to add – will define the fundamental character of the chocolate. By the time this stage is done, what was once bitter, fibrous cocoa nibs has become a glossy, brown liquid with the consistency of honey. It's untempered, warm, and aromatic – if you dipped a spoon in for a taste, it would coat your mouth with a harsh, somewhat acidic chocolate flavor, a bit unrefined and tongue-coating. That's because we have one more critical refinement to go: conching.

CONCHING: Smoothing, Mellowing, and Rounding Out Flavor

The conching process revolutionized chocolate into the silky confection we know today. Before conching, chocolate was coarse and gritty. After conching, it became velvety smooth and more mellow in taste. The term comes from the Spanish word "concha" (shell), describing the shape of Rodolphe Lindt's original vessel, which resembled a conch shell. Lindt developed this process in 1879 in Bern, Switzerland.

But what exactly happens in this step? Conching is essentially the controlled stirring, aerating, and agitation of liquid chocolate for an extended time under gentle heat. By continuing to churn the chocolate (which by now includes cocoa solids, cocoa butter, sugar, and any added milk or flavoring) for many hours, several things happen. Excess moisture left from the grinding stage evaporates off. Volatile acids – leftovers from fermentation that can cause sharp or sour notes – are driven out as vapor.

The constant friction and mixing help coat every tiny particle of cocoa and sugar with cocoa butter, further refining the texture and creating that luxurious mouthfeel. In effect, conching acts like a polishing tumbler for flavor and texture, taking the roughly ground chocolate and refining it into something much more exquisite.

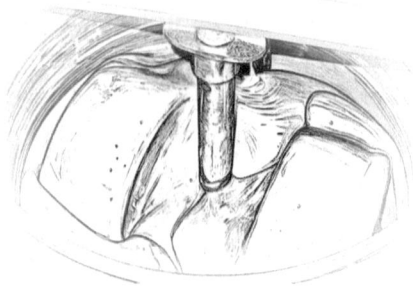

Conching: the process that refines the soul of chocolate.

Artisan approaches to conching vary greatly, and this is where a chocolate maker's philosophy often shines. Some makers conch for 48 or 72 hours straight, believing that a long conche yields the silkiest texture and most rounded flavor profile, with minimal bitterness.

Others may conch only briefly or even effectively skip a dedicated conching step (especially if they're using a melanger that has already been running a long time grinding) in order to preserve some of the more vibrant, fleeting top-note flavors of the cacao. Too long a conche, they argue, and you might lose certain fruity or floral notes; too short, and the chocolate might retain a rough edge or acrid bite.

Deciding the ideal conche time is part science, part art, and part personal style. The environment during conching is important too: the chocolate is kept warm (often around 50°C / 122°F) so it stays liquid and reactive. Large chocolate manufacturers have big steel conches that can process hundreds of kilograms at once, sometimes in open troughs that let the chocolate breathe; small makers might conche in tabletop machines or the same grinder used earlier.

From a sensory standpoint, conching fills the workshop with an irresistible perfume – gone are the sharp acidic hints, replaced by deep, harmonious chocolate aromas that make your mouth water. If you taste the chocolate at intervals during conching, you'd notice its evolution: early on it might taste harsh or inconsistent, but hour by hour it becomes smoother, milder, more homogeneous, and more refined on the palate.

This is also the stage where a chocolate maker will do a lot of tasting and adjusting. If something seems a bit flat, they might add a touch of high-quality cocoa butter to elevate the creaminess. If the flavor isn't sweet enough (perhaps the cacao is exceptionally bold), a bit more sugar could be added and dissolved through.

Generally, though, by the end of conching, all the ingredients have fully married. The chocolate is wonderfully liquid, glistening, and aromatic, with a complex flavor that reflects its cacao origin but without any one jarring note. The texture is almost there – but not quite a finished bar. For the chocolate to truly become what you snap and savor as a bar, it needs one final technical treatment: tempering.

TEMPERING: The Crystal Dance

Before chocolate can be molded into its final form, it must undergo tempering—a carefully controlled process of heating and cooling that aligns the cocoa butter crystals into a stable structure. This is what gives fine chocolate its satisfying snap and glossy sheen. The science and art of this remarkable process is explored in full detail in a later chapter.

MOLDING: Giving Chocolate Its Form

With the chocolate now smoothly conched, properly tempered, and ready to go, the next step is delightfully tactile: molding. This is where the liquid chocolate is poured into shapes – whether it be the classic rectangular bar mold, a delicate bonbon shell, or any number of creative forms artisans dream up. For a simple bar, chocolatiers use sturdy polycarbonate or silicone molds that are scrupulously clean and often slightly warm (to help the chocolate flow and settle evenly). They ladle or pump the tempered chocolate into each mold cavity, usually on a vibrating table or while tapping the mold gently. The vibrations and taps are important: they force any trapped air bubbles to rise to the surface and pop, ensuring a solid, flawless finished chocolate without holes or gaps. The chocolate fills every corner and engraving of the mold (many molds are embossed with the chocolatier's logo or artistic designs that will imprint on the bar's surface).

In a large chocolate factory, molding is an automated assembly line: spinning spouts deposit precise portions of chocolate into hundreds of molds that convey along vibrating belts and then travel through cooling tunnels. In a small workshop, molding is more intimate – you might see rows of molds being filled by hand and a chocolatier peering and thumping each one to chase out bubbles. Despite the high-tech possibilities, many fine chocolate makers stick to hand-molding because it allows for careful attention to detail, and frankly it's one of the joys of the craft to handle liquid chocolate in its gorgeous final state.

Once poured and leveled, the molds are cooled to let the chocolate solidify. Cooling might be done at room temperature or in a dedicated cooling cabinet at around 15°C (59°F) for a slower set that can enhance shine. As the chocolate cools, you can actually see it changing: it goes from glossy wet to a matte finish and then detaches slightly from the mold as it contracts. For an onlooker, the moment of truth comes when the mold is flipped over and the bars or figures drop out with a firm tap.

A well-tempered, well-molded chocolate will release cleanly and have a lustrous sheen and sharp detail. The undersides of the bars, which were against the mold's smooth surface, gleam like mirrors. The room fills with a rich chocolate fragrance intensified by the slight warmth remaining in the freshly solidified bars. Now you have a recognizable chocolate bar – but it's not quite finished. The final step in this long journey is to protect and present the fruits of all this labor.

Wrapping: The Final Touch

From the tropics to tempering, the cocoa bean's journey culminates in a beautifully molded chocolate bar. Yet one vital aspect remains before it reaches the eager chocolate lover: packaging. Wrapping a chocolate bar is both a practical necessity and a part of the overall experience. A fine chocolate bar is often dressed in multiple layers: an inner wrap (foil or plastic lined paper, sometimes even biodegradable film) that hugs the chocolate, and an outer wrapper or box that provides information and visual appeal. This dual approach harks back to traditions over a century old – since the early 1900s, chocolate bars have been commonly enveloped in foil to preserve freshness, then enclosed in a paper band or box.

Many companies have elevated wrapping to an art form. They choose materials that protect the bar from moisture, light, and absorbing external odors (chocolate is very sensitive to picking up surrounding smells). They also consider sustainability, increasingly opting for compostable or recyclable wraps that reflect the ecological care that often goes into sourcing their cacao.

Picture an artisan wrapping session: a stack of dull-gold foil sheets and a pile of freshly unmolded bars. Each bar is carefully placed on the foil, which is then folded tightly along the bar's edges, creasing neatly as if wrapping a precious gift. With each fold, the crinkle of foil is accompanied by the soft snap of the bar confirming its solidity.

Once swaddled in foil to lock in the aroma, the bar might slide into a chic paper sleeve or receive a hand-applied label. These wrappers often tell a story of their own – vibrant designs that echo the cacao's origin (perhaps motifs of Ghanaian textiles or Amazonian fauna), or refined minimalist packages that let a small window reveal the chocolate itself. Some include notes about the cacao variety, percentage, tasting notes, or a snippet about the farmers who grew the beans, reinforcing the connection between the finished product and its exotic beginnings.

For a chocolate lover, the unwrapping is a moment of anticipation and delight: you unfold the paper and foil to release that first burst of chocolate aroma that has been trapped inside – a moment that signals the finale of the bean's long voyage and the beginning of your personal sensory experience. The packaging may be modern and sophisticated, but it's also a nod to tradition: in earlier times, chocolate was a luxury often given as a gift, and a beautifully wrapped bar continues that legacy of honoring chocolate as something special. In essence, wrapping is the chocolate's debut outfit, preparing it to meet the world. It preserves the craftsmanship that went into the bar and offers a hint of the pleasure to come.

~

From Bean to Bliss

The life of a cocoa bean is a tale of transformation – a journey almost as complex and rich as the flavors of the chocolate itself. It begins in tropical orchards where nature imbues each bean with potential: influenced by the variety of the cacao tree, the terroir of the soil, the whim of weather. Through careful harvest and traditional fermentation methods, that potential is coaxed into reality as precursors of flavor. Sun drying, done as it has been for centuries, further develops the bean and readies it for the wider world. Across continents the beans travel, carrying with them the whisper of their origin, to meet the ingenuity of chocolate makers who apply heat, rhythm, and patience to turn raw earthiness into refined indulgence.

Each stage – roasting, grinding, conching, tempering, molding – is a chapter in the bean's story and leaves its mark on the final chocolate. Roasting adds the voice of warmth, singing out notes of nut, fruit, or caramel. Grinding and conching add the velvety texture and harmonize flavors, much like a long decanting mellows a fine wine. Tempering and molding lend the polish and form that delight the eyes and ears (that unmistakable snap!) as much as the tongue.

Throughout this journey, the interplay of traditional wisdom and modern artisan techniques is constant. Cacao farmers employ practices learned from their ancestors, even as some innovators bring new ideas to fermentation and post-harvest handling. Chocolate artisans embrace modern equipment to refine textures yet often uphold or revive old-world methods – from stone grinding to hand-tempering – when those best serve the flavor. It's a delicate balance of science and art, precision and passion.

For chocolate lovers enjoying a gourmet bar, understanding this journey enriches the tasting experience. The fruity zing you detect in a single-origin dark chocolate might hark back to a particular fermentation quirk on a remote farm. The silky melt and nuanced aroma are the direct result of hours of patient conching and the exacting tempering dance. The bright snap and glossy finish speak to skilled hands and keen eyes at the tempering stage. Even the intricate wrapper might connect you to the story of that bar's creation, perhaps illustrating the Amazon jungle or the faces of the farming cooperative that grew the beans.

In the end, a piece of fine chocolate is much more than a sweet treat; it's the culmination of a global saga and a labor of love. The next time you let a square of dark chocolate luxuriously dissolve on your tongue, take a moment to savor not just its taste but its story. From a cacao blossom in a faraway rainforest to the craftsmanship in a chocolatier's kitchen, so much had to happen for that morsel to exist. This "secret life" of cocoa beans – hidden behind every chocolate bar – is what makes gourmet chocolate truly worth appreciating. It's a story of nature's bounty, human dedication, and the magical combination of the two. And for those who are enchanted by chocolate, knowing the journey from tropical fruit to wrapped confection makes each bite even more profound – a little moment of wonder at how something so complex can taste so blissfully sublime.

10

FERMENTATION MASTERS: THE INVISIBLE ALCHEMISTS OF FLAVOR

Chocolate's irresistible flavor — its rich aroma, nuanced sweetness, and hints of fruit or flowers — owes much to an invisible army of helpers. Long before a silky chocolate bar melts in your mouth, tiny microbes have been hard at work transforming bitter raw cocoa seeds into the flavorful cocoa beans that chocolatiers prize. In the steamy tropics where cocoa is grown, these microbes are the true "fermentation masters," orchestrating a biological synthesis that gives chocolate its complexity. For chocolate lovers, understanding this hidden stage of chocolate-making offers a new appreciation of how much flavor is crafted not by sugar or cocoa alone, but by yeasts and bacteria living on the cocoa farm.

From Bitter Seeds to Bliss: The Crucial Fermentation Step

When cocoa pods are harvested, the journey to chocolate has only just begun. Inside each pod are dozens of almond-sized cocoa beans coated in a sweet white pulp. Fresh out of the pod, cocoa beans taste nothing like chocolate — in fact, they are highly bitter, astringent, and basically inedible. It turns out that fermentation is the key to unlocking their potential. Farmers have known for millennia that fermenting the beans after harvest is essential to develop chocolate flavor.

In a typical traditional process, farmers scoop out the moist beans and pile them into boxes or heaps, often lined and covered with banana leaves. This begins the fermentation stage, which usually lasts about five to seven days. At first, it might look like a simple waiting period where the beans are just sitting around. But peel back those banana leaves, and you'll find a miniature ecosystem heating up. The sticky pulp around the beans is teeming with sugars and acids, and within hours it becomes the playground for wild microorganisms from the surrounding environment.

Underneath these banana leaves, a microbial inferno is raging.
Yeasts and bacteria raise the temperature to 122°F, killing the bean
and birthing the chocolate flavor.

Despite all the advances in food technology, cocoa fermentation is still done much as it was centuries ago: relying on natural microbes in the environment. Farmers don't typically add anything — they trust nature to take its course, letting indigenous yeasts and bacteria colonize the pile. As one food microbiologist quipped, "we're still doing chocolate the good old-fashioned way because people love the way it tastes." Indeed, this time-honored step has a huge impact on the taste of the final product. Over the next several days, an invisible transformation occurs: the pulp breaks down, the beans undergo chemical changes, and a wealth of flavor precursors are created. By the end of fermentation, those once-bitter seeds have been chemically primed to become the chocolate we know and love after roasting.

A Microscopic Assembly Line: Yeasts and Bacteria at Work

What's happening inside a cocoa fermentation pile is akin to a carefully choreographed dance of microbes, each group taking turns and creating conditions for the next. In fact, the process unfolds in three main phases, led by different sets of microorganisms, each contributing unique ingredients to the flavor mix:

- Yeasts – The First Wave: In the initial day of fermentation, wild yeasts are the first to feast. The bean heap is dense and low in oxygen, a perfect playground for yeasts that thrive in such environments. Drawn by the sugary pulp, a diversity of yeasts begin converting sugars into alcohol (ethanol) and carbon dioxide. As they gobble up pulp sugars, yeasts also produce small amounts of flavorful molecules like esters (which can smell fruity or floral). This yeast party generates heat; within about 24 hours, the fermenting mass can reach temperatures around 40°–45°C (104°–113°F). That heat is not just a byproduct — it's crucial. Warming up the beans helps kickstart chemical reactions inside and will eventually kill the cocoa seed embryo, preventing germination and freeing the bean's internal enzymes to create flavor precursors. In essence, the yeasts set the stage: they reduce the pulp, produce alcohol and heat, and create an environment for the next microbes to thrive.
- Lactic Acid Bacteria – The Second Act: After a day or two, as the pulp breaks down and the heap is stirred or naturally aerated, oxygen begins to seep in, and conditions shift. Now it's the turn of lactic acid bacteria (LAB). These bacteria (the same kind that sour milk into yogurt or cabbage into kimchi) flourish and start consuming the sugars and byproducts the yeasts left behind. LAB produce lactic acid (hence their name) and other compounds. This acid starts to further ferment the

pulp and penetrate the beans. The presence of oxygen also allows some metabolic pathways that weren't possible earlier. During this phase, the heap might not heat up much more, but the chemical environment is changing: acids accumulating, pH dropping in parts of the pulp, and new metabolites forming. The lactic acid bacteria help continue breaking down bean pulp and generate compounds that will later contribute subtle flavor notes. They're effectively building on the foundation the yeasts established, softening the bean pulp matrix and preparing for the final microbial group.

- Acetic Acid Bacteria – The Final Transformation: With more air coming in (often farmers will turn the fermenting beans after a couple of days to introduce oxygen), acetic acid bacteria (AAB) take center stage. These bacteria love oxygen and use it to convert the ethanol (from the yeast phase) into acetic acid — essentially producing vinegar inside the cocoa heap. You might even catch a sharp vinegar scent wafting from a ferment at this stage. The acetic acid bacteria drive the temperature even higher, often peaking at 45°–50°C (up to about 122°F). The production of acetic acid, combined with the heat, is what truly kills off the cocoa beans' living tissue. The bean cells burst, and their internal contents begin to break down. While "killing" the beans sounds extreme, it's exactly what's needed: the death of the beans triggers the release of enzymes that start generating flavor precursors. Inside each bean, the high temperature and acidic conditions cause proteins to break into amino acids and peptides, and complex carbohydrates to break into simpler sugars. Two special protein-cutting enzymes (activated by the acidity) start producing what will become chocolate's flavor building blocks. Meanwhile, the acetic acid bacteria themselves also produce various metabolites and volatiles. The heap at this point is a hot, acidic stew of microbes, each group feeding on what the previous ones produced in a neat ecological relay.

Throughout these stages, other microbes join the mix in smaller supporting roles — from other yeast species to various bacterial strains — each nibbling on specific compounds and contributing their own minor flavor inputs. It's a lively microbial ecology, a succession where one community paves the way for the next.

==

THE INVISIBLE ASSEMBLY LINE: A FERMENTATION TIMELINE

Flavor isn't born; it's grown. Here is the 7-day schedule of the microbes that make chocolate taste like chocolate.

- **Days 1–2: The Party (Yeasts)**
  - The Fuel: Sugar-rich pulp.
  - The Action: Yeasts convert sugar into alcohol.
  - The Result: Heat rises. The bean dies (preventing germination). Fruity and floral notes are born.
- **Days 3–4: The Sour Turn (Lactic Acid Bacteria)**
  - The Fuel: Changing acidity levels.
  - The Action: Bacteria consume leftover sugar and citric acid.
  - The Result: The pulp breaks down and liquefies. Creamy, yogurt-like flavor notes develop.
- **Days 5–7: The Finish (Acetic Acid Bacteria)**
  - The Fuel: Alcohol and oxygen (from turning the pile).
  - The Action: Bacteria convert alcohol into acetic acid (vinegar).
  - The Result: Intense heat (122°F). Cell walls break down, mixing substrates to create the deep "chocolate" precursors.

==

By the end of the week, the feast is over: the sugars of the pulp are largely gone (and with them the pulp itself melts away or drains off as liquid), the beans have been fully fermented (and died in the process), and the microbial party winds down as the environment becomes inhospitable (all food used up, temperature cooling, beans now acidic and drying out). The once-white, slimy heap has turned into a mass of brown, fragrant fermented cocoa beans. Now they're ready for the next steps: farmers will spread the fermented beans in the sun to dry, and eventually the beans will be roasted, ground, and made into chocolate.

CRAFTING COMPLEXITY: **How Fermentation Unlocks Flavor**

Why go through all this microbial mayhem? Because fermentation utterly transforms the chemistry of cocoa, and flavor is all about chemistry. Before fermentation, a raw cocoa bean is full of compounds that taste bitter and unpleasant — notably a lot of polyphenols (tannins) that make your mouth pucker.

Fermentation causes many of those bitter compounds to diminish or bind up, reducing astringency. More importantly, fermentation creates a treasure trove of new molecules that will become the signature flavors and aromas of chocolate.

Inside the beans, the death and breakdown of cells release amino acids, peptides, and reducing sugars from proteins and starches. These are exactly the ingredients needed for the famous Maillard reaction that occurs later during roasting — the reaction that produces the browned flavors in cooked foods.

Thanks to fermentation, when the beans are roasted, those free amino acids and sugars will react to form hundreds of flavor compounds, including many that we associate with a chocolatey aroma (like rich nutty, caramel, and roasted notes). In fact, it's often said that without fermentation, you simply can't get real chocolate flavor — unfermented beans, even if roasted, taste flat, overly bitter, or like burnt vegetables.

Fermentation does more than just set up the precursors for roasting. The microbes themselves also create volatile flavor compounds during fermentation. As the Fungi and bacteria metabolize the pulp, they release alcohols, organic acids, esters, ketones, and aldehydes into the fermenting mass.

For example, yeasts might produce fruity ester molecules (like isoamyl acetate, which has a banana-like aroma, or ethyl acetate with a sweet, fruity smell). Lactic acid bacteria can contribute mild buttery or yogurt-like notes. Acetic acid bacteria generate acetic acid (vinegar), which in careful balance adds a desirable sharpness and complexity (too much would be unpleasant, but just enough gives bright notes).

By the time fermentation is complete, the beans are imbued with a medley of these microbial metabolites. Many of these volatiles will linger through the drying and roasting process, adding to the final aroma. Others react during roasting to form new flavor compounds.

The result of this microbial collaboration is astounding: chocolate is one of the most chemically complex foods we know. Scientists have identified hundreds of distinct flavor compounds in chocolate — by some counts, over 600 different volatile compounds in a well-fermented, roasted cocoa bean.

This diversity easily rivals that of famed complex products like wine or coffee. (For comparison, a glass of wine or a cup of coffee might each contain a few hundred aroma compounds; chocolate holds its own or surpasses them.) This complexity is why chocolate's flavor can be so rich and multidimensional. It's why you might detect hints of vanilla, red fruit, blossoms, nuts, or even caramel in a high-quality dark chocolate, even if no such ingredients were added — the magic happened inside the bean, courtesy of fermentation.

One expert who studies chocolate chemistry noted that chocolate's astounding flavor complexity "largely comes from fermentation." The irony is delicious: the same fermenting process that gives us pungent, sour foods like kimchi or yogurt is also behind the sweetness and allure of chocolate.

The hundreds of flavor molecules generated and unlocked by fermentation are what make chocolate's taste so captivating to our senses. So the next time a piece of chocolate overwhelms you with its aroma, remember that tiny microbes helped paint that flavor palette.

Terroir in a Cocoa Pod: Microbes Make the Difference

Beyond just making flavor possible, fermentation also makes flavor variable. If you've ever savored different single-origin chocolates (say, one from Madagascar known for its citrusy zing vs. one from Ecuador with deep floral notes), you've experienced how chocolate carries a terroir — a sense of place, much like wine does. Part of that is due to climate, soil, and cocoa bean genetics. But an often underestimated factor is the unique community of microbes that perform the fermentation in each locale.

Because cocoa fermentations rely on spontaneous, wild microbes, the exact mix of yeast and bacterial species can differ from farm to farm, valley to valley. The ambient environment contributes microorganisms — from the soil, from the surfaces of cocoa pods, even carried by insects attracted to the pulp. As a result, each fermentation is a little bit different.

One farm might have more of a certain wild yeast strain that produces extra fruity esters, while another farm's fermentation might be dominated by slightly different microbes that lean toward more acidic or nutty flavor precursors. These microbial differences can translate into subtle differences in the flavor profile of the beans after roasting.

Scientists in recent years have begun cataloguing the microbial ecosystems of cocoa fermentations around the world. They find that while the general pattern (yeast then bacteria succession) is consistent, the species present can vary by region or even by season. For example, yeasts of the genus Saccharomyces (famous for bread and beer) are common in many cocoa ferments, but in some regions wild yeasts like Hanseniaspora or Pichia might dominate early on. Similarly, the dominant lactic acid bacteria might be Lactobacillus fermentum on one continent versus Leuconostoc or others elsewhere. Each of these species can have different metabolic quirks, producing slightly different sets of flavor compounds.

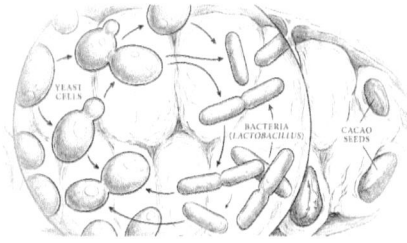

The invisible alchemists: Wild yeasts consume the sugary pulp of the fruit, creating the alcohol and acids necessary to transform the bitter seed.

Moreover, the dynamics of fermentation — how fast it heats up, how quickly pH changes, how long each phase lasts — can influence flavor. For instance, if a fermentation runs too hot too fast, it might kill beans prematurely or evaporate away some fragrant compounds; if it stays too cool or doesn't get enough oxygen at the right time, certain flavor notes might never develop.

Experienced cocoa farmers are in effect fermentation masters themselves, knowing when to mix or aerate the beans, when to extend fermentation or stop it, to achieve desired results. Traditionally, farmers have learned through experience that, say, fermenting for six days and turning the beans twice yields better flavor than four days with no turning.

In making those judgment calls, they are indirectly managing the microbial action (giving oxygen to the acetic acid bacteria at the right moment, for example). The skill of fermentation is often a defining factor in the quality of cocoa from a given farm.

All this means that fermentation adds a layer of local character to cocoa. Microbes are a part of the terroir. In fact, researchers have observed that fine flavor cacao — the kind used for premium chocolates with florals and fruit notes — often owes its distinguishing aromas to the specific mix of wild microbes present during fermentation.

In one recent study, scientists compared fermentations on different Colombian cocoa farms: two farms known for producing exquisitely aromatic cocoa and one producing more ordinary "bulk" cocoa. They discovered that the microbial communities in the fine-flavor fermentations had distinct species and progressed differently, resulting in beans with more nuanced flavor compounds (like extra floral and berry notes).

The bulk cocoa's fermentation, while still successful in making edible beans, was less varied in microbes and ultimately in flavor complexity — "more monotone," as the researchers described it. This kind of evidence underscores how wild fermentation can fine-tune flavor in ways that even the cocoa plant's genetics might not. Some scientists go so far as to suggest that fermentation can have a bigger impact on chocolate flavor than the particular variety of cocoa bean itself.

For chocolate aficionados, this interplay of microbes adds to the romance of single-origin chocolate. Just as a wine lover might appreciate that a Burgundy Pinot Noir is touched by the native yeasts of French vineyards, a chocolate connoisseur can appreciate that a 70% dark from Madagascar owes some of its bright fruity punch to the local microbiome that fermented those beans. The flavor in your favorite chocolate bar is, in a very real sense, a gift of a tiny corner of the world's microbial flora.

∽

SCIENCE MEETS ART: Tinkering with Fermentation for the Future

Despite the wonders of natural fermentation, it's not without challenges. Relying on wild microbes means inconsistency — results can vary from batch to batch. For large-scale chocolate producers, inconsistency is risky, and for farmers, a "bad ferment" can mean lower quality beans and lower prices. Moreover, the fermentation step is something of a black box that occurs on farms, often with little control. Recognizing how pivotal fermentation is, scientists and chocolate makers have been experimenting with ways to guide or enhance the process, effectively asking: *Can we make the microbes do an even better job, or ensure they do it every time?*

One approach has been to develop starter cultures for cocoa fermentation — much like how winemakers add selected yeast to grape juice, or brewers add specific yeast to beer wort. Researchers have isolated strains of yeast and bacteria that seem to be key "flavor makers." For example, certain yeast strains are especially good at pumping out fruity esters.

In experimental trials, inoculating cocoa bean heaps with a selected yeast strain (instead of leaving it entirely to chance) has yielded beans that produce chocolate with noticeably different flavor profiles. In one notable experiment, fermentation was kickstarted with a particular Pichia kluyveri yeast (known from tropical fruit fermentations). The inoculated batch generated more pronounced fruity and floral notes in the finished chocolate, and was even rated as less astringent than the naturally fermented batch. By tweaking which microbes lead the fermentation, scientists found they could tilt the flavor outcome – more of one note, less of another.

Beyond yeasts, specialized blends of bacteria have been tested too.

Given the results, companies and researchers are intrigued by the idea of a "defined microbial community": a cocktail of a few best-performing yeast and bacterial species that could be added to cocoa beans to reliably produce gourmet flavors.

In a recent breakthrough study, a team of scientists assembled a mix of microbes that successfully mimicked the fermentation from a top-quality farm. The lab-fermented beans, using this controlled culture, surprised tasters by exhibiting many of the same coveted notes — orange blossom, berry, tropical fruit, floral hints — found in the farm's chocolate.

This suggests that we might not be far from being able to engineer fermentations for specific flavor outcomes. Imagine tailoring a fermentation recipe to create a chocolate that naturally carries a jasmine aroma or extra caramel depth, simply by choosing the right microbial "chef."

However, this idea of highly controlled fermentation is not universally welcomed in the chocolate world. Artisan and small-batch chocolate makers, in particular, often value the uniqueness that comes from traditional fermentation.

Some worry that if everyone started using the same microbial starter packs, flavor profiles could become uniform and "homogenized," losing the charm of terroir. There's also pride and craft at stake: for many fine chocolate producers, the ferment is an art that shouldn't be overtaken by laboratory concoctions.

As two craft chocolate makers in England remarked when asked about microbial additives, such designer fermentation cocktails would likely be rejected by the craft chocolate community, since good farming and careful traditional practices already yield great tasting chocolate without needing a biotech assist. They fear it might encourage a one-size-fits-all approach and even cover up for poor harvest practices.

Scientists acknowledge these concerns. Tinkering with microbial balance is tricky — too much of a given compound, and a delightful aroma can turn into an overpowering stink. Interestingly, the wild fermentation might naturally strike a balance that our human-designed mixtures could overshoot.

One microbiologist noted that the yeasts in spontaneous fermentations seem to produce flavor compounds at levels that sit right below the human threshold of "too much"; push beyond that, and the chocolate could taste off.

There's also the ecological angle: a laboratory mix might not perform the same way on every farm, especially when facing competition from robust native microbes adapted to that locale. In some cases, the local microbes could simply outcompete the introduced ones, making starters ineffective. In others, introduced strains could dominate but at the expense of some subtle local flair.

The future of cocoa fermentation will likely strike a balance between tradition and technology. On one hand, understanding the microbial ecology in detail can help farmers troubleshoot and improve their fermentations (for instance, recognizing a problematic bacteria that's causing off-flavors and finding ways to minimize it, or adjusting aeration timing to favor certain microbes).

On the other hand, judicious use of starters or microbial management might help regions with less consistent fermentation weather, or new cocoa-growing areas, to produce high-quality beans.

There's even talk of developing bioreactors for cocoa fermentation: imagine stainless steel vats or controlled chambers where cocoa beans ferment under monitored conditions, perhaps useful in places where traditional heap fermentation isn't feasible. Yet, even with high-tech interventions, the heart of the process remains the same ancient dance of biology.

THE MASTERS Behind Every Bite

In the end, every piece of chocolate carries the story of a grand microbial adventure. It's quite wondrous when you think about it: the luxuriant taste that we associate with comfort and indulgence is, at its core, the product of microbial growth and decay on a tropical farm, orchestrated by tiny organisms we can't see.

These microbial maestros have been performing their symphony since humans first started making chocolate thousands of years ago, and they continue to do so today largely in the same way. The farmers who cultivate cocoa have learned to work with these unseen partners, becoming masters of fermentation themselves to coax the best from their crop. And as scientists deepen our understanding, we're discovering just how much finesse and complexity these microbes contribute.

For chocolate lovers, knowing this backstory adds a new layer of appreciation. Next time you unwrap a chocolate bar, take a moment to inhale its aroma. Those notes of fruit, flower, earth, or nut didn't just come from the cacao tree — they were crafted by an ecosystem of yeasts and bacteria collaborating in a box or heap on some distant farm. With every smooth bite that melts on your tongue, you're not just tasting cocoa and sugar; you're tasting the results of fermentation alchemy.

The microbes may be invisible, but their signature is on every delightful flavor note. They truly are the fermentation masters behind the scenes, turning ordinary cocoa beans into the chocolate we adore. And for that, chocolate lovers around the world have many reasons to be grateful to our microscopic friends. Enjoying a square of fine chocolate is, in a way, raising a toast to the tiny life forms that made it all possible — a delicious collaboration between human hands and microbial magic.

11

CHOCOLATE'S SHADOW PLANTS: GUARDIANS, PARASITES, AND IMPOSTORS

T o understand the life of a cacao tree, you must understand that it is fighting a war. It stands in the humid understory of the tropics, surrounded by enemies that want to strangle, starve, or mimic it. This is not a passive garden; it is a slow-motion battlefield.

The most insidious enemy does not have teeth or claws; it has roots. The parasitic mistletoe (Tapinanthus) is the vampire of the cocoa farm. Birds deposit its sticky seeds onto the cacao branches, where they germinate and drill into the bark, tapping directly into the tree's vascular system. It bypasses the soil entirely, drinking the cacao tree's lifeblood—its water and nutrients— straight from the vein. If the farmer does not cut this vampire out by hand, the branch withers, the pods shrivel, and the harvest dies. In the shadow of the cocoa tree, survival is a contact sport.

THE ALLIES ABOVE: Shade Trees That Shape Chocolate's Flavor

On a humid afternoon in southern Mexico, an elderly cacao farmer strides beneath a green canopy, her machete in hand. Above her, the sun is filtered through the leaves of orange and banana trees. She pauses to gently pat the trunk of a young cacao tree, one of hundreds growing in the dappled light. "Nunca solo," she says softly – "never alone." For over

50 years, she has cultivated cacao under the embrace of a jungle garden. Banana plants, orange and mango trees, even passionfruit vines weave through her cacao grove. She insists that cacao should never be grown in an open field, exposed to the sky. The neighboring trees, she believes, lend their own character to the cacao: their presence keeps the soil moist and the air cool, and perhaps even whispers subtle flavor into the beans. As she tells it, *those surrounding plants share their spirit with the chocolate.* Whether or not science can measure it, generations of traditional growers agree that cacao develops best in companionship.

This scene could be from Chiapas, Mexico, or from Ecuador, or Cameroon – anywhere cacao farmers have learned the value of shade. The cacao tree (*Theobroma cacao*) is, by its nature, an understory tree. In its original home, the Amazon rainforest, wild cacao thrived in the dim understory, sheltered by towering hardwoods and draped in vines. Early planters of cacao realized that young cacao seedlings are delicate, easily scorched by direct sun. So they planted "nurse trees" to protect the cacao in its youth. In Ghana and Ivory Coast, for example, farmers interplant cacao with fast-growing plantains or bananas.

The broad banana leaves spread above the tender saplings, casting mottled shade and shielding them from harsh sun and gusty winds. As a bonus, the farmers harvest bunches of plantains to eat or sell while the cacao slowly matures. In Latin America, cacao is often cradled under the feathery canopy of leguminous trees like *Inga* or *Gliricidia*. *Gliricidia sepium*, fittingly nicknamed "Madre de Cacao" (Mother of Cacao), is a favored companion: it grows quickly, fixes nitrogen in the soil to fertilize the ground, and can be pruned to provide mulch and regulate shade.

In traditional agroforests of Central America, towering fruit trees such as mango, avocado, or breadfruit often stand guard over cacao groves, providing food, timber, and habitat for wildlife, all while moderating the microclimate that cacao relies on.

Beyond simply protecting cacao, shade trees profoundly shape how cacao grows – and even how it tastes. Imagine two cacao farms: one a clearing under the blazing tropical sun, the other a glade of mixed trees and cacao. In the sun-blasted plantation, cacao pods may ripen faster, but the trees are often stressed.

Hot, direct sun can cause cacao trees to shed leaves to conserve moisture, and the developing beans inside the pods may turn out smaller and more bitter. By contrast, under a gentle canopy of shade, cacao trees lead a less stressful life. The shade buffers extreme temperatures, preventing sunburn and moisture loss. The soil stays cooler and richer in organic matter thanks to fallen leaves from the canopy.

Cacao pods in the shade tend to develop more slowly and evenly, allowing complex flavors to mature. Farmers and chocolate makers have observed that beans from shade-grown cacao can have more nuanced flavors – a bit less bitterness and acidity, and sometimes more of the fruity or floral notes that connoisseurs prize. It's a subtle art: too much shade, and the cacao yields may drop or diseases might linger in the damp; too little shade, and the trees are stressed and the flavors turn flat or harsh.

The ideal is a dappled light, about 30-50% shade, where sun and shadow dance on the cacao leaves through the day. Under such conditions, the cacao's "soul" seems to come alive. One cacao scholar described shade trees as "shaping the soul of cacao" – the canopy above doesn't just shield the tree, it influences everything from bean size to the cocktail of sugars, fats, and acids inside each bean that will later ferment into chocolate.

There is even a belief among cacao growers (like that wise woman in Chiapas) that the type of shade tree can impart specific hints of flavor to cacao. For instance, some farmers swear that cacao grown alongside citrus trees picks up a whisper of citrus brightness, or that cacao under avocado will have a certain smooth richness. Scientific evidence for direct flavor transfer is scant – it's more likely the effect of microclimate and soil – but the anecdotes persist, adding a romantic mystique. At the very least, these interplanted orchards produce cacao with a sense of place.

Just as wine enthusiasts speak of *terroir* (the environment's effect on grapes), chocolate lovers are starting to realize that a cacao tree's neighbors leave an imprint on the beans. A cacao pod maturing under the canopy of a rainforested valley, with wild nutmeg and orchids nearby, might develop differently than one in a regimented monoculture. In Papua New Guinea, for example, cacao is often grown near smoke-drying fires and can take on a smoky overtone. In contrast, cacao intercropped with fruit trees in a vibrant agroforest might carry subtle fruity aromas.

Economic and ecological benefits flow from these "chocolate shade" systems as well. In Indonesia, many smallholder farmers grow cacao under the fronds of coconut palms. The tall coconuts provide intermittent shade and an extra income (coconuts for copra or oil) while the understory cacao provides the main cash crop – a clever dual harvest from the same land.

In the Amazon, indigenous communities traditionally left the forest intact, planting cacao in the understory along with other useful crops, essentially creating a human-managed forest that yields chocolate, fruits, medicines and more. Such diversified farms are more resilient: if a disease hits cacao, the farmer still has other produce; if cocoa prices fall, the shade trees (some of which are valuable hardwoods) can be a savings account, sold for timber in a pinch. Meanwhile, the very presence of diverse shade species helps keep pests in balance and can reduce the need for chemical fertilizers by naturally enriching the soil.

Perhaps nowhere is the wisdom of shade more evident than in Brazil's Atlantic Forest, where a system called *cabruca* has been practiced for over two centuries. In *cabruca* agroforestry, farmers do not fell all the native trees. Instead, they thin the jungle understory and plant cacao right under the towering forest trees that remain. Imagine walking in what feels like primary rainforest – lianas hanging, toucans flapping overhead – and then noticing yellow and red cacao pods sprouting from tree trunks all around you. That is a cabruca cacao grove.

This method allowed southern Bahia's cacao region to flourish without sacrificing the rainforest; in fact, cacao became a guardian of the forest, since landowners preserved woods as their productive asset. Under the emerald cathedral of the Atlantic Forest, cacao coexisted with a teeming community of plants and animals – from orchids and bromeliads clinging to branches above, to monkeys, bats, and brilliant blue butterflies attracted by the mix of fruiting trees.

Old photographs and accounts describe these cacao forests alive with biodiversity. Farmers learned that cacao yields could be decent under such shade, and the quality high, even if the absolute output per hectare was lower than in full-sun plantations. The trade-off was worth it: the canopy protected the cacao from intense sun and dry winds, and the forest litter fed the soil.

When a devastating fungal disease called witch's broom struck Bahia's cacao in the 1990s, it ravaged the plantations mercilessly. Many farms were abandoned or converted to other uses. Yet, in recent years, there's a renaissance of the cabruca idea. Researchers and environmentalists are working with farmers to rejuvenate these shade-grown cacao systems, seeing them as a way to restore lost forest cover and also produce high-quality cocoa.

The notion is simple: a chocolate forest is more sustainable than a sun-baked monoculture. In an era of climate change, shade trees also buffer cacao from heat spikes and droughts, giving hope that chocolate can endure in a warming world.

In short, cacao's leafy companions overhead – the coconuts and bananas, ingas and mangoes, oaks and cedars – are more than just background characters. They are protectors, providers, and even flavor influencers. They form a living umbrella that shelters the "food of the gods" as it grows. Every time we bite into a fine chocolate, we might spare a thought for the unseen guardians above the cacao, whose quiet presence may have subtly shaped the taste we cherish.

Silent Invaders: **The Vampire of the Canopy**

Not all of cacao's neighbors are benevolent. In West Africa, farmers wage a constant war against mistletoe (Tapinanthus spp.). Unlike the festive holiday sprig, this variety is a botanical vampire. Birds deposit its sticky seeds onto cacao branches, where they germinate and sink root-like haustoria deep into the wood, tapping into the tree's plumbing. It is a "silent killer," siphoning off water and nutrients until the branch withers and snaps. For the farmer, there is no chemical cure—only the vigilant, labor-intensive work of pruning the parasites by hand before they bleed the orchard dry.

Fungi and insects also plague cacao – witches' broom fungus, frosty pod rot, cacao mirid bugs – but these are not *plants*, so they are outside our botanical detective scope. It is sobering, though, to consider that cacao lives besieged by organisms that want to consume it. From microscopic fungal spores to obvious vines and mistletoes, the threats abound.

The parasitic plants are especially intriguing because they are visible, plant-against-plant adversaries, almost like a slow-motion strangulation or poisoning happening in the canopy. One might walk under a cacao tree and not realize an assassin is perched among the leaves above. In West Africa, some farmers refer to mistletoe infestations as a "cancer" on their cacao, something malignant growing within that must be cut away for the tree to recover.

Despite the challenges, these plant parasites can be managed with knowledge and care. Researchers are studying whether certain shade tree selections or farm layouts can minimize mistletoe spread – for instance, planting cacao in rows might make it easier to inspect and prune, and perhaps some tree species are less likely to harbor mistletoe-seeding birds than others.

There's even exploration of biological control: could a pest or disease of mistletoe be introduced to help farmers? It's a tricky proposition, since you wouldn't want to unleash a new problem into the ecosystem. For now, the trusty machete and pruning saw are the cacao farmer's best defense against the *shadowy invaders* entwined in their trees.

In our detective tale, if the shade trees are cacao's guardian angels, then parasitic plants like mistletoe are the stealthy thieves in the night – quietly, persistently robbing cacao of vitality. The battle between them is fought in the heights of the canopy and in the hidden tissues under bark.

Every cacao farmer who has heaved a sigh of relief after cutting away a mistletoe can attest: not all of cacao's green neighbors are friends. Some, like this "kiss of death" mistletoe, must be vigilantly snipped out to keep the chocolate dreams alive.

Impostors Among the Trees: Cacao's Look-Alike Species

Our botanical mystery grows deeper when we consider that even identifying the true cacao tree has not always been straightforward. Deep in the Amazon rainforest, an early 20th-century botanist slogs through sweltering swamps, intent on finding wild cacao relatives. He spots a small tree with glossy, drooping leaves and bright pods dangling from its trunk. Success!

==

THE GARDENER'S GUIDE: FRIENDS & FOES

A cacao tree cannot survive alone. Know who to plant and who to prune.

The Friends (Plant These):

- Banana/Plantain: The "Nurse Tree." Its giant leaves protect young cacao seedlings from the scorching sun.
- Legumes (Inga/Gliricidia): The "Fertilizer." These trees pull nitrogen from the air and fix it into the soil, feeding the cacao roots.
- Midges: The "Pollinator." Not a plant, but they need rotting leaf litter on the floor to breed. Don't sweep the jungle clean!

The Foes (Cut These):

- Mistletoe: The "Vampire." It taps into the branch and sucks out the sap.
- Strangler Fig: The "Constrictor." It wraps around the trunk and slowly chokes the host tree.

==

He thinks he's found a wild cacao (Theobroma cacao) far from any farm. But when he cracks open a pod, he's puzzled: instead of the familiar purple-tinted cacao seeds, he finds snowy white seeds inside. The pulp tastes sweet and fragrant, but different. This isn't the cacao that makes chocolate – it's an impostor, a close cousin now known as *Theobroma bicolor*. In local parlance it's called macambo or jaguar cacao, and while it belongs to the chocolate tree's family, it yields a very different treasure.

Throughout the tropics of the Americas, there are a number of "chocolate doppelgängers" – plants that look remarkably like Theobroma cacao, or were historically mistaken for it, yet are separate species with their own identities. The genus *Theobroma* itself contains around two dozen species, often referred to as cacao's cousins. They evolved in the same forests, often side by side, and some are so similar in appearance that even indigenous peoples and early explorers had to distinguish carefully between them.

One of the most intriguing is Jaguar cacao (Theobroma bicolor). At a glance, a Jaguar cacao tree could fool an untrained eye: it has comparable foliage and grows in the same environments as chocolate cacao. Its pods are slightly different – generally larger, with a more elongated football shape and a rough, mottled surface. When ripe, they might turn yellowish-white or remain a pale green, rather than the golden-orange of many cacao pods.

Crack one open, and you'll see why it earned the name "Jaguar": the large seeds inside are pure white with dark speckles, reminiscent of a jaguar's spots. The ancient Maya and other Mesoamerican cultures knew Jaguar cacao well (they called it *pataxte* or *balamte'* among other names) and used it alongside regular cacao. However, *pataxte* was often considered inferior for making the prized chocolate drink – it lacks the intense bitter cocoa flavor of true cacao. Jaguar cacao seeds have a milder, nutty taste, more like a neutral almond or cashew note, with far less of the caffeine and theobromine that give cacao its kick.

Nonetheless, the Maya found a special role for this impostor: they would mix Jaguar cacao seeds into cacao drinks to create a luxurious foamy head on top. In fact, *Theobroma bicolor* has a higher fat content that whips up into a stable froth, so it was added to enhance the *frothiness* of ceremonial chocolate beverages. Some anthropologists think that certain hieroglyphs on ancient Maya pottery – long thought to just mean "cacao" – actually differentiate between regular cacao and *pataxte*, suggesting the two were often paired in recipes.

Spanish colonizers, encountering these drinks, were perplexed by this "white cacao" that didn't taste quite like chocolate. For a time, there was confusion in Europe as to whether this was a variety of cacao or a completely different plant. Eventually, botanists gave Jaguar cacao its own name and classification, but even into the 20th century it remained obscure to science. Only in recent decades have chocolate enthusiasts "rediscovered" Jaguar cacao, experimenting with its seeds to create a kind of white chocolate or *"bicolate."* It's still a rarity – a shadow of chocolate rather than the real thing – but it stands as a living reminder that not everything called cacao is created equal.

Theobroma bicolor, *or Jaguar Cacao. A cousin of chocolate with white, waxy seeds, used by the Maya to create the prized foam on their drinks.*

Another notable look-alike lurks deeper in the Amazon basin: Cupuaçu (Theobroma grandiflorum), often dubbed *the cacao cousin of Brazil.* A cupuaçu tree is a dead ringer for a cacao tree in many respects – similar height, similar glossy leaves that flush red when young – but it was long misidentified by outsiders. Indigenous peoples of the Amazon knew it as a distinct species, prized not for its seeds but for its pulp.

The pods of cupuaçu are what give it away: they are larger and more ovoid than cacao pods, with a fuzzy, thick brown skin that looks almost like a russet potato or a small rugby ball. Inside, instead of a sweet white pulp clinging to bitter seeds (as in cacao), cupuaçu's pulp is the main delight – creamy white, aromatic, and intensely fruity, like a mix of pineapple, pear, and banana flavors. Amazonians crack open cupuaçu pods to suck the pulp or make delicious juices, ice creams, and desserts.

The seeds themselves are quite similar to cacao seeds, and interestingly can be fermented and roasted to produce a kind of chocolate-like product. Some Brazilian chocolatiers have experimented with making "cupulate", a cupuaçu chocolate. It doesn't taste quite the same – it's often described as more tangy or earthy – and it lacks the strong cocoa aroma.

Still, in a pinch, one could grind cupuaçu seeds and get a passable cocoa substitute. There was even a small controversy in the early 2000s when a Japanese company attempted to patent cupuaçu products in international markets, seeing it as the next trendy superfood or chocolate alternative.

Brazil fought back, asserting cupuaçu as part of their cultural heritage and biodiversity. Today, cupuaçu is gaining global attention not as an impostor chocolate, but as a unique fruit in its own right – yet its close relationship to cacao means farmers sometimes accidentally mix them up.

There are anecdotes of growers trying to graft cacao onto cupuaçu rootstock, or vice versa, to see if they can confer disease resistance, since cupuaçu is relatively hardy against some pests. In the wild, a newcomer might walk past a cupuaçu tree and mistake it for an odd variety of cacao until they see the huge fuzzy pod.

The cast of cacao doppelgängers continues: *Theobroma subincanum*, *Theobroma speciosum*, *Herrania purpurea* (often called "Monkey cacao"), and others. Monkey cacao, in the genus *Herrania*, is a curious one – its pods are long, ribbed, and red or yellow, looking like some fantasy version of a cacao pod.

While not in the exact same genus, it's a close relative and sometimes shares habitat with cacao. Locals called it "monkey cacao" because monkeys and rodents love to crack open its thin pods and eat the pulp, even if humans didn't cultivate it. Botanists in the 1800s occasionally mislabeled such specimens as variants of cacao until careful study proved otherwise.

Why do these look-alikes matter? For one, they have led to mix-ups in both cultivation and science. A farmer might inadvertently grow a non-cacao species thinking it's the real deal (especially if someone sold them seeds of *T. bicolor* under the assumption it was just a different type of cacao).

This is rare, but imagine the surprise when after years of growth, the trees produce pods with useless (for chocolate) seeds! On the scientific front, preserving wild cacao relatives has become important for genetic diversity. Those impostors might carry genes that could help the cultivated cacao down the line – perhaps resistance to a disease or tolerance to different climates.

So, botanists now scour the same forests where those species lurk, this time intentionally seeking them out rather than avoiding them. The line between "supporting" and "mimicking" can blur here: the impostor species don't directly help cacao, but they could indirectly support its future through breeding research.

From a cultural perspective, the existence of look-alike cacao relatives adds rich texture to the chocolate story. In pre-Columbian times, people in Central and South America knew many "cacaos."

They understood their differences and uses: one for the sacred bitter drink, another for a foamy festive beverage, another as a tasty fruit. When Europeans arrived, some nuance was lost as they fixated on *Theobroma cacao* as *the* chocolate tree.

It's tantalizing to think of early explorers stumbling upon a wild Jaguar cacao and puzzling over why the chocolate they made from it tasted so weak – perhaps prompting further expeditions to find the "true" cacao. Indeed, we might say these impostors played a bit of hide-and-seek with us in history, contributing to the aura of mystery around tropical forests: in the dense jungle, even a familiar treasure like cacao can wear a different face.

Next time you peel open a chocolate bar, consider that there are other trees out there, bearing pods and seeds that look a lot like cacao but aren't quite. They inhabit the shadow realm of chocolate: close enough to be kin, sometimes masquerading as the real thing, yet ultimately revealing their own unique identities.

These botanical doppelgängers enrich the narrative of cacao by reminding us that nature always holds more surprises – not just one "food of the gods," but a pantheon of them hidden in the green gloom of the forest.

The Forest Partners: Companion Flora for Thriving Cacao Farms

In a thriving cacao farm that resembles a natural forest, every plant –

from the highest canopy giant to the tiniest fern on the forest floor – plays a part in the success of the chocolate crop. Picture a cacao agroforest in the hills of Ecuador: a mosaic of greenery where cacao trees blend into a living tapestry of other vegetation. Slender papaya trees and bushy coffee shrubs grow between the cacao trunks.

A towering Albizia tree (a native rainforest species) stretches above, its umbrella-like crown providing mottled shade. Pepper vines spiral around some cacao stems, and pineapples or taro root cluster at the base, covering the ground. The air is humid and alive with the drone of insects and the calls of distant birds. Dead leaves and cacao pod husks carpet the soil, slowly decomposing into rich humus. This is not chaos – it's a carefully balanced orchestra of life, orchestrated by farmers who understand that cacao thrives best as part of an ecosystem, not in isolation.

Modern agriculture often preaches control: neat rows, weed-free plots, single crops for efficiency. But cacao, by its very biology and heritage, lends itself to polyculture and biodiversity. The small, gnat-sized flies that pollinate cacao (often called midges) are a prime example. These midges are the unsung heroes of every chocolate bar – without them, cacao flowers would rarely turn into pods.

And what do these midges need for their own life cycle? Moisture and decaying organic matter. In a sterile plantation where all leaf litter is cleared and there are no shady damp thickets, midge populations plummet. But in a farm that retains a layer of fallen leaves, that piles discarded cacao pods in between trees to rot, and that maybe has a little stream or pond nearby, midges find plenty of breeding sites.

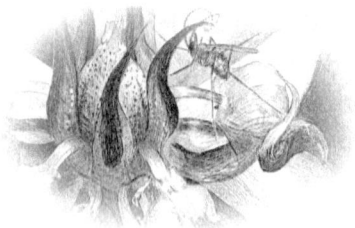

No midge, no chocolate. This pinhead-sized fly is the only creature small enough to navigate the complex labyrinth of the cacao flower to pollinate it.

Some species of cacao-pollinating midges lay eggs in the decomposing banana trunks or in fungal growth on the forest floor. That provides a direct clue to farmers: if you want good pollination, leave some rotting vegetation around!

Indeed, recent research demonstrated that something as simple as increasing the leaf litter on the ground can boost natural pollinator numbers and result in significantly higher yields of cacao. One study across multiple countries found that when they hand-pollinated flowers (simulating perfect pollination), yields shot up by 20% – meaning most farms were not reaching their potential due to pollination shortfall.

The recommendation was clear: encourage the natural pollinators by keeping a farm "messy" in the right ways – more organic litter, taller shade trees to keep humidity, and fewer chemical sprays that might harm the delicate insects. In essence, the forest floor itself is a crucial companion to cacao: it must be alive and thriving, not swept clean.

Companion flora can also provide natural pest control. In a diverse cacao garden, you might find that some trees house colonies of ants that patrol the cacao for caterpillars, or that certain flowers attract predator insects or birds that eat cacao pests.

For instance, some farmers allow patches of bush or specific flowering plants on the margins of their cacao plots to support bees, wasps, and other insects that, while visiting those flowers, might also prey on pests like mealybugs or shield bugs that attack cacao pods. Tall shade trees can serve as perches for birds and bats, many of which are insectivores that nightly feast on moths and beetles that could be harmful to cacao.

Even the choice of shade species matters: a citrus or guava tree in the mix might lure fruit-eating birds and bats that incidentally also devour insects. Some pioneering farmers in Asia have experimented with planting nectar-rich shrubs or lemongrass in cacao rows to repel certain pests or to confuse them with strong scents. While not all such methods are scientifically proven, the underlying principle is sound – biodiversity tends to create checks and balances.

A cacao monoculture is like an all-you-can-eat buffet for any specialist pest or disease that loves cacao; a mixed cacao forest is a more challenging, dynamic environment where pests have more predators and the spread of any one problem can be slowed.

Soil health is another area where companion plants shine. Many cacao-growing regions have nutrient-poor soils (for instance, much of West Africa's cocoa belt is on old, weathered soils that can be low in nitrogen). Traditionally, in a forest setting, trees like legumes fix nitrogen, and the constant rain of leaves and twigs creates a fertile topsoil that cacao can tap into.

By mimicking this, farmers plant cover crops and mulch. Some will sow a low-growing legume ground cover (like pueraria or a local bean) to cover bare soil, add nitrogen, and suppress weeds. Others heap the discarded cacao pod shells around the base of trees – rather than treat them as waste, they become slow-release fertilizer as they break down, returning potassium and other minerals to the earth. Certain companion trees are especially valued as "fertilizer trees": *Albizia* and *Flemingia* in Asia, or *Erythrina* (a coral tree) and *Inga* in Latin America, all known to enrich soil with nitrogen or abundant leaf drop.

In some innovative farms, gliricidia trees are pollarded (cut back) regularly, and their lopped branches are laid around cacao trunks to decompose – a method of in-situ composting. The cacao farm thus feeds itself in a cycle, much like a natural forest would.

Cultural wisdom often encapsulates these ideas in simple ways. A saying among some Latin American cacao farmers goes: *"Cacao se cría con sus amigos"* – "Cacao grows up with its friends." Those "friends" include not just the big shade trees but all the living elements around it. In parts of the Philippines and Indonesia, coconut and cacao are called a "marriage" – the tall, airy coconut palms happily share sunlight with the shorter, shade-craving cacao beneath.

In West Africa, a common practice is to intercrop young cacao with food crops like yams, cassava, or maize for the first few years. This not only gives farmers sustenance and income while the cacao is immature, but the intercrops can provide partial shade and keep the ground covered.

As the cacao trees grow larger and form their own canopy, the temporary companions are harvested and phased out, to be replaced by more permanent shade trees if needed. The result is a dynamic succession that transitions from mixed food forest to a cacao-dominant agroforest.

Even the forest at the farm's edges or nearby plays a role. Studies have found that cacao farms adjacent to patches of natural forest tend to have higher yields and fewer pest issues. Why? The forest is a reservoir of beneficial species: it's home to a larger pool of pollinators, it harbors predators that wander into the farm, and it maintains climate stability (cooler temperatures, regular rainfall patterns, etc.).

One researcher described natural forest as a "service provider" to cacao farms – essentially a neighbor whose influence spills over the fence in positive ways. This has bolstered arguments for landscape-level conservation, where protecting wild forest is seen as not just an environmental goal but an agricultural strategy to keep the surrounding cacao farms productive and resilient.

In our detective story analogy, if shade trees are cacao's kindly guardians and parasites are its stealthy enemies, then companion flora are its supportive community – the ensemble cast that sets the stage for cacao's success. They don't get individual credit on the chocolate bar label, but without them the star of the show would falter.

A cacao tree alone, in a bare field, is an orphan in a hostile world. But a cacao tree surrounded by supportive plants is part of a robust network: it can lean on others and, in turn, drop its own leaves and fruits to feed the system. The "forest farm" concept essentially means farming in a way that emulates a natural forest, leveraging the ancient partnerships between species that have co-evolved over millennia. Cacao evolved under the canopy with a rich undergrowth around – that is its comfort zone.

As consumers clamor for sustainable and ethical chocolate, more attention is being paid to these agroforestry methods. Some craft chocolate makers will talk about the specific farm where the cacao grew, describing how it was "shade-grown under citrus and hardwoods" or how the farmer uses permaculture principles.

These details resonate because they promise not just good ecology but often superior flavor (back to our flavor discussion – healthy, unstressed trees yield better beans). We begin to realize that the taste and tale of chocolate is really the taste and tale of an entire plant community. It's the product of cacao and banana and mango and mystic little flies and friendly fungi and rich leaf litter all working in concert.

A Tapestry of Chocolate's Green Allies and Enemies

Every luscious bite of chocolate carries echoes of a far-away landscape – not just the cacao tree, but its whole entourage of shadow plants. In the shadows we found the benevolent shade givers, quietly influencing chocolate's quality and ensuring the cacao's survival through tough climates.

We uncovered the parasitic infiltrators, reminding us that even in Eden, there are serpents in the branches that must be kept at bay. We met the look-alikes and botanical cousins, those tricksters of the tropics, showing that cacao has a larger family than we knew, with its own hidden gifts. And we saw how the chorus of companion plants creates a living symphony around cacao, a symphony that yields both abundance and resilience.

The world of chocolate is richer and more complex than a single type of tree in a plantation. It's a botanical detective story with twists: A mistletoe might be silently draining the life from a tree that otherwise looked fine; an entire harvest might depend on leaving a few wildflowers or weeds alone to shelter pollinators; a farmer's fortune might turn on planting a row of shade trees today that will only tower decades later for the next generation; a chocolate bar's award-winning flavor might owe a nod to the orange blossoms or avocado leaves that perfumed the cacao grove where it was born.

For chocolate enthusiasts, knowing these backstories deepens the appreciation of that familiar treat. One can savor not just the notes of red fruit or nuts in a fine dark chocolate, but also the knowledge that perhaps those notes were midwifed by a nurturing rainforest canopy or a biodiverse garden teeming with unseen helpers.

Each cacao farm or forest has its own web of life, and in that web, chocolate's shadow plants play decisive roles. In the grand drama of bringing cacao from pod to palate, they are the supporting characters that rarely get standing ovations, yet the show could not go on without them.

So, the next time you unwrap a chocolate bar, consider it an offering not just of Theobroma cacao, but of an entire botanical community. In that smooth square of chocolate lies the ghost of a banana tree that once shaded the cacao, the essence of rich loamy compost that fed its roots, the memory of the vines that twined around its trunk, and the vigilance of a farmer who guarded it from parasites. Chocolate is the fruit of an ecosystem as much as of a tree.

In both wild forests and cultivated groves around the world, cacao's neighbors – supportive, threatening, and mimicking alike – continue to shape the destiny of chocolate. Understanding and respecting these relationships is not only a journey into fascinating ecology and history, it's also a roadmap for sustaining chocolate's future. After all, to truly help cacao thrive, we must embrace the whole community of life in its shadows, ensuring that the story of chocolate remains a symphony and not a solo.

12

THE ARKS OF CACAO: THE PERILOUS EXPEDITIONS OF F.J. POUND

T he heat on the Nanay River in April does not merely sit on the skin; it presses down with a physical weight, a suffocating blanket of humidity that turns the air into soup. Deep in the Peruvian Amazon, thousands of miles from the manicured lawns of the Imperial College of Tropical Agriculture in Trinidad, Dr. F.J. Pound sat in the stern of a hollowed-out dugout canoe. His white linen shirt, long since stained with river mud and sweat, clung to his back. Around him, the jungle screamed—a cacophony of howler monkeys, cicadas, and the splash of unseen things slipping into the water.

It was 1938. Pound, a British agronomist with the build of a rugby player and the obsessive focus of a detective, was not looking for gold, rubber, or lost cities. He was hunting for a ghost. For weeks, he and his small team of local guides had poled their way up the twisting tributaries of the upper Amazon, battling malaria, dysentery, and the constant threat of capsizing in rapids. They stopped at every riverside settlement, every indigenous clearing, asking the same question: *Where are the trees that do not die?*

*Pound travels deep into the Amazon searching for resilient cacao. His
journey underscores the urgency behind saving threatened plantations.*

Pound was chasing a theory that his peers called desperate and his
critics called suicidal. He believed that somewhere in this "Green Hell"—
the ancestral birthplace of *Theobroma cacao*—there existed wild cacao
trees that had naturally evolved immunity to the fungal plague
destroying the world's chocolate supply. He was looking for a genetic
needle in the largest botanical haystack on Earth. If he failed, the chocolate industry of the Caribbean faced extinction. If he succeeded, he
would change the genetic destiny of chocolate forever.

THE COLLAPSE of the Pearl

To understand the sheer desperation that drove a Cambridge-
educated scientist into a dugout canoe, one must understand the cata-
strophe unfolding back in Trinidad. In the early 20th century, Trinidad
was the "Pearl of the Caribbean," the jewel in the crown of the British
chocolate empire. It was famous for its Trinitario beans—a natural
hybrid of the delicate Criollo and the hardy Forastero—which possessed
a complex flavor profile of fruit and spice that European chocolatiers
coveted.

But in 1928, a shadow fell over the island's plantations. Farmers
began reporting strange, chaotic growths on their cacao trees. Instead of
graceful branches, the trees sprouted dense, broom-like clusters of green
shoots that looked like old witches' brooms. These shoots drained the

tree's energy, leaving it exhausted. Pods turned hard and stony, or rotted into black mush before they could ripen.

The culprit was *Moniliophthora perniciosa*, a basidiomycete fungus. Its spores traveled on the wind, invisible and unstoppable. It was named Witches' Broom disease, and it was a death sentence. By the mid-1930s, Trinidad's cocoa production had plummeted by nearly 50%. Plantations that had stood for generations were reduced to ghost forests of dead wood. The economy of the island teetered on collapse.

A dead cacao grove shows the catastrophic effects of Witches' Broom. The disease's impact explains the desperate need for genetic rescue.

Science had failed to stop the spread. Fungicides washed away in the tropical rains. Pruning the infected "brooms"—the standard recommendation—was labor-intensive and ultimately futile; a single overlook broom could release millions of spores. The British colonial government was in a panic. The chocolate giants of England—Cadbury, Rowntree, Fry—saw their supply of high-quality beans evaporating. They needed a miracle.

The Theory of Co-Evolution

F.J. Pound was a man of science, but he possessed the soul of an explorer. Appointed to the Cacao Research Scheme in Trinidad, he looked at the devastation and formulated a radical hypothesis based on the principles of evolution.

He knew that Witches' Broom was endemic to the Amazon basin. Yet, wild cacao still grew there. How? Pound theorized that the fungus and the tree had co-evolved over millennia in the Amazonian rainforest. In the brutal logic of nature, an evolutionary arms race would have occurred: as the fungus became more deadly, certain wild cacao trees would have mutated to develop immunity. The trees in Trinidad, descendants of a narrow genetic lineage brought by colonizers, had no such defense. They were sitting ducks.

But in the wild Amazon, Pound argued, there must be survivors— trees standing healthy amidst the rot, their DNA shielding them from the spores. If he could find those trees, harvest their budwood, and bring it back to Trinidad alive, he could cross-breed that resistance into the local crop. He wasn't trying to cure the disease; he was trying to breed a better victim.

It was a sound biological theory, but the logistics were a nightmare. The Amazon basin is roughly the size of the continental United States. Pound was proposing to find specific individual trees in a wilderness that was largely unmapped and biologically hostile.

The First Foray: 1937

Pound launched his first expedition in 1937. It was a reconnaissance mission, a test of endurance designed to trace the path of the disease to its source. He started in Ecuador, traversing the Andes mountains by donkey on terrifyingly narrow paths where a single slip meant death in the gorge below. He descended into the humid lowlands, following the river systems that fed into the Amazon.

His journals from this trip read less like agronomy reports and more like an adventure novel. He describes sleeping in hammocks slung between trees, listening to the cough of jaguars in the darkness. He recounts the relentless assault of insects—sweat bees that swarmed the eyes, mosquitoes that carried malaria, and ants whose bite felt like fire. Food was often scarce; the team survived on yucca, river fish, and whatever canned rations they had dragged with them.

Pound developed a system of interrogation. At every village, he would ask the locals about their wild cacao. He wasn't interested in the trees that produced the most fruit or the sweetest pulp—traits farmers usually prized. He asked for the *cacáo de monte* (wild cacao) that didn't get the "escoba de bruja" (witches' broom).

Time and again, he would trek miles into the bush to inspect a grove, only to find the wild trees riddled with brooms, infected and dying. The disease was everywhere. It seemed to have conquered the Amazon completely. But Pound refused to turn back. He pushed deeper, following the Ucayali river, then the Marañón, moving into the headwaters where the biodiversity was densest. He was mapping the enemy's territory, looking for a fortress that could withstand it.

By the end of 1937, battered and exhausted, Pound returned to Trinidad empty-handed in terms of a cure, but armed with knowledge. He had confirmed that the disease was rampant in the western Amazon, but he had also seen variation. Some trees were sicker than others. The resistance existed; he just hadn't found the immune "super-tree" yet. He needed to go back, and he needed to go further.

The Ghost of the Nanay

In April 1938, F.J. Pound returned to the Amazon. This time, he was not just scouting; he was hunting. Armed with the knowledge from his previous trip, he focused his efforts on the headwaters of the Amazon River in Peru, a region so biologically dense it was considered a "center of diversity" for the cacao species.

He established a base camp in Iquitos, a rubber-boom city that sat like an island of civilization in a sea of jungle. From there, he launched a series of forays up the tributaries that fed the mighty river. The most promising leads pointed him toward the Nanay River, a winding, blackwater tributary that snaked through the lore of local farmers. They spoke of *cacáo* trees that grew wild on the riverbanks, surviving floods and pests without human intervention.

The journey up the Nanay was grueling. Pound and his team traveled in dugout canoes, poling against the current for days. The heat was relentless, and the threat of malaria was constant. But as they pushed further upstream, beyond the last settlements, they began to see something remarkable.

On the muddy banks, amidst the tangle of vines and undergrowth, stood wild cacao trees. Unlike the sickly, broom-infested specimens he had seen elsewhere, these trees were vigorous. Their canopies were full and green. Their trunks were free of the chaotic, vegetative brooms that signaled infection.

Pound scrambled up the muddy banks to inspect them. He found pods that were structurally different from the cultivated varieties back in Trinidad—smaller, rounder, with a thicker husk and smooth yellow skin. To a chocolatier, they might have looked unimpressive compared to the large, colorful Trinitario pods. But to Pound, they looked like salvation. These trees were living in the heart of the disease zone, surrounded by spores, yet they were thriving.

He cataloged the population meticulously. One particular tree stood out for its total lack of infection. He labeled it Scavina 6 (SCA-6). It was not a majestic giant; it was a scrappy survivor. Pound realized he had found the genetic "Adam"—a tree that had evolved a natural shield against the fungus.

Pound finds a healthy wild cacao tree amid widespread disease. This single survivor becomes the foundation for future resistance breeding.

The Wardian Case: A Lifeboat for Plants

Finding the tree was only the first victory. The greater challenge was getting it out.

Pound needed to transport live genetic material—budwood (branches with buds suitable for grafting)—from the interior of Peru to the island of Trinidad. The journey would take weeks, involving canoe travel downriver to Iquitos, a steamer voyage down the Amazon to the Atlantic coast of Brazil, and finally a sea crossing to the Caribbean.

Cut branches are fragile. If they dried out, they would die. If they got too wet, they would rot. If they got too hot, they would cook. In 1938, there was no refrigeration, no overnight air freight.

Pound turned to a Victorian invention: the Wardian Case.

Invented in the 19th century by Dr. Nathaniel Bagshaw Ward, the Wardian case was essentially a portable, sealed greenhouse made of wood and glass. It was designed to create a self-sustaining microclimate. Inside the sealed case, moisture transpired by the plant leaves would condense on the glass walls during the cool of the night and rain back down onto the soil during the heat of the day. This closed water loop allowed plants to survive for months without fresh water.

Pound modified the cases for the tropics. He packed the cuttings in moist moss and charcoal to prevent mold. He instructed his team to keep the cases shaded from the direct equatorial sun while in the canoes, yet ensure they received enough indirect light to keep the buds alive.

The return journey was a race against rot. Pound nursed the cuttings like infants. Every day, he checked the humidity levels, wiping condensation from the glass to prevent magnifying the sun's rays. He battled fungal outbreaks inside the cases, removing any cutting that showed signs of decay to save the rest.

When the steamer finally docked in Port of Spain, Trinidad, Pound unloaded his cargo. He had left with empty boxes and a theory. He returned with the genetic future of chocolate.

The Great Cross-Breeding

The arrival of the Scavina clones was the turning point in the war against Witches' Broom. The material Pound collected became the foundation of the International Cocoa Genebank in Trinidad, which remains the most important repository of cacao genetics in the world today.

Scientists tend curated cacao varieties at a modern genebank. Pound's collected genetics now safeguard the future of global chocolate.

Breeders immediately began the slow work of hybridization. They took the hardy, disease-resistant Scavina 6 and crossed it with the flavor-rich but fragile Trinitario trees (specifically the Imperial College Selections, or ICS).

The results were transformative. The offspring—known as the TSH varieties (Trinidad Selected Hybrids)—inherited the best of both parents. They had the robust immune system of the Amazonian wild tree and the fine flavor profile of the Caribbean heirloom.

Farmers in Trinidad began replanting their decimated orchards with these new super-trees. Slowly, the "ghost forests" of dead cacao began to green again. Yields recovered. The industry was saved from total collapse.

The Legacy of Scavina 6

F.J. Pound did not live to see the full extent of his triumph. The rigors of his expeditions took a severe toll on his health. He died in 1949, at the young age of 41, likely from complications related to the illnesses he contracted in the jungle.

But his legacy is written in the DNA of nearly every chocolate bar we eat today. In the decades that followed, scientists discovered that the Scavina 6 gene was a "super-gene" for resistance. It was so effective that it was shared globally.

Today, if you analyze the genome of cacao trees growing in West Africa, Indonesia, or Brazil, you will often find traces of the genetic lineage that Pound pulled out of the Peruvian mud in 1938. The vast majority of the world's disease-resistant cacao stock can trace its ancestry back to those few canoe-loads of budwood.

Scavina 6 is the matriarch of modern chocolate. It is the reason we can still enjoy affordable chocolate bars despite the constant assault of pathogens. F.J. Pound's expedition proved that the solution to agriculture's biggest threats often lies in nature's own library, waiting for someone brave enough to go and find it.

The Global Genetic Dominoes

The arrival of the Scavina cuttings in Trinidad in 1938 was not the end of the expedition, but the beginning of an urgent, multi-decade breeding program. The fragile, imported budwood was immediately grafted onto hardy rootstock at the Imperial College of Tropical Agriculture (ICTA). Pound's mission was to breed the immunity of the wild Amazonian survivor into the delicate, flavorful Trinitario varieties that defined Caribbean excellence.

The initial crosses were painstaking, yielding a new genetic goldmine designated as Trinidad Selected Hybrids (TSH). These TSH varieties were a fusion: they possessed the disease-resistant toughness of the Scavina parent and the nuanced flavor potential of the Trinitario. Crucially, the genetic traits for disease resistance were found to be complex, requiring careful selection to ensure that the delicate flavor compounds—the notes of red fruit, spice, and jasmine prized by European chocolatiers—were not lost to the blunt, acidic flavor often associated with high-yield Amazonian strains.

THE SEED of Global Salvation

The work Pound began ensured Trinidad's immediate survival, but the impact of the Scavina genetics quickly spread far beyond the Caribbean. As Witches' Broom continued its relentless march across Latin America and other fungal diseases like Black Pod and Frosty Pod threatened production worldwide, the global cacao industry desperately needed resistant stock.

The Scavina 6 gene proved to be a "super-gene," providing robust protection against multiple pathogens. The TSH hybrids became the backbone of breeding programs across the globe:

- Latin America: Breeders used the TSH lines to fortify new varieties against Witches' Broom and Frosty Pod, saving large-scale commercial production in Ecuador and Brazil.
- West Africa and Asia: Though these regions did not initially face Witches' Broom, they incorporated the TSH lines to boost overall hardiness and increase yield, preparing the stock for the eventual arrival of the devastating fungal plagues.

Today, the genetic fingerprint of F.J. Pound's Amazonian finds is woven into the DNA of the vast majority of the world's commercial cacao. Every time a chocolate bar is sold, whether a mass-market treat from West Africa or a fine-flavor bar from Indonesia, its very existence is owed a debt to the durability inherited from those few fragile cuttings that survived the long journey down the Nanay River.

THE ARK's Modern Mandate

The cuttings Pound brought back became the nucleus of the International Cocoa Genebank (ICG) in St. Augustine, Trinidad. The ICG is often referred to as the "Noah's Ark" for chocolate, holding the most diverse collection of living cacao trees on the planet. The Genebank's function today is monumental, serving as the world's genetic insurance policy against future disasters.

- The Living Library: The ICG currently maintains over 2,400 unique varieties of *Theobroma cacao*, grown as live trees because cacao seeds cannot survive conventional freezing methods. This collection includes ancient heirloom Criollos, resilient Amazonian Forasteros, and the key TSH hybrids.
- Targeting New Threats: Genebank researchers continually screen this collection for new defenses against emerging diseases, such as the *Cacao Swollen Shoot Virus* (CSSV) that threatens West Africa, and the challenge of heavy metal uptake in the soil. The Genebank has already identified rare genotypes that avoid absorbing cadmium from contaminated soils—a critical trait for food safety that is now being bred into commercial lines.
- Genome Mapping: As detailed in Chapter 13, the genomic sequencing revolution of the 21st century relies heavily on the biodiversity preserved in the ICG. Scientists use the diverse genetic lines collected by Pound and subsequent explorers as a reference map to isolate disease resistance and flavor genes, accelerating the creation of new, climate-resilient cacao varieties.

Pound's legacy is the recognition that the key to modern agriculture is genetic depth. His journey proved that preserving the wild, sometimes low-yielding, genetic strains is not a hobby; it is a necessity for food security in a changing world.

THE COST of Discovery

For all his monumental contribution, F.J. Pound died with little fame or fortune. He returned from the jungle, a world-class scientist who had achieved the impossible, only to face the bureaucracy of colonial agricultural life.

His rigorous expeditions, constantly battling malaria and dysentery without the benefit of modern medicine, took a severe toll on his constitution. He died tragically young in 1949, at the age of 41, before the true, global impact of the Scavina clones was fully realized. His name does not adorn chocolate wrappers, and few consumers know the extent of his sacrifice.

He traded his health for an idea, venturing into the remote Amazonian labyrinth to fulfill a mandate for an industry that failed to adequately acknowledge his monumental contribution during his lifetime.

Every time we bite into a chocolate bar today, we are enjoying a small piece of Pound's Ark. We are tasting the flavor of the Caribbean, protected by the hardiness of the Amazon, a synergy made possible by one man's courage and scientific conviction. His journey proves that the most valuable treasure in the tropics is often not the gold that glitters, but the genetic material that can save an entire industry

13

THE GENOME REVOLUTION: REWRITING THE DNA OF CHOCOLATE

I magine the year 2050. The supermarket candy aisle is half-empty. A standard chocolate bar costs $25. In West Africa, millions of acres of former farmland are dust bowls, the heat having risen too high to support the delicate Theobroma cacao. This is not the plot of a dystopian novel; it is the trajectory of current climate models.

CACAO IS AN EVOLUTIONARY WIMP. It has zero tolerance for drought and succumbs to fungal spores that travel on the wind. For centuries, we relied on a genetic bottleneck, cloning the same productive but fragile trees. Now, as the planet warms and pathogens like the Swollen Shoot Virus mutate, we are facing a "Chocolate Cliff"—a point of no return where global demand permanently outstrips what the dying trees can produce. To stop this, scientists had to do something radical: they had to hack the code of the tree itself.

A Fragile Tree in Peril

It's hard to imagine that the future of chocolate could be at risk, yet the cacao tree has always been vulnerable. Cacao thrives only in narrow conditions: the shady understory of tropical rainforests, within a band 20 degrees north or south of the Equator. It wilts if temperatures climb too high or rainfall falters. And worse, cacao is constantly stalked by blights and pests.

Farmers have a grim, evocative lexicon for these threats: *Witches' Broom, Frosty Pod, Black Pod, Swollen Shoot*. Each name is a nightmare. Witches' broom disease, caused by a fungus that likely coevolved with cacao in the Amazon, makes branches sprout deformed tangles of stems – the "brooms" – sucking life from the tree. Frosty pod, a cousin fungus, erupts across the surface of pods in a white, powdery crust, rotting the beans inside.

Black pod disease turns the fruit black and foul. And the swollen shoot virus, spread by tiny mealybugs, invisibly infects trees for years, slowly strangling them from within until their trunks swell and crack.

For decades, these plagues have periodically ravaged cacao heartlands. In Ghana – the world's second largest cocoa producer – outbreaks of swollen shoot disease first discovered in the 1930s have never fully gone away.

By the 1960s, it had decimated Ghana's yields, contributing to a collapse in production that shook the cocoa market. In the 1980s, a severe resurgence of the virus, coupled with drought, forced farmers to fell and burn countless trees; Ghana's cocoa output plummeted, and with it the nation's economy trembled. Across the ocean in Brazil, another chocolate powerhouse, an even more dramatic disaster was unfolding.

In the late 1980s, witches' broom fungus invaded the cacao groves of Bahia. This rich agricultural region, which once made Brazil the world's number two cocoa producer, saw its orchards overrun in just a few years. Ghostly groves of leafless branches and fungal spores replaced what had been emerald canopies dotted with red-gold pods. By the 1990s, Brazil's cocoa harvest had collapsed by more than half, devastating rural communities. Many still call it "the chocolate apocalypse."

These crises exposed a dire truth: the global chocolate supply rests on a narrow genetic base. Cacao has a surprisingly shallow family tree on today's farms. Though the plant originated in the upper Amazon with myriad wild varieties, the cacao grown commercially around the world descends from just a few lineages.

In the 18th and 19th centuries, colonial planters spread cacao from its native Americas to Africa and Asia – but they carried only a handful of pods across the oceans. In West Africa, for example, virtually all the millions of cacao trees stem from a few seeds of a type called Forastero (specifically the "Amelonado" strain) that were brought from Brazil and São Tomé.

This gave great yields and hardiness, so it flourished – but it was just one branch of cacao's diversity. Earlier chapters detail the strengths and weaknesses of Criollo, Forastero, and their hybrid offshoots; here the focus shifts to what decades of narrow selection mean for global resilience.

The urgency to save cacao from its own success – from the genetic narrowness that made it profitable – started to dawn on scientists and the chocolate industry alike. If chocolate was to survive the 21st century, cacao would need to be armed with stronger genes. Disease resistance, climate resilience, flavor preservation, biodiversity – all hung in the balance.

The solution would have to be global and visionary. It would require not just traditional crop breeding, but cutting-edge science and unprecedented international collaboration. Thus began the cacao genome revolution: an effort to decode, preserve, and manipulate the genetic blueprint of cacao. It's a story spanning rainforest expeditions, high-tech laboratories, ancient trees and modern corporations – all converging to secure the future of chocolate.

Guardians of a Lost Genetic Heritage

The foundation for the genome revolution was laid decades earlier by the agricultural adventurers described in the previous chapter. The work of pioneers like F.J. Pound, who scoured the Amazon for resistant wild cacao in the 1930s, proved that the solution to cacao's fragility lay in its ancestral genetics. The material they collected—including the legendary Scavina 6—became the backbone of modern breeding. However, traditional cross-breeding was slow, and pathogens were evolving faster than botanists could work. To secure the future, science needed to move from physical expeditions to genetic ones.

To conserve all this genetic wealth, international cacao genebanks were established as living libraries of the crop's diversity. Nowhere is this more impressive than at the International Cocoa Genebank in Trinidad (ICG). Hidden in the verdant fields of the University of the West Indies' research center, the ICG is often called *Noah's Ark for chocolate*. Here, about 2,400 unique varieties of cacao are grown in one expansive garden – the most diverse cacao collection on the planet.

Each tree in Trinidad's genebank has a story: some were rescued from a riverbank deep in the Peruvian jungle; others are descendants of ancient Mayan orchards. Walking through the ICG, you can spot trees with slender yellow pods, squat green pods, or even cherry-red pods covered in spiky protuberances. Some yield beans with intense fine aromas of jasmine or nuts; others carry genes that make them impervious to particular fungi. "It's a wishing well," says Dr. Pathmanathan Umaharan, the genebank's director.

Whenever a new threat or challenge emerges – a virulent fungus, a soil toxin, a climate extreme – chances are that the cure lies somewhere among these trees. Indeed, the Trinidad collection has given rise to many success stories. When cadmium contamination recently threatened cacao exports (as certain soils cause cacao to uptake this heavy metal into beans, running afoul of food safety limits), researchers screened the collection and found a rare genotype whose roots avoid absorbing cadmium. That trait is now being bred into commercial lines.

In Central America, another key sanctuary is CATIE, the Tropical Agricultural Research and Higher Education Center in Costa Rica. At CATIE's sprawling farm, over 1,100 distinct cacao types are maintained, representing clones from throughout the Americas and West Africa. Tall shade trees arch over the plots, mimicking the rainforest canopy.

Here too, diversity is on full display – from venerable heirloom Criollos once cherished by Maya kings, to new hybrids developed by modern scientists. CATIE's international collection, like Trinidad's, has been built over decades through global exchanges of seeds and cuttings. Notably, because cacao seeds cannot survive drying or freezing like typical seed bank specimens, these collections must be kept alive as trees, requiring constant care.

They are vulnerable to hurricanes, droughts, or disease outbreaks themselves. Protecting them is an ongoing challenge. As Dr. Umaharan poignantly notes, these genebanks are the last refuge for cacao's gene pool – and "the arks of chocolate must not sink."

The work at Trinidad, CATIE, and similar institutes is largely unsung, but it laid the foundation for the genome revolution. Preserving genes is one step; the next was learning how to read and deploy them in the most efficient way possible. By the turn of the millennium, the time was ripe for cacao to enter the age of genomics.

CRACKING the Chocolate Code

For years before the breakthrough, scientists had been collecting clues: unexplained patterns of disease resistance, flavor differences between cacao families, and the stubborn fragility of the crop across continents. Each anomaly pointed toward a deeper story written in DNA, but without the genome, breeders and farmers were fighting blind. The sequencing race that followed was not a scientific indulgence—it was a desperate attempt to understand a crop whose survival would determine the future of chocolate itself.

In September 2010, a small group of scientists and executives gathered at a press event and made an astonishing announcement: the genome of the cacao tree had been sequenced and assembled. This achievement was the culmination of years of quiet effort by an international consortium – and an unlikely alliance of industry and academia.

The project had all the elements of a biotech thriller. On one side was Mars, Incorporated, the American confectionery giant behind M&Ms, Snickers, and countless chocolate treats. Mars had a clear business interest: the company relies on a stable cocoa supply, and threats to cacao are threats to their bottom line. But under the leadership of Mars's chief agricultural officer, Dr. Howard-Yana Shapiro, the company also had a vision of "applying the best of science to an underserved crop."

Mars committed substantial funding and insisted the results be made public for all.

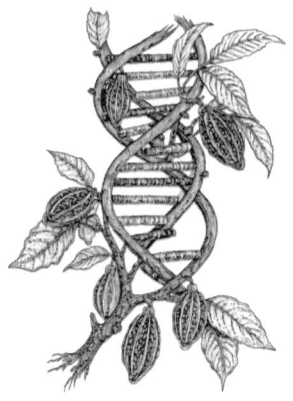

In 2010, the cacao genome was fully sequenced, giving scientists a map to breed trees resistant to climate change and blight without sacrificing flavor.

One arm of the sequencing effort formed in the United States, where Mars partnered with the USDA's Miami-based ARS laboratories. Molecular biologist David Kuhn led the team responsible for decoding Matina 1-6, a rugged Forastero variety that anchors much of the world's cocoa production.

To process the millions of DNA fragments, the group enlisted IBM's Blue Gene supercomputer—one of the most powerful machines of its time—bringing industrial-scale computing to a crop long considered too minor for such attention.

Meanwhile, a competing effort had formed, creating a "race to the genome" reminiscent of the Human Genome Project. While the Mars/USDA team focused on the hardy *Matina 1-6* (a Forastero type dominant in commercial production), a rival consortium involving Hershey's, Penn State University, and the French agency CIRAD set their sights on the "Prince of Cacao"—the rare and delicate *Criollo*. By sequencing a heritage Criollo variety collected in Belize, this second team aimed to uncover the specific genetic architecture of fine flavor. The simultaneous completion of both projects allowed scientists to compare the robust engine of the Foras-tero against the delicate machinery of the Criollo, revealing the trade-offs between disease resistance and flavor complexity. But in truth, the cacao scientists maintained a spirit of collaboration. Dozens of researchers from around 20 institutions and six countries contributed.

The DNA itself was extracted from cacao leaves and then shattered into millions of fragments for sequencing. As the data poured in, bioin-formaticians assembled the fragments back together like a colossal jigsaw puzzle – the cacao genome contains 10 chromosomes and roughly 420 million DNA base pairs—an immense biological puzzle whose assembly demanded the combined power of supercomputing and painstaking genetic analysis.

Dr. Mark Guiltinan, a plant molecular biologist at Penn State on the Criollo project, likened the task of genome assembly to "an art form" requiring equal parts computing power and genetic savvy.

When both teams completed their assemblies, the outlines of cacao's genetic story came sharply into view. Matina revealed the rugged resilience that had made it a global workhorse, while Criollo exposed the fragile, intricate chemistry behind its legendary flavor. The two genomes shared most of their DNA, yet their differences were decisive: small variations that shaped how each tree resisted disease, produced aroma compounds, or adapted to its environment. For breeders, this was the closest thing to an instruction manual cacao had ever had.

Crucially, all of the genome data was released into the public domain, posted openly to global databases where scientists, breeders, and farmers could access it without restriction—an unprecedented act of transparency in crop research. Anyone, from an Ivory Coast agronomist to a boutique cacao farmer in Hawaii, could access cacao's genetic code. This open-science approach, championed by Mars and the academic partners, meant the genome wouldn't sit behind patents or paywalls.

A new era had begun: cacao could finally be bred not by trial-and-error or intuition, but by hard genetic evidence. Instead of relying solely on observation and years of field trials to determine whether a new cacao cross held promise, scientists could search directly for genetic markers—molecular signposts that reveal whether a seedling carries a desired trait long before it bears its first pod.

This method—known as marker-assisted selection—had already reshaped the breeding of corn and rice, and now promised to do the same for cacao. Now cacao would get the same boost. As Guiltinan put it, the goal wasn't to genetically engineer chocolate bars, but to give traditional breeders a high-tech map to speed up their work.

The genome breakthrough also yielded deeper scientific insights. Researchers noted that cultivated cacao varieties displayed pockets of alarmingly low genetic diversity—clear genetic fingerprints of the crop's narrow escape from its Amazonian birthplace. And because the major pathogens that plague cacao—such as witches' broom and frosty pod rot—had also been sequenced by plant pathologists, scientists could, for the first time, compare the genomes of cacao and its enemies.

They began to map, gene by gene, how cacao defends itself during infection and which fungal genes orchestrate the most destructive attacks—an arms race written in DNA. This arms-race in code could reveal new ways to fortify cacao's defenses.

Yet even as the scientific community celebrated, a harder truth emerged: a sequenced genome does not save a single cacao tree. The real challenge lay ahead—translating this avalanche of data into living plants that could survive the heat, pests, and diseases that were already reshaping cacao-growing regions. The genome was the map, but the journey had barely begun.

Breeding for a Sweeter Future

With the cacao genome in hand, plant breeders around the world leapt into action to create the next generation of cacao trees. In West Africa—where more than 70% of the world's cocoa is grown—national institutes and USDA-backed programs focused urgently on traits that could counter the region's most devastating diseases: swollen shoot virus and black pod rot.

Using DNA markers, researchers could identify seedlings that carried genetic resistance—traits often inherited from long-ago Amazonian ancestors—and select them in the nursery years before disease could strike, rather than waiting years for those trees to mature and be tested by exposure. This shaved years off the breeding cycle. In

Ghana and Ivory Coast, trials of new hybrids are underway that promise not only higher yields but also built-in resistance to viral infection, potentially saving millions of trees from the ax.

Cloning chocolate: Farmers graft branches of flavorful "heirloom" varieties onto robust root systems to ensure the tree survives while producing superior beans.

In Latin America, breeders faced the twin terrors of witches' broom and frosty pod. They turned to the gene bank reserves: varieties like Scavina 6, a legendary Upper Amazon cacao genotype known for its strong defense against witches' broom, became a popular parent in crosses. Before genome mapping, Scavina's resistance gene was used, but often at the cost of other traits like flavor.

Now, scientists can combine multiple resistance genes – for different diseases – into one plant, while monitoring that flavor genes remain intact. In Ecuador and Peru, researchers are working to marry the disease-resistant toughness of high-yield hybrids like CCN-51 with the fine flavor of traditional strains.

They scour seedlings' DNA for markers associated with desirable flavor precursors, ensuring those aren't lost in the quest for resilience. Even flavor itself is getting demystified: some genes influencing the cacao butter content and aromatic compounds have been pinpointed, giving breeders clues on maintaining or even enhancing taste.

The stakes are high – no chocolate lover wants a future of plentiful cocoa that tastes bland. The holy grail is a tree that resists disease, yields generously, withstands climate stress, and produces exceptional flavor— all in a single plant. Breeders often quip that achieving this balance is like trying to breed a racehorse that's also as tough as a mule. Progress is incremental, but accelerating thanks to the genome tools.

==

THE BREEDER'S WISHLIST: BUILDING THE PERFECT TREE
   If scientists could design a tree from scratch, it would look like this:

- The Shield: Immune to Witches' Broom and Frosty Pod (fungal killers).
- The Stature: Short and bushy (Dwarf). Easier to harvest by hand without ladders.
- The Yield: Produces 50+ pods a year (vs. the standard 20).
- The Flavor: Must taste like fruit and nuts, not "acidic dirt" (the flaw of current high-yield clones).

==

Profiles of the people leading this charge show a passionate, almost missionary zeal. In a Pennsylvania lab, Dr. Siela Maximova tends to petri dishes of tiny cacao embryos, coaxing them to grow into saplings after experimental crosses – her team's innovations in tissue culture have made it easier to propagate new hybrids en masse.

In France, CIRAD scientists travel frequently to Côte d'Ivoire, working alongside local agronomists to test French-developed varieties in African soils, bridging languages, climates, and agricultural traditions through a shared commitment to sustainable cocoa. At the USDA's facility in Miami, David Kuhn and colleagues continue to update the cacao DNA database as new genetic variants are discovered, essentially maintaining a living genetic encyclopedia of cacao—an evolving reference that breeders around the world consult like scripture.

And in the green hills of Costa Rica, an old-school plant breeder at CATIE might walk through a test plot, chewing on a raw cacao bean to get a hint of its bitterness or floral notes, even as he checks his tablet displaying the genetic marker profile of that very tree. The merging of traditional knowledge and modern genomics is creating something new: the art and science of cacao improvement.

There have been setbacks and lessons. Early on, it became clear that even with genomic insight, nature can surprise breeders. Some gene combinations don't work as expected in the field due to environmental factors we don't yet understand. And pathogens themselves evolve – a fungus might overcome a single resistance gene after a few years, which is why stacking multiple resistance traits is crucial.

This is why safeguarding cacao's biodiversity is essential: each additional genetic lineage expands the crop's ability to withstand evolving diseases, shifting climates, and unforeseen stresses. The genome revolution hasn't replaced the need for those cacao "arks"; it has actually made them more valuable by highlighting which rare genes they hold and deploying them more intelligently.

Every cacao farmer ultimately benefits from this network of science – even if they might not realize the new trees in their field were crafted with the help of a supercomputer and a gene bank thousands of miles away.

From Genome to Genome Editing

As remarkable as the breeding advances have been, some visionaries have set their sights on an even more direct approach: genome editing. Why wait for slow breeding cycles, they argue, if we can tweak the cacao's own DNA precisely to improve it?

In a pristine lab at the Innovative Genomics Institute in California, rows of cacao seedlings grow not in soil, but in sterile gel inside test tubes. These seedlings are special – their DNA has been subtly altered using the CRISPR-Cas9 gene editing tool. Here, plant biologist Myeong-Je Cho and colleagues work under the guidance of Nobel laureate Jennifer Doudna, the co-inventor of CRISPR. In partnership with Mars, they began experimenting with editing cacao genes around 2017.

The first targets: genes that influence drought tolerance and disease resistance. By knocking out or modifying certain genes, they aim to create cacao trees that can thrive in a hotter, drier climate, or that become immune to viruses.

The vision is bold: cacao that could be planted in new regions or remain productive despite climate change, ensuring chocolate doesn't become a casualty of the warming planet. Mars's long-term commitment – including a pledge of $1 billion toward sustainability research –

signaled how seriously the industry takes these threats. "Chocolate is forever, right?" one headline quipped – the implication being that it won't be unless we act. Mars and others want to make sure it is.

By 2025, the gene-editing effort took a further leap. Mars announced a partnership with a leading agricultural biotech startup to fast-track CRISPR-enhanced cacao. The company licensed cutting-edge CRISPR technology to specifically address cacao's most pressing issues.

The director of plant science at Mars, Dr. Carl Jones, explained that the aim is to help cacao "adapt to climate challenges, disease pressures, and resource constraints" in ways traditional breeding might not achieve quickly enough.

One can imagine a not-too-distant future where a cacao tree is edited to resist the swollen shoot virus – the genetic tweak might involve inserting a fragment of a native resistant gene from a wild cacao into a high-yield variety's genome, conferring full immunity.

Or perhaps a gene that regulates the plant's response to heat stress is adjusted so that pods set even when temperatures spike. Unlike older genetic modification (transgenics), which introduces foreign genes from other species, CRISPR edits the plant's existing DNA. Because no foreign genetic material is added, some regulatory bodies, particularly in the U.S., view these crops differently than traditional GMOs, framing the process as accelerated natural selection.

Still, the prospect of gene-edited chocolate raises questions. Will consumers accept it? Mars is betting yes – or that they may not even need to know if regulations classify these edits as conventional breeding. Some scientists caution that biology is complex: one edited trait could have ripple effects on flavor or ecology. "Finding the right blend of flavors, while ensuring disease resistance, rapid growth and high productivity, isn't easy," one researcher noted, underscoring that even with CRISPR's precision, cacao's genome has trade-offs we don't fully grasp. Despite these debates, field trials for edited cacao are likely on the horizon. If successful, they could complement the slower breeding efforts and serve as a sort of genetic insurance policy for the crop.

==

BIOTECH EXPLAINED: HOW CRISPR WORKS

It isn't "Franken-food." It is a pair of molecular scissors.

- **The Tool:** CRISPR-Cas9 is an enzyme that acts like a "Find and Replace" function for DNA.
- **The Process:** Scientists program it to find a specific gene (e.g., the gene that makes a tree susceptible to virus).
- **The Edit:** The enzyme snips that gene out. The plant repairs the cut, but the "weakness" is gone. No foreign DNA is added.

==

A New Dawn for Chocolate

On a late summer morning in Trinidad, Dr. Umaharan strolls through the cocoa genebank after a night of heavy rain. The air is thick with petrichor and the faint sweet smell of ripe cacao fruit. He stops before a particular tree – a scraggly, inconspicuous specimen with mottled pods. This is an old Upper Amazon genotype, hardly used in any plantation, but DNA tests show it carries a gene that could hold the key to defeating frosty pod disease. Nearby, a young researcher is tagging flowers on a different tree, carefully pollinating by hand and tying little identifying ribbons. That tree, a descendant of a Criollo, has outstanding flavor. The hope is that its offspring, crossed with a disease-resistant parent, will combine the best of both. It's painstaking work – but now they have the genome data to know which seedlings from this cross to nurture.

In a very different scene halfway around the world, under the fluorescent lights of a climate-controlled growth chamber, stand row upon row of knee-high cacao plants whose leaves have a slight golden hue – a sign of an edited gene affecting chlorophyll, intentionally done to test the CRISPR system. A technician checks each for any abnormal growth, then makes notes on a tablet. So far, so good. These could be the first generation of climate-resilient cacao, engineered to prosper where their ancestors would have withered. If they pass more tests, they might be headed to a field in Côte d'Ivoire or Indonesia, heralding a new era in cacao farming.

The cacao genome revolution is not one single event but an ongoing saga – a blend of conservation, innovation, and determination. It links the deep past to the unfolding future. Think of the ancient cacao groves where Maya priests once prayed to the cacao spirit for bountiful harvests. Those priests could not have imagined DNA sequencers or gene editing, but they understood the sacred importance of this plant. Today's scientists and farmers, in their own way, carry on that reverence. They peer through microscopes and pore over computer screens with the same hope: to keep the cacao tree healthy and abundant for generations to come.

The stakes could not be more human. Millions of smallholder farmers in West Africa, Asia, and Latin America depend on cacao for their livelihoods. Whole national economies rely on its export. And for the rest of us, cacao provides small daily joys – a piece of chocolate that melts on the tongue, a beloved flavor that has journeyed from a tropical pod to our palate. Preserving that joy against threats like blight and climate change is both a scientific challenge and a moral one.

As we look ahead, we can imagine the year 2050: a farmer walking through a thriving cocoa orchard that grows where previously it was too hot or dry. The trees are bearing plentiful pods, and he knows these particular trees won't easily fall to disease – they were bred and even gene-edited for exactly that resilience. The pods he harvests carry the classic rich cocoa taste that his grandparents remember, because the breeders made sure not to lose the fine flavor genes in the process. In a distant lab, some of the very scientists who helped create these trees might be enjoying a chocolate bar made from that farmer's crop, marveling at how far things have come.

From the brink of collapse in the 1980s to the high-tech rescue missions of today, cacao has been on a remarkable journey. It has survived fungal plagues, navigated genetic bottlenecks, and now is entering a renaissance of genomic enlightenment. The cacao genome revolution is ensuring that the story of chocolate will go on – richer, more sustainable, and perhaps even sweeter than before. In saving the cacao tree, we are, in a sense, decoding and safeguarding a small but beloved piece of our global heritage. And that is truly a heroic enterprise worth savoring.

14

GROWING GREEN COCOA:
SUSTAINABILITY AND
THE FUTURE OF FARMING

magine walking through a lush cacao grove at dawn. Sunlight filters through a canopy of towering trees, illuminating clusters of ripening cocoa pods in dappled gold and crimson. The air is alive with the chirps of birds and the faint sweet scent of fermenting cocoa. This serene scene is worlds away from the harsh reality that many cocoa farms have faced – but it offers a glimpse of chocolate's sustainable future.

IN RECENT YEARS, the chocolate industry has begun a quiet revolution. Chocolate lovers and makers alike are realizing that the story behind our favorite treat is as important as its taste. Across the tropics, forward-thinking farmers, companies, and consumers are working to grow "green" cocoa – cacao that is cultivated and processed in harmony with the environment and with respect for the people who produce it.

The journey isn't simple. It's a story of challenges and change, of ancient farming wisdom rediscovered, of new innovations from farm to factory, and of chocolate enthusiasts using their purchasing power to demand better. Let's unwrap this rich narrative of how sustainability is shaping chocolate's future.

. . .

THE BITTER SIDE of Cocoa

The global demand for chocolate has cast a long shadow on the tiny cacao farms scattered through equatorial forests that are the source of much of the the world's cacao supply. In West Africa – which grows about three-quarters of the world's cocoa – expanding cocoa plantations have often come at the cost of priceless tropical rainforest. In countries like Côte d'Ivoire and Ghana, vast swaths of forest were cleared over past decades to make way for cocoa trees.

This deforestation not only erases habitat for endangered species, it also disrupts local climate and soil health. When diverse jungles turn into single-crop monoculture farms, biodiversity plummets. Birds, insects, and other wildlife that once thrived in cocoa's shade vanish when the shade itself is gone.

The soil, no longer protected by a canopy or enriched by a mix of plant life, becomes exhausted. Without the natural cover, farmers often rely on more fertilizers and pesticides to coax yields from the weakened earth. The result is a cycle that further harms rivers, soil life, and surrounding communities.

Climate change pours additional heat on this already strained system. Cacao trees are fussy; they need specific temperatures and moisture levels to flourish. As global temperatures rise, the threat to cacao becomes existential. Climatologists have drawn a sobering line in the sand: the year 2050. According to models from the Intergovernmental Panel on Climate Change (IPCC), if current warming trends continue, the optimal altitude for growing cacao in West Africa will rise from 350 to 1,500 feet.

The problem? Most of West Africa is flat. By 2050, the lush, humid belt that currently supplies the world's chocolate could bake into a savannah, rendering the crop—and the livelihoods of two million farmers—biologically impossible. We are not just facing a bad harvest; we are facing an extinction event for the industry as we know it.

==

THE 2050 PLEDGE: FUTURE-PROOFING YOUR CHOCOLATE

The most powerful tool for sustainability is your wallet. Here are three actions to support the tree.

- DEMAND SHADE-GROWN: Buy brands committed to Agroforestry systems. This is the single best way to combat climate stress and deforestation at the farm level.
- PAY THE DIFFERENTIAL: Actively seek brands that pay a price premium or Direct Trade rate, not just the commodity price. Low prices force farmers to clear-cut forest for more land.
- UPGRADE YOUR APPETITE: Prioritize Darker Chocolate (70%+). This increases demand for cocoa solids and reduces the volume needed, easing global supply pressure.

==

A DISEASE OUTBREAK or dry spell can ruin a harvest and push farmers to the brink. In some areas, farmers are even attempting to plant cocoa at higher elevations or moving into new regions, which sometimes means cutting down more forest. Thus, climate change and deforestation can form a vicious circle.

The challenges aren't just environmental – they're deeply ethical as well. The chocolate we enjoy is largely the product of millions of small-holder farmers, many of whom live in poverty. The price of cocoa on the world market has often been so low that farming families struggle to cover basic needs. I

t's common to find cocoa farming communities lacking electricity, schools, or clean water, even as their crop feeds a $100-billion chocolate industry worldwide. This imbalance in wealth and power has led to troubling labor practices. In the most extreme cases, children end up working long days on cocoa farms instead of going to school, and instances of forced labor have been documented.

Recent estimates suggest that well over a million children in West

Africa perform hazardous work on cocoa farms. These kids might wield machetes to crack pods or spray chemicals without protection – tasks no child should have to do. The root cause is economic desperation: when prices for cocoa are too low, farmers cannot afford to hire adult labor or implement safer practices, so the whole family must pitch in to survive.

This bitter side of cocoa's supply chain leaves a bad taste. Deforestation, climate pressures, exploitative labor – they all pose serious threats to the future of chocolate. Yet, across the globe, a movement is growing to address these issues head-on. From the heart of Africa to the islands of Asia, people are proving that cocoa can be grown in a way that nurtures the land and uplifts farming communities. The next sections will delve into how sustainable practices and passionate change-makers are transforming the cocoa sector from the ground up.

Cultivating a Greener Cocoa: Sustainable Farming Practices

Turning the tide from destructive farming to a sustainable model starts at the farm level. Around the world, farmers and agronomists are reviving smarter, greener ways to grow cacao. Many of these methods actually hark back to traditional practices, now supported by modern science. Here are some key sustainable practices taking root in cacao fields:

- The Carbon Credit Economy: Sustainability is no longer just about charity; it is becoming a financial asset. As global corporations race to reach "Net Zero" emissions, cacao farms are becoming valuable carbon sinks. Tech-forward cooperatives are now mapping trees via satellite. If a farmer can prove—through aerial data—that they have maintained canopy cover rather than clear-cutting, they can sell "Carbon Credits" to heavy polluters in the West. This turns the shade tree from a biological necessity into a second cash crop. The farmer gets paid for the cocoa they grow *and* the carbon they store, creating a powerful financial incentive to keep the rainforest standing.

- Biodiversity Conservation: Hand-in-hand with agroforestry comes an emphasis on preserving biodiversity on farms. Instead of a sterile plantation of only cocoa trees, sustainable farms cultivate a variety of plants. Some farmers grow food crops alongside cacao – cassava, maize, or vegetables – which improves food security and income diversity for the family. Others maintain strips of natural vegetation or leave big old forest trees standing among the cocoa. These pockets of life serve as corridors for wildlife and reservoirs of genetic diversity. They also help with pest control: for example, birds and bats living in shade trees gobble up insects that might otherwise damage cocoa pods. Even the soil biodiversity improves; worms and microbes thrive when organic matter returns to the earth. By treating the farm as an ecosystem rather than a factory, farmers create conditions where nature's services (like pollination, pest reduction, and soil fertility) shoulder some of the workload. In Madagascar, for instance, some cocoa growers take pride in the fact that their groves also host vanilla orchids, pepper vines, or medicinal plants. A single farm might shelter dozens of species – including, famously, the lemurs that sometimes leap through Madagascar's cacao orchards – turning cocoa cultivation into an act of conservation.
- Regenerative Agriculture: Sustainability goes beyond preventing harm – it's also about restoring what's been lost. Enter regenerative agriculture, a philosophy of farming that aims to rebuild soil health, increase biodiversity, and capture carbon in the ground. For cocoa farmers, regenerative practices include mulching fields with fallen leaves and cocoa pod husks (instead of burning them), planting cover crops to prevent erosion, and using natural compost or manure to enrich the soil. Some farmers are experimenting with dynamic agroforestry, a regenerative system where cacao is one part of a constantly evolving mix of trees and shrubs that can restore degraded land. The results can be dramatic: soils once hardened and depleted start teeming with life and

nutrients again, yielding better harvests without heavy
chemical use. Carbon sequestration is another bonus –
healthy cacao agroforests act like little carbon sinks, locking
away CO_2 in tree trunks and soils, which helps in the fight
against climate change. In Ecuador, innovative projects have
even planted cacao as a tool to reforest former cattle pasture.
Young cacao trees grow under the protection of fast-growing
pioneer trees; over time a multi-layered forest develops, and
what starts as a cocoa farm ends up looking and functioning
like a young rainforest. This kind of regenerative cacao
farming not only produces fine cocoa beans, but also leaves
the land richer and more resilient than before.

- Farmer Cooperatives and Fair Livelihoods: Sustainability isn't
  solely about ecology – it's also about economics and equity.
  Around the cocoa-growing world, farmers are coming
  together to form cooperatives and community organizations.
  By banding together, small-scale farmers increase their
  bargaining power when selling beans, invest collectively in
  tools and training, and share knowledge about sustainable
  techniques. Cooperatives often provide education on crop
  diversification, fermentation methods to improve bean
  quality, and ways to navigate market prices. Importantly,
  many co-ops are dedicated to ethical trade, cutting out
  exploitative middlemen and ensuring farmers receive a
  higher share of the chocolate dollar. In Ghana, for example,
  one famous cooperative became co-owners of a global
  chocolate brand – a groundbreaking model that gives farmers
  a voice and stake in the final product. Such arrangements
  empower farmers to prioritize long-term sustainability
  because they're not just price-takers at the mercy of volatile
  markets. Earning a better income means families can afford
  to keep children in school and hire adult labor, breaking the
  cycle of poverty-driven child labor. Furthermore, cooperatives
  often reinvest in their communities: building local schools,
  clinics, or providing crop insurance and pension plans for
  members. In essence, social sustainability underpins

environmental sustainability – when farming families have stability and hope for the future, they are far more likely to care for their land and cocoa trees with an eye toward the next generation.

From shaded groves teeming with life to organized farmer groups, these sustainable farming practices are like rays of sunshine breaking through the canopy. They show that cocoa can be grown in a way that enriches the soil, protects forests, and allows farming families to thrive. But what does this look like in practice on the ground? Let's journey to a few cacao-growing regions to see how these ideas are transforming real communities and landscapes.

GHANA: Reviving Forest-Friendly Cocoa Farming

West Africa's Ghana is synonymous with cocoa – "cocoa is Ghana, and Ghana is cocoa," as the local saying goes. Yet along with neighboring Côte d'Ivoire, Ghana has wrestled with the dark sides of cocoa farming: dwindling forests and entrenched farmer poverty. Now, a wave of change is bringing new life to Ghana's cocoa belt by looking to the past for inspiration. Generations ago, Ghana's cocoa farmers grew their crops under the rainforest canopy, and many are reviving that tradition today.

Sustainable chocolate mimics the rainforest. Cacao thrives best when planted in the shade of taller timber and fruit trees, creating a biodiverse home for birds and pollinators.

In southern Ghana, one might visit a cocoa farm that feels like a mini-forest: tall shade trees such as odum and cedrella rise above a lower layer of cocoa, plantains, and citrus trees. Sunbeams peek through rustling leaves, and you can hear insects buzzing lazily in the afternoon heat. This isn't just a pretty vision – it's a climate-smart strategy. The shade trees cool the farm (a blessing as average temperatures climb) and their fallen leaves act as natural fertilizer for the cocoa.

On a farm like this, the cocoa trees are less stressed and more resistant to drought. Farmers also gain extra sources of food and income – bananas, oranges, timber, or charcoal – all from the shade-providing plants. One Ghanaian farmer quipped that his cocoa "now grows with companions instead of alone," and those companions have made all the difference in keeping his farm productive year-round.

Beyond re-greening the farms, Ghana is also tackling sustainability through community innovation. A heartwarming example comes from a rural community in Ghana's Eastern Region, where a husband-and-wife farming team, Alex and Georgina, decided to try something unusual: beekeeping on their cocoa plot. Initially, they were nervous – Would the bees sting their kids? Could they manage the hives? – but they received training and encouragement from a local sustainability initiative.

They planted wildflower shrubs and protected a few old forest trees on their land to give the bees a healthy habitat. Fast forward a year, and their small farm has been utterly transformed. The bees happily pollinate the cacao flowers, leading to more plentiful pods at harvest. The flowering trees and shrubs provide forage for the bees and in return enrich the soil with fallen organic matter.

Alex and Georgina now harvest not just cocoa, but pure golden honey which they can sell for extra income. "The hives have brought us more than just honey," Georgina says with a proud smile. "Our cocoa pods grew bigger and healthier this year, and we earn money from two sources."

This integrated approach – cocoa trees, shade trees, and bees working in harmony – encapsulates the win-win outcomes that sustainability efforts are yielding across Ghana. Yield increases, diversified income, and the restoration of nature's balance on the farm have given these farmers newfound optimism.

Integrated farming: Farmers in Ghana are introducing beehives to
their cocoa groves. The bees pollinate crops and provide honey,
creating a second income stream.

On a broader scale, Ghana has joined international pledges to end deforestation linked to cocoa. The government, major chocolate companies, and NGOs are collaborating on programs to distribute shade tree seedlings, train farmers in agroforestry, and monitor forest cover via satellite to curb illegal expansion into protected areas.

Farmer cooperatives in Ghana are also very active; some have obtained Fairtrade or Rainforest Alliance certifications, signaling to buyers that their cocoa meets certain environmental and social standards. All these efforts are like seeds planted in Ghana's rich soil – they are beginning to grow into a more sustainable cocoa sector. The hope is that Ghana can be a model, proving that one of the world's top cocoa producers can find a balance where forests, farmers, and chocolate lovers all win.

ECUADOR: Cacao Heritage Meets Conservation

Travel across the Atlantic to Ecuador, and you find a cacao story steeped in history and flavor. Ecuador is often called the birthplace of cacao; indigenous communities here have cultivated cacao for millennia, and the country is famed for its *Arriba Nacional* beans with their delicate floral aroma.

But Ecuador's rainforests, including parts of the Amazon, have faced pressures from agriculture and development, and cocoa farming hasn't been innocent in that. The future of Ecuador's cacao lies in honoring its heritage while innovating to protect the forests that make this land so special.

In the Upper Amazon of Ecuador, indigenous Kichwa farmers still practice a traditional form of agroforestry known as the *chakra* system. A chakra is like a garden of Eden – a biodiverse parcel of land where cacao trees grow intermixed with banana, cassava, corn, hardwood trees, medicinal plants, and more.

Wander through a chakra farm and you'll see cacao pods dangling next to bunches of ripe plantains; vines of vanilla and black pepper coil around trunks, and colorful heliconia flowers attract hummingbirds. This sustainable approach goes back generations, and it's brilliantly resilient. The mix of crops means families have food security and multiple income streams, and the forest cover stays largely intact.

One Kichwa farmer explained that when he walks through his chakra, he feels pride knowing that it provides almost everything his family needs while looking almost like wild forest. In terms of conservation, these farms serve as important buffer zones around primary rainforest, creating a gradual transition rather than a hard edge of deforestation.

Projects in Ecuador are now supporting such indigenous practices by offering training on organic cocoa cultivation and helping these farmers get premiums for their high-quality cacao. By valuing the traditional knowledge embedded in the chakra, conservationists are finding an ally in local culture to save forests.

Ecuador is also home to some cutting-edge sustainability experiments. On the coastal plains, where sun-tolerant hybrid cacao varieties once fueled large-scale monocultures (and consequent deforestation), some entrepreneurs are flipping the script. One notable initiative involves reforesting degraded farmland with native tree species and cacao – essentially using cacao as a driver of reforestation.

Young cacao trees are planted amidst tropical hardwood saplings. As the forest matures, the cacao benefits from the shade and rich soil, and the surrounding forest benefits from having an economic crop integrated, which deters future clear-cutting.

Early results have been inspiring: previously eroded lands are turning green again, local farmers earn income from the cocoa and from fruits or timber of companion trees, and wildlife is gradually returning. This kind of regenerative cacao farming is not just a theory; it's happening on the ground. For example, in one such project a farmer might plant cacao alongside balsa and citrus trees on former pasture.

Within a few years, the area transforms into a young forest that sequesters carbon and shelters sloths, birds, and insects – all while yielding fine cacao for premium chocolate. It's a powerful demonstration that cacao, often blamed for deforestation, can be marshaled as a tool for re-greening the earth.

In the realm of ethics and economics, Ecuadorian cocoa is taking steps forward too. There's a strong push for traceability and quality. Many farmers are part of cooperatives that ferment and dry beans centrally to maintain high quality, and some are now exporting directly to craft chocolate makers worldwide.

A few local chocolate companies in Ecuador have adopted a bean-to-bar model at origin, which means they produce finished chocolate within the country. This keeps more value with the farming communities and cuts down the carbon footprint of shipping bulk beans overseas.

One luxury chocolate brand in Ecuador even partners with a conservation NGO – for every bar sold, they fund the planting of trees in the very regions where their cacao is sourced. Stories like these show how Ecuador's deep-rooted love of cacao is evolving hand-in-hand with a commitment to preserve its incomparable forests and biodiversity. The result is chocolate that doesn't just taste incredible, but carries within it the richness of a thriving ecosystem.

MADAGASCAR: Cacao in Harmony with the Land of Lemurs

Madagascar, the large island off Africa's east coast, is renowned for its one-of-a-kind wildlife and vanilla-scented air. It also produces a tiny fraction of the world's cocoa, but that cocoa has an outsized reputation among chocolate aficionados for its unique, fruity flavor profile. What's more, some of the most inspiring sustainability stories percolate from this Indian Ocean gem, where cacao grows in balance with nature and communities find new hope in chocolate.

Most of Madagascar's cacao comes from the Sambirano Valley in the northwest of the island. Here, the cacao is often grown on small family farms that resemble flourishing gardens. Picture a Malagasy cacao plot:

you'll see cacao trees with their red and orange pods nestled under taller shade like mango, jackfruit, or indigenous trees. You'll likely smell the sweet fragrance of nearby ylang-ylang flowers (used in perfumes) or vanilla vines that some farmers cultivate alongside cacao.

The air rings with the sounds of cicadas and distant calls of birds – and perhaps, if you're lucky and quiet, you might spot a lemur watching from a high branch, big eyes peering curiously at the human tending the cocoa below. This interwoven diversity is not by accident; Malagasy farmers have learned that their cocoa thrives best with some natural shade and companionship.

The island's long isolation has created delicate ecosystems, and farmers generally understand that protecting their forest fragments and soil is crucial. They often use organic practices by default, recycling cacao pod husks as compost and avoiding expensive chemicals. After all, many farms are so remote that pesticides and fertilizers are hard to come by – a challenge that has become an ecological advantage.

One remarkable initiative in Madagascar is the push to produce chocolate locally and ethically. Traditionally, Madagascar exported its fine cacao beans to Europe. But over the last decade or two, a few social enterprises have set up chocolate factories right in Madagascar, closer to the farmers.

One such company not only sources directly from hundreds of Malagasy smallholders, paying them well above market rate, but also manufactures the finished bars in Madagascar's capital. By doing so, they create skilled jobs locally (from chocolate makers to wrapper designers) and keep a greater share of profit in-country.

This "value addition at origin" model has had ripple effects: farmers now have a stable buyer who rewards quality and sustainability, and they receive training in farm rehabilitation, pruning, and fermentation techniques to ensure consistency. Moreover, because the chocolate is sold with a compelling story – single-origin, heirloom cacao grown in harmony with Madagascar's environment – global consumers pay a premium, which flows back to the producers.

The brand's success has inspired others and shown the world that an African country can produce gourmet chocolate, not just raw cocoa.

From a conservation standpoint, this approach reduces pressure on land. When farmers earn more from the same plot of cacao, they are less tempted to slash-and-burn new land to plant additional crops.

Some farmers who partner with local chocolate makers have agreements to practice reforestation – for example, planting a number of native trees each year on their property, or protecting a nearby riverbank with vegetation.

The presence of high-value cocoa that depends on the area's biodiversity becomes an incentive to preserve that biodiversity. In essence, a bar of Madagascar chocolate today might symbolize a safe haven for lemurs or a patch of forest not cut down. It's a powerful synergy: the island's exotic ecology imparts rare flavor notes to the chocolate (many tasters detect hints of citrus and red berries in Madagascar cacao), and the premium earned from those beans helps ensure the ecology remains intact.

Madagascar's experience, though on a smaller scale, serves as a beacon. It shows that even in a country struggling with poverty and deforestation, sustainable cocoa can take root and flourish.

By safeguarding their environment and investing in local chocolate production, Malagasy farmers and entrepreneurs are proving that chocolate can indeed be a force for good – a force that protects the very enchantment (be it a lemur's call or a rainforest bloom) that makes their cocoa so exceptional.

VIETNAM: A New Frontier for Ethical Chocolate

Not long ago, Vietnam was not even on the map of cocoa producers. But in the last two decades, this Southeast Asian nation – better known for coffee and rice – has quietly emerged as an unexpected player in the chocolate world. With its tropical climate and enterprising farmers, Vietnam is turning out to be a new frontier for sustainable, ethical chocolate, carving a niche with distinctive flavors and progressive practices.

Cocoa was introduced to Vietnam only in the 20th century, but it's in the 21st century that it really took off. Much of Vietnam's cacao is grown in the Mekong Delta and the Central Highlands. What makes Vietnam's approach interesting is how farmers have integrated cacao into existing farming systems. In the lush Mekong Delta, for example, it's common to see cacao trees planted in the shade of towering coconut palms.

This dual-crop model – cacao intercropped with coconuts – has been a win-win. The tall coconut trees provide ample shade for the cacao (and drop leaves that enrich the soil), while the cacao offers farmers an extra source of income without requiring more land. One farmer in Ben Tre province joked that his cacao trees are "earning money during the coconut trees' nap time," since coconuts alone left parts of his orchard's potential untapped.

The government and agricultural experts have promoted this model, noting that a hectare of coconut-cacao interplanting can significantly increase a family's earnings versus coconuts alone. It's a strategy of diversification that boosts resilience: if coconut prices slump or a storm harms one crop, the other can carry them through.

And unlike clear-cut monocultures, these mixed orchards keep the delta green and biodiverse. You might walk through a Vietnamese cacao-coconut grove and see chickens scratching at fallen leaves or hear the croak of frogs in irrigation canals – signs of a healthy, mixed farming ecosystem.

Sustainability in Vietnam's cocoa story extends beyond farming methods. The rise of bean-to-bar chocolate makers in the country has been a game changer. A handful of passionate artisans in Vietnam decided to make high-quality chocolate using local cacao, rather than seeing all the good beans exported.

They established small factories to roast and grind beans from specific provinces, each batch of chocolate highlighting a "terroir" – be it the robust, spicy notes from Dak Lak or the bright, fruity profile from Tien Giang. Crucially, these makers work directly with farmers, often paying premium prices for well-fermented, organic cacao. They visit farms, share feedback on bean quality, and sometimes even provide financing for farm improvements or fermentation equipment.

This direct trade approach builds trust and incentivizes sustainable farming; a farmer knows that better environmental stewardship and post-harvest care will be rewarded by a long-term purchasing relationship with the chocolate maker.

In one case, a cooperative of farmers in Ba Ria province received technical help to transition to organic practices, after which a Vietnamese chocolate company began buying their entire output at a generous price. Such partnerships are still growing, but they hint at a future where Vietnamese cacao could be synonymous with quality and ethics.

Another innovation from Vietnam is the use of cacao byproducts. Some communities have started processing the sweet white pulp that surrounds cacao beans – a typically discarded byproduct – into refreshing drinks and confections for the local market. By making full use of the cacao fruit (not just the beans), farmers create extra value and reduce waste. It's the kind of resourcefulness that aligns perfectly with sustainability principles.

Additionally, Vietnam's entry into cocoa has been marked by a strong emphasis on learning and adapting global best practices quickly. From the get-go, many Vietnamese farmers accessed training on agroforestry, grafting high-yield cacao varieties onto hardy rootstocks, and proper fermentation techniques.

The country even has an annual cocoa conference where farmers and entrepreneurs swap knowledge on everything from pest control without pesticides to developing eco-friendly packaging for their chocolate bars.

Vietnam's journey is proof that it's never too late to do cocoa right. By blending cocoa into their existing agro-ecosystems and focusing on ethical, high-quality production, Vietnam's cocoa pioneers are avoiding many of the pitfalls experienced elsewhere. For chocolate enthusiasts, the result is exciting: new flavors to explore, and the satisfaction of knowing these bars come from a supply chain that values farmers and forests.

Vietnam's example might well inspire other emerging regions to leapfrog straight into sustainable cocoa farming, showing that the newest chapter in chocolate's history can also be one of its greenest.

FROM BEAN TO WRAPPER: Sustainable Innovations

Sustainability isn't just growing cacao the right way – it extends to how chocolate is produced, packaged, and delivered to sweet-toothed consumers. After cocoa beans leave the farm, there are many steps before they become chocolate bars, and each step is an opportunity to reduce waste and environmental impact. In recent years, the chocolate industry has seen an influx of innovations aimed at making the entire journey from bean to wrapper more eco-friendly.

One exciting area of innovation is in using the whole cacao fruit. Typically, when farmers crack open a cacao pod, they scoop out the beans and the rest – the sticky pulp, pod husk, and cocoa bean shells – is thrown away.

Astonishingly, about three-quarters of the cacao pod by weight is not the beans themselves. Traditionally that biomass has been left to rot on the farm or tossed in a pile at the chocolate factory. But now, creative minds are finding uses for these so-called wastes. For instance, the sweet cacao pulp that surrounds the beans is being turned into juices, jams, and even a natural sweetener for chocolates. In some West African countries, entrepreneurs collect cacao pulp from fermentaries to bottle a refreshing juice that provides farmers extra income.

Researchers have also discovered that the pod husks can be composted into rich organic fertilizer or processed into biochar, a form of charcoal that, when added to soil, boosts fertility and locks away carbon. In one innovative project, cacao pod husks are used as fuel in biomass generators to produce electricity for rural communities – turning what was garbage into green energy.

And what about the papery shells that come off roasted cacao beans during winnowing? Those cocoa shells are finding a second life too: breweries steep them to make cocoa-infused beer, gardeners use them as mulch to suppress weeds, and some companies are even milling them into high-fiber cocoa flour for baking.

Perhaps most impressive of all, scientists recently developed a method to incorporate ground cacao pod fibers back into chocolate, creating a finished chocolate bar that includes ingredients from what normally would be scrap. This "whole-fruit chocolate" has more fiber and less sugar, and it means fewer truckloads of waste leaving the factory. Imagine a future where every part of the cacao harvest becomes something useful – that future is on the horizon.

==

DON'T TOSS THE HUSKS: BREW CACAO TEA

Sustainability starts in your kitchen. After roasting beans (or buying nibs), you are often left with papery shells. This is not trash; it is "The Mayan Tea."

- The Recipe:
  - Take 2 tablespoons of clean, roasted cacao shells.
  - Steep in 8oz of boiling water for 5–7 minutes.
  - Add a splash of almond milk or a teaspoon of agave.
- The Taste: It tastes like a delicate chocolate tea with zero fat and a gentle theobromine buzz. It is the ultimate zero-waste drink.

==

Chocolate manufacturing itself is also getting a green makeover. Chocolate factories, especially artisanal makers, are adopting cleaner energy and smarter processes. In Switzerland and the UK, a few chocolate factories have installed solar panels on their roofs, harnessing the sun to power their roasters and grinders (how fitting, to use sunshine to create chocolate that originally grew under the sun!).

Some larger companies invest in wind farms or solar farms to offset the energy used in their confectionery plants. Energy efficiency is another focus: modern machinery can grind cocoa nibs into silky liquor using less electricity than older models, and heat exchangers reclaim warmth from roasting machines to heat other parts of the facility or even nearby homes. At a factory in Ghana, engineers implemented a system to burn cacao shells – yes, those same shells mentioned above – in a boiler, generating steam that powers the cocoa bean drying process.

This reduces reliance on fossil fuels and cleverly uses a byproduct that used to just go to waste. Water conservation efforts are also in play; some cocoa processing units recycle water used in cleaning equipment or cooling, cutting down on overall usage. Step by step, these improvements shrink the carbon footprint and resource needs of making chocolate, which is good news for the planet.

Now let's talk about that final layer every chocolate bar comes in: packaging. Historically, chocolates have been wrapped in a mix of plastic, foil, and paper – much of which ends up in landfills or as litter. But no aspect of chocolate is too small to escape the sustainability rethink. Packaging is undergoing a revolution of its own. Many chocolate companies are switching to compostable or biodegradable wrappers made from plant-based films. These materials might be derived from cellulose (like wood pulp or corn starch) or even seaweed.

They look and act much like plastic to keep chocolate fresh, but when disposed of properly they break down into harmless organic matter. In grocery aisles today you can find chocolate bars sealed in translucent compostable foils inside recycled paper boxes decorated with soy-based inks – every element designed to minimize environmental harm.

Some brands have eliminated the plastic inner wrapper entirely, opting for just one layer of thick paper that is recyclable or compostable yet still keeps the chocolate safe. Upcycling is a buzzword in packaging too. Remember those cacao bean shells and husks?

A few innovative companies are pulping them into paper to create rustic-looking chocolate boxes and labels – literally packaging chocolate in its own skin! This upcycled paper not only reduces waste but also gives chocolate lovers a tangible connection to the cacao plant with every unboxing.

There are even experiments in edible packaging: imagine a chocolate bar wrapped in a thin film made of cacao byproducts or other edible material, so you could theoretically eat the wrapper (or at least toss it in your compost with zero waste).

While still niche, edible wrappers speak to the creativity being unleashed in solving the packaging problem. Additionally, some chocolatiers are trying a minimalist approach – selling bars in reusable tins or jars, or encouraging customers to buy unwrapped chocolates in bulk with their own containers, similar to how one might refill coffee beans or grains.

The key challenge with sustainable packaging is to maintain the quality of the chocolate (protecting it from moisture, oxygen, and light) while cutting down on plastic and waste. With technology improving, that balance is increasingly achievable. Customers, especially younger, eco-conscious ones, are responding with enthusiasm – many say they prefer brands that show responsibility in packaging and will even pay a bit more for it.

All these innovations, from all-parts-used cacao to solar-powered production to zero-waste packaging, are aligning to redefine what it means to make chocolate. It's a nod to the idea that sustainability doesn't end at the farm gate; it must carry through the entire lifecycle of chocolate.

And encouragingly, it seems to be a case where tradition and technology are working together: some of the greenest ideas (like using cacao husks for fertilizer) are what farmers have done for ages, while others (like bio-based edible film or carbon-neutral factories) are products of modern science. Together, they're helping ensure that our enjoyment of chocolate leaves behind as little environmental impact as possible – just the foil crinkle and a happy memory of sweetness.

CONSCIOUS CONSUMERS: **The New Ingredient in Chocolate's Future**

Who ultimately has the power to ensure chocolate is sustainable? The simple answer: all of us who eat it. In the journey towards greener cocoa and ethical chocolate, conscious consumers have emerged as one of the most influential forces. Our collective choices – in supermarkets, gourmet shops, and online – are sending a loud and clear message to the industry: we want chocolate that we can feel good about, not just indulge in.

The rise of the conscious chocolate consumer can be seen in the proliferation of labels and certifications on chocolate bars. More people now look for badges like Fair Trade, Rainforest Alliance, or Organic when choosing their sweet treat.

These logos aren't just box-ticking; they signal that the product meets certain standards for environmental care and farmer well-being. Buying a Fair Trade chocolate bar, for instance, means the consumer is supporting a system where farmers received a minimum price and an additional premium for community development.

Opting for a Rainforest Alliance bar indicates that the cocoa was grown with an eye to conserving forests and wildlife. Even though such certifications aren't perfect, they reflect a demand from shoppers for transparency and accountability in the cocoa supply chain.

In response, major chocolate manufacturers have had to step up their game, announcing plans to trace their cocoa to the source and eliminate deforestation and child labor. A decade ago, these kinds of commitments were rare; today, they're increasingly seen as baseline expectations – and that's largely thanks to consumer pressure and awareness.

==

DECODER RING: WHAT THE LOGOS ACTUALLY MEAN
Not all stamps are equal.

Choose the one that matches your values.

- Fairtrade (The People): Guarantees a Minimum Price for farmers to protect against market crashes. Focus: Poverty alleviation.
- Rainforest Alliance (The Planet): Focuses on Biodiversity and shade coverage. Does not guarantee a minimum price for the farmer. Focus: Ecology.
- USDA Organic (The Chemicals): Zero synthetic pesticides or fertilizers. It says nothing about labor conditions or wages.
- B Corp (The Company): Certifies the entire company, not just the bar. Measures social and environmental performance.

==

Beyond certifications, the ethos of "bean-to-bar" and "direct trade" has caught the imagination of chocolate lovers. These terms often mean that a chocolate maker sources beans straight from specific farmers or cooperatives, forging personal relationships and often paying above-market prices for exceptional quality and sustainable practices.

While bean-to-bar chocolate started as a small artisanal movement, it has grown into a significant segment of the market because consumers crave that connection to origin. It's similar to the way coffee drinkers became interested in single-origin brews and knowing the farmer's story.

With chocolate, when people read on a package that the bar inside came from, say, a single estate in Tanzania where agroforestry is practiced, or from a women-led cooperative in Peru that invests in local schools – it adds depth to the tasting experience.

It transforms a simple snack into a narrative of culture, ecology, and ethics. And people are willing to support that with their wallets. The success of many small craft chocolate brands with strong direct-trade models demonstrates that a segment of consumers actively seeks out chocolate that aligns with their values.

Conscious consumers are also engaging with chocolate's sustainability through education and advocacy. Initiatives like "Chocolate Scorecards" and documentary films about the cocoa industry have armed enthusiasts with knowledge about which companies are leading and which are lagging on issues like deforestation or farmer income.

In an age of social media, bad press travels fast – if a big brand is linked to a human rights scandal or forest destruction, consumers will hear about it and some will turn away in disgust. Conversely, brands that pioneer positive change (like achieving carbon-neutral production or launching a program to give farming communities ownership stakes) often earn public praise and fierce loyalty from ethically-minded customers.

Even specialty chocolate shops and chocolatiers report more customers asking questions: *"Where do the beans for this truffle come from?"* *"Is this cacao sourced ethically?"* Just the fact that such questions are being posed regularly is pushing retailers to stock better options and know their supply chains in detail.

Perhaps one of the most heartening shifts is the idea of quality over quantity. Instead of mindlessly munching through a cheap candy bar, some consumers are choosing to savor a smaller amount of higher-quality, ethical chocolate.

This aligns perfectly with sustainability. Fine chocolate made from well-treated lands and workers might cost a bit more, but if the market increasingly favors it, companies large and small will pivot to meet that demand.

Already, we've seen some of the biggest chocolate companies invest in sustainability programs, from distributing millions of tree seedlings to farming communities to funding schooling and childcare in cocoa regions, to experimenting with plant-based alternatives and carbon offset projects. These corporations recognize that the future market belongs to brands that can prove they are part of the solution, not the problem.

Finally, conscious consumerism in chocolate is spilling over into policy. In Europe and the United States, citizens' concern about deforestation and child labor in products has catalyzed new regulations.

For example, the European Union is gearing up to enforce rules that would ban imports of cocoa (and other commodities) linked to deforestation or illegal labor. Voters and consumers pushed for these laws, essentially saying: "We don't want our guilty pleasure to secretly be guilty of hurting people or the planet." When such laws come into effect, they will compel all players in the chocolate industry to adhere to higher standards – a huge win driven in large part by public sentiment and advocacy.

In summary, conscious consumers have become a vital ingredient in chocolate's sustainable future. Every time we choose a chocolate bar that supports fair wages, or rainforest protection, or innovative farming, we are adding momentum to a global shift. It's reminiscent of how consumer demand helped drive dolphin-safe tuna or fair-trade coffee into the mainstream. With chocolate, that momentum is now unmistakable.

And this is empowering: it means that even the small act of enjoying a treat can be connected to positive change. Chocolate lovers aren't just passive indulgers anymore – we are active participants in shaping an industry that can hopefully be as sweet for those who produce it as it is for those who consume it.

∾

Savoring a Sustainable Future

From the cocoa groves of Ghana to the boutique chocolate shops of Saigon, a sustainable future for chocolate is slowly but surely being molded. It's a future where a chocolate bar might carry the story of regenerated forests in Ecuador, cleaner rivers in Ghana, empowered farming cooperatives in Madagascar, and innovative compostable packaging from a high-tech lab. It's a future where the simple joy of tasting chocolate is amplified by the knowledge that this joy wasn't built on somebody else's suffering or a scar on the Earth.

Getting there is not without challenges. The legacy issues of deforestation, climate change, and social injustice in cocoa won't disappear overnight. There are still many farmers struggling to earn a living wage, and still forests in peril from agricultural expansion. But the momentum has shifted.

The conversation in the chocolate world today is fundamentally different than it was a generation ago – sustainability has moved from a niche concern to a central imperative. And this change is driven by a diverse coalition: scientists developing agroforestry techniques that boost yields naturally, grassroots organizers training farmers in new skills, companies large and small experimenting with greener methods, and consumers using their voices and dollars to reward what's right.

For chocolate companies (like us) writing on these topics, it's also a call to action and a commitment. We share these stories not only to inform and inspire our readers, but to hold ourselves accountable to the promise of growing green cocoa.

As a chocolate lover reading this, you are part of the narrative too. Next time you unwrap a bar, take a moment to taste the possibilities: the hint of biodiversity in a shade-grown cacao, the extra depth knowing the farmer's name, the lack of guilt seeing a compostable wrapper. Each of these details is a brick in the road toward chocolate's sustainable future.

In the end, perhaps the greatest lesson of "growing green cocoa" is that farming and business as usual is not the only path. There is an alternative – one that is kinder to the earth and more just to those who work it. The journey to sustainable chocolate is about rekindling a respect for the origins of our food, and an understanding that even something as delightful as chocolate has consequences and responsibilities attached.

The good news is that with every new sapling planted in an agroforest, every fair trade premium paid, every eco-friendly innovation and conscious choice, we are rewriting chocolate's story for the better.

The future of chocolate is being shaped now, in real time, by all these efforts. It's a future where the chocolate we adore doesn't have to come at the cost of forests felled or farmers short-changed. Instead, every creamy, rich bite can be a celebration – of sustainability, of collaboration, and of hope.

That truly is chocolate's sweetest promise: that we can indulge our love for it while nurturing the world that makes it possible. Let's grow this green future together, one cocoa bean and one chocolate bar at a time. Enjoy, consciously and wholeheartedly, the sweetness that's on the horizon.

15

THE CHOCOLATE CLOCK: HOW
TIME TRANSFORMS FLAVOR

I magine a lone chocolate bar resting in a dark cupboard, patiently waiting. Day by day, week by week, something subtle is happening inside that glossy wrapper. Time, often an unnoticed ingredient, is quietly working its magic on the chocolate. Much like a winemaker cellaring a fine vintage or a cheesemaker aging a prized wheel, a chocolatier (and even the avid chocolate lover at home) can enlist time to transform flavor. The result? A journey in taste that unfolds slowly, revealing new notes and nuances that weren't there before, or softening edges that once seemed sharp. In the world of cacao, the passage of time can be a gentle alchemy – one that turns youthful vibrancy into mellow harmony, and simple sweetness into a symphony of complex flavors.

BUT how exactly does time change chocolate's flavor? And what does it mean to savor a piece of "vintage" chocolate versus a fresh one? To explore these questions, we'll wind back the chocolate clock and look at each tick of time's influence – from the moment cocoa beans are fermented at origin, to the months (or even years) a finished bar might rest before being unwrapped. Along the way, we'll draw parallels to aged wines, cheeses, and spirits, and delve into the science and poetry of what unfolds as chocolate ages. So get comfortable and prepare to indulge in a different kind of tasting experience – one that proves that in the realm of fine chocolate, time may be the most under-appreciated flavor of all.

AGING AT THE SOURCE: **Beans in Waiting**

Long before a chocolate bar melts on your tongue, its story begins on a cocoa farm. Freshly harvested cacao beans undergo fermentation and drying – crucial steps that develop the bean's flavor. Yet even after they're dried to a papery crisp, the journey isn't over. In many traditional practices, farmers and chocolate makers allow cocoa beans to "rest" or age for weeks or months before they are roasted and made into chocolate. Why wait? Because freshly dried beans can be too *green* – their flavors chaotic or overly sharp, with grassy or sour notes from fermentation still lingering. Just as a young wine might taste harsh before it mellows, cocoa beans often need a bit of breathing time.

==

THE FRESHNESS CLOCK: HOW LONG DOES IT LAST?

Chocolate is stable, but not immortal. Here is the lifespan of a bar stored at 65°F.

- White Chocolate: 6–8 Months. (High dairy fat content goes rancid fastest).
- Milk Chocolate: 1 Year. (The milk solids eventually stale).
- Dark Chocolate: 2+ Years. (With no dairy, the antioxidants preserve the fat).

==

During this post-fermentation rest, the beans quietly continue to mature. Harsh acids that developed in fermentation (like acetic acid, the vinegar-like byproduct of cacao fermentation) slowly evaporate or neutralize. Some of the more aggressive aromas fade into the background.

What emerges is a more stable, rounded flavor potential ready for roasting. Farmers and makers have long observed that beans roasted too soon after drying can produce chocolate that tastes off – imagine hints of yeast or damp cardboard – whereas beans aged a month or two tend to create a cleaner, richer flavor. In essence, the beans are exhaling their last volatile sighs of youth, settling into a steadier flavor profile.

It's a delicate balance: given too much time in poor conditions, beans could develop mold or lose some of their desirable aromas. Good storage is key – burlap or airtight bags, cool and dry environments. Under the watchful eye of a careful grower, however, this aging period for beans can be a quiet enhancer, ensuring that by the time the cacao is roasted and refined, it starts from a place of flavorful harmony. It's the first tick of the chocolate clock – a pause that makes all the difference in what comes next.

THE MAKER'S PATIENCE: Aging Chocolate During Production

Once those cocoa beans have been roasted, ground, and conched into silky chocolate, you might think the work is done. Not quite! Many craft chocolate makers know that time can play a role even after the chocolate is made but before it's molded into bars. In chocolate workshops from Menlo Park to Madagascar, it's not uncommon to see blocks of untempered chocolate or filled chocolate vats set aside for a rest, much like bread dough rising slowly.

Why would a chocolate maker intentionally delay finalizing their bars? Because flavor continues to evolve in this stage too. When chocolate comes fresh out of the grinder and refiner, it can be *intense*.

Imagine a just-baked cake that needs to cool – freshly made chocolate can have volatile compounds still buzzing from the roasting and conching process. By storing the liquid chocolate (or solidified blocks of it) for a few weeks or even a few months, makers allow those flavors to "marry" and mellow. Unwanted notes (perhaps a wisp of smoke or a spike of sourness) may drift away, while the pleasant cocoa notes develop greater depth and cohesion.

This practice is akin to letting a stew sit overnight: the flavors seem to blend and deepen with a bit of rest. Some makers refer to this as aging the chocolate mass. They might store untempered chocolate in large blocks, wrapped tightly, for 30, 60, or even 180 days.

When the time is right, they'll gently re-warm, temper (crystallize the cocoa butter for a shiny snap), and mold the bars. Skeptics note that any flavors gained could potentially be lost during reheating and tempering, but many artisans swear they can taste the difference – a rounder profile, a smoother finish.

Others take a different approach: they age already-tempered chocolate. In this case, a maker tempers the chocolate to the proper solid form, perhaps pouring it into large molds or slabs, and then tucks it away for a while longer. The thought here is that as the cocoa butter crystallizes fully and stably over weeks, it can "lock in" subtle flavor improvements.

Tempered chocolate is quite solid and less porous, so changes are slower – but proponents say it still benefits from a few weeks of rest to reach its peak. In fact, many small-batch makers will taste their bars right off the production line, then again after a month on the shelf, and note differences. By the time we consumers tear open the wrapper, that bar might already have had its built-in "aging" period to settle into its best self.

The Vintage Bar: Does Finished Chocolate Improve with Age?

This is the question that sparks lively debate among chocolate lovers: Once a chocolate bar is made and wrapped, what happens if you simply let it sit for months or even years? Fine wines often get better with age – developing complexity as tannins soften and new flavor notes emerge – but does chocolate follow the same path? The answer: *sometimes*, and it depends on many factors.

First, let's set the stage: we're talking about dark chocolate bars with no perishable ingredients (no fresh creams or nuts that could truly spoil). A solid dark chocolate, properly stored, can last a long time – it doesn't "rot" like fresh food. But its flavor will not remain static. Like a mischievous spirit in the cellar, time will nudge and tease the flavor profile in quiet ways.

Many aficionados have conducted "vertical tastings" of chocolate, comparing, say, a bar made from the same batch of cocoa but one tasted fresh in 2023 and another square saved until 2025. What they report would intrigue any food lover. Over time, certain flavors may mellow: a bar that once screamed with bright, sharp notes (imagine zingy citrus or aggressive roast bitterness) might, after two years, taste gentler, more integrated.

The sharp edges are sanded down; the overall impression can become smoother or more rounded. You might find that what was once a punch of tart red fruit has calmed into a warm dried-fruit sweetness, while undertones of honey or leather that were barely noticeable before have come forward.

On the other hand, not all changes are for the better – and this is where aging chocolate is a bit of a gamble. Some of the most volatile aromatic compounds, which often carry those high floral or fruity notes, will diminish over time.

A chocolate celebrated for delicate jasmine, fresh banana, or wild raspberry hints might lose some of that spark after years in storage, leaving a simpler profile behind. In wine terms, it's as if the bright young fruit has faded, and if nothing interesting replaces it, the chocolate can taste flat or "hollow" compared to its youth.

There's also the risk of flavor staleness: notes of cardboard or faint waxiness that can creep in if a bar sits too long or isn't stored perfectly. Like a story repeated one too many times, the flavor can become muted.

Storage conditions play a huge role here. A well-aged chocolate is usually one kept from heat, moisture, and strong odors, ideally in an airtight container in a cool, consistent environment. Under these conditions, a dark chocolate bar can age gracefully for a few years, much like a book preserved on a shelf, pages yellowing gently but story intact.

If temperature swings or humidity intrude, however, the chocolate may develop "bloom" – a dusty white film of sugar or fat crystals rising to the surface. While bloom isn't dangerous and doesn't mean the chocolate is rotten, it definitely interferes with texture (making it dry or crumbly) and can accelerate flavor loss. In short, aging a chocolate bar is an art and a bit of luck: do it right, and you might unveil hidden treasures of flavor; do it poorly, and you end up with a faded glory.

==

HOW TO BUILD A VINTAGE LIBRARY
  Yes, you can age chocolate. No, you can't just leave it in a drawer.

- The Candidates: Only age High-Percentage Dark Chocolate (70%+). Milk and White chocolate have dairy fats that go rancid quickly. Dark chocolate is stable.
- The Vessel: Use an airtight container (glass Tupperware or a tin). Throw in a silica gel packet (saved from a shoe box) to absorb humidity and prevent Sugar Bloom.
- The Environment: Store in a cool, dark place (60-65°F). A wine fridge is ideal. A basement shelf is good. A kitchen cupboard near the stove is fatal.
- The Wait: Taste a piece now. Seal it. Wait 12 months. Taste again. Look for softened acidity and mellowed tannins.

==

FOR THOSE WILLING TO take the chance, aging a chocolate bar at home can be an exercise in patience and curiosity. Tuck away two or three of your favorite dark chocolate bars in a cool, dry spot. Wait six months, a year, or more. Then compare them with a fresh bar of the same kind. The differences – however subtle or significant – can be fascinating.

You'll develop a new appreciation for the living nature of chocolate flavor, even in something as solid and "finished" as a chocolate bar. In fact, some craft chocolate companies have started to label their bars by harvest year (similar to wine vintages) or even release limited "aged" editions, inviting chocolate lovers to experience the timeline of taste.

PARALLELS IN TIME: **Wine, Cheese, and the Chocolate Connection**
  It's natural to draw parallels between aged chocolate and other aged delicacies we know and love. Fine wine is the classic example – we treasure vintages, celebrate the transformations that occur in a bottle over decades. Tannins polymerize and soften, new aroma layers (like dried

fig, tobacco, or earthy truffle) appear, and a great aged wine can deliver a tapestry of flavor that a young wine only hints at.

Artisan cheese follows a similar principle: a young cheddar might be mild and smooth, but an aged cheddar, left to mature in caves for a year or two, becomes sharp, crumbly, with crystal bursts of concentrated flavor. Whiskies and spirits sit for ages in wooden barrels, where time and oak together create caramel richness and mellow warmth out of raw fiery distillate. Even foods like traditional balsamic vinegar or cured ham rely on long aging to reach their peak.

Borrowing from winemakers, some craft chocolatiers now age their nibs in used bourbon or rum barrels to infuse the chocolate with notes of oak and vanilla.

So, can chocolate join this pantheon of delectables improved by time? The answer is a qualified yes – but chocolate's journey is a bit different. Unlike wine or cheese, a chocolate bar isn't fermenting or alive with microbes once it's made. Its aging is more about subtle chemical shifts and the slow movement of molecules within a very stable solid matrix.

Think of chocolate as a time capsule of its making: all the flavor compounds formed during fermentation and roasting are locked in at the moment the bar solidifies. Time doesn't create new flavors in chocolate the way it might in cheese (where molds and bacteria actively create new tastes), but it can re-balance what's there. It's as if the flavor orchestra, initially with some instruments blaring and others muted, gradually finds its harmony over time.

Chocolate also contains a large amount of fat (cocoa butter) which, when properly crystallized, keeps everything in place. Over time, that fat can undergo a type of transformation too – a slow migration or re-crystallization that can affect texture and how flavor is released.

In a well-tempered dark chocolate bar, the primary cocoa butter crystals (called Form V in chocolate chemistry) are very stable, giving the bar its snap and gloss. Given enough time, some of those crystals may shift toward an even more stable form (Form VI), which can make the bar a bit firmer or drier to the bite. In the wine analogy, this is not like wine's tannins transforming (chocolate's equivalent of tannins are polyphenols, which largely stay the same), but more like the liquid wine gradually precipitating sediments or changing mouthfeel.

Importantly, these changes in the fat structure can alter how the flavor compounds are perceived – maybe they don't burst out as quickly, which can make the flavor seem slower, deeper, more lasting but less bright.

Another parallel is the concept of vintage and terroir. Every harvest of cacao beans is unique – affected by that year's rainfall, sun, soil, and fermentation quirks. Just as wine lovers compare a 2018 and 2019 Cabernet from the same vineyard, chocolate lovers can explore different harvest years from the same farm.

Aging comes into play because a bar made from, say, the 2020 harvest and then stored until 2025 is both a time capsule of that year and an example of what time has done to it. In this way, chocolate absolutely shares the romance of wine: the notion that certain years, kept and savored later, offer a taste of history. A "vintage chocolate" might be prized not for a higher value in resale (as in wine auctions) but for the sheer experience of tasting how that bar from years ago presents itself now.

Finally, consider the parallel of barrel-aging, a common practice in spirits and increasingly an experimental one in chocolate. Some innovative chocolate makers have borrowed a trick from whiskey: they age cacao nibs or even whole bars in barrels that once held bourbon, rum, or wine.

The wood and leftover spirits impart extra layers of flavor – a whisper of smoky oak, a breath of ripe cherries or whiskey warmth – as the chocolate sits for months. This is time plus an aromatic friend at work, rather than time alone, but it underscores the same theme: flavor evolves with patience.

The result can be wonderfully complex chocolate that carries echoes of a distillery or winery, a true fusion of aging techniques. While barrel-aging is a deliberate infusion of outside flavors, it still relies on time to transfer and integrate those notes, proving once again that chocolate's relationship with time is multifaceted and exciting.

THE SCIENCE OF SLOW FLAVOR: **What's Happening Inside?**

Peering deeper into the chocolate as it ages, we find a host of quiet chemical and physical changes. You don't need a PhD to appreciate aged chocolate, but understanding the science can certainly deepen your wonder. Here are some of the key processes that time influences in a chocolate bar:

- Volatile Aroma Compounds: These are the tiny molecules that produce the glorious scents and top-notes of chocolate – think fruity esters, flowery aldehydes, nutty pyrazines. "Volatile" means they are prone to evaporate. Over time, some of these drift away or chemically break down. For example, a bar that initially smells very fruity might lose some of those high notes as the fruity esters dissipate. This doesn't mean the chocolate becomes flavorless; rather, the balance of aromas shifts. The more stable, deeper compounds (like rich caramel-like notes or roasted tones) start to dominate over the lighter ones that have quietly exited. In practical terms, time can reduce sharpness (like sour vinegar hints, which come from acetic acid, a volatile compound) and reduce strong florals, potentially revealing underlying chocolate, nut, or spice flavors more clearly.
- Cocoa Butter Crystallization: As mentioned, cocoa butter – the fat in chocolate – crystallizes in a particular form when

chocolate is tempered. Initially, not 100% of the fat is in the most stable form; tempering gets most of it, but some fraction of cocoa butter is still adjusting. With time, cocoa butter slowly continues to rearrange into a more stable crystalline network. Think of it like a jar of honey that crystallizes over time – it becomes more solid. In chocolate, this slow crystallization can make an older bar a touch firmer, less meltingly creamy. The upside is it often gives a very clean snap and a more slow-release melt, which some tasters feel prolongs the flavor on the palate, focusing on base notes. The downside is if it goes too far (or fluctuates with heat), you might see fat bloom – the white haze of fat crystals surfacing. Under stable, cool conditions, however, you usually won't see bloom, just a gradual tightening of texture.

- Oxidation and Maillard Reactions: Chocolate contains not just fat and aroma compounds but also proteins, sugars, and polyphenols (antioxidants). Over long periods, particularly if exposed to oxygen and not perfectly sealed, a bit of oxidation can occur. This might diminish antioxidants and potentially create very slight oxidative flavors (sometimes described as papery or stale at extremes). However, chocolate has a lot of natural antioxidants (it's rich in cocoa polyphenols), which generally protect it from significant oxidation for quite a long time. There's also the potential for very slow Maillard reactions continuing – the same "browning" chemistry between sugars and amino acids that occurs during roasting. At room temperature, Maillard reaction proceeds at a snail's pace, but over a span of years, who knows? It could contribute to subtle changes like the development of deeper caramel tones or a loss of sweetness perception as compounds interact. This area is still being explored by food scientists, but it's fascinating to think that a chocolate bar might be very gradually "cooking" in flavor even as it sits undisturbed in its wrapper.
- Flavor Integration: Not a single chemical process, but worth noting: as volatile notes soften and certain compounds

diminish, the overall flavor profile can taste more integrated. Early on, you might have been able to pick out distinct flavor bursts (a flash of cherry, a spike of oak, a finish of bitterness). After aging, these elements might have woven together into a tapestry that's harder to tease apart – you just taste "chocolate... plus something complex" without as many jagged peaks. Some describe aged chocolate's flavor as more unified or coherent, which can be delightful, though others might miss the fireworks of the fresh bar's individual notes.

In summary, the science of chocolate aging is about *subtraction and addition*: subtract a little of the volatile, edgy compounds, add a bit of polymerization and crystallization to bind things together. The result is neither uniformly good nor bad – it's simply different. Each bar will have its own journey, and tiny differences in formulation or storage will steer that journey down different paths. This is what makes the subject so intriguing. We're only beginning to scientifically map how time transforms chocolate, but as chocolate lovers, we can taste those transformations firsthand and revel in the mystery and the mastery of time.

Savoring the Years: **Tasting Aged Chocolate vs. Fresh Chocolate**
There's a special pleasure in tasting an older chocolate alongside a fresh one. It's a bit like meeting an old friend after years apart and comparing memories with the present moment. Let's paint a picture of such an experience:

You unwrap a bar of 85% dark chocolate that was made last month. The aroma hits your nose in a burst: bright red fruit, like sour cherry and raspberry, with a flirtation of rose petal and a crackle of roasted coffee. The first bite is lively – the acidity dances on your tongue, carrying those fruit notes high and clear. There's a hint of bitterness that prickles at the finish, giving it a wild, untamed character. This fresh chocolate feels young and spirited, an exuberant song hitting some high notes even if it's a bit loud at moments.

Next to it, you unwrap a bar from the exact same batch that you've kept sealed for two years. The look is slightly different – perhaps the color is a shade deeper, the snap of the break is a tad harder. As you inhale, you notice the aroma is more shy at first; no big burst, but what wafts up is lower in tone: think warm woods, gentle spice, maybe a raisin-like sweetness.

When you taste it, the immediate impression is soft and round. Those sharp fruity acids have quieted down to a gentle tartness, more like dried cherry than fresh. The bitterness has smoothed out, now more of a dark espresso note that fades into cocoa richness. New flavors might surprise you – is that a whisper of vanilla or whiskey barrel you detect, even though none was added?

Perhaps the slow creaming of the cocoa butter and faint oxidation created a nuance reminiscent of vanilla or oak. The aged chocolate's texture feels a bit drier on the tongue, but it melts into a long, lingering finish of deep cocoa that stays with you, like the final resonant note of a piano.

Like wine, high-quality dark chocolate can change over time. While it doesn't "age" for decades, a year of rest can mellow acidity and integrate flavors.

The difference is intriguing. The fresh bar was bright, assertive, and dynamic; the aged bar is mellow, enigmatic, and cohesive. Neither is categorically "better" – it's a matter of personal taste, much like preferring a fresh, fruity Beaujolais versus a mature, velvety Bordeaux. What's undeniable is that they are distinct experiences, even though they started from the same recipe.

Emotionally, tasting aged chocolate can be a bit of a romantic affair. There's the anticipation built over months or years of waiting – a quiet excitement in finally unveiling what time has done. There's nostalgia too: if it's a bar you loved when it was fresh, tasting it aged brings a flood of memories of that first encounter, now overlaid with the new sensations.

Some chocolate enthusiasts describe aged chocolate tasting as almost meditative – it encourages slow savoring, as if you're conversing with the chocolate, hearing what it has to say after a long silence. Fresh chocolate shouts its story at once; aged chocolate sits you down by a fireside and tells you its tale gradually.

For those who really want to immerse in this, you might host a "chocolate age vertical" tasting. Select a particular fine chocolate bar and acquire multiple copies. Enjoy one immediately. Stow the others away with dates marked – one for six months later, one for a year later, maybe more.

When the dates come due, bring them out and taste in sequence: freshest to oldest. It's a flavor time machine. You might find the six-month bar has lost a bit of edge and gained a friendly warmth. The one-year bar might taste quite different – perhaps a note that was minor became major. It's not unlike watching a child grow into an adult in accelerated time; certain traits fade, others strengthen.

Such an exercise not only delights the senses but also connects you more deeply to chocolate's life cycle. You start to appreciate that a chocolate bar is not a static object but an evolving story.

It also fosters patience – a virtue any chocolate lover finds hard when faced with delicious treats. By deliberately waiting to eat a chocolate bar, you heighten the eventual pleasure and satisfy more than just a craving; you satisfy curiosity and a sense of discovery.

Embracing the Chocolate Clock

In the end, the relationship between time and chocolate is a love story of sorts – sometimes tumultuous, sometimes harmonious, always intriguing. Time can be the benevolent caretaker that smooths a chocolate's rough edges and deepens its character, or it can be the silent thief that steals away the delicate perfumes of youth.

The "chocolate clock" is always ticking, from the farm where cacao beans rest after fermentation, to the workshop where chocolate is set aside to mature, to the pantry shelf where a chocolate lover might squirrel away a special bar for a future occasion. Each tick and tock brings tiny changes.

For the general chocolate lover, you don't need to become a chemist or start hoarding bars for decades to appreciate this phenomenon. Simply being aware that time is an ingredient can enrich your enjoyment.

Next time you taste a fine single-origin chocolate, try to imagine how it might evolve over the coming months: Which notes would you miss if they faded? Which ones might emerge more boldly? If you have the willpower, save a bit and revisit it later to see. Treat chocolate a little like wine or cheese – something that can indeed have a vintage and a journey through time – and you'll find yourself experiencing your favorite treat in a new light.

The Chocolate Clock invites you to slow down and taste the moment *and* the months and years within each bite. Whether you're nibbling a bar that was made last week or unwrapping one you've saved for a special day, remember that time has touched it.

Just as importantly, remember to give yourself time when enjoying it. Let it melt slowly on your tongue, close your eyes, and search for the layers of flavor – some bright, some deep, some whispering from the past. In doing so, you become part of the chocolate's journey through time, a journey that makes the simple act of eating a piece of chocolate feel just a little bit magical.

So here's to vintage chocolate, to patience and curiosity, and to the ever-ticking chocolate clock that connects past, present, and future in one delicious square. Time truly can change the flavor of cacao – and with an attuned palate and an open mind, every taste can be a revelation. Enjoy the journey, one delicious moment at a time.

==

THE 1-YEAR VINTAGE CHALLENGE

Do not just read about time; taste it.

- **The Setup:**
    - Buy two identical bars of high-quality 70% dark chocolate (avoid inclusions like nuts or fruit).
    - Day 1: Eat half of the first bar. Write down three adjectives describing the acidity (e.g., "Sharp," "Citrusy," "Bright").
    - The Vault: Vacuum seal the second bar (or wrap it tightly in foil and place it in a Ziploc bag with the air squeezed out). Place it in a cool, dark cupboard. Do not touch it.
    - Day 365: Buy a new fresh bar of the same brand.
    - Open your "Vault" bar.
- **The Tasting:**
    - Taste the Fresh Bar first, then the Aged Bar.
    - You will notice the Aged Bar has lost its "high notes"—the sharp fruitiness—but gained a mellow, fudge-like bass note.
    - You have just tasted the physics of flavor dissipation.

==

PART III

FLAVOR, SENSORY SCIENCE, AND
THE PSYCHOLOGY OF TASTE

16

THE ARCHITECTURE OF FLAVOR: TASTE, TEXTURE, AND STRUCTURE

I *magine unwrapping a piece of fine chocolate and letting it rest on your tongue. The first impression is sweet, yes – but then comes a rush of deeper sensations. There's a warmth of roasted nuts and coffee, whispers of fruit and flowers, a silky melt that caresses the mouth, and an aroma so enchanting it seems to bypass your taste buds and go straight to nostalgia. Chocolate's flavor is a symphony, and sweetness is just the opening note. What lies beyond is a fascinating mix of chemistry, biology, and even a bit of memory and emotion. A snap, a melt, a rush of deep cocoa and caramel on the tongue – biting into a chocolate bar is a small everyday luxury. For a moment, time slows as the square of chocolate yields to warmth, releasing a bouquet of aromas and a silky cascade of flavor. But behind that simple pleasure lies an intricate synthesis of art and science.*

A CHOCOLATE BAR may look uniform and straightforward, yet it is anything but simple. It is the culmination of a journey that spans equatorial cacao farms and hi-tech kitchens, ancient techniques and modern innovations. In this exploration, we examine what makes chocolate tick: how its flavor is built from the ground up, what gives it that luscious texture, and how its internal structure makes the magic possible.

Whether you prefer dark, milk, white, or the new blush of ruby chocolate, understanding the science of chocolate flavor will deepen your appreciation for every bite.

PART I: THE ARCHITECTURE OF FLAVOR

FROM BEAN to Bliss

The unmistakable flavor of chocolate is one of the most complex and beloved in the world. It can be decadent and fudgy, or hauntingly bittersweet. It can carry bright notes of red fruit, mellow hints of honey and vanilla, or deep tones of roasted coffee and nuts. How does a cacao bean – bitter, astringent, and practically inedible on its own – transform into the symphony of flavors we recognize as chocolate? The answer begins with fermentation and roasting – processes explored in detail earlier in the book. These foundational stages create the chemical precursors that make chocolate's flavor possible. Here, we focus on what happens after: how processing, ingredients, and our own senses shape the final taste experience.

THE MAILLARD MAGIC of Roasting

After fermentation and drying, cocoa beans travel to the chocolate maker's facility, where they encounter serious heat. Roasting is where the magic of chemistry fully unlocks the flavor within those beans. In large drum roasters or ovens, cocoa beans are heated to roughly 120–150°C (248–302°F). This high heat triggers the Maillard reaction—the same cascade of browning reactions between amino acids and sugars discussed in our look at fermentation—which is essential for developing the bean's final character..

For the roast master, this process is auditory as much as it is olfactory. Just as popcorn pops, cacao beans make a distinctive sound as they roast. As the internal water turns to steam and pressure builds, the beans let out a series of sharp, rhythmic cracks. This "popping" is a crucial sensory cue, signaling that the shell has loosened from the nib and the chemical transformation is reaching its peak. It is the sound of flavor being born.

The Maillard reaction is the same process that gives us the delectable flavors of seared steak, toasted bread crust, and roasted coffee. In cocoa, it produces a symphony of new flavor molecules. As the beans roast, they start to exude the rich, unmistakable aroma of chocolate – a smell so heavenly that many chocolate lovers would count it among their favorite scents on Earth. Notes of caramel, malt, and nuts develop, layering on top of the cocoa's intrinsic character. Hints of vanilla, spice, or fruit might also appear, depending on the bean's origin and how it was fermented.

Roasting is an art as much as a science. A light roast might last only a short time at a gentler heat, preserving more of the bean's delicate floral or fruity notes – imagine a chocolate that surprises you with whispers of berries or jasmine alongside the cocoa. A dark roast, on the other hand, might push the beans to a deeper, more robust flavor – think of the deep cocoa notes with a backdrop of toasted nuttiness or a touch of smokiness. However, roast too dark or too long and you risk driving off some of the nuanced aromatics or introducing charred flavors.

The Maillard Reaction: The moment heat turns amino acids and sugars into the complex "browning" flavors of nuts, toast, and coffee.

CONCHING: **The Happy Accident That Created Velvet**

Roasted cocoa nibs are ground into a paste (cocoa mass) and often mixed with sugar and other ingredients. But historically, this mixture was gritty, acidic, and rough on the tongue. The transformation of this coarse paste into the silky chocolate we know today is due to a process called conching—a discovery that remains one of the great legends of chocolate history.

In 1879, Rodolphe Lindt, a Swiss chocolatier, was struggling to make his chocolate palatable. At the time, chocolate was brittle and required chewing; it did not melt. As the story goes, Lindt left a mixing machine running over a weekend—either by accident or a hunch. The machine rocked the chocolate back and forth for 72 straight hours.

When he returned on Monday morning, he expected to find a ruined, burnt mess. Instead, he found a miracle. The friction had generated gentle heat, keeping the chocolate liquid, while the relentless motion had pulverized the particles. He dipped a spoon into the vat and found it didn't crumble; it flowed. He had created the world's first chocolat fondant, or melting chocolate.

So what exactly happens during this "accidental" process? Conching is essentially the controlled stirring, agitating, and aerating of liquid chocolate under heat. This mechanical kneading performs three critical functions that define the final flavor:

- Texture Refinement: It polishes the cocoa and sugar particles until they are microscopically smooth, coating every jagged edge in a layer of cocoa butter to create a velvety mouthfeel.
- Flavor Aeration: The heat and airflow act like a decanter for wine. They drive off volatile acids (like acetic acid leftover from fermentation) and moisture. This mellows the flavor, stripping away the sharp, vinegar-like notes and allowing the deeper cocoa aromas to shine.
- Chemical Development: It promotes the Maillard reaction, deepening the caramel and roasted notes within the chocolate.

~

CHOCOLATIERS TODAY TREAT CONCHING as a stylistic choice. A long conche (up to 72 hours) yields a mild, ultra-smooth chocolate with subdued acidity. A shorter conche might preserve the bright, fruity tang of a single-origin bean. It is the step that turns a rough ingredient into a refined luxury.

CACAO ORIGINS: Genetics and Terroir

Even before processing plays its role, there's something fundamentally baked into chocolate's taste: the very genetics of the cacao bean and the environment in which it grew. Not all cocoa beans are created equal – in fact, there are several major varieties of Theobroma cacao, each with distinct flavor potentials. Take Criollo cacao, for example.

This heirloom variety is often called the "prince of cocoa" for its delicate and complex flavor profile. Criollo beans, which are relatively rare, can produce chocolate with tantalizing notes of fruit, flowers, nuts, and an almost perfumed quality, with very low bitterness. If you've ever had a single-origin bar that tasted remarkably of blueberries or jasmine, it might have been Criollo.

On the other end is Forastero, the workhorse variety that constitutes the majority of the world's cocoa production (especially in West Africa). Forastero beans are robust and hardy, but their flavor is usually described as classic "chocolatey" but simpler – strong cocoa base notes, more bitterness, and less of the high floral notes.

In between lies Trinitario, a hybrid of Criollo and Forastero, which inherits some of Criollo's finesse and some of Forastero's strength. Trinitario cocoas can vary widely in flavor, from earthy and nutty to bright and fruity, depending on the mix of genetics and how they're processed. Genetics give each bean a flavor blueprint, but terroir – the influence of the environment – writes its own chapter in the flavor story.

Chocolate aficionados often compare cacao to wine grapes in this respect. The term "terroir" encompasses soil composition, climate, rainfall, altitude, and even the surrounding flora and fauna. All these factors subtly affect the taste of the beans.

Consider cocoa from Madagascar: this island's beans, often of Trinitario lineage, are famous for bright, fruity flavors – imagine hints of citrus, cherry, or berries naturally infused by the cocoa itself. Some say it's the island's soil and microclimate that contribute to this distinctive tang. Meanwhile, beans from Ghana (largely Forastero) might give you a very deep, classic cocoa flavor with a nutty, earthy character – perfect as a base in blends.

==

DO THE MATH: DECODING THE WRAPPER
What are you actually eating? Here is the breakdown of a typical bar.

If the label says: 70% DARK CHOCOLATE

- 70% comes from the Cacao Bean: This is a mix of Cocoa Solids (flavor/fiber) and Cocoa Butter (fat/texture).
- 30% is Sugar: The remaining weight is almost entirely sweetener.
- <1% is "Helper" Ingredients: Usually Vanilla (flavor) and Lecithin (an emulsifier for smoothness).

Note: A "100% Bar" contains zero sugar. It is pure ground bean.

==

A Mosaic of Over 600 Compounds
The flavor of a chocolate bar doesn't come down to a single compound or note – it is a complex architecture of hundreds of aromatic molecules working in concert. Scientists have identified over 600 distinct flavor compounds in chocolate, one of the most chemically complex foods we eat. But the average chocolate lover's experience is more poetic than scientific: we perceive a handful of dominant notes that define the chocolate's character. F

or instance, a bite of a 70% dark chocolate might unfold like this: first a deep roasted cocoa taste, then a wave of dry fruitiness like raisins or plums, underpinned by a gentle bitterness and a hint of earthy depth. If it's a single-origin bar, you might catch unique accents – maybe a Madagascar dark chocolate surprises you with bright cherry and citrus tang, whereas an Ecuadorian bar might resonate with floral jasmine or a smoky undertone.

This complexity is a large part of chocolate's allure: it can be comfort food or connoisseur's delight, childhood candy or gourmet delicacy, all depending on how those flavor elements are composed.

PART II: THE MOUTHFEEL OF PERFECTION

FROM GRITTY to Silky

If flavor is the soul of a chocolate bar, texture is its seductive body – the physical experience that carries the flavor to our senses. Consider the pleasing snap when you break a good chocolate bar. That crisp sound is the first hint of quality, telegraphing the bar's firm solidity. Then place a piece on your tongue. A well-made chocolate will melt smoothly, gradually, without grittiness, transforming from a hard solid to a velvety liquid that coats your mouth. This luxurious mouthfeel is the result of meticulous engineering.

The earliest chocolate bars were nothing like the creamy confections we know today. J.S. Fry's first chocolate bar in 1847, while revolutionary as a solid eating chocolate, was described as gritty – the sugar and cocoa particles were large and rough. It would take another few decades and the development of the conching process to refine that grainy paste into a smooth delight. Particle size is a key factor in chocolate texture.

In a finished chocolate bar, solid particles of cocoa (and sugar, and milk powder if present) are dispersed in a continuous phase of fat (cocoa butter). If those particles are too large – say, 50 microns or more – the tongue can detect them as grainy or sandy. As we discussed earlier, modern premium chocolate is ground so finely that the particles are often smaller than 20 microns, well below the threshold of our tongue's perception. This fine grinding, combined with conching, erases the coarse roughness and produces a chocolate that feels silky.

The Magic of Cocoa Butter

Just as important as particle size is the unique melting property of cocoa butter. Cocoa butter is a remarkable fat: it melts at around 34°C (93°F), which is just below human body temperature. That means a piece of solid chocolate will remain firm at room temperature, but the moment it enters your mouth (around 37°C) it begins to liquefy. This is why chocolate literally "melts in your mouth."

===

SENSORY TEST: THE MELTING RACE

Is your chocolate high quality? Your body heat will tell you the truth.

- **The Setup:** Take one piece of High-End Couverture (Real Cocoa Butter) and one piece of Cheap Halloween Candy (Vegetable Oil/Compound).
- **The Test:** Place one in the palm of your left hand, and one in your right. Close your fists. Count to 20.
- **The Result:**
  - Real Chocolate: Will be a puddle. Cocoa butter melts at 93°F.
  - Fake Chocolate: Will still be solid or soft. Vegetable oils have higher melting points to extend shelf life.

===

The smooth melt is a hallmark of high-quality chocolate. There's a natural thrill to feeling a hard chunk metamorphose into a silky pool on your tongue. And as it melts, it releases those flavor compounds we talked about, coating the tongue and reaching the nasal passages.

It's a perfect delivery mechanism. However, that perfect melt only happens if the chocolate is in the right crystalline form. A well-tempered chocolate bar that's been stored properly will melt evenly and slowly.

Have you ever left a chocolate bar in a hot car and then cooled it again, only to find it soft, chalky, or with a white film on it? That is chocolate that has "bloomed" or lost its temper – the fat crystals have reorganized improperly. Such a bar often feels waxy or crumbly and may shatter or bend rather than snapping cleanly.

THE SENSORY ELEMENTS of Texture

Texture isn't just one thing – it's a combination of sensations. First, there's hardness or firmness at room temperature. A dark chocolate bar, especially one high in cocoa content, tends to be quite firm and gives a very sharp snap when broken.

Milk chocolate, on the other hand, is typically softer; it yields more easily under your teeth and might have a gentler snap or even just a soft break. This difference comes from composition: milk chocolate contains milk fat, which is softer and melts at a lower temperature than cocoa butter.

Then there's the snap and bite. Snap is a pleasure not just for the ears but for the teeth; it's the first textural interaction. A crisp snap signals a well-tempered chocolate with a dense matrix of stable crystals. It sets expectations: you anticipate a clean break and a smooth melt. Temperature and shape play roles too.

Place a thin flake of chocolate on your tongue and it will melt almost instantly, releasing flavor in a burst. A thicker chunk takes longer, creating a more extended creamy experience. This is why even the shape and thickness of a chocolate bar are deliberate design choices – they impact how quickly the chocolate melts and how the flavor is delivered.

PART III: INSIDE THE CHOCOLATE BAR

THE MICROSTRUCTURE: Crystals and Cocoa Butter Matrix

Beneath the flavor and the feel of a chocolate bar lies an invisible world of structure. At its heart, a solid chocolate bar is a feat of materials science. Think of it this way: you have dry particles (cocoa solids from the cocoa mass, plus sugar crystals, and in milk chocolate also milk powder particles) that need to be combined with fat (cocoa butter) into a solid form. Chocolate is essentially a suspension of particles in a fat.

When in liquid form (above the melting point of cocoa butter), it's a free-flowing suspension, albeit a thick one. When it solidifies, it's the cocoa butter that sets into a matrix, locking all the other particles in place.

==

BRAIN HACK: THE SHAPE OF TASTE

Does a circle taste sweeter than a square? Try this trick.

- The Setup: Take two pieces of the same chocolate. Cut one into a jagged, sharp shard. Melt the other slightly and mold it into a round droplet.
- The Test: Eat the round piece first, then the sharp one.
- The Result: Your brain associates roundness with sweetness (the "Bouba" effect) and sharp angles with bitterness (the "Kiki" effect). The round piece will almost always taste sweeter.

==

The key is that cocoa butter is polymorphic—it can solidify in many different ways. If left to its own devices, it will settle into a loose, unstable structure that crumbles and looks dull. The chocolatier's goal is to force the butter into a specific, tight alignment that yields a glossy finish and a sharp snap. (We will explore the deep physics of these crystal forms, specifically the elusive "Form V," in the next chapter).

Achieving Form V is the goal of tempering – the controlled cooling and agitation process chocolatiers use to pre-crystallize cocoa butter in the right form. In a perfectly tempered chocolate bar, the microstructure is a uniform network of interlocking cocoa butter crystals (mostly Form V) that hold all the solid particles in a tight, ordered lattice. Sugar and cocoa particles are distributed evenly, each coated by fat and integrated into the structure. This uniformity is what gives a bar its even color, sheen, and snap.

THE VARIETIES: **Dark, Milk, White, and Ruby**

Now consider a milk chocolate. The added dairy fundamentally changes the flavor landscape. Milk contains lactose (a sugar) and proteins that, when conched and cooked with cocoa, produce delicious caramelized notes.

Many European milk chocolates use a technique called the "crumb" process – mixing cocoa with sugar and condensed milk, then drying it into a crumb before refining – which yields a distinctive cooked milk flavor reminiscent of dulce de leche or butterscotch.

Then there's white chocolate, the outlier that some chocolate purists love to hate. While purists often scoff, white chocolate *is* technically chocolate by legal and chemical standards, provided it contains at least 20% cocoa butter.

It lacks the non-fat cocoa solids (which hold the brown color and bitter antioxidants), but it retains the specific fat crystal structure that gives chocolate its unique melting properties.

==

MYTH-BUSTER: YES, WHITE CHOCOLATE IS REAL

Stop the snobbery. White chocolate is not "fake"—it just lacks the solids.

- **The Science:** A cacao bean is roughly 50% fat (cocoa butter) and 50% solid (cocoa powder).
  - Dark Chocolate: Contains both the fat and the solid.
- White Chocolate: Contains only the fat (cocoa butter), plus sugar and milk.
- **The Verdict:** Because it is made from the fat of the cacao bean, it is botanically chocolate. If it uses vegetable oil instead of cocoa butter? That is fake. Look for "Cocoa Butter" as the first ingredient.

==

QUALITY WHITE CHOCOLATE has a subtly cocoa-buttery aroma, which can hint at dairy and vanilla. Its flavor is dominantly sweet and milky, often with added vanilla to boost appeal. And now we arrive at the newest chapter in chocolate flavor: ruby chocolate.

Unveiled in 2017 by a Belgian-Swiss company after a decade of development, ruby chocolate is often touted as the "fourth type" of chocolate (after dark, milk, and white). Its appearance is striking – a naturally pink hue – and its taste is unlike its siblings. Bite into a piece of ruby chocolate and you'll notice a bright, tangy fruitiness, as if berries were somehow blended in (though they are not). Ruby chocolate is made from special cocoa beans (nicknamed "ruby beans") that, through a particular process kept partly secret, preserve natural red-purple pigments and tart flavor compounds that ordinary processing would oxidize or destroy.

PART IV: FLAVOR AND THE BRAIN

THE SYMPHONY of the Senses

Tasting chocolate is a multi-sensory experience, engaging smell, taste, touch, and even sight and sound. To truly understand why chocolate tastes the way it does, we have to consider how it interacts with our senses. Aroma is perhaps the unsung hero of chocolate tasting.

Our tongue perceives basic tastes (sweet, bitter, sour, salty, umami), but our nose perceives the character of what we're eating. When you place a piece of chocolate in your mouth and begin to let it melt, volatile aroma molecules are released and travel up the back of your throat to the olfactory receptors in your nasal cavity (this is called retronasal olfaction).

The result is that you "smell" the chocolate as you taste it, and your brain combines these signals into what we experience as flavor. Chocolate's aroma is incredibly complex: chemists have identified over 600 different volatile compounds in cocoa and chocolate. Not all of these have a strong smell, but the dozens that do create a tapestry of scent.

There are pyrazines that give roasted, nutty notes (a bit like the smell of toasted bread or popcorn). There are aldehydes that can smell sweet or buttery (some of the same compounds you find in vanilla or butter). There are traces of fruity esters, floral terpenes, even a slight grassy note or a hint of sour acidity lingering from fermentation.

If you doubt aroma's importance, try this experiment: pinch your nose closed and eat a piece of chocolate. You'll taste sweetness and a bit of bitterness, but much of the nuance will be missing. Release your nose mid-taste and suddenly the full flavor blooms. That is the power of aroma.

Taste, Smell, and Chocolate Emotions

Why do we crave chocolate? Why does just the thought of it bring a smile to so many faces? The answer lies not just in chemistry or the senses, but in our brains and emotions. Chocolate's flavor doesn't just tickle the taste buds – it taps into the brain's reward system and our emotional memory in powerful ways. Consider what happens as you taste a piece of chocolate.

Your tongue's taste receptors register the sweetness, which immediately signals to the brain: energy! sweetness! good! – an evolutionary reward response. At the same time, other receptors pick up bitterness from the cacao. Interestingly, bitter taste in nature often warns of toxins, but in the case of chocolate (and coffee, for that matter), a little bitterness adds depth and intrigue to the flavor. Now think about smell and memory.

The olfactory bulbs (which process smell) are directly connected to the limbic system, which includes the amygdala and hippocampus – key centers for emotion and memory. This direct wiring is why a whiff of a particular scent can suddenly flood you with a vivid memory or feeling.

With chocolate, there's often a lifetime of positive associations built in: perhaps the smell of brownies in your mother's kitchen, or the foil-wrapped chocolate egg you got one joyful Easter, or the heart-shaped box of chocolates from a fond valentine. All these factors – the taste receptors, the smell and memory link, the brain's chemical response – converge when you eat chocolate.

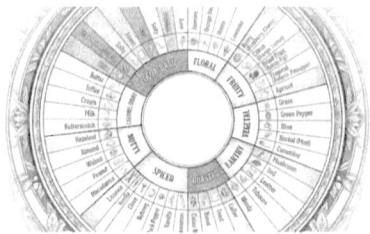

The Chocolate Flavor Wheel helps tasters identify specific notes. To
use it, imagine starting at the center with broad categories like
'Fruit' or 'Roast,' and moving outward to the specific edges to find
'Red Berry' or 'Burnt Coffee.' A single bar can contain over 600
distinct volatile aroma compounds—more than red wine.

The technical might describe it as "a stimulation of the opioid
receptor system" or "activation of the mesolimbic reward pathway," but
we feel it simply as pleasure, comfort, even love. Chocolate has been
called "happiness you can eat." In the context of science, these grand
descriptions start to make sense.

Beyond Sweetness, Beyond Ordinary

From the precise roast that browns beans to aromatic perfection, to
the chocolate factory where they are refined into silky bliss, and finally
to the complex orchestra of our senses and brain – we see that chocolate's flavor is so much more than sugar on the tongue. Sweetness is just
one instrument in a rich ensemble.

The true taste of chocolate is built on a foundation of fermented
fruitiness and browned caramel notes, shaped by choices in craft and
origin, delivered through melt and aroma, and received with memories
and emotions that amplify its delight. Next time you bite into a piece of
chocolate, take a moment to appreciate the journey that little square has
been through. Notice the snap as you break it, inhale its bouquet, let it
dissolve slowly, and see what flavors unfold.

You might detect a hint of the tropical rainforest in its exotic notes or
a ghost of roast like a distant campfire. You might feel a wave of calm or
joy as the flavor settles in.

That is chocolate moving beyond sweetness into the realm of experience. It's science and art working together: microbiology giving us those

precursors, chemistry giving us the roast aromas, physics and engineering giving us the texture, and human biology translating it all into pure pleasure. Chocolate tastes the way it does because it is, quite literally, a product of all these elements.

It's a convergence of nature and nurture, of bean and process, of senses and soul. This is what makes chocolate unique and perhaps why it holds a special place in our hearts (and on our taste buds). It's not just a treat – it's a testament to how complex and wonderful flavor can be. Beyond sweetness, there's a whole world inside a piece of chocolate, and that world is what makes each bite so irresistibly captivating.

17

THE PHYSICS OF THE SNAP: CRYSTALS, POLYMORPHS, AND TEMPERING

I t starts with a snap. That crisp, decisive break when you bite into a fine chocolate bar or snap a piece in half between your fingers – it's a sound and sensation cherished by chocolate lovers. Equally alluring is the glossy sheen that catches your eye, and the silky melt that follows on your tongue. These qualities of great chocolate are no happy accident of nature. They are the result of precise craftsmanship and science – the art and engineering of tempering. Tempering chocolate is a process that transforms melted cocoa into a solid of exquisite texture and appearance. Beneath the surface, it's a story of crystals and polymorphs, of trial and error by confectioners of old, and of modern science explaining an age-old culinary mystery. In this in-depth journey, we'll explore how tempering was discovered, the fascinating crystalline behavior of cocoa butter, and how mastering it engineers that perfect snap. It's a tale blending history, chemistry, and a touch of culinary magic – one that every chocolate lover can appreciate with each delightful bite.

A Brief History of Tempering

Chocolate wasn't always the glossy confection we know today. For much of its history, chocolate was consumed as a drink or a gritty paste. The ancient Maya and Aztecs prepared rich cacao beverages, but the idea of a shiny, solid chocolate bar came much later. In fact, the very first solid eating chocolate is credited to J. S. Fry & Sons in 1847, when they mixed cacao powder, sugar, and melted cocoa butter to create a moldable paste.

That Victorian-era chocolate was revolutionary but had room for improvement – early bars could be coarse, crumbly, or develop a dull, dusty look over time. As the 19th century progressed and chocolate making blossomed (with innovations like conching creating smoother chocolate), chocolatiers began noticing that how chocolate cooled after melting made a big difference in its quality.

By the late 1800s, confectioners were on a quest for a consistently shiny, firm chocolate that not only tasted delicious but also looked appealing and could be stored without developing flaws. Swiss chocolate makers, in particular, led the charge.

Jean Tobler, a chocolatier in Bern (later famous for the Toblerone), is often credited in the 1890s with pioneering a special cooling technique – what we now call tempering – to give his chocolate bars a lustrous finish and satisfying snap. In those days, this was an art learned through practice: chocolate was heated, cooled, and re-warmed in careful sequences, even if the makers didn't fully understand the science behind it.

By the early 20th century, tempering became more widely adopted in Europe as chocolatiers shared methods to prevent the dreaded "bloom" (that whitish film or streaks that can appear on chocolate). By 1931, the process of tempering was formally described in industrial chocolate production as a way to control bloom and achieve a crisp, glossy product. However, even then, chocolatiers only knew *that* it worked; it wasn't until decades later that scientists unraveled *how* it worked on a molecular level.

The mid-20th century brought deeper scientific insight. Food scientists began studying the structure of cocoa butter, the fat in chocolate, to explain why tempered chocolate behaved differently than untempered. By the 1960s and 1970s, using techniques like X-ray diffraction, researchers discovered that cocoa butter can solidify in multiple forms – a phenomenon known as polymorphism. This was the key to tempering.

The practices that innovators like Tobler had developed by intuition were finally being explained in terms of different crystal structures of fat.

It validated what the best chocolatiers already knew: if you cool choco-late just right, you get the prize – a stable, glossy, delectable chocolate – and if you don't, the chocolate can end up soft, mottled, or prone to melting.

Thus, through a blend of empirical craft and later scientific valida-tion, tempering became an indispensable step in chocolate making. Today, every gourmet chocolatier and large chocolate factory alike relies on tempering to ensure their products are as beautiful to behold as they are delicious to eat.

Cocoa Butter's Secret: Polymorphs and Crystal Magic

What exactly makes tempering so important? The answer lies in the unique nature of cocoa butter, the fat that makes up the majority of a chocolate's lipid content. Unlike most fats you might cook with, cocoa butter is polymorphic – meaning it can solidify into several different crystalline arrangements.

Think of it as fat molecules playing Tetris: they can stack together in different patterns, forming crystals of varying stability. In fact, cocoa butter is known to form six distinct crystal types, traditionally labeled Form I through Form VI. Ideally, we want Form V (Beta), which orga-nizes the fatty acids into a tight, stable lattice that reflects light uniformly. Each of these forms has different properties – different melting points, hardness, and stability.

Only one of these forms is the golden ticket for perfect chocolate: Form V. When chocolate solidifies primarily in Form V, it emerges firm and snaps cleanly, appears shiny, and melts desirably close to body temperature (around 33-34 °C, or ~93 °F, just below human body temper-ature – that's why a well-tempered chocolate melts so luxuriously in your mouth but stays solid on the table).

Form V crystals pack the cocoa butter molecules in a tight, orderly fashion, making the chocolate bar hard enough to break crisply and giving it that mirror-like gloss that reflects light beautifully. They're also relatively stable, so the chocolate won't immediately revert or "bloom".

By contrast, the other forms (I through IV, and even Form VI) are less ideal. For example, Form I (sometimes called the gamma form) forms if chocolate cools very quickly – it's soft, unstable, and melts in your hand almost immediately. Forms II, III, and IV (various intermediate "alpha" and "beta-prime" crystals) are a bit more firm but still give chocolate a lackluster, matte appearance and a soft bite with no real snap.

They also tend to be unstable at room temperature – over time, they will reorganize into higher forms. Form VI, interestingly, is actually more stable than Form V but forms only over a long period (several months) as Form V slowly transforms. Form VI has a slightly higher melting point (around 36 °C, ~97 °F) and when it appears, it often brings an unwelcome guest: fat bloom. Form VI crystals can cluster in a way that makes fat visibly separate on the surface, producing that chalky white coating.

Chocolate polymorphism: Cocoa butter can harden into six different crystal shapes. Only one (Form V) is stable; the others result in soft, crumbly chocolate that melts in your hand.

In essence, if melted chocolate is allowed to solidify willy-nilly, you get a hodgepodge of crystal forms. The texture suffers (maybe it's crumbly or too soft), the appearance dulls, and worse, the cocoa butter might soon migrate or re-crystallize in spots, creating those grey or white streaks known as bloom.

This is why that untempered chocolate bar you left in a warm car and then re-solidified looks so unappetizingly mottled – it solidified without control, and unstable crystals eventually let the fat separate out. Good tempering is all about controlling crystallization: encouraging the cocoa butter to form ample Form V crystals as it sets, and eliminating the other forms as much as possible.

The science behind this polymorphic behavior is fascinating. Cocoa butter is composed of a mixture of triglycerides (fat molecules) primarily derived from stearic, palmitic, and oleic acids. These molecules can pack together in different alignments.

Form V (the desired form) is a type of crystal packing that happens to be both fairly dense and stable but not the absolute densest. It's sometimes referred to as the "β form".

It provides a great balance: stable enough to give a long shelf life and resist bloom for a reasonable time, but not so stable that it raises the melting point too high. Form VI (the so-called "β_1" or super-beta form) is the densest, most stable arrangement – but if chocolate turns into Form VI, it becomes hard, dry-looking, and loses that lovely mouthfeel (and as mentioned, often gets bloom).

That usually happens only after long storage or incorrect handling, even with tempered chocolate. The goal of tempering is to pre-set the stage for Form V. When done correctly, tempering leaves a chocolate with a kind of "crystal memory" – a small fraction (maybe a few percent) of its fat solidified as Form V crystals, evenly dispersed. These serve as seeds or nuclei.

As the rest of the liquid chocolate cools around those seeds, it mimics that structure and also solidifies into Form V. The result? A bar or bonbon that is almost entirely Form V crystalline cocoa butter. It will be delectably firm and snappy, glossy to the eye, and will largely resist developing bloom.

This microstructure is like an invisible scaffold that holds all the cocoa solids, sugar, and flavor components in a tight network. When you crack a well-tempered chocolate, you're essentially hearing the break of that well-formed crystal lattice. And when it melts in your mouth, it does so uniformly, releasing flavor in a smooth, even way – no graininess, no waxy residue, just a clean melt.

How Tempering Works: The Art and Engineering of Snap

Tempering is the act of giving chocolate a new memory. First, every existing crystal—stable or unstable—is melted away, leaving the cocoa butter in its most fluid, chaotic state. Then the temperature is guided downward with exquisite care, encouraging only the strongest and most desirable crystals to form.

==

THE CRYSTAL LADDER: A CHEAT SHEET

Cocoa butter is a shapeshifter. It can solidify into six different structures, but only one is "chocolate."

- **Form I & II (The Mush)**
  - Melting Point: 17°C (63°F)
  - Texture: Soft, crumbly, melts in your hand instantly.
  - Cause: Created by rapid, uncontrolled cooling.
- **Form III & IV (The Dull)**
  - Melting Point: 25°C (77°F)
  - Texture: Firm but snaps poorly. Matte finish.
  - Cause: Cooling at room temperature without tempering.
- **Form V (The Prize)**
  - Melting Point: 34°C (94°F - Body Temp)
  - Texture: Glossy shine, sharp "snap," melts smoothly.
  - Cause: The target of tempering.
- **Form VI (The Bloom)**
  - Melting Point: 36°C (97°F)
  - Texture: Hard and waxy. White streaks (bloom) appear.
  - Cause: Occurs after months of storage or heat damage.

==

A final gentle warming removes the remaining unstable structures. Whether done by hand on a marble slab or in the steel chamber of an automated tempering machine, the goal is the same: a network of perfect Form V crystals ready to snap cleanly and melt flawlessly:

- Melting – First, the chocolate is slowly heated to a high temperature (typically around 45-50 °C, or about 113-122 °F for dark chocolate; a bit lower for milk or white chocolate) until *all* the existing fat crystals have melted. This "resets" the chocolate's crystal structure entirely. At this stage, the chocolate is a uniform liquid, free of any solid cocoa butter crystals – essentially a blank slate. It's critical not to overheat (burnt chocolate is unrecoverable), but you must exceed the highest melting point of cocoa butter's forms (Form VI melts around 36 °C, so going to ~45 °C ensures even the most stable crystals are gone).

- Cooling/Seeding – Next, the melted chocolate is cooled down carefully to somewhere in the high 20s °C (around 26-28 °C, roughly 80-82 °F). This can be done by stirring the chocolate in a cool environment, working it on a cold surface (like the classic marble slab method), or just by slowly stirring in a bowl off heat. As the temperature drops, cocoa butter will start to crystallize. At this stage, without intervention, a mix of Forms IV and V (and some others) will nucleate. The chocolatier's job here is to encourage Form V to form. In traditional hand-tempering, for example, about two-thirds of the chocolate may be poured onto a marble slab and spread back and forth with a spatula – this cools it rapidly and, through constant motion, creates lots of tiny crystal "seeds". Some of those seeds will be Form V. The goal is to generate a critical mass of desirable crystals without letting the mass get so cold that it solidifies completely or forms too many unstable crystals.

- Rewarming – Now comes the crucial trick. The chocolate, which at this point has begun to thicken as crystals form, is warmed back up gently to a moderate working temperature (for dark chocolate, typically around 31 °C, or about 88 °F; a couple degrees lower for milk or white chocolate which have dairy fats and lower cocoa butter content). This heating is just enough to *melt away* the unwanted, unstable crystal forms (like Forms IV, III, etc.), which have lower melting points, while not melting the Form V crystals that have a slightly higher melting threshold. It's a bit like pruning a bonsai tree —you trim away the bad and keep the good. Visualize the process as a U-shaped curve: you melt high (the top of the U), cool deep to form crystals (the bottom), and gently warm back up to the working temperature (halfway up the right side). After this step, if done correctly, what remains is a smooth, still-liquid chocolate that contains a dispersed population of hardy Form V seed crystals and nothing else. The chocolate is now in temper, though still fluid.

- Setting – Finally, the tempered chocolate is ready to be formed. Whether it's being poured into molds to make bars, enrobing a candy center, or being dipped for truffles, the chocolate at this point will solidify on cooling into that gorgeous Form V-dominant solid. As it cools to room temperature, those seed crystals guide the formation of the rest of the cocoa butter into the same structure. The result hardens relatively quickly into a firm piece with a glossy finish. One can usually tell almost immediately if the tempering was successful – properly tempered chocolate sets evenly and detaches from molds easily (it even shrinks just a tiny bit as the crystal lattice forms, pulling away from the mold). If it was not successful, the chocolate might remain tacky or soft for a long time, or set with streaks.

This process can be temperamental (pardon the pun). If the temperature goes a bit too high in the rewarm, you can accidentally destroy your good seeds and knock the chocolate *out* of temper – meaning you have to start over. If you don't warm it enough, you might leave in too many unstable crystals that will cause trouble later.

That's why chocolatiers measure temperatures so closely and often test their tempered chocolate before committing a whole batch to molding. A classic test is to dip a knife or paper edge into the chocolate and see if it solidifies with a uniform gloss within a few minutes at room temperature. If it does, the temper is right; if it looks dull or marbled, something's off.

∾

```
================================================
```

PRO TECHNIQUE: THE "KNIFE TEST"

Is your chocolate in temper? Don't guess. Do this.

1. Dip the tip of a clean metal knife into your melted chocolate.
2. Set it down on the counter (room temp, roughly 68°F/20°C).
3. The Stopwatch: Watch it for 3 minutes.

<u>The Verdict:</u>

Good Temper: It sets to a satin sheen within 3 minutes.

Bad Temper: If it is still wet, sticky, or spotty after 3 minutes, you must re-seed. Do not pour your molds yet!

```
================================================
```

FOR ARTISANAL MAKERS, METHODS LIKE "TABLING" (the marble slab technique described above) or the seeding method (adding finely chopped tempered chocolate or a chunk of special cocoa butter known to be in Form V into the melted chocolate to kickstart crystal seeding) are common.

In large-scale factories, sophisticated tempering machines take care of this dance: they have temperature-controlled coils and stirring paddles that precisely cool and rewarm the chocolate. Imagine a machine that continuously circulates melted chocolate through cooled pipes to generate crystals, then through a warming zone to melt the undesirables, all timed perfectly – that's essentially what an industrial continuous temperer does.

These machines churn out perfectly tempered chocolate en masse, making it possible for every chocolate bar on a store shelf to have that ideal snap and shine.

Whether by hand or machine, tempering is a delicate balancing act. The engineering of the snap requires controlling variables like temperature, time, and agitation. Even humidity or stray water can wreak havoc (a drop of water can cause the chocolate to seize and ruin the texture, though that's a different issue from crystallization). But when done right, tempering yields chocolate that is the pinnacle of the craft – a product that not only delights the taste buds but is also structurally optimized for our sensory pleasure.

===

KITCHEN CHEMISTRY: WHY CHOCOLATE "SEIZES"
Warning: Water is the enemy of melted chocolate.

- **The Phenomenon:** You are melting chocolate. A single drop of water splashes in. Suddenly, the liquid pool turns into a hard, gritty, unworkable paste.
- **The Science:** Chocolate is dry particles (cocoa/sugar) suspended in fat (cocoa butter). It is a "dry" liquid. When you add a tiny bit of water, the sugar crystals attract it immediately. They glue themselves together, separating from the fat and forming a concrete-like clump.
- **The Fix:** You must do the unthinkable: Add MORE water (or cream). By flooding the mixture, you dissolve the sugar clumps and create a ganache. You can't use it for molding anymore, but it makes a great sauce.

===

What tempering ultimately creates is structure—an invisible architecture that determines how chocolate looks, feels, breaks, and melts. A bar that has been tempered properly carries a kind of internal coherence, its crystal network uniform and resilient.

A bar that hasn't will tell you immediately: in its dull surface, its soft bend, or its uneven melt. Understanding why this structure matters reveals why tempering is central to chocolate craft.

WHY TEMPERING MATTERS: Snap, Shine, and Shelf Life

Why go through all this trouble? If you've ever compared a high-quality couverture chocolate bar to a cheap, waxy candy coating, you know the answer. Tempering greatly impacts three key aspects of the final chocolate: its appearance, its texture (snap and mouthfeel), and its stability.

First, the appearance: well-tempered chocolate has a uniform, glossy sheen. It catches the light in a way that immediately signals "delicious" to our brains (akin to how a fresh glaze on a doughnut might entice us). Untempered or poorly tempered chocolate looks dull or mottled.

This isn't just aesthetic; in the world of confectionery, people truly "eat with their eyes" first. A shiny chocolate truffle or bar just looks more appetizing than one with a grey cast. High-end chocolatiers pride themselves on that mirror finish, and it's only achievable through tempering. In competitions or evaluations, the shine of a chocolate is actually a scored criterion.

Next, the snap: this is the hallmark tactile experience of quality chocolate. Break a piece of a well-tempered dark chocolate bar – you'll hear a sharp, clear snap. That sound comes from the fracture of a rigid, well-arranged crystal network. It also indicates the chocolate is hard enough to break cleanly.

In contrast, chocolate that isn't tempered will often just bend or break with a dull thud, crumbling without a clean line. The *engineering* behind the snap is essentially the creation of a rigid structure at the microscopic level.

Interestingly, the snap can even be measured – chocolatiers sometimes speak of a "snap test," and scientists have used texture analyzers to quantify the force needed to break chocolate or the acoustic profile of the snap. A tempered chocolate bar will require more force to break (hence the crisp snap sound) than an untempered one, which might yield or crumble quietly.

Beyond sound, this structure also contributes to a creamy melt in the mouth rather than a grainy one. Because tempered chocolate is a solid continuous network, it melts uniformly and slowly, giving a smooth mouthfeel. Untempered chocolate, containing many crystal forms and often microscopic phase separation, can feel waxy or greasy as it softens, and may not melt as evenly on the tongue.

Tempering on marble. By manipulating the temperature, the
chocolatier forces the cocoa butter to crystallize into "Form V," the
only structure that yields a glossy shine and sharp snap.

Finally, shelf life and stability: proper tempering significantly improves how well chocolate keeps. A tempered chocolate bar stored in a cool, dry place can look and taste good for months. Without tempering, chocolate is prone to fat bloom – those white streaks or blotches of cocoa butter that mar the surface.

While bloom is not mold and not harmful, it certainly makes the chocolate look unappealing and changes the texture (bloomed chocolate can be dry or chalky on the outside). Bloom happens when unstable crystal forms in the chocolate re-melt or transform and allow fat to migrate to the surface, where it re-crystallizes in a rough, diffuse way. Tempering minimizes this by starting the chocolate off in the most stable form (Form V).

Over time, even tempered chocolate can eventually develop some bloom – especially if exposed to heat fluctuations – because Form V will very slowly transition to Form VI and push a bit of fat out. But this process is slow; a well-tempered chocolate might take many months or years to show bloom, whereas an untempered one could bloom in days or weeks.

===

KITCHEN HACK: SAVING BLOOMED CHOCOLATE
Your chocolate has turned white and chalky. Is it ruined? No.

- **The Diagnosis:** It is not mold. It is just cocoa butter that has separated and hardened on the surface. It is safe to eat, but the texture is gritty.
- **The Fix:** Do not eat it raw. Melt it down.
- **The Use:** Once melted, the fat reintegrates. Use bloomed chocolate for:
  - Brownies: The batter hides the texture.
  - Hot Cocoa: Whisking it into hot milk re-emulsifies the fat.
  - Ganache: The heavy cream will smooth out the grit.

===

ADDITIONALLY, tempered chocolate resists melting at moderate room temperatures better than untempered (since Form V melts at a relatively higher temp than the lower forms). That's why a tempered chocolate bar might survive a mildly warm day intact, whereas an untempered one might get soft or misshapen quickly.

Tempering also affects how chocolates are handled in confectionery. A tempered chocolate coating will set quickly and contract slightly, which means coated candies or molded chocolates release easily from their molds. Without temper, chocolate might stick to molds or need refrigeration to force it to set, and even then it can come out with blemishes.

Professional chocolatiers rely on tempering to create those beautifully smooth shells of bonbons and chocolate figures with intricate details intact. It's worth noting that achieving temper in chocolate has been such a crucial factor that alternatives have been developed for less meticulous applications.

So-called "compound chocolate" or coating wafers use different fats (like vegetable oils or fractionated palm kernel oil) that don't have the tempering requirements of cocoa butter. These are used for ease – you can simply melt and use them without worrying about temper. But the trade-off is in quality: the melt-in-your-mouth feel isn't the same, and the snap is usually softer.

Real chocolate purists can often tell when a coating isn't true tempered cocoa butter chocolate. There really is a unique sensory magic to tempered chocolate that substitutes can't quite replicate.

==

KITCHEN PHYSICS: THE "MAGIC SHELL" HACK

Recreate the childhood nostalgia of instant-hard-shell ice cream topping using fat chemistry.

- **The Ratio:**
  - 1 cup Chocolate Chips
  - 2 tablespoons Refined Coconut Oil
- **The Science:**
  - Coconut oil is solid at room temperature but melts at 76°F. When you mix it with chocolate, you lower the chocolate's viscosity (making it pourable) but raise its sensitivity to cold.
- **The Method:**
  - Pour over ice cream.
  - Watch as the thermal shock freezes the saturated fats instantly.
  - Crack with a spoon.

==

A Blend of Art and Science

To anyone watching, tempering looks almost meditative: slow, deliberate strokes that guide the chocolate across a cool surface as its sheen shifts moment by moment. A skilled chocolatier reads these cues instinctively—the subtle thickening at the edges, the soft satin finish, the way it clings to a spatula.

But intuition is only the visible half of the craft. Beneath those motions lies a precise manipulation of cocoa butter's crystalline forms, a choreography of thermodynamics that decides whether the final chocolate will gleam, snap, and melt with perfection. Tempering is where sensory intuition meets molecular engineering.

The terminology even overlaps with metallurgy: *tempering* in metallurgy also involves controlled heating and cooling (though in steel, tempering actually softens a quenched metal to make it less brittle; whereas in chocolate, tempering hardens the product to make it more crisp).

In both cases, it's about getting the microstructure right. Some chocolatiers like to think of themselves as the metallurgists of the culinary world, turning a molten state into a finely structured solid. Instead of steel's martensite or austenite, they speak of Form V crystals and beta prime. And instead of a blade that can hold an edge, the end result is a confection that can hold a shine and snap exquisitely.

Over the years, improvements and tweaks have been discovered. For instance, food scientists have developed specialty fats and even minor additives to assist tempering. One technique uses a pinch of powdered cocoa butter crystals (commercially known products like Mycryo) which are essentially pure Form V seeds – you stir them into melted chocolate to quickly induce temper.

There's ongoing research into using certain phospholipids or other lipids to guide cocoa butter into the right form more easily, which could simplify tempering or make it more robust to temperature fluctuations. However, purists often stick to the classic methods, which are very effective when done right. After all, tempering has been working since the days of Jean Tobler with essentially just two ingredients: chocolate and controlled heat.

For the general chocolate enthusiast, understanding tempering can enhance appreciation of fine chocolate. The next time you snap a piece of glossy dark chocolate, you might pause to consider that inside that simple pleasure was a complex orchestration: the grower who fermented and dried the cacao beans, the makers who roasted and refined them, and finally the chocolatier who tempered the chocolate to perfection. Each snap is the echo of that expertise. It's what separates a dull candy bar that leaves a waxy residue from a radiant piece of chocolate that cracks briskly and then melts sumptuously in your mouth.

===

KITCHEN SCIENCE: THE "SEEDING" HACK

You don't need a marble slab to temper chocolate. You just need physics.

The Concept: If you melt chocolate completely, you destroy the good crystals (Form V). If you add a piece of solid, tempered chocolate to the melted pool, it acts as a "seed" crystal, teaching the liquid fat how to restructure itself correctly as it cools.

The Protocol:

- Melt: Melt 2/3 of your dark chocolate in a bowl until smooth (approx. 115°F / 46°C).
- Seed: Remove from heat. Toss in the remaining 1/3 of solid, unmelted chocolate chunks.
- Stir: Stir constantly until the solid chunks dissolve and the temperature drops to 88°F / 31°C.
- Test: Dip a spoon in. If it hardens glossy within 3 minutes, you have successfully engineered Form V crystals.

===

THE LEGACY of Tempering

In the grand timeline of chocolate – from ancient Mesoamerican cacao rituals to the artisan chocolate bars of today – tempering is a relatively recent chapter, but an indispensable one. It exemplifies how an empirical discovery in a confectionery kitchen evolved into a scientific understanding. The fact that a substance as common as cocoa butter can crystallize in six different ways still feels a bit magical, almost like chocolate's secret life revealed. Tempering is the key that unlocks the best of what chocolate can be.

In modern chocolate factories, tempering is just one step on the assembly line, often taken for granted now that machines handle it. But in smaller ateliers and home kitchens, learning to temper by hand is almost a rite of passage for serious chocolate makers. It can be frustrating at first – failed tempers are common for beginners, resulting in chocolate that blooms or doesn't set. But with practice, one develops that knack, and it's immensely satisfying to turn out batch after batch of glistening, crisp chocolates. It gives a deeper appreciation for those beautiful bonbons in the shop window or the perfectly snappy holiday chocolate bark.

From a storytelling perspective, tempering also humanizes chocolate-making. It reminds us that even with today's technology, making great chocolate isn't just pressing a button. It requires understanding your material intimately. The techniques invented over a century ago still hold up as the best way to tease out cocoa butter's finest form. Science has explained the "why," but the execution remains a craft.

So, the next time you enjoy a piece of chocolate that *snaps* just right, take a moment to savor not just the taste but the journey that piece has undergone. The gloss and snap in your hand are the culmination of growers, inventors, and scientists spanning continents and centuries. It's crystallized history and chemistry in one delicious moment. Tempering is the science that makes chocolate shine – literally and figuratively. And for us chocolate lovers, it's the reason that a simple bite can engage so many senses at once: sight, sound, touch, and of course, taste. That is the hidden genius in a well-tempered piece of chocolate – a small marvel of engineering that makes the experience of chocolate truly snap.

==

TECH HACK: TEMPERING WITH SOUS VIDE

The foolproof method. No stirring, no mess, perfect crystals every time.

- **The Setup:**
  - Seal chocolate in a vacuum bag or Ziploc (remove all air).
  - Set your Sous Vide water bath to 88°F (31°C) for Dark Chocolate.
- **The Process:**
  - Drop the bag in.
  - Walk away.
  - Wait 20 minutes.
- **The Result:**
  - The water holds the chocolate exactly at the crystallization point of Form V.
  - It will stay in perfect temper for hours as long as it sits in the water.
  - Snipping the corner turns the bag into a piping tool.

==

18

THE ART OF TASTING:
SUPER-TASTERS AND THE
PSYCHOLOGY OF FLAVOR

O*n a misty equatorial morning, deep in a Venezuelan cacao grove, Ed Seguine kneels beside a heap of fermenting cocoa beans. Steam rises from the pile's rich auburn mass as he plunges his hands in and lifts a scoop to his nose. He closes his eyes and inhales slowly. A small circle of farmers watches in anticipation. After a long moment, Seguine smiles. "Black cherry and plum... with a whisper of tobacco," he murmurs, describing the invisible tapestry of aromas wafting from the beans. The farmers exchange glances of surprise—they smelled only the sharp tang of vinegar from fermentation. But Seguine's face is alight with discovery. In that brief inhale, he has divined a world of flavor possibilities lurking within their crop, subtle notes that most of us would never detect.*

Meanwhile, in a quiet tasting room across the world, a small square of dark chocolate is held up to the light. A connoisseur studies its glossy sheen and listens for a sharp snap as it breaks, a telltale sign of expert tempering. She closes her eyes and inhales deeply; in that aroma she detects hints of roasted coffee, dried cherry, and maybe a whiff of leather. Finally, she lets the chocolate melt slowly on her tongue, noting how the flavors unfold. Around the table, fellow devotees murmur in agreement about the bar's "bright fruitiness" and "silky mouthfeel." This isn't a wine tasting or a coffee cupping—it's a chocolate tasting. And the people assembled are part of a growing movement that treats a simple chocolate bar with the same reverence and scrutiny as a fine vintage wine.

THESE TWO SCENES, the flavor expert in the field and the connoisseur in the tasting room—represent two sides of the same coin: the art and science of tasting chocolate. One involves individuals with extraordinary, almost superhuman sensory abilities who guide the industry from farm to factory.

The other involves a passionate culture of enthusiasts who have elevated chocolate appreciation into a sophisticated pursuit. Together, they are transforming how we understand, evaluate, and ultimately enjoy this ancient, beloved food.

THE BIOLOGY of Extraordinary Tasters

What sets the "chocolate whisperers" apart from the rest of us? In large part, it comes down to biology—and a bit of serendipity. Some people are born with super-taster genes or an abundance of taste buds, granting them a vivid tasting experience from an early age.

Scientists estimate about one in four people is a super-taster, with an unusually high density of fungiform papillae (the tiny bumps on your tongue that house taste buds). If you've ever met someone who finds broccoli intolerably bitter, black coffee undrinkable, or who insists they can taste minor differences in mineral water, they might just be a super-taster.

The term, coined by psychologist Dr. Linda Bartoshuk, describes individuals whose sense of taste for certain flavors is far more sensitive than average. They literally live in a heightened taste world: sweets taste sweeter, salt saltier, and bitters exponentially more bitter.

Importantly, super-tasters don't just react to one flavor. Research shows they perceive all taste qualities—sweet, sour, bitter, salty, umami—more intensely. This intensity stems from anatomy. With up to twice the number of taste buds crowding their tongues, super-tasters have more receptors sending signals to the brain with every bite.

Imagine tasting in high-definition compared to the rest of us in standard resolution. That amplification can be overwhelming—many super-tasters avoid strong bitter foods like grapefruit or dark leafy greens, since to them the bitterness can be almost painful. But in the right context, that same sensitivity can become a superpower for detecting subtle gastronomic nuances.

90% of flavor is smell. Tasters rub the chocolate to release volatile oils before eating, engaging the nose to detect fruit and floral notes the tongue cannot taste.

Yet taste buds alone don't paint the full flavor picture. In fact, upwards of 80% of what we perceive as "flavor" comes from our sense of smell. Our tongues can only detect the five basic tastes; all the enchanting notes of cherries, vanilla, jasmine, hazelnut, and hundreds of other flavor nuances in chocolate are actually aromas, sensed by the olfactory receptors in our nasal passages.

When you bite into a piece of chocolate, volatile aroma compounds flood up the back of your throat to your nose in what scientists call retronasal olfaction. It's essentially smelling from the inside. A person with an extremely keen sense of smell—sometimes called a "super-smeller"—might therefore perceive far more complexity in a chocolate than someone with an ordinary nose, even if their tongues were identical.

This is why when a bad cold stuffs up your nose, even the richest dark chocolate tastes flat and bland: you've lost the aromas. Extraordinary tasters seem to have both ends of the equation maxed out —discerning tongues and sensitive noses—plus the brain wiring to interpret and catalog all those signals. Some have genetic advantages;

others have simply trained themselves through years of focused practice. Many likely have a bit of both.

Crucially, the brain plays interpreter, combining taste and smell into one seamless sensation. In these gifted individuals, it's as if the brain's flavor orchestra has more musicians and a stricter conductor. Some are even neurodivergent, with atypical neurological wiring that lends a unique edge to sensing flavor.

There are autistic tasters who report heightened sensory acuity— noticing patterns and details in flavor others gloss over—or people with synesthesia who literally see or hear flavors as colors and music, adding an extra dimension to their tasting notes.

One celebrated wine expert with synesthesia famously experiences flavor as shapes and colors; we can only imagine how a bar of single-origin dark chocolate might appear in her mind's eye—perhaps a burst of purple prism for a Peruvian cacao or undulating golden lines for a caramelized white chocolate. Such cross-wiring can make flavor perception a multi-sensory panorama.

Meet the Chocolate Whisperers

Among this exceptional cohort, each "chocolate whisperer" hones their gift in distinct ways. Some, like Ed Seguine, apply it out in the field and lab, working directly with cacao beans. Others, like professional chocolate sommeliers, use it to curate transcendent tasting experiences for the rest of us, or to create imaginative new chocolate pairings.

Still others work behind the scenes in R&D labs, quietly safeguarding quality in each batch of truffles or crafting the next award-winning bar. They can pinpoint origins blindfolded, discern defects in a single nibble, and articulate the ineffable: the floral hint of an Ecuadorian Nacional bean or the warm spice undertone of an island Trinitario. In doing so, these extraordinary palates are quietly shaping what we taste and treasure in the world's finest chocolate.

Ed Seguine: The Field Expert

Ed Seguine has decades of experience in both industrial chocolate R&D and artisan chocolate making. These days he runs a consultancy advising cacao producers and premium chocolatiers on flavor. He travels to cocoa farms in Latin America, Africa, and Asia, often arriving with a mobile "flavor lab" in his backpack: small grinders, an alcohol burner, test tubes. He will ferment tiny batches of beans in the field to compare methods, roast samples over a flame, and mix up miniature chocolate liquor on the spot to taste. All this is to help farmers understand and improve the flavor potential of their beans.

In regions where growers historically focused only on yield or disease resistance, Seguine and colleagues have introduced a new vocabulary: hints of jasmine, panela (brown sugar), pineapple, almond, leather, oak. These are words never before associated with raw cocoa beans, but once farmers hear them from a flavor expert, it clicks. They begin to realize their beans aren't just a commodity—they are ingredients with terroir and character that, if nurtured, could fetch higher prices from fine chocolate makers.

Ed Seguine

Seguine even chairs an international "fine cacao" panel that formally evaluates which cocoas merit designation as Fine or Flavor grade (a status that helps farmers market to premium buyers). Under his leadership, this panel might cup and taste hundreds of cocoa liquors from around the globe.

He's developed a charming shorthand for breeders trying to create better cocoa varieties: green light for ones with great flavor, red light for ones that taste poor. "Green light means this tastes so good you really ought to keep it in the breeding mix," he explains to breeders, "and red light means I don't care if this tree is a miracle of disease resistance—if it tastes bad, drop it!" By tirelessly championing flavor, these experts are influencing which types of cacao get planted and preserved.

Genevieve Leloup: The Chocolate Sommelier

In a cozy tasting room in New York City, Genevieve Leloup prepares to introduce a dozen students to flavors they've never encountered. On the table before her lie treasures of the tropical rainforest: a fresh yellow cacao pod, a dish of sticky sweet white cacao pulp, and neat squares of fine dark chocolate made from rare cacao varieties.

Genevieve, a certified chocolate taster and self-styled chocolate sommelier, has made it her mission to open people's senses to the full spectrum of cacao—from the tangy fruit that encases the beans to the fragrant chocolate it becomes.

Dressed smartly and with an air of warm enthusiasm, Genevieve could be mistaken for a wine sommelier about to unveil a flight of Grand Cru Burgundies. Indeed, her approach borrows from wine education. She asks her students to first examine the chocolate squares for a glossy shine and even color, then to inhale deeply and describe what they smell.

The room fills with the soft sound of sniffing and murmured observations: "I get raisins... and something floral." She grins and encourages them: "Yes! Perhaps orange blossom? Or honeysuckle?" They sip lukewarm water, cleansing their palates as they would between wine samples. Finally, they snap the pieces in half—listening for the crisp "snap" that well-tempered chocolate makes—and let the pieces melt on their tongues.

Genevieve Leloup

For Genevieve, chocolate tasting has been a lifelong passion. Born to a Swiss mother and Belgian father, she jokes that chocolate runs in her veins. "Chocolate is hugely important in my family... it's a ritual after every meal, and we'd share and talk about it," she recalls. Even as a little girl, she would sample different chocolate bars with her parents and critique them. By her teenage years, she could discern the subtle differences between a Lindt 70% cacao bar and a Valrhona 70% bar—differences most casual chocolate eaters would miss entirely. One might carry whispers of citrus and vanilla, while the other tasted deeper, earthier. She didn't have terminology for it yet, but her palate was already in training.

One of her signature achievements has been unlocking the potential of fresh cacao fruit pulp—the sweet, tangy white flesh that surrounds cocoa beans, typically discarded after fermentation. Many have never tasted this perfumed nectar (often called baba de cacao); those who do are astonished that it's part of chocolate's journey.

Genevieve fell in love with the pulp's delicate flavor—a beguiling mix of lychee, citrus, and jasmine—and she wondered if she could capture that essence in a confection. The result: cacao pulp truffles and bonbons that burst with the bright tropical fruitiness of fresh cacao, balanced by just enough rich chocolate to remind you they're siblings. At her tasting events, these inventive treats often steal the show. "So this is what choco-late tastes like before it's chocolate!" people exclaim, eyes wide in wonder.

FACTORY PANELS: **The Guardians of Quality**

If mavericks like Genevieve bring chocolate's poetry to the people, others apply their heightened senses behind factory doors to ensure quality and consistency in our favorite treats. In northern Italy, in the small town of None, a renowned gourmet chocolate company called Domori runs one of the strictest tasting panels in the industry. Here, a group of expert tasters—many of them longtime employees—convene every two weeks in a quiet, fluorescent-lit room that smells faintly of cocoa and coffee. They are the gatekeepers of Domori's famed chocolate, and nothing escapes their scrutiny.

Domori was founded by Gianluca Franzoni with a mission to revive ultra-aromatic heirloom cacaos like Criollo. To do so, Franzoni knew flavor had to lead. Thus, the tasting panel was born—an internal sensory team trained to evaluate every incoming batch of cacao beans and every prototype chocolate recipe. No machine can replicate the multi-sensory analysis performed by these tasters.

They sit around a table with clipboards and small cups of samples. First come the cacao beans themselves, roasted and cracked into nibs. The panelists sift through them, judging appearance and roasting level, and especially the aroma: they're checking that fermentation was done just right on the farm, because improperly fermented beans can ruin flavor.

They chew a few nibs thoughtfully, letting the bitter paste spread over their tongues, identifying off-notes (excess acid? smoke? mold?) or promising hints (perhaps a floral sweetness signaling top-quality Criol-lo). Only if the beans pass muster will Domori even consider buying that lot.

Next, the real fun begins: tasting the chocolate made from those beans. The panel examines the snap—a good clean crack! indicating proper tempering. They breathe in the bar's fragrance and jot down impressions: "plum, cream, faint wood smoke." They place a square on their tongues and close their eyes. In silence, they let it melt, probing for texture (smooth or gritty? silky or waxy?), for flavor development (Does the initial bitterness give way to fruitiness? Is there a crescendo of nuttiness at the end?), and for balance. Each taster captures "a thousand nuances, aftertastes, strengths, and weaknesses" on the scorecard in front of them.

It's a high-stakes sensory exam, and this rigorous process ensures Domori's chocolates remain superlative. In fact, the tasting panel's decision effectively comes before any business decision. They will only sign contracts with cocoa suppliers or green-light new products if the panel's palates are happy. In a sense, these anonymous tasters hold power akin to that of a wine château's master blender or a perfumery's "nez" (nose). Through disciplined sensory evaluation, they guard the company's reputation and push quality ever higher.

The Rise of Chocolate Connoisseurship

Just a generation ago, the idea of scoring a chocolate on a 100-point scale or describing its flavor notes in poetic detail might have sounded absurd. Chocolate was candy—a beloved treat, to be sure—but not an object of sophisticated analysis. Yet today, a segment of chocolate lovers has elevated tasting into an art and science. They pursue the perfect bar, swap detailed tasting notes, attend guided pairing sessions, and debate whether a Madagascar cacao's tart berry notes outshine the deep earthy tones of a Venezuelan bar. This passionate connoisseurship comes with its own rituals, vocabulary, and even a bit of controversy.

Today's chocolate connoisseur is as passionate and discerning as any wine sommelier or coffee geek. There is now a thriving community around fine chocolate. There are chocolate festivals and fairs in major cities where craft chocolate makers showcase their bars much like wineries at a tasting room. At these events, enthusiasts mill about comparing notes on the latest single-origin finds. Workshops teach novices how to taste chocolate properly, guiding them through flights of samples that illustrate the differences between, say, a tangy Tanzanian cacao and a smoky Indonesian one. Specialty shops and cacao-focused boutiques have opened, offering curated selections of bars from around the world—often complete with tasting notes on each product.

The language here is telling. Borrowing from the wine and coffee worlds, chocolate connoisseurs speak in tasting notes and percentages, reveling in the fine distinctions of flavor and mouthfeel. A general chocolate lover might say, "I like dark chocolate" or "I prefer milk chocolate." The connoisseur goes further: "I'm partial to Madagascan 70% dark, for its red fruit acidity," or "This Dominican 80% has a wonderful leather and tobacco undertone balanced by dried fig sweetness." To some, it might seem overly specific—even pretentious. But to those in the know, these descriptors capture very real differences. With over 600 distinct flavor compounds identified in cocoa, fine chocolate can exhibit an astonishing range of aromas: from berries, citrus, and tropical fruits to nuts, spices, flowers, wood, and beyond.

The rise of the modern chocolate connoisseur has also given birth to formal structures for evaluating and credentialing expertise. There are now international chocolate competitions—such as the International Chocolate Awards or the Academy of Chocolate Awards—where expert judges convene to taste and rank products from dozens of makers. These judges often come from backgrounds in pastry, wine, or sensory science, and they taste blind (samples are unlabeled) to ensure objectivity. Winning a gold or silver in these contests can put a small chocolatier on the map and instantly signal to connoisseurs that a bar is worth seeking out.

In addition, educational programs for chocolate tasting have emerged. Organizations and schools now offer courses where one can learn to become a certified chocolate taster or even a chocolate sommelier of sorts. These courses cover the intricacies of cacao agriculture, processing, the chemistry of flavor, and lots of guided tasting practice. Trainees calibrate their palates to detect subtle differences and learn a shared vocabulary for describing chocolate. This standardization helps the community communicate: when one taster says a bar has a "clean fermentation" or "notes of jammy fruit," others know exactly what that means.

==

THE TASTING THESAURUS: FINDING THE WORDS
Struggling to name that flavor? Scan this list to pinpoint the note.

- **If you taste FRUIT:**
  - Bright/Acidic: Raspberry, Citrus, Green Apple, Passion Fruit.
  - Dark/Dried: Raisin, Prune, Fig, Black Cherry.
- **If you taste EARTH:**
  - Forest: Mushroom, Moss, Fresh Soil, Truffle.
  - Woody: Cedar, Oak, Pencil Shavings, Bamboo.
- **If you taste ROAST:**
  - Sweet: Caramel, Molasses, Toffee, Malt.
  - Savory: Coffee, Toast, Smoke, Leather, Tobacco.
- **If you taste SPICE:**
  - Warm: Cinnamon, Clove, Nutmeg, Vanilla.
  - Herbal: Mint, Grass, Green Tea, Licorice.

==

THE TASTING RITUAL: A Systematic Approach
So, what exactly do chocolate connoisseurs do when they taste? Much like a wine tasting or a coffee cupping, chocolate tasting involves a ritualized process to ensure every aspect of the experience is evaluated. The sequence engages all five senses in a structured way:

- Visual Inspection: First, the chocolate is examined with the eyes. Aficionados check the color and surface. Is it a rich mahogany brown or reddish or almost black? Is the bar's finish glossy and free of blemishes or bloom (the white sugar or fat crystals that sometimes appear)? Fine chocolate, well-tempered, often has an attractive sheen and a uniform color.

- The Snap Test: Next, many tasters actually listen to the chocolate. They hold a piece near their ear and break it. A clear, crisp "snap!" indicates good tempering—the crystalline structure of the cocoa butter is properly aligned, a sign of skillful processing and freshness. A soft or dull break might suggest a poorer temper or an older bar. This step is a nod to the multi-sensory nature of tasting: even sound plays a part.

- Aroma Assessment: Before tasting, the piece of chocolate is brought to the nose. Smelling chocolate can reveal a surprising array of scents. Connoisseurs often close their eyes to focus on aroma. They may detect notes like vanilla, caramel, leather, earth, cherry, or even odd hints like olive or cheese—cacao is complex! Some tasters rub the chocolate slightly to warm it and release more aroma. This is the time to form initial impressions: Does the smell promise intensity or subtlety? Is it mostly sweet cocoa or are there distinct aromatic notes dancing out?

- Tasting (Flavor and Texture): Now comes the main event. The chocolate is placed on the tongue and allowed to melt gradually. Patience is key—instead of chomping away, connoisseurs let the melt do the work, sometimes pressing the chocolate to the roof of the mouth to help it dissolve. As it melts, they pay attention to texture (technically called mouthfeel). Is it buttery smooth, indicating a lengthy conching and fine particle size? Or perhaps intentionally rustic and slightly gritty, offering a different kind of tactile experience? They also notice if it's creamy (especially in milk chocolate with added dairy) or if it feels drying or astringent.

- As the chocolate melts, flavors start to bloom. A fine chocolate often has a flavor arc—a beginning, middle, and finish. For instance, the first taste might be bright and acidic (imagine a zing of citrus), then it may evolve into something deeper like roasted coffee or malt, and finally leave a gentle whisper of, say, dried fruit sweetness in the aftertaste. Tasters try to parse these stages. They also judge the balance of flavors: is the bitterness harmonious with the sweetness? Does any flavor

dominate or do they complement each other? Noticing small
details is the connoisseur's joy: maybe a fleeting hint of violet
floral somewhere in the middle, or a walnut-like nuttiness
that lingers.

- Finish and Aftertaste: After swallowing (or sometimes
  politely spitting, if it's a professional marathon tasting to
  avoid palate fatigue), the taster focuses on the aftertaste. How
  long do the pleasant flavors linger on the palate? This length
  is a mark of quality—a long, satisfying finish is prized. They
  also check if any off-notes emerge late (for example, a waxy or
  soapy note might indicate poor-quality fat used, or a burnt
  note might suggest over-roasting). A great chocolate leaves
  you with clean, echoing flavors that make you want another
  bite; a lesser one might fade fast or leave a cloying or odd
  residue.

Scoring Systems: Translating Sensation into Numbers

Throughout this ritual, serious tasters often take notes. They might
jot down descriptors ("red currant, toast, olive, cream") or score various
aspects of the chocolate. Many connoisseurs and competitions employ
scoring systems to rate what they taste.

While there's no single universal system (unlike, say, wine's popular
100-point scale, though some apply that to chocolate too), a number of
chocolate enthusiasts and competitions use structured score sheets.
These typically break down the evaluation into components:

- Appearance & Snap (10 points) – evaluating visual appeal and
  the quality of the snap sound/texture.
- Aroma (10 points) – intensity and quality of the scent,
  complexity of aroma notes.
- Texture/Mouthfeel (10 points) – smoothness, melting quality,
  and overall feel on the tongue.
- Flavor (often the most important category, 10 points) –
  judging complexity, balance, intensity, purity of flavor.

- Sweetness/Acidity/Balance (10 points) – assessing if the sweetness level and any acidic tang are in harmony.
- Finish/Length (10 points) – quality of the aftertaste and how long the flavor positively persists.
- Overall Enjoyment (10 points) – a catch-all subjective score for the overall impression and pleasure derived.

Each taster might tweak the categories and weights to their preference. Some add specific points for creativity or complexity, or deduct points for defects (like a hint of mold, smoke, or improper fermentation flavors). But the goal is usually the same: to translate a multi-sensory experience into a semi-objective rating that can be compared and communicated.

Consider a scenario: a judge at a chocolate competition picks up a sample—it's a 70% dark from, say, Ecuador. It has a beautiful reddish-brown hue and a sharp snap (score high on appearance). The aroma is potent: rich cocoa with floral undertones (score well on aroma). On tasting, it's incredibly smooth and melts like butter (full points on texture).

The flavor starts earthy and woody, then blooms into a blackberry-like fruitiness with a hint of jasmine tea—it's unusual and enchanting, with a balanced sweetness and just a mild bitterness (flavor and balance get high marks). The finish is long and pleasant, with the floral note gently fading after a good minute (high score on finish). The judge's personal overall enjoyment is very high. They tally the points—perhaps it comes out to a 94/100, an outstanding score—likely a gold medal contender.

==

THE TASTING SCORECARD: RATE IT LIKE A PRO
  Copy this template to judge your next bar. Maximum Score: 50.

- **Appearance (1-5):**
  - Look for: Glossy shine, no white streaks (bloom), rich color.
  - Deduct for: Scuffs, bubbles, dullness.
- **The Snap (1-5):**
  - Listen for: A crisp, sharp sound when broken.
  - Deduct for: A dull thud or crumbling (indicates poor tempering).
- **Aroma (1-10):**
  - Smell for: Complexity. Do you smell fruit? Earth? Spice?
  - Deduct for: Weak scent, burnt rubber, or smoke.
- **Mouthfeel (1-10):**
  - Feel for: Silkiness. It should melt evenly like butter.
  - Deduct for: Grittiness, waxiness, or slime.
- **Flavor & Finish (1-20):**
  - Taste for: Balance of sweet/bitter. A long, pleasant aftertaste.
  - Deduct for: Metallic tang, astringency (drying), or flavor that vanishes instantly.

==

IT'S worth noting that despite these attempts at objectivity, tasting is inherently subjective. The same chocolate might score differently with another well-trained taster—perhaps they are more sensitive to a certain bitter note and would mark it down, or maybe they love the earthy profile even more and score it higher. Connoisseurs recognize this; many will stress that their scores are an attempt to be fair and consistent, but not a definitive verdict from on high.

. . .

TASTING WITH THE BRAIN: **The Psychology Behind Flavor**

As the connoisseurs parse every note and assign scores, a fascinating question arises: how much of this experience is "real," in the sense of being driven by the chocolate's chemistry, and how much is happening in our minds? The field of sensory science and psychology of tasting has some illuminating answers—and humbling ones, too—that show just how subjective flavor can be.

First, it's crucial to understand that what we call flavor is largely a creation of the brain. Our tongue's taste buds detect only a handful of basic tastes: sweet, sour, salty, bitter, and the savory taste known as umami. All the intricate flavors—the raspberry, the cinnamon, the jasmine, the caramel—these aren't literally "tastes" in the strict sense; they are perceived through our sense of smell.

When we eat, aromatic molecules from the food travel to our olfactory receptors in the nasal cavity (this is called retronasal olfaction). The brain takes those smell signals and combines them with the tongue's taste signals, plus input about texture and temperature, to produce a unified perception of flavor.

In essence, flavor lives in the mind, an interpretation of various sensory inputs. That's why when you have a head cold and your nose is stuffed, chocolate (or any food) tastes bland—you've lost the aroma part of flavor.

For chocolate, this means that the bar's chemical compounds might be identical for two people, but their brains could interpret the flavor differently. One person may be more attuned to certain aroma molecules while another is sensitive to different ones.

There are even genetic differences at play: for example, some people have gene variants that make them especially sensitive to bitterness or certain aromas. So a very bitter 85% cacao might be pleasantly intense for one taster and unbearably harsh for another, purely due to their biological makeup. Acknowledging this variability is part of the psychology of tasting—everyone's reality of flavor can be slightly different.

Experience and training further shape perception. A novice chocolate eater might just register "rich cocoa taste" when eating a complex dark bar, whereas a trained palate has a mental library of reference flavors to draw on: they've smelled and tasted pure ingredients like blackcurrant, smoke, violet, or malt in isolation or in other foods, so they can recognize those nuances within the chocolate.

Psychologists and food scientists have noted a phenomenon: if you have a name for a flavor and have experienced it before, you can detect it more readily. This is why building a vocabulary via tasting notes and aroma training kits (yes, those exist for chocolate, similar to wine aroma kits) can actually improve one's ability to discern flavors. It's less about developing some superhuman tongue and more about teaching the brain to notice and categorize what it was perhaps overlooking.

===

DEFECT DETECTIVE: WHAT WENT WRONG?
Does your chocolate taste "off"? Here is how to diagnose the crime.

- **The Flaw:** It smells like Ham or Smoke.
  - The Culprit: Improper Drying. The beans were likely dried over an open wood fire instead of the sun, absorbing the smoke.
- **The Flaw:** It tastes like Mold or Musty Basement.
  - The Culprit: Humidity. The beans weren't dried enough (under 7% moisture) before shipping, allowing fungus to grow inside.
- **The Flaw:** It tastes Sour or Vinegary.
  - The Culprit: Rushed Conching. The manufacturer didn't conche (mix/aerate) the chocolate long enough to evaporate the natural acetic acids from fermentation.
- **The Flaw:** It feels Gritty or Sandy.
  - The Culprit: Sugar Bloom. Moisture touched the bar, dissolving the sugar crystals, which then re-hardened into large, rough grains.

===

IN OTHER WORDS, part of connoisseurship is training your brain—and once trained, you genuinely experience more facets of the chocolate than you did as a casual eater. However, our brains can also be misled. This is where the psychology gets really intriguing. One of the biggest factors influencing taste is expectation. If you expect something to taste a certain way, that expectation can directly color your perception. For instance, if you're told a chocolate is a top-award winner or extremely expensive, you might unconsciously prime yourself to find it exceptional.

Classic experiments in the wine world demonstrated this: experts were given the same wine in two different bottles, one labeled as a cheap table wine and one as a prestigious grand cru. The tasters described the "grand cru" with far more laudatory terms and scored it higher, while dismissing the "cheap" one—even though the wines were identical. Their expectations shaped their experience profoundly.

In chocolate, similar dynamics occur. The power of suggestion is strong. If someone at a tasting mentions "I get a hint of banana here," suddenly others might notice it too—not because it magically appeared, but because our attention was directed towards that particular nuance.

The extrinsic cues around a chocolate also set up expectations that sway our senses. Take packaging and branding: a bar wrapped in matte black paper with gold lettering, sold in a chic boutique, telegraphs luxury and quality. A no-frills wrapper from a drugstore, not so much.

Research has shown that people's brains respond differently even before tasting based on such cues. A 2019 study, for example, found that participants reported enjoying the same chocolate more when it was presented in an elegant, high-end wrapper versus a plain one. The packaging evoked positive emotions and anticipation, which then made the actual tasting feel better—essentially a placebo effect via design and marketing.

Remarkably, even our other senses can cross-wire into taste. Experiments by psychologists (often in collaboration with chefs) have shown that certain sounds or music can heighten specific taste perceptions. For instance, high-pitched musical notes tend to accentuate sweetness, while low bass notes can emphasize bitterness. In one such study, people tasting chocolate in a shop reported it as more flavorful and enjoyable when listening to music that was designed to complement the chocolate, versus tasting in silence or with mismatched music.

They even were willing to pay more for the chocolate paired with the "right" sound environment. Similarly, visual ambiance—lighting color, plate design—can sway taste. A piece of chocolate served on a gleaming white plate in a softly lit room might "taste" subtly different (better) than the same piece eaten under harsh fluorescent lights. These effects aren't massive, but they are measurable. The brain blends all sensory inputs to inform the eating experience.

For the chocolate connoisseur, being aware of these biases is crucial. It's akin to a scientist controlling variables in an experiment. That's why formal tastings have protocols: often blind tasting (so brand and price are unknown), using neutral, clear or white plates (so color cues don't intrude), cleansing the palate with water or crackers between samples, and tasting in a quiet, neutral-smelling environment.

The brain blends auditory and gustatory inputs, allowing "sweet"
sounds to measurably alter the tasting experience.

Judges might even take breaks and come back to samples at different times of day to avoid the effects of palate fatigue or fluctuating hunger. Despite these efforts, subtle biases can creep in—maybe a judge prefers the fruity profile and thus is kinder to those bars, or maybe after tasting ten samples, the eleventh (if it's the last) gets a bit of subconscious "this is the finale" bump in enjoyment.

In fact, one psychological finding dubbed the "last piece effect" demonstrated that people in a study rated a piece of chocolate more highly when they were told "this is the last one" compared to when they thought it was just another in an ongoing sequence. The mere knowledge of finality added a kind of extra savor.

TRAINING THE PALATE: **From Casual Eater to Connoisseur**

Are chocolate whisperers simply born with it, or can one become a discerning taster through training? The answer is a mix of nature and nurture. While certain genetic traits (like the bitter-taste gene TAS2R38 or overall taste bud count) set the stage, even the most gifted palate must be carefully cultivated to reach an extraordinary level. Think of it like musical talent: perfect pitch might be inborn, but even a prodigy must practice scales for years to become a maestro.

Professional sensory scientists and flavor educators have, over time, demystified some of the training methods that can turn an average Joe into a discerning taster—or a super talent into a veritable flavor oracle. One key element is building a library of known aromas and tastes in one's memory. This is why wine sommeliers famously sniff vials of pure scent compounds (like blackcurrant, pepper, or citrus zest) to memorize them. In the chocolate world, similar practices are used. Trainees might start with the basic tastes: sipping dilute solutions of quinine (bitter), sugar (sweet), salt, and citric acid (sour) to calibrate their tongue's sensitivity and learn to quantify intensity.

Then comes aroma training: smelling and tasting reference samples of flavors commonly found in chocolate. For instance, an instructor might have students smell actual vanilla pods, roasted hazelnuts, dried cherries, and freshly brewed coffee—then give them chocolates that exhibit each of those notes to see if they can link the aroma to the chocolate's flavor.

Over time, patterns emerge: Madagascar-grown cacao often carries bright berry and citrus notes; Venezuelan Chuao cacao is famed for its red fruit and nuts; Ghana's classic Forastero beans have a deep cocoa "chocolatey" base note but fewer high florals. By consciously tasting and mentally cataloguing dozens of chocolates side by side, a taster trains their brain to quickly recognize origin signatures and quality markers.

Formal educational programs have arisen to standardize this learning. The International Institute of Chocolate and Cacao Tasting (IICCT) now offers the world's first accredited certifications in chocolate tasting, with multi-level courses hosted in cities from London and New York to Tokyo and Bangalore.

In these classes, aspiring chocolate connoisseurs spend intensive days tasting upwards of 9 or 10 single-origin bars, practicing descriptive vocabulary (is that note more like dried fig or fresh date? Does the finish remind you of green tea or perhaps olive oil?), and learning the impact of processing variables. They discover, for instance, how a lighter roast can preserve a cacao's hidden floral tones, or how fermenting beans for seven days versus five can dramatically boost acidity and fruity flavors.

One might wonder: do super-tasters ever suffer sensory overload? The answer is yes—tasting fatigue is real. Just as a perfumer might lose acuity after smelling dozens of fragrances, a chocolate taster's palate can get saturated after too many samples.

That's why the pros set limits and rituals. Georg Bernardini, a German chocolate critic who famously evaluated over 6,000 chocolates from 70 countries to write an encyclopedic guide, would schedule two dedicated tasting sessions a day: one in late morning, one in mid-afternoon (when the palate is freshest). He learned to stop when his taste buds felt dulled and would sometimes take a "reset" day of plain foods to recalibrate.

Even with precautions, a finely trained palate can be a double-edged sword. Consider the case of Georg Bernardini confronting a sub-par chocolate: his sensitivity made the flaws unmissable and frankly unbearable. He once recounted trying a high-end Icelandic bean-to-bar chocolate that had a heavy smoke contamination. The smoky taste was so intense to him that he literally could not swallow it. "It was like my mouth was full of ham," he shuddered, describing how the bar's intended flavor of cacao was completely overwhelmed by acrid smoke notes.

Similarly, Bernardini didn't mince words when he reviewed mass-market chocolates. A Hershey's milk chocolate bar, he pronounced "extremely rancid—cheesy... inedible," detecting off-flavors of spoiled dairy that average consumers, accustomed to the brand, might not consciously notice. The point is, to an extraordinary taster, defects in chocolate shout loudly. Their very acuity that makes great chocolate transcendent also makes bad chocolate truly horrific. It's the curse of a super-palate: once you've perceived fine nuance, you can't un-taste mediocrity.

Shaping the Industry: From Farm to Finished Bar

The influence of these expert tasters reverberates far beyond sensory labs and private tastings—it's quietly shaping the evolution of chocolate itself. In an era when chocolate is becoming as complex and celebrated as wine, the guidance of super-palates is helping farmers, makers, and even chefs push boundaries and raise standards. The high-end chocolate industry today leans on its sensory experts at every step from bean to bar.

When Ed Seguine sniffed out those notes of cherry and tobacco in Venezuelan cacao, he wasn't just showing off—he was giving the farmers valuable feedback about their crop's quality. His guidance helps them understand that their beans aren't just a commodity—they are ingredients with terroir and character.

For instance, one high-yield variety called CCN-51 produces tons of beans but with such mediocre taste that Seguine has likened its chocolate to "acidic dirt." Thanks to pressure from the fine flavor movement, some farmers are now intercropping or replacing CCN-51 with heritage strains that, while less productive, yield far superior flavor. In short, the chocolate whisperers are literally changing the agricultural landscape, bean by bean, aroma by aroma.

Inside the innovation kitchens of gourmet chocolate houses, having a super-taster on the team can make the difference between a good product and a transcendent one. These experts lend their palates and creative vision to blend cacao origins, develop new recipes, and even pair chocolate with other ingredients in groundbreaking ways. Take, for example, the trend of single-origin chocolate bars—bars made from beans from one region or even one farm, much like single-vineyard wines. It was the discerning palates of chocolate makers and tasters that revealed how different a Madagascar bar tastes from a Venezuelan one, and advocated for preserving those unique profiles rather than mixing them all together. Now, origin-driven bars are a staple of every fine chocolate line.

Another realm the chocolate whisperers are revolutionizing is how we enjoy chocolate in combination with other foods and drinks. Just as sommeliers have long paired wines with meals, now chocolate tastings are being paired with everything from whiskey to cheese to tea. Who devises these novel pairings? Often it's the chocolate sensory experts.

They apply their deep flavor knowledge to find complementary or contrasting matches that elevate both elements. For example, a super-taster might know that a particular Venezuelan dark chocolate has prominent dried fruit and tobacco notes. They might then suggest pairing it with a smoky single-malt whisky from Islay—the peat in the whisky resonates with the chocolate's tobacco note, while the chocolate's sweetness softens the whisky's burn. The two together create a synergy that makes aficionados swoon.

==

THE SPIRIT GUIDE: RULES OF ENGAGEMENT

Pairing wine and chocolate is harder than it looks. Follow these two laws to avoid disaster.

- **Law 1:** The Sweetness Rule The drink must be sweeter than the chocolate.
    - The Mistake: Pairing dry red wine (Cabernet) with sweet milk chocolate. The wine will taste sour and metallic.
    - The Fix: Pair dry reds with High% Dark Chocolate. Pair Milk Chocolate with Port or Sherry.
- **Law 2:** The Intensity Match Light spirits get drowned by dark chocolate.
    - White Chocolate goes with Gin or Fruity White Wines.
    - Milk Chocolate goes with Rum or Merlot.
    - Dark Chocolate goes with Peaty Scotch or Bourbon.

==

ONE INNOVATIVE PAIRING that emerged recently was matching chocolate with specialty coffee. Since both chocolate and coffee are complex, roasted products of tropical beans, a number of sensory specialists (often Q-graders from coffee teaming up with chocolate tasters) have had a field day selecting, say, a fruity Ethiopian coffee to sip alongside a tangy Ugandan chocolate, or a deep earthy Sumatran coffee with a malty Papua New Guinea chocolate. The layers of flavor build and echo each other. High-end restaurants have begun employing such experts to design chocolate tasting menus and cocktails as well. What all this points to is that these extraordinary tasters are not just passively describing chocolate; they are actively expanding the ways we experience it.

The Allure and the Absurd

By now, it's clear that chocolate connoisseurship involves much more than simply liking chocolate. It's a hobby, a science, a bit of an art, and for some, nearly a lifestyle. What drives people to go to such lengths—and what might be the downsides? The allure of joining this "cult" is multifaceted.

At heart, connoisseurship is about enriching enjoyment. If you adore chocolate, learning to taste it the way experts do can feel like discovering a new dimension in something familiar. It's akin to moving from listening to music in the background to really hearing the notes and instruments.

That first time you detect a nuanced flavor in chocolate ("Wow, there really is a hint of pineapple here!") can be eye-opening. Connoisseurship invites you to slow down and be present with the food. In our fast-paced world, that alone can be a rewarding form of mindfulness. Many enthusiasts describe tasting fine chocolate as almost meditative—you have to be patient, attentive, and immerse yourself in the senses.

There's also the joy of learning and discovery. The world of chocolate is broad and rich. As you delve into it, you learn about far-flung places where cacao grows: the rainforests of Ecuador, the highlands of Madagascar, the jungles of Belize.

You learn about how fermentation techniques or roasting levels influence flavor. You begin to recognize brands and makers, developing favorites and understanding their philosophies. This can be intellectually stimulating—it's an ever-ending journey, because there's always a new origin, a new harvest, or an experimental process to try.

The line between genuine appreciation and obsession is thin.
Connoisseurship invites us to treat a simple square of chocolate
with the same rigor one might apply to a fine wine or a rare antique.

Connoisseurship also comes with a sense of community. Enthusiasts bond over shared passions. The cult of chocolate connoisseurs might be global, but it's tight-knit in its own way. Members trade bars via mail across continents, write blogs that others follow, and attend the same festivals or events yearly like reunions. There is a camaraderie in collectively chasing the next great taste. Much like collectors of rare books or vintage wines, chocolate aficionados enjoy comparing finds and marveling at each other's prized possessions (like a bar made from cacao of an almost extinct variety, or one aged for 10 years).

However, every cult has its potential excesses, and chocolate connoisseurship is no exception. It's worth acknowledging the criticisms and pitfalls. To some observers, the level of analysis and flowery language used by connoisseurs veers into the pretentious. There's the classic image of the snobbish wine taster pontificating about "oaken bouquet with a hint of gooseberry and an impertinent finish."

Chocolate tasters can sound similar, rhapsodizing about "luscious top notes of passionfruit and a beguiling smokiness on the mid-palate." For an average person who just thinks "Mmm, that's yummy chocolate," this might seem over-the-top.

There's some truth to the idea that connoisseurs sometimes overthink things. When you're dissecting a beloved food to this degree, you risk losing the forest for the trees. One might get so caught up in detecting notes and comparing percentages that the simple pleasure of letting a piece of chocolate melt in your mouth gets intellectualized to the point of abstraction.

It's important, even for the devoted taster, to occasionally step back and just enjoy the treat without analysis—to remember why you fell in love with chocolate in the first place. Some connoisseurs have a rule: when they encounter a truly sublime chocolate, they'll do the formal tasting for a piece or two, then stop taking notes and just savor the rest without distraction, allowing joy to take over from judgment.

All these quirks of the mind don't invalidate connoisseurship—if anything, they deepen the intrigue. Knowing that our perception is part biology, part psychology underscores why tasting is such a personal experience. It also highlights why two chocolate experts might genuinely disagree about a chocolate's merits and yet both be right in their own subjective realities. The best tasters acknowledge these factors with a dose of humility. The phrase "your mileage may vary" applies strongly to taste. One taster's 9/10 is another's 7/10, and that's okay.

SAVOR IT: **A New Appreciation**

Back in the Venezuelan grove, the sun has climbed and the heat of midday intensifies the heady perfume of fermenting cacao. Ed Seguine wraps up his notes for the farmers: which lots sing with fruitiness and deserve a gentler roast, which might need an extra day of fermentation next time to mellow an astringent edge.

Before he leaves, he breaks open one more bean and hands half to the lead farmer's elderly father—a man who has grown cacao here for 50 years but seldom, until now, tasted the nuances of his own crop. Together they chew the raw bean. The old man's eyes widen; he grins in surprise. "Banana... I taste ripe banana!" he exclaims in Spanish, delighted at this realization. Seguine chuckles and nods—he tastes it too. In that moment, knowledge passes directly through flavor: the farmer will never ferment his beans quite the same way again, now that he's glimpsed the delicate sweetness that can be preserved.

This scene, and countless like it, illustrates the quiet revolution wrought by the chocolate whisperers and connoisseurs. They remind us that flavor is a language, one that can be learned and shared. By listening to their heightened senses, we too learn to slow down and taste more deeply. A square of dark chocolate is no longer just a candy or a quick snack; it can transport us to a Sumatran rainforest or a Malagasy hillside through its notes. The work of these sensory experts ultimately enhances our appreciation as consumers. Thanks to them, origin labels now read like wine appellations, and we find ourselves detecting, perhaps for the first time, that hint of violet in our Peru 70% bar or the whisper of spice in our Ecuador truffle.

For the general chocolate-loving public, you don't have to be a professional taster or join a club to take a page from the connoisseurs' book. The next time you treat yourself to a nice chocolate, try slowing down and tasting it mindfully. Notice its color, listen for the snap, breathe in its aroma.

Let it melt and see if you can identify one or two flavor notes beyond "chocolatey." You might surprise yourself—hey, there is a nutty or fruity hint! Doing this won't turn a casual snack into a laborious analysis; rather, it can make a small piece of chocolate far more satisfying than a whole bar mindlessly chomped.

The cult of connoisseurship has, in a way, done us all a favor by revealing how much there is to appreciate in chocolate. They've shown that chocolate isn't just candy for children or a guilt-laden indulgence— it can be as nuanced as wine, as worthy of appreciation as a gourmet cheese or single-origin coffee.

Through their obsessive experiments and discussions, they've mapped out the dimensions of chocolate flavor and the workings of our own senses. We've learned that our experience of taste is part physics and part psychology, that our brains can be both a tasting supercomputer and a trickster, and that sharing tasting experiences can build connections and knowledge.

So, is chocolate connoisseurship a kind of cult? Perhaps it is, in the sense that it has ardent believers, rituals, and an esoteric body of knowledge. But it's a welcoming cult, one that anyone with a genuine love of chocolate can join simply by being curious and open to learning. There's no secret handshake required—maybe just a willingness to close your eyes and concentrate the next time a square of dark chocolate begins to soften on your tongue.

In the end, whether you consider yourself a connoisseur or just an occasional chocolate dabbler, the core message might be the same: savor it. A square of chocolate can be a fleeting snack or it can be a gateway to momentary bliss—the choice is in how we experience it. The connoisseurs choose bliss through knowledge and awareness. Even if you never take notes or care about cacao percentages, adopting just a bit of their mindful approach can enrich your enjoyment.

===

MASTERCLASS: HOW TO HOST A CHOCOLATE TASTING

Turn this book into a gathering. Here are the Rules of Engagement.

- **The Order of Operations:** Always taste from lowest cocoa percentage to highest (e.g., 60% -> 70% -> 85%). If you taste the bitterest bar first, you will blow out your palate and the lighter bars will taste like sugar.
- **The Palate Cleansers:** Do not use wine or coffee; they compete with the cocoa. The professional standard is room temperature water and plain polenta (cornmeal) crackers or slices of Granny Smith apple to scrub the tongue.
- **The Blind Reveal:** Break the bars into pieces before guests arrive and place them on numbered sheets of paper. Hide the wrappers. Biases are real—people will rate a fancy label higher than a plain one. Let the flavor speak first.

===

In an age of convenience and standardized foods, these individuals stand apart, almost like throwbacks to an era of guild artisans—people whose craft is not building or painting, but perceiving ephemeral qualities and preserving them for our enjoyment.

Their value is recognized in small circles, but perhaps unsung among the broader public. Yet every chocoholic owes them a debt. The astonishing diversity of fine chocolate today, the thrilling new flavors and ever-improving quality, are in large part the result of their passionate, tireless tasting.

The chocolate whisperers will continue doing what they do best—scouring the globe for rare cacao jewels, coaxing the finest flavors from each batch, and teaching us to savor the difference. The connoisseurs will keep pursuing the perfect bar, building communities around shared passions, and revealing to newcomers the hidden poetry in each bite. And if we listen closely to these extraordinary palates, we just might hear chocolate whisper back to us, revealing its secrets one sublime flavor note at a time.

Just be warned: once you've tasted chocolate with a connoisseur's mindset, even the simplest candy bar might never taste the same again. In a good way. Enjoy the journey, and let the chocolate cultivate your senses.

19

BEYOND SWEET AND BITTER: UMAMI, KOKUMI, AND PHANTOM FLAVORS

W*hen you bite into a square of fine dark chocolate and let it dissolve on your tongue, waves of flavor unfold. First comes the familiar bittersweet cocoa hit, followed by subtler whispers— maybe a fruity tang like cherries or a floral hint reminiscent of jasmine. There's often a nutty roast and a vanilla sweetness lingering in the background. But beyond these recognizable notes lies something more mysterious: fleeting sensations you can sense but not quite name. A ghost of spice? A trace of earthiness or fresh-cut grass? These are the phantom flavors of chocolate—the secretive molecules that tease our senses and yet largely evade scientific identification.*

CHOCOLATE'S FLAVOR is a complex orchestration of hundreds of chemical compounds, and even with modern chemistry's best efforts, a few of those instrumental notes remain unknown. Yet in recent years, scientists and chefs have begun exploring another frontier entirely: the savory, mouth-filling depth that has always been there, just not consciously recognized. This "fifth taste" is known as umami, a Japanese term meaning "essence of deliciousness," and its enigmatic ally, kokumi—the so-called "taste of richness." Together, these ideas are reshaping our understanding of chocolate, pushing it into bold and uncharted territory.

A Mosaic of Flavor Molecules

Chocolate is often described as having one flavor—"chocolate"—but in reality it's a mosaic composed of many individual aromas and tastes. As we explored in the architecture of flavor, chocolate contains a staggering array of volatile compounds. Researchers have cataloged hundreds of these molecules contributing to its smell alone.

These volatiles are tiny molecules that easily evaporate into the air, carrying aroma to our nose. Each one has a distinct scent if sniffed in isolation: amazingly, the roster includes molecules that smell like peaches, cooked cabbage, raw beef fat, potato chips, earthy soil, honey, and even human sweat (specifically isovaleric acid).

Not exactly the kinds of smells you'd associate with a luscious chocolate bar! Yet in the peculiar chemistry of flavor, when all these disparate aromas merge, they produce the familiar delicious character of chocolate. Together, hundreds of oddball smells melt into one harmonious blend that we instantly recognize as that cocoa-rich goodness.

Food chemists have been cataloguing these flavor molecules for decades. They've identified acids that lend tanginess, pyrazines that give roasted, nutty notes, esters that impart fruity tones, and terpenes that add sweet floral hints.

By now, virtually every major component of chocolate's aroma has been detected and named—from acetic acid (which smells like vinegar) to 2,3,5-trimethylpyrazine (which has a toasty, cocoa-like scent) and linalool (a sweet floral aroma). But here's the twist: even the most "chocolatey" of these individual compounds doesn't smell like chocolate on its own.

There isn't one single molecule that we can point to and say "this is the smell of chocolate." As Dr. David Salt, a plant scientist who studies cocoa, puts it, "There isn't a molecule in cacao beans that's chocolate flavor. The overall 'chocolatiness' is a bouquet of different compounds." In other words, chocolate flavor is an ensemble cast—a product of many molecules interacting, rather than a solo act.

```
==================================================
```

CHEMISTRY CLASS: THE MOLECULE MATCHER

When you taste a flavor, you are actually smelling a chemical. Here is the translation key.

- **Pyrazines = "The Roast"**
  - Smells like: Popcorn, Toast, Peanut Butter.
  - Source: Created by heat during roasting (Maillard reaction).
- **Esters = "The Fruit"**
  - Smells like: Banana, Pineapple, Honey.
  - Source: Created by yeast during fermentation.
- **Linalool = "The Flower"**
  - Smells like: Froot Loops, Lavender, Rose.
  - Source: Native to the cacao flower itself (especially in Arriba Nacional beans).
- **Acetic Acid = "The Tang"**
  - Smells like: Vinegar.
  - Source: Created by bacteria in the final stage of fermentation. If it's too strong, the beans weren't aerated enough.

```
==================================================
```

In fact, scientists have shown just how crucial the combination is. In one remarkable experiment, researchers in Germany took a list of 25 of cocoa's key aroma chemicals—culled from those hundreds—and mixed them together in the lab.

This custom blend included substances with unappetizing descriptors like sweaty, cabbage-like, and meaty. The result? To everyone's surprise, the mixture smelled just like chocolate. By contrast, if you sniffed any one of those ingredients alone, you'd never associate it with a chocolate bar. "The mixture smells completely different from the individual constituents," notes Dr. Peter Schieberle, a leading food chemist who helped pioneer these studies. "At the moment, there is no way to predict how the final mixture will smell." The chocolate aroma seems to emerge only when the right pieces are in place together—a fragrant mosaic assembled by our brains.

THE SCIENCE of Flavor Perception

How is it that a jumble of odd volatile molecules—some smelling of sweat or cooked cabbage—can collectively create the heavenly aroma of chocolate? The answer lies in the way our sensory system processes smells and tastes. Humans have hundreds of odor receptors in the nose, each a special protein tuned to detect certain molecular features.

When you inhale the vapors rising from a melting piece of chocolate, molecules waft into your nasal cavity and bind to these receptors in various combinations. Each aroma compound triggers a specific set of receptors, like a key fitting into locks. Signals from those receptors travel to the brain, where they are integrated into what we perceive as a distinct smell.

Crucially, when multiple aroma compounds hit our nose at once—as they do when enjoying chocolate—our brain doesn't register each one separately. Instead, it assembles a composite sensation out of all the signals. "By the time you put four chemicals together, your brain can no longer separate them into components," explains Gary Reineccius, a flavor scientist at the University of Minnesota. "It forms a new, unified perception that you can't recognize as any of those individual aromas."

In other words, the brain performs a kind of olfactory blending, creating a singular "chocolate" impression from many inputs. The upshot is that chocolate flavor exists as a whole in our minds, even though it's made of many parts. We experience chocolate not as a list of discrete smells (a bit of this, a hint of that), but as one deliciously coherent flavor.

Flavor perception doesn't end with the nose, of course. Taste buds on our tongue contribute basic tastes (sweet, bitter, sour, etc.), and other senses like touch play a role (think of the creamy melt or astringent drying sensation of chocolate). In chocolate's case, the taste side is relatively straightforward: sugar provides sweetness; theobromine and caffeine (natural stimulants in cocoa) lend a gentle bitterness; and polyphenols (antioxidant compounds) create some bitterness and astringency, that dry-mouth feel.

But much of what we call flavor—especially the nuanced differences between a fruity chocolate versus a nutty or floral one—comes from aromas detected in the nose. In fact, if you pinch your nose while eating chocolate, you mostly taste sweetness and bitterness; only when you release your nose and breathe do the rich aromatic layers bloom.

Chocolate provides a perfect demonstration of the retronasal mechanism explored in previous chapters. As the cocoa butter melts, it releases its payload of volatile aroma molecules, which rise through the back of the throat to strike the nasal receptors from the inside. This is why experts always advise savoring chocolate slowly.

The candy's high fat content (cocoa butter) holds onto aroma compounds and then liberates them gradually at mouth temperature. "Chocolate's flavor comes out as it melts," says Dr. Schieberle. "When you put chocolate in your mouth, a chemical reaction happens. Some people just bite and swallow, but if you do that, the reaction doesn't have time to happen, and you lose a lot of flavor." Instead, letting chocolate languorously dissolve gives your taste buds and nose time to catch every flavor note.

Discovering the Fifth Taste: Umami in Chocolate

For most of us, chocolate has long been synonymous with sweetness. From childhood memories of milk chocolate bars to the grown-up allure of bittersweet truffles, the taste of chocolate seemed firmly planted in the realms of sweet and bitter, perhaps with a pinch of salt on top. But as chefs and food scientists dive deeper into the science of taste, they're discovering that chocolate has a hidden side—a savory, mouth-filling depth that has always been there, just not consciously recognized.

The story of umami in the modern culinary world began over a century ago. In 1908, a Japanese chemist named Kikunae Ikeda identified a distinct savory taste in kombu seaweed broth that did not fit the classic four tastes (sweet, salty, sour, bitter). He named this taste umami, and soon isolated glutamate as the amino acid responsible for it.

For decades, umami was often associated with Asian cuisine—the satisfying savoriness in soy sauce, miso soup, aged fish sauce, mush-rooms, and parmesan cheese. It wasn't until much later, around the early 2000s, that Western scientists and chefs fully acknowledged umami as a fundamental taste perceived by specialized receptors on our tongue. Today umami is celebrated as the "fifth taste," found in foods all over the world. But what does it have to do with chocolate, a food mostly consumed in sweet contexts?

At first glance, chocolate doesn't scream "savory." A square of dark chocolate pleases us with a balance of bitterness and sweetness; a creamy milk chocolate delights with sugar and fat. Yet, if you savor a high-quality dark chocolate or a complex cocoa beverage, you might notice something else lurking under the cocoa and caramel notes—a sort of mouth-filling satisfaction, a depth that is reminiscent of a well-seasoned dish or a sip of rich coffee.

This is where umami subtly enters the picture. While cocoa beans themselves are not loaded with glutamate like, say, tomatoes or cheese, the fermentation and roasting processes that turn cacao into chocolate generate a symphony of flavor compounds. Among these can be trace amounts of amino acids and small peptides that contribute to savoriness.

Moreover, chocolate often naturally contains minor notes that we describe in surprising ways: ever caught a hint of earthiness or something almost like black olives or aged wine in a very dark single-origin chocolate? Those nuanced notes can be analogous to the savory flavors in other fermented foods.

Historically, chocolate actually began as a much less sugary affair. The ancient civilizations of Mesoamerica drank chocolate as a bitter, spiced beverage—often mixed with chili, cornmeal, and aromatic herbs. These early chocolate drinks were foamy, bitter, and complex, bearing little resemblance to the candy-sweet hot cocoa of today. In those preparations, chocolate's inherent bitterness and richness were the stars, sometimes accompanied by a peppery kick and thickened with maize.

One could argue that these preparations leaned into chocolate's savory qualities; they certainly weren't trying to make it a dessert. In a sense, the original chocolate experience was closer to a savory soup than a sweet milkshake. Over time, of course, sugar entered the equation and our palates came to expect chocolate as a treat firmly planted in the sweet category.

Now, in the 21st century, we've gone full circle to an extent—bringing back savory elements into chocolate, but armed with the language and science of taste. When we talk about umami in chocolate today, it's not about making chocolate overtly salty or meaty. It's about recognizing and enhancing those background notes that give chocolate a roundness and completeness.

Think of the way a pinch of salt in a brownie recipe makes the chocolate taste more vibrant—that's a simple example of leveraging our taste biology (salt reduces bitterness and enhances overall flavor). Umami works in a similar way, but with even more intriguing results: it can amplify the natural flavors and add a lingering, mouth-watering satisfaction.

CHOCOLATE'S HIDDEN Savory Side

The modern palate has been gradually prepared for this evolution. Over the past couple of decades, we've seen a rise in sweet-and-salty combinations and other unlikely pairings becoming mainstream. Sea salt caramels and salted chocolate bars, which were once novel, are now beloved staples. That little crunch of flaky salt on a truffle or caramel doesn't make the candy taste salty; rather, it heightens the other flavors and curbs excessive sweetness. This was an important step in opening consumers' minds—and taste buds—to the idea that a touch of savory could improve a sweet treat.

From there, bolder experiments gained traction. Pioneering chocolatiers began to play with savory inclusions in their confections. One famous example is the bacon chocolate phenomenon. A luxury chocolate brand introduced a milk chocolate bar studded with crispy bacon bits, and what sounded like a prank at first turned into a cult hit. Why? The smoky, umami-rich flavor of bacon paired with sweet chocolate created something utterly craveable—a balance of sweet, salty, fatty, and savory that hit every pleasure point on the tongue.

Likewise, chocolate-covered pretzels, once a niche item, married the toasty, savory notes of pretzel with chocolate's richness and became a household snack. Each of these combinations succeeded by leveraging umami or its close cousins in some form. Bacon brings meaty umami compounds; pretzels bring malted grain notes and salt.

Inspired by such successes, chefs started venturing further. If salt and bacon work, what about other sources of umami? Enter ingredients like miso, soy sauce, malt, cheese, and even mushrooms into the dessert lexicon. It may sound like a dare, but these have all been used—with remarkable results—in the hands of creative professionals. Home cooks began hearing about these tricks through food media. F

For instance, an article in Bon Appétit not long ago extolled the virtues of adding a splash of soy sauce to chocolate brownie batter. The writer discovered this hack serendipitously one night and found that replacing the usual pinch of salt with soy sauce gave the brownies "a serious depth of flavor and a delicious savoriness that salt alone couldn't achieve." The idea is that soy sauce (essentially fermented soybeans and wheat) delivers saltiness plus a dose of pure umami. Used judiciously, it doesn't make the dessert taste like stir-fry; it simply underscores the cocoa with an earthy, savory base note.

Similarly, miso—the fermented soybean paste ubiquitous in Japanese cuisine—has found its way into pastry kitchens around the world. Pastry chefs have discovered that a tablespoon of mild miso can transform chocolate confections. Why miso? Think of miso as a cousin of salted caramel, but on steroids. It provides saltiness, yes, but also a funkiness and depth from fermentation that plain salt lacks.

Jessie Sheehan, a baker and cookbook author, has called miso the "underrated ingredient your chocolate desserts need." She points out that if you love what a pinch of flaky salt does to a chocolate cookie, miso might be your new best friend in baking. It can be melted into butter for brownies, whisked into ganache for truffles, or blended into cream for a chocolate mousse. The result is a dessert that has people furrowing their brows in delight—"What is that flavor?"—even though they likely can't identify the miso. It makes the chocolate taste more complex, balancing the bitterness and sugar with something almost savory, almost tangy, utterly delicious.

And it's not just soy-based ingredients. Consider Marmite—the famed British yeast extract spread known for its intense umami and saltiness. A few years ago, an award-winning chocolatier in London named Paul A. Young was dared to make a Marmite-infused chocolate truffle. The idea raised eyebrows (Marmite is so polarizing that Brits famously say "you'll love it or hate it"), but he went for it. The result? A dark chocolate ganache kissed with just enough Marmite to accentuate the cocoa. To everyone's surprise, the Marmite truffle became a best-seller in his shop. Eaters raved that it didn't taste of yeast or anything odd —it just tasted like the most chocolatey chocolate truffle ever, with a long, savory finish.

Then there are the boldest moves—ones that truly blur the line between dinner and dessert. A renowned food writer recounted sampling a chocolate truffle made with fish sauce at a culinary confer-ence. Yes, fish sauce, the intensely aromatic fermented liquid that gives Southeast Asian dishes their savory punch.

It sounds outrageous, but the chef's reasoning was sound: high-quality fish sauce is essentially a super-concentrated umami liquid (anchovies fermented over months until they release a salty, glutamate-rich nectar). Used sparingly, it can season a dish much like salt, but with extra complexity.

In that truffle, the fish sauce didn't announce itself; there was no fishy taste at all. It simply deepened the cocoa flavor and added a long, mouth-coating savoriness to each bite. The taster described it as giving the chocolate "just a little bit more depth," noting that chocolate, which undergoes fermentation in its making, has some kinship with fish sauce, another fermented product.

THE PHANTOM FLAVORS: Molecules We Cannot Name

Despite identifying hundreds of compounds in cocoa, scientists have not caught them all. Every so often in the laboratory, a flavor chemist analyzing a chocolate will stumble upon an aroma they can clearly smell —but whose source they can't pinpoint. These are chocolate's phantom flavor molecules: elusive chemicals that make their presence known to the human nose yet elude analytical instruments and databases. They are the aromatic equivalent of ghosts—sensed but not seen.

Consider an example from a scientific study in 2008. A team of researchers was examining the aroma of chocolates made from Ghanaian cocoa beans. Using a technique called GC-Olfactometry— essentially a gas chromatograph that lets a human sniff individual compounds as they emerge—they catalogued the key odors contributing to the chocolate's smell.

Among the usual suspects (like the familiar roasted and sweet notes) they encountered one particularly striking smell: a note described as "grassy/lettuce-like," which seemed important to the overall aroma character.

But when they tried to match this odor to known chemicals, they hit a dead end. It didn't correspond clearly to any compound in their library, and its precise identity remained unidentified. In other words, the scientists knew the smell was there—their noses detected it strongly—but they couldn't determine what molecule caused it. It was a phantom, a nameless wisp hiding in the verdant lettuce scent.

Leap forward to 2019, and another intriguing case emerges. In that year, German researchers at the Technical University of Munich conducted an in-depth "sensomics" analysis on high-cocoa dark chocolates. By this time, analytical technology had advanced and you might think nothing in chocolate's aroma could surprise us.

The team identified 50 distinct odor-active compounds rising from the chocolate samples. Forty-seven of them were successfully identified and named—a who's who of chocolate aromatics. But three compounds defied identification. They were detected by their smell and by their chromatographic presence, yet scientists couldn't chemically identify or match them to any known substance. What were they like?

The researchers noted the descriptors: one gave a strong fruity, sweaty, pungent smell; another had a meaty, savory, seasoning-like aroma; and the third had a fruity aroma with a tropical nuance.

These ghost compounds were clearly contributing to the chocolate's aroma profile—possibly providing subtle notes that enrich the cocoa, or perhaps influencing the perception of other flavors by contrast. And yet, at the chemical level they remain cipherous. We know they exist, because trained sniffers can consistently sense them in the aroma extracts. But we don't yet know their names, structures, or origins.

Why are these molecules so hard to identify? The challenges are numerous. For one, these phantom compounds often occur in extremely low concentrations—maybe just a few parts per billion in the chocolate. That's enough for the human nose to detect (since our olfactory system can be incredibly sensitive to certain odors) but it pushes the limits of our machines.

Instruments like mass spectrometers might pick up only a weak signal, or none at all, from such trace components. Additionally, some molecules are just chemically tricky: they might be highly reactive or unstable, breaking down during the analysis process. Imagine trying to catch a snowflake on your tongue—by the time you examine it closely, it's melted away. Similarly, a fragile aroma compound might decompose under the heat of a gas chromatograph or upon exposure to oxygen, leaving only a fleeting trace that something was there.

Another issue is the vastness of chemical space. The unknown chocolate odorants could be molecules that have simply never been catalogued before. Flavor chemists rely on databases of mass spectral signatures and known compounds to identify substances. If a particular molecule isn't in any database (because it's never been synthesized or reported), identifying it is like looking up a word that isn't in the dictionary. You're left puzzling over fragments and inferencing what it might be.

Then there's the possibility that some phantom flavors aren't from a single molecule at all, but from a combination. Recall that flavor notes can emerge from synergy: two or three compounds together might create a new aroma impression that none of them has alone. Our analytical instruments, however, typically isolate and measure compounds one by one. If the "note" disappears when the mixture is separated, one might erroneously conclude a single mysterious compound was responsible, when in fact it was a harmonious duet. The phantom might be a ghost that vanishes under interrogation, because its identity was essentially "the sum of parts."

∾

ENTER KOKUMI: The Sixth Taste Sensation

Alongside the umami revolution in chocolate is the rise of kokumi, a concept that might be the next big thing in flavor science. If umami is the fifth basic taste, some researchers have proposed kokumi as a candidate for the "sixth taste." However, kokumi is a bit different from the other five tastes because it doesn't have a distinct flavor of its own. Instead, kokumi is often described as the taste of "heartiness" or "richness." It's that quality of a slow-cooked stew that coats your mouth, the depth of a long-aged cheese, the satisfying body of a well-aged wine. The term kokumi itself means "rich taste" in Japanese.

Molecular harmony: Dark chocolate and blue cheese share over 70 distinct flavor compounds, making them a chemically perfect, if surprising, pairing.

Scientists discovered kokumi by studying certain molecules—notably gamma-glutamyl peptides—found in foods like garlic, onions, yeast, and fermented foods. These molecules don't trigger the sweet, sour, salty, bitter, or umami receptors directly.

Rather, they activate calcium receptors on the tongue, which in turn modulate our taste perception, making flavors seem rounder and longer-lasting. In practical terms, when a kokumi compound is present, sweet tastes taste sweeter, salty tastes taste saltier, and umami tastes taste more savory—all without adding more sugar, salt, or MSG. Kokumi is like an enhancer of everything, a booster that adds "volume" to the flavor orchestra. Think of it as turning a two-dimensional flavor into three-dimensional.

What does kokumi have to do with chocolate? Quite a lot, it turns out, especially in how we experience chocolate's flavor and texture. When we describe a luxurious chocolate as "creamy," "velvety," or "full-bodied," we're partly talking about kokumi effects.

A high-quality dark chocolate has an almost tongue-coating feel and a lingering flavor that stays minutes after the bite—that's not just the cocoa butter richness, but also certain peptides generated during fermentation and roasting that inherently have kokumi properties. In fact, one reason a long-fermented, well-roasted cocoa bean from, say, a single estate chocolate bar tastes so layered and lingering is that it likely contains more of these flavor-enhancing compounds, compared to a bulk processed cheap chocolate which might taste flat. So even before scientists gave it a name, kokumi was quietly at work in our favorite chocolate experiences.

Today, food scientists and ingredient companies are isolating kokumi compounds and producing them as additives to help manufacturers create richer flavor without relying on time-consuming traditional methods. In the context of chocolate and cocoa products, this has exciting implications. Imagine a ready-to-mix hot cocoa powder that, even when made with water, tastes as satisfying as if it were made with milk and simmered gently—kokumi enhancers could make that possible by adding mouthfeel and depth.

Large food companies have started experimenting with kokumi in chocolate beverages and protein shakes, finding that it can make a low-fat chocolate protein drink taste more "indulgent" and "authentic". Kokumi ingredients have been used to boost cheap cocoa, making it taste more like a premium, high-cocoa-content product by amplifying the roast notes and adding a lingering finish that normally comes from long conching and higher cocoa butter.

Chefs, too, are learning about kokumi and incorporating it in more natural ways. Instead of using a purified kokumi additive, a chef might use kokumi-rich foods to achieve the effect. For instance, adding a bit of aged Gouda (a cheese high in kokumi peptides) into a chocolate spread can surprisingly enhance the chocolaty notes without making it taste "cheesy"—the kokumi from the cheese just rounds out the flavor. Or a chef might simmer cocoa nibs in a broth with kombu (sea kelp, high in glutamates and kokumi compounds) to create a savory chocolate sauce for a meat dish, harnessing kokumi to meld the flavors together. Some forward-thinking baristas are even adding a drop of shio-koji (a fermented rice marinade rich in kokumi) to mochas and hot chocolates, finding that it magically boosts the creamy mouthfeel and makes the chocolate flavor pop, all without identifiable new flavors.

What kokumi ultimately offers to chocolate is a kind of flavor alchemy: it can make something taste like it's been developed longer, cooked or aged, even when it hasn't. It's a way of layering in time, so to speak. This is why it's often called the "new flavor frontier"—we are just beginning to understand how to use it.

While the average home baker might not be sprinkling pure kokumi powder in their brownie mix anytime soon, they are likely already bene-fiting from kokumi when they use ingredients like browned butter, aged spirits (think rum or bourbon added to chocolate desserts), or even slow-roasted nuts. All those things are rich in kokumi compounds and add to the luxurious taste.

FROM CRAFT TO CHEMISTRY: Decoding Chocolate's Secrets

For most of its history, chocolate was an art and a craft, developed by sensory intuition and tradition rather than scientific analysis. The ancient Mesoamericans who first fermented cacao beans and the European chocolatiers who later refined the process knew that certain steps—fermenting the pulp-covered beans for days, roasting them over heat, grinding and conching the paste—yielded a delicious product. But they could not have told you about pyrazines or esters or Maillard reaction pathways. Flavor chemistry was a black box.

It wasn't until the mid-20th century that technology started to catch up. The invention of gas chromatography (GC) and later mass spectrometry (MS) revolutionized flavor science.

Suddenly, chemists had tools to separate the volatile oils from cocoa, break them into individual components, and identify those components by their molecular fingerprints. In the 1960s and 70s, researchers began publishing the first lists of aroma compounds found in cocoa and choco-late. They found pyrazines, formed during roasting, which had nutty and coffee-like smells. They found esters and aldehydes that offered fruity and floral notes. They confirmed the presence of short-chain acids from fermentation (like acetic and butyric acid) contributing pungency or tang. Each discovery was a small piece of the puzzle.

By the 1990s, the picture had become much fuller. Pioneers like Peter Schieberle and his colleagues applied ever-more sophisticated methods to identify and quantify the volatiles in chocolate. They also introduced approaches like Aroma Extract Dilution Analysis (AEDA), which helps rank which compounds have the strongest influence on aroma by seri-ally diluting an aroma extract and seeing which smells still come through.

This pinpointed the "odor-active" compounds—those likely to matter most to what we smell. It turned out that out of the hundreds of volatiles, perhaps a few dozen were really pulling the weight in creating the recognizable chocolate aroma.

One of the landmark achievements of this era was the creation of the chocolate recombination experiment—mixing the 20-30 key aroma compounds to recreate a convincing chocolate scent. When sensory panelists failed to distinguish the lab-made aroma from real chocolate, it proved scientists had identified the major players. This "flavor blueprint" marked a triumph of analytical food chemistry.

In one fascinating discovery, scientists found that certain cyclic dipeptides (formed during cocoa fermentation and roasting) can create desirable mouthfeels—a kind of subtle savoriness or kokumi effect that makes chocolate taste richer and smoother without adding sweetness.

These were entirely "new" taste molecules in the context of choco-late, unknown in earlier decades. For instance, by tweaking the roasting process (adding a little sugar during the Dutching process, which is an alkali treatment), Schieberle's lab demonstrated the formation of previ-ously unknown taste-active compounds that gave a "velvety mouthfeel" to the chocolate. They essentially discovered new flavor compounds by modifying the process, highlighting how much there is still to learn.

Chefs and Chocolate Makers Push Boundaries

What started as avant-garde experiments in high-end kitchens and indie chocolate shops has now grown into a bona fide trend in the culinary world. Chefs and chocolate makers across the globe are embracing umami and kokumi to craft novel taste experiences. From pâtissiers in Paris to bean-to-bar chocolate artisans in Tokyo, the idea of savory complexity in chocolate is catching on.

In the realm of professional pastry and confections, many chefs view these ingredients as part of an expanded palette of flavors. A pastry chef might reach for a jar of tahini (sesame paste) or peanut butter to add a nutty umami note to a chocolate tart. Another chef might experiment with aged balsamic vinegar or soy reduction in a chocolate sauce to serve with roasted fruit—the acidity and umami combining to brighten and deepen the chocolate simultaneously.

One trend in upscale restaurants is serving savory chocolate courses as either an appetizer or a cheese course: think a disk of barely sweetened dark chocolate ganache topped with olive oil, sea salt, and a few shavings of aged parmesan cheese or truffle (the aromatic fungus, not the chocolate candy). It sounds daring, but diners are loving these unexpected combinations. The umami of the cheese or truffle brings out the fruity, nutty notes in the chocolate. Instead of clashing, the flavors find harmony on the tongue.

Chocolatiers—those who make gourmet chocolates and bars—are also innovating by incorporating umami-laden ingredients into their creations. For example, a bean-to-bar chocolate maker in Japan wanted to meld Japanese culinary tradition with chocolate. He created a dark chocolate bar blended with shiitake mushroom powder, aiming to let customers "enjoy the umami of Japan in a chocolate bar."

The shiitake, rich in natural glutamates, adds a subtle earthy savoriness to the chocolate. Tasters of this unique bar report that it has an extra dimension—the usual plum-like fruitiness and honey notes of the Bolivian cacao are still there, but alongside them is a gentle savory undertone that makes the flavor feel fuller and longer-lasting.

Not to be outdone, Western craft chocolate makers are on the move as well. In the United States, the craft chocolate company Raaka in Brooklyn teamed up with famed chef David Chang's Momofuku brand to create a limited-edition "Miso Potato Chip" chocolate bar. This bar blended unroasted dark chocolate with Momofuku's tangy chickpea miso and bits of crunchy potato chips.

The first test batches, they admitted, were almost too shockingly savory—miso's potency can surprise—but by adding the salty potato chips, they struck the right balance of flavor and fun. The final product delivered the transcendent umami of miso wrapped in smooth chocolate, punctuated by a familiar salty crunch. It sold out quickly, twice over, as curious chocolate lovers snapped it up.

At the same time, mainstream confectionery in some parts of the world has also dabbled in this space. In Japan, which often leads the charge in unusual candy flavors, even mass-market chocolates have tried incorporating umami.

There have been regional Kit Kat bars flavored with soy sauce, which surprisingly taste more like a salted caramel white chocolate than anything overtly soy. The soy sauce provides a toasted, salty-sweet note that resembles brown sugar or butterscotch, showing how an umami element can be translated into a widely appealing candy flavor.

A SYMPHONY OF FLAVOR: Tasting the Future of Chocolate

So, how does chocolate enhanced with umami or kokumi actually taste? It's easy to talk about "depth" and "complexity" in the abstract, but the real test is on the tongue. Imagine for a moment sitting at a dessert tasting where the chef presents two versions of a classic chocolate pudding. The first is a traditional recipe—cocoa, milk, sugar, eggs—straightforward and sweet. The second looks identical, but the chef explains it has a special twist: a touch of soy sauce and a hint of kombu extract were cooked into the mix.

You take a spoonful of the first pudding: it's lovely, chocolaty, familiar. Then you cleanse your palate and try the second. This pudding's texture feels just a bit more indulgent, coating your mouth in a silkier way. The chocolate flavor seems bolder; there's a pronounced cocoa note at the front, but then it blooms into something almost like toasted nuts and caramel as you swallow.

There's a lingering aftertaste that reminds you of the satisfaction after finishing a good latte or a bite of cheesecake—that sort of umami sigh of contentment. It's not that it tastes salty or soy-flavored—it doesn't. It just tastes, well, more. More chocolaty, more rounded, with the sweetness in check and the flavor lasting longer. That is the kokumi and umami effect in action.

Or picture breaking a piece of an artisan dark chocolate bar that has been made with shiitake mushrooms. The chocolate snaps, dark and glossy, and as it melts on your tongue you get the usual rush of bittersweet chocolate.

Then, an unexpected hint of something savory emerges. It's subtle—a whisper of earthiness, like the smell of a forest after rain, or the memory of a well-aged red wine. You might not immediately think "mushroom," but you do notice the bar has a distinctive savory edge that amplifies the fruitiness of the cacao. The next time you have a plain chocolate bar, you find yourself missing that extra layer that the umami provided.

We can also talk about pairings. Chocolate and cheese might sound odd at first, but at a flavor level it makes perfect sense. Aged cheeses like Parmesan or sharp cheddar are umami powerhouses, rich in the same kind of savory compounds found in soy or miso. Dark chocolate, especially around 70% cacao, has a robust flavor that can stand up to those cheeses.

When you taste a sliver of Parmesan together with a piece of dark chocolate, something fascinating happens: the salty crystals in the cheese highlight the chocolate's sweetness, and the chocolate's bitterness tones down the cheese's funk. They meet in the middle with a nutty, fruity harmony that is really delightful. Add a sip of a fortified wine like sherry or port (also full of umami and kokumi from its aging process) and you have a trifecta of complex flavors feeding off each other.

THE UNFINISHED SYMPHONY

After all the studies, charts, and chemical analyses, one could ask: does it matter if we name every last molecule in chocolate? In a practical sense, chocolate will continue to delight regardless of whether we've formally catalogued phantom compounds X, Y, and Z. Yet, for scientists and flavor enthusiasts, these mysteries are irresistible. Each unidentified flavor molecule is a reminder that our sensory world is richer than our scientific lexicon. There's something almost poetic in the idea that in a well-known treat like chocolate—a product humans have been making for centuries—there are still secrets to be uncovered.

Kokumi, or "rich taste," is achieved by adding savory ferments like miso or soy sauce to chocolate, deepening the flavor profile without adding sugar.

THE SEARCH for chocolate's phantom flavors is more than an academic exercise. It speaks to a broader human quest: to understand the things that give us pleasure on a molecular level. Already, this journey has taught us incredible things. We've learned that flavor is an emergent property, born from the marriage of chemistry and biology—the compounds in the food and the receptors in our nose and mouth. We've discovered that what we experience as one flavor (like "chocolate") is really a symphony of many notes, and that our brain is the composer weaving them together.

Practically, unlocking every flavor component could help make chocolate even better. It could lead to new ways to process cocoa to accentuate those elusive notes or to preserve flavors that are currently lost in standard production. It could aid in breeding new cacao varieties that naturally produce higher levels of desirable aromatics.

And it could allow the creation of even more authentic chocolate flavors for use in foods where using real cocoa isn't feasible. Imagine being able to recreate the aroma of a rare, exquisite chocolate in a pastry without actually using that chocolate, by blending all its known aromatic molecules—that's the kind of possibility complete knowledge offers.

Importantly, umami and kokumi also align with efforts to make healthier yet still delicious chocolate products. Since these taste enhancers can boost perception of sweetness and richness, a chocolate bar with a bit of kokumi might need less sugar to satisfy our cravings, or a reduced-fat chocolate milk could still taste whole.

Food scientists are already researching how a pinch of MSG (a pure umami compound) or kokumi-rich extracts in a low-sugar chocolate pudding might trick our taste buds into thinking it's just as indulgent as the original recipe. Early results are promising: test consumers often report such products as tasting even better than the full-sugar versions, because the flavor is more rounded and satisfying, not just sweet. In a world increasingly concerned with sugar intake and processed ingredients, the idea that "more flavor" can equal "less sugar" is a compelling one.

For home cooks and chocolate enthusiasts, the adventure is just beginning as well. The barrier to entry to play with these flavors is actually quite low—you probably have some umami-rich ingredients in your kitchen already. Next time you bake brownies or a chocolate cake, you could try the trick of adding a teaspoon of soy sauce or a tablespoon of miso to the batter and see how it transforms the outcome.

Or sprinkle a tiny bit of instant espresso powder and a dash of cinnamon (both of which surprisingly enhance savory notes) to deepen a chocolate frosting. Even something as simple as finishing homemade chocolate fudge with a few grains of coarse sea salt and a drizzle of olive oil can mimic that kokumi effect and leave your friends wondering what gourmet chocolatier you visited.

Ultimately, the journey into umami, kokumi, and chocolate's phantom flavors is expanding our appreciation of chocolate as a full-spectrum food. Chocolate isn't just a vehicle for sugar or a one-note treat; it's a complex product of nature and craft that can engage all of our taste receptors.

By exploring the fifth taste of umami in chocolate, pushing into kokumi's new flavor frontier, and hunting for those elusive phantom molecules, we are finding that chocolate can be as dynamic and multidimensional as a fine wine or a gourmet cheese. Each bite can carry multiple layers of taste: sweet, yes, but also bitter, acidic, savory, and enriched with that ineffable "oomph" that kokumi provides.

===

THE SECRET INGREDIENT: UMAMI RATIOS

Want your homemade brownies to taste expensive? Add "the funk."

- **The Miso Trick (For Cookies)**
  - The Ratio: Swap 1 tablespoon of butter for 1 tablespoon of White Miso paste.
  - The Result: A salty-sweet depth that mimics caramel.
- **The Soy Sauce Hack (For Brownies)**
  - The Ratio: Add 1 teaspoon of Soy Sauce to your batter.
  - The Result: It acts like salt, but richer. It amplifies the "fudgy" flavor without tasting like Asian food.
- **The Balsamic Splash (For Strawberry-Choc)**
  - The Ratio: Macerate berries in 1 tablespoon of Balsamic Vinegar before dipping in chocolate.
  - The Result: The acid cuts the fat; the sweetness bridges the gap.

===

The storytelling of flavor is richer now: we can talk about a single chocolate bonbon the way one might describe a dish—"It starts with a hit of brightness (a touch of passion fruit maybe), then the cocoa notes come through, and there's a gentle savory roundness in the finish that just lasts and lasts." That kind of poetic tasting note was not associated with chocolate in the past, but it's becoming possible and common as we play with these new ingredients and deepen our scientific understanding.

From ancient bitter brews to modern umami truffles, chocolate's flavor journey continues to evolve. The fifth taste, umami, has taught us that a hint of savoriness can make sweet chocolate sing, and kokumi promises a future where even a tiny square of chocolate can deliver a symphony of taste that lingers long after it melts away.

Meanwhile, phantom flavors remind us that in a food as beloved and studied as chocolate, undiscovered molecules are still lurking—perhaps new keys to unlocking flavors we haven't even experienced in isolation. Chefs and chocolate makers are embracing these tools to surprise and delight us, crafting confections that break the rules in the most delicious ways.

So the next time you let a piece of fine chocolate melt slowly on your tongue, consider the layers of discovery and mystery it contains. From the rainforest-grown cacao bean, through fermenters and roasters, into the chemist's lab and onto your palate, chocolate's flavor has been shaped by countless hands and minds.

We've identified nearly all of the ingredients of its essence, natural and even synthetic, but a few phantoms still dance in the background. And perhaps that's fitting. Chocolate has always had an aura of the enchanting and addictive. Knowing that there are flavor molecules in it that we can detect but not fully identify adds to its enchantment—a reminder that even in our highly analyzed world, some secrets are deliciously slow to give themselves up.

In the end, chocolate's hidden dimensions—its phantom flavors, its umami depth, its kokumi richness—invite us to enjoy the mystery. Science will continue to chase those ghosts, and one day we'll likely name them and know them. Until then, they remain a subtle whisper in the aroma, an extra magic in every bite—part of the soul of chocolate that keeps us coming back for more. So go ahead, taste the fifth (and maybe sixth) taste in your chocolate. You just might discover a whole new reason to love this ancient, beloved food all over again.

SONIC SEASONING: HOW SOUND SHAPES THE TASTE OF CHOCOLATE

I n a dimly lit concert hall, an audience sits in perfect silence as a conductor lifts his baton. At that precise moment, each guest places a piece of chocolate on their tongue. The first notes—a bright shimmer of violins—float into the room, and the chocolate seems to grow sweeter, almost blooming with the music. Minutes later, the orchestra descends into a darker, brooding passage, and the next bite of chocolate tastes unmistakably more bitter. The room doesn't react with surprise; they react with recognition. Everyone can feel that the flavor has changed, even though the chocolate hasn't. This is not illusion or theatrics, but a carefully crafted experiment in how sound reshapes taste—an emerging collaboration between chocolatiers, neuroscientists, and musicians exploring the hidden harmonies between ear and palate.

WHAT FEELS LIKE MAGIC IS, in fact, a frontier of sensory science. Researchers around the world are uncovering the ways sound frequencies, rhythms, and textures can shift our perception of sweetness, bitterness, and richness. Chocolate—complex, emotionally charged, and deeply tied to memory—has become an ideal test case. From concert halls to sensory labs, the pursuit is the same: to understand how sound infiltrates taste, and how our brains blend these senses into a single, seamless experience.

The Science of Sonic Seasoning

To understand how this works, scientists point to an emerging field known as crossmodal perception—the study of how our senses collaborate rather than operate alone. The brain does not treat taste, sound, smell, or sight as separate channels; instead, it blends them into a unified experience, allowing one sense to subtly steer another. This is why the crunch of chocolate coating can make freshness feel more vivid, why a mellow soundtrack can smooth the edges of bitterness, and why certain melodies seem to brighten the perceived sweetness of cacao. Flavor, in other words, is not just tasted—it is orchestrated.

One of the earliest and most elegant demonstrations came from a laboratory experiment involving a single piece of dark chocolate. Volunteers tasted identical samples while wearing headphones that played shifting soundscapes. High, delicate chimes made the chocolate seem fruitier and brighter; low, rumbling tones drew out its bitterness and depth. Nothing in the chocolate had changed—only the music. Yet the brain recalibrated the entire experience, proof that flavor perception can be guided as surely as lighting can guide the mood of a room. Something about those sonic qualities primed the tasters' brains to focus on certain flavor notes in the chocolate.

Part of the effect comes from the way our brains naturally link sensory qualities. We describe tastes with musical metaphors—sharp, flat, smooth, bright—because these sensations genuinely overlap in our perception. Experiments show that people consistently match certain sounds with certain flavors, even without training.

These shared mappings form an unconscious sensory language that sonic seasoning taps into. Scientific experiments confirm that many people share similar cross-sensory mappings. In fact, you don't need to have the rare condition of synesthesia to sense that, say, a brassy trombone note feels "bitter" or a delicate flute melody seems "sweet."

Sonic Seasoning: Research shows that high-pitched sounds can
make chocolate taste sweeter, while low-frequency bass tones
accentuate bitterness.

OUR AUDITORY SYSTEM and taste system might seem like apples and
oranges, but in the brain they collaborate more than we realize. High-
frequency sounds (think of the bright trill of a piccolo or the chiming of
a high piano key) tend to be mentally linked with sweetness and light,
delicate flavors.

Low-frequency sounds (like the rumble of a bass or the drone of a
cello's lowest string) are linked with heavier, bitter, or umami flavors.
These associations may stem from real patterns in nature – for instance,
many sweet foods (like ripe fruits) might evoke higher-pitched sounds in
our environment (birds chirping in fruit trees?), while bitter, earthy foods
could be subconsciously tied to deeper, earthier sounds.

Or it might simply be the way our language and culture have evolved
to pair concepts (we talk about "high notes" in flavor or "bass notes" in a
sauce). Whatever the origin, the effect is measurable: change the soundtrack, and you can change the taste.

SWEET NOTES VS. Bitter Tones

To understand how specific sound qualities tweak our taste buds,
let's break down what scientists have found. Here are some sonic ingredients and the flavor notes they tend to enhance:

- High-Pitched Tones (Treble) – Enhances sweetness and bright flavors. For example, tinkling bells, violins playing in a high register, or a melody on a flute can make a piece of dark chocolate seem milder and sweeter. In studies, participants consistently rated chocolates as sweeter when listening to music dominated by high-frequency sounds. It's as if those sugary high notes trick the brain into finding more sugar in the food.
- Low-Pitched Tones (Bass) – Emphasizes bitterness and depth. Deep bass notes, like those from a bass guitar, cello, or brass instruments (tubas, trombones), tend to draw out the bitterness or robust savory aspects. A chocolate's darker, earthy cacao flavors can feel amplified under a rumbling soundtrack. Some experiments even found that people perceived more bitterness in coffee or chocolate when low drone-like notes played in the background.
- Smooth, Continuous Sounds (Legato) – Enhances creaminess and roundness. When music is flowing and legato (notes connected smoothly), with gentle consonant harmonies, foods like milk chocolate or creamy desserts are often rated creamier and more pleasurable. One study used a "creamy" music track featuring sustained, consonant chords and found that listeners felt a chocolate truffle had a silkier texture and sweeter taste compared to eating it in silence or with harsher sounds.
- Abrupt, Staccato Sounds – Accentuates crispness or crunch and can increase perception of bitterness or sharpness. Music that is percussive, jagged, or dissonant can make textures seem harder or flavors more intense. For instance, a chaotic, staccato piece might make a brittle toffee feel extra crunchy or a bitter taste feel even more bitter. Researchers have used "rough" soundtracks with stuttering, disjointed noise and found chocolates tasted more bitter and less creamy.
- Consonant vs. Dissonant Music – Influences pleasantness. Consonant music (notes that harmonize nicely) generally enhances enjoyment and can make flavors seem more

palatable, whereas deliberately dissonant music might make even a sweet treat feel slightly less pleasant. In one quirky experiment, people enjoyed a bite of milk chocolate more when it was accompanied by mellow jazz than when abrasive hip-hop was playing, suggesting the genre or harmony of music influences the overall pleasure of tasting.

Interestingly, these effects can occur even though the food itself doesn't change at all – only your brain's perception of it does. When you hear a high tinkling piano, your brain might "hear" sweetness and actually adjust how it processes the signals coming from your tongue, dialing up the sweet receptors. When a low bass vibrates around you, perhaps your brain pays more attention to bitter flavor components. It's almost like an auditory illusion that works on your taste buds. And the differences aren't just in your head; in blind taste-tests, significant numbers of people report these shifts in flavor intensity, proving this is a reproducible phenomenon.

Scientists in Europe have been at the forefront of this research. In Belgium, one chocolatier even collaborated with a team of academics to create specific music for his chocolates. In their trials, a piece of dark, 70% cacao chocolate was perceived as noticeably sweeter when participants listened to a specially composed "sweet soundtrack" full of high-pitched, resonant notes. That same chocolate tasted a lot more bitter when the subjects listened to a "bitter soundtrack" dominated by low, resonant tones.

The music effectively acted like a seasoning – sprinkle on some treble, and voila, the bitterness is tamed by perceived sweetness. In another experiment, people ate identical pieces of chocolate while listening to two tunes: one was a "creamy" melody (soft and flowing), the other a "rough" composition (sharp and percussive). The tasters overwhelmingly said the chocolate felt creamier and sweeter with the creamy music, and more bitter with the rough music, regardless of the actual chocolate's cacao content. What's more, these effects held true across various types of chocolate – whether it was a crunchy 80% dark or a smooth 70% ganache, the music's character shifted how it was experienced.

~

ORCHESTRATING FLAVOR: When Chefs and Composers Collide

The science is intriguing, but how do we apply it in real life? Enter the world of flavor composers and adventurous chefs who are turning research findings into sensory feasts. The concert scene described earlier actually comes from a composition called "Symphonic Chocolates." Written by the Canadian composer Maxime Goulet, *Symphonic Chocolates* is an orchestral suite explicitly designed to be paired with chocolate tasting. Goulet crafted four short musical movements, each inspired by a different chocolate flavor, and audiences are given chocolates to eat in sync with each movement.

Imagine attending such a concert: for the Caramel Chocolate movement, the orchestra plays a gentle, enveloping theme – long, silky strings and mellow tones that mirror caramel's buttery sweetness. Next comes Dark Chocolate, set to an intense tango-like habanera. The music is passionate and slightly edgy, with a few dissonant chords adding a "spiced bitterness," just like a high-cacao chocolate that's seductive yet a touch bitter. The third piece, Mint Chocolate, might surprise you with its delicate, frosty notes – perhaps flutes or chimes creating a sense of coolness, as if the sound itself carried a whiff of mint's freshness.

Finally, the Coffee-Infused Chocolate movement concludes the suite with an energetic burst – an espresso tempo with a Brazilian flair, say a samba or bossa nova rhythm played by rhythmic strings and percussion, capturing the invigorating jolt of coffee and the rich roast of cacao. During each movement, you savor the corresponding chocolate, letting the live music wash over you. By the end, you've experienced chocolate in a way you never did before – *tasting* the music and *hearing* the flavors in a harmonious blend.

This innovative concert has been performed with live orchestras, and also packaged as a special box set (complete with chocolates and a recording of the music) so people can try it at home. It's a brilliant example of how knowing the sonic-taste connection allows artists to compose flavor experiences, almost like a sommelier pairing wine with food, but here the composer pairs melodies with cocoa.

Chocolatiers themselves are getting musical as well. In the UK, a major chocolate brand recently enlisted a University of Bristol researcher and composer, Dr. Natalie Hyacinth, to create what they called the "sweetest song in the world." Hyacinth dove into decades of sensory science studies and then wrote a 90-second musical piece designed specifically to be heard while eating the company's milk chocolate. Her composition featured lilting piano notes to enhance perceived sweetness, layered with soft harp chords to impart a creamy, smooth mouthfeel.

Even the tempo was chosen thoughtfully: she set the rhythm to about 78 beats per minute, roughly the same pace at which a bite of chocolate melts in your mouth. The idea was to synchronize the music's progression with the chocolate's texture journey, from solid to silky liquid. In trials, tasters reported the chocolate did indeed seem sweeter and more enjoyable when savored with the song versus in silence. Hyacinth noted that this kind of multi-sensory approach "engages all the senses" and can make a simple chocolate break feel more immersive and relaxing – essentially turning a casual snack into a mini symphony of flavor and sound.

Smaller artisan chocolatiers are also experimenting with these ideas. One high-end chocolate shop in Belgium known for daring flavors offered customers a chance to taste their pralines while listening to curated soundtracks over headphones in-store. Customers might try a raspberry ganache while a bright, tinkling piano tune plays, then sample a single-origin dark chocolate from Madagascar while a piece of music with deep drums or chanting sets a more primal tone. The feedback has been enthusiastic: people often describe the chocolates "coming alive" in new ways when paired with the right music. It's as if the confectioners are composing a soundtrack for your taste buds – and in a sense, they are. We've long known chocolatiers as artists of flavor and texture; now they are becoming DJs and composers, engineering the audio environment in which their creations sing.

Even outside of formal experiments, many of us have experienced the difference that ambiance can make. Consider a romantic restaurant playing soft jazz – the dessert might just feel a tad more luscious. Or think about how a fun pop song at a party can make even ordinary snacks taste a bit better, simply because you're in a happier mood. Some chocolate makers have begun recommending playlist pairings for their bars, much like a wine might come with a suggestion for a cheese pairing. The idea is catching on that choosing the right music is part of the tasting ritual.

WHEN SOUND BECOMES TASTE: **Insights from Synesthesia**

For most of us, pairing music with flavor is a novel thrill – our senses cooperating in new ways. For a rare few, the link between sound and taste is not subtle at all—it is constant. These individuals experience synesthesia, a neurological condition in which a sound can trigger a flavor as vividly as if they had tasted it. A cello's low C might bring the unmistakable rush of dark chocolate; a bright piano chord might spark a flash of citrus. This is not metaphor but perception, and it offers a window into how deeply intertwined our senses truly are.

===

SENSORY TRIVIA: THE CRUNCH TEST

Sound affects texture. Your brain "hears" freshness.

- **The Science:** Experiments have shown that when a consumer bites a potato chip or a chocolate-covered pretzel, the loudness and pitch of the crunch directly correlates to the perceived freshness.
- **The Trick:** If you play a recording of a louder, higher-pitched crunch sound while someone eats a stale chip, they will rate the chip as significantly fresher than it is.

Your brain trusts your ears over your tongue.

===

One synesthetic musician described how the sound of certain chords would evoke flavors of different candies for her, making composing music a strangely culinary experience. Another synesthete, the president of a synesthesia association, has said that hearing everyday sounds (like a car horn or a piece of music) can spontaneously trigger tastes like toast or coffee in his mouth. This rare blending of senses might give us a clue to why even non-synesthetes respond to sonic seasoning. In the synesthetic brain, there are literal cross-talks between sensory regions – taste, sound, color, etc., are more intertwined. In the rest of us, the connections aren't as direct, but we still have subconscious links – perhaps remnants of the same pathways.

Even if you don't physically taste chocolate when you hear a trombone, you might metaphorically *agree* that a trombone sounds "bitter" or a piccolo sounds "sweet." In fact, experiments have shown that non-synesthetic people consistently pair certain musical tones with taste descriptors in a synesthesia-like way. For example, when asked to match basic tastes with musical instruments, a majority might match sourness with a dissonant violin screech, sweetness with a gentle piano or bells, bitterness with a low brass note.

These findings suggest that on some level, our brains naturally align flavor and sound qualities, almost as if we each have a bit of synesthetic wiring within us. It's this natural overlap that sonic seasoning exploits. In essence, the new research and gastronomic tricks are giving ordinary people a taste of synesthesia. You can momentarily experience what it's like when sound and taste merge, by simply putting on a thoughtfully chosen piece of music while you eat.

Understanding synesthesia also underscores how subjective flavor can be. Taste isn't just a chemical sense happening on your tongue; it's a construction in the brain, influenced by expectations, memories, visuals, aromas, and now we know, soundscapes too. As one famous chef, Heston Blumenthal, has put it, "sound is the forgotten flavor sense."

Blumenthal, known for his experimental approach to dining, famously created a seafood dish called "Sound of the Sea" which is served with an iPod playing actual ocean sounds. Diners reported that the fresh oysters and seaweed in the dish tasted notably "brinier" and more oceanic when accompanied by the crashing of waves and distant calls of seagulls. The sound triggered memories and feelings that enhanced the saltiness and overall marine flavor of the food. In a way, that's synesthesia-by-design: using sound to evoke the full context of a flavor in the mind.

~

Sound Engineering for Your Palate

Beyond composed music, consider the everyday sound engineering that goes into our food experiences. Restaurants, food companies, and even airlines are paying attention to how background noise and specifically engineered sounds impact taste.

Take the example of airplane food: Ever wonder why tomato juice or a Bloody Mary cocktail is so popular at 30,000 feet? It turns out the constant loud background noise of an airplane cabin (around 80-85 decibels of engine roar) actually dulls certain taste receptors – notably, it reduces our sensitivity to sweetness and salt. That's why airline food is often criticized as bland unless it's over-salted or over-sweetened on purpose.

Meanwhile, that same noise seems to enhance umami flavors, making a savory, spiced tomato juice particularly satisfying in the air when it might not be on the ground. One Oxford University researcher, Professor Charles Spence, has advised that if you want your airline meal to taste better, put on noise-cancelling headphones and listen to music you love.

By cutting out the harsh noise and adding pleasant sounds, you can recover some of your taste perception and enjoyment. In fact, he notes that simply liking the music you hear can boost how much you like the food you're eating – our emotions and senses are tightly linked.

Spence's lab has demonstrated that unpleasant noise can ruin a meal even if the food is great, whereas a pleasing sound environment boosts our enjoyment. This is leading to a new appreciation among restaurateurs and food producers for the *soundscape* of eating. High-end restaurants might curate their playlists or the acoustics of the dining room as carefully as they do the wine list.

Have you noticed how many coffee shops choose mellow, soft music in the morning? It's not just to create a mood; they likely know that gentle background music can make that latte and croissant feel extra soothing (and perhaps encourage you to linger and spend more). Conversely, fast-food outlets often play upbeat, loud music during rush hour – it might not enhance taste per se, but it speeds up eating and turnover, showing that sound can influence behavior around food as well.

Food companies also engineer sound into the product itself. Think about the crispy crunch of a potato chip – that's a sound we associate with freshness. Experiments have shown that if you alter the sound of a chip's crunch (for example, by playing a recording of a crunch at a higher or lower pitch), you can make people perceive a stale chip as fresher or a fresh chip as staler than it really is.

Snack companies strive to create the perfect crunch sound in their chips and crackers because the moment you bite in, that sound is part of the flavor impression. Chocolate, being generally a quiet food, doesn't have an inherent sound when you eat it (aside from a soft snap when you break it). But some chocolatiers have started to think about the wrappers and boxes: the rustle of the foil, the gentle snap of a chocolate bar segment breaking, these are subtle auditory cues that can influence perceived quality. A crisp, clean snap sound implies a well-tempered, high-quality chocolate. A crinkly luxurious wrapper might subconsciously prime you for a richer taste.

Advertising and branding have also jumped on the sonic bandwagon. There are now ice cream commercials that eschew jingly music and instead amplify the *sound* of a spoon scraping through creamy ice cream or the crunch of the chocolate shell on a bar – because hearing those sounds makes viewers almost *feel* the taste and texture, making the product more tempting. Some whiskey distilleries have created tasting experiences where you sip a whiskey while listening to audio of a crackling fire and low throbbing tones to bring out the smoky, peaty flavors. It's all about matching the sensory inputs to create a more convincing overall impression.

In many ways, sound engineering for taste is about setting the stage for flavor. Just as lighting can make a dish look more appetizing and plating design can guide your eyes, sound provides context and suggests what you should notice. A chaotic, noisy environment tells your brain "don't focus on subtlety," so you may miss the delicate notes of a fine chocolate. A complementary soundtrack, however, whispers to your brain "pay attention, this is sweet and delightful," and your taste perception follows that lead.

. . .

The Art and Science of Musical Pairing

What started as a curious niche of food science – playing with sound and taste – has grown into a broader art of musical pairing. Think of it as similar to pairing wine with food, except here the "wine" is a song or a symphony that complements the flavor profile of the dish. Pioneers in this space, like Professor Spence and others, have collaborated with chefs, bartenders, and even winemakers to explore ideal pairings.

For instance, certain wines seem to truly shine with specific musical backdrops: a velvety Merlot might reveal richer berry notes when enjoyed with a smooth, romantic jazz ballad; a crisp Sauvignon Blanc might taste even crisper and more refreshing when paired with a bright, uptempo classical piece, say Vivaldi's Spring. In one study, people described a Cabernet Sauvignon as more "powerful and heavy" when drinking it to the bombastic strains of Carl Orff's Carmina Burana, whereas the same wine felt more "subtle and refined" when sipped to a gentle waltz by Tchaikovsky. The wine hadn't changed – the music simply framed its attributes in a different light, much like how a gold frame can bring out different hues in a painting.

Closer to the world of chocolate, craft beer brewers have experimented with musical pairings as well. Stouts and porters, with their coffee and chocolate notes, often pair wonderfully with deep, bass-heavy music or something with a slow, steady beat that matches the sip's lingering finish. Meanwhile, a fruity chocolate-infused ale might go well with something fun and poppy to highlight the sweet highlights. It's all very experimental, but that's the fun of it – flavor pairing with music is as much art as science. There isn't a strict right or wrong; it's about the experience you want to create.

What makes musical pairing particularly special is the personal dimension. Everyone's taste in music differs, just as their taste in food does. So part of the equation is finding a combination that resonates with the individual. Researchers have noted that if you love a song, that positive emotion can spill over and make whatever you're eating more enjoyable. So while there are general trends (high notes sweet, low notes bitter), the *best* pairing might also depend on your personal music preferences. A die-hard heavy metal fan might actually relish their dessert more with shredding guitars in the background, even if traditionally one might recommend a mellow tune for sweetness. The science provides the broad brushstrokes, but personal experimentation fills in the details.

And indeed, we are all invited to be experimenters in this field. It doesn't take a lab or an orchestra to try it out – you can become a flavor DJ in your own kitchen. The next time you have a rich dark chocolate at home, try creating your own "flavor soundtrack": put on a playlist that starts with some deep, bass-heavy music and then shifts to something light and whimsical.

Taste the chocolate through the transition. Does it seem to evolve in tandem with the music? Or pour two small cups of hot chocolate; enjoy one with quiet classical music and the other with the noise of your TV in the background, and see which one feels more flavorful. You might be surprised at how much the soundscape shapes your perception of even familiar foods.

Savoring a Multi-sensory Future

As chefs, chocolatiers, and musicians experiment, a new kind of culinary artistry is taking shape—one in which flavor is composed, not just crafted. These collaborations blend emotion with science, turning each bite of chocolate into an experience guided not only by ingredients, but by atmosphere, memory, and sound.

The exploration of sound and taste is still relatively new, and it's exciting to imagine where it might lead. High-end restaurants could soon employ sound sommeliers – experts who craft playlists to pair with each course of a tasting menu. Your dessert might arrive with a pair of headphones delivering a bespoke melody timed to the dessert's melting pattern (as Galaxy's research hinted). Specialty food producers might include QR codes on packaging that link to "flavor playlists" for you to play as you enjoy the product. Perhaps one day, grocery stores will subtly play certain background notes in the chocolate aisle to subliminally influence which bar you perceive as most delicious!

Composers and chocolatiers are now collaborating to create "edible
concerts," where the music is timed to change the perception of the
chocolate melting in the listener's mouth.

ON A MORE PROFOUND LEVEL, this convergence of senses prompts us to
appreciate the complexity of our perception. Taste is not an isolated
sense; it's deeply integrated with our other ways of experiencing the
world. This is why the realm of sensory culture – from synesthetic art
installations to scientific food labs – feels so rich with possibility. Musicians might start thinking like flavorists, and chefs might compose meals
as if they were symphonies. We might discover new combinations that
elevate simple foods into unforgettable experiences, just by adding the
right auditory ingredient.

In the meantime, the next time you treat yourself to a piece of chocolate, give a little thought to the sounds around you. Try nibbling it in
silence, and then with your favorite song playing. Try a bite with a classical piano piece, then another bite with a bass-heavy electronic track.
You'll be conducting your own little experiment in sonic seasoning. You
may find that the chocolate tastes subtly different each time – perhaps a
bit sweeter with the music on, or more bitter with that rumbling bass. At
the very least, you'll have turned a simple snack into an immersive experience. After all, when it comes to savoring life's pleasures, why not
engage all our senses? As the worlds of music and gastronomy continue
to intertwine, our future might be filled with flavor symphonies and

edible melodies – truly a sweet sound to look forward to. Enjoy the show, and bon appétit!

==

DIY SENSORY EXPERIMENT: THE SOUNDTRACK OF FLAVOR

Don't just take our word for it. Grab a piece of dark chocolate, open your music app, and try this experiment.

- **Step 1:** The Sweetness Test Put a piece of chocolate on your tongue. Search for and play a song featuring high-pitched piano or wind chimes (e.g., "Clair de Lune" by Debussy). Observe: Does the bitterness fade? Does the chocolate suddenly taste sweeter?
- **Step 2:** The Bitterness Test Take a sip of water. Put a second piece of chocolate on your tongue. Switch to a track with deep bass or heavy brass (e.g., a cello solo or low-frequency electronic drone). Observe: Does the cocoa roast suddenly feel heavier and more bitter?

==

21

THE CHEMISTRY OF PAIRING: WHY BACON AND CHOCOLATE JUST WORK

The kitchen of *The Fat Duck* in Bray, England, is less a restaurant galley and more a high-stakes laboratory. It is 1999, and Heston Blumenthal—the bespectacled alchemist of modern cuisine—is wrestling with a flavor paradox. He is trying to understand the nature of salt.

Blumenthal knows that salt is a flavor magnifier. He knows it suppresses bitterness and elevates sweetness. But he is hunting for something more specific: a partner for caviar. He tastes the briny, metallic pop of the sturgeon roe. He pairs it with melon. It works, but it is expected. He pairs it with cucumber. Boring. Then, acting on a whim driven by the molecular structure of the ingredients, he reaches for a disc of high-quality white chocolate.

It is a combination that should be repulsive. White chocolate is fatty, vanilla-laden, and cloying. Caviar is fishy, sharp, and oceanic. The culinary dogma of the 20th century dictates that these two ingredients occupy opposite ends of the gastronomic universe.

Blumenthal places the roe on the chocolate and tastes.

The reaction is immediate and confusing. It is not disgusting. It is... electric. The rich, coating fat of the cocoa butter melts, carrying the vanilla notes across the tongue. As the caviar pearls burst, their salinity cuts through the fat like a laser. But there is something else—a third flavor, a ghostly harmony that rises where the two ingredients meet. It tastes seamlessly correct, as if they were harvested from the same strange tree.

A bold pairing of caviar atop white chocolate captures the moment chefs first trusted chemistry over intuition. Shared aroma molecules reveal why flavors that seem incompatible can harmonize.

Baffled, Blumenthal calls François Benzi, a flavor chemist at the Swiss perfume and flavor house Firmenich. He describes the sensation. Benzi, a man of science, does not talk about "mouthfeel" or "culinary tradition." He turns to the gas chromatograph—a machine that vaporizes food to analyze its volatile molecular fingerprint.

Benzi runs the samples. The machine spits out the data, revealing the invisible architecture of the ingredients. And there it is, buried in the spectral lines: *trimethylamine*. It turns out that caviar and white chocolate both contain high levels of trimethylamines, a class of organic compounds associated with savory, fishy, and nutty aromas. To the tongue, they are opposites. To the nose—and the brain—they are siblings.

This moment popularized the "Food Pairing Hypothesis," bringing a scientific framework previously restricted to flavor labs into the culinary mainstream. It moved cooking from the realm of intuition to the realm of molecular engineering. It posed a radical question: What if our favorite combinations—strawberries and cream, bacon and eggs—aren't just cultural habits, but chemical equations waiting to be solved? And if we solve them, what other monstrous, beautiful pairings are hiding in the data?

· · ·

THE ARCHITECTURE of Affinity

To understand why bacon and chocolate—or white chocolate and caviar—work, we must first abandon the idea that we taste with our tongues. As explored in the sensory science chapters, the tongue is a crude instrument, capable only of detecting the "Big Five" (sweet, sour, salty, bitter, umami). The true heavy lifting is done by the olfactory bulb.

A flavor chemist identifies a shared aroma compound linking caviar and white chocolate. This molecular overlap explains why their unlikely harmony works on the palate.

Flavor is, chemically speaking, a collection of volatile organic compounds (VOCs). These are light, flighty molecules that evaporate from food, travel through the retro-nasal passage at the back of the throat, and hit the smell receptors. A single strawberry contains over 350 of these volatile compounds. A roasted cocoa bean contains over 600.

For centuries, chefs paired food based on intuition and geography. Tomatoes go with basil because they grow in the same Italian soil. Lamb goes with rosemary because the sheep graze near the bushes. This is the "what grows together, goes together" philosophy.

But the Food Pairing Hypothesis, formalized by researchers like Benzi and later network scientists like Albert-László Barabási, proposes a different law: Ingredients taste good together when they share key flavor compounds.

It is a game of molecular matching. If Ingredient A contains a high concentration of *Compound X*, and Ingredient B also contains *Compound X*, the brain perceives a bridge between them. The shock of the new ingredient is mitigated by the familiarity of the shared molecule. In the case of Heston's epiphany, the bridge was trimethylamine. But in the world of dark chocolate, the bridges are far more complex, linking the cocoa bean to ingredients that seem to have no business in a dessert shop.

THE MAILLARD TWINS: Chocolate and Coffee

Let us begin with the most famous power couple in culinary history: Mocha. The combination of chocolate and coffee is so ubiquitous that we rarely stop to ask *why* it works. They are both bitter. They are both roasted. Logically, they should compete, creating an acrid, overwhelming bitterness. Yet, they harmonize.

The secret lies in the violence of heat.

Both the cacao bean and the coffee bean undergo the Maillard reaction. As detailed in Chapter 16, this chemical browning process generates the specific family of molecules responsible for savory depth: pyrazines.

Pyrazines are the scent of "brown." They are responsible for the aromas of toasted bread, roasted nuts, seared steak, and popcorn.

- Roasted Coffee is dominated by 2-*furfurylthiol* (roast/smoke) and various methylpyrazines.
- Roasted Cocoa is dominated by *tetramethylpyrazine* and *trimethylpyrazine* (nutty/cocoa/earthy).

When you sip a mocha, your brain is not processing two distinct flavors. It is processing a massive overdose of pyrazines. Because the molecular structures are so similar, the brain stacks them. The nutty, earthy notes of the chocolate reinforce the roasted, toasted notes of the coffee.

FURTHERMORE, they engage in a relationship known as flavor modulation. Coffee contains chlorogenic acid, which is intensely bitter. Chocolate contains fat (cocoa butter) and sugar. When combined, the fat coats the tongue, physically blocking some of the bitter receptors, while the sugar distracts the brain. The result is that the chocolate makes the coffee taste smoother, while the coffee makes the chocolate taste deeper. They are chemically codependent.

THE BLUE CHEESE Anomaly

If coffee is the safe bet, Blue Cheese is the high-stakes gamble.

In 2004, the food pairing website (founded by bio-engineer Bernard Lahousse) published a graph that scandalized the pastry world. It showed a thick, undeniable line connecting Dark Chocolate and Roquefort cheese.

Chefs were skeptical. Blue cheese is pungent, salty, and funky—the antithesis of dessert. But those who tried it—melting a square of 70% dark chocolate on a tongue coated with Stilton—were stunned. The pairing was not just edible; it was profound.

The chemical bridge here is a group of molecules called methyl ketones.

- In Blue Cheese: The mold *Penicillium roqueforti* breaks down fatty acids into methyl ketones (specifically 2-heptanone and 2-nonanone), which give the cheese its spicy, metallic, fruity funk.
- In Dark Chocolate: The fermentation of cocoa beans (specifically the aerobic phase) and the subsequent roasting process produce... the exact same methyl ketones.

When you eat them together, the brain recognizes the ketones in the cheese and the ketones in the chocolate as the same signal. The "funk" of the cheese merges with the "fruity/fermented" notes of the cacao.

Simultaneously, the creaminess of the cheese mirrors the melt of the cocoa butter. The salt in the cheese acts as a signal amplifier (a phenomenon we will explore in Part II), suppressing the bitterness of the cacao and allowing its natural fruitiness to explode. It is a pairing that works because, chemically, blue cheese is just "savory chocolate," and dark chocolate is just "sweet cheese."

THE SALT BRIDGE and the Bacon Convergence

If the "Shared Compound" theory explains why ingredients that smell alike taste good together, it fails to explain the most addictive pairing in the modern pantry: Salt and Chocolate.

Salt has no aroma. It has no volatile organic compounds to share with cocoa. By the logic of the gas chromatograph, salt and chocolate should be strangers. Yet, when a flake of Maldon sea salt lands on a dark chocolate truffle, the flavor does not just change; it expands. The chocolate tastes more like chocolate.

The secret here lies not in the nose, but in the biology of the tongue. It is a phenomenon known as Signal Amplification.

For decades, scientists believed that sugar receptors and salt receptors operated independently. But recent research into the SGLT1 (Sodium-Glucose Linked Transporter 1) receptor has revealed a biological synergy. This receptor, found in the sweet-tasting cells of the tongue, effectively uses sodium as a "battery" to transport glucose into the cell.

When you eat sweet chocolate in the absence of salt, your sugar receptors fire at a standard rate. When you introduce salt, the SGLT1 receptors activate, supercharging the cell's ability to register sweetness. The salt acts as a volume knob, turning the sweetness up without adding more sugar.

But salt performs a second, equally vital function in chocolate pairing: Suppression.

At low concentrations, sodium ions suppress the transduction of bitter compounds. Dark chocolate is naturally bitter due to the presence of theobromine and polyphenols. By sprinkling salt on a 70% bar, you are chemically muting the bitterness, which allows the brain to perceive the subtle fruit and floral notes that were previously drowned out by the bitter noise. The result is a flavor profile that feels "rounder" and more robust.

A chocolatier blends crispy bacon with milk chocolate in an experiment that defies culinary expectations. The combination succeeds by uniting sugar, fat, and salt in a powerful sensory triad.

THE BACON PHENOMENON

This understanding of salt paves the way for the most polarizing, yet scientifically sound, craze of the 21st century: The Bacon Chocolate Bar.

When luxury chocolatiers first began enrobing hickory-smoked bacon in milk chocolate, it was dismissed as a novelty stunt. But the pairing stuck because it hits a "Bliss Point" trifecta that the human brain finds nearly impossible to resist: Sugar, Fat, and Salt.

However, the chemistry goes deeper than mere macronutrients. The affinity between bacon and chocolate is a masterclass in the Maillard Reaction interacting with Thiamine Degradation.

1. The Maillard Bridge: As discussed in Part I, roasted cocoa is rich in pyrazines. Fried bacon is also rich in pyrazines, created when the proteins in the meat brown in the pan. The brain recognizes this shared "roast" profile.

2. The Thiamine Connection: Pork is high in thiamine (Vitamin B1). When bacon is cooked, the thiamine degrades into sulfur-containing compounds (thiols) that give bacon its distinct meaty, savory aroma. Surprisingly, trace amounts of

similar sulfur compounds are generated during the fermentation of cocoa beans. This creates a faint, subterranean link between the "funk" of the meat and the "funk" of the cocoa.

3. The Fat Interaction: Bacon fat is roughly 40% saturated fat and 50% monounsaturated oleic acid. Cocoa butter is similarly composed of stearic and oleic acids. Because the lipid profiles are compatible, they melt at similar rates in the mouth, preventing the waxy separation that occurs when mixing chocolate with incompatible oils.

The final piece of the puzzle is Dynamic Contrast. Food scientists argue that the brain stops registering a flavor if it is continuous (a phenomenon called sensory adaptation). A solid block of chocolate eventually becomes boring to the neuron. But bacon adds a "crunch-melt" cycle. The hard crunch of the cured meat interrupts the smooth melt of the chocolate, resetting the brain's attention and forcing it to re-evaluate the flavor with every bite.

THE CHILI PARADOX: The Chemistry of Pain

If bacon is about comfort, Chili Chocolate is about danger.

The pairing of cacao and capsicum is the oldest in the book, dating back to the Aztec *cacahuatl*. But why do humans enjoy hurting them-selves with dessert? The answer lies in the interaction between Capsaicin (the spicy molecule) and Casein (milk protein) or Cocoa Butter (fat). Capsaicin is a hydrophobic (oil-loving) molecule. It does not dissolve in water; it dissolves in fat.

When you eat a chili pepper alone, the capsaicin binds tightly to the TRPV1 pain receptors on the tongue, sending a signal of "HEAT" to the brain. Water washes over it without dislodging it.

When you eat chili infused into chocolate, the abundant cocoa butter acts as a solvent. It creates a "time-release" mechanism. The fat coats the tongue, creating a buffer zone that slows down the binding of the capsaicin. Instead of a sharp, immediate burn, the heat builds in a slow, glowing crescendo.

Simultaneously, the sugar in the chocolate triggers the release of endogenous opioids (endorphins) in the brain to block the "pain" of the spice. The result is a neurochemical rollercoaster: the chili sends a danger signal, the brain releases natural painkillers, and the sugar provides a dopamine reward. It is a thrill ride for the trigeminal nerve.

THE CONTRAST THEORY: West vs. East

While the "Shared Compound" hypothesis (like Heston Blumenthal's white chocolate and caviar) dominates Western food science, it is not the only law of the land. In 2011, network scientists analyzing over 50,000 recipes discovered a startling cultural divide.

- North American and Western European cuisines tend to pair ingredients that share flavor compounds (e.g., Chocolate + Peanut Butter).
- East Asian and Southern Indian cuisines tend to pair ingredients that have contrasting flavor compounds.

This explains why chocolate has struggled to find a foothold in traditional Asian savory cooking, where the goal is often to avoid overlapping flavors. However, it also explains the success of Mole in Mexico.

Mole is a "negative pairing" masterpiece. The bitter, fatty, roasted notes of the chocolate share almost no DNA with the sharp, vegetal heat of the chilies or the pungent bite of the onions and garlic. They sit on opposite sides of the flavor spectrum. By occupying different frequency bands, they prevent the dish from becoming "muddy." The chocolate provides the bass, the chili provides the treble, and because they don't overlap, the brain can hear the entire orchestra clearly.

THE FRONTIER of Weird Science

If salt and chili are the entry-level drugs of chocolate pairing, Cauliflower is the deep end.

In 2005, Heston Blumenthal struck again. He served a dish of cauliflower risotto with chocolate jelly. Diners were perplexed, but the science was sound. It turns out that roasted cauliflower and cocoa beans share a hidden chemical bond: Isothiocyanates and Sulfides.

Specifically, when cauliflower is caramelized (roasted until brown), it develops nutty, toasted notes derived from the Maillard reaction. But it also retains sulfurous compounds (dimethyl sulfide) that give it its vegetable pungency. Cocoa contains trace amounts of these same sulfides, remnants of the fermentation process where amino acids were broken down.

When eaten together, the brain latches onto the "toasted nut" profile they share, while the sulfur compounds provide a savory depth that prevents the chocolate from tasting cloying. It is a pairing that tastes like "earth"—a grounding, resonant flavor that bridges the vegetable garden and the candy shop.

THE BLACK GARLIC Miracle

Perhaps no ingredient exemplifies the "shared compound" success story better than Black Garlic.

Black garlic is not a specific variety of garlic; it is regular garlic that has been aged for weeks at varying temperatures and humidity. This process is not fermentation (which requires microbes), but a slow-motion Maillard reaction. The enzymes break down the sharp, biting allicin (the compound that gives raw garlic its heat) and convert starches into sugars.

The result is a clove that is jet-black, soft as jelly, and tastes of balsamic vinegar, tamarind, and molasses.

When paired with dark chocolate, the chemistry is nearly perfect.

- Melanoidins: Both black garlic and dark chocolate are packed with melanoidins, the brown polymers formed during browning reactions. This gives them a shared "dark/roasted" flavor backbone.
- Acidity: The natural acidity of the black garlic mirrors the fruit acidity found in fine-flavor cacao (like the berry notes of Madagascan beans).

- Umami: As explored in Chapter 19, the savory glutamate hit of the garlic amplifies the chocolate's richness without adding salt.

Chefs have used this to create "Black Garlic Truffles" that taste less like garlic bread and more like an intensely complex, aged balsamic caramel. It is a pairing that relies on time—both ingredients require weeks or months of processing to develop the flavor bridge that connects them.

THE ALGORITHM as Chef

The future of flavor pairing is no longer being written by chefs in kitchens; it is being written by neural networks in server rooms.

In 2012, IBM unveiled "Chef Watson," an AI designed to analyze the chemical composition of ingredients and propose recipes that had never existed before. Watson digested databases containing thousands of volatile compounds and millions of existing recipes. Its goal was to find ingredients that shared high concentrations of flavor molecules but were rarely combined in human culture.

The machine spat out suggestions that sounded like hallucinations:

- Chocolate and Beef: Based on shared roasted notes and fat solubility.
- Chocolate and Smoked Eel: Based on trimethylamine and phenolic smoke compounds.
- Chocolate and Soy Sauce: Based on the "Kokumi" effect (richness) and salt-sugar synergy.

One of Watson's most famous creations was a Chocolate-Chili-Meat dish that scientifically optimized the savory depth of mole without adhering to Mexican tradition.

This marks a shift in the philosophy of taste. For millennia, we paired food based on what grew nearby (Terroir). In the 20th century, we paired food based on what chefs intuited (Art). In the 21st century, we are pairing food based on what the data dictates (Science).

∾

The Limits of Chemistry

However, there is a danger in relying solely on the gas chromatograph. Chemistry can tell us that White Chocolate and Caviar share amines, but it cannot predict if the *texture* of fish eggs popping in vanilla fat will make a diner gag.

Science can explain *why* a pairing works after the fact, but it struggles to predict the emotional resonance of a dish. Bacon and chocolate works not just because of pyrazines, but because it feels transgressive—it breaks the rules of breakfast and dessert. Chili and chocolate works because the endorphin rush feels like a thrill.

The magic of pairing lies in that gap between the molecule and the mind. It is the moment where the brain, confronted with two things that should not go together, finds a hidden harmony and signals a spark of delight. It is the chemistry of surprise.

PART IV

ART, CULTURE, AND THE
AESTHETICS OF DESIRE

22

CHOCOLATE AS ART:
EDIBLE SCULPTURE AND
CULINARY ILLUSION

T he air inside the exhibition hall isn't sweet; it is tense. It smells
of ozone, the metallic tang of dry ice, and the heavy scent of
warm cocoa butter. *On a raised platform, a competitor from Japan
is holding his breath. He is standing before a six-foot-tall structure that resembles a steampunk clock tower, gears interlocking in a defiance of gravity. But it
is not made of brass or wood. It is made entirely of tempered chocolate.*

The clock on the wall ticks down: two minutes remaining. The chef
reaches for a canister of "cold spray"—compressed food-grade refrig-
erant—to weld a final fern to the apex. His hands tremble. It is a physio-
logical reaction to the adrenaline, but in this arena, a tremor can be fatal.
The stage lights are blazing, raising the ambient temperature on the
platform to 24°C (75°F). For the audience, it is warm; for the sculpture, it
is a death zone. The crystal lattice of the chocolate is softening. The
structural integrity of the thermal welds is failing.

Suddenly, a sharp, sickening crack echoes through the microphone
system like a gunshot. It is the sound of thermal shock. A cantilevered
wing on the tower shears off, plummeting to the floor where it shatters
into a thousand glossy shards. A collective gasp sucks the air out of the
room. The chef freezes, staring at the ruin of three days' labor. In the
world of high-end chocolate art, there is no eraser, no "undo" button.

There is only the unforgiving physics of fat crystallization. This is not dessert. This is extreme engineering performed without a safety net.

While the world eats chocolate for comfort, a rarefied cadre of artisans treats it as a structural building material, pushing it to limits that seem biologically impossible. They are the chocolate illusionists, the sculptors of the sweet, who have transformed the pastry arts into a discipline that sits somewhere between architecture and magic. To understand their world, we must look past the flavor and examine the chocolate bar as a brick, a beam, and a canvas.

THE PHYSICS OF FRAGILITY: Chocolate as a Building Material

Marble is passive; stone waits to be carved. Chocolate is chemically active. It is a material that wants to move.

As explored in Chapter 17, structural integrity relies entirely on the tensile strength of Form V crystals. This crystal form provides the rigidity necessary to support weight. However, the material has a fatal flaw: its shear strength is incredibly low compared to its compressive strength.

A column of tempered chocolate can support a surprising amount of vertical weight—some chocolatiers have built stools and tables that can support a human adult. But apply a lateral force—a twist or a bend—and the material fails instantly. This makes creating dynamic, gravity-defying shapes a nightmare.

Furthermore, the "cement" used in chocolate architecture is simply more chocolate. To join two pieces, the artist applies a thin layer of tempered chocolate (at roughly 32°C) to the joint. They blast the joint with cold spray (often -50°C) to create an instant, albeit brittle, thermal weld. If the room heats up, the sculpture expands while the frozen joint remains rigid. The resulting stress causes the fractures that haunt competitors' nightmares.

Structural Integrity: The challenge of chocolate sculpture is overcoming the material's fragility and low shear strength to create dynamic forms, requiring chocolatiers to calculate loads and use internal armatures like civil engineers.

The chocolate artist must therefore think like a civil engineer. They calculate loads and fulcrums. They use internal armatures—hidden skeletons made of dense, untempered chocolate—to bear the weight of the decorative outer shell. They understand that white chocolate, which lacks the fibrous cocoa solids of dark chocolate, is more elastic and better for ribbons, while dark chocolate is more rigid and better for structural beams.

THE LINEAGE OF the Pièce Montée

This obsession with edible architecture is not a modern invention; it is the continuation of a lineage that dates back to the courts of Europe. The concept of the *pièce montée* (literally "mounted piece") was popularized in the early 19th century by Marie-Antoine Carême, the first "celebrity chef." Carême studied architecture before he studied pastry, and he famously declared that architecture was the noblest of the arts, and pastry was its highest form.

However, Carême worked primarily with sugar paste (pastillage) and marzipan. Chocolate, in the 1800s, was still coarse and difficult to temper. Only after the invention of the conche and refined tempering techniques did chocolate become a viable sculpting medium.

The shift from sugar to chocolate as the primary medium for show-pieces occurred largely in the late 20th century, driven by the rise of the *Coupe du Monde de la Pâtisserie* (World Pastry Cup). Pastry chefs realized that chocolate offered a unique advantage over sugar: it could be carved. Sugar work is additive—you pull and blow molten sugar into shapes. Chocolate work can be subtractive. You can cast a massive block of chocolate and hack away at it, revealing a form inside just as Michelangelo liberated David from the marble.

THE MODERN ALCHEMIST'S Toolkit

Today's chocolate sculptors have traded the copper pot for the machine shop. Walk into the atelier of a master like Amaury Guichon, and you will see tools that belong in a garage, not a kitchen.

- The Lathe and the Drill: To create perfectly symmetrical shapes—cylinders, spheres, table legs—artists now cast massive logs of chocolate and mount them on wood-turning lathes. As the chocolate log spins at high RPM, the chef uses metal gouges to carve intricate grooves and patterns. The friction of the tool melts the chocolate surface slightly, which immediately re-hardens, leaving a polished, machine-perfect finish that looks like mahogany or plastic.
- The Water Jet: For intricate latticework that would shatter under a knife, some high-end ateliers use computer-controlled water jets. These machines blast a stream of water at high pressure to cut precise gears, logos, or lace patterns out of chocolate sheets.
- The Acetate and the Illusion: The secret weapon of the chocolate shine is acetate. Chocolate poured onto a rough surface will dry matte. Chocolate poured onto a mirror-smooth surface will dry with a mirror finish. Artists cast chocolate onto sheets of flexible plastic (acetate) to create ribbons that look like satin or panels that look like glass. By manipulating the surface texture of the mold, they can mimic almost any material. A wire brush on semi-set chocolate

creates "wood grain." A crumpled ball of aluminum foil pressed into wet chocolate creates "stone." Cocoa powder dusted over a surface creates "rust" or "velvet".

The goal is *trompe-l'œil*. When Amaury Guichon creates a life-sized chocolate motorcycle, complete with tires and engine block, he isn't just making a cake.; he is performing a feat of material mimicry. The tires look like rubber because he has abraded the chocolate surface; the gas tank gleams like chrome because he has used edible silver luster dust on a perfectly tempered shell.

This technical wizardry serves a philosophical purpose. By forcing chocolate to look like iron, wood, or leather, the artist creates a moment of cognitive dissonance. When the viewer finally sees the object cut or bitten, the shattering of the illusion creates a sense of wonder. The rusty wrench dissolves into cocoa; the rubber tire snaps with the crisp sound of high-quality dark chocolate.

Nature's Mirror and the Coliseum of Cocoa

While the architects of chocolate build towers that defy gravity, a different school of artists has turned its gaze inward, seeking not to build larger, but to build *truer*. This is the movement of "Edible Nature," a philosophy that rejects the abstract geometries of traditional French pastry in favor of a radical, deceptive realism.

At the forefront of this movement is *trompe-l'œil*. In the past, a lemon tart looked like a tart: a crust, a filling, a meringue. Today, thanks to pioneers like Cédric Grolet, a lemon tart looks exactly, terrifyingly, like a lemon.

The Hyper-Realist Revolution

Imagine walking into a patisserie and seeing a crate of peaches. They have the fuzzy, variegated skin of a fruit plucked from a tree in Provence. They have the irregular shape, the slight bruising, the matte finish of nature. But when you slice one open, there is no pit. Instead, there is a core of coulant (liquid fruit compote) surrounded by a light-as-air ganache montée, all encased in a shell of cocoa butter so thin it shatters like eggshell.

This is the new frontier of chocolate sculpting: creating the "uncanny valley" of food.

The challenge here isn't load-bearing weight, but surface texture. Chocolate is naturally glossy; nature is matte, fuzzy, pitted, or waxy. To achieve these textures, chocolatiers have had to invent entirely new finishing techniques.

- The Velour Effect: To create the fuzzy texture of a peach or the soft nap of a mossy log, chefs use a technique called "flocking" or "velour." They load a spray gun with a mixture of 50% chocolate and 50% cocoa butter, heated to exactly 40°C. They then spray this mixture onto a frozen mousse cake (at -18°C).
- The physics of the collision are violent. The hot liquid hits the freezing surface and crystallizes instantly, before it can spread into a smooth film. It freezes into millions of microscopic droplets, creating a pebbled, velvet-like texture. By adjusting the nozzle pressure and the temperature differential, the artist can mimic anything from the fuzz of an apricot to the rough bark of a pine tree.
- The Skin of the Fruit: For smooth-skinned fruits like cherries or apples, the challenge is the opposite: creating a skin that looks organic, not plastic. The chef must dip the frozen mousse center into a colored cocoa butter glaze. The dip must be timed to the millisecond. Too long, and the heat of the dip melts the mousse. Too short, and the shell is too thin to hold the filling. Once dipped, the "fruit" is often hand-painted or airbrushed with natural dyes to add the imperfections that signal reality—the brown spots on a banana, the blush on a pear. This is art that relies on the brain's pattern recognition. If the chocolate apple has a perfectly convincing blemish, the brain forgives the fact that it smells like vanilla instead of orchard fruit.

THE COLISEUM OF COCOA: The World Chocolate Masters

If the boutique is the gallery of chocolate art, the competition circuit is its gladiator arena. The pinnacle of this world is the *World Chocolate Masters* (WCM), a triennial event held in Paris that is widely considered the most grueling pastry competition on Earth.

To understand the WCM, you must discard the image of a cozy bake-off. This is an industrial design competition fought with food. National champions from twenty countries—Japan, France, USA, Italy, and more —gather in a stadium-like hall filled with roaring crowds, commentators, and cameras.

For three days, these chefs endure a mental and physical marathon. They must produce a massive artistic showpiece (often exceeding two meters in height), a range of molded bonbons, a "fresh" pastry, and a "snack on the go," all adhering to a strict theme like "Futropolis" or "The Cocoa of Tomorrow."

THE ENGINEERING of Stress

The environment of the competition is designed to test the chocolate as much as the chef. The lights are hot. The air conditioning struggles against the heat generated by twenty tempering machines. The floor vibrates with the footsteps of judges.

In this hostile environment, the structural integrity of the showpiece is the primary source of drama. Competitors often spend months, or even years, calculating the center of gravity of their sculptures. They bring blueprints that look like they belong to NASA. They design internal lattices of chocolate "rebar" to prevent collapse.

Yet, disaster is a spectator sport. There is a specific, haunting sound known to every attendee of the WCM: the *crack*. It usually happens in the final hour. A chef attempts to lift a heavy chocolate sphere onto a slender pedestal. The thermal stress of his hands, combined with the micro-vibrations of the table, causes a catastrophic failure in the crystal lattice. The sculpture shatters.

In 2013, the Mexican contestant's massive Aztec-themed statue collapsed minutes before the buzzer. In 2018, a cantilevered futuristic cityscape sheared off its base. The tragedy is absolute: points are deducted not just for the missing piece, but for the "cleanliness of the station," which is now covered in debris. The chef must finish the competition knowing they have already lost, a psychological torture that separates the masters from the amateurs.

The Taste of Adrenaline

While the showpieces garner the Instagram likes, the tasting portion of the competition is where the true alchemy happens. Here, the art must dissolve.

The judges are looking for something called the "flavor journey." It is not enough for a bonbon to taste good; it must tell a story. A winning chocolate might start with a sharp hit of yuzu acidity (Head Note), transition into a creamy hazelnut praline (Heart Note), and finish with the lingering, earthy bitterness of a single-origin Papua New Guinea dark chocolate (Base Note).

Creating this arc requires a deep knowledge of aroma volatility. The chef knows that fruit acids hit the tongue fast and vanish, while fats coat the mouth and linger. They layer these sensations like a composer layers instruments.

In the high-pressure environment of the WCM, chefs often push the boundaries of savory-sweet pairings—using tobacco, miso, or black garlic to impress judges whose palates are fatigued by sugar. It is a high-stakes gamble. A truffle flavored with smoked hay and caramelized white chocolate might win the "Best Bonbon" award, or it might be spat out by a traditionalist judge.

The Price of Perfection

The world of chocolate art is one of immense waste and immense beauty. A showpiece for the World Chocolate Masters might consume 100 kilograms of high-quality couverture—chocolate that could have made 2,000 gourmet bars. After the competition, these sculptures are often displayed for a few days until the fat blooms and the dust settles, and then they are destroyed. They are melted down (if the chocolate is clean enough) or simply discarded.

This ephemerality is part of the allure. Unlike a bronze statue that will last for millennia, a chocolate sculpture is a flower. It blooms for a moment of perfection, defying heat and gravity, and then it is gone. For the artist, the value lies not in the object, but in the mastery required to bring it into existence, however briefly, before the laws of thermodynamics reclaim it.

THE DIGITAL FOUNDRY and the Post-Human Sculptor

In a quiet laboratory in Zurich, a nozzle moves silently across a build plate. It is not extruding plastic or metal, but tempered dark chocolate. Layer by layer, a shape begins to emerge—a complex, twisted lattice that looks less like a dessert and more like a magnified bone structure or a coral reef.

No knife could carve this. No silicone mold could cast it; the undercuts are too deep, the geometry too interlocking. It exists only because a computer dreamt it up and a robot built it.

This is the frontier of the "Digital Foundry," where the chisel has been replaced by the CAD (Computer-Aided Design) file. As chocolate art moves into the future, the boundary between the pastry chef and the industrial designer is dissolving.

THE IMPOSSIBLE GEOMETRY of 3D Printing

For centuries, chocolate art was limited by the laws of molding. To make a shape, you had to be able to pull a mold away from it. This rule dictated the visual language of chocolate: smooth curves, tapered angles, and solid volumes.

3D printing shattered that rule. By using Fused Deposition Modeling (FDM) adapted for food, artists can now create shapes with internal voids, interlocking moving parts, and mathematical fractals.

3D-Printed Chocolate: Using FDM, artists create shapes with internal voids and complex fractals, pushing the limits of chocolate art beyond traditional molding.

The engineering challenge is immense. Unlike plastic filament, which sets instantly at 200°C, chocolate melts at 32°C and solidifies slowly. To print it, the machine must maintain a "Goldilocks zone" of thermal precision—fluid enough to flow, yet cool enough for the previous layer to support the new weight. If the ambient temperature shifts by two degrees, the sculpture collapses into a puddle.

Pioneers like the Dutch design studio Michiel Cornelissen or the researchers at the Singapore University of Technology and Design have pushed this technology to create "edible mathematics." They print gyroid structures—infinite, non-intersecting surfaces—that have a crunch unlike any molded bar because the texture is derived from the air pockets inside the print, not just the ingredients.

Generative Design: The Algorithm as Sous-Chef

The next leap goes beyond just printing shapes; it involves using algorithms to *design* them. This is the realm of "Generative Design."

Instead of a human drawing a shape, the artist inputs parameters into software: "Create a support column that is 20cm tall, uses minimum material, and resembles a tree root." The computer then runs thousands of simulations, evolving a structure that meets the criteria.

The resulting forms are often alien and organic, mimicking the cellular growth of plants or the weave of muscle fibers. When executed in chocolate, these forms have a disturbing beauty. They look grown, not made.

In high-end dining, this allows for a new level of customization. A chef can scan a diner's face and print a chocolate cameo in real-time. They can create a dessert that is structurally engineered to collapse at the precise moment a hot sauce is poured over it, a pre-programmed structural failure that serves as kinetic theater.

THE PHILOSOPHICAL CRISIS: **Hand vs. Machine**

This technological explosion has sparked a philosophical crisis in the world of fine pastry. If a robot sculpts the chocolate, is it still art?

Traditionalists argue the soul of the *pièce montée* lies in the struggle of the human hand—the sweat on the brow, the trembling fingers welding a joint. They see 3D printing as a sterilization of the craft, reducing the chef to a machine operator.

However, the futurists argue that the machine frees the artist. By offloading the repetitive labor of tempering and stacking to a robot, the chef is free to become an architect of flavor and form. They argue that the tool does not matter; only the vision does. Was the Pantheon less art because the Romans used cranes?

THE EPHEMERAL ARCHIVE

There is one final irony to the digitization of chocolate art. For the first time in history, these fleeting masterpieces can be saved.

In the past, a World Champion's sculpture existed for a week before rotting or melting. Today, those sculptures are scanned using LiDAR (Light Detection and Ranging). Their digital twins are preserved in the cloud, immortalizing every scratch, texture, and fracture.

We can now 3D print a replica of a prize-winning sculpture from 2015. But here lies the paradox: A plastic replica lasts forever, but it is dead. The chocolate original was alive because it was doomed.

~

The Sweetest Vanishing Act

Whether carved by a knife-wielding genius in Paris or extruded by a robotic arm in Zurich, chocolate art remains defined by a single, unchangeable truth: it is food.

No matter how tall the tower, how realistic the fruit, or how complex the fractal, the destiny of chocolate is to be eaten. Its beauty is inextricably tied to its destruction. The snap of the structure, the shattering of the illusion, the melting of the medium on the tongue—this is the final act of the performance.

Chocolate art reminds us that possession is temporary. The only way to truly keep it is to consume it. In a world obsessed with permanence, the chocolate sculptor teaches us the value of the moment—building castles of sugar and cocoa just to watch them fall, leaving nothing behind but a memory of sweetness.

23

THE CHEF'S CHOCOLATE: SAVORY INNOVATIONS AND AVANT-GARDE CUISINE

I*n a hushed, candlelit dining room, a chef steps forward with a microplane grater and a bar of 80% cacao. Diners look on curiously as he showers bitter chocolate shavings over roasted quail and wilted cabbage. The aroma that rises is earthy and unexpected. This isn't dessert; it's the main course. Across the culinary world, a quiet revolution is afoot. Chocolate—long worshipped in candy shops and pastry kitchens—is emerging as a high-art ingredient in savory cuisine, adding intrigue and luxury to dishes in ways most chocolate lovers have never imagined.*

THE SAVORY SIDE OF CHOCOLATE: **Ancient Roots, New Inspirations**

Chocolate's journey beyond the dessert cart is, in fact, a return to its roots. Centuries before it was ever sweetened, cacao was treated as a sacred spice and a savory staple. The Mayans and Aztecs drank chocolate with spices and chile, believing it to be a gift from the gods.

In Europe, once cacao arrived from the New World, adventurous cooks in Baroque kitchens slipped chocolate into game stews and ragouts. In eighteenth-century Italy, a dash of chocolate might enrich a wild boar sauce or lend silkiness to a simmering polenta.

It was a hidden luxury, a chef's secret for depth and shine. Over time, chocolate became pigeonholed as a confection—synonymous with candy bars and cake. But today's chefs are looking backward to move forward, drawing on those global traditions to inspire something boldly new.

In Mexico, the practice of using chocolate in savory cooking never truly faded. Now it's a clarion call for modern chefs seeking complexity. Nowhere is this more evident than in Oaxaca, often called the culinary heart of Mexico.

In rustic Oaxacan markets, you can find villagers grinding roasted cacao beans on stone metates, blending them with toasted chiles, garlic, nuts, and ancient spices. The result is mole negro, the midnight-dark sauce that might dress a turkey or enchiladas at a celebration.

Taste a true mole and you notice a whisper of chocolate—just enough to bind and mellow the chili heat, not enough to dominate. It's a symphony of flavors with cacao as the quiet conductor. This tradition inspires contemporary masters: celebrated Mexican chefs have made mole the star of tasting menus from Mexico City to Manhattan, proving that chocolate in a sauce can be as nuanced as any Bordeaux in a reduction.

Mole and Beyond: Latin America's Gift to Savory Chocolate

Mexican mole is just the beginning of chocolate's Latin repertoire. Across Latin America, chocolate finds its way into marinades, stews, and rubs in imaginative ways. In Veracruz, a rich chocolate-and-chile sauce might be used to braise pork for a celebratory stew known as *asado de bodas*.

In the American Southwest, home cooks slip a square of dark chocolate into pots of chili con carne, letting it melt into the tomatoes and cumin to add a mysterious richness. "It's my secret ingredient," one chef confides—an old trick to give the chili a deeper backbone and a hint of smokiness. Even an everyday barbecue sauce can get the cacao treatment: a spoonful of cocoa powder stirred into a chipotle-laced sauce lends a subtle bitter edge that makes grilled ribs sing.

==

THE PITMASTER'S SECRET: "BLACK GOLD" RUB

Cocoa powder adds a dark, earthy bark to meat that smoke alone cannot achieve.

The Mix:

- 2 tbsp Unsweetened Cocoa Powder (The bitter base)
- 1 tbsp Brown Sugar (The caramelization)
- 1 tbsp Smoked Paprika (The heat)
- 1 tsp Sea Salt & Black Pepper
- 1/2 tsp Ground Coffee (The booster)

The Method: Rub generously onto Steak, Pork Ribs, or Venison 30 minutes before grilling. The cocoa butter in the powder will render, creating a dark, savory crust.

==

MODERN CHEFS with Latin American roots are taking these ideas to new heights. Consider a dish that turned heads at Cantina La Martina just outside Philadelphia: short ribs braised in hibiscus and Mexican chocolate. Chef Dionicio Jiménez, originally from Puebla, Mexico, slow-cooks beef short ribs in a broth steeped with dried hibiscus flowers (for tart acidity) and chunks of Oaxacan chocolate (for complexity and color). The meat emerges dark, fork-tender, with a mole-like depth.

In a bold twist, he serves it atop creamy Italian risotto, scattering tangy queso añejo cheese on top. The result is a cross-cultural marriage of flavors: Italian comfort meets Oaxacan soul. Diners may not pinpoint "chocolate" at first bite, but they marvel at the dish's unique warmth and complexity. That is the magic of savory chocolate—it works behind the scenes, making familiar flavors feel intriguingly new.

Latin America also offers up less expected chocolate pairings. In Peru and Ecuador, visionary chefs experiment with the cacao fruit itself—the sweet-tart white pulp that encases cocoa beans. They ferment it into

vinegars or syrups to dress salads and seafood, bringing a floral brightness with just a hint of cocoa essence.

And in a playful take on a Middle Eastern classic, one inventive
Mexican chef created a white chocolate–avocado hummus, drawing on
the creamy cocoa butter of white chocolate to enrich the dip without
overwhelming it. These creations pay homage to the idea that chocolate,
in all its forms, can be as versatile as chile or citrus, ready to enhance any
flavor profile.

Chocolate as a spice: In Mexican Mole, cacao is used not for
sweetness, but to provide a bitter, earthy backbone to a complex
sauce of chilies and nuts.

OLD WORLD ALCHEMY: European Traditions Reborn

Meanwhile, Europe's own savory chocolate traditions have been
quietly simmering back to life. In Renaissance Italy, cooks in the courts
of Tuscany and Venice stirred chocolate into meat sauces and even into
pasta dough.

That heritage lives on today in the hands of modern Italian chefs,
who are rediscovering chocolate as a spice in their repertoire. Walk into
a trattoria in Umbria during hunting season, and you might find a nod to
nonna's old recipe: tender wild hare braised "in dolce forte", an
agrodolce stew sweetened with raisins, vinegar, and a piece of dark

chocolate to thicken the sauce. The chocolate doesn't make the dish sugary; rather it deepens the flavors—like a bass note rounding out a chord.

In New York City, Italian chefs are taking those age-old ideas and giving them a contemporary polish. At the legendary Felidia, diners swoon over cocoa ravioli—thin pasta tinted with cocoa, filled with velvety butternut squash and fresh burrata cheese, finished in sage-infused brown butter.

The pasta's subtle chocolate bitterness accentuates the sweetness of squash, creating a perfect autumnal harmony. A few blocks away, another restaurant twirls out plates of cacao pappardelle: wide, dark ribbons of pasta made with pure unsweetened cocoa, tossed in a slow-simmered Chianti and short rib ragù. The chef explains that this dish was inspired by a Renaissance preservation method of marinating meat in wine.

By adding cacao to the mix, he found a "unique twist on a classic," balancing the Chianti's tannic bite with the cocoa's faint sweetness. The sauce clings to those chocolate-colored noodles, every bite a play of bitter, savory, and sweet. It's Italian comfort food—just reframed.

Even classic European sauces have quietly welcomed chocolate back into their embrace. In France, a traditional civet of venison might hide a few squares of dark chocolate, melted in at the very end to give the sauce a glossy sheen and velvety texture. This trick, once recommended by Auguste Escoffier himself, imparts a luxurious mouthfeel—a *silkiness* that lingers on the palate.

And in Spain's Catalonia region, the grandmothers still remember adding a pinch of chocolate to their picada—a pesto-like finishing paste of almonds, herbs, and garlic used to thicken stews. In an updated homage to that Catalan tradition, one Barcelona-inspired bistro serves charred cauliflower with a chocolate-almond picada sauce, the nutty cocoa notes playing off the vegetable's sweetness.

These dishes might sound avant-garde, but they are grounded in something old and human: a craving for balance. Chocolate, used judiciously, can balance savory flavors the way salt or acid does. European chefs are embracing that notion anew, treating chocolate not as a confection, but as a tool for complexity.

~

Modernist Magic: Unlikely Pairings and New Techniques

If tradition showed chefs the way, innovation beckoned them further. In the past two decades, a wave of modernist chefs—part scientists, part artists—have pushed chocolate to the edge of imagination. They're deconstructing it, re-forming it, pairing it with ingredients few of us would ever dream to match.

Take white chocolate, that oft-maligned sweet, which contains no bitter cocoa solids at all—just cocoa butter, milk, and sugar. Long relegated to candy store novelty, white chocolate has found redemption in the savory kitchen. Chefs realized that, at its core, white chocolate is a rich dairy fat that can behave much like butter or cream.

The slight sweetness and silky texture make it a surprising ally for savory flavors. In Los Angeles, one farm-to-table chef recalls an unlikely inspiration: a white chocolate macadamia cookie. From that memory he devised a chilled English pea salad strewn with white chocolate "snow" —white chocolate frozen and grated over the peas like delicate flakes.

A drizzle of sherry vinegar consommé melts the flakes just enough to coat the peas in a glossy, creamy sheen. The dish arrives looking like a spring garden after a light snow, and tastes like one too: sweet peas and mint, pops of sea salt, and a gentle, nutty sweetness in the background that makes diners pause between bites to ponder, *what is that flavor?*

On the opposite coast, in New York, Chef Ken Oringer drew inspiration from the experimental kitchens of Spain and Britain to create something truly extravagant: caviar with white chocolate. At his tapas bar, he roasts white chocolate in a low oven until it caramelizes into a golden "dulce de leche," intensifying its milky sweetness.

He then dollops that alongside briny Osetra caviar on a grilled baguette, finishing with a dab of tangy yogurt and a sliver of charred lemon. The first time this combination appeared, even foodie cynics were astonished: the burst of salty roe against the buttery caramel white chocolate is an indulgent ballet of ocean and candy store, somehow in perfect step.

This dish is a direct culinary descendant of the molecular breakthroughs explored in Chapter 21, taking the science of the "Food Pairing

Hypothesis" out of the lab and translating it into a bustling tapas bar experience.The modernist love affair with chocolate doesn't stop at curious pairings. It extends to textures and techniques that transform chocolate into forms you'd never expect. In Washington D.C., a Belgian-born chef created a sensation with lobster poached in white chocolate butter. He blends good white chocolate into warm butter, creating a sauce base that's aromatic with vanilla. Plump lobster meat is gently poached in this medium, emerging tender and faintly sweet, served with a bright passionfruit sabayon and charred grapefruit. The cocoa butter in the chocolate enriches the lobster like no ordinary butter could, giving it a satin finish that tastes opulent and just a little sweet against the tart fruit accents.

At a cutting-edge Miami resort, a young chef who started in the pastry kitchen turned octopus into art. He slow-cooks Spanish octopus sous-vide until meltingly tender, then whips up a white chocolate-infused foam to accompany it. To make this foam, he caramelizes white chocolate for hours until it's amber and complex, then blends it with brown butter and artichoke into an airy froth.

Spoon this tangy, buttery foam over a slice of octopus with a sliver of salty jamón, and something alchemical happens: the octopus tastes richer, the ham tastes sweeter, and the whole bite dissolves like oceanic candy on the tongue. Such dishes blur the boundary between savory and sweet so completely that those words cease to matter—what matters is that it's delicious.

And for a true avant-garde spectacle, consider a dish from a Michelin-starred table in Chicago: foie gras with a white chocolate noodle. The chef wanted to serve his silky foie gras torchon (usually an appetizer) later in the meal, closer to dessert, and needed a bridge to carry it there.

His solution was to literally gel white chocolate and cream into the shape of a noodle—using a touch of agar agar to set it—and coil it atop the medallion of foie gras. When the dish is served, the diners see what looks like a delicate tagliatelle or a curl of ivory. But as the "noodle" hits the warmth of the tongue, it miraculously melts, mingling with the lush foie gras and a scatter of macerated strawberries and fennel blossoms.

The cocoa butter adds an ethereal richness that helps the foie gras transition toward the meal's sweeter finale, while subtle notes of cumin and olive crumble bring it back to earth. It's playful, sensual, and totally unexpected—exactly the point of modernist cuisine.

Heston Blumenthal's famous discovery: The fatty, creamy notes of white chocolate pair perfectly with the briny pop of caviar.

Texture, Technique, and the Artistry of Chocolate

Why are today's chefs so enamored with using chocolate in these unconventional ways? The answer lies in chocolate's incredible versatility. It can be liquid or solid, bitter or sweet, rich or subtle, depending on how it's handled. In the savory kitchen, this makes chocolate a shape-shifter—a palette of textures and tones that a creative chef can deploy like a painter with oils.

One key aspect is texture. Chocolate can add body and silkiness to sauces that is hard to achieve with anything else. A dark chocolate square or a spoonful of cocoa powder stirred into a braising liquid acts as a natural emulsifier, binding water and fat, tightening a sauce without flour or cream.

This is why a beef stew with a bit of chocolate can feel velvety on the tongue, each bite coating the mouth in a lingering richness. A classic French jus or an Italian ragù enriched with a hint of cocoa feels complete, its flavors married together in a way you can't quite explain until you know the secret. Chefs prize this effect; as one put it, "chocolate gives a sauce a sheen and cohesion that's just *sexy*."

===

THE CHEF'S SECRET: THE GOLDEN RATIOS

Texture is just math. Memorize these ratios of Chocolate : Cream to master any dessert.

- **1 : 1 (The Truffle):** Equal parts chocolate and heavy cream. Creates a firm, scoopable ganache for truffles.
- **2 : 1 (The Glaze):** Two parts chocolate to one part cream. Creates a glossy, pourable coating that sets firm on cakes.
- **1 : 2 (The Mousse):** One part chocolate to two parts cream. Creates a light, airy whip for fillings and piping.

===

TEXTURE ISN'T ONLY about thickness, though—it's also about crunch, air, and surprise. Consider cacao nibs, the dry-roasted pieces of the cocoa bean. They are intensely aromatic and bitter, like coffee beans in bite-sized form. Pastry chefs have long sprinkled nibs on desserts for crunch, but savory chefs have discovered their power too.

You might find nibs acting as a spice, ground with sea salt and paprika to rim the crust of a seared tuna steak, giving an unexpected cocoa bite to the first mouthful. Or nibs candied lightly in soy and mirin to form a brittle crumble over a bowl of mushroom congee, adding a crackling texture and an umami depth.

Even something as simple as a salad can get the cacao treatment: one chef shaves cured ham over arugula and then tosses in a handful of toasted cacao nibs, their nutty crunch standing in for croutons. The diners get peppery greens, salty ham, and then the nibs—their taste morphing from nutty to a gentle chocolate bitterness as you chew. It's subtle, but transformative; you realize a few nibs can carry the aroma of a whole chocolate bar without any sweetness at all.

Then there are the smoked and infused forms of chocolate. Think of a chef using the shells of roasted cocoa beans as fuel for smoking duck breast or eggplant. As the shells smolder, they release a toasty, cocoa-laced smoke that perfumes the food with a haunting hint of chocolate.

At a boutique BBQ joint, the pitmaster might mix cocoa husks with mesquite wood, the resulting smoke giving his brisket a mysterious dark warmth. And in some forward-thinking bars, mixologists have captured "chocolate smoke" under glass to unveil with a flourish—imagine a Manhattan cocktail that arrives swirling with vapors of burnt cocoa, teasing your nose before you take a sip.

==

BAR HACK: HOW TO "FAT-WASH" BOURBON

Want chocolate whiskey without the sugary syrup? Use science.

- **The Infusion:** Melt 2 oz of dark chocolate or cocoa butter. Pour it into a jar with 8 oz of Bourbon. Shake well.
- **The Freeze:** Let it sit for 4 hours, then put the jar in the freezer overnight. The fat will rise to the top and freeze into a solid puck.
- **The Strain:** Poke a hole in the fat cap and pour the liquid through a coffee filter.

The Result: You are left with a crystal-clear whiskey that has the silky mouthfeel and roasted aroma of chocolate, but none of the mess.

==

Infusions are another frontier. Cocoa butter, the fat in chocolate, is a prized medium for carrying flavor. Innovative chefs melt cocoa butter and infuse it with herbs or spices to create chocolate-scented oils.

A few drops of cocoa butter infused with rosemary might finish a roasted carrot soup, adding gloss and a faint chocolaty aroma that marries beautifully with the sweet carrots. And in the realm of fermentation, some chefs are treating cacao like soybeans or barley, creating what can only be described as chocolate miso.

By inoculating crushed cacao nibs with koji culture and salt, they coax it to ferment into a paste that's profoundly savory and aromatic.

The resulting cacao miso paste can be swirled into broths or brushed on meats as a marinade, lending a deep, umami-rich chocolate note that is more akin to soy sauce than candy. It's a full circle moment—recognizing that chocolate itself is a fermented food, and pushing that process further to bridge cuisines.

One Japanese-Italian fusion restaurant in California brushes cacao miso onto grilled eggplant, in a clever riff on classic miso-glazed eggplant. It arrives glistening and browned, with an aroma that is equal parts salty, savory, and faintly cocoa. The taste is extraordinary: the eggplant's flesh is creamy and smoky, the glaze is sweet, salty, and just a touch bitter from the chocolate. It's an umami bomb with a whisper of dessert.

==

KITCHEN MAGIC: THE ONE-INGREDIENT MOUSSE

Physics allows you to make mousse without cream or eggs. It is pure chocolate texture.

- **The Science:** By whisking melted chocolate over ice, you trap air and rapidly crystallize the fat, creating a stable foam.
- **The Method:**
  - Melt 1 cup of Dark Chocolate with 3/4 cup of Water in a bowl.
  - Place that bowl inside a larger bowl filled with Ice and Water (an ice bath).
  - Whisk by hand vigorously for 3–5 minutes.
  - Watch closely. The liquid will suddenly thicken into a dense, luxurious mousse. Stop whisking immediately or it will turn grainy!

==

Throughout these experiments, chefs maintain a guiding principle: balance. Chocolate in a savory dish should never clobber you over the head. It's there to enhance and deepen, not dominate. Much like a squeeze of lemon or a splash of fish sauce, a little can go a long way. Too much, and the dish veers into strange territory.

The best chefs use chocolate with a restrained hand, as a high note or a bass line rather than the whole melody. When done right, the diner might not even realize chocolate is in the mix until it's revealed—or until a familiar, pleasant aftertaste cues a memory of a favorite dark chocolate bar savored long ago.

A New Flavor Frontier: Chocolate as High Art Ingredient

From the low-lit test kitchens of avant-garde restaurants to the homely stewpots of traditional cooks, chocolate is being reborn as something more than a sweet treat. It has become a medium for artistry, a link between cultures, a bridge between taste sensations. Chefs today speak of chocolate the way a painter might speak of color or a composer of sound—an element to play with, to provoke emotion and surprise. It's a way to add *mystery* to a sauce, *luxury* to a protein, or an *element of whimsy* to a plate.

The beauty of this movement is how accessible it can be. You don't need a chemistry degree or a siphon gun to appreciate or even attempt savory chocolate cooking. Any home cook can take a cue from the pros: stir a spoonful of cocoa into your next pot of chili, and see how it adds depth.

Whisk a bit of melted dark chocolate into a red wine pan sauce and marvel at the sheen and complexity it brings. Even something as simple as a good olive oil with a pinch of cocoa powder can dress roasted root vegetables, accentuating their sweetness and adding a hint of earthy drama.

For the dining public, these innovations mean that chocolate is more omnipresent—and more exciting—than ever. You might find yourself savoring a cacao-braised short rib tamale at a food festival, or enjoying a tasting menu where every course has a subtle cacao touch, from the salad to the soup to the roast and beyond.

You may not identify each instance of chocolate immediately, but you'll sense it in the way the dish makes you feel comforted and intrigued all at once. And when the chef finally sends you a cocoa-dusted truffle or a cup of spiced hot chocolate at meal's end, you appreciate the journey that chocolate has taken you on throughout the evening.

===

MENU: A DINNER IN DARKNESS

A conceptual menu inspired by the avant-garde techniques in this chapter. Do not serve dessert first.

- **The Appetizer:** White Chocolate & Caviar on Grilled Baguette (Inspired by Chef Ken Oringer. The salty roe cuts the fatty sweetness of roasted white chocolate.)
- **The Main Course:** Cocoa-Rubbed Short Ribs with Hibiscus Reduction (Inspired by Oaxacan mole. Bitter 100% cacao acts as a spice rub, creating a bark that seals in the meat's juices.)
- **The Salad Course:** Arugula with Cured Ham & Cacao Nibs (A textural study. Toasted nibs replace croutons, providing a crunchy, nutty counterpoint to the peppery greens.)
- **The Finale:** Blue Cheese & Dark Chocolate Truffle (The "Umami Bomb." A ganache infused with pungent blue cheese —a pairing made possible by the shared methyl ketones explored in Chapter 21—bridging the gap between cheese course and dessert.)

===

Luxurious food and culture have always gone hand in hand with storytelling, and chocolate brings a rich narrative to the table. It carries whispers of Mesoamerican rituals, echoes of European feasts, and now, the bold signatures of modern artists in chef's whites. With detailed, vivid strokes, today's culinary creators are painting with chocolate in unprecedented ways.

The next time you sit down to a beautifully crafted meal, keep an eye (and nose) out for that hint of cocoa in the air or on the plate. In an era when culinary artists use chocolate in ways you'd never imagined, a simple cocoa bean's journey from bitter pod to savory masterpiece is a story of creativity, culture, and pure culinary magic. Bon appétit, and let the chocolate surprise you.

24

THE FOLEY ARTIST'S TRUFFLE: ENGINEERING APPETITE ON SCREEN

*T*he camera's lens moves in, slowly, inexorably, towards a chocolate *truffle resting on a silver dish. The lighting on Soundstage 7 in Burbank is blistering, designed to create a perfect, cinematic glow. The chocolate—a sphere dusted with cocoa powder—glistens with an unattainable, mirror-like sheen. The actor reaches for the confection, and in the hush of the set, the audience is meant to feel a deep, primal surge of craving. This chapter explores a different kind of science: not the botany of the bean, but the engineering of desire.*

Yet, this moment of profound appetite appeal is a calculated lie, built on engineering and deception. While the camera sees perfection, the reality is a desperate battle against thermodynamics. The chocolate truffle, a prop meant to symbolize indulgence, is biologically and structurally hostile to the act of filming. The high-powered tungsten lights, designed to make the cocoa look rich and mahogany, generate enough radiant heat to turn the air immediately surrounding the prop into a microclimate exceeding 40°C (104°F).

The pure cocoa butter crystal lattice, the very molecular structure that gives real chocolate its snap and its sublime melt, collapses instantly under this thermal stress. Within minutes, the Form V crystals dissolve, forcing the fat to the surface and replacing the mirror-like sheen with an unappetizing, oily film known as "fat bloom." The pristine sphere warps into a greasy smear. The cinematographer demands that the prop be rigid, glossy, and unchanging for hours; the cocoa bean insists that it must melt at body temperature. This fundamental conflict between biological reality and cinematic necessity is the core challenge of food styling in Hollywood.

A plating of luxurious truffles is filmed under intense studio lights to appear luxurious. Its perfection is the result of careful technical staging.

The Formulation of Stunt Chocolate

To create a chocolate prop that survives the set, food stylists must become materials scientists, engineering a Stunt Double that mimics the optical properties of chocolate but possesses the thermal stability of plastic. This material must not just look right; it must adhere to strict Continuity rules—the cardinal rule of filmmaking that demands every prop look identical across dozens of takes and complex cuts.

The Stunt Chocolate formula is a carefully balanced compromise between Prop-Grade (non-edible, maximum durability) and Actor-Grade (edible, necessary for bite scenes).

PROP-GRADE STUNT CHOCOLATE (The Non-Melt)

For wide shots, background props, or anything that must stand for hours, the core is typically composed of ingredients with a high concentration of saturated fatty acids and waxes:

- Waxy Coatings: The primary structure often utilizes compound coatings—the same "fake" chocolate discussed in Chapter 17. By replacing temperamental cocoa butter with fractionated palm kernel oil or lauric fats, prop masters create a material that mimics the look of chocolate but possesses a much higher melting point. These fats have a rigid crystalline structure that remains stable at temperatures up to 55°C (130°F).
- Color and Texture: Carob powder (for color) is mixed with food-grade paraffin wax or beeswax (for texture and rigidity) and titanium dioxide (for opacity). This blend is stable, durable, and provides the dark, matte base required for lighting.

Actor-Grade Stunt Chocolate (The Bite)

When the actor must bite or break the prop, the material needs to be chemically safe and pliable enough to create a realistic tooth mark without shattering.

- The Pliable Core: The internal structure is often a dense paste of powdered sugar, corn syrup, and vegetable shortening. This mixture is then colored with a dark cocoa powder. It holds a tooth impression perfectly for continuity shots (the mark doesn't fade) but provides no waxy resistance.
- The Quick-Set Shell: The outer shell, visible to the camera, must still snap. This is achieved by coating the prop in a thin layer of high-ratio shortening blended with specialized cocoa butter replacers (CBRs) designed for instant, high-temperature crystallization.

THE RESULTING Stunt Chocolate is a chemical marvel—it is structurally rigid, optically appealing, and utterly flavorless. It is engineered to defy the very purpose of chocolate.

~

A stylist crafts durable chocolate props that withstand heat and handling. These engineered fakes replace real chocolate during long film shoots.

THE VISCOSITY PROBLEM: The Hydraulics of the Pour

The cinematographer's desire for the perfect, mesmerizing flow of liquid chocolate—the "curtain of silk" seen in high-speed commercials—is a struggle against the physics of non-Newtonian fluids.

Real melted chocolate is a Bingham plastic. It has a yield stress, meaning it must be pushed with a certain force before it begins to flow, and its viscosity changes with temperature and shear rate (how fast it's stirred). This results in a flow that is often lumpy, unpredictable, and separates under the high-speed cameras.

To create the perfect cinematic pour, stylists rely on hydrocolloids and specialized thickeners that provide high viscosity without the stickiness or separation of cocoa butter.

- Methylcellulose and Xanthan Gum: These compounds (commonly used in food science for their gelling properties) are mixed with food coloring, titanium dioxide, and a tiny amount of natural cocoa powder. The mixture achieves a smooth, heavy, high-surface-tension flow that allows the liquid to fold over itself in heavy, unbroken ribbons without splashing. This creates the visual implication of density and richness.
- Glycerin and Silicone: For fluid dynamics shots where the liquid is meant to look *perpetually* flowing (such as a chocolate fountain), prop masters often circulate mixtures of silicone, acrylic paint, or colored industrial oil. This synthetic sludge possesses a controllable flow rate and is completely impervious to spoilage or temperature, providing a predictable, controllable fluid that behaves exactly how the director wants it to behave.

This fluid engineering is critical because the audience's subconscious links the viscosity of the pour to the richness of the product. A thick, slow, even pour signals high-quality cocoa butter and high caloric density—a visual promise of opulence.

Technicians create a flawless chocolate ribbon using specialized thickeners. The smooth pour seen in ads is often a scientific fabrication.

THE AUDITORY DECEPTION

If the visual cue confirms the chocolate's richness, the auditory cue confirms its freshness and quality. The high-frequency snap of the chocolate bar is an auditory signal that registers in the brain as rigidity, indicating a proper temper and structural integrity.

THE ACOUSTIC PHYSICS of the Snap

Capturing the actual sound of a human biting into chocolate is notoriously difficult. The acoustics of the human mouth dampen the noise, resulting in a low-frequency, wet, squishy sound that is unappealing to the audience. To solve this, sound designers (Foley artists) must invent a sound that triggers the brain's expectation of crispness.

The ideal snap sound for cinematic chocolate is a sharp, high-frequency crack, typically in the 2,000–4,000 Hertz (2-4 kHz) range. This specific acoustic profile is what the brain associates with the successful fracture of a perfectly stable crystalline structure—the structure that makes food fresh and crisp.

- The Celery Hack: The most famous trick utilizes frozen vegetables. Snapping a frozen stalk of celery creates a sharp, jagged crack because the frozen water expands, tensioning the cellulose fibers until they shatter. This acoustic profile mimics the fracture of a perfect cocoa butter lattice almost exactly.
- The Crunch: For the sound of biting into a dense cluster (like a chocolate-covered nut or brittle), Foley artists might crush eggshells wrapped in a damp chamois cloth (the cloth muffles the low-frequency eggshell crunch but preserves the high-frequency brittle crack) or bite into dry pasta and nuts separately, mixing the sounds in post-production.
- The Squelch: For the deep, satisfying squish of a dense ganache center, Foley artists often record the sound of squeezing a tub of thick hand cream or soft mud, which conveys density and moisture better than a microphone pointed at an actual truffle.

THESE INVENTED sounds bypass the reality of the food and deliver an auditory illusion of perfection directly to the viewer's sensory cortex.

A Foley artist breaks celery to mimic the crisp snap of chocolate. Sound design substitutes real chocolate noise with more reliable stand-ins.

THE MULTI-LAYERED SOUNDSCAPE of Savoring

A single bite of chocolate in a film or commercial is a symphony of at least four recorded tracks:

1. The Approach: (Sound Design) The crisp, high-frequency snap (celery).
2. The Contact: (Sound Design) The soft, bass-heavy sound of the chocolate being crushed (recorded walnuts or dry pasta).
3. The Melt/Moisture: (Foley) The wet, squelching sound of the tongue and palate (recording of the Foley artist slowly sucking on ice or squeezing a sponge).
4. The Reaction: (Dialogue Track) The actor's sigh or approving murmur.

THIS MULTI-LAYERED APPROACH ensures that even the unconscious process of *savoring* is amplified and dramatized, creating an irresistible auditory signal of satisfaction and richness.

THE MIRROR NEURON Response

The most potent tool in cinematic chocolate is its use as a psychological device. It is a symbol of forbidden pleasure, excess, and primal appetite.

The intensity of craving experienced by the audience is rooted in the Mirror Neuron system. When a camera focuses on an actor slowly and sensually savoring a bite of chocolate, the neurons in the viewer's brain that would fire if *they* were performing that action also fire. This subconscious mirroring triggers the viewer's own salivary glands and jaw muscles, creating a real, physical sensation of hunger and desire.

The scene's effectiveness is directly proportional to the actor's commitment to the sensory illusion. The moment of savoring is often extended in slow motion, focusing intensely on the actor's closed eyes, the slight dilation of their pupils (a genuine sign of pleasure), and the slow dissolution of the prop in their mouth. This technical amplification forces the viewer to mirror the pleasure, translating the visual act into a visceral craving.

COLOR SCIENCE and the Warmth Bias

Color grading, the final post-production process, is used to introduce an emotional bias that enhances appetite.

- Warmth and Safety: Colorists deliberately increase the color temperature of the footage, boosting the reds, yellows, and ambers. In neuroscience, these warm colors are associated with physical comfort, safety (fire/sun), and ripeness. This creates a warmth bias where the brain associates the image of the chocolate with a physical feeling of coziness and security.
- The Kelvin Shift: The chocolate itself is often shifted from a neutral 5500K (daylight white) toward the warm end (3200K–

4000K, or golden light). This shift ensures that the chocolate reads as *richly caramelized* and *perfectly roasted* rather than raw or dull.

The visual language of craving, therefore, is engineered to bypass cultural taste preferences and appeal directly to the reptilian brain's desire for warmth and caloric density.

Chocolate as a Plot Device

In cinema, chocolate is rarely just a snack; it is often a moral or spiritual metaphor.

- Sin and Gluttony: In films like *Matilda* (where the cake is a weapon) or *Se7en* (where a gluttonous character is force-fed), chocolate represents unchecked desire and moral failure. The camera focuses on the *excess*—the overwhelming density, the sticky mess—forcing the viewer's appetite to transition from desire into disgust.
- Redemption and Passion: In *Chocolat*, the confectionery shop serves as a spiritual anchor, challenging the cold piety of the town. The chocolate's texture—silky, smooth, often spiced— symbolizes Vianne's passion and the town's buried emotional life. The visual language of the shop (bathed in golden light, contrasting with the town

's cold blue) is designed to signal the warmth of sensual indulgence.

The technical brilliance of the prop is thus required to uphold a significant narrative weight. The non-melting cake must endure an hour of filming to carry the entire moral struggle of the character.

The Ethics of Illusion

The use of chemically engineered props raises a complicated ethical question for the audience. Is it deceptive to make food look better than it is?

For the food industry, this practice is a fundamental part of the cinematic contract. The director's job is not to serve the viewer a meal, but to sell them an idea. The chocolate on screen is a Platonic ideal—an object of flawless perfection that can only exist in the mind and on the screen, not in the real world.

The ultimate irony of cinematic chocolate is that the more appetizing it appears, the more inedible it is. The high-gloss sheen is often permanent; the perfect snap is a trick of acoustics; and the sublime melt is a lie of chemical engineering. The truth of the truffle is that it must be hard, tasteless, and chemically resilient to convince the human psyche that it is soft, delicious, and fragile.

The Foley artist's truffle is a monument to our own sensory suggestibility—a reminder that in the search for pleasure, our eyes and ears are often more easily convinced than our tongue.

25

THE CHOCOLATE LANGUAGE: LINGUISTICS, MYTH, AND ETYMOLOGY

E*very chocolate lover knows the bliss of tasting a silky square of dark cacao or sipping a rich cup of cocoa. But hidden in that everyday indulgence is a lexicon of stories as layered and rich as a bonbon assortment. The language surrounding chocolate—its very name, its terminology, even the mythical tales tied to its words—reveals a history of kings and gods, of global journeys and happy accidents. From ancient temples to modern cafes, chocolate's vocabulary tells a story about human civilization itself. In this long-form exploration, we'll unwrap the origins of chocolate's most delicious words, tracing how linguistics and legend have flavored the way we talk about our favorite treat.*

Ancient Roots: Cacao in Myth and Language

Long before "chocolate" became a word on anyone's lips, there was *cacao*. The cacao tree is native to the tropical Americas, and by 3,000 years ago it was already being cultivated by early Mesoamerican civilizations.

The Olmec people of present-day Mexico are often credited as the first to domesticate the cacao plant. We don't know what the Olmec called it, but they passed their cacao cultivation and terminology to those who followed. The Maya, for instance, prized cacao so highly that it became both a luxury crop and a currency.

The Classic Maya word for cacao was recorded as "kakaw" (often written in glyphs as symbols sounding like *ka-ka-wa*), and cacao beans were used as money—literally small change that could buy food or pay tribute. In ancient Maya art, kings are often depicted drinking cacao, and their ceramic drinking vessels were inscribed with hieroglyphs declaring them to be for *kakaw*. In other words, chocolate had its own language in the Maya world, written right onto royal cups.

Cacao held deep mythic significance. The Maya offered cacao in rituals and saw the cacao pod as symbolically connected to the human heart, with the cacao drink's color linked to blood in sacrificial ceremonies.

In Mayan tradition, chocolate was more than food—it was communion. In fact, one Mayan Quiché expression, *chokola'j*, means "to drink chocolate together." It's a beautiful notion that the very act of sharing a chocolate drink gave rise to a word about community and togetherness. Some scholars have mused that this could even be an origin of the word "chocolate" itself, as we'll soon explore. Among the Aztecs of Central Mexico, who inherited the love of cacao from earlier cultures, chocolate was likewise dubbed the "drink of nobles" and was strictly an elite affair.

Aztec warriors, priests, and emperors consumed a bitter, spiced cacao beverage known for its invigorating effect. By the time the Aztec Empire flourished in the 15th century, cacao beans were flowing in from tribute-paying regions, filling imperial storehouses alongside gold and jewels.

THE GLYPH in the Stone

The linguistic detective story of chocolate begins not with a spoken word, but with a picture. Epigraphers decoding Classic Maya script found a recurring glyph on ceramic vessels: a fish-like head (the sound "ka") followed by a comb-like fin (the sound "wa"). When repeated, it read *ka-ka-wa*.

This linguistic evidence changed our understanding of history. It proved that the word *cacao* was not an Aztec invention, but a loan-word inherited from the Maya, who likely borrowed it from the even older Mixe-Zoquean languages of the Olmecs (dating back to 1000 BCE).

This endurance is remarkable. Empires rose and fell, cities were burned and abandoned, but the phonemes *ka-ka-wa* survived virtually unchanged for three millennia. It is one of the oldest continuously spoken words in the Americas. When you say "cacao" today, you are speaking a ghost language, uttering the exact syllables that an Olmec farmer used to describe his harvest three thousand years ago.

From "Xocolatl" to Chocolate

The very word *chocolate* is a linguistic confection of its own—a blend of sounds and cultures that crossed oceans. English *chocolate* comes from Spanish *chocolate*, which in turn was born during the Spanish conquest of the Americas in the 1500s. But how did the Spanish coin that word? The answer is a bit complicated, and as bitter-sweet as chocolate itself.

For many years, a charming story circulated that *chocolate* comes from the Aztec/Nahuatl word "xocolatl," often said to mean "bitter water" (from *xococ*, sour or bitter, and *atl*, water). This explanation certainly *sounds* plausible: the Aztec chocolate drink was bitter, and it was essentially a flavored water of cacao. The idea took hold so firmly that you'll still find it in books and even the names of trendy chocolate shops.

However, modern linguists and historians have peeled back the layers of this tale and found that "xocolatl" might be more myth than fact. In Nahuatl sources from the time of the Spanish conquest, a word like xocolatl is conspicuously absent. The word xococ in Nahuatl actually means sour, not bitter, and was used to describe fermented maize gruels. Furthermore, the Aztec elite preferred their drink sweet or spicy, not sour. So, if the Aztecs didn't call their chocolate "bitter water," where did the word *chocolate* really come from?

The evidence suggests the Aztec word for the cherished cacao drink was "cacahuatl," literally "cacao water." This term is clearly related to *cacao* (the bean) plus *atl* (water). It rolls off the tongue similarly to many other Nahuatl words for beverages (for example, *atole* is a corn gruel, and *pulque* was octli atl, the agave drink).

The Spanish, in their early encounters, used *cacahuatl* or just *cacao* to refer to the beverage. But here they encountered a linguistic quirk: in Spanish, *caca* is a crude word for feces. Understandably, Spanish colonizers were a bit uncomfortable marketing a delectable new drink with a name that began with "caca." One theory proposes that this vulgar coincidence spurred a search for an alternative name.

Enter the mingling of languages: The Spanish had allies and subjects among various indigenous peoples, including the Maya further south. The Maya often consumed their cacao hot, unlike the Aztecs who usually drank it cold. In the Mayan languages, one word for hot is *chokol*.

According to a theory popularized by scholars Sophie and Michael Coe, the Spanish cleverly combined the Maya term *chokol* (hot) with the Nahuatl *atl* (water) to forge a new hybrid word: "chocolatl." In essence, they may have created a name that meant "hot water" to describe the hot chocolate they grew fond of, sidestepping the awkward *caca*. This mixed-linguistic origin story is compelling because it mirrors the mixed cultural reality of colonial Mexico: Spanish conquerors adopting an indigenous drink, modifying it to their tastes (adding sugar and spices, serving it warm), and even naming it through a fusion of indigenous languages. It's a delicious piece of historical wordplay: *chocolate* as a product of cross-cultural blending, just like the drink itself.

Another intriguing possibility emerges from the Nahuatl language alone. Some linguists have pointed out that many modern dialects of Nahuatl (and related languages) use words like *chikolatl* or *chokolaj* for chocolate, suggesting the original Nahuatl term might have had a "ch" sound instead of "x."

Why would that be? Nahuatl has a word *chicoli* (or *chikolli*), referring to the wooden stirring stick—the ancestor of the *molinillo*—used to froth the drink. A recent hypothesis posits that the original term could have been "chicolatl," meaning "stirred drink" or "beaten drink," highlighting the distinctive preparation of chocolate with a foaming stick.

Imagine an Aztec chocolatier whisking the cacao mixture to a foam and naming the concoction after the very action that made it delicious. This theory aligns with the deep cultural reverence for the drink's frothy head, which persisted for centuries. If *chicolatl* was indeed the word, it would have easily been heard by Spanish ears as the familiar-sounding *chocolatl*, leading to the Spanish *chocolate*.

In truth, we may never pinpoint the exact moment or mechanism by which *chocolatl* became the go-to term in New Spain (colonial Mexico). It could be the Spanish heard a version with *ch* from some dialect or neighboring language. Or they might have engineered it themselves from pieces of words, as the Coes argue. What we do know is that by the late 1500s, Spaniards in Mexico were calling the drink "chocolate," and they carried this word back to Europe along with shipments of cacao.

The first European references to *chocolate* as a drink appear in the 16th century, and by the 17th century *chocolate* was a fashionable beverage name in Spanish, Italian, French, and English parlors. The word was exotic but easy enough to say, and it spread even faster than the treat itself. Each language gave it a slight twist—French turned it to *chocolat*, the Italians *cioccolata*, the Germans *Schokolade*. In every tongue, it became synonymous with a little piece of Eden in a cup or on a plate.

The iconography of the Aztec world. Linguists believe the modern word 'chocolate' evolved from the Aztec's Nahuatl language— possibly from *chicolatl*, meaning 'beaten drink,' a reference to the prized foam atop their cacao.

Cacao vs. Cocoa: A Tale of Two Words

While *chocolate* was making its grand tour of Europe, the earlier word *cacao* took a quieter path—and underwent its own transformation. The Spanish word *cacao* came directly from indigenous languages (likely from the Maya or Olmec via Nahuatl *cacahuatl*). It referred to the cacao bean and the raw material used to make chocolate. Early English texts in the 1600s did use the word *cacao* (sometimes spelled *cacoa* or *cacaoa*) when describing the exotic beans from the New World. However, as English speakers became more familiar with the product, a funny thing happened: *cacao* got munged into *cocoa*.

Linguistically, *cocoa* is essentially an English accident. Scholars believe that English traders and writers heard the word *cacao* but transposed the letters (perhaps thinking it was pronounced similarly to *coco* as in coconut).

By the late 17th century, English texts were routinely spelling it *cocoa*. The two vowels in the middle flipped places, and somehow this misspelling stuck. It's a bit ironic: a whole industry today distinguishes between *cacao* (usually referring to the raw bean or minimally processed nibs) and *cocoa* (often meaning the processed powder or mass-produced products). But etymologically, they are the same word—*cocoa* is just *cacao* in a quirky mirror. English is one of the few languages that made this switch; most others kept a form of *cacao*.

The persistence of *cocoa* in English might also be because it was easier to say and already vaguely familiar (the word *coco* in Spanish, meaning coconut, was known, and *cocoa* sounds warm and cozy). By the time of Samuel Johnson's 1755 dictionary, "Cocoa" was defined as the dried seed of the cacao tree used to make chocolate.

Interestingly, as knowledge of chocolate grew, the scientific naming of the plant—*Theobroma cacao*—enshrined its divine reputation in Latin, ensuring the plant's mythic status would survive the transition into the age of science.

And *cacao* was enshrined in science as the species name, ensuring that term would never disappear completely. In recent years, especially among artisanal chocolate makers and nutrition circles, there's been a small renaissance of using 'cacao' to refer to the agricultural crop and the raw bean, distinguishing it from 'cocoa,' which implies the processed powder. This linguistic shift reclaims the original word from which the industry sprang.

So next time you ponder buying "cacao nibs" instead of "cocoa nibs," remember: you're really circling back to a 3,000-year-old term, reconnecting with the Olmec, Maya, and Aztec who first gave us this gift.

===

SPEAKING CHOCOLATE: A PRONUNCIATION KEY

Don't just eat it; say it right.

- **Xocolatl (Sho-ko-la-tl):** The ancient Nahuatl ancestor of the word. Note the "sh" sound at the start.
- **Cacahuatl (Ka-ka-watl):** The Aztec word for "cacao water."
- **Gianduja (Jan-doo-yah):** The Italian hazelnut-chocolate paste. The "G" is soft, like "geometry."
- **Couverture (Koo-ver-chure):** High-fat professional chocolate used for coating. French for "blanket" or "covering."
- **Theobroma (Theo-bro-ma):** Greek for "Food of the Gods."

===

A WORLD of Chocolate Words

As chocolate culture blossomed worldwide, it brought forth a bouquet of new terms, each with its own story. The *language of chocolate* expanded beyond the basics of *cacao* and *chocolate* to include the processes, people, and confections that define our experience of this treat. Understanding these terms is like learning the dialect of a chocolate lover. Let's sample a few of the most flavorful entries in the chocolate lexicon:

- Chocolatier – This French-origin word literally means a person who makes or sells chocolate (*chocolat*, plus the *-ier* suffix for a profession). It entered English in the early 20th century as fine European-style chocolate making took hold. To call someone a chocolatier evokes images of a craftsman, a bit of Old World artistry behind the candy counter. The rise of the *chocolatier* reflects how chocolate shifted from a homemade drink or apothecary's mixture into a gourmet art.

- Conching – Smooth chocolate as we know it today owes its texture to a process called conching, invented in 1879 by Swiss chocolatier Rudolph Lindt. The word *conch* comes from the Spanish *concha*, meaning shell. Lindt's innovation wasn't just mechanical; it was linguistic. The machine's granite bed was curved like a giant seashell, inspiring the name conche (Spanish for shell). While the machine revolutionized texture, the name immortalized the vessel shape itself, turning a marine noun into a culinary verb. Thus, a term from the ocean was repurposed into chocolate language. If you ever see "conched for 72 hours" on a chocolate label, now you know the poetic origin of that term.

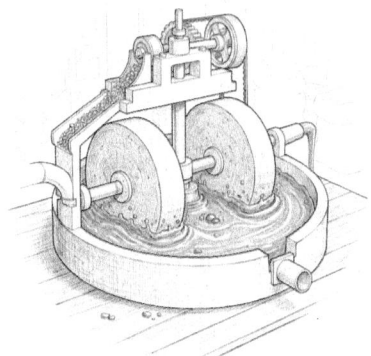

Heavy granite wheels rotate steadily within the melanger, grinding and aerating the warm chocolate liquor to refine its texture and develop complex flavors.

- Temper – To make a chocolate bar snappy and shiny, chocolatiers must temper the chocolate, carefully controlling its temperature to arrange the cocoa butter crystals. The term *temper* here is just a common English word meaning to moderate or bring into balance (the same root as "temperament"). While not exotic in origin, it's an old word that found new significance in the chocolate world. When you hear of "tempered chocolate," it's all about the language of chemistry meeting culinary craft—balancing something's "temper" to make it stable.

- Criollo, Forastero, Trinitario – These are the names of the primary varieties of cacao beans, and they carry a legacy of colonial history. *Criollo* is Spanish for "native" or "of the colony" (literally "Creole"), and in cacao it refers to the prized ancient varieties first cultivated in Central America. True criollo cacao is delicate, flavorful, and was the original chocolate of kings, but it's finicky to grow. *Forastero* means "foreigner" or "outsider" in Spanish, and it was the name given to hardier cacao that came from "elsewhere" – in practice, the Amazon basin. Forastero became the bulk crop of African and Brazilian plantations (it's more robust and higher-yield, but generally less nuanced in flavor). When a natural hybrid of Criollo and Forastero emerged on the island of Trinidad in the 18th century (after a storm decimated criollo orchards and new plantings crossed with imported forastero), it was dubbed *Trinitario* after its island of origin. These terms reflect how European colonizers categorized cacao much like people – natives, foreigners, and mixed – a little linguistic capsule of New World history. To this day, chocolate experts speak of criollo beans in reverent tones, and the very words hint at old tales of exploration and agriculture.

- Praline – Today a *praline* might mean a filled chocolate bonbon in Belgium, a caramelized nut in France, or a creamy pecan patty in New Orleans. But the word's origin is distinctly aristocratic. In 17th-century France, the personal chef of a certain Marshal Du Plessis-Praslin invented a crunchy almond-and-caramel sweet. He named the confection for his patron, the Marshal – hence *praline* (originally *praslin*). The recipe evolved and spread; French settlers took it to Louisiana, where pecans replaced almonds and cream was added, creating the Southern praline. Meanwhile, in Belgium, *praline* came to mean those elegant filled chocolates (since one of the first Belgian chocolate makers, Jean Neuhaus, adopted the term for his filled bonbons in 1912). What a journey for a word: from a nobleman's kitchen through continents and centuries, now broadly associated with chocolate indulgence in various forms.

- Ganache – Silky, rich chocolate ganache (that mixture of chocolate and cream at the heart of truffles and cakes) has an origin story as smooth as its texture. Legend holds that around the 1850s, a young apprentice in a Parisian pâtisserie accidentally spilled scalding cream into a vat of precious chocolate. His furious master shouted "Ganache!"—a colloquial insult meaning "idiot" or "blockhead." Facing the hot mess, the chefs found that the chocolate and cream, instead of ruining, had emulsified into a glossy, velvety mixture. What began as a mistake became a cornerstone of dessert craft. In a wry twist, the very word for "fool" became the name of a genius invention. Next time you bite into a chocolate truffle and the center melts in your mouth, you're tasting a happy accident immortalized in language.

- Truffle – Speaking of truffles, why do we call those chocolate spheres by the name of a prized fungus dug up by pigs in the forest? The answer lies in appearance. Sometime in the late 1800s or early 1900s, as confectioners were experimenting with rolling ganache into bite-sized balls, someone had the idea to dust them in cocoa powder (or sometimes ground nuts). The result was a lump of chocolate that looked strikingly like a dirt-covered truffle mushroom. The whimsical name stuck. A simple metaphor—*it looks like a truffle, let's call it a truffle!*—gave us a word that now instantly means "decadent chocolate ball" to anyone with a sweet tooth. The chocolate truffle's name is a tiny tribute to the power of culinary imagination: even language is an ingredient in creating allure.

Decadent truffles dusted with cocoa powder

- Gianduja – This term may be less familiar unless you're a Nutella fan or an Italian chocolate aficionado. Gianduja (or gianduia) is a blend of chocolate and hazelnut paste, invented in the Piedmont region of Italy during the Napoleonic era. With British blockades causing cocoa shortages, resourceful chocolatiers in Turin extended their precious chocolate supply by mixing it with finely ground local hazelnuts, creating a delicious new concoction. They named it after Gianduja, a jovial masked character in Piedmontese carnival folk theater who represented the archetypal local peasant. Legend has it that during a Carnival celebration around 1865, chocolate makers distributed hazelnut-chocolate treats wrapped in foil depicting Gianduja's face, cementing the association. Thus, a comedic figure from Italian culture lent his name to a recipe born of hardship but destined for greatness. Today gianduja is revered, proof that even constraints (and a bit of humor) can enrich the language of chocolate.
- Chocoholic, Chocolate Box, and other cultural terms – As chocolate ingrained itself in modern life, new words and idioms sprouted in the vernacular. Coinage of the term chocoholic is often credited to a 1968 headline, playfully combining 'chocolate' and 'alcoholic' (patterned after "alcoholic")—a testament to how consuming chocolate was humorously likened to a delightful dependency. The phrase "like a kid in a candy store" captures chocolate's place in

childhood bliss, while "life is like a box of chocolates – you never know what you're gonna get," a line from Forrest Gump, became a metaphor for life's surprises. In British English, calling something "chocolate-box" (as in "a chocolate-box village") means it's picture-perfect and perhaps a bit too quaint or pretty—an allusion to the idyllic paintings that adorned chocolate boxes in Victorian times. Even love hasn't escaped chocolate's linguistic sway: how many of our expressions of affection, from heart-shaped boxes to chocolate-dipped strawberries, rely on the unspoken language of chocolate to convey sweetness?

===

THE PHRASEBOOK: HOW TO ORDER LOCALLY
Don't ask for "Hot Cocoa." Ask for the legend.

- **In Paris:** "Un Chocolat Chaud l'Africain, s'il vous plaît." (The super-thick, almost pudding-like dark chocolate served at Angelina).
- **In Turin:** "Un Bicerin, per favore." (A layered glass of espresso, hot chocolate, and cold milk foam).
- **In Oaxaca:** "Un Chocolate de Agua, por favor." (The traditional pre-Hispanic preparation: water-based, spiced, and frothy).
- **In Vienna:** "Eine Heiße Schokolade mit Schlag, bitte." (Hot chocolate with a mountain of whipped cream).

===

MYTHS, Metaphors, and the Ongoing Story
Tracing the linguistics and lore of chocolate words shows us how tightly language, culture, and beloved foods interweave. Each term carries echoes of discovery, conquest, innovation, and joy. When we say

the word *chocolate* today, we invoke ancient Mesoamerican tongues and the voices of Spanish conquerors; we summon up myths of gods and the experiments of chefs; we hint at bitterness and sweetness all at once. Few foods have a vocabulary so romantic and storied.

The mythic origins behind chocolate's words continue to enchant us. We still refer to chocolate as a gift from the gods (just check any Valentine's marketing), an almost sacred indulgence. We tell and retell the legend of Quetzalcóatl's divine generosity and perhaps feel a tiny connection to those ancient rituals when we savor a cup of hot cocoa on a cold night.

The terminology of chocolate-making, from conching to tempering, reminds us that human ingenuity transformed a bitter seed into a confectionary art, and that each innovation left its mark in language. The fact that a slip of the hand gave us *ganache*, or that an aristocrat's name lives on in *praline*, adds a sense of whimsy and humanity to the candy we love.

What's also striking is how chocolate's language spans the globe. It is inherently multicultural: *cacao* might hail from the Olmec or Maya, *chocolate* from a Nahuatl-Maya-Spanish mashup, *gianduja* from Italian lore, *Schokolade* and *chocolat* from European adaptations, and so on. Yet all these words center on the same essence—the same cherished substance that conquers all hearts. In learning the etymology of chocolate terms, we end up learning a little world history and anthropology along the way. It's a gentle reminder that simple pleasures often hide rich complexities.

And the story isn't over. As chocolate continues to evolve in our era—from single-origin craft bars to sustainably traded cacao—new phrases and concepts join the lexicon: *bean-to-bar*, *fair trade*, *cocoa percentage*, *grand cru chocolate*. The language of chocolate grows just like a living tree, sprouting new expressions with each generation of chocolate lovers and makers. Who knows what new chocolate words await us in the future? Perhaps a century from now, linguists will marvel at how *chocoholic* or *bean-to-bar* entered common speech.

In the end, the "chocolate language" is one of indulgence and imagination. It's the shared vocabulary that lets us praise and savor one of life's great delights. Next time you enjoy a piece of chocolate, consider the words that melt alongside it on your tongue. From *kakaw* whispered in ancient prayers to *chocolate* exclaimed in delight today, these words are part of the flavor. The language of chocolate is yet another reason why this food is special—every bite is a taste of history, myth, and linguistic artistry. And that is truly something to savor.

PART V

POWER, SCANDAL, ECONOMICS,
AND THE UNDERGROUND WORLD

26

THE HEIRLOOM HUNTERS: THE RACE TO SAVE THE WORLD'S RAREST CACAO

T he flight from Quito was delayed, giving the customs officers extra time. In the luggage screening room, a suitcase sat open on a metal table. Inside, tucked between layers of muddy trekking clothes and field notebooks, were six football-shaped pods wrapped in damp newspaper. To the untrained eye, they looked like spoiling fruit. To the botanist standing nervously nearby, they were the Holy Grail.

These weren't just snacks for the flight; they were genetic samples of a rare cacao variety harvested from a remote valley days earlier—a variety thought to be extinct for a century. The botanist, funded by a European chocolate conglomerate, insisted they were for academic study. The officials saw it differently: this was an act of biopiracy—an attempt to smuggle out a national treasure that could be cloned, patented, and monetized thousands of miles away, cutting the country of origin out of the loop forever.

THIS TENSE STANDOFF is the front line of a modern botanical war. While the world consumes millions of tons of industrial chocolate annually, a shadow race is underway to control the genetic future of the crop. From the cloud forests of Peru to the high-tech nurseries of Southeast Asia, "heirloom hunters" are scouring the earth for the last surviving strands of legendary cacao. It is a story where adventure meets avarice, and where a single twig can be worth a fortune.

THE VILLAIN: The Rise of CCN-51

To understand the intensity of this hunt, one must first understand the enemy. For the last century, the global chocolate industry has been fighting a war against nature, and for a long time, flavor was the casualty.

In the 1960s, a brilliant but pragmatic Ecuadorian agronomist named Homero Castro set out to save the cacao industry from fungal blight. He successfully cross-bred several strains to create a "super-tree"—a hybrid that was resistant to disease, grew fast, and produced massive, heavy pods packed with fat-rich beans. He named it Colección Castro Naranjal 51, or CCN-51.

Agronomically, it was a miracle. It saved farmers from ruin. But gastronomically, it was a disaster. Chocolate makers found that CCN-51 lacked the floral, nutty, and fruity nuances of traditional cacao. In fact, unfermented, it tasted acidic and flat; some experts famously described its flavor profile as highly astringent, chemically bitter, and reminiscent of "acidic dirt."Yet, because it was so profitable, CCN-51 conquered the tropics. It swept through Ecuador, replacing ancient groves of fine-flavor trees with endless rows of this industrial workhorse.

By the year 2000, experts feared that the "Grand Crus" of cacao— ancient lineages like Pure Nacional and Porcelana—had been cross-pollinated into oblivion.

To understand the magnitude of this loss, one must visualize the family tree of cacao. At the trunk is the ancient Amazonian ancestor. One major branch, the Forastero, grew thick and hardy, spreading across the lower Amazon and eventually dominating Africa; it is the robust, albeit often bitter, workhorse of the world. A delicate, slender branch split off early and migrated north to Central America: the Criollo. This is the 'Prince of Cacao'—frail, prone to disease, but possessed of an exquisite, complex flavor profile lacking in bitterness. Later, on the island of Trinidad, these two estranged branches reunited to create the Trinitario, a natural hybrid combining Forastero's strength with Criollo's finesse.

Rare, ancient lineages still survive in isolated pockets of the Americas, forming the genetic foundation for today's fine-flavor cacao. The world was awash in industrial chocolate, but it was losing its soul. This genetic erosion birthed a new generation of Heirloom Hunters. Walking in the muddy footsteps of F.J. Pound—the agronomist whose perilous 1930s expeditions were chronicled in Chapter 12—this modern ragtag group of botanists and adventurers is dedicated to finding the survivors before they disappear forever.

===

FLAVOR POLICE: HOW TO SPOT "CLONE" CACAO

Is your expensive bar actually made from cheap CCN-51? Taste for these flaws.

The "Acidic Dirt" Test: Heirloom cacao is acidic like fruit (citrus, berry). CCN-51 is acidic like vinegar or chemicals. If the acidity hurts the back of your throat, it is likely a clone.

The Astringency: High-yield clones often lack fat content. If the chocolate sucks the moisture out of your mouth (high astringency) and lacks a long finish, it is likely industrial filler.

The "Cardboard" Note: Fine cacao lingers. Clone cacao often vanishes quickly, leaving a flat, paper-like aftertaste.

===

THE MIRACLE of the Marañón Canyon

No discovery illustrates the stakes better than the resurrection of Pure Nacional, a variety of cacao that was essentially the lost legend of the chocolate world.

In the 19th century, Ecuador was the world's premier source of fine chocolate, thanks to the Nacional bean. It was famous for its "Arriba" flavor—a distinct floral note of orange blossom and lilac that no other bean possessed. But in 1916, a fungal plague known as Witches' Broom swept through the region, decimating the orchards. To save the industry, resistant foreign varieties were introduced, diluting the gene pool. For decades, chocolate historians wrote that Pure Nacional was extinct.

==

THE FAMILY TREE: KNOW YOUR BEANS

Not all cacao is created equal. Here is the genetic hierarchy.

<u>The Ancestor</u>

- Curaray (Amazon Basin): The ancient mother of all cacao.

<u>The Three Main Branches</u>

- Criollo (The Prince):
    - Traits: Fragile, white seeds, low bitterness, complex fruit/floral notes.
    - Famous Offspring: Porcelana, Chuao.
- Forastero (The Workhorse):
    - Traits: Robust, purple seeds, high bitterness, classic "cocoa" flavor.
    - Famous Offspring: Amelonado, CCN-51.
- Trinitario (The Hybrid):
    - Traits: A natural cross of Criollo + Forastero. Combines flavor with hardiness.

<u>The Lost Heirloom</u>

- Nacional (The Ghost):
    - Traits: Native to Ecuador. Famous for "Arriba" floral scent. Thought extinct until 2009.

==

THEN, in 2007, two Americans—Dan Pearson and Brian Horsley—were sourcing bananas and supplies for a mining camp in the remote Marañón Canyon of northern Peru. This canyon is a geographical fortress: surrounded by Andean walls, it has its own microclimate and had been isolated from the rest of the agricultural world for decades.

In the backyard of a local farmer named Don Fortunato, Pearson spotted a strange tree. It was gnarled, old, and bearing pods with a smooth, yellow skin. When they cracked one open, the wet seeds inside weren't the usual purple of industrial cacao. They were pure, porcelain white.

White seeds are the genetic marker of the purest, most delicate cacao—specifically, the mutation associated with the ancient Nacional line. Pearson and Horsley sent leaf samples to the USDA's genetic lab in Maryland for testing. The results stunned the scientific community: this was a 100% genetic match for the ancient Pure Nacional. They named the resulting chocolate "Fortunato No. 4" in honor of the farmer, giving the world a taste of a ghost. It was a population that had survived in isolation at the foot of the Andes for nearly a century, shielded by the canyon walls from the blights and hybridizations that destroyed its cousins in Ecuador.

The discovery was a triumph for biodiversity, but it ignited a frenzy. Suddenly, the chocolate world turned its eyes to the Marañón. It proved that "extinct" varieties might still be hiding in the wild, waiting for someone to walk deep enough into the jungle to find them.

Pure Nacional Cacao: The rare, white-seeded pods of the ancient Nacional line, thought to be extinct, rediscovered in a remote Peruvian canyon.

THE WHITE GOLD OF VENEZUELA: Porcelana

While the Nacional was found by chance, other heirlooms are hunted with maps and historical ledgers. In the region south of Lake Maracaibo in Venezuela lies the ancestral home of Porcelana—arguably the most famous and fragile cacao in history.

Porcelana gets its name from the translucent, white appearance of its seeds, which look like unbaked porcelain clay. Unlike robust industrial beans, Porcelana trees are frail. They are prone to disease and produce few pods. But the chocolate they yield is extraordinary: incredibly smooth, with notes of cream, strawberries, and toasted bread, and almost no bitterness.

For centuries, European kings paid premiums to secure the Porcelana harvest. But the oil boom in Venezuela and the spread of heartier hybrids pushed Porcelana to the brink. By the 1990s, it existed mostly in research stations.

Recently, a quiet movement of Venezuelan agronomists and Italian chocolatiers (notably the company Amedei, and later others) began a project to rehabilitate the Porcelana. They didn't just buy beans; they funded the restoration of the genetic stock. It was a race against time and politics. Working in a region often unstable due to economic crisis, these hunters had to convince farmers that growing a low-yield, high-maintenance tree was worth it.

They succeeded by decoupling the price of Porcelana from the commodity market, paying farmers nearly ten times the going rate for bulk cocoa. Today, a bar of pure Porcelana is one of the most expensive chocolates on earth—often fetching over $20 for a 50-gram bar—a testament to the fact that flavor, when rare enough, becomes a luxury asset.

BIOPIRACY: The Shadow Economy of Seeds

The race to find these trees has a dark side. In the age of empire, plant hunters like Sir Hans Sloane or Robert Fortune openly took seeds from colonies to build industries elsewhere (rubber from Brazil to Asia, tea from China to India). Today, however, nations assert "genetic sovereignty." International treaties like the Nagoya Protocol dictate that genetic resources belong to the country of origin, and any use of them must come with profit-sharing agreements.

But the law stops at the border, and enforcement is difficult in the jungle. This has given rise to a modern form of smuggling. "Crop scouts" working for private interests reportedly tour remote villages in Latin America and West Africa. They aren't looking to buy tons of beans; they are looking for "budwood"—small branches that can be grafted onto rootstock.

A single branch, wrapped in moist cotton and slipped into a backpack, is all it takes. Once smuggled out, that branch can be taken to a private greenhouse in a country with laxer regulations. Through grafting and propagation, that single stolen branch can be multiplied into an orchard of thousands of trees within a few years. The result? A company could release a "Single Origin Ecuador" chocolate bar grown entirely in a greenhouse in Southeast Asia, with no money returning to the Ecuadorian farmers who stewarded that variety for generations.

This fear was crystalized by the Cupuaçu Affair in the early 2000s. As detailed in Chapter 11, a Japanese company attempted to patent the Cupuaçu fruit, effectively trying to trademark a food source indigenous to the Amazon. The resulting "Cupuaçu is Ours" campaign overturned the patents, but the lesson stuck: if you don't protect your plants, someone else will try to own them.

The Guardians: Conservation vs. Commerce

Caught in the crossfire of this genetic arms race are the indigenous communities and smallholder farmers who have lived with these trees for centuries. For them, cacao is not just a genetic asset; it is an ancestor.

In the Beni department of Bolivia, indigenous collectors harvest "wild cacao islands"—natural groves that grow without human intervention in the Amazon floodplains. These beans are tiny, about half the size of commercial beans, and difficult to process. But they possess flavors of wild honey and herbs that cannot be replicated in a farm setting. In Peru, the Awajún people cultivate "grandfathers"—massive, old-growth cacao trees in their forest gardens that tower forty feet high.

The **Cupuaçu Fruit**: A cousin of cacao, this Amazonian fruit
became the center of a major international controversy when a
foreign company attempted to patent it, sparking a successful
Brazilian campaign to protect its indigenous ownership.

These communities are the true guardians of diversity. While corporate hunters seek specific traits to extract and clone, these farmers
protect the entire ecosystem. They know that the flavor doesn't just come
from the DNA; it comes from the soil, the shade trees, and the specific
fermentation rituals passed down by their elders.

Conservation groups are now racing to support these communities
before the biopirates or the loggers get there. Initiatives like the Heirloom Cacao Preservation Fund work to genetically map these trees in
situ (in their original place), giving the farmers certification and market
access so they can earn a living by keeping the trees standing.

The Taste of a Survivor

The era of the Heirloom Hunter is far from over. As climate change
threatens conventional crops, the search for wild, resilient, and flavorful
genes is accelerating. Every unmapped valley in the Amazon might hold
the next great chocolate discovery—or the next great legal battle.

For the chocolate lover, this adds a layer of profound depth to the tasting experience. When you unwrap a bar labeled "Wild Beni," "Pure Nacional," or "Chuao," you are not just tasting a confection. You are tasting a survivor. You are tasting a genetic line that endured blights and deforestation, that was hidden by geography or protected by a village, and that may have been the subject of a high-stakes international tug-of-war.

It is a flavor that reminds us that the most precious things in the world cannot be manufactured; they can only be found, and if we are not careful, lost.

27

THE BITTER CODE:
ESPIONAGE, CIPHERS, AND
SECRET COMMUNICATION

I n a dimly lit London salon in the 1700s, the air is rich with the scent of hot chocolate and candle smoke. Gentlemen huddle in a corner, whispering treason. Fast forward to World War II, and a young codebreaker at Bletchley Park scribbles furiously on a chocolate bar wrapper, racing to decode a Nazi message. Throughout history, chocolate has been more than a sweet treat or luxury indulgence – it's been an accomplice in espionage, a cover for clandestine plots, and even a weapon in disguise. This is the little-known story of how a simple cup of cacao became entwined with secret messages and cryptographic breakthroughs, a tale where Sherlock Holmes meets The Imitation Game, but edible.

Cacao Couriers and Colonial Secrets

Our journey begins in the age of empires. In the 16th and 17th centuries, chocolate was a *secret* the Spanish Empire tried desperately to keep. After conquistadors brought cocoa beans from the New World, Spain held a monopoly on this exotic product.

For nearly a century, Spain had guarded the preparation of cacao as a state secret, restricting the privilege to nobility and monks. But controlling chocolate meant controlling a lucrative trade and a source of power, and such monopolies rarely last.

But secrets rarely stay buried. By the 1600s, rival European powers and opportunistic smugglers were scheming to get their hands on cacao. Enter the courier networks and merchant spies: agents who realized that a shipment of cacao could double as a stealth messaging service. Sacks of cocoa beans became an ideal cover to hide letters or ciphered documents; after all, who would suspect *mundane cocoa* of concealing treason?

In ports and marketplaces from Veracruz to Seville, barrels labeled *"cacao"* might contain hidden correspondence nestled among the beans. Merchants, pirates, and monks alike learned that a few sheets of parchment could be slipped under a false bottom of a crate or inside a hardened cake of chocolate, safely ferrying secrets across oceans.

==

THE PIRATE WHO BURNED A CHOCOLATE FORTUNE

In 1579, English privateer Sir Francis Drake captured a Spanish ship expecting chests of gold and silver. Instead, his crew found tons of strange, dark beans in the hold. Mistaking the cacao beans for worthless "sheep droppings," the frustrated pirates burned the entire cargo. Little did they know they'd just incinerated a small fortune in chocolate – and helped Spain keep its prized secret a little while longer.

==

These early chapters set the stage for chocolate as a vehicle of secrecy. A simple sack of cocoa could slip past checkpoints better than a satchel of letters marked "Top Secret." Whether tucked in a merchant's caravan or a ship's cargo hold, chocolate became a trusty cloak-and-dagger tool – delicious to consume, and even more useful to conceal.

HOT CHOCOLATE and Hotbeds of Sedition

As chocolate migrated into Europe's elite circles, it found a new role: lubricating the plots and schemes of revolutionaries. Nowhere was this more evident than in the famed chocolate houses of 17th and 18th century London. These were fashionable gentlemen's clubs where the wealthy sipped premium hot chocolate and gossiped – or, just as often, conspired. The brew in their porcelain cups might be sweetened with sugar and cinnamon, but the talk could turn bitter with treason.

As explored in earlier chapters, London's chocolate houses—such as White's, Ozinda's, and The Cocoa Tree—were celebrated for their social exclusivity and high-stakes gambling. But for the intelligence community of the 18th century, these establishments served a darker, more functional purpose: they were the ideal operational cover. In the noise and smoke of the salon, distinct factions claimed different territories—White's for the Tories, St. James's for the Whigs—allowing agents to easily locate their targets. Jacobite rebels and government spies mingled freely in these spaces, their treasonous conversations masked by the clatter of porcelain and the haze of tobacco smoke.

The Cocoa Tree on St. James's Street was not merely a social club; it reportedly housed a physical infrastructure for espionage, including a secret escape tunnel—a "bolt hole"—allowing plotters to flee King Charles II's officers during raids. In this era, a cup of chocolate was the ultimate prop for the undercover agent. It was an innocent luxury that granted access to the most dangerous conversations in the Empire, transforming the chocolate house from a venue of leisure into a nerve center of surveillance and survival.

One could argue that modern intelligence culture – the art of gathering secrets in plain sight – was foreshadowed by those cocoa-fueled meetings. The next time you enjoy a hot chocolate, picture radical ideas and clandestine alliances swirling in the cup – as they often did in eighteenth-century London.

～

London's **Cocoa Tree on St. James's Street:** The luxurious and
seemingly innocent façade of an 18th-century chocolate house,
which doubled as a nerve center for political plotting and
espionage.

HIDDEN MESSAGES AND SMUGGLERS' Tricks

Not all secret chocolate operations happened in grand salons. Some
took place on the high seas and in colonial warehouses, where smugglers and couriers honed crafty methods to hide information inside
chocolate itself. If the previous era was about talking conspiracies over
chocolate, this one was about encoding conspiracies into chocolate.

One clever technique involved using hardened chocolate or cocoa
butter as a physical medium for messages. For example, a courier
carrying an incriminating letter might bury it in a block of pressed
cacao, the kind used to make drinking chocolate. The letter, wrapped in
oilskin, would be shoved into a hollowed-out portion of the solid cocoa
cake, then resealed.

To any inspector, it looked like an ordinary brick of chocolate –
nothing worth confiscating (besides, who would destroy such a luxury
on a hunch?). Once safely delivered, the recipient could melt the cacao
block and extract the hidden note. In an age when wax tablets and
carved ivory were also used to conceal writings, chocolate was just
another ingenious vehicle for *steganography*, the art of secret hiding
places.

===

DIY SPYCRAFT: THE "DEAD DROP" BAR
Hide a secret message inside a solid bar, just like a colonial smuggler.

- The Method:
- The Shell: Pour tempered chocolate into a mold, filling it halfway. Tilt it to coat the sides. Chill until set.
- The Payload: Write a note on small paper. Fold it tight and wrap it in wax paper or foil (to prevent oil absorption). Place it in the center.
- The Seal: Pour fresh melted chocolate over the hidden package to fill the mold. Level it off.
- The Reveal: When the recipient breaks the bar, the "treasure" is revealed inside the solid block.

===

Smugglers, too, found chocolate useful for concealing codes and signals. A sack of cocoa beans might include a few odd items that carried meaning to those in the know – perhaps a uniquely marked bean or a paper with a sequence of cacao trading numbers that actually corresponded to a secret rendezvous date. Some colonial records hint that pirate crews developed simple ciphers based on cocoa cargo counts ("shipments of X beans" as code for amounts of gunpowder or troops). And in the age of high piracy, more than one undercover agent posed as a *cacao trader* to slip in and out of ports undetected. After all, a merchant bargaining over cocoa aroused less suspicion than a diplomat carrying letters.

Chocolate even intersected with religious secrecy and identity. In the Spanish Inquisition era, secret Jews (*crypto-Jews*) living in New Spain would sometimes use chocolate as a kind of cultural code. Records tell of a noblewoman in Mexico who offered a visitor a cup of chocolate; when he refused to drink it (perhaps fearing it wasn't kosher), she instantly realized he shared her hidden faith. A simple chocolate refusal became a covert handshake, identifying friend from foe without a word spoken. In this way, chocolate's role as a social staple made it an *unlikely cipher* for signaling insider status among the persecuted – a sweet stand-in for a secret handshake.

From colonial smugglers hiding gold and letters in cacao sacks to subversive signals stirred into hot cocoa, the cacao bean carried a lot more than flavor. It carried information – and sometimes the fate of empires – within its bitter, unassuming shell.

War and Peace Through Chocolate

By the 20th century, chocolate had earned a place in every soldier's ration kit and every civilian's heart. It was energy, comfort, and a taste of home. But even on the brutal front lines of world wars, chocolate continued its secret double life – boosting morale in the clear light of day, and trading in subterfuge after dark.

One of the most touching episodes came during World War I, echoing a royal precedent set by Queen Victoria during the Boer War in 1900. Just as the Queen had commissioned personalized tins for her troops (some of which survive, unopened, to this day), the city of York in December 1914 sent special tins of chocolate to all its sons fighting on the front.The effect was magical. War-weary Yorkshire lads in trenches and training camps savored the unexpected gift – a moment of sweetness amid the mud and misery.

In return, over 250 of them penned thankful replies, letters so heart-felt they earned a nickname: the "Chocolate Letters." These letters, preserved by the York museum, speak to how a simple treat can carry profound emotional messages. *"I feel I ought to send my very best thanks for the nice box of chocolate I received so unexpectedly,"* one soldier wrote from the front, before closing with a line that tugs at the heart even a century later:

"I shall prize the box as long as God spares me." – Gunner Henry Bailey, in a 1915 letter thanking his hometown for a gift of chocolate.

These were not coded messages in the cryptographic sense, but they were *messages borne of chocolate* nonetheless – notes of hope and gratitude riding on the coattails of a candy tin. The people of York had effectively used chocolate as a communication medium to boost morale, and the soldiers' replies showed how powerful that gesture had been.

World War II, however, shifted the scene from heartfelt letters to deadly intrigue. The same war that produced Alan Turing and the Enigma codebreakers also produced one of the most bizarre espionage gadgets in history: the exploding chocolate bar. In 1943, British intelligence MI5 uncovered a Nazi plot so diabolical it sounded like a dark fairytale.

German saboteurs had designed an *apparently ordinary* chocolate bar – black foil wrapping, gold lettering and all – that concealed a slab of high explosive. If an unsuspecting British VIP (perhaps Winston Churchill, known for his sweet tooth) tried to snap a piece off, a hidden charge would ignite after a seven-second fuse, blowing the chocolate – and the eater – to pieces. Designed to mimic the popular luxury brand "Peter's Chocolate," this weapon was a testament to how literally explosive chocolate's role in warfare had become.

==

DECLASSIFIED: THE EXPLODING BAR BLUEPRINT

British Intelligence MI5 discovered the mechanism inside the "Peter's Chocolate" bomb. Here is how it worked.

- **The Coating:** A thin layer of real dark chocolate (to pass visual inspection).
- **The Body:** A steel chassis hidden beneath the candy shell.
- **The Trigger:** A canvas strap attached to the end of the bar.
- **The Action:** Breaking the chocolate "snap" pulled the canvas strap, releasing a striker.
- **The Fuse:** A 7-second delay before the high-explosive charge detonated.

==

THANKFULLY, Allied spies foiled the plan before the lethal candy bar ever found its way to Churchill's desk. But the mere existence of such a device proved that in war, even innocent confectionery could not be trusted. "Death by chocolate," usually a joking phrase, was suddenly a very real threat.

Allied forces, for their part, used chocolate in more benevolent covert ways. American and British commanders sometimes hid escape tools inside chocolate bars shipped to POWs – a compass here, a tiny file there – banking on the enemy's obliviousness or the prisoners' resourcefulness. And on the home front, British candy manufacturers developed unappetizing high-cocoa bars (ironically called "Excellence" or "Special Chocolate") as part of survival kits for agents in the field. These bars were so bitter and dense that you'd only eat them in an absolute emergency – which made them perfect for secret messages too. A spy could scratch a note on the hard surface of such a bar or use its unwrapped foil as signal mirror, then simply eat the evidence if danger approached. Chocolate had become standard issue gear for the shadow warriors of WWII.

CRACKING Codes Over Cocoa

Amid all these clandestine uses of chocolate, perhaps its most surprising role was in pure cryptography – the science of secret codes. The image of bespectacled codebreakers poring over strange ciphers might seem worlds away from anything as frivolous as chocolate. But at Bletchley Park, the top-secret British codebreaking center during World War II, the worlds of sweet cocoa and high mathematics did intersect. Long, grueling hours deciphering enemy communications required quick energy and comfort, and the staff famously guzzled endless cups of tea. Less famous is the fact that chocolate bars were a prized snack among the codebreakers – a little sugar boost to keep the brain whirring during a midnight shift decoding Enigma ciphers.

One young woman at Bletchley, however, found chocolate useful for more than staving off hunger. Mavis Batey, a 19-year-old cryptanalyst, made history in 1941 by cracking a crucial Italian naval code, helping set up the Royal Navy's victory at Matapan. But her legend includes a quirky detail that has become part of Bletchley folklore. As the story goes, Mavis had so few writing supplies on hand during one breakthrough moment that she grabbed the wrapper of a chocolate bar on her desk and began scrawling down preliminary decryptions on the foil. While the physical wrapper was never preserved, the anecdote endures as a testament to the high-pressure improvisation of the codebreakers.

Whether by coincidence or fate, that chocolate-fueled effort paid off – she deciphered the message in record time (just minutes), giving the Allies vital information about an impending Italian attack. The tale of the *chocolate wrapper code-crack* became part of Bletchley lore, a reminder that genius can improvise with whatever materials are at hand. In Mavis's case, a late-night candy bar turned into an unlikely decryption pad that helped change the course of the war.

A true Bletchley Park legend: Mavis Batey, the 19-year-old
cryptanalyst who made history by cracking Italian naval codes and
turning the tide at Matapan. Her quick thinking and unwavering
dedication were instrumental in the Allied victory.

The connections didn't end there. In the later stages of WWII, British codebreakers were hunting for any edge to break the latest German ciphers. One idea hatched involved printing subtle code hints on the packaging of soldier's rations, including chocolate. The notion was to embed a string of seemingly random letters or patterns on a chocolate bar wrapper, which Allied soldiers in the field would recognize as guidance for using a new cipher system (but to the enemy, it looked like part of the design or an innocuous lot number).

There are hints in declassified files that some British special ops units received maps or coded instructions concealed in the labels of their ration chocolates. If captured, the enemy might devour the chocolate and discard the wrapper none the wiser, while the Allied trooper had already memorized the hidden message. It was low-tech steganography – hiding secrets in plain sight – and chocolate was an ideal delivery vehicle. After all, who would suspect a candy wrapper of carrying military intelligence?

In the annals of cryptography, such tricks are a footnote compared to the famous Enigma machine or Navajo code talkers. But they illustrate an important point: the craft of secret communication often exploits the everyday and ordinary. A coded message on elegant stationery screams "important – examine me!" But a coded message on a crumpled chocolate wrapper whispers "nothing to see here – just a snack." Time and again, those whispering messages proved more effective.

A Sweet Tooth for Secrets

From the cobblestone alleys of Baroque Europe to the battlefields of modern wars, chocolate has shadowed the world of secret communication in unexpected ways. It has been a carrier of hidden letters, a meeting place for conspirators, a medium for coded ink and signals, a bribery tool, a morale booster, and on occasion, a literal explosive device.

In each role, chocolate's disarming nature – its familiarity and innocence – has been its greatest strength. No one looks twice at a cup of cocoa or a box of bonbons, and that is precisely why, under the right circumstances, they became the perfect foil for intrigue.

It's a niche slice of history, to be sure. Great battles were not decided *solely* by candy, and spies didn't base whole careers on desserts. But it's fascinating to realize that the bitter complexity of espionage found a home in something as universally beloved as chocolate. Like a detective novel's red herring, chocolate drew attention one way while hiding something in plain sight. Like a good cipher, it masked meaning with flavor and appearance.

Next time you enjoy a piece of chocolate, consider the rich legacy behind that sweetness. Think of the intrepid couriers who slipped documents into cocoa sacks, or the plotters swapping passwords in a cocoa parlor. Think of weary soldiers writing grateful letters home after a taste of chocolate on the front, and brilliant codebreakers crunching on candy as they unravel enemy secrets.

The history of cryptography and secret communication is full of ingenious tools and unsung heroes; improbably, chocolate has been both. It just goes to show: sometimes the key to a great mystery isn't a magnifying glass or a supercomputer – sometimes it's a simple cup of chocolate, steaming quietly at the center of the plot, waiting for those clever enough to sip its secrets.

28

BOOM AND BUST: THE VOLATILE ECONOMICS OF BROWN GOLD

B y the 17th century, cacao had already transformed from a sacred Mesoamerican treasure into Europe's newest obsession. But choco-late's ascent was only beginning. As demand grew, so did the scramble for supply—and with it came speculation, fortune-seeking, and market frenzies that would shape nations. The pursuit of "brown gold" proved as volatile as any precious metal rush, with fortunes made and lost on the whims of weather, disease, and distant trading floors.

YET BEHIND THE boom lay a darker reality. The labor that made cocoa profitable in early plantations was often forced. Enslaved Africans were brought to work the cacao haciendas of Venezuela, New Spain, and the Caribbean. The pursuit was brutal: tropical diseases, punishing heat, and long hours plagued the workforce. Cocoa's first gold rush thus enriched European merchants and colonial elites while the enslaved and indigenous laborers paid a heavy price. This troubling foundation would echo through later chapters of cocoa's history, as cycles of boom and bust continually intertwined wealth and hardship.

. . .

The 19th-Century Chocolate Revolution

For much of the 1700s, chocolate remained a luxury indulgence—a rich drink for aristocrats or a medicine for the ailing. That began to change in the 19th century, when the Industrial Revolution met the cacao bean. A series of inventions transformed chocolate into an affordable treat for the masses. Suddenly, chocolate wasn't just for sipping in gilded salons; it was a snack that middle-class families and even children could enjoy. Demand for cocoa beans exploded as candy went mainstream.

This surge in appetite set off a global scramble for supply. Europe's confectioners and nascent chocolate companies—Cadbury, Nestlé, Lindt, Hershey—needed reliable, massive quantities of cocoa. It was an energy rush, akin to drilling for oil but to feed candy factories.

Until about 1850, the world's supply mostly came from a patchwork of tropical American sources: Venezuela's plantations, Ecuador's coastal orchards, and Brazil's Bahia region. Now, with the market growing, every cacao-producing region kicked into high gear.

Latin America's Brown Gold

One epicenter of the 19th-century boom was Ecuador. By mid-century, the nation realized its coastal climate was ideal for Theobroma cacao. Small farmers and businessmen alike planted trees across the fertile Guayas river basin. The world's hunger for chocolate was so insatiable that by the 1890s, cacao made up over half of Ecuador's exports.

The port city of Guayaquil transformed into a thriving boomtown, its docks piled high with burlap sacks of beans destined for New York, Amsterdam, and London. An upper class of exporters arose—Ecuadorian "cacao barons" who built mansions and founded banks with their profits. They called the bean pepa de oro, or "grain of gold." For a few glorious decades, Ecuador was the world's leading producer, its flavor-rich Arriba variety coveted by chocolate makers everywhere.

South of Ecuador, Brazil saw a similar rush in its Bahia state. Pioneers had introduced cacao to Bahia's rainforests in the late 1700s, but it was in the late 1800s that the industry truly ignited. By the turn of the 20th century, the region around the town of Ilhéus was flush with wealth

—a tropics-tinted mirror of a California gold rush town. Plantation owners, often called "colonels," lived extravagantly. Their rivalries and romances became the stuff of Brazilian legend, immortalized by novelist Jorge Amado in stories of obsession, violence, and greed amid the groves.

For Bahia and Ecuador alike, the boom brought prosperity, but it also sowed the seeds of future turmoil. Monoculture wealth is fragile. In Ecuador, the golden years ended abruptly around 1916 when Witches' Broom disease decimated the legendary "Pure Nacional" orchards.

The biological disaster triggered an economic one: production collapsed just as cheaper African cocoa began glutting the market. The country's economy nosedived, and wealthy families went bankrupt overnight. The once-bustling wharves of Guayaquil fell quiet as the global trade shifted east to Africa.

The lush rainforests of Brazil and Ecuador were ideal environments for growing cacao due to its delicate nature, which thrives under the protective shade of taller trees.

West Africa's Cocoa Frontier

Just as Latin America's bonanza began to falter, a new frontier opened. In the late 19th century, European colonial powers introduced the cacao tree to their West African territories, imagining neat plantations supplying the empires. But what actually happened was unprecedented: local African farmers embraced the crop with entrepreneurial fervor, kicking off one of history's most dramatic agricultural shifts.

The Gold Coast (modern Ghana) offers the most vivid example. In 1879, a blacksmith named Tetteh Quarshie returned to the Gold Coast from the Spanish island of Fernando Po, stealthily carrying a few cacao pods. He planted these seeds on his farm outside Accra. Those trees flourished, and word spread of this promising new crop.

Villagers in the Gold Coast—everyone from tribal chiefs to families —started carving new farms out of the rainforests, planting thousands, then millions of trees. By 1910, a mere three decades after Quarshie's experiment, the Gold Coast was exporting a staggering 40,000 tons of cocoa a year, suddenly becoming the largest producer on the planet.

One British official marveled in 1938 that this growth "has no parallel in the world," noting that in just forty years Ghana went from zero to supplying roughly 40% of the world's cocoa—all of it grown by small, independent African farmers.

THE GREAT DEPRESSION's Bitter Lesson

However, the volatility of the market soon caught up with the farmers. By the late 1920s, overproduction drove cocoa prices to extreme lows. The situation reached a breaking point during the Great Depression. As economic turmoil spread worldwide in the early 1930s, the price offered for cocoa beans sank so low that many West African farmers could not even cover their costs. In despair, some farmers burned or abandoned their cocoa farms.

In the Gold Coast, growers organized the famous 'Cocoa Hold-Up' of 1930-31. It was essentially a farmers' strike; they refused to sell their beans to British trading firms unless they received a better price.

Mountains of cocoa piled up unsold as farmers held out for relief. The colonial government eventually intervened with minor concessions, but the incident revealed how cocoa—once a symbol of easy wealth— could become a source of economic anguish for those at the bottom of the supply chain.

THE IVORY COAST Miracle

When Ghana became the first sub-Saharan African nation to gain independence in 1957, it was a land built on cocoa wealth. But a neighbor would soon eclipse it.

Ivory Coast, under President Félix Houphouët-Boigny after its 1960 independence, pursued a policy of aggressively expanding cocoa and coffee production. He encouraged migrants from poorer, landlocked African countries to come help clear the forests and plant cacao. New boomtowns sprouted in the western forests. Under Houphouët-Boigny's leadership, Ivory Coast enjoyed a "cocoa miracle" in the 1960s and '70s: the country paved highways, built one of Africa's most modern city skylines, and attained a relatively high per capita income.

By the 1980s, Ivory Coast surpassed Ghana as the world's top producer, a title it holds to this day. In some Ivorian villages, it wasn't uncommon to hear stories of farmers becoming "cocoa millionaires" overnight when a good harvest coincided with high global prices.

THE 1970s FEVER: Speculation Runs Wild

Cocoa proved to be a textbook example of a boom-and-bust commodity. In the 1970s, the world experienced a commodity price explosion. Inflation was high, and raw materials were seen as prime investments. Between 1971 and 1977, the price of cocoa beans skyrocketed more than tenfold, reaching levels never seen before. By 1977, cocoa hit around $5,000 per metric ton.

A media panic erupted about a coming "chocolate bar crisis." The speculative boom was driven partly by real supply issues—bad weather and disease—but largely by investors piling into commodity markets. Cocoa had become the new gold, with traders in London and New York shouting orders as frantically as if they were trading oil bullion.

President Houphouët-Boigny tracked prices with the intensity of a stockbroker; his nation's fortunes were so intertwined with the commodity that the price ticker might as well have been monitoring his own heartbeat.

==

WALL STREET DICTIONARY: TALK LIKE A TRADER
Cocoa is a gamble. Here are the rules of the casino.

- **The Spot Price:** The cost to buy a ton of cocoa right now (cash in hand).
- **The Future:** A contract to buy cocoa at a set price months from now. Farmers use this to lock in income; speculators use it to bet.
- **The Bull:** A trader betting the price will go UP (e.g., due to drought).
- **The Bear:** A trader betting the price will go DOWN (e.g., due to a surplus harvest).
- **The Glut:** When supply exceeds demand, crashing the price (as seen in 1984).

==

THE GREAT CACAO Collapse of 1984

However, as often happens with commodity booms, the feast was followed by a dramatic famine. Farmers worldwide, encouraged by the high prices of the 70s, had expanded their plantings. By 1984, a series of bumper crops flooded the market. Ivory Coast, Brazil, Malaysia, Ecuador, and Indonesia all harvested record volumes.

Warehouses brimmed. Chocolate manufacturers suddenly had more than enough supply, and the price plummeted. What had been selling for over $5,000/ton sank to around $1,500 by the mid-1980s.

The impact in West Africa was devastating. In Ivory Coast, the collapse meant the primary source of national income evaporated. President Houphouët-Boigny grew increasingly paranoid, suspecting that foreign traders were manipulating the market to keep African nations poor. In Ghana, the situation was even worse; a mix of mismanagement and the catastrophic bushfires of 1983 had already reduced output to a fifty-year low.

. . .

THE WITHHOLDING GAMBIT: **A One-Nation Cartel**

Desperate times breed desperate measures. In 1987, President Houphouët-Boigny declared economic war on the global market. He announced that Ivory Coast would boycott the market, refusing to export a single bean until prices rose. It was a bold attempt to form a one-nation cocoa cartel.

For a time, beans simply piled up. Through 1987 and 1988, ships at Ivorian ports sat empty while huge burlap sacks filled warehouses to the rafters. Nearly 135,000 tons of cocoa—almost a quarter of the country's annual harvest—were withheld. But the scheme failed to ripple the global price. Other countries like Malaysia and Indonesia were happy to fill the gap, and big chocolate manufacturers simply drew down their own stockpiles.

VICTIMS OF A FINANCIAL **Tailspin**

The standoff destroyed the Ivorian economy. The state marketing board (Caistab) still had to pay local farmers a guaranteed price—about 65 cents per pound, the highest in the world—even though no export revenue was coming in. The treasury bled dry.

In remote towns, unscrupulous middlemen took advantage of the chaos. Some foreign traders offered to buy beans for rock-bottom unofficial prices, paying in IOUs or even counterfeit paper scrip instead of real money.

Thousands of farmers, desperate to unload a perishable crop, accepted these worthless promissory notes—only to find the buyers vanished overnight. In one district, a notorious case saw a trader flee after buying up cocoa with IOUs; enraged farmers were left with neither money nor their cocoa.

Reports trickled into Abidjan of violent reprisals in some villages. Whispered stories spoke of vigilante justice and bodies of swindling agents found in the bush. Bitterness flared. Cocoa, once the proud engine of prosperity, had become a source of misery and anger.

By early 1989, reality could no longer be denied. Ivory Coast capitulated. The great cocoa mountain was sold off at rock-bottom prices, incurring massive losses. The "Cocoa Miracle" was officially over.

===

THE MONEY TRAIL: WHO GETS WHAT?

If you pay $4.00 for a mass-market chocolate bar, here is where your money vanishes.

- Retailer & Taxes: $1.44 (36%) – The store makes the biggest cut.
- Manufacturer: $1.40 (35%) – Marketing, R&D, and profit margins.
- Ingredient Costs: $0.48 (12%) – Sugar, milk, vanilla, and lecithin.
- Transport & Grinding: $0.40 (10%) – Shipping and factory processing.
- The Cocoa Farmer: $0.28 (7%) – The person who grew the tree gets the crumbs.

===

SPECULATION in the Modern Age

The volatility did not end in the 80s. In 2010, a legendary episode unfolded that seemed ripped from a financial thriller. A British commodities trader named Anthony Ward quietly amassed a gigantic stockpile of cocoa beans, eventually controlling an estimated 240,000 tons—about 7% of the world's annual production—through purchases on the London exchange.

Ward's move was an attempt to corner the market, creating an artificial shortage to drive prices up. The press nicknamed him "Chocfinger," after the Bond villain Goldfinger. For a time, cocoa futures spiked, sending panic through chocolate manufacturers. It was a stark reminder that even in the digital age, this age-old commodity could inspire bold, almost romantic gambits to make a fortune.

As of the mid-2020s, the market has entered uncharted territory. Between 2023 and 2024, cocoa prices didn't just rise; they tripled, shattering historical records to breach $10,000 per metric ton. Fueled by catastrophic harvest failures in West Africa and climate-induced shortages, industry experts are no longer calling it a squeeze—they are calling it a structural deficit. Once again, the pattern asserts itself: high prices prompt talk of expansion, perhaps pushing the agricultural frontier further into the forests of the Philippines or Papua New Guinea.

The story of cocoa economics is one of frenzied highs and crushing lows. It is a tale where boomtowns rise and fall on the fickle price of a bean, and where fortune-seekers take the form of Spanish conquistadors, African pioneers, and Wall Street traders. In these booms and busts, some found sweet success—building cities and nations on the back of chocolate—while others tasted only bitterness.

29

THE CHOCOLATE NOMAD:
FOLLOWING THE HARVEST
ACROSS CONTINENTS

I n the predawn hush of a West African forest, a small camp stirs to life among the cocoa trees. A makeshift shelter of tarpaulin and bamboo protects the Konaté family as they huddle around a glowing charcoal fire. Beneath a makeshift shelter of tarpaulin and bamboo, the Konaté family huddles around a glowing charcoal fire. A pot of porridge bubbles as 12-year-old Awa Konaté sleepily rubs her eyes. Today will be like every other day for the past two months: as the first light filters through the canopy, Awa and her parents will fan out into the lush green gloom, baskets in hand, to harvest cocoa pods. They are far from their home, living in a temporary camp set up for the harvest season. By sunrise, the quiet forest will echo with the thunk of machetes striking husks and the laughter and calls of dozens of other migrant families scattered through the plantation, all part of the annual ritual of the cocoa harvest.

THE KONATÉS ARE CHOCOLATE NOMADS – families who follow the ripening of cacao pods as diligently as birds following the seasons. Each year, they journey hundreds of miles from their drought-scarred home in northern Mali to the humid cocoa-growing regions of Côte d'Ivoire.

They travel in packed buses and rattling trucks, carrying only what they need: cooking pots, mats to sleep on, and simple tools. When they arrive at a cocoa farm that needs extra hands, they construct a temporary village on the margins of the fields. During harvest months, these makeshift communities of tents and huts spring up amid the plantations, then vanish with hardly a trace once the work is done. It's a hard life on the move, dictated by the flowering and fruiting of the cacao trees, but for thousands of families like the Konatés, it has become a way of life – one that spans countries and even continents in the global pursuit of chocolate.

Life on the Cocoa Trail

Under the dense shade of cocoa orchards, the day's labor unfolds in a steady, rhythmic cadence. Awa's father, Mamadou, uses a long-handled knife to slice ripe golden cacao pods off the tree trunks, careful not to damage the flowering buds that will become next season's crop. Awa and her mother gather the fallen pods and crack them open with practiced whacks of a machete.

==

TOOLS OF THE TRADE

The harvest is manual labor. No machines can navigate the jungle floor.

- **The Go-To-Hell (The Harvesting Hook):** A curved blade on a long pole used to slice pods from the high canopy without damaging the delicate bark.
- **The Machete (The Cracker):** Used to slice the thick husk open. One wrong move damages the beans inside—or the hand holding the pod.
- **The Banana Leaf (The Oven):** Not a tool, but essential. Beans are heaped on these leaves to ferment. The leaves trap the heat (up to 50°C) that creates the chocolate flavor.

==

. . .

INSIDE EACH GOURD-LIKE **cacao** pod lies a cluster of damp white beans –
cacao seeds enveloped in sweet, sticky pulp. The air fills with the tangy-
sweet smell of fermenting fruit as families pile the wet seeds into
baskets. Later, the beans will be fermented under banana leaves and
dried under the sun on woven mats. But the Konatés will not be around
by then – their job is to bring in the harvest, and once the trees have
been stripped of pods, the family will move on.

For generations, families across West Africa have migrated with the
cocoa harvest in search of opportunity. In Côte d'Ivoire, the world's
leading cocoa producer, seasonal workers from Mali, Burkina Faso,
Guinea and beyond make up a significant portion of the workforce on
cocoa plantations. Some are entire families, while others are fathers and
older sons who leave younger children and grandparents behind in the
village.

They come because back home the rains have been fickle, the crops
meager, and there are few ways to earn cash. Word travels that cocoa
farms in the south need labor right after the rainy season, when the pods
are heavy and plentiful. And so, each year after their own subsistence
crops are harvested, waves of migrant farmers trek down from the
savannas and Sahel into the emerald forests, joining the cocoa caravan.

Life on the cocoa trail is a mix of hope and hardship. On one hand,
there is the promise of income – perhaps a few hundred dollars for
weeks of work, money that can keep a family fed and clothed, maybe pay
school fees or buy a small parcel of land someday. On the other hand,
the challenges are immense. The Konatés and others like them often
sleep in open-sided huts with thatched roofs that barely keep out the
torrential rains.

They have no electricity or clean water; at night, the darkness is
absolute save for flickering lanterns. Malaria-bearing mosquitoes
whine in the humid air. Medical care is distant, so a machete gash or a
bout of dysentery can be life-threatening. Yet Mamadou and his wife,
Aissatou, endure these privations for the sake of that cocoa income.
"We barely survive doing this," Mamadou says quietly as he slings a
sack of freshly harvested pods over his shoulder. "But if we stay home,

we have nothing. Here, at least we can earn something for our children."

By noon, the tropical sun hangs high and heavy. The families take a brief break, gathering under a giant shade tree at the edge of the farm. Awa plays with other children, tossing around a few cocoa pods as improvised toys. Her mother ladles out spicy peanut stew over cassava fufu from a communal pot – a simple but filling lunch for the exhausted laborers.

The conversation among the adults is in a babel of languages: Bambara from Mali, Mooré from Burkina, Dioula and Baoulé from Côte d'Ivoire. These harvest camps are a cultural melting pot. Strangers from different countries become neighbors and allies. They swap stories of home and news from afar. An elder from Burkina strums a homemade guitar and sings a wistful song about the rains back in his village. For a moment, weary faces brighten. In this transient community, bound together by work and fate, there is a sense of solidarity. Each family here has undertaken the same gamble – leaving home to follow the cocoa, hoping it will reward their sacrifice.

As the midday heat ebbs, the workers return to the groves for the afternoon push. There is urgency in the air; the harvest season is short, and they must gather every pod they can. Children like Awa work alongside their parents. She deftly scoops cocoa beans from cracked pods and heaps them into a wooden bucket. At twelve years old, she knows how to handle a machete almost as well as the adults – a skill she learned out of necessity.

Here, the line between work and childhood blurs. Awa chats with her friend Salif as they work; he is a few years older and dreams of one day seeing the big coastal city, Abidjan, though he's not entirely sure where it is. Neither Awa nor Salif has set foot in a school in months. In theory, this is "temporary" – they will catch up on lessons when back home – but reality often proves otherwise. Many children of the cocoa trails fall permanently behind in their education. One young migrant from Burkina Faso, who came to Ivory Coast to find schooling, admitted with a sad smile that he hadn't attended classes in five years; the quest for a better life through cocoa had instead trapped him in an endless harvest cycle.

Young harvesters contribute labor to the afternoon shift; for many
children on the cocoa trails, the demands of the fields often replace
the classroom.

As dusk approaches, the day's haul of cocoa beans is heaped into a
fermenting pit and covered with banana leaves. The rich scent of
fermenting pulp mixes with the woodsmoke drifting from the cooking
fires. The Konatés trudge back to their tent, bodies aching and sticky
with sweat. They will sleep early, under a mosquito net patched with
string, so they can rise before dawn and begin again. In a week or two,
this farm's harvest will be done. Mamadou will carefully tally their earnings – perhaps by the kilogram of beans collected or a flat season rate
promised by the farm owner.

Then the family will decide: head home with their hard-won pay, or
join another harvest farther east, where the pods are just reaching peak
ripeness. In this way, some families manage to string together back-to-
back harvests, roaming from one region's cocoa belt to another's,
following the staggered calendar of the crop.

Their journey might take them from Ivory Coast into neighboring
Ghana, or down into Cameroon – even, for the most adventurous, across
the ocean to Brazil or Ecuador if opportunities arose and visas weren't
such an impossible dream. In reality, few can afford such far-flung travel,
but the notion that "somewhere else, the cocoa is waiting" persists as a
tantalizing idea.

A TRADITION with Deep Roots

The concept of following harvests is as old as agriculture itself. But
following the cocoa has a particularly rich and bittersweet history. Long
before families like the Konatés crisscrossed West Africa chasing

seasonal work, the cocoa bean had itself traveled across the world on the backs of human migration – some voluntary, much of it forced. The story of chocolate is entwined with journeys of explorers, colonists, slaves, and farmers moving across continents.

Cacao, the source of chocolate, is native to the rainforests of Central and South America. In ancient times, the Maya and Aztec people cultivated cocoa trees in their homelands and celebrated chocolate as "the sacred cacao".

While these early farmers weren't nomadic in harvesting – they tended their trees in place – cocoa's value set it moving along trade routes. By the 16th century, Spanish conquerors became the first "chocolate nomads" of a sort, carrying sacks of cocoa beans across the Atlantic to Europe and later transplanting the trees to new colonies.

By the 17th and 18th centuries, the Spanish, Dutch, and Portuguese had introduced cocoa cultivation to the Old World tropics: islands in the Caribbean, the Philippines, Indonesia, West Africa. With these seeds and saplings came people – often African slaves or indentured servants – forced to migrate to where cocoa would grow.

In the 19th century, the center of gravity for cocoa production shifted across the Atlantic to West Africa. As detailed in the earlier chronicle of boom and bust, this transition was initially marred by the use of forced labor on islands like São Tomé. However, as the industry moved to the mainland, it sparked a different kind of movement: the voluntary migration of farmers chasing the "brown gold."

As cocoa took root in West Africa, it sparked a wave of internal migration. Farmers from coastal regions and neighboring territories ventured into the interior forests to establish farms, mirroring the legendary journey of Tetteh Quarshie, whose initial planting of cocoa seeds near Accra had ignited the region's agricultural revolution.

In the 1920s and 1930s, young men ventured into sparsely populated interior forests to stake out cocoa farms. They hacked villages out of the wilderness, planted cocoa seedlings, and waited years for the first pod. Often these were not temporary migrations but one-way journeys—pioneers establishing new cocoa communities.

In Ivory Coast, migration for cocoa became a cornerstone of the nation's growth. After independence in 1960, the Ivorian government actively encouraged workers from abroad to immigrate and farm cocoa and coffee. Throughout the 1960s and 70s, tens of thousands of families from Burkina Faso, Mali, and Guinea moved into Ivory Coast's forests, drawn by the chance to become landowners and cash-crop farmers.

Many Ivorian landowners welcomed them, leasing out plots in exchange for a share of the crop. Entire villages of foreign-born cocoa farmers blossomed in the Ivorian countryside. For a while it was a win-win: Ivory Coast's cocoa production surged to number one in the world, and the migrant families earned far more than they could back home. But over time, this influx created tension. By the 1990s, land grew scarce and economic woes fanned xenophobic flames. Migrant farmers who had lived in Ivory Coast for decades suddenly found themselves disparaged as outsiders.

Access to land and nationality became explosive issues, contributing to civil conflicts in the 2000s. Even so, the seasonal flow of labor never truly stopped. To this day, as each cocoa season arrives, new faces show up in the old camps – the pull of a paying harvest proving stronger than political turbulence.

A Shared Harvest: Since 1960, migrant families from Burkina Faso, Mali, and Guinea have traveled to the Ivory Coast to cultivate cocoa, a labor flow that fueled the nation's rise to the world's top producer.

JOURNEYS ACROSS CONTINENTS

Although West Africa produces the lion's share of the world's cocoa and thus sees the most extensive harvest migrations, it is far from the only place where chocolate nomads roam. Cocoa's orbit spans the equatorial band around the globe, and wherever the pods ripen, people will travel for the work. In Latin America and Asia, similar stories unfold amid different landscapes and cultures.

Consider Indonesia, the largest cocoa producer in Asia. In the late 20th century, the country experienced a cocoa boom that transformed lives and landscapes – and uprooted families. Sulawesi, a sprawling Indonesian island, went from almost no cocoa in the 1970s to becoming a global cacao hotspot by the 1990s.

How? Small farmers embraced the crop after seeing its profitability, and a wave of migrants from other islands, especially densely populated Java, answered the call of this chocolate frontier. Families packed their belongings onto boats and ferries bound for Sulawesi's green interior. They cleared patches of rainforest to plant cocoa, often learning techniques from those who came before.

These Javanese migrants were not following a seasonal harvest and then going home; like earlier African pioneers, they relocated to chase a dream of cocoa riches. For a time, many prospered as yields soared. Sulawesi became synonymous with mass-produced cocoa. But booms can bust. By the 2000s, pests and disease attacked the cocoa trees, yields dropped, and global prices stagnated. Some settlers cut down their cocoa and left in search of the next opportunity elsewhere – perhaps oil palm plantations or gold mines – a new kind of nomadism spurred by the fickle fortunes of farming.

Yet many stayed, adapting by diversifying crops or improving their cocoa methods. The legacy is visible today: central Sulawesi's hills are quilted with small cocoa plots, and one can still meet old Javanese couples who recall their migration decades ago, and whose children and grandchildren carry on the cocoa farming tradition on Sulawesi soil.

On the other side of the world, in the lush Amazon basin of South America, cocoa has been both a traditional crop and a new promise. In Ecuador and Peru, indigenous communities have grown cacao for generations, often in wild or semiwild groves mixed under the rainforest canopy. These farmers traditionally didn't need to migrate; the cocoa grew in their backyard forests as part of a diverse ecosystem.

But economic pressures and opportunities have introduced a degree of mobility here as well. In Peru's eastern lowlands, for instance, the past twenty years have seen a significant shift: thousands of Andean families from highland regions have moved into the tropical foothills, encouraged by government programs to cultivate cacao instead of coca (the raw plant used for cocaine). For these families, it's a voluntary migration away from the troubles of the illicit drug economy towards the hope of stable, legal income through cocoa.

===

SOCIAL IMPACT: FROM COCAINE TO CHOCOLATE
In Peru, the "Chocolate Nomad" story is often one of survival.

- **The Trade:** Farmers in the Amazon foothills historically grew Coca (for the illegal drug trade) because it paid well. But it brought violence and cartels.
- **The Switch:** Government programs now subsidize Cacao saplings
  - The Result: Farmers earn a legal, safe living.
  - The Flavor: The same soil that grew potent coca now grows award-winning "Fine Flavor" cacao, prized by French chocolatiers.

===

THEY ARRIVE in humid valleys like San Martín and Huánuco, often with little more than a few sacks of clothes and some farming tools, and learn to tend cacao trees on assigned plots of land. Life is not easy – the jungle soil can be capricious, unfamiliar pests attack the crops, and newcomers face the isolation of living in frontier settlements hacked out of dense forest. Some give up and return to their mountain homes. But many persevere, forming cooperatives, building new communities literally rooted in cacao. They take pride in producing fine-flavor cocoa coveted by artisanal chocolate makers. In a sense, they have become nomads by circumstance, leaving ancestral lands to follow the call of a different harvest, one that might secure a better future for their children.

EVEN WITHIN ESTABLISHED cocoa-growing countries like Brazil or Mexico, there is movement tied to the crop. In Brazil's Bahia region, once the powerhouse of cocoa production in the Americas, colonels (cocoa plantation owners) historically employed entire colônia of workers – families who lived on the estate year-round.

Those workers didn't migrate seasonally; they were bound to the land in a feudal arrangement, often for generations, until a devastating blight (witches' broom disease) in the 1990s collapsed the industry and sent thousands of laborers scattering to find other work. Now, Brazil's cocoa revival in the Amazonian north has attracted some of those uprooted families to venture into new plantations in Pará and Rondônia, repeating the cycle of internal migration.

In Central America, a country like Nicaragua sees internal migrants from drier western regions move to its humid Atlantic coast to farm cacao under reforestation initiatives. And in the Caribbean, a place like the Dominican Republic – one of the largest organic cocoa exporters – relies mostly on local family farms, but occasionally Haitian workers cross the border seeking jobs in the cocoa drying and processing facilities, a small parallel to the much larger migrations for coffee and sugarcane in that region.

Different lands, different circumstances – yet a common thread runs through these stories. Whether it's West African villagers, Indonesian islanders, or Peruvian highlanders, families across continents are drawn by the prospect (or simply the necessity) of making a living from the chocolate trade. They pack their lives into bundles and set off, following the scent of opportunity that wafts from the cacao pod.

TRIALS AND TRIUMPHS on the Road

The life of a chocolate nomad is fraught with challenges that outsiders can scarcely imagine. The work itself is physically punishing. Harvesting cocoa is not a mechanized process – it is done almost exactly as it was a hundred years ago, by hand with knife and machete. Each ripe pod must be cut down individually. A strong worker might harvest hundreds of pods in a day, swinging a sharpened blade attached to a pole to reach those higher up, then stooping to gather them. Arms tire, necks crane, and feet squelch in the mud of the plantation floor.

To understand the toll, one must feel the weight of the machete after hour ten. The handle becomes slick with sweat and sap, turning every swing into a battle for grip. The pod breaking is a violent, percussive rhythm that reverberates through the skeletal system. One elder harvester described the sensation not as pain, but as a vibration that settles in the elbows and never leaves, a permanent hum of the harvest lodged in the bone.

When a pod cracks open, it doesn't just release beans; it releases a spray of mucilage that attracts biting midges, covering the worker in a sticky, itchy second skin. The work doesn't end when the sun sets; often, by flashlight or firelight, workers continue to heap, ferment, or transport beans into the night if rain threatens to spoil the crop. It's common to see scars on the shins and hands of veteran harvesters – etched stories of slipped machetes and thorny vines.

Beyond the labor itself, there are the dangers of the environment. In the steamy jungles, venomous snakes sometimes coil around the branches or hide under fallen leaves, startling unwary pickers. Malaria and other tropical diseases lurk. For families on the move, healthcare is often an afterthought; an illness can turn dire out in the field. Then there's the ever-present threat of exploitation. Many migrant harvesters are at the mercy of middlemen and farm owners for wages.

Some landowners pay a fixed sum per season, others by the quantity of beans gathered. Either way, the balance of power seldom favors the laborer. It's not unheard of for unscrupulous farm managers to undercount the sacks of dried beans or inflate deductions for food and lodging before paying the workers. A family might work a whole season only to find their earnings whittled away by debts – perhaps for advances taken to pay for the journey south, or inflated prices for rice and provisions bought on credit at the farm's trading post. In extreme cases, this system can resemble the indentures of old, binding workers in a cycle of owing and laboring.

Child labor is another painful reality. While cocoa farming is often a family endeavor in one's own plot, on commercial plantations the use of children as workers remains widespread despite international scrutiny.

Families who migrate together typically have little choice but to have their children help; there's no school in the middle of the forest camp, and idle supervision is a luxury they can't afford when everyone must contribute.

Beyond the harvest: A worker navigates the perils of the jungle while families await the tally at the trading post, where the balance of power rarely favors the laborer.

Some parents also believe it's a necessary apprenticeship for the child – teaching them the skills to survive in a world that hasn't offered them much else. Yet the cost is high: lost education, and the risk of injury from sharp tools and heavy loads at a tender age.

Numerous human rights reports over the years have chronicled the haunting sight of children carrying sacks of cocoa beans almost as big as themselves, or wielding machetes to split pods, their small bodies marked by scars and calluses. It is a bitter irony that these children often have never tasted a chocolate bar. In many cocoa-growing communities, chocolate is an exotic luxury, restricted not just by poverty but by physics. Without a reliable "cold chain" of refrigerated transport and storage, a chocolate bar would melt into a puddle in the tropical heat long before it reached the village shop.

And yet, amid these trials, there are triumphs and moments of sweetness in the lives of the chocolate nomads. There is the satisfaction of a good harvest – when the rains have been kind, the pods abundant, and the quality of beans high.

On such years, a family might earn enough to actually get ahead a little. Perhaps Mamadou and Aissatou Konaté manage to save up to buy a motorbike, making next year's travels easier than cramming into an overloaded truck. Maybe they afford a few more goats or a new tin roof for their house back home.

In some cases, after years of seasonal migrations, a family can accumulate enough money or goodwill with a landowner to secure their own small plot of cocoa trees. That is often the ultimate dream – to stop wandering and become a settled farmer, modestly prosperous, sending one's children to school and eventually passing on a cocoa orchard to them. A few do achieve it, effectively graduating from laborer to landholder. Their journey may still have started on the rough road of migrant harvesting, but it culminates in a place they can finally call home.

In the camps, there is also a strong sense of community and culture that uplifts spirits. Storytelling is a favorite pastime when the day's work is done. Under starry skies, elders recount folktales – some about clever spiders and proud lions from West African lore, others more recent and true, like how "Grandpa Amadou" first came to this very farm as a young man and ended up saving enough to send his daughter to university.

There are jokes and banter in multiple tongues, and in the absence of televisions or phones, people truly talk to each other. Music and dance often weave into camp life; someone produces a djembe drum or simply claps a rhythm, and soon a circle of dancers – children and grown-ups alike – will hop and sway, their laughter echoing among the cocoa trees.

These joyous moments are brief respites from toil, but they create bonds that can last a lifetime. It's not uncommon for families that met in a harvest camp to keep in touch over years, attending each other's weddings and funerals, considering themselves kin forged by the shared experience of the road.

Moreover, the knowledge exchanged in these roving communities can be invaluable. Farmers swap tips on everything from combating cocoa diseases to recipes for cooking the wild bushmeat one might trap in the forest. In recent times, some NGOs and agricultural extension workers have started visiting migrant camps to teach better farming practices or literacy classes at night.

While still rare, such efforts plant seeds of change. In one camp in Ghana, for example, a volunteer teacher traveling with a church group started a tiny makeshift school under a mango tree, inviting the migrant children for a couple of hours each evening. Twelve-year-old Awa learned to read simple sentences in those twilight classes, kindling dreams that perhaps she could continue her education if her family settles one day. These glimmers of hope can sustain the spirit even when conditions are harsh.

The Rhythm of the Seasons, the Uncertainty of the Future

From October's heavy rains to July's drying winds, the harvest seasons roll on, and with them roll the feet of the nomads. There is a certain rhythm to the year for those who follow the cocoa. Generally, the main harvest in West Africa begins around the end of the rainy season – roughly October – and runs through December or January.

Then a smaller "light" harvest might come around May or June. In South America, near the equator, harvest times often complement this: some regions peak in April and May, another small crop in late year. Southeast Asia's cocoa seasons can differ again. For the truly adventurous and well-connected worker, it's theoretically possible to hopscotch between harvests across the globe, never really stopping.

A veteran harvester half-jokes that if he ever won the lottery (a fanciful notion, as he's never bought a ticket), he'd buy plane tickets to follow cocoa around the world – "Ivory Coast in November, Brazil in March, Indonesia in July, back to Ghana by October" – an endless loop chasing the ripening pods and fair weather. But of course, for the real nomads, air travel is beyond imagination; their migrations are overland, incremental, and bounded by what they can afford and where they can get permits to work.

The future of these families is caught in a web of larger forces. Climate change, for one, looms as a formidable challenge. Cocoa is finicky about climate – too much heat or too little rain can ruin a crop. In recent years, extreme weather has begun to disrupt the predictability of harvest seasons. Droughts have withered cocoa pods in Ghana; unseasonal heavy rains have caused black rot on Ivory Coast farms; shifting weather patterns confuse the trees, leading to patchier yields.

For families who depend on moving to where the harvest is, such uncertainty can be devastating. One year, they might arrive in a region

only to find the harvest came early and is mostly done, or failed alto-
gether. Then they must roam further, seeking any farm that still needs
labor.

==

THE GLOBAL CLOCK: WHEN IS HARVEST?
Cocoa never stops. Somewhere in the world, the pods are ripe.

- **October–March:** West Africa (The Main Crop). Massive
  harvests in Ghana and Côte d'Ivoire feed the world's bulk
  supply.
- **April–August:** Latin America (The Fly Crop). Ecuador and
  Peru harvest their fine-flavor beans.
- **September–December:** Asia. Indonesia and Vietnam hit
  their peak production.
- **Year-Round:** The Equator. Farms exactly on the equator (like
  Colombia) often have a continuous, slow trickle of ripe pods.

==

Climate change might, ironically, create even more nomads – as
previously fertile areas become less reliable, workers may have to travel
farther or move into new, more remote zones (often clearing more forest
in the process) to find viable cocoa. The map of the chocolate harvest is
slowly being redrawn by temperature and rainfall, and the people will
follow, as they always have, but with greater strain.

Another factor is the shifting economics of the chocolate industry.
There is growing awareness, at least in international discourse, of the
plight of cocoa farmers and laborers. Talk of "sustainable chocolate" and
fair trade practices has grown louder.

Governments in Ivory Coast and Ghana have even tried in recent
years to negotiate higher prices for their cocoa to better support farmers.
If prices paid to farmers were to rise significantly, perhaps the smallholders could afford to hire local labor at decent wages, alleviating some
need for entire families to migrate in desperation. Perhaps more schools

and services could reach cocoa communities so that children like Awa wouldn't have to trade textbooks for machetes.

These are hopeful possibilities, but the imbalance of power – between poor cocoa-growing regions and wealthy chocolate-consuming nations – remains vast. For now, each chocolate bar sold in a shiny wrapper still carries only a few cents of income for those at the bottom of the supply chain. Until that changes, poverty will continue to drive the migrations.

The next generation of would-be chocolate nomads may also chart a different course. Many young people from traditional farming families express reluctance to endure the same hardships as their parents. In a Malian village that has sent seasonal workers to Ivory Coast for decades, a 19-year-old aspiring mechanic shakes his head when asked if he'll ever join the cocoa caravan. "Maybe when I was little, I thought I would go with my father," he says, "but now I have other plans.

I've been to the city, I've seen there are other ways to live." If enough youth choose urban jobs or other trades, a labor shortage could hit cocoa farms. In fact, some regions are already seeing aging farmer populations with fewer young replacements. This might force changes – possibly higher wages to attract workers, or attempts at mechanization (though cocoa harvesting remains stubbornly difficult to automate given the scattered pods under dense shade).

It might also lead to more migration from even poorer areas – an influx of new nomads from places wracked by conflict or climate disaster, willing to do the work others shun. The cycle of who follows the harvest could shift, but the fundamental dynamic – people moving in search of a livelihood – will persist.

Still, there are rays of optimism. Various initiatives aim to improve conditions for migratory farm families. Some cooperatives in West Africa have started providing mobile clinics that travel to remote farms during harvest, so that migrant workers can get basic healthcare and their children vaccinated.

Rays of hope in the harvest: mobile clinics and traveling teachers
bring stability to the fields, while digital connectivity empowers
workers to build a safety net across distances.

Pilot programs in Côte d'Ivoire are experimenting with portable schooling – essentially a traveling teacher who moves with clusters of migrant children, ensuring they don't fall too far behind in reading and math during harvest months. In an age of mobile phones, even nomadic communities are not as isolated as before. Farmers now share information via WhatsApp, warning each other of regions where work is scarce or celebrating when prices rise.

Such connectivity can prevent the worst exploitation, as word spreads fast if a certain farm owner failed to pay or mistreated workers. The nomads are, in a way, organizing, even if informally – building a support network across distance.

A Harvest of Stories

Night has fallen again on the cocoa camp. The final pods have been collected, and the Konaté family is preparing to depart at first light. Their harvest here is finished; ahead lies a journey back home to Mali. The children chatter excitedly at the prospect of seeing their village again, of sleeping in their own hut and playing under the familiar old baobab tree by their compound.

Awa cradles a small treasure in her hands – a dried cocoa pod she kept as a souvenir. To her, it's more than a pod; it's a reminder of months spent in a faraway forest, of the friends she made from other lands, of the work she did that helped her family earn their keep. She has seen more of the world by age 12 than many might in a lifetime, though much of it was under the canopy of cacao leaves.

As Awa drifts to sleep on her mat, she wonders if they will come back next year. Her parents have murmured about possibly staying home if they can manage, perhaps trying a new trading business with the money they saved. But Awa isn't sure – she senses the pull of the cocoa is not so easily escaped.

Across the globe, countless stories echo the Konatés' experience, each with its unique details. In one story, a young father in Sulawesi recalls arriving in a jungle with nothing and now standing amid a thriving cocoa orchard he planted himself – hardship blossomed into success.

In another, a grandmother in Ghana remembers as a girl walking for days behind her parents, carrying a bundle of cassava and a basket of cocoa pods on her head, forging a path that her own children later followed in her footsteps. There are stories of heartbreak too – a boy injured by a falling pod who never fully recovered, a family that got cheated out of their pay and had to beg for transport home. These narratives seldom make the headlines, yet they quietly form the backbone of the chocolate industry.

Every time we unwrap a chocolate bar or savor a piece of dark truffle, we partake in these journeys. The sweetness on our tongue is built on the labor of families moving through tropical nights and dawns, navigating muddy roads and border checkpoints, chasing a crop that in turn chases the rains.

The modern convenience of having chocolate year-round, from dozens of countries, is made possible by an intricate human ballet: as one region's season ends, another begins, and there are always hands ready to pick up the work. We rarely see those hands, much less the faces of the children and parents and grandparents whose lives revolve around the rhythms of cacao. They remain, by and large, invisible nomads, even as their collective effort spans continents and feeds a global appetite.

Yet, change may come if we start to value the human story as much as the product. Perhaps the term "chocolate nomad" will one day be a relic of the past – a chapter in history when people had to wander for work in the chocolate trade – because future generations managed to root cocoa farming in stability and fairness. In the meantime, however, the nomads are still out there, moving with the seasons.

The next time you bite into a piece of chocolate, think of dawn breaking in a distant orchard and a family rising from sleep under a canvas sheet. Think of Awa and Mamadou and Aissatou, and millions like them, whose journey from farm to farm, harvest to harvest, carries the gift of cocoa to the world. Inside each chocolate bar lies not just the flavor of cocoa, but the spirit of perseverance and hope of the families who follow the harvest across horizons – a rich, complex story as bitter-sweet as chocolate itself.

30

GREAT RIVALRIES: BITTER FEUDS
AND FLAVOR SUPREMACY

It's a bitter irony that one of the world's sweetest delights has a history steeped in rivalry, intrigue, and ideological clashes. In Roald Dahl's Charlie and the Chocolate Factory, the eccentric Willy Wonka frets about spies sent by rival confectioners to steal his secrets. This whimsical plot was inspired by very real events: in Dahl's schoolboy days, Britain's top chocolate makers were known to infiltrate each other's factories in a clandestine battle for sweet supremacy.

For centuries, chocolate's greatest innovations and most iconic brands have been driven by intense competition – sometimes friendly, sometimes ferocious – among visionary chocolatiers. From the genteel Quaker businessmen of Victorian England to the brash American moguls of the 20th century, the saga of chocolate's evolution is a tale of bitter feuds, competing philosophies, and an unrelenting quest to conquer taste buds around the world.

THE QUAKER ORIGINS of a Sweet Industry

The modern chocolate industry was born in an unlikely crucible of piety and social conscience. In the early 19th century, a group of British Quakers – families named Cadbury, Fry, and Rowntree – launched businesses to offer an alternative to the era's real vice: alcohol. As devout Quakers barred from many professions, they turned to commerce, and cocoa was seen as a healthful, morally upright drink that could wean the working class off gin. In 1824,

John Cadbury opened a small shop in Birmingham selling tea, coffee, and "drinking chocolate." He and his fellow Quakers viewed business as a means to improve society. Profit was welcome, but ethical practices and charity were paramount. This noble outlook set the stage for a distinctly principled kind of corporate rivalry.

Cadbury's early years were a struggle for purity in an age of adulteration. Some less scrupulous makers were bulking out cocoa powder with everything from ground brick to sawdust. Determined to offer a pure product, Cadbury championed quality even at higher cost.

Likewise, in Bristol, the Fry family – another Quaker clan – had been grinding cocoa since the 1700s and shared these ethical standards. In 1847, Joseph Fry scored a breakthrough by producing the world's first proper chocolate bar, blending cocoa powder, sugar, and cocoa butter into a solid confection. This was a milestone – chocolate was no longer just a drink. The race was on to develop new forms and flavors, and the Quaker chocolatiers led the charge.

Yet Quaker business rivalry was anything but cutthroat. The Cadburys, Frys, and another Quaker-founded firm, Rowntree's of York, were part of a close-knit community. They attended the same meetings, sometimes intermarried, and even cooperated on big issues like campaigning against the use of slave labor on cocoa plantations. Still, in the marketplace they were fierce competitors, each striving to outdo the others with a better cocoa press or a smoother chocolate recipe.

In the 1860s, Cadbury leapfrogged rivals by acquiring the revolutionary Van Houten cocoa press technology. That press removed excess cocoa butter from the beans, yielding fine cocoa powder and paving the way for easily molded chocolate bars. Armed with this technology, Cadbury could make chocolate that was more consistent and silky than many competitors' gritty concoctions. The Quaker brethren had no qualms "poaching" good ideas to gain an edge – always, of course, in service of quality and honesty.

By the late 19th century, Cadbury had emerged as a leader in the British market, renowned for pure cocoa and innovative products. One of their best-sellers was a simple box of chocolates called "Cadbury's Cocoa Essence," marketed with the slogan "Absolutely Pure – Therefore Best." Over in York, the Rowntree company (founded in 1862 by Henry Rowntree) was up-and-coming, expanding from grocery goods into chocolate. Though sharing the Quaker ethos, Rowntree's placed a greater emphasis on experimental new sweets and marketing flair.

They launched pastilles, gums, and chocolate-covered biscuits, cultivating a reputation for creativity. Meanwhile, J.S. Fry & Sons in Bristol continued to develop their own chocolate brands, including the first mass-produced chocolate bar and later the iconic Fry's Turkish Delight. A three-way rivalry was taking shape in Britain – fought not with dirty tricks (at least initially) but with the Quaker weapons of quality, integrity, and industrious innovation.

The War for the Wrapper: Branding as a Weapon

While the Quaker families shared a philosophy of moral obligation toward their workers, they were ruthless in their battle for the consumer's eye. The rivalry between Cadbury and Rowntree birthed modern food marketing.

In the early 1900s, chocolate was sold in loose chunks or plain blocks. Cadbury changed the game by understanding the power of the brand. They introduced a distinctive royal purple to wrap their Dairy Milk bars. It was a masterstroke of psychology, associating their chocolate with royalty and luxury.

Rowntree's countered not with colors, but with concepts. They realized they couldn't beat Cadbury on "creaminess," so they targeted "convenience." They marketed the KitKat not just as a sweet, but as a utility —a companion for the "break." This created a schism in the industry that exists to this day: Chocolate as *Indulgence* (Cadbury) versus Chocolate as *Snack* (Rowntree). This philosophical divergence drove their rivalry for decades, turning the candy aisle into a battlefield of psychological cues.

Of course, altruism alone didn't win market share; innovation did. By the turn of the century, the chocolate business was booming, and competitors sprang up beyond the Quaker circle. Cadbury's commitment to quality was tested in the late 1800s by a scandal over adulterated cocoa beans sourced from Portuguese West Africa, which turned out to be harvested by enslaved workers.

Horrified, the Cadburys and Rowntrees joined forces to reform the supply chain, even sending investigators abroad and ultimately boycotting slave-grown cocoa. This episode demonstrated that even amid rivalry, shared values could triumph – a stark contrast to the more ruthless corporate battles to come.

Having navigated that moral crisis, Cadbury scored a commercial triumph in 1905 with the debut of Dairy Milk chocolate. By using a higher proportion of milk than any rival had dared, Cadbury produced a rich, creamy bar that was an instant sensation. Dairy Milk was marketed with the slogan "a glass and a half of milk in every bar," reinforcing an image of wholesome indulgence.

The new recipe gave Cadbury a decisive lead in the British chocolate wars: by the outbreak of World War I, Dairy Milk was outselling all competitors and defined the taste of British milk chocolate. Rowntree's, which lacked a milk chocolate blockbuster, saw its fortunes wane in comparison. For a time, it seemed Cadbury had vanquished its local foes by sheer force of flavor.

But the war and its aftermath leveled the playing field. Cocoa and sugar were rationed, forcing companies to make drastic pivots. Rowntree's was even compelled to temporarily abandon its signature recipe due to milk shortages, selling a dark chocolate version under a plain blue wrapper known as the "Blue Label" Kit Kat to manage consumer expectations. In the 1920s, Rowntree's was teetering – a distant second to Cadbury in chocolates, with an aging product line.Enter a visionary named George Harris, a dynamic marketing director at Rowntree's. Harris recognized that directly imitating Cadbury's Dairy Milk was a losing battle.

Instead, he pushed Rowntree's to invent entirely new types of chocolate treats. His first masterstroke was Black Magic in 1933 – a stylish box of assorted chocolates for gifting, designed through extensive consumer research. It was a hit. Harris then green-lit two bold new products in 1935: the KitKat (a light wafer biscuit covered in chocolate, sold as a convenient "snack" bar) and the Aero (an aerated chocolate bar filled with tiny bubbles). These novel creations, backed by clever advertising, tapped into consumers' desire for variety and fun.

By 1936, for the first time in decades, Rowntree's sales began to seriously threaten Cadbury's dominance. The lesson was clear: you could not topple a giant like Dairy Milk with a copycat – you needed to change the game.

The "Blue Label" Kit Kat (c. 1942). Due to wartime milk rationing, Rowntree's was forced to alter their recipe to dark chocolate and temporarily replace their signature red packaging with a blue wrapper to mark the change.

THE RACE for Flavor and Innovation

Meanwhile, a parallel chocolate revolution had been unfolding on the European continent, spurring another kind of rivalry – an arms race in technical innovation and flavor finesse. Throughout the 19th century, the Swiss, French, and Dutch chocolatiers vied to create ever smoother, tastier chocolate. In Switzerland, Daniel Peter, working with Henri Nestlé (inventor of condensed milk), finally perfected the recipe for milk chocolate in 1875.

By drying and mixing milk with cocoa liquor and sugar, Peter produced a solid milk chocolate that was much smoother and milkier than any British "chocolate with milk" that had come before. The Swiss had effectively thrown down the gauntlet to the world: this was how chocolate should taste – rich, creamy, and sweet.

Swiss confectioners continued pushing boundaries with new

processing techniques. The development of conching—which transformed gritty paste into silky chocolate—gave certain manufacturers a
significant competitive advantage that others scrambled to replicate.
Suddenly, any chocolatier still producing coarse, rough chocolate was
behind the times.

The rivalry now was not only between companies, but between
methods. Those who innovated (or quickly copied innovations) leaped
ahead, while others fell by the wayside. In France, the Menier family had
pioneered large-scale mechanized chocolate production and were wrapping chocolate bars in eye-catching labels by mid-century, setting
marketing trends that British and American firms would later follow.

Across the chocolate-making world, ideas were cross-pollinating: one
breakthrough in Holland or Switzerland would spur a response in
England or America. Everyone, it seemed, was chasing the ultimate goal
– the smoothest, most delicious chocolate imaginable.

By the early 20th century, as knowledge spread, the playing field in
terms of technique was leveling out. Conching, milk formulas, better
presses – these became standard tools of the trade. So chocolatiers
turned to other means to gain an edge: branding and new flavors. Here
again, rivalry pushed creativity.

If one company introduced a chocolate studded with hazelnuts, a
rival would debut one with almonds. If a French chocolatier created delicate praline-filled bonbons (as Jean Neuhaus did in Belgium in 1912,
inventing the first hard chocolate shell pralines), competitors from
London to New York raced to offer their own assorted chocolate boxes.
With each new confection – caramel-filled bars, fruit crèmes, crispy rice
chocolate (such as Nestlé's Crunch bar of 1938, swiftly answered by
Hershey's Krackel) – the competition intensified. Consumers reaped the
rewards of this delicious one-upmanship: more variety and better taste
than ever before.

Candy Spies and the Battle for Britain

As the 20th century progressed, the stakes grew higher. The chocolate market was a substantial industry, and the genteel cooperation of

the Quaker founding fathers gave way to something more aggressive. Nowhere was this more evident than in Britain during the interwar period, where the *Chocolate Wars* between Cadbury and Rowntree escalated into a full-on rivalry – complete with espionage.

Both companies had become household names, employing thousands and spreading their reach across the British Empire. With so much to lose or gain, each was obsessed with the other's moves. Rumors swirled of secret informants and stolen recipes. In fact, it became an industrial legend that Cadbury and Rowntree routinely planted spies in each other's factories—a corporate paranoia so deep that companies hired private detectives and kept new product development under a veil of absolute darkness.In the 1920s and 30s, you'd sooner get into Fort Knox than pry into the goings-on in a confectionery R&D lab.

This climate of paranoia bore fruit in rapid innovation. After the success of KitKat and Aero, Rowntree's continued to gamble on new ideas, launching Smarties (sugar-coated chocolate buttons) in 1937 and polishing off a minty chocolate marvel called After Eight in 1962. Cadbury answered in kind, introducing the Flake bar (1920), the Crunchie honeycomb bar (with a partner company in 1929), and throughout the 20th century expanding its line of fruit-and-nut chocolates and assorted Milk Tray confections.

Each tried to outmaneuver the other with advertising too. Rowntree's famously coined the slogan "Have a Break, Have a KitKat," embedding their product into British culture as the go-to snack with your tea break. Cadbury countered by marketing chocolate not just as candy but as an experience of comfort and joy – who can forget the cheeky *"Everyone's a Fruit and Nutcase"* jingle or the mysterious Milk Tray Man delivering chocolates by stealth?

The rivalry was heated, but it spurred both companies to refine not only their flavors but their image. By mid-century, Cadbury was synonymous with creamy, family-friendly indulgence, while Rowntree's products stood for playful fun and youthful energy.

Yet an unexpected challenger was about to crash this British party – an American upstart with a very different philosophy. In 1932, an ambitious young man named Forrest Mars Sr. arrived in London with a chip on his shoulder and a head full of ideas. Forrest was the estranged son of Frank Mars, a self-made candy king from Minnesota who had found success in the U.S. with the Milky Way bar.

After a bitter falling-out with his father, Forrest left the comfort of the family firm and set up his own operation in England to prove his mettle. In the London suburb of Slough, he founded Mars Limited and launched a new bar tailored to British tastes – the Mars Bar (a caramel-and-nougat bar similar to the American Milky Way, but marketed as a substantial snack "to help you work, rest, and play"). With this one product, Forrest Mars planted a flag on Cadbury's turf, and he had no intention of stopping there.

Ruthlessly efficient and relentlessly focused, Mars ran his factory with military precision. He studied production lines, eliminated waste, and kept formulas secret. Unlike the Quaker firms, Mars had no qualms about profit-driven pragmatism. Price competition, hard bargaining with suppliers, aggressive advertising – these were his tools. British competitors were quickly unnerved by Mars's unflinching approach.

The *chocolate cold war* had begun in earnest: Cadbury vs. Rowntree vs. Mars – three giants with three very different philosophies colliding in postwar Britain.

Mars's arrival brought new dimensions to the rivalry. Cadbury and Rowntree, for all their competition, had been bound by a certain gentlemanly decorum and shared values. Forrest Mars cared for neither. He believed in winning, full stop. If his rivals built model villages, Mars built an empire of secrecy. His company famously refused any publicity or interviews, and even decades later, the Mars family kept details of their operations under wraps. But the products spoke loudly.

Mars introduced Britons to Maltesers (chocolate malted-milk balls) and a smooth Galaxy milk chocolate bar (known elsewhere as Dove), directly challenging Cadbury's Dairy Milk with a silkier texture. With substantial funds behind it, Mars blitzed the airwaves and billboards with punchy, promise-driven campaigns that made Cadbury's nostalgia look old-fashioned. Suddenly, Cadbury's advertising, which leaned on nostalgia and whimsy, looked old-fashioned next to Mars's punchy, promise-driven campaigns.

The British chocolate market in the 1970s and 80s became a fierce battleground. Each holiday was an opportunity to one-up the other – Cadbury cultivated the Easter egg tradition and later the gooey Creme Egg, Mars pushed into Christmas selection boxes and anytime treats.

Supermarkets stocked rival armies of candy bars: Crunchie vs. Mars Bar, KitKat vs. Twix (Mars's chocolate-coated biscuit bar), Smarties vs. M&M's (which Mars introduced to the UK). It was a fight for shelf space and hearts. Through it all, Cadbury and Rowntree never forgot their philanthropic roots – they still prided themselves on charitable works and fair dealing – but they had to adopt some of Mars's hard-nosed tactics or risk defeat. By the late 1980s, this three-way rivalry reached a dramatic turning point through corporate twists of fate that few had foreseen.

```
=================================================
```

CORPORATE DNA: THE THREE KINGS

How the giants conquered the world using three different philosophies.

- **Cadbury (The Quaker Moralist):**
  - The Philosophy: "Business for Society."
  - The Strategy: Built model villages (Bournville) and focused on "Purity" to win trust.
  - The Legacy: Dairy Milk (Comfort/Luxury).
- **Mars (The Efficient Warrior):**
  - The Philosophy: "Efficiency and Secrecy."
  - The Strategy: Ruthless optimization, military precision, and global expansion.
  - The Legacy: Snickers/M&Ms (Fuel/Energy).
- **Hershey (The Utopian Builder):**
  - The Philosophy: "Community First."
  - The Strategy: Mass production to lower costs, funding a town and orphanage with the profits.
  - The Legacy: The Hershey Bar (Accessibility/Americana).

```
=================================================
```

~

Hershey vs. Mars: A Duel in the New World

Even as the battles raged in Europe, across the ocean another epic rivalry was taking shape – one that would pit two very different American titans head-to-head and ultimately reshape the global industry. The protagonists could not have been more different: Milton Hershey, the kindly, idealistic founder of The Hershey Chocolate Company, and Forrest Mars Sr., the driven, often ruthless architect of Mars, Incorporated. Their clash would become the stuff of business legend, casting them in many observers' eyes as chocolate's very own embodiment of good vs. evil.

Milton Hershey's journey into chocolate began with a stroke of inspiration at the 1893 Chicago World's Fair, where he marveled at a European exhibitor's chocolate-making machinery. At the time, Hershey was a successful caramel producer, but he foresaw that chocolate was the future.

He bought the necessary equipment on the spot and shipped it home to Pennsylvania. By 1900, he had sold his caramel business and was churning out the first Hershey's Milk Chocolate Bars, determined to make this once-luxurious Swiss treat affordable to the common man. In 1903, Hershey broke ground on a new factory in rural Derry Township and went on to build a whole town around it – Hershey, Pennsylvania, a direct homage to Cadbury's Bournville.

Hershey's model town featured comfortable homes for workers, trolley cars, a public school, a library, and eventually even an amusement park. Workers earned decent wages and enjoyed unheard-of benefits, all under the benevolent gaze of "Mr. Hershey," who wandered the factory floor in his white suit, knowing many employees by name. Childless, Milton and his wife founded a residential school for orphaned boys in 1909, endowing it with most of their wealth.

The *Hershey Industrial School* (today the Milton Hershey School) still exists, funded by the trust that owns a controlling stake in the company. In short, Milton Hershey was more than a businessman – he was a philanthropist who used chocolate to attempt a miniature utopia in the

Pennsylvania countryside. His company's motto might as well have been *doing well by doing good*.

A Town Built on Chocolate: Milton Hershey designed his model community down to the smallest detail, including Kisses-shaped streetlights.

This impulse to build a utopia was not unique to Hershey; it was a transatlantic contest of benevolence. Decades earlier in England, the Cadbury family had built Bournville, a "garden village" designed to save workers from the grime of industrial Birmingham. But while Bournville was rooted in Quaker temperance (famously banning pubs), Hershey's town was built on American optimism, complete with an amusement park, a trolley system, and streetlights shaped like foil-wrapped Kisses. Both men used chocolate wealth to sculpt the physical world, creating company towns that stood as monuments to their divergent ideals: one distinctively British and moralistic, the other bold, entertaining, and quintessentially American.

For decades, Hershey enjoyed uncontested dominance in the American chocolate scene. Its flagship chocolate bar – often simply called "The Great American Chocolate Bar" – became an icon. Hershey's Kisses (introduced in 1907) were a delight, and the company even supplied chocolate rations to U.S. troops in both World Wars. Hershey's approach to business was old-fashioned: focus on a few core products, maintain quality, don't take on debt, and avoid dirty competition. In fact, under Milton Hershey, the company refused to spend a penny on advertising, feeling the product should speak for itself. It was a tranquil chocolate kingdom – but one that was about to be disrupted by the very same Forrest Mars who had shaken up Britain.

Forrest Mars's return to the United States in the late 1930s set the stage for a showdown. After his father Frank's death, Forrest took control of Mars, Inc. and immediately began applying the rigorous methods that had fueled his UK venture. One of his first challenges was this: Mars's American business still bought its chocolate coating from none other than Hershey.

In a remarkable arrangement, the Mars company's early hits – the Milky Way and Snickers bars – were essentially collaborations, with Hershey supplying the chocolate that enrobed Mars's nougat and caramel. Forrest Mars had no intention of remaining dependent on a rival, however amicable that long-standing relationship had been. He stunned Hershey's executives by cutting off all purchases and investing heavily to produce Mars's own chocolate from scratch.

At the same time, he identified an ingenious way to leverage Hershey's strength for his own gain: in 1941, anticipating wartime rationing, Forrest approached Bruce Murrie – son of Hershey's president – to propose a new candy venture. Legend holds that during the Spanish Civil War, Forrest Mars observed soldiers eating pellets of chocolate encased in a hard sugar shell—a design that prevented the candy from melting in the Iberian heat.

He immediately recognized the military utility. He wanted to produce these "chocolate Midgets," but he needed steady supplies of chocolate and sugar, which were about to be tightly controlled by the government in World War II.

War Candy: M&Ms were originally sold in cardboard tubes and included in soldier rations because they resisted melting in the heat.

The solution was as bold as it was shrewd: Forrest Mars offered Bruce Murrie a 20% stake in the new candy, to be called M&M's (for Mars & Murrie), in exchange for Hershey's support. The Hershey company, effectively, would ensure M&M's had all the raw materials it needed – a guarantee no other competitor could get during rationing.

The deal was struck, and soon M&M's (packaged in convenient cardboard tubes) were being shipped exclusively to American G.I.s overseas as part of their rations. "Melts in your mouth, not in your hand," the advertising would later boast – a slogan that became legend.

As for Milton Hershey's company, it found itself in the awkward position of enabling what would become its fiercest rival. By war's end, American soldiers were coming home hooked on M&M's, and Mars was primed to launch them to the public. In 1948, with sugar rationing over, Forrest wasted no time in buying out Bruce Murrie's share and kicking the Hershey partner to the curb. M&M's was now 100% Mars's property – and Hershey had inadvertently nurtured the seed of its own looming downfall.

===

BUSINESS STRATEGY: THE M&M ALLIANCE

The most famous candy in the world was born from a temporary truce between enemies.

- **The Problem:** WWII rationing meant Mars couldn't get raw ingredients.
- **The Deal:** Forrest Mars partnered with Bruce Murrie (son of the Hershey president).
- **The Name:** "M&M" stands for Mars and Murrie.
- **The Payoff:** Hershey supplied the chocolate; Mars supplied the tech.

===

Once rationing ended, Mars bought Murrie out and took total control.What followed in the post-war decades was a titanic duel for America's sweet tooth. Mars rolled out a procession of hit products: the M&M's line expanded with peanuts, then other colors and flavors; the Three Musketeers bar, Skittles candies, and more.

Hershey, initially slow to react, stayed with its knitting: Hershey bars, Kisses, and a few new tries like the Hershey's Special Dark bar. Hershey did make one brilliant move in 1963 by acquiring the H.B. Reese Candy Company, makers of Reese's Peanut Butter Cups – a beloved candy that combined peanut butter and chocolate. The Reese's cup, created by a former Hershey employee turned rival, would become Hershey's greatest strategic weapon against Mars. To this day, it remains the best-selling candy brand in the United States, a peanut-butter-filled fortress that Mars has never managed to breach despite decades of attempts.

Still, by the early 1960s, Hershey's complacency was apparent. The company was still run in the spirit of Milton Hershey – cautious, community-minded, content with its dominant market share and high quality. Advertising was minimal; marketing strategy was stuck in a bygone era. Mars, by contrast, was hungry and unsentimental. Forrest Mars referred to Hershey as "the sleeping giant." He was determined to shake it awake – or shove it aside.

The 1960s became Hershey's trial by fire. Forrest Mars unleashed a full frontal assault: investing in state-of-the-art factories, flooding TV and print with advertisements, and introducing new candies to exploit any gap in Hershey's lineup. Mars's corporate culture, intense and top-secret, contrasted sharply with Hershey's paternalistic town-hall vibe. Employees at Hershey still felt they were part of a family; employees at Mars felt they were part of a war.

Under the pressure of Mars's onslaught, Hershey began to lose ground. By decade's end, Mars had nearly pulled even in U.S. chocolate sales. The once-unassailable Hershey empire was wobbling, its share of the market shrinking year by year. There was even talk in the Hershey boardroom that the company's survival was at stake if they didn't modernize.

Thus, the great Hershey vs. Mars rivalry forced a reckoning. In the 1970s, Hershey's management brought in outside talent and adopted many of Mars's tactics. They began regular advertising for the first time, launched new products (like the KitKat bar in the U.S. under license, and later the Take5 and Whatchamacallit bars), and diversified into things like cookies and crackers.

The company also gradually shifted away from the all-encompassing social benefits Milton Hershey had provided. The free housing, schools, and other perks in the town of Hershey were reduced or ended as the company focused more on efficiency and profit – much to the dismay of locals, but signaling that Hershey was entering the late-20th-century corporate reality at last.

Forrest Mars, having disrupted the industry and reached the top ranks of global wealth, stepped back from day-to-day operations in the late 1970s (passing leadership to his children). Milton Hershey had long since passed away in 1945, his name and legacy now an indelible part of American folklore. The rivalry their companies began would continue into the new millennium, but by the 1990s Hershey and Mars had settled into an uneasy duopoly in the U.S. market – together controlling the lion's share of candy sales, but each remaining fiercely competitive.

Their styles were still night and day: Hershey, a publicly traded company controlled by a charitable trust, still emphasized community and tradition in its branding (think of the nostalgic Christmas ads of Hershey's Kisses ringing like bells). Mars, entirely private and family-owned, maintained its aura of mystery while pushing a global expansion and snapping up other brands (including Wrigley's gum in 2008) to become the world's largest confectioner. If Hershey was the heart of chocolate in America, Mars had become the muscle.

Global Conquests and Modern Showdowns

As the 20th century gave way to the 21st, the chocolate world saw its once-distinct fiefdoms merge into a truly global market – and with globalization came a new wave of rivalries, takeovers, and shifting alliances. The old Quaker companies of Britain would face their destinies in this new era, and new players from Europe would rise to stand alongside the American giants.

One of the most significant developments was the dramatic end of the independent British chocolate makers. In 1988, Rowntree – the company that had so ingeniously fought back against Cadbury with KitKats and Aeros – fell prey to a takeover.

It wasn't Cadbury who conquered them, but Swiss food behemoth Nestlé. The acquisition was like a changing of the guard: the venerable

Rowntree name (and with it, beloved brands like KitKat, Smarties, and After Eight) passed into foreign hands, ending over a century of family ownership.

Nestlé's victory in that bidding war highlighted how international the chocolate business had become – even a company from a small town in York was now part of a multinational portfolio. For a time, Nestlé seemed poised to challenge Mars for global preeminence, assembling a stable of brands across continents.

Cadbury, on the other hand, survived the 20th century still under British control and even prospered, expanding its reach into Asia, Africa, and the Americas (often becoming the leading brand in former British colonies where the Cadbury name had long been established).

Cadbury had merged with the drinks company Schweppes in the 1960s, but chocolate remained its soul. The company continued to innovate gently – introducing the world's first chocolate bar with a filled center (Cadbury Crème Eggs became a phenomenon), playing with new flavors of Dairy Milk, and acquiring smaller firms to boost its candy range (like Fry's, which Cadbury had actually merged with as far back as 1919, and later the U.S. candy brand Adams in the 2000s).

Through it all, Cadbury projected an image of quintessential British sweetness and benevolence – its founding principles kept alive in philanthropic projects and a generally warm, family-friendly brand aura.

The Modern Era Begins: In 1971, the product was officially renamed the 'Cadbury Creme Egg,' transitioning from the earlier Fry's branding.

Perhaps that's why it came as such a shock to Britain when, in 2009, Cadbury found itself the target of a hostile takeover by the American food conglomerate Kraft Foods. The battle was intense and emotional.

Cadbury's management initially resisted fiercely – supported by British public opinion, which was largely aghast that a treasured national company might be swallowed by a foreign corporation known mostly for processed cheese and Oreos.

Kraft's CEO, Irene Rosenfeld, argued that the combined company would create synergies and global growth, but critics saw it as an old story of financial muscle overpowering heritage and values. Despite public protests and even debates in Parliament, Cadbury's defenses fell. In early 2010, Kraft succeeded in purchasing Cadbury for around £11.5 billion.

The purple-wrapped Dairy Milk bars that had once been the pride of a Quaker family business now became assets in a vast, impersonal multinational. It was a bittersweet end to an era – a "bitter feud" in its own right, pitting Cadbury's independent legacy against Kraft's corporate might.

The aftermath of that deal saw Kraft split off its global snack and candy business into a new company, Mondelez International, which today houses Cadbury as one of its premier brands. And interestingly, Mondelez soon found itself facing off with Hershey in a peculiar transatlantic rivalry: because Hershey holds the license to produce Cadbury products in the United States (a relationship dating back to a partnership with Cadbury long ago), disputes have arisen over whose Cadbury chocolate is "real" and whether Brits can import their beloved UK-made Cadbury bars into America.

In 2015, Hershey famously sued to stop imports of British Cadbury chocolate, citing trademark infringement, much to the outrage of British expats and chocolate connoisseurs in the States. The feud highlighted a fundamental difference in philosophy: British Cadbury's recipe uses liquid milk heated with sugar for a caramelized creaminess.

Hershey, by contrast, uses a process (lipolysis) that stabilizes the milk but produces butyric acid, giving the American bar its characteristic tangy, slightly sour profile that loyalists love and detractors question. The question of which tastes better is a matter of national loyalty – and it proves that even after acquisitions and globalization, rivalries over taste and tradition remain potent.

Amid all these changes, new champions have risen in Europe as well.

The Ferrero family of Italy, makers of Nutella and Ferrero Rocher, built a confectionery empire in the late 20th century by going against the conventional wisdom. The Ferrero legacy began in 1946 with Pietro Ferrero, who faced a post-war cocoa shortage. To stretch his limited supply, he combined a small amount of cocoa with the abundant hazelnuts of Piedmont to create 'Pasta Gianduja,' a solid loaf. Later, he tweaked the recipe to be spreadable, calling it *Supercrema*—the direct ancestor of Nutella. His son Michele later refined this into a global empire.

For decades, Ferrero avoided the high-profile rivalries, preferring to fly under the radar. But by the 2010s, Ferrero had grown into a global powerhouse second only to Mars in candy revenue, even quietly acquiring former Nestlé brands like Butterfinger and BabyRuth in the U.S. Ferrero's rise is another testament to how a singular vision – in this case, the pursuit of a particular flavor profile (the combination of rich cocoa and roasted hazelnut which Italians adore) – can challenge established giants. It's quite poetic that while everyone else was fighting over chocolate bars and market share, Ferrero conquered by creating an addiction to a chocolate spread that people would slather on their breakfast toast.

We also see the Swiss firm Lindt & Sprüngli staking a claim in the modern premium chocolate market. Through the late 20th century, Lindt transformed from a continental luxury brand into a worldwide ambassador of Swiss chocolate excellence. They opened boutiques, pushed their Lindor truffles as affordable luxuries, and acquired other brands like California's Ghirardelli.

Lindt's rivalry has been less with any single company and more with the notion of mediocrity – they have long sought to convert milk chocolate lovers to a smoother, higher-cacao experience, competing on quality in a market flooded with cheaper candy. In that sense, Lindt (and other gourmet chocolatiers from Belgium, France, and beyond) form another front in the chocolate wars: mass vs. class. By the 21st century, a discerning segment of consumers began gravitating toward small-batch, single-origin dark chocolates made by artisan makers.

These craft chocolate makers – the modern "master chocolatiers" working on a smaller scale – inherently set themselves up in rivalry against the "Big Chocolate" of Mars, Mondelez, Hershey, Nestlé, and Ferrero. The feud here is philosophical: bean-to-bar purity and ethical sourcing versus massive volume and cost efficiency. While this battle is still playing out, it echoes the very earliest chocolate rivalries when purity and ethics were on the line. It seems the more things change, the more they stay the same.

~

A Legacy Etched in Chocolate

After centuries of conquest and competition, what has emerged is a chocolate landscape rich and diverse – a direct result of those bitter feuds and clashing philosophies. The winners and losers of individual battles have mattered less, in the long run, than the innovations they spawned.

Thanks to rivalries, we have milk chocolate and dark, bars filled with caramel or cookie pieces, truffles that melt in your mouth, and candies that can travel to war or space without melting at all. Each leap forward in flavor or texture was driven by someone striving to outdo someone else: a smoother process, a richer recipe, a smarter marketing hook.

The personalities behind these struggles have become legends in their own right. Milton Hershey and Forrest Mars – one remembered as a benevolent dreamer, the other as an exacting empire-builder – both irrevocably shaped how the world enjoys candy. The Cadbury brothers and the Rowntrees proved that business can have a conscience, even as they fought for market primacy.

Their legacy lives on every time a Dairy Milk or KitKat is unwrapped during a work break or a holiday gathering. And those Quaker pioneers might find some satisfaction in the fact that, even as their companies were absorbed by bigger fish, the debate they started about the soul of business carries on. Are companies beholden only to profit, or also to people? In the chocolate world, we've seen models for both, each successful on its own terms.

In the end, chocolate's great rivalries have done more than create corporate winners and losers – they've given us an endless assortment of treats and stories to savor. Whether you prefer the simple nostalgia of a

Hershey bar, the creamy comfort of Cadbury, the playful crunch of an M&M or KitKat, or an elegant Lindt truffle, you are enjoying the spoils of wars fought long ago (and some still being fought).

The feuds were often bitter, but they pushed chocolatiers to be better – to dream up wilder flavors, craft smoother confections, and package joy in ever more delectable ways. The next time you indulge in a piece of chocolate, you might taste a hint of that history: the inventiveness, the passion, and yes, the competitive fire that have fueled chocolate's rise from an everyday drink to a global obsession. In a world of constant change, one thing remains sweetly consistent: whenever chocolate lovers benefit, chances are a rivalry was the secret ingredient.

31

THE DARK SIDE: FRAUD, SMUGGLING, AND THE SHADOW ECONOMY

T wo scenes unfold simultaneously, thousands of miles apart, yet connected by the same humble bean.

In a quiet laboratory tucked behind a gourmet chocolatier's shop, a chemist carefully tests a selection of 'premium' chocolate bars. What she discovers sends shockwaves through the confectionery world: not all that glitters is pure cacao. Some of these luxury-labeled bars—priced and marketed as the finest, most authentic chocolate—are hiding a dark secret. The ingredients don't match their labels. Exotic single-origin claims smell fishy, and subtle flavor notes hint at adulteration.

Midnight, somewhere near the Ghana–Togo border: A battered minibus rattles down a dusty road, its driver nervously eyeing the rearview mirror. The vehicle looks ordinary enough, packed with sacks of cassava and yams—but hidden in a secret compartment beneath the roof are dozens of burlap bags filled with cocoa beans. Suddenly, flashing headlights appear. Uniformed officers from Ghana's National Anti-Cocoa Smuggling Taskforce flag the minibus to a stop. In the ensuing search, they clamber onto the roof and expose the illicit cargo: sixteen 110-pound bags of cocoa, carefully concealed.

. . .

THESE ARE the two faces of chocolate's shadow economy—fraud and smuggling—twin plagues that have haunted the cacao trade since its earliest days. Together, they form a silent scandal that cheats consumers, robs farmers of fair payment, and funnels billions of dollars into the hands of unscrupulous middlemen and criminal networks.

A hidden lab reveals how scientific testing exposes adulterated chocolate.
Even the most luxurious bars can hide deceptive ingredients.

THE GREAT CHOCOLATE Fraud

Under the shop's low ambient light, the chemist furrows her brow at the data in front of her. One bar, advertised boldly as a '70% single-origin dark chocolate' from a fabled cacao-growing region, contains unexpected compounds under analysis. The ratios of cocoa butter to cocoa solids are wrong. Even more troubling, traces of a vegetable oil—something that has no business being in a pure chocolate bar—turn up in the test results. Could this pricey 'artisan' bar have been bulked up with something cheaper?

She runs the tests again, and again the results challenge the label's claims. This isn't a one-off fluke—patterns begin to emerge. The same anomalies show up in other samples labeled as 'exclusive' or 'bean-to-bar' chocolates. Recent research in the food industry suggests that about one in ten food and drink products worldwide is adulterated or mislabeled. Chocolate, it seems, is no exception, especially among high-end bars that command a premium for supposedly ethical or rare ingredients. The more money at stake, the greater the temptation to cheat.

Alarmed by the lab results, the chemist confides in a trusted ally—a veteran food safety inspector renowned for his dogged investigations.

This food-safety sleuth has chased fraud in everything from fake olive oil to phony truffle shavings.

When he hears the chemist's findings, he agrees: this chocolate case warrants a closer look. The pair begin poring over labels, ingredient lists, and supply chain documents for the suspect bars, comparing what's on paper with what's in the chocolate. The deeper they dig, the clearer it becomes: the chemist's discovery is likely the tip of a very large, very cocoa-dusted iceberg.

The Whistleblower's Revelation

Just as the sleuth and chemist ramp up their inquiry, a cryptic message arrives from overseas. It's from an industry insider—a whistle-blower who has worked for years at a major cocoa exporter. Using careful, coded language, the insider hints at systematic deceit in the trade. He describes cocoa beans from ordinary farms being re-labeled as prized 'single-estate' lots, and shipments of bulk cacao quietly mixed with rarer, high-flavor beans to inflate profits.

'They'd take sacks of our standard beans and sprinkle a few premium ones on top for show,' he writes. 'Then they'd mark the whole lot as fine flavor cacao from a special origin.' In essence, buyers further down the line were paying for top-shelf quality but receiving a diluted product—a blend that was part genuine, part imposter.

This type of deception has a name: Economically Motivated Adulteration (EMA). It is a $40 billion global problem, but it is not a new one. As we saw in Chapter 2, even the Aztecs battled counterfeiters who filled empty cacao shells with clay. Today, the methods have evolved from mud to vegetable fats, but the intent remains the same. Chocolate is in the same high-risk category as extra virgin olive oil, honey, and truffle oil.

The logic of the fraudster is simple arithmetic. Cacao butter is the most expensive fat in the confectionary world. Palm oil and shea butter are cheap. If a factory can replace just 5% of the cocoa butter with a cheaper substitute and hide it within a complex flavor profile, they can save millions of dollars a year.

The consumer's palate is easily tricked; the mass spectrometer is not. But until someone tests the bar, the profit margin is pure gold. Today's scams include passing off low-grade cacao as elite varieties or mixing cheap fillers into what's sold as pure, high-cocoa chocolate.

Secrets in the Supply Chain

A major breakthrough comes in a bustling port city's warehouse district, where the air smells of cocoa and seawater. Here, the team watches pallets of jute sacks being loaded off cargo ships. Each sack bears a printed label—declarations like 'Ecuador – Arriba Nacional, Grade 1' or 'Single Origin: Ivory Coast.' In theory, a bag labeled with a specific origin and grade should contain exactly that and nothing else. But the investigators notice subtle inconsistencies. In one warehouse, they spot a stack of sacks with overwritten labels—as if someone had stamped a new origin on top of a previous one.

The real proof comes when they obtain samples from one of these suspect shipments and send them to a specialized lab for genetic analysis. Thanks to a recently developed cocoa DNA 'fingerprinting' technique, scientists can pinpoint a cacao bean's varietal lineage—and even its geographic origin—by analyzing its genetic markers.

A week later, the lab report comes back with damning results. The beans in a sack purportedly from a single-origin lot in Peru show DNA markers that don't match Peruvian cacao at all. In fact, they closely resemble hybrid beans common in West Africa. Another sample labeled 'Madagascar boutique estate' turns out to be a mix of varieties, some of which likely came from commodity farms in different countries.

The complexity of the global cocoa supply chain makes it ripe for these kinds of tricks. From remote plantations, beans pass through many hands—local collectors, middlemen, exporters, importers, processors—and at each step there's room for an unscrupulous player to slip in something, relabel something, or quietly mix lots together. Even well-intentioned certifications like 'Organic' or 'Fair Trade' can be gamed. An organic or fair-trade label commands higher prices, making it a tantalizing target for fraud.

∾

Officers reveal smuggled cocoa hidden in a minibus roof compartment. The discovery highlights the complex networks behind illegal bean trafficking.

CHEAPER INGREDIENTS, Costly Lies

Mislabeling the origin of cacao is one form of deceit; adulterating the chocolate itself is another, often more blatant, form. During a covert visit to a small chocolate manufacturing plant, the sleuth observes something he wasn't meant to see.

A production worker, glancing furtively over his shoulder, dumps a bucket of pale, waxy solid chunks into a melting tank that's supposed to contain only pure cocoa butter and cocoa mass. Later, the team manages to obtain a sample of that mystery ingredient and have it analyzed. The verdict: it's vegetable fat, likely palm oil-based.

By law in many regions—a standard fought for in the "Chocolate Wars" detailed in Chapter 32—only a very small amount of alternative vegetable fat (usually up to 5%) is allowed in products sold as chocolate, and even then it must be disclosed on the label. Using more than that, or failing to disclose it, is outright fraud. Beyond the legal issues, adding a cheap fat dilutes the rich flavor and smooth texture that true chocolate lovers expect from a high-quality bar. It's a deceptive shortcut to boost margin.

And it's not just fats that are being swapped or added. The investigation uncovers other instances of adulteration. Some supposedly high-grade cocoa powder on the market is being secretly cut with cheaper substances to increase volume.

A worker secretly adds cheap fats into a chocolate vat, showing how fraud often begins on the factory floor. The scene illustrates the ease with which purity can be compromised.

One common trick is blending cocoa powder with carob powder—a low-cost chocolate substitute that can mimic cocoa's color and a hint of its taste when mixed in moderate amounts. In another case, a chocolate hazelnut spread that claimed to use only costly cocoa and real vanilla was found to include coloured starch and artificial flavorings to imitate the appearance and aroma of richer ingredients.

COUNTERFEIT CONFECTIONS

As the investigation widens, the trail of fraud leads from factory formulas to something even more brazen: counterfeit chocolate bars on store shelves. These aren't just misformulated chocolates hidden behind legitimate brands, but outright fake products packaged to look like famous brands.

In a crowded street market one Saturday, the sleuth comes upon a stall selling what appear at first glance to be popular brand-name chocolates. Among the assorted bars, one catches his eye immediately—a bright wrapper proclaiming 'Wonka Bar' in swirling candy-font letters. Fans of Charlie and the Chocolate Factory might squeal with joy at the sight, but the sleuth knows that no legitimate Wonka Bars are in production these days.

It turns out fake 'Wonka' bars have been flooding markets in the UK and beyond, piggybacking on the whimsical appeal of the brand. In December 2023, Britain's Food Standards Agency (FSA) sounded the alarm on a surge of bogus chocolate bars imitating various well-known names, specifically citing the danger of unregistered allergens in counterfeit "Wonka" bars sold online.

One particularly bizarre knock-off capitalized on the viral popularity of an energy drink brand called Prime—wrappers for 'Prime chocolate bars' appeared, despite the real company having never made a chocolate product at all. These counterfeit bars are often churned out by unlicensed, underground operators who pay little heed to hygiene or food safety laws.

Bogus Branding. These unlicensed bars piggyback on the whimsy of the Wonka name but bypass essential food safety regulations, serving as prime examples of the "bogus chocolate" epidemic flagged by the FSA.

An FSA official publicly warned that these were not just copyright infringements, but biological hazards. 'You don't know what's in them... There could be a food safety risk, especially for those with food intolerances or allergies.' Those words proved painfully true. These unregulated novelty bars often bypass the strict allergen controls of legitimate factories, turning a childhood fantasy wrapper into a potential medical emergency.

The previous year, dozens of fake Wonka Bars were seized after authorities discovered they contained undeclared allergens—ingredients like nuts and milk that weren't listed anywhere on the phony labels. For someone with a serious allergy, a single bite of those fraudulent chocolates could have meant a trip to the emergency room, or worse.

In one especially shocking case a few years back, a batch of counterfeit chocolate products imported from China was found to be infested with live worms. A video from the bust showed customs officers opening golden foil boxes—made to resemble those of a famous hazelnut chocolate brand—only to reveal squirming white larvae crawling among the chocolates.

French authorities seized over 10 tons of these low-grade counterfeit chocolates ahead of the holiday season one year, goods that would have been worth hundreds of thousands of dollars on the black market.

THE SMUGGLING SURGE

While fraud corrupts what's inside the chocolate bar, another shadow economy operates on an even grander scale: the smuggling of raw cacao beans across international borders. Cocoa—the raw heartbeat of chocolate—is West Africa's lifeblood. Ghana and Côte d'Ivoire together produce nearly two-thirds of the world's cocoa beans.

Yet in recent years, a shadow economy has exploded around this commodity. Smuggling rings spirit cocoa across porous borders under cover of night. Middlemen whisper secret deals in border villages. Countless tons of beans 'disappear' from official supply chains, reappearing in neighboring countries' ledgers as if by magic.

At the heart of this surge is a simple economic lure: price. Ghana and Ivory Coast maintain fixed farmgate prices for cocoa, guaranteeing farmers a set rate each season. The policy is meant to protect growers from volatile global markets. But when world cocoa prices soar—as they have in recent years, reaching their highest levels in over four decades—those fixed local prices start to look like a bad deal.

In late 2024, for example, Ghana's official price to farmers was around $3,000 per ton. But just across the border in Togo—a country without a fixed price, where the market floats freely—traders were suddenly paying the equivalent of $5,000 or more per ton. For a struggling farmer, that gap is enormous.

'I have expenses to take care of,' says Joshua Dogboe, a cocoa grower from eastern Ghana's Volta region. Last year, Dogboe delivered his harvest to Ghana's state buyer and waited weeks for payment that never arrived; the government-run cocoa board was mired in debt and late in paying farmers. Now, Dogboe admits, if unofficial buyers come with cash on the spot, offering higher prices, he's ready to sell 'quickly, before they disappear.' He knows it's illegal. He also knows it might be the only way to make ends meet this season.

Dogboe's dilemma is shared by thousands. Ghana's Cocoa Board (known as COCOBOD) estimates that in the past two years alone, the country lost nearly half a million tonnes of cocoa to smuggling—roughly a fifth of its total output. That equates to over $1 billion in lost revenue that never passed through official hands.

THE CHOCOLATE CARTELS

What's striking is how organized and brazen these operations have become. 'It's not just farmers carrying a few bags on bicycles or motorbikes anymore,' notes Abu Seidu, who leads a cocoa task force in Ghana's Volta region. 'Now you see a heavy-duty tipper truck loaded with cocoa, with a pile of stone chippings on top as disguise.' During one recent patrol, Seidu's team stopped a truck that appeared to be transporting gravel from a quarry—only to uncover hundreds of sacks of cocoa hidden beneath the top layer of rocks. 'If you catch a truck with 800, 500, or even 200 bags,' Seidu says, 'it tells you someone is aggregating the cocoa... It's now an organized cartel.'

Indeed, law enforcement officials suspect that sophisticated trafficking syndicates are bankrolling much of this trade. According to intelligence gathered in Ghana, some of the most active cocoa-smuggling rings are operated or financed by foreign businessmen and shadowy intermediaries based in Togo and other neighboring states. Investigators have traced links to individuals from Lebanon, China, France, and even Russia, who have set up shop just over the border.

These middlemen provide the cash up front to buy large quantities of beans from farmers, arrange the logistics of transport, and then funnel the contraband cocoa into the global market—often mislabeling its origin to evade detection.

There have even been hints of geopolitical intrigue. In Ghana, **Joseph Boahen Aidoo**, the chief executive of COCOBOD, raised eyebrows when he publicly suggested that elements of Russia's Wagner

Group—the infamous mercenary network—were involved in cocoa smuggling in Africa. Aidoo alleged that the group was bypassing sanctions by buying up illicit Ivorian and Ghanaian beans through proxy traders to fund their operations. While hard evidence is scarce and some analysts remain skeptical, the mere suggestion underscores how valuable cocoa has become on the global stage.

Seeds of Wrath: A History of Contraband Cacao

If all this sounds like a storyline ripped from a modern war on drugs, it might come as a surprise that cocoa smuggling is hardly new. Wherever there have been profits to be made from cocoa, there have been those willing to bend or break the law to get a bigger share of the spoils.

Travel back three centuries to the Spanish Empire in the Americas, and you'll find one of the earliest 'chocolate wars' playing out. In the 1700s, Spain jealously guarded its New World cacao sources—in colonies like Venezuela, where the prized beans from Caracas and Maracaibo were as valuable as gold in European markets. The Spanish crown granted monopolies to chartered companies to control the cocoa trade, forbidding any unauthorized selling of cacao to foreign powers. But local planters bristled under what they saw as unfairly low prices. And just offshore, lurking in the Eastern Caribbean, were eager buyers: Dutch, British, and French traders who would pay handsomely, no questions asked, for smuggled Spanish cacao.

A clandestine trade blossomed. Venezuelan cacao farmers covertly sent boatloads of cocoa beans to nearby Dutch islands like Curaçao, or to British Jamaica, trading in secret coves and hidden inlets under the cover of darkness. By the mid-18th century, historians estimate that millions of pounds of Venezuelan cacao—some accounts say between three and four million pounds annually—were quietly being siphoned onto the Dutch black market, feeding the burgeoning chocolate demand in Amsterdam and London.

Cacao farmers confront colonial officials over unfair trade controls. Their revolt shows how deeply chocolate economics shaped political resistance.

In April 1749, tensions boiled over into outright rebellion. Led by a charismatic planter named Juan Francisco de León, Venezuelan cacao growers rose up in anger against the monopoly company's stranglehold and low prices. For years, many had quietly enriched themselves by selling to smugglers.

Now they took to the streets of Caracas, armed and determined to expel the hated company. The rebellion was eventually quashed by Spanish forces, but it forced reforms; the monopoly loosened its grip slightly and raised prices to placate growers. It's a vivid historical echo of what's happening in West Africa today: when farmers feel cheated by official channels, the black market offers an outlet—albeit a dangerous one—for their frustration.

Meanwhile, far to the north, in the Anglo-American colonies, cocoa smuggling took on a swashbuckling, piratical flair. In the 1730s and 1740s, New England merchants traded for high-quality cacao from Dutch Suriname or French Martinique, skirting British import taxes and navigation laws.

Some even mixed this with the nefarious slave trade, creating a triad of contraband: New England rum and fish traded for enslaved Africans in West Africa, transported to Suriname and exchanged for cacao, which was then smuggled back to North America or Europe.

. . .

Conflict Cocoa

Just as 'blood diamonds' fueled conflicts in Sierra Leone and Congo, one could speak of 'conflict cocoa' in Ivory Coast's turmoil. During Ivory Coast's civil war in 2010–2011, rebel militias controlling the western regions reportedly smuggled tens of thousands of tons of cocoa out through Liberia to fund their arms purchases. Those former rebels-turned-smugglers became a kind of criminal cartel themselves after the war, using networks of army checkpoints and bribed officials to skim off cocoa profits long into the peace.

The cocoa black market often goes hand-in-hand with other illicit activities. In some cases, child labor and trafficking intersect with these informal networks—traffickers might smuggle vulnerable children from impoverished neighboring countries into Ivory Coast or Ghana to work on cocoa farms, especially if the farms are off the radar of authorities due to illicit trading. And if a farmer decides to sell to a smuggler, they're unlikely to report or seek help for abused or trafficked laborers, for fear of exposing their own illegal sales.

Additionally, a lucrative smuggling trade can breed corruption: local officials or border guards might be bribed to turn a blind eye, under-mining governance and the rule of law in fragile communities. A Ghanaian police inspector was arrested last year after he was found escorting a truck packed with contraband cocoa—allegedly ensuring its safe passage for a cut of the profits. These stories sow mistrust, painting law enforcement as complicit, and make honest farmers wonder why they too shouldn't bend the rules when those tasked with upholding them are on the take.

Victims of the Chocolate Con

The stakes in chocolate's shadow economy go far beyond some connoisseurs overpaying for mediocre candy. Public health is on the line. The adulteration of chocolate isn't just about taste and money—it can introduce ingredients that certain people can't safely eat. Think of those undeclared allergens in the fake Wonka bars: a parent might unknowingly give what looks like a normal chocolate treat to a child with a nut allergy, not realizing it's laced with cheap nut powder used as filler. The result could be a life-threatening allergic reaction.

On the flip side of the supply chain, consider the cocoa farmers and honest chocolate makers who become collateral damage in this fraud. When a gourmet bar is 'cut' with inferior ingredients or its origin misrepresented, the honest producers are undercut and undermined.

Farmers who toil to cultivate high-quality, heirloom cacao—carefully fermenting and drying the beans for optimal flavor, often as part of traditions passed down through generations—depend on the premium prices that authentic fine chocolate can command. But if buyers and consumers start to doubt every claim on a label, suspecting that 'Madagascar' or 'Venezuela Criollo' might just be a marketing ploy, the market for fine cacao falters.

The whistleblower—the man who helped crack the fraud case open—knows these human stakes all too well. He comes from a family of cocoa growers and feels the pain in his bones. 'My father grows cacao the traditional way,' he says softly, fidgeting with a cacao pod plucked from his family farm. 'He ferments it just right, takes such pride in it... but he gets pennies. Meanwhile, I saw traders mixing his beans with others and selling some story about "legacy cacao" to naïve buyers. It made me sick.'

The victims of smuggling are likewise the small farmers and the legitimate economies of producing nations. When beans are sold illicitly, farmers remain in the shadows, often underpaid even by the smugglers, with no access to the benefits that come from selling through official channels—like potential bonuses, pension schemes, or support programs from cocoa boards. They also risk severe penalties if caught—prison sentences of five to ten years in Ghana, for instance, for anyone convicted of cocoa smuggling. That's a harsh fate for a farmer whose only crime is seeking a better price for his hard-grown harvest.

FIGHTING BACK: **Technology and Transparency**

Amidst the anger and betrayal, there is also determination. Scientists and regulators see an opportunity to right these wrongs. New testing technologies are offering ways to verify what's in a chocolate bar beyond what the label says. The DNA analysis used to uncover bean origins is one tool in the arsenal. Another is cutting-edge spectroscopy devices that can scan a chocolate or cocoa powder and instantly flag unusual ingredients or contaminants by their spectral signature.

One researcher explained that these innovations could be game-changers: currently, a DNA test can cost hundreds of dollars per sample, but if the technology becomes more accessible and cheaper, a chocolate maker—or even a curious consumer—could authenticate a bar's origin or detect adulteration on the spot. As these tests become more widespread, it will be much harder for fraudsters to get away with their schemes. Imagine a future in which you could scan a QR code on a chocolate bar and see the full journey of the ingredients, verified by independent audits and scientific tests. In that world, chocolate counterfeiting and adulteration would have no hiding place.

A startup company is even exploring blockchain-based ledgers for cacao shipments—imagine being able to trace every box of beans via an incorruptible digital record, making it nearly impossible to surreptitiously mix or alter a batch without leaving a telltale trace.

Switzerland, famed as a chocolate-making hub but with no cocoa trees of its own, has offered technical assistance to Ghana to improve traceability systems. In Ghana, pilot programs are training farmers to use electronic scales and record purchases digitally. Ivory Coast has considered GPS tracking units on trucks hauling cocoa, to ensure they don't wander off approved routes to clandestine border crossings.

Battling the Bitter Aftertaste

While law enforcement and border patrols remain crucial, many experts argue that the real antidote to cocoa's dark side is economic, not just criminal. As one development specialist puts it, 'If a farmer can earn a decent living selling legally, the incentive to smuggle evaporates.' In practice, that means raising farmgate prices to more competitive levels, paying farmers on time, and reducing the costs they shoulder for fertilizer, tools, and other inputs.

In 2019, Côte d'Ivoire and Ghana, tired of seeing their farmers remain impoverished while global chocolate giants raked in profits, banded together to create a joint initiative often dubbed an 'OPEC for cocoa.'

They agreed to coordinate on pricing and introduced a premium called the Living Income Differential (LID)—essentially a surcharge of $400 per ton on cocoa sales, intended to raise farmer incomes. For the first time, the two rivals—normally competitors for buyers—were acting in concert like a classic commodity cartel.

There have been some moves to address immediate crises. In late 2024, when Ghanaian farmers grew restless and even threatened mass smuggling as a form of protest, the government took notice. Ghana's finance ministry made the unusual decision to increase the fixed cocoa price mid-season, bumping it up by 12% to appease farmers after Ivory Coast preemptively raised its own price. It was a temporary fix, but it sent a message that farmer voices—and the specter of them taking their crops underground—carried weight.

Perhaps the most nuanced approach is tackling the root cause: farmer poverty and overreliance on a single crop. Diversification programs are being promoted, encouraging cocoa farmers to intercrop with other plants or develop side businesses, so a slump in cocoa price isn't a ruinous blow. Some NGOs help organize village savings and loan associations, giving farmers a financial cushion and reducing the temptation to accept a smuggler's quick cash.

What Chocolate Lovers Can Do

For now, what can a chocolate lover do? There's no foolproof method to guarantee a treat is legit, but experts suggest a few steps that can tilt the odds in your favor and support integrity in the industry.

Buy from reputable makers or sellers. Well-known chocolatiers or retailers with a reputation to protect are far less likely to risk selling fraudulent products. If you're eyeing a rare origin or high-priced chocolate from an unfamiliar source and the deal seems too good to be true, trust your instincts—it probably is too good to be true.

Read labels closely. If the package says 'chocolatey' or 'chocolate flavored' instead of just 'chocolate,' that's a red flag—it often indicates the product isn't real chocolate at all. Be wary of vague language or an overly long list of ingredients on what should be a simple dark chocolate bar. High-quality chocolate is usually pretty minimal in ingredients: cocoa mass, cocoa butter, sugar, maybe vanilla and lecithin.

Trust your palate and your gut. If a so-called premium bar tastes oddly waxy, overly sweet, or just not as rich as you'd expect, don't be afraid to question it. Texture and mouthfeel are often the biggest giveaways of subpar or adulterated chocolate—real chocolate made with pure cocoa butter should start melting the moment you touch it and feel luscious, not plasticky.

With so many choices, knowing how to spot true quality in
chocolate becomes essential for a truly satisfying treat.

Know your chocolatier when possible. The closer you can buy to the source, the better. If you have access to bean-to-bar chocolate makers who are transparent about their process, consider supporting them. Many craft chocolate makers take pride in forging direct relationships with cacao farmers and will happily share details about origin, processing, and even lab results for their bars.

A BITTERSWEET LEGACY

One might wonder, as they unwrap a chocolate bar or sip a cup of cocoa, why this beloved treat so often seems to carry a bitter aftertaste of exploitation—child labor, deforestation, and now fraud, smuggling, and cartels. The truth is, chocolate's supply chain has always been complex and fraught with inequality. The dark side of chocolate today is but the latest chapter in a long story of people fighting—sometimes literally—over who gets to profit from this cherished commodity.

==

THE ETHICAL BUYER'S CHEAT SHEET

Labels can be lying. Here is your 3-second audit to avoid fraud and slavery.

- **1. The Price Test:**
  - Is it under $3 for a bar? RED FLAG. Cheap chocolate usually relies on underpaid labor or cheap filler fats.
- **2. The Ingredient Audit:**
  - Does it say "chocolatey coating" or "vegetable fat"? FAKE. Put it back.
  - Are there more than 5 ingredients? CAUTION. High-quality chocolate needs only beans, sugar, and maybe butter/lecithin.
- **3. The Origin Check:**
  - Does it list a specific country (e.g., "Madagascar") or just "West Africa"? SPECIFIC IS BETTER.
  - Does it say "Direct Trade"? GOLD STANDARD. This usually means the maker visited the farm and paid above market rate.

==

From colonial planters skirting imperial decrees to modern farmers defying their governments' pricing schemes, the protagonists are often the same: those at the bottom rungs trying to claim a fair share of the wealth that cocoa can create. The antagonists, too, follow a familiar pattern: powerful entities determined to maximize their own gain, laws and ethics be damned. Caught in between are individuals simply trying to survive or thrive in the system they're born into—a Ghanaian farmer weighing whether to sell to an illegal buyer to feed his family this year, or a Venezuelan campesino in 1740 weighing whether to load his mule and sneak off to the Dutch trader who pays in silver coin.

The Great Chocolate Fraud raises tough questions about truth and transparency in our food system. Consumers understandably feel betrayed. If you can't trust the label on a ten-dollar artisanal bar of chocolate, what does that say about all the other foods in your pantry? The lesson here isn't to give up on chocolate—it's to demand honesty and accountability from farm to factory to store.

It is easy to enjoy a piece of chocolate without a thought for the journey of its ingredients. Yet, embedded in that rich flavor is a global drama—one that involves smuggling plots and fraud schemes in real-life chocolate wars. The next time you indulge in a truffle or a cup of hot cocoa, consider the far-away struggles that help keep that supply steady and affordable. The world of chocolate isn't only sweet delight; it's also clandestine deals on moonlit nights and a fight for economic justice that spans generations.

IN THE END, the story of fraud, smuggling, black markets, and informal economies in chocolate is a reminder that even the most ordinary pleasures often have extraordinary backstories. The battle against chocolate's dark side will likely persist until the deeper issues are resolved. Until then, the wars in the shadows rage on, leaving us to savor each bite of chocolate with perhaps a bit more appreciation of the complex network of human endeavor, desire, and ingenuity that makes it possible. The taste is sweet, but the struggle to bring it to our lips is anything but simple.

32

THE COCOA DIRECTIVE: THE THIRTY-YEAR WAR FOR THE SOUL OF CHOCOLATE

*T*he war began not with a gunshot, but with a refusal. In 1973, the United Kingdom, along with Ireland and Denmark, formally joined the European Economic Community (EEC), the precursor to the European Union. It was a moment of political unification, a knitting together of economies to prevent future conflicts. But in the cargo holds of British trucks and the pantries of British expats, a contraband item was being smuggled across the Channel. It was purple-wrapped, rectangular, and utterly beloved by the British public. It was a bar of Cadbury Dairy Milk.

To the British, this was the quintessential taste of home: creamy, sweet, and comforting. But to the customs officers and food regulators of France, Belgium, and West Germany, it was an imposter. Under the strict food purity laws of the Continental bloc, the British bar was legally forbidden from bearing the name "chocolate." It contained a foreign substance, an ingredient that the purists viewed as a culinary heresy: unadulterated vegetable fat.

Thus began the longest, most bitter dispute in the history of European food law. Known to bureaucrats as the Cocoa Directive Conflict and to the press as the Chocolate War, this thirty-year saga paralyzed the European Parliament, pitted nation against nation, and exposed the deep cultural rifts between the industrial pragmatism of the North and the gastronomic idealism of the South.

At the heart of the conflict was a question that seems simple but is fraught with billion-dollar implications: Is chocolate defined by its ingredients, or by the pleasure it provides?

The Cult of Cocoa Butter

To understand why this war was fought with such ferocity, one must first understand the substance at the center of the battlefield: cocoa butter.

Cocoa butter is a freak of nature. In the world of edible fats, it is unique. Most animal fats (like lard) are solid at room temperature but greasy; most vegetable oils (like olive or canola) are liquid. Cocoa butter, however, occupies a miraculous middle ground. It is crystalline and brittle at 20°C (68°F), providing the structural rigidity that gives a chocolate bar its satisfying "snap." Yet, its melting point is razor-sharp, sitting exactly between 33°C and 34°C (roughly 93°F).

This thermal threshold is just a few degrees below the internal temperature of the human mouth (37°C). This means that when a piece of pure chocolate is placed on the tongue, it does not just soften; it undergoes a rapid phase change from solid to liquid. This phase change absorbs latent heat from the mouth, creating a physical cooling sensation—a refreshing, silky cascade that chocolatiers call "the melt."

For the chocolate purists of Belgium, France, Switzerland, and Germany, this physical property was the soul of chocolate. Their legal codes, dating back to the 19th century, were explicit: for a product to be called chocolate, the only fat it could contain was the fat extracted from the cocoa bean itself.

To these nations, cocoa butter was expensive, difficult to work with, and temperamental—but it was non-negotiable. It represented the integrity of the craft.

～

THE RISE of the Vegetable Fat

Across the English Channel, the history of chocolate had taken a different trajectory. While the French and Belgians were refining dark, high-cocoa couverture for the aristocracy, the British Quaker industrialists—the Cadburys, the Rowntrees, the Frys—were trying to mass-produce a treat for the working class.

In the late 19th and early 20th centuries, British manufacturers faced a problem. Cocoa butter was the most expensive component of the bean. To make chocolate affordable for the factory worker, and to make it stable enough to sit on a shop shelf in summer without turning into a puddle, they needed a stabilizer.

They found their answer in the colonies. The British Empire provided access to a variety of tropical fats—shea butter from West Africa, illipe from Borneo, sal from India, and palm oil from Malaysia. British chemists discovered that by blending small amounts of these vegetable fats (up to 5%) with cocoa butter, they could achieve several industrial advantages:

- Cost Reduction: Vegetable fats were significantly cheaper than cocoa butter.
- Bloom Resistance: The addition of these fats helped prevent fat bloom (the white streaking caused by cocoa butter separating).
- Texture Modification: It created a slightly softer, more malleable bar that was less brittle and easier to mold.

For decades, the British public happily consumed this product. They did not care about the crystal lattice structure of triglycerides; they cared that it was sweet, milky, and affordable. When the UK joined the EEC in 1973, they assumed their chocolate would join them.

They were wrong. The French and Belgians, protecting their own high-end chocolate industries, refused to recognize the British product. They demanded that British chocolate be sold in Europe under a derogatory label: "Vegelate," "Fat-based Fantasy," or simply "Chocolate Substitute."

The British were outraged. To tell a nation that its beloved Dairy

Milk was actually "Vegelate" was a cultural insult of the highest order. The battle lines were drawn.

The Chemistry of Betrayal

The war might have remained a diplomatic spat if not for the rapid advancement of food chemistry. In the 1970s and 80s, the science of fat took a quantum leap forward.

In the early days, the vegetable fats added to chocolate were merely fillers. They were chemically distinct from cocoa butter and often resulted in a waxy mouthfeel (the dreaded "candle wax" texture). But as the Chocolate War heated up, major industrial lipid companies like Unilever and Fuji Oil began developing a new generation of fats known as Cocoa Butter Equivalents (CBEs).

To create a CBE, scientists analyzed the molecular fingerprint of cocoa butter. They found it was composed primarily of three triglycerides: POP (Palmitic-Oleic-Palmitic), POS (Palmitic-Oleic-Stearic), and SOS (Stearic-Oleic-Stearic).

Using a sophisticated process called fractionation, chemists could take palm oil (rich in POP) and shea butter (rich in SOS) and isolate the specific fractions that matched cocoa butter. By blending these fractions in precise ratios, they could engineer a fat that was chemically almost identical to cocoa butter.

This terrified the purists. The old vegetable fats were easy to spot— they tasted bad. But CBEs were stealth agents. They snapped like cocoa butter. They melted like cocoa butter. They crystallized in the same polymorphic forms. In a blind taste test, even experts struggled to tell the difference between a bar made with 100% cocoa butter and one made with 95% cocoa butter and 5% CBE.

To the Traditionalist bloc (France, Belgium), this was not progress; it was the ultimate fraud. It meant that multinational corporations could dilute their chocolate with cheaper fats, increase their profit margins, and the consumer would never know. They argued that legalizing CBEs would trigger a "race to the bottom," forcing high-quality artisan producers out of business as they struggled to compete with cheaper, engineered industrial chocolate.

. . .

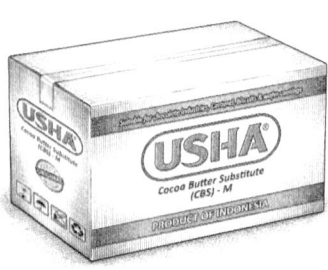

The European Union Directive 2000/36/EC (left) harmonized
standards across Europe, legally permitting the addition of up to 5%
vegetable fats other than cocoa butter. This ruling opened the door
for wider use of Cocoa Butter Substitutes (CBS) and Equivalents
(right) in products labeled as chocolate, a point of contention for
traditional purists.

THE GEOPOLITICS of the Shea Nut

The Chocolate War was not just fought in European courtrooms; it
had ripples that reached deep into the African savannah.

As the debate raged, a new and unexpected coalition entered the fray.
The proponents of vegetable fat (led by the UK) argued that allowing
CBEs was actually a humanitarian act. They pointed to the source of
these alternative fats: the shea tree (*Vitellaria paradoxa*).

The shea tree grows wild across the Sahel belt of Africa—from
Senegal in the west to Sudan in the east. The harvesting of shea nuts is
an industry almost entirely dominated by women. In rural communities
in Burkina Faso and northern Ghana, collecting and processing shea
nuts is one of the few sources of independent cash income for women.

Lobbyists for the industrial chocolate giants weaponized this fact,
creating one of the strangest alliances in political history. Suddenly,
multinational corporations like Mars and Nestlé found themselves
marching in lockstep with women's rights groups and development
NGOs. They argued that by banning vegetable fats, the European
purists were effectively impoverishing African women. This moral
leverage painted the "100% Cocoa Butter" rule not as a standard of

quality, but as Eurocentric protectionism that hurt the developing world.

On the other side of the trench were the cocoa-producing nations—Côte d'Ivoire and Ghana. They viewed the rise of CBEs as an existential threat. Cocoa butter is the most valuable part of the cocoa bean (often trading at two to three times the price of the cocoa solids). If Europe allowed manufacturers to replace 5% of that cocoa butter with shea or palm oil, the global demand for cocoa beans would plummet.

Wild shea trees (*Vitellaria paradoxa*) dotting the arid savanna of the Sahel belt.

The International Cocoa Organization (ICCO) crunched the numbers. They estimated that if the 5% rule were applied across the EU, the demand for cocoa beans would drop by 200,000 tons per year. Prices would crash. The economies of West Africa, already fragile, would shatter.

The European Parliament found itself trapped in a moral pincer movement.

- Vote "Yes" to Vegetable Fats: You support the British industry and the women of the Sahel, but you betray the cocoa farmers of the Ivory Coast and the culinary heritage of France.
- Vote "No" to Vegetable Fats: You protect the purity of chocolate and the cocoa market, but you alienate the UK and destroy the market for shea nuts.

THE LOBBYING BLITZ: 1996–2000

By the late 1990s, the deadlock had to be broken. The European Union was expanding, and the single market could not function if a Mars Bar was legal in London but illegal in Madrid.

The lobbying effort that descended on Brussels was unprecedented in the history of food. It involved everyone from the Prime Minister of the UK to the President of France.

THE PURIST ARGUMENT: Led by France and Belgium, the purists launched a campaign focused on "Gastronomic Integrity." They argued that chocolate was one of the few remaining food products with a standard of identity that meant something. To allow vegetable fat was to open the floodgates. If 5% was allowed today, why not 10% tomorrow? Why not 50%? They warned of the "Americanization" of European food —a slide toward bland, standardized, chemically engineered calories.

They proposed a compromise that the British found insulting: British chocolate could be sold in Europe, but it could not be called "Chocolate." It had to be labeled "Family Milk Chocolate" or "Chocolate with High Milk Content." The British press had a field day, mocking the "Euro-crats" who wanted to rename their national treat.

THE INDUSTRIAL ARGUMENT: The multinational corporations (Nestlé, Mars, Mondelez/Kraft, Ferrero) formed a powerful bloc called CAOBISCO. Their argument was one of technological necessity. They claimed that CBEs were not just about cost—they were about functionality.

- In the warmer climates of Southern Europe, 100% cocoa butter chocolate melted too easily on the shelf. CBEs raised the melting point slightly, keeping the chocolate firm.
- CBEs allowed for harder textures and better gloss retention in complex filled pralines.

They pushed for a "harmonization" of the rules: allow 5% vegetable fat across all of Europe, but mandate clear labeling so the consumer could choose.

THE ENDGAME: Directive 2000/36/EC

After thirty years of arguing, twenty years of legal battles, and ten years of intense lobbying, the war ended on June 23, 2000. The European Parliament voted to adopt Directive 2000/36/EC. It was a compromise that left scars on both sides, but it established the definition of chocolate that governs the world today.

THE VERDICT:

- The 5% Rule: Member states were free to authorize the addition of vegetable fats to chocolate products, up to a maximum of 5% of the finished product's weight.
- The Approved List: Not just any fat could be used. The Directive established a strict list of six exotic tropical fats (CBEs) that were chemically similar to cocoa butter:
  - Illipe (Borneo)
  - Palm oil (Tropics)
  - Sal (India)
  - Shea (West Africa)
  - Kokum gurgi (India)
  - Mango kernel (Asia)
- The Labeling Mandate:
  - This was the victory for the purists. Any product containing vegetable fats had to bear a conspicuous, clearly legible statement on the label: "Contains vegetable fats in addition to cocoa butter."
  - This statement had to be near the list of ingredients but distinct from it.
  - Cheap fats like coconut oil or hydrogenated fats remained banned in real chocolate.

. . .

THE AFTERMATH: **A Divided Landscape**

The Directive came into full force in 2003. The predicted apocalypse of the cocoa market did not happen, nor did the complete degradation of chocolate quality—at least not immediately. Instead, the market bifurcated.

- **The Mass Market:** The giant multinationals (Cadbury, Nestlé, Mars) largely adopted the 5% rule. They reformulated recipes across Europe to standardize production. If you buy a standard candy bar in a gas station in Berlin or London today, flip it over. You will likely see palm or shea oil in the ingredients list. To the average consumer grabbing a snack, the change was imperceptible.
- **The Premium Market:** For the artisan chocolatiers of Belgium and France, the Directive became a marketing weapon. They doubled down on purity. They created a new seal of quality: **"AMCAO"** (Artisans du Monde pour un Chocolat Authentique et Original). Labels began to proudly proclaim **"Pure Cocoa Butter"** or **"100% Cocoa Butter."**

The war had an unintended consequence: it educated the consumer. Before the Directive, few people knew what was in their chocolate. The controversy forced the public to learn about cocoa butter, vegetable fats, and percentages. It laid the groundwork for the modern craft chocolate movement.

Today, a savvy chocolate lover knows that the "Contains vegetable fats" disclaimer is the dividing line. It separates the "candy" from the "chocolate," the industrial snack from the gastronomic experience. The war is legally over, but the skirmish for quality continues in the grocery aisle every day.

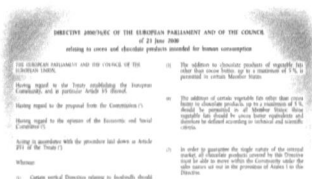

The Treaty of Versailles for Candy. The opening text of Directive
2000/36/EC, passed in June 2000. This legal document ended the
thirty-year "Chocolate War," creating a compromise that allowed up
to 5% vegetable fats in chocolate sold across the European Union—
saving British chocolate from the indignity of being labeled
"Vegelate."

The Cocoa Directive remains a fascinating case study in the intersection of law and taste. It proved that in the modern world, "authenticity"
is not a natural state, but a negotiated legal term, defined by the friction
between the artisan's pride and the corporation's profit.

===

SENSORY AUDIT: THE WAX TEST

Is your chocolate pure, or did they use the "5% Vegetable Fat"
loophole?

- **The Science:** Cocoa butter melts clean at body temperature.
  Vegetable fats (Palm/Shea) often have higher melting points
  to prevent smearing.
- **The Test:** Place a piece of chocolate on the roof of your
  mouth. Do not chew.
- **Pure Chocolate:** Dissolves completely into liquid.
- **Vegetable Fat:** Leaves a lingering, waxy film that feels like a
  candle. It coats the tongue and dulls the flavor.

===

PART VI

INNOVATION, TECHNOLOGY, AND THE FUTURE OF CHOCOLATE

33

THE WHITE CHOCOLATE PARADOX: AN ORIGIN STORY OF WASTE

I n the pantheon of confectionery, white chocolate is the divisive sibling. To the purist, it is an abomination—a cloying, pale impostor that has stripped the cacao bean of its soul (the dark, bitter cocoa solids) and left behind only a sugary ghost. Culinary critics have long dismissed it as "waxy children's food," while legal regulators in Europe and America spent decades arguing over whether it even deserved the name "chocolate."

YET, to dismiss white chocolate is to misunderstand one of the greatest triumphs of industrial efficiency in food history. The existence of the white bar is not due to a chef's sudden desire for a vanilla-forward flavor profile, nor a confectioner's artistic whim. It was born from industrial desperation.

white chocolate is the delicious solution to a massive logistical nightmare... It is a product of pure engineering, a story of how the industry took a byproduct—once used primarily for suppositories and skin ointments—and repurposed it into a global luxury.

THE GREAT DIVORCE of 1828

To understand the paradox of white chocolate, we must return to the pivotal moment when the cacao bean was split in two. For thousands of years, consuming chocolate meant consuming the whole bean. The Maya and Aztecs ground the roasted nibs into a dense paste, mixed it with water and spices, and drank the suspension. It was gritty, fatty, and heavy. Because the cacao bean is roughly 50% fat, early European drinkers often complained that the heavy grease floated to the top of their cups, making the beverage unpalatable to the refined aristocratic palate.

The turning point came in 1828, in the Netherlands. Casparus van Houten Sr. patented the hydraulic cocoa press, a machine capable of exerting immense pressure on the ground cocoa mass. The press squeezed the life out of the bean, separating it into two distinct commodities:

- The Press Cake: A dry, rock-hard disc that could be pulverized into fine, water-soluble cocoa powder. This was the prize. It made drinking chocolate cheap, instant, and light. It democratized chocolate, moving it from the palaces to the pantries of the working class.
- The Butter: A yellow, viscous oil that oozed out of the press and solidified into hard, ivory blocks of cocoa butter.

Van Houten's invention was a miracle for drinking chocolate, but it created a massive economic imbalance. For every pound of cocoa powder produced for the booming beverage market, the factory produced roughly a pound of cocoa butter as a byproduct.

In the mid-19th century, this fat was largely a nuisance. While some of it could be added back into cocoa mass to create solid dark chocolate bars (which require extra fat to be moldable), the demand for drinking powder far outstripped the demand for eating chocolate. As factories across Europe ramped up powder production to feed the armies and laborers of the Industrial Revolution, warehouses began to fill with blocks of ivory fat. They were sitting on a mountain of caloric energy with no obvious culinary use.

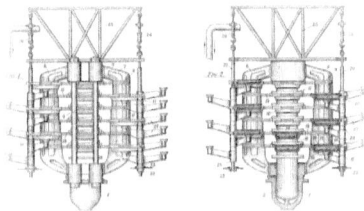

Patent diagrams illustrating the internal mechanism of the
hydraulic cocoa press, patented by the Van Houten family in 1828.
This invention allowed for the efficient separation of cocoa butter
from cocoa solids for the first time.

From Ointments to Edibles: The Search for a Use

For decades, this surplus cocoa butter led a double life. Because it melts at body temperature (approx. 34°C/93°F) and is shelf-stable, it became a darling of the pharmaceutical and cosmetic industries, rather than the food industry.

If you walked into a Victorian apothecary, you would not find cocoa butter in the candy aisle. You would find it in the back room, being molded into suppositories. Its unique melting curve—solid at room temperature, liquid inside the body—made it the perfect delivery vehicle for medicine. It was also whipped into skin creams, balms, and salves to treat everything from stretch marks to burns.

But for the chocolate giants, selling fat to pharmacists was not enough to clear the inventory. The volume of waste was too high. They needed a way to get people to eat it.

The challenge was flavor. Pure cocoa butter is remarkably bland. Natural, undeodorized cocoa butter has a faint, nutty, chocolatey aroma, but almost no taste on the tongue. It possesses the texture of chocolate—the snap and the melt—but none of the bitterness, acidity, or fruitiness that gives cacao its character. To a 19th-century palate accustomed to strong spices and robust flavors, eating a block of fat was repulsive.

· · ·

THE NESTLÉ INTERVENTION: 1936

The breakthrough finally arrived in the 1930s, spearheaded by the Swiss giant Nestlé. Nestlé was uniquely positioned to solve this problem. The company was already a master of milk technology. Decades earlier, Henri Nestlé had revolutionized infant formula, and Daniel Peter had figured out how to use condensed milk to create milk chocolate. In the 1930s, Nestlé faced two surpluses simultaneously: an excess of cocoa butter from its chocolate processing, and an excess of milk powder from its dairy division.

The chemists at Nestlé realized that while cocoa butter lacked flavor, it possessed an incredible ability to carry flavor. It was a neutral, creamy canvas. If they could suspend the milk powder and sugar within the matrix of cocoa butter, the fat would provide the luxurious "melt," while the dairy and sugar would provide the taste.

In 1936, Nestlé launched the Galak bar in Continental Europe. Almost simultaneously, they introduced the same formula to the UK market under the name Milkybar. It was the first commercially successful white chocolate.

It was a feat of engineering disguised as a treat. By removing the cocoa solids, Nestlé removed the bitterness and the stimulants (theobromine and caffeine). What remained was a product that was essentially "solidified sweet cream." It was positioned not as a luxury for adults, but as a healthy, energy-rich treat for children—pure, white, and associated with the wholesomeness of milk rather than the dark stimulation of cocoa.

The paradox was complete: The industry had taken its waste product, mixed it with cheap sugar and milk, and rebranded it as a premium novelty.

THE ANATOMY OF A GHOST: Why It Behaves Differently

To the professional chocolatier, white chocolate is a completely different beast than its dark or milk siblings. Working with it requires a different set of instincts because, chemically, it is missing the structural "skeleton" of the cacao bean.

==

THE BIRTH OF THE MILKYBAR

The original white chocolate. Nestlé launched the Milkybar (known
as Galak in mainland Europe) in 1936 to utilize a massive surplus of
cocoa butter and milk powder. Early packaging marketed the bar
not as a luxury indulgence, but as a "healthy," energy-rich
supplement for children.

The first white chocolate wasn't a luxury; it was a vitamin supplement.

- 1930s: Nestlé sits on a surplus of milk powder and cocoa butter.
- 1936: They launch the Galak (Milkybar) in Europe.
- The Pitch: Marketing materials focused on "The Goodness of Milk" and Vitamin D, positioning it as a healthy energy bar for children rather than a candy.

==

IN DARK CHOCOLATE, the microscopic cocoa solids (the fiber) act as insulators and structural supports. They help the bar hold its shape and resist heat. White chocolate lacks this fiber. It is essentially a suspension of sugar crystals and milk proteins floating in a pool of fat.

This lack of solids makes white chocolate incredibly volatile in the kitchen. Dark chocolate can be melted at temperatures up to 50°C (120°F) without significant damage. White chocolate, however, becomes unstable at just 44°C (110°F). If you overheat it by even a degree, the milk proteins can scorch and the structure seizes, turning the smooth liquid into a gritty, unworkable paste. It demands a gentle touch, earning it a reputation among chefs as temperamental and unforgiving.

However, its chemical neutrality is also its superpower. Cocoa butter is lipophilic—it loves to bond with other fats and oils. Because white chocolate doesn't have the overwhelming flavor of roasted cacao to compete with, it is the perfect vehicle for delicate, fat-soluble flavors that would otherwise be drowned out.

This is why white chocolate is the medium of choice for adventurous chocolatiers using matcha, saffron, rose, or freeze-dried fruits. Dark chocolate forces you to fight the cocoa flavor; white chocolate steps aside and lets the infusion shine. It is the culinary equivalent of a blank canvas, waiting for pigment.

THE WAR ON "FAKE" White Chocolate

If white chocolate has a bad reputation today, it is largely due to a second wave of industrial intervention that occurred in the late 20th century: the rise of compound coating.

As cocoa butter prices continued to rise (eventually becoming the most expensive component of the bean, often double the price of cocoa powder), manufacturers sought to cut costs. They realized they could mimic the texture of white chocolate using hydrogenated palm kernel oil, coconut oil, or other vegetable fats.

These products flooded the market, often labeled as "White Confection," "Almond Bark," or "White Morsels." They looked like white chocolate, but they did not melt like it. Vegetable oils have a higher melting point and leave a waxy, greasy residue on the roof of the mouth. They lack the clean "snap" of real cocoa butter.

This created a generation of consumers who believed they hated white chocolate, when in fact, they had never tasted it. They had tasted sweetened vegetable shortening.

The legal battles to protect the definition of white chocolate were fierce, mirroring the "Chocolate Wars" over vegetable fats in Europe (detailed earlier in this chapter) and the Quaker rivalries of the 19th century (see Chapter 30). In the United States, the FDA did not establish a formal Standard of Identity for "white chocolate" until 2002. Before that ruling, the market was the Wild West, with manufacturers freely substituting vegetable fats without penalty. Today, the regulations are strict: to be legally labeled "White Chocolate," a product must contain at least 20% cocoa butter by weight. If it contains vegetable oil fillers, it cannot bear the name.

The Maillard Renaissance: Caramelizing the Ghost

In the 21st century, white chocolate is undergoing a renaissance, driven by a happy accident in a professional kitchen.

In 2012, Frédéric Bau, a pastry chef at the famed French chocolate company Valrhona, accidentally left a batch of white chocolate in a bain-marie (water bath) for too long. He forgot about it for nearly ten hours. When he returned, he expected to find a burnt, ruined mess. Instead, he found gold.

The heat had triggered the Maillard reaction—that same browning magic we saw in the roasting of cocoa beans. Here, the amino acids in the milk proteins reacted with the sugars, slowly caramelizing the chocolate. The color had turned a deep, toffee blonde.

The flavor had transformed from simple sugary milk to a complex profile of shortbread, toasted biscuit, and roasted salt. Bau refined the process and Valrhona released "Dulcey," the world's first "Blond Chocolate."

This discovery changed the narrative. It proved that white chocolate had hidden potential. It wasn't just a carrier for other flavors; it had a dormant complex flavor of its own, waiting to be unlocked by heat. Today, "roasted" or "caramelized" white chocolate is a staple in high-end pastry, bridging the gap between the dark chocolate snob and the white chocolate lover.

A Product of Pure Engineering

The white chocolate bar is a testament to human ingenuity. It is a product that exists only because we invented a machine to destroy the cocoa bean, and then invented a recipe to salvage the wreckage.

It challenges our definitions of "natural." A dark chocolate bar can be made with stone tools in the middle of the jungle. A white chocolate bar cannot. It requires the industrial separation of fat, the dehydration of milk, the refining of sugar, and the precise conching of the mixture. It is a processed food in the truest sense of the word, yet when made with pure ingredients, it offers a sensory experience that nature alone cannot provide.

It offers a melt that is unparalleled, a texture that is pure velvet. It captures the physical pleasure of chocolate—the thermodynamics of the fat—without the chemical stimulation of the cocoa solids.

So, the next time a purist scoffs at a bar of white chocolate, remember its history. It is the ghost of the bean, resurrected by science. It is the edible evidence that in the right hands, even industrial waste can be turned into gold.

===

KITCHEN ALCHEMY: ROASTED WHITE CHOCOLATE

White chocolate is full of sugar and milk protein. If you bake it, it doesn't melt—it caramelizes.

- **The Method:**
  - Spread chopped white chocolate on a baking sheet.
  - Bake at 250°F (120°C).
  - Stir every 10 minutes.
  - The Transformation: Over 45–60 minutes, it will turn from ivory to golden peanut-butter color.
- **The Taste:** It loses its cloying sweetness and tastes like salted caramel, toffee, and shortbread. Use it in cookies or ganache.

===

34

THE HACKER'S NOOTROPIC: SILICON VALLEY'S OBSESSION WITH CACAO

L ate at night in a Palo Alto co-working space, the glow of multiple monitors reflects off tired eyes. Empty cold-brew bottles litter the desks. But instead of reaching for another cup of coffee or an energy drink, a young software engineer unwraps a small bar of deep, dark chocolate. The first bite is rich and bitter-sweet. Almost immediately, a subtle wave of alertness and comfort washes over her. Around the room, similar scenes play out: a tech founder nibbles cocoa nib granola, a product manager passes around artisanal chocolate squares in a meeting, and a group of hackers at a hackathon pop caffeinated chocolate-covered espresso beans like chips. In Silicon Valley today, chocolate isn't just a candy or dessert – it's brain fuel. The tech world has fallen head over heels for cocoa as a cognitive pick-me-up, blending pleasure with productivity in a way that only this culture could.

The Rise of Chocolate as Tech's Brain Fuel

In an industry infamous for marathon coding sessions and relentless innovation, professionals have long sought the perfect stimulant. For decades, coffee was the undisputed king of Silicon Valley's stimulant scene – the archetypal image of a bleary-eyed programmer glued to a screen with a mug of java at hand is practically a cliché. But in recent years, a challenger has emerged to join coffee at the desk: dark chocolate.

Walk into the micro-kitchens of a major tech company's campus and alongside the espresso machines and kombucha taps, you might find jars of gourmet chocolate squares or trail mix studded with cocoa nibs. At Google's sprawling offices, for example, employees famously enjoy free snacks; until health initiatives kicked in, this even included colorful bowls of M&Ms. These days, the trend skews toward high-cacao dark chocolates as a "better-for-you" indulgence to satisfy the afternoon slump. The message is clear – a little chocolate can brighten your mood and sharpen your mind, without the jittery overload of a sixth cup of coffee.

The embrace of chocolate goes beyond the 9-to-5 office routine and into the adrenaline-fueled world of hackathons and startup all-nighters. At hackathons – those weekend-long programming competitions often running overnight – organizers have learned that providing sugary soda and pizza isn't enough; participants crave something that keeps them alert *and* feeling good.

Enter chocolate bars spiked with caffeine and bitter cacao energy bites. "Everyone there ate nothing but pizza and caffeinated chocolate bars while downing as many Cokes as they could stomach," one hackathon volunteer observed about the ravenous scene at a university coding event. It turns out that a few bites of chocolate can deliver a quick boost: the sugar offers immediate energy, while the cocoa's natural stimulants provide sustained mental stimulation.

Some hackathon veterans swear by chocolate as their secret weapon – a handful of chocolate-covered espresso beans to keep the code flowing at 3 AM, or an " Awake" chocolate bar (a brand infused with as much caffeine as a cup of coffee) to power through the final presentation prep. In these intense moments, chocolate has proven its merit as both a comfort and a catalyst.

Even in more everyday settings, the culture of Silicon Valley has woven chocolate into its fabric. Tech workers proudly display premium chocolate brands on their desks the way others might show off fine wines. It's not uncommon to hear a UX designer mention that a square of 85% cocoa chocolate is their "afternoon brain booster," or see a CTO stash a bag of cacao nibs in their laptop bag for a quick concentration snack.

The Coder's Crunch: Tech workers have embraced cacao nibs as a
jitter-free alternative to coffee for sustaining focus.

The general sentiment is that dark chocolate is a kind of guilt-free indulgence – a treat that feels decadent but is intellectually justified by its purported health benefits. After all, if it potentially improves focus and mood (more on that shortly), why not make it a staple of the work-day? Chocolate has essentially been reframed in tech culture: from candy to cognitive fuel.

This shift in attitude reflects a broader trend in Silicon Valley: the blending of wellness and work performance. Just as open-office plans now include meditation rooms and nap pods for optimal productivity, the snack choices have upgraded from pure junk food to "smart snacks." Dark chocolate sits proudly in that category – delicious, yes, but also dense with compounds that promise to supercharge your brain (or so devotees believe).

THE NOOTROPIC OF Choice

In the optimization-obsessed culture of Silicon Valley, food is rarely just fuel; it is a tool for performance. Coffee has long been the engineer's drug of choice, but caffeine comes with a crash. This is where high-percentage dark chocolate has found its niche as the perfect "flow state" food.

Tech workers treat cacao less like a candy and more like a nootropic —a cognitive enhancer. The appeal lies in the specific interplay of theo-bromine and caffeine. Unlike the jagged spike of an espresso shot, cacao offers a smoother, sustained lift. It is the difference between a sprint and a marathon. For a coder facing a twelve-hour debugging session, that steady hum of alertness is invaluable.

This utility has rebranded chocolate in the breakrooms of San Francisco. It is no longer a guilty pleasure to be hidden in a desk drawer; it is a productivity hack, displayed proudly alongside standing desks and noise-canceling headphones. The darker the bar, the more serious the user. In this circle, 90% cacao isn't bitter; it's efficient.

Of course, not all chocolate is created equal. The tech crowd's love is specifically for dark, high-cacao chocolate – usually 70% cacao content and above – and often minimally processed or "bean-to-bar" artisanal types. This matters because the benefits we're talking about come from the cacao itself.

Milk chocolate or candy bars packed with sugar and fillers contain far less of the actual cocoa solids (and the good stuff within them). Many mass-market chocolates also use a process called "Dutching" (alkalizing the cocoa) to reduce bitterness, which unfortunately strips away many flavanols. So, the Silicon Valley chocolate aficionados are careful: they go for organic, raw or lightly processed dark chocolate, sometimes single-origin bars that highlight how much pure cacao they carry.

These are the bars that might taste a bit bitter or intense to the uninitiated, but to the believers, that intensity is the taste of potency. In their view, a 85% dark chocolate bar is essentially an edible nootropic – a cognitive enhancer wrapped in foil.

BIOHACKERS and the Cult of Cacao

No exploration of Silicon Valley's nutritional obsessions would be complete without visiting the world of biohackers – those individuals, often tech entrepreneurs or investors themselves, who experiment with diets and supplements to optimize health and performance. In recent years, biohackers have become some of the most vocal champions of dark chocolate and cocoa. To them, high-quality chocolate isn't just a sweet; it's a strategic tool in their regimen for a sharper mind and even a longer life.

===

THE CHEMISTRY OF JOY: A USER'S GUIDE

Why does chocolate make you feel this way? Meet the molecules (detailed further in Chapter 5).

- Theobromine (The Flow State): As noted in our look at medicinal cacao, this vasodilator offers a smoother ride than caffeine. For the coder, this means increased blood flow and alertness without the 'crash' associated with coffee.
- Anandamide (The Bliss Molecule): Named after the Sanskrit word for "joy," this lipid binds to cannabinoid receptors in the brain, mimicking the "runner's high."
- Phenylethylamine (The Love Drug): The same chemical released when you fall in love. It triggers a release of endorphins and dopamine.
- Flavanols (The Brain Food): These antioxidants increase blood flow to the hippocampus, potentially boosting memory and reaction time.

==

TAKE DAVE ASPREY, for example – the tech entrepreneur-turned-nutrition guru famous for Bulletproof Coffee and the entire "biohacking" movement. Asprey has unabashedly endorsed dark chocolate as a daily health food. "Dark chocolate and green tea are on my list of health-boosting superfoods," he declares, pointing to their high levels of polyphenols (those antioxidant compounds). Asprey built a philosophy that you don't have to punish yourself with bland foods to be healthy; instead, he argues, you must "reframe delicious foods that are healthy for you."

In his words: *"You don't get to be a better person by denying yourself. The way you win is by reframing delicious foods that are healthy for you."* Chocolate, with its rich flavor and beneficial compounds, exemplifies this idea. He often cites how the polyphenols in dark chocolate can support energy and even *"hack your willpower"* by making you feel satisfied. In the

Bulletproof diet world, a piece of organic dark chocolate (preferably sugar-free or lightly sweetened with something natural) is a perfectly acceptable – even encouraged – treat, because it feeds your brain and body useful nutrients. Asprey's embrace of chocolate has undoubtedly influenced thousands of health-conscious tech workers to view a few squares of dark chocolate in the afternoon not as cheating on their diet, but as a smart choice.

Another leading figure in this arena is Bryan Johnson, a tech multimillionaire who made headlines by spending millions annually on a quest to reverse aging. Johnson's intense health regimen, called "Blueprint," is a data-driven attempt to optimize every facet of his biology – and it prominently features cocoa.

In 2024, he revealed that he incorporates pure, high-flavanol cocoa powder into his daily diet as a supplement for neuroprotection and overall health. Johnson isn't munching Hershey bars; we're talking about essentially 100% unsweetened cocoa. He sources what he claims is the world's best cocoa – rigorously tested to be free of heavy metals and unusually rich in flavanols – and stirs it into his foods and drinks each day. Why go to such lengths? Johnson points to research on flavanols' benefits: improved vascular function, reduced inflammation, and potentially a lower risk of age-related cognitive decline.

For a longevity enthusiast, cocoa offers a cocktail of brain-friendly molecules that align with the goal of staying mentally sharp into old age. He even warns that not all cocoa powder is created equal; typical store-bought cocoa might have contaminants like lead or cadmium (there was indeed public concern after some 2022 reports on heavy metals in chocolate).

So, he approached cocoa sourcing with a true Silicon Valley, problem-solving mindset: test everything, find the purest supply, and share the data. *"When you go to the store, you have no idea what you're buying. It could be really dirty... We test [our cocoa] before we buy it, we test it when it's in our warehouse, and then we share the results. This is how the world should function,"* Johnson proclaimed, effectively applying quality assurance principles from tech to his personal nutrition.

In his kitchen, cocoa powder has become as indispensable as a multivitamin. He mixes it into a daily "nutty pudding" (a concoction of nuts and nutrients) and even into his coffee. With a smile, he admits that the only danger is how delicious it is: one bite of this cocoa-infused healthy Nutella-like spread, and it's hard to stop.

==

RECIPE: THE "FOCUS FUEL" BARK

A high-fat, low-sugar "nootropic" snack inspired by Silicon Valley biohackers.

- **Ingredients:**
  - 4 oz 100% Cacao (Unsweetened).
  - 2 tbsp Coconut Oil (MCTs for brain energy).
  - 1 tbsp Almond Butter (Satiety).
  - 1/2 tsp Sea Salt (Electrolytes).
  - Optional: A pinch of stevia or monk fruit.
- **Instructions:**
  - Melt the cacao and oil together gently.
  - Stir in the nut butter until smooth.
  - Pour onto parchment paper and sprinkle with salt.
  - Freeze for 20 minutes. Break into shards. Eat one when your brain fogs.

==

Biohackers aren't alone. Tim Ferriss, another well-known tech personality and author of *The 4-Hour Body*, has often sung the praises of low-sugar dark chocolate as a smart snack, noting its appetite-suppressing qualities and healthy fats which can be compatible with ketogenic diets popular in tech circles.

Many people striving for ketosis (a metabolic state favored for fat loss and mental clarity) discover that a few squares of ultra-dark chocolate can satisfy cravings without causing a big carb spike – it's practically the only "dessert" allowed in strict paleo or keto diets.

Thus, dark chocolate has become a darling of the "eating for productivity" crowd, right alongside grass-fed butter and MCT oil. It's common to find recipes on biohacker forums for chocolate fat bombs (little sugar-free fudge bites loaded with cocoa and good fats) or to hear about entrepreneurs who start their day with a "cacao smoothie" instead of a Frappuccino.

The enthusiasm reaches into mental health and stress management as well. Tech life can be mentally taxing, and some have found that incorporating a mindful chocolate ritual helps them unwind or reset during a busy day.

A product manager at a fast-paced startup might take a ten-minute break to slowly savor a piece of 90% dark chocolate, almost like a meditation, letting the complexity of flavors unfold. This mindful tasting can have a calming effect, easing anxiety and providing a moment of joy. In a culture where burnout is a real risk, such small pleasures double as preventive self-care.

Hackathons, All-Nighters, and the Sweet Edge

On the front lines of Silicon Valley's innovation – those legendary hackathons and crunch-time sprints – chocolate has earned a reputation as a true MVP. To appreciate its role, imagine a classic hackathon scenario: Teams of young programmers have 24 or 36 hours to create a prototype from scratch.

They're typically fueled by adrenaline, ambition, and a questionable amount of caffeine. Yet, as night wears on, energy flags and minds wander. The savviest participants come prepared not just with laptops and cables, but with snacks engineered for endurance. Sure, energy drinks and coffee abound, but too much and hands start shaking and hearts pounding. That's where chocolate shines.

The scene around 2:00 AM often includes wrappers of energy chocolate bars scattered among keyboards. These specialty bars – some provided by sponsors, others brought by participants – often advertise a blend of chocolate with added caffeine or vitamins.

One popular brand simply called Awake offers bars and bites where each serving packs the same caffeine as a cup of coffee, cleverly delivered in rich chocolate that's far more palatable than yet another bitter espresso shot. Hackers report that eating these keep them awake enough to code, but also oddly comforted. There's something psychologically uplifting about tasting chocolate when you're stressed or exhausted; it's like a little morale boost that says "you got this, keep going."

In the quieter corners, you might find a group of coders passing around a bag of chocolate-covered espresso beans – essentially coffee you can crunch on. They joke that it's "chewing their coffee" and appreciate that a handful of these crunchy delights can spike their focus when the screen starts blurring.

Others prefer a more natural route: trail mix with a heavy dose of dark chocolate chunks and almonds, or protein bars drizzled with cocoa. The combination of some protein, healthy fat, and dark chocolate's stimulants keeps their blood sugar stable while still offering a cognitive kick. This is key – pure sugar can make you crash, but chocolate's mix of fats and low glycemic sweetness (in dark varieties) provides a slower burn of energy.

Anecdotes from hackathon veterans underscore how chocolate often makes the difference in the final stretch. "At 5 AM, our code was a mess and everyone was nodding off. Then someone opened a pack of double-chocolate brownies from a local bakery – not exactly health food, but at that point it was magical.

Fifteen minutes after devouring them, we were debugging with fresh eyes and actually laughing again," one startup engineer recalls with a laugh. It's not that the chocolate gave them new skills, of course, but the mental reset – a rush of blood sugar, the awakening jolt of cocoa's stimulants, and frankly the emotional lift of a tasty treat – helped them push through. In Silicon Valley's ethos of maximizing performance, sometimes strategic indulgence is part of the toolkit.

Even outside of hackathon settings, the broader tech community has taken note of how effective chocolate can be during any intense work session. It's become common to keep some form of chocolate at one's desk for emergencies – whether it's a bar of artisanal 80% cacao picked up from a boutique shop, or just a pack of fun-sized dark chocolate pieces.

A mid-afternoon piece of chocolate can feel like a reward and a recharge simultaneously. Some programmers quip that debugging code is 10% skill and 90% refusing to give up – and a little sugar and cocoa can supply the will to keep going. As one popular coding humor meme puts it: *"I'm powered by chocolate and sheer determination."*

Techies Turned Chocolatiers

Silicon Valley's love affair with chocolate runs so deep that it's not only being consumed en masse – some tech professionals have literally transformed into chocolate makers. In a region defined by innovation, a number of former coders and engineers have pivoted from bytes to bars, applying high-tech thinking to the ancient art of chocolate-making. The result has been a mini-boom in artisanal, bean-to-bar chocolate companies founded or funded by tech alumni, effectively merging the worlds of cocoa and code.

One of the most famous examples is Dandelion Chocolate, a beloved craft chocolate maker based in San Francisco. It was started by Todd Masonis, a Stanford-educated engineer who had co-founded the tech startup Plaxo (an early social networking address book) and sold it to Comcast in 2008 for a sum reportedly around $150–170 million. Flush with success and resources, Masonis could have launched another software venture, but instead he took a detour that surprised his peers.

After some soul-searching and travels – which included touring small chocolate factories in Europe – he fell in love with the challenge of making truly great chocolate. In 2010, he and his friend Cameron Ring (also from the Plaxo team) founded Dandelion in a Mission District garage, channeling their tech-honed obsession for problem-solving into perfecting chocolate.

Walking into Dandelion's flagship factory-café today, you can immediately sense the almost geeky attention to detail. The aroma of roasting cacao fills the air, and behind the counter you might see sophisticated machinery grinding nibs in precise rotations. The process is laid bare for visitors, much like an open-source project on GitHub, inviting questions and sharing knowledge of how chocolate is made from scratch. Masonis approaches chocolate with an engineer's mindset: experimentation, measurement, iteration.

He's known to meticulously tweak roasting times or refining speeds to coax different flavors from the beans, akin to optimizing an algorithm.

The company sources cacao beans directly from farmers around the world, and every batch is treated like a unique science experiment – data is collected, variables adjusted, outcomes tasted and logged.

This methodical approach paid off as Dandelion's chocolate earned international accolades for its purity and flavor. Masonis himself is often on the factory floor, in casual startup attire but with the aura of Willy Wonka. *"I eat chocolate every day,"* he admits cheerfully – a true believer living his dream. His goal isn't just to enjoy chocolate, but to "disrupt" the sweets industry with a model of small-batch, high-quality production and direct trade ethics (very much a Silicon Valley way of thinking applied to chocolate).

Dandelion is not alone. Consider TCHO Chocolate – another Bay Area company explicitly blending technology and chocolate. TCHO was co-founded by Louis Rossetto, the founding editor of *Wired* magazine, and Timothy Childs, a former NASA technologist. From the outset, TCHO branded itself as "a technology company in the chocolate industry."

In its early days around 2005-2007, TCHO's factory was outfitted with sensors and remote monitoring systems that would make any IT admin proud. In one anecdote, Childs rigged up his chocolate-making equipment so he could check on a conche (a machine that refines chocolate) via webcam and even adjust settings from his smartphone in the middle of the night. The image of a chocolate machine quietly churning at 4 AM while a programmer-half-turned-chocolatier fine-tunes it remotely from home could not be more Silicon Valley.

TCHO applied the same rigor to flavor analysis: they developed a flavor wheel (borrowing concepts from wine and coffee tasting) and even worked on software to help growers and makers optimize the taste profiles of cacao. By infusing chocolate-making with a dose of Silicon Valley's tech and data culture, TCHO aimed to solve specific problems (like how to get consistent quality and specific flavor notes) and push the frontier of what great chocolate could be.

The marriage of tech and chocolate isn't just limited to production techniques; it's also evident in the ethos and community around these companies. Both Dandelion and TCHO, for instance, embraced open knowledge sharing – Dandelion's founders published a book detailing their process, and they host tours and talks. This mirrors the open-source mindset of many software developers.

The Bay Area's techies-turned-chocolatiers often say they were drawn to chocolate because it's *"the perfect mix of science, art, and passion,"* a phrase that wouldn't sound out of place describing a beautiful piece of code. And just as importantly, they saw an opportunity to innovate. Much as a startup might look at an established industry and see ineffi-ciencies to disrupt, these founders looked at big chocolate (the Mars and Hershey's of the world) and saw a lack of transparency in sourcing and a stagnation in quality. They set out to change that with direct farmer part-nerships, ethical sourcing (some talk about blockchain for supply chain tracking, naturally), and obsessive quality control – all very aligned with Silicon Valley values.

This phenomenon isn't isolated. Numerous other tech veterans have dabbled in chocolate entrepreneurship or investing. There's a joke that starting a craft chocolate business is the new "starting a vineyard" for the Silicon Valley elite – a tangible, sensory venture as a counterpoint to the digital world.

For example, former engineers from companies like Google and Facebook have been known to start small chocolate companies or cacao farms in exotic locations. The result is that the San Francisco Bay Area has become a hotspot for craft chocolate innovation, boasting many small brands that cater to the discerning tastes (and wallets) of tech connoisseurs. Some of these gourmet bars cost as much as fancy bottles of wine, and yet they sell quite well locally. It appears that when tech people become passionate about something, they don't hesitate to turn it into a startup and push boundaries – chocolate included.

Investing in Brainy Chocolate Innovations

Silicon Valley's romance with chocolate isn't just cultural or anec-dotal – it's also financial. In the last few years, venture capital and angel investors (including some big names in tech) have started funding a wave of functional chocolate startups and related innovations. In true Silicon Valley fashion, entrepreneurs are asking: how can we *optimize* chocolate for even better brain benefits or wellness? And investors are betting millions on the answers.

One striking example is the company Alice Mushrooms, founded in 2022. This startup created a line of chocolate bars laced with medicinal mushrooms and other nootropic (brain-enhancing) ingredients. The idea is to deliver benefits like improved focus or reduced stress in the familiar, delightful format of a chocolate bar.

By 2024, Alice Mushrooms had caught the attention of serious investors: they secured funding from venture capital firms like L Catterton (known for backing health and wellness brands) and even celebrity investors such as actors Zac Efron and Kevin Hart. The money is being used to scale up production of these "better-for-you" chocolates, which promise consumers not just a tasty treat but an "experience" – think of a chocolate bar that might help you sleep, or another that might give you a gentle brain boost during the workday.

With flashy marketing and partnerships with trendy grocers (one bar became a hit at Los Angeles' health-centric Erewhon market), Alice Mushrooms saw a reported 175% growth year-over-year and is expanding nationwide. Clearly, the concept of functional chocolate resonates beyond just the hardcore coder crowd; there's mainstream curiosity about confections that can double as supplements.

Functional Confectionery: Startups are blending nootropic mushrooms with chocolate to create snacks that promise cognitive benefits.

They're not alone. The market for what some call "functional confectionery" is heating up. Another startup, fittingly named The Functional Chocolate Company, has developed a range of chocolate bars each targeting a different need – one for energy, one for calm, one for focus, etc.

They managed to get their products into big retailers like Target and Vitamin Shoppe, signaling that chocolate as wellness is going mass-market. Then there's AWAKE Chocolate, a brand that pioneered caffeinated chocolate bites a decade ago and remains popular among students and professionals. They raised around $3.6 million to expand distribution, proving that investors see value in the simple premise that many people would rather eat their caffeine than drink it.

Perhaps the most notable success is Mid-Day Squares, a company that makes a sort of protein-packed chocolate snack bar. Founded by young entrepreneurs (outside Silicon Valley, in this case Canada), Mid-Day Squares positioned their bars as the perfect afternoon snack to replace unhealthy cookies or candy – high in protein and fiber, low in sugar, but with a chocolate core that makes them crave-worthy. The product struck a chord, especially with fitness enthusiasts and yes, busy professionals looking for convenient brain fuel. They've secured over $17 million in funding and reportedly sell over 50,000 bars daily. Such numbers and cash infusions indicate that "smart chocolate" is not a niche fad but a burgeoning industry segment.

The wellness world is also merging with the beauty world in choco-late form. A company called Sourse has created "chocolate vitamins" – essentially candy-coated supplements (like vitamin D or collagen) in the guise of chocolate bites. In just one year, Sourse hit $2 million in sales and even landed their products on the shelves of Sephora, a beauty retailer, framing them as edible skincare. This trend – sometimes dubbed "snackable wellness" – aligns perfectly with the Silicon Valley approach of efficiency. Why take a bitter pill when you can get the same supplement in a sweet chocolatey bite? It's health hacking for the taste buds, and investors are on board with it.

And let's not forget the frontier science angle: some tech startups are even exploring lab-grown cocoa or cacao alternatives in anticipation of future supply constraints or ethical issues in chocolate farming. One company, California Cultured, has been working on culturing cacao cells (essentially brewing chocolate in a bioreactor) to create chocolate without the cacao plantations – a moonshot idea that could appeal to environmental and ethical sensibilities.

The Atlantic dubbed this trend "Silicon Valley is coming for your chocolate," highlighting how startups aim to *disrupt* even the cacao bean through biotech. While that's still in R&D and not yet on our shelves, it shows the extent of the intellectual and financial capital being poured into the world of chocolate.

All these ventures underscore a larger point: Silicon Valley sees chocolate as a platform for innovation. Whether it's enhancing chocolate with new ingredients, optimizing its production with technology, or reinventing it entirely, the tech mindset is being applied with full force.

And why not? Chocolate sits at a lucrative intersection of big markets – food, wellness, even indulgence. If you can pitch a product that taps into people's love for chocolate *and* their desire to be healthier or smarter, you've got a compelling story for investors. The result is that being a chocolate entrepreneur in the 2020s might involve as much lab work or clinical research as it does culinary skill.

For the general public, this means an ever-growing array of brain-boosting chocolate products to choose from. Want your daily multivitamin? Have a chocolate. Need a pre-workout energy kick? Try a cacao-mushroom truffle. Stressed at work? Melt a calming herbal-infused chocolate square in your mouth. It's a delicious feedback loop: demand from health-conscious consumers (which certainly includes tech workers) drives innovation in functional chocolate, which in turn reinforces the idea that chocolate is a legitimate vehicle for self-improvement.

A Sweet Future for Silicon Valley and Chocolate

From the coding trenches to venture capital boardrooms, from biohacker labs to bean-to-bar factories, chocolate has ingrained itself into the heart of Silicon Valley's culture of self-optimization and innovation. What started perhaps as a quirky preference – the programmer with a sweet tooth who claimed chocolate helped him concentrate – has evolved into a full-fledged movement. Silicon Valley fell in love with chocolate as brain fuel, and it shows no sign of falling out of love anytime soon.

The power of this relationship lies in the optimization of pleasure. Tech denizens have managed to justify their indulgence with quantifiable data and in doing so, they've shed a lot of the guilt that people sometimes associate with eating chocolate. In a way, it's a reframing: rather than "sneaking" a piece of candy, a programmer feels proud about choosing a few squares of organic dark chocolate – it's practically part of the work strategy.

That positive feedback encourages more interest, more sharing of favorite brands and tips, and suddenly you have a community of chocolate enthusiasts swapping notes much like open-source developers swap code. Visit any Silicon Valley office chat channel and you might find a lively debate on which local chocolatier makes the best 100% cacao bar, or whether adding a spoon of raw cacao to one's morning smoothie beats a standard Americano for brain clarity. These are not hypotheticals; they're real conversations that reflect how normalized the idea of chocolate-as-fuel has become.

Certainly, moderation remains key. Even dark chocolate carries calories, and too much sugar (for those not sticking to ultra-dark) can negate the benefits. The health-conscious tech crowd is aware of this – hence the focus on portions, purity, and often pairing chocolate with nuts or other healthy foods.

Some enthusiasts like Bryan Johnson caution about heavy metals and emphasize the importance of sourcing, showing that the love for chocolate doesn't blind them to potential downsides. If anything, it motivates them to solve those downsides (with testing, alternative ingredients, etc.), as we've seen.

It's also worth noting that chocolate's appeal in Silicon Valley isn't solely about molecular brain hacks. There is a human, emotional element. The tech industry is high-stress and often abstract – working long hours with code and algorithms can feel disconnected from tangible reality. Chocolate, on the other hand, is sensual, immediate, and universally comforting. In a place that constantly reaches for the future, a piece of chocolate can momentarily anchor you in the present, delighting your senses. It's a bridge between the ultra-analytical life and the simple joys of being human. As one software engineer put it, "Biting into a good dark chocolate reminds me that life has simple pleasures. It keeps me sane on crazy days." That psychological comfort shouldn't be underestimated; a happy worker is often a more creative and productive one.

Looking ahead, the trend of cocoa-fueled creativity seems likely to grow. With remote work becoming more common, people have greater flexibility in their snacking and energy habits at home – and many have discovered that keeping high-quality chocolate at their desk is an essential part of their home office setup.

Online communities for developers and entrepreneurs continue to share scientific articles about cocoa's effects, new chocolate product reviews, and even chocolate tasting meetups (virtual or in-person). The crossover between tech meetups and foodie culture means you might soon find a "coder chocolate tasting night" where algorithms and origins are discussed with equal passion.

And as the wellness movement keeps booming, chocolate sits in a sweet spot (pun intended) of being both an indulgence and a functional food. It's not outlandish to imagine future tech offices where the free snack bar includes brain-boosting chocolate truffles custom-formulated by the company's nutritionist, or AI-personalized chocolate supplements where you input your biometrics and get a daily chocolate with tailored vitamins and compounds. Silicon Valley would absolutely be the place for that kind of Willy Wonka-meets-IBM scenario.

In the end, the love story between Silicon Valley and chocolate is a reminder that even in one of the world's most advanced, cutting-edge communities, people still cherish something as ancient and earthy as the cacao bean. The Aztec emperors drank cacao to enhance their vigor; centuries later, the leaders of the tech revolution are munching it to sharpen their wits. The context changes, but the core idea is the same: chocolate makes us feel energized, focused, and happy.

So the next time you see a hard-working developer break into a smile as they unwrap a bar of dark chocolate at midnight, you'll know it's not just a snack – it's a secret weapon, a ritual, a small act of self-care, and a spark for innovation all at once. In Silicon Valley, the code may be complex, but the fuel can be as simple as a square of cocoa. And as long as there are problems to solve and code to compile, you can bet there will be chocolate close at hand, helping to fuel the brains that just might change the world – one sweet bite at a time.

35

GREAT EXPERIMENTS:
THE CHOCOLATE TEAPOT
AND OTHER INVENTIONS

I magine a teapot that should not exist—fragile, meltable, and entirely made of chocolate—yet managing to pour a perfect cup of steaming tea. In 2014, a British chocolatier proved it could be done, turning a centuries-old idiom on its head and setting the tone for chocolate's long history of improbable inventions.

This spirit of playful ingenuity threads through some of chocolate's strangest chapters: booby-trapped wartime candy bars, holographic confections created with lasers, and scientific breakthroughs sparked by nothing more than a bar melting in someone's pocket. Some experiments reshaped industries; others fizzled into obscurity. But all of them illuminate a singular truth: chocolate invites curiosity in a way few substances do, inspiring inventors to push the boundaries of the possible simply because the medium itself is irresistible.

ACROSS CENTURIES, chocolate has served as drink, medicine, luxury, and comfort, but it has also been an unusually fertile playground for experimentation. Inventors, soldiers, chemists, engineers, and artists have treated chocolate not merely as a food but as a material—one that can be shaped, tested, engineered, and repurposed.

In their hands, chocolate has been strengthened for battlefields, altered for medical trials, stretched into art installations, and used to solve physics problems. Over and over, people have pushed chocolate beyond its traditional identity, discovering along the way that its quirks and complexities often lead to surprising breakthroughs.

To understand chocolate's role in invention, we have to look at the moments when curiosity collided with accident, ambition, or pure eccentricity. These are not the stories you find in recipe books or culinary histories, but the odd, brilliant, and often hilarious experiments that reveal how far people have been willing to go with chocolate in hand. What follows is a tour through the breakthroughs no one planned, the failures that taught more than they promised, and the strange prototypes that remind us innovation often begins with play.

The Accidental Breakthroughs

Some experiments happen because someone sets out to bend chocolate into a new form. Others happen because chocolate simply happens to be there at the right (or wrong) moment. Few substances have played supporting roles in scientific breakthroughs as unexpectedly as chocolate, and one of the most influential examples began not in a kitchen, but in a radar lab during World War II.

In the annals of scientific discovery, few origin stories are as charming (and gooey) as the invention of the microwave oven. The hero of this tale was Percy Spencer, an American engineer working for the Raytheon company in 1945. Spencer was an expert in radar technology, churning out high-power magnetrons for Allied forces during World War II.

One day, as legend has it, he paused near an active radar set with a Mr. Goodbar (a peanut cluster bar) in his pocket. He felt a strange sensation, reached into his pocket, and found the peanuts had survived, but the chocolate had pooled into a warm, sticky smear.

Intrigued, Spencer didn't scold himself for a laundry mishap – he immediately suspected the magnetron's radio waves were responsible. To test his idea, he sent for some unpopped popcorn and held the kernels in front of the device. Sure enough, they began popping and flying around the lab. By the end of the day, Spencer realized that high-frequency microwaves could cook food rapidly, and the seeds of a kitchen revolution were planted thanks to that melted chocolate.

Building on this cocoa-catalyzed epiphany, Spencer and his colleagues rushed to develop the world's first microwave oven. It was a monstrous thing at first – over five feet tall, weighing about 750 pounds, and water-cooled – but it worked. Within two years, Raytheon patented the invention and started marketing it (initially under the name "Radarange").

Those early microwaves were expensive and bulky, finding homes only in restaurants and ships, and some called them a commercial failure at first. But over the following decades the technology shrank and improved, until the microwave oven became a kitchen staple worldwide. And to think, it all began with a happy accident involving a chocolate bar in a scientist's pocket. Chocolate quite literally changed the course of culinary technology in the 20th century by sparking this accidental breakthrough.

Chocolate has crept into scientific experiments in other quirky ways as well. Physics teachers have long known a sweet trick for measuring the speed of light using nothing more than a microwave oven and a flat bar of chocolate.

Without rotation, the microwave's electromagnetic waves create "hot spots" that melt the chocolate at specific intervals. By measuring the distance between melted spots (which corresponds to half the wavelength of the microwaves) and multiplying by the oven's frequency, students can calculate the speed of light to astonishing accuracy – about 300,000 kilometers per second – all while filling the lab with the delicious smell of warm chocolate. It's a high-school science project staple that demonstrates serious physics with a dash of dessert. Once again, chocolate proves to be more than just a treat: it can literally help illuminate fundamental constants of the universe.

==

KITCHEN PHYSICS: MEASURE THE SPEED OF LIGHT

Replicate Percy Spencer's discovery. You need a microwave, a ruler, and a large chocolate bar.

- **The Prep:** Remove the rotating turntable from your microwave (this is crucial). Place the chocolate bar on a paper plate in the center.
- **The Zap:** Heat on high for 20 seconds. You want it to soften, not liquify.
- **The Math:** Find the two melted "hot spots." Measure the distance between their centers in centimeters.
- **The Formula:** Distance x 2 (to derive the full wavelength) x 2,450,000,000 (standard microwave frequency).
- **The Result:** The number should be roughly 29,979,245,800 cm/s—the speed of light.

==

FROM THE MICROWAVE oven to the ubiquitous cookie jar, these episodes remind us that experimentation is often messy – literally so when melted chocolate is involved – but can yield game-changing results. Chocolate, with its unique properties and universal appeal, has a way of enticing people to try odd things, occasionally leading to breakthroughs that leave a lasting impact on science and society.

War and Chocolate: Bombs, Rations, and Moral Boosters

During World War II, chocolate found itself at the center of some of the conflict's strangest and most secret experiments. On one hand it was a weapon of war, on the other a vital source of energy for troops – and in each case, it prompted inventive solutions that ranged from deadly to simply hard to swallow.

While the Axis powers experimented with lethal saboteur devices—like the exploding "Peter's Chocolate" bomb detailed in Chapter 27—the Allied forces faced a different challenge: logistics. As American and British soldiers marched into battle, their governments searched for the ideal compact, high-energy food to include in field rations. Chocolate, dense in calories and loved by troops, was a natural choice—but it had drawbacks.

It could melt into a mess in hot climates, and if it tasted too good, soldiers might snack on their emergency rations rather than saving them for true emergencies. So the U.S. Army turned to the Hershey Chocolate Corporation with an unusual request: create a chocolate bar for soldiers that "can withstand high temperatures and tastes just a little better than a boiled potato." That last specification was quite deliberate – they wanted something nutritious but not so delicious that troops would be tempted to eat their rations before they needed them.

Hershey's chemists and chocolatiers got to work and, by 1937, delivered the result: the D Ration Bar. It was a far cry from a creamy Hershey's milk chocolate sold in stores. This bar was a compact 4-ounce brick of extremely dark chocolate fortified with oats and other ingredients.

It was designed to not melt easily and to deliver a whopping 600+ calories for sustenance. Soldiers quickly discovered the Army had gotten exactly what it asked for. The D Ration was so hard it often required a knife to cut, and so bitter that many gagged it down or tossed it away despite orders.

Designed to be Disliked: The Army requested a bar that tasted "a little better than a boiled potato" so soldiers wouldn't eat it as a snack.

BUT THE BAR did the job: it could endure tropical heat and provided vital energy when there was nothing else to eat. Over the course of the war, billions of these ration bars were produced, earning nicknames like "Hitler's Secret Weapon" among troops (a wry reference to how unpalatable they were).

Hershey later improved the formula slightly with a Tropical Chocolate Bar, a version even more heat-resistant for Pacific theatre troops, though it still wasn't winning any candy awards. These experimental chocolates were failed inventions only in a culinary sense – as military technology, they were a success, keeping countless soldiers on their feet during grueling campaigns.

==

KITCHEN PROJECT: THE MODERN "D-RATION"

The original WWII ration tasted like "a boiled potato." Here is a version that survives the heat but actually tastes good. Perfect for hiking.

Ingredients:

- 4 oz Dark Chocolate (melted)
- 1/2 cup Oat Flour (for density/calories)
- 1 tbsp Honey (preservative/energy)
- 1 tbsp Coconut Oil (stabilizer)

Instructions:

- Mix all ingredients into a thick, heavy paste.
- Press firmly into a small rectangular mold.
- Let set. The result is a dense, high-energy brick that resists melting in your pocket.

==

Beyond rations, chocolate played other supportive roles. It was included in British and American soldiers' field kits not just for calories but for morale – a taste of home on the front lines. The mere presence of a piece of chocolate could comfort a war-weary fighter.

Recognizing this, the Red Cross and various military charities often distributed chocolate bars to troops as treats or on holidays. Thus, another "experiment" emerged: using chocolate as psychological sustenance. It wasn't patented or secret, but it was powerfully effective. For many veterans, memories of tearing open a crinkled wrapper in a foxhole – savoring a small moment of sweetness amid the bitterness of war – became one of the most poignant symbols of relief.

World War II also spurred innovative manufacturing around chocolate. By necessity, Hershey had to develop new production methods to mass-produce the unusually thick D Ration paste and pour it into molds by hand. Elsewhere, British chocolatiers like Cadbury worked on creating "ration chocolate" that used limited luxury ingredients, leading to new techniques in flavoring and stretching supplies.

Some of those improvisations in emulsifying or processing cocoa would quietly influence post-war candy making. In a sense, wartime chocolate technology forged a bridge to the modern energy bar and survival food industry. Today's hikers with their foil-wrapped energy squares or marathon runners with their high-calorie bars might owe a nod to those hard chocolate rations of the 1940s – they showed that sometimes a "failed" candy (in terms of flavor) could be a highly successful invention in purpose.

Perhaps no story from the war captures the dual nature of chocolate better than a moment reported during the liberation of a concentration camp in 1945. As survivors emerged, starved and weak, Allied soldiers shared the only provisions they had on hand – chocolate bars from their rations.

In those instances, chocolate was literally life-saving, a bridge from horror to hope. It's a stark contrast to that deadly Nazi bomb. Chocolate could kill, and chocolate could save. It was all a matter of how humans harnessed it. And harness it they did, in some of the most imaginative (and sometimes disturbingly imaginative) ways during the war.

~

The Chocolate Teapot and Other Edible Engineering Wonders

The age-old idiom "as useful as a chocolate teapot" suggests something laughably impractical. For ages, this phrase was a British go-to for dismissing useless ideas. But in recent years, a few enterprising souls turned the joke into a genuine engineering puzzle. It started as a whimsical experiment by some science enthusiasts. In 2008, a team affiliated with the University of Cambridge (featured on the BBC's "Naked Scientists" program) set out to calculate just how thick the walls of a chocolate teapot would need to be to hold hot tea. They poured molten chocolate into molds, experimented with different thicknesses, and even built partial chocolate "walls" to test against boiling water.

The science behind it was intriguing: chocolate doesn't melt all at once; it softens in stages depending on its cocoa butter content and how heat is applied. There was a sweet spot (pun intended) where a thick chocolate wall could absorb some heat, soften slightly, but not collapse entirely – at least not immediately. Through trial and error, they determined that if the chocolate teapot were made with sufficiently thick, sturdy walls, it could indeed contain hot water long enough to brew tea and pour one cup before structural integrity gave way.

The result of their kitchen-lab tinkering? A partially successful chocolate teapot – not efficient for daily use, surely, but not completely useless either. The experiments showed that the idiom might need a tweak: a chocolate teapot *can* be useful, if engineered with care (and consumed quickly thereafter!).

This playful scientific curiosity soon caught the attention of professional chocolatiers. Nestlé's Product Technology Centre in York, England – a research hub devoted to confectionery – took up the challenge. In 2014, Nestlé's master chocolatier John Costello unveiled a fully functional chocolate teapot that had been rigorously designed to meet real teapot expectations.

The team chose a special dark chocolate with 65% cocoa solids. While the cocoa butter still melts at the same temperature, the lower fat content created a much higher viscosity and a denser structural lattice. This density provided the necessary thermal mass to absorb the heat of the tea without immediately losing structural integrity. They cast the pot with extra-thick walls and a broad shape. In demonstrations, this chocolate teapot successfully brewed tea for two minutes and then poured out a proper cuppa, all without springing a leak or dissolving into sludge. It worked because of thermal mass: the thick walls acted as an insulator, absorbing the heat of the water slowly enough that the inner layer merely softened while the outer structural integrity held firm. It was an edible engineering marvel – the impossible made possible by understanding chocolate's thermodynamics.

Useful After All: Engineers proved that with thick enough walls, a chocolate teapot can actually brew tea—if you drink it fast.

The chocolate teapot, of course, was never meant to spawn a new line of cookware. It was more of a celebration of chocolate's versatility and a clever bit of science communication. Videos of the feat went viral among chocolate lovers and science buffs alike.

The teapot would ultimately cool and harden with tea still inside, making subsequent brews impractical – and eventually someone was bound to break off a delicious spout or lid for a snack. But none of that detracted from the delight: a phrase had been defied, and chocolate once again proved itself a material of surprising depth (literally, in this case – those walls were thick!).

This wasn't the only time chocolate served as a medium for structural or mechanical experiments. We've seen chocolate bridges and chocolate houses constructed as publicity stunts or seasonal attractions, testing the limits of what chocolate sculptures can do.

In 2011, to celebrate its 100th anniversary, the town of Lititz, Pennsylvania (home of Wilbur Chocolate) built a huge chocolate train, complete with engine and caboose, showcasing the strength of well-tempered chocolate to hold intricate shapes. Around the world, pastry chefs routinely compete to create record-breaking chocolate buildings – life-size cabins or elaborate architectural replicas – often reinforcing the chocolate with internal frames or using varying cocoa butter percentages to achieve different hardness levels.

These projects are half engineering, half art, and while they're not "inventions" in the patent sense, they push the boundaries of chocolate as a building material. Sure, a chocolate skyscraper would collapse under its own weight long before topping out, but a careful design and a cool room can yield a multi-story chocolate sculpture that stands tall for days.

In the realm of scientific exploration, one fascinating experiment used chocolate to illustrate geological processes. Geologists sometimes pour melted chocolate on blocks of ice to simulate how lava flows on glaciers (a way to study volcanic interactions with ice in places like Iceland). The chocolate solidifies into craggy formations, helping researchers visualize the patterns. It's an inventive analog model – and perhaps the most delicious-smelling lab setup imaginable.

These unusual uses highlight a broader point: chocolate isn't just candy; it's a complex material. It melts at just below body temperature, can be molded when tempered correctly, and transitions through multiple crystalline phases as it cools.

Understanding these properties enables wacky ideas like teapots and record-setting sculptures to work (at least for a short while). And even when a concept is destined to collapse – say, a chocolate chair that inevitably buckles – the attempt yields insight (and probably a tasty cleanup). The chocolate teapot's journey from idiom to reality exemplifies how a dash of humor and a bit of scientific rigor can transform a silly idea into a memorable, educative experiment.

PATENTLY BIZARRE: **Strange Chocolate Patents and Projects**

Innovation in the chocolate world isn't confined to pranks and one-off stunts – it's often formalized in patents and trademarks as inventors and companies try to protect their unusual chocolate ideas. A survey of the patent archives and recent industry news reveals some truly peculiar chocolate-related inventions, ranging from the ingenious to the eyebrow-raising.

One particularly charming patent comes from a company called Chocolate Graphics International. In the early 2000s, they secured a suite of international patents for a computer-controlled process described as "communicating via chocolate." Their technology treated chocolate like printer ink, allowing for a resolution of detail previously impossible with standard molding. Their technology treated chocolate like printer ink, allowing for a resolution of detail previously impossible with standard molding—essentially, 'communicating via chocolate."

What does that mean? Essentially, they figured out how to use laser technology to print messages and images onto the surface of chocolate, using chocolate itself as the "ink." With precise lasers, they etch text or photos in contrasting shades on a chocolate's surface without any paper or frosting.

The result can be a fully edible business card, wedding invitation, portrait, or even QR code – all made of chocolate. At their production peak, CGI claimed they could churn out 150,000 personalized chocolates a day for clients, turning candy into a delicious messaging medium. It's the kind of idea that would make Willy Wonka proud: edible communication, where you can read it and eat it too. While this invention might not have revolutionized the world, it certainly sweetened it for those who received a marriage proposal or holiday greeting literally written in chocolate.

Another set of patents, filed in 2006 by a U.S. company called New World Enterprises, focused on using chocolate in an unexpected way: as a delivery system for nutrients and medications. The idea was to harness chocolate's appealing taste and chemical properties to make vitamins or even medicines more palatable.

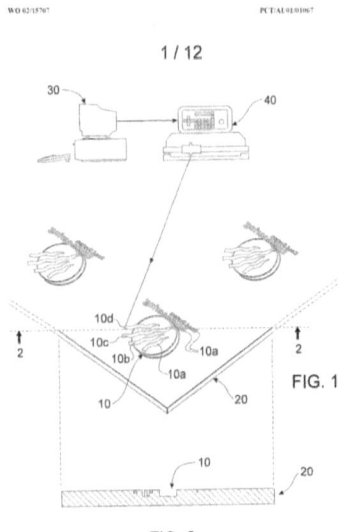

Schematic from Chocolate Graphics International's patented
process showing how digital artwork is translated into a mould that
embosses raised designs directly into chocolate—an early blueprint
for 'communicating via chocolate.'

THEY RESEARCHED how chocolate's natural compounds affect mood and
energy, and explored formulations that could give a health boost without
the usual sugar and fat. The ultimate creation was a kind of dietary
chocolate supplement – something that mimicked the taste and pleasure
of chocolate but enriched with vitamins and minus the guilt. Essentially,
NWE tried to invent "chocolate that's good for you" in a literal sense.

Whether or not these supplements took off in the market, the patents
underscore a long-standing truth: people want to have their chocolate
and eat it, too – without the downsides. And if that means patenting a
process to cram nutrients into a chocolate-like matrix or use cocoa
compounds to mask medicine's bitterness, so be it. It's an ongoing area of
innovation; even today, researchers publish studies on fortifying chocolate with everything from protein to probiotics. It seems the only thing
better than chocolate is chocolate that doubles as a health food (if only
our taste buds could be so lucky on a broad scale).

Not to be outdone in creativity, the global chocolate industry heavy-weights have also filed their share of unusual patents. Swiss-based Barry Callebaut, one of the largest chocolate manufacturers in the world, secured a patent in the 2010s for an all-natural purple chocolate – yes, purple.

The patent, with the somewhat dry title "Process for making red or purple cocoa material," detailed a method of processing cocoa beans in such a way that the resulting chocolate retains a naturally reddish-purple hue without any dyes. Why purple? It turns out some cocoa beans, when minimally fermented and specially treated, exhibit a ruby or purple tone (and Barry Callebaut indeed launched "Ruby chocolate" as the fourth type of chocolate – after dark, milk, and white – touting its unique berry-fruit flavor and rosy color). The patent acknowledged that "some consumers desire cocoa products of a different color" – a delightful understatement speaking to our endless appetite for novelty.

Purple chocolate was essentially an invention of Instagram age: a visually striking new chocolate experience. It made quite a splash in gourmet circles upon its debut, and though it's not as widely known as milk or dark chocolate, ruby/purple chocolate is gradually finding its niche, from high-end confectionery to baking competitions. It's a reminder that even after 3,000+ years of chocolate history, there are new shades and flavors to be discovered – and patented.

Color isn't the only thing companies fight over; even the shape of a chocolate bar can be serious business. In the UK, confectionery giant Cadbury once famously tried to trademark the particular purple color of its Dairy Milk wrappers – a battle that rival Nestlé fought in court for years. And Nestlé, for its part, attempted to trademark the distinctive shape of the KitKat bar (those four joined fingers) in various markets.

These moves led to protracted legal tussles, with debates over whether a color or a simple shape could truly be owned as intellectual property. In one odd case, Nestlé did succeed in patenting a specific chocolate shape for a product – not a functional invention, but a design. Starbucks, the coffee chain, also secured a design patent for a unique mold of a chocolate they give out (an angular, stylized shape, to elevate their brand's visual identity).

It might seem strange to seek monopoly rights on something as simple as a chunk of chocolate, but in the fiercely competitive candy world, even a trivial difference can be marketed as a signature style worth protecting. So yes, there exists a patent purely for a piece of chocolate's look – a kind of aesthetic patent that speaks to chocolate's cultural cachet as much as its taste.

On the more whimsical end, one of the weirdest patents in the chocolate realm addresses a problem few knew existed: how to keep your chocolate from visibly melting on a hot day. Companies like Nestlé and Hershey have both researched heat-resistant chocolates for decades, trying various tricks – adding tropical fats, altering particle sizes, incorporating edible fibers – to raise the melting point.

Nestlé filed a patent for a process involving adding certain plant fibers to chocolate so it could resist heat up to 40°C (104°F) or more without turning to goo. The target market was largely countries with hot climates, where traditional chocolate struggles. While not exactly bizarre (there's clear practical value), the image of a candy bar that won't melt even under a summer sun almost feels like a child's fantasy ("Mom, my chocolate stayed solid in my pocket all afternoon!").

To achieve it, scientists essentially reinvent aspects of chocolate's chemistry – a reminder that even a classic product is constantly evolving in labs behind the scenes. Hershey during WWII had an experimental "Tropical Chocolate" for the Pacific, as noted earlier, but today's food technologists are refining those ideas to bring a stable chocolate to store shelves worldwide. Maybe one day, the dreaded experience of opening a melted candy bar will be as outdated as dialing up the internet.

Perhaps the quirkiest modern invention wasn't a patent but a product: the chocolate inhaler. Yes, you read that right – a device that allows one to breathe in chocolate. This contraption, called "Le Whif," emerged around 2009 from the mind of Harvard professor David Edwards and his collaborators in Paris. Le Whif looked like a little lipstick tube; inside, it contained powdered chocolate. By puffing on it, a user got a tiny burst of cocoa flavor delivered to their tongue and olfactory senses – chocolate without actually eating chocolate.

Chocolate Inhaler: Le Whif, a quirky product invented by Harvard professor David Edwards in 2009, contained powdered chocolate in a lipstick-like tube, allowing users to breathe in the flavor without consumption.

The creators pitched it as a zero-calorie chocolate experience, an intersection of molecular gastronomy and gadgetry. It sounded like something straight out of Willy Wonka's lab: imagine quelling your chocolate cravings with a quick inhale rather than a 300-calorie bar. The product did garner attention and some initial sales in Europe, but it also raised a lot of eyebrows (and, reportedly, a lot of coughs – early users sometimes sputtered on the fine particles).

Culturally, some found it too absurd: why deny yourself the pleasure of actually *eating* chocolate and feeling it melt on your tongue? Critics asked, "Do we not still have taste buds? Who wants to inhale their dessert?" The chocolate inhaler, despite its innovation, never became a mainstream hit. Production was limited, and it quietly faded away after the initial novelty wore off. In retrospect, Le Whif was a failed invention, but a fascinating one.

It challenged the boundary of what "eating" means and poked fun at our dieting paradoxes – giving chocoholics a guilt-free fix that, ultimately, just wasn't as satisfying as the real thing. Still, one can find its legacy in the trend of "breathable flavors" and cocktail vaporizers that pop up in avant-garde restaurants. Chalk it up as yet another strange path that chocolate-inspired creativity has taken us down.

These patents and products – from edible holograms to nutrient bars to inhalable cocoa – show that the world of chocolate is not just grandmas baking brownies. It's high-tech, cutthroat, and often downright peculiar. For every beloved bar on the shelf, there's a string of experiments behind it, many of which never see the light of day. And yet, inventors keep experimenting, filing papers, and tinkering in kitchens and labs, convinced they might just mold the next big thing in chocolate. As long as people adore chocolate (which shows no sign of stopping), the incentive to innovate with it – however oddly – will persist. And that means more weird patents are surely on the way.

Cars, Couture, and Beyond: Chocolate's Final Frontiers

If you thought chocolate's weird journey was confined to kitchens, laboratories, and battlefields – think again. Our final stop on this grand tour of chocolate experiments ventures into environments where you'd least expect to find a smear of cocoa: the racetrack, and even the edges of space.

Chocolate-Powered Speed: The "WorldFirst" Formula 3 racing car, developed by Warwick University in 2009, ran on biodiesel made from chocolate factory waste (cocoa butter oils), demonstrating the surprising final frontier of chocolate's utility.

Let's start with the racetrack. In 2009, a team of British engineers at Warwick University unveiled what was touted as the world's first chocolate-powered race car. This Formula 3 vehicle, dubbed the "WorldFirst" racing car, was an eco-engineering marvel and a bit of a prank on traditional motorsports. Its diesel engine was tuned to run on biodiesel derived from chocolate factory waste – essentially leftover cocoa butter oils that weren't suitable for confectionery. In effect, it drank chocolate to zoom around.

And zoom it did: the car could reach speeds near 150 mph, proving that sweet fuels could be serious. Moreover, the car's construction was a feast of sustainable materials. The steering wheel was made from carrot fibers, the seats from soybean oil foam, and the body panels from potato starch and flax fiber. Even the brake pads had cashew nut shells in them. The entire design was 95% biodegradable.

It's as if someone challenged a bunch of engineers to make a fruit-and-veg salad that could beat a Ferrari off the starting line – and they garnished it with chocolate for good measure. The project was partly a publicity stunt to showcase green tech in the automotive industry, but it was also a genuine research effort. They had proven that cocoa biodiesel was viable as a fuel.

However, when it came time to actually race, the chocolate car hit a snag: Formula 3 regulations didn't allow biodiesel fuel in competition at that time. So this blazing fast, earth-friendly machine could only perform in exhibition, not in actual F3 races. It's a classic example of a brilliant invention held back not by physics or engineering, but by rules that hadn't caught up with innovation.

Regardless, the chocolate race car made headlines worldwide and captured imaginations. It prompted many people to realize that waste from making chocolate bars and Easter eggs could find a second life powering vehicles. Today, research into biofuels often includes oddball sources like coffee grounds, algae, and yes, chocolate waste. Perhaps in the future, fleets of delivery trucks or farm equipment will quietly run on the energy of repurposed candy factory discards. Should that day come, we might remember the WorldFirst car as a pioneer – a flashy proof-of-concept that even the need for speed can have a sweet tooth.

Walking the Runway: The Chocolate Dress

Perhaps the most ephemeral of all chocolate experiments occurs annually in Paris at the *Salon du Chocolat*, where chocolatiers team up with fashion designers to create haute couture you can eat.

Engineering a chocolate dress is a battle against thermodynamics. The body heat of the model is enough to melt the garment. To solve this, designers have invented techniques like spraying chocolate onto tulle netting, creating flexible "scales" of ganache, or tempering chocolate so hard it acts like rigid armor. These creations exist for only a few hours under the hot stage lights—a fleeting, decadent experiment in functional art that pushes the structural properties of cocoa butter to their absolute limit.

Back on Earth, chocolate also finds itself in experimental realms like medicine and psychology. Researchers have tried using chocolate's scent and compounds to trigger cognitive or mood responses. There have been hospital studies examining if the smell of chocolate could reduce stress or if a little chocolate on the tongue before certain medical procedures calms patients' nerves.

These are soft experiments – not the flashy kind with patents – but they show how deeply chocolate is woven into human experience. We instinctively turn to it for comfort, so scientists can't help but probe that connection. One whimsical study even involved using chocolate to model blood flow in medical training, since melted chocolate has a viscosity not unlike blood (and it's safer to handle in classroom demos). It's messy, sure, but any med student would prefer cleaning chocolate off their lab coat to actual bodily fluids.

Even the art world has joined in the experimental love affair. Edible chocolate records have been made that can play music on a turntable – at least for a few spins until the needle wears down the grooves (and you inevitably nibble the disc). A famous example is when a creative designer named Erika Marthins in 2017 produced a playable vinyl record made of chocolate as part of a culinary art project in Switzerland.

She recorded a classic space-age pop song onto a chocolate disc and successfully played it, the sound warbling as the stylus carved through the chocolate. Listeners could literally hear the music *and* smell the dessert at the same time. It was ephemeral – play it a few times and the record degrades – but that was the point, to savor the fleeting moment.

Similarly, chocolate has been used to create film negatives for pinhole cameras (developing an image on a thin chocolate layer – the results are faint but discernible) and even to make circuitry (researchers once printed a simple electrical circuit on a chocolate bar with conductive edible ink, as a novelty to show edible electronics).

These strange creations exist somewhere between engineering and art, revealing how chocolate invites a level of experimentation few materials can match. Each invention—practical, whimsical, or downright absurd—demonstrates how easily chocolate slips across boundaries, inspiring ideas that would never surface with any other ingredient. The question isn't whether people will push chocolate further, but how soon the next improbable idea will appear.

A Legacy of Sweet Experimentation

Looking across these stories, a pattern emerges: chocolate has always been more than nourishment or indulgence. Its physical quirks, emotional resonance, and cultural ubiquity make it a uniquely fertile material for invention. Chocolate melts predictably, solidifies cleanly, carries aroma vividly, and invites both precision and play. That combination has sparked breakthroughs big and small—from microwave ovens to military rations to edible electronics—and has inspired countless ideas that never made it past the prototype stage. Even the failures matter: each odd experiment pushes someone else toward the next discovery.

There's also a charming human thread through all this: optimism and playfulness. Who but an optimist looks at a chocolate bar and imagines it might launch rockets or cure diseases or brew tea? Who but a playful spirit attempts to refine the melting points and structures of chocolate as if forging a spacecraft part? Chocolate, by virtue of being a beloved indulgence, invites a bit of whimsy into the sterile halls of R&D. It reminds engineers and chefs alike that innovation can be fun – even a little ridiculous – and still matter. You can almost picture all the madcap moments: the chuckle of surprise Percy Spencer had seeing gooey chocolate on his uniform, the grins in the lab when a teapot of cocoa goodness survived the boiling water test, or the incredulous laughter of race mechanics fueling a car with what looks (and smells) like dessert syrup.

For the general audience that loves chocolate, knowing these stories deepens the appreciation for that next bite of candy. There's history and daring in chocolate's taste. The trivial-seeming chocolate bar is a product of centuries of experiment – some serious, some silly, all driven by the craving to do more with this ingredient. Next time you unwrap your favorite bar, consider the countless trials that made it possible:

The ancient Mesoamerican who first ground cocoa beans and mixed them with spices in an experimental drink; the 18th-century pharmacist who pressed cocoa butter into a cake, inadvertently paving the way for solid chocolate; the factory tinkerer who perfected the conching machine for smooth texture; and the marketing maven who thought to include a collectible trading card in a chocolate box, innovating how we consume content with candy (yes, that happened too!). And in our era, the experiments continue – maybe a new failed invention is happening right now in some confectionery lab, destined to be a quirky footnote or perhaps the next big food craze.

Chocolate's great experiments remind us that even the most commonplace pleasures can launch extraordinary journeys. Whether it's a lifesaving tool, a weapon of intrigue, a scientific apparatus, or a work of art, chocolate has worn all these hats and more. Its failures are often as fascinating as its successes – and sometimes it's hard to tell which was which until years later. In the end, every melted mess and every eureka moment has added to the richness of chocolate's story.

Chocolate's strangest experiments remind us that innovation often begins with curiosity, not practicality. Ideas that once seemed laughable —brewing tea in a chocolate teapot, printing music onto chocolate vinyl, or discovering new technologies thanks to a melted candy bar—show how imagination can reshape both desserts and devices. The next time a chocolate bar melts in your pocket or an idea seems too peculiar to pursue, remember these stories. Chocolate has proved that even the most unlikely experiments can lead somewhere remarkable. The world changes one bold, playful idea at a time—and chocolate has never been afraid to lead the way.

36

THE MACHINE AGE: ROBOTICS AND THE FACTORY OF THE FUTURE

At a chocolate factory in Austria, a visitor stands behind the glass barrier and watches a robotic arm pour molten chocolate with a precision no human hand could match. In seconds the machine shifts to smoothing molds, tapping them, and lifting newly formed pralines with a flourish that almost looks intentional—an echo of craft embedded in code. Nearby, another robot sorts confections with an elegance that borders on choreography. This seamless fusion of performance and production signals a new era in chocolate making: a Machine Age defined not by cold efficiency, but by the merging of tradition, artistry, and automation.

CHOCOLATE REMAINS STEEPED IN NOSTALGIA, but the industry that produces it is undergoing a transformation far louder than it first appears. Across continents, small workshops and mega-factories alike are turning to robotics, artificial intelligence, and networked machines to handle tasks once entrusted to expert hands. The motivation is not merely speed or volume—it is consistency, precision, and the possibility of enhancing chocolate's sensory magic through technological control. The question is no longer whether automation belongs in chocolate making, but how it will reshape the craft at every level.

This long-form exploration will dive into how automation is sweeping through the chocolate industry worldwide, how these technologies are affecting flavor and craftsmanship, and how age-old traditions are adapting to this new world. Grab a piece of your favorite chocolate, and let's peel back the wrapper on the factories of the future.

Yet for all its futuristic gloss, the rise of chocolate automation is ultimately a human story—of engineers trying to preserve flavor through precision, of workers displaced or retrained by machines, and of chocolatiers wrestling with the boundaries between craft and code. Framed this way, the Machine Age becomes less about robots replacing humans and more about the changing relationship between people, technology, and taste.

A GLOBAL SHIFT in Chocolate Production

Step onto the floor of a modern chocolate factory and the first sensation is not sweetness but rhythm: conveyor belts gliding, robotic arms turning with almost balletic precision, and machines coordinating movements once carried out by teams of skilled workers. Automation is no longer an experiment or novelty—it is the baseline architecture of chocolate production worldwide, stretching from American megaplants to European confectionery houses to Asia's high-tech manufacturing hubs.

In the United States, the shift toward flexible, modular manufacturing has accelerated dramatically. Companies like Hershey have begun replacing traditional linear production lines with clusters of robotic, self-contained units that can switch tasks in seconds. This approach mirrors the adaptability of small craft producers while retaining the throughput of industrial giants—an early sign that automation can expand creative possibilities rather than limit them.

This modular design means the factory can switch between making different chocolate bars on the fly, with minimal downtime for cleaning and recalibration. One minute the line might be wrapping a run of special dark chocolate bars, and soon after it could be molding and filling a batch of cookies-and-cream bars.

Such agility is a departure from the old model of chocolate manufacturing that prized relentless uniformity and volume above all. Hershey's goal with this project is to respond faster to changing consumer tastes—getting new flavors or limited editions to market quickly—without sacrificing efficiency. Robotics are crucial here: robotic arms and automated guided systems handle the quick changeovers and precise movements needed for a more diverse production schedule. In essence, automation is allowing a very large chocolate maker to behave more like a nimble craft producer, scaling variety without losing scale.

Across the Atlantic, Europe's chocolate industry is also adapting, albeit a bit more cautiously. Europe is home to some of the world's oldest chocolatiers in countries like Switzerland, Belgium, France, and Italy. These companies have rich traditions and in many cases still emphasize hand craftsmanship in their branding.

Perhaps as a result, full-on robotics adoption has been a slower burn. Recent industry estimates suggest that only about one in ten food and confectionery producers in Europe currently employ robotics on their production lines. But that minority is steadily growing.

Labor shortages and the rising cost of skilled workers are motivating European confectioners to explore automation. At the same time, consumer demand is shifting: retailers want a greater variety of products, seasonal specialties, and even personalized chocolates, which can be challenging to produce with purely manual methods. Robotics firms in Europe report increasing inquiries from chocolate companies looking for flexible packaging solutions and efficient ways to handle many product variations.

For instance, an executive at a German robotics provider noted that confectionery manufacturers are struggling to find enough workers for repetitive tasks like packing bonbons into trays, and robots are an attractive solution. In one example, a renowned Belgian chocolate brand recently introduced robotic "picker" systems in its packing department. These robots use cameras and sensors to recognize assorted chocolates on a conveyor and gently pick and place them into fancy assorted gift boxes. They can even be programmed to ensure that each box gets the right mix of truffles and pralines, a job that used to be done by teams of workers hand-packing each selection. The robots never get tired, never drop a chocolate, and can work around the clock if needed. This careful automation of packing delicate treats shows how Europe's chocolatiers are starting to blend Old World quality with new technology in areas invisible to the customer.

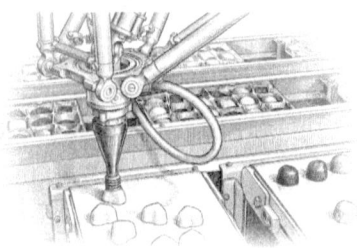

Precision: Robots now handle the tempering and sorting tasks, performing with a consistency that human hands cannot match.

Meanwhile, the Asia-Pacific region is experiencing a boom in "smart" chocolate factories. Countries such as China, India, and Japan have rapidly growing chocolate markets, and companies there are building state-of-the-art production lines from the ground up. Many of these new factories are being outfitted with the latest automation tech from day one. Analysts predict double-digit annual growth in adoption of automation and robotics in Asia's food processing sector in the coming years, and chocolate is no exception.

Governments and corporations alike are investing in advanced manufacturing as part of broader economic development strategies. For example, a major chocolate producer in China opened a facility that uses robotic arms to handle almost every step of production, from stirring giant vats of cocoa mixture to palletizing finished cases of chocolate bars.

In Japan, known for its love of both technology and elegant sweets, you can find famously precise robots working in chocolate packaging—and even entertaining visitors in flagship stores by making confections on the spot. One famous Japanese chocolatier, for instance, has a storefront where visitors watch a robotic system pipe patterns onto candies and drizzle ribbons of chocolate with artistry that rivals human pâtissiers.

These sorts of installations are part practical manufacturing, part public relations—showcasing how futuristic tech can produce something as joyful and traditionally handcrafted as chocolate. The message is clear across Asia: automation is not seen as the enemy of quality, but as a means to achieve consistency and scale up production to meet surging demand for chocolate among a growing middle class.

In Latin America, a region crucial to the chocolate ecosystem (as it includes many cocoa-growing countries as well as emerging chocolate manufacturers), automation is also making inroads. In Mexico, one of the country's largest chocolate producers, which is part of the Colombia-based food conglomerate Grupo Nutresa, has modernized its factories with robotics specifically to tackle a bottleneck in its operations: packaging. The company's chocolate bars and confections, such as hazelnut-filled treats and peanut-coated candy bars, used to rely on intensive manual labor at the end of the production line to sort, pack, and box the products.

As volumes grew, this became unsustainable. In recent years, Nutresa's Mexico division partnered with an Italian automation firm to install a new packaging line powered by robotic arms and intelligent vision systems. Now, as chocolates move off the wrapping machines, swift robotic arms identify each piece and place them into trays and cartons at blinding speed. The system was designed to be versatile: it can pack chocolates in different arrangements and counts depending on whether the batch is destined for a wholesale bulk order, a supermarket variety pack, or a membership club store pallet.

This flexibility has allowed the factory to increase its output without exhausting its workforce. In fact, the initial concern that robots would replace human workers did not fully materialize; instead, the company reports that workers who used to do the laborious packing by hand have been retrained to oversee the robots, manage quality control, or handle other growing areas of the business.

Similar stories are unfolding in Brazil, Argentina, and other countries where chocolate consumption and local production are rising: automation is being adopted not just by the world's largest multinationals but also by regional players aiming to modernize and compete.

Taken together, these examples show a global trend: the chocolate industry is embracing automation to reimagine how factories operate, though each region might be at a different stage of the journey. But what does all this high-tech change mean for the chocolate itself—and for the people and traditions behind it? To answer that, we need to step inside the factory and see exactly what these robots and smart systems are doing.

THE ERA OF **Digital Chocolate**

While traditional factories focus on volume, the cutting edge of automation is focused on the impossible. We have entered the era of 3D-printed chocolate.

In specialized micro-factories, robotic nozzles extrude tempered chocolate layer by layer. This process is agonizingly slow—taking hours to print a complex structure that a mold could produce in seconds—which currently restricts the technology to high-end customization rather than mass market distribution. However, it allows for building geometries that no mold could ever release. These printers allow for internal lattices, hollow fractals, and personalized shapes scanned from a customer's own design.

This technology is shifting the industry from "mass production" to "mass customization." Imagine ordering a dessert that is structurally engineered to collapse in a specific way upon the first bite, or a chocolate bar printed with your own name embossed in the structure, not just the surface. The machine age isn't just about making the same bar faster; it's about making bars that human hands literally cannot shape.

THE AI CHOCOLATIER

Beyond shape, machines are now learning to taste. Major manufacturers are deploying "Electronic Tongues"—sensors comprising lipid/polymer membranes that can detect bitterness, astringency, and sweetness with higher sensitivity than a human palate.

These AI systems analyze flavor trends from social media and search data, then cross-reference them with chemical databases to invent new recipes. In 2022, the Finnish dairy Valio released 'The Bar'—a milk chocolate designed entirely by an AI. The algorithm analyzed 1.5 million consumer reviews to determine the statistically perfect ratio of cocoa to milk.

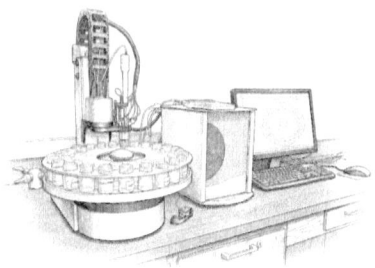

Digital Tasters: Electronic tongues use sensors to detect bitterness and astringency with a sensitivity that surpasses human biology.

The machine age isn't just about making the same bar faster; it's about algorithms dreaming up bars that humans haven't thought of yet. All these elements—precise mixing, smart conching, robotic molding, machine vision quality checks, and automated packing—come together to form what industry insiders call the smart chocolate factory.

It's a facility where every step is monitored, data is collected continuously, and many decisions are made by algorithms or robots in real time. If a machine down the line senses a slight temperature fluctuation that could affect tempering, it can signal upstream equipment to adjust cooling rates instantly. If an automated system detects that one particular product is running low in the warehouse, the factory can seamlessly schedule a new production run of that item, since retooling is so quick now.

Some of the most advanced manufacturers are even implementing digital twins – virtual models of their production lines that allow them to simulate changes or predict problems before they happen in the real factory.

For example, Mars, Incorporated (maker of M&Ms, Snickers, and more) has been working on a "factory of the future" initiative using artificial intelligence and digital modeling. The aim is to virtually test tweaks in the process (say, a new recipe or a speed increase on a line) to foresee any quality issues or bottlenecks, without risking real downtime or waste. It's a far cry from the days when making a new chocolate product meant weeks of trial and error and many scrapped batches.

Stepping into these automated factories can feel almost like entering Willy Wonka's imaginary chocolate works, but instead of whimsical Oompa-Loompas, there are whirring robots and silent automated systems doing the work. As impressive as this high-tech production is, it inevitably raises a question: what about the flavor and soul of the chocolate being made? Is a robot-made chocolate bar as good as one crafted by human hands? And what happens to the artistry and tradition of chocolate-making in such a setting? These questions get to the heart of the debate about automation in food: efficiency and consistency are great, but not if they come at the cost of quality or character. Let's examine how automation is affecting the flavor of chocolate and the craftsmanship behind it.

The Uncanny Valley of Flavor

Despite these advances, robots have a fatal flaw: they have no soul. Or, more scientifically, they have no culture. An "Electronic Tongue" can detect sweetness, but it cannot detect nostalgia. It cannot understand why a slightly gritty texture might remind a Mexican grandmother of her childhood stone-ground chocolate, or why a certain level of bitterness appeals to a craft beer drinker in Portland but repels a sweet-tooth in Tokyo.

AI can optimize for the average palate, creating a statistically perfect chocolate that offends no one and delights no one. This is the "Uncanny Valley" of industrial food: products that are technically flawless but emotionally hollow. The future of chocolate may be robotic, but the soul of chocolate remains stubbornly biological.

Efficiency vs. Flavor: Does Automation Change the Taste?

For any chocolate lover, the proof is ultimately in the taste. All the robotics and automation in the world wouldn't be welcome if they produced chocolate that was bland or inferior. So, how does the march of machines impact the flavor and overall quality of chocolate? The answer is a nuanced one: in many ways automation is enhancing consistency and unlocking new possibilities for flavor optimization, but there's also a tension between mass efficiency and the small-batch craftsmanship that can yield unique flavors.

On the positive side, automated systems can refine the control of flavor-critical steps beyond what even skilled humans can do. Take roasting, for example. The flavor of chocolate begins with how you roast the cocoa beans to develop aroma and taste. Traditional roasting was often done by sight, smell, and timing based on a roast master's intuition.

While many experts still roast by craft, automated roasters with smart controls can roast each batch of beans with a customized profile, ensuring that the beans hit the exact flavor notes desired (fruity, nutty, malty, etc.) without going overboard. Computers don't get distracted or have an "off day" – if programmed correctly, they'll execute the roast profile precisely time after time. This means a company can maintain the signature taste of its chocolate year-round, even as harvests and bean origins change, by tweaking the program rather than relying on manual adjustments. Consistency is a key virtue: your favorite chocolate bar should taste the same every time you buy it, and automation helps guarantee that level of quality control.

Beyond consistency, automation and AI-driven analysis are helping chocolatiers experiment with new flavors in a more systematic way. In the past, developing a new chocolate recipe or flavor was largely a trial-and-error process, guided by expertise and palate. Now, some companies use data and algorithms to assist flavor development.

They can analyze the chemical makeup of different cocoa beans, for instance, and use software to predict how those beans will respond to certain roasting or conching conditions. AI can even suggest blends of beans or ingredient ratios to achieve a target flavor profile. This doesn't mean a computer is replacing a chocolatier's creative touch, but it gives them powerful tools to narrow down the infinite choices in crafting a new product.

Big chocolate makers like Barry Callebaut (a huge Swiss chocolate supplier) have been investing in such technology to help their food-scientist chocolatiers create recipes that maximize certain flavor attributes. The benefit for consumers could be more delicious and diverse chocolate options – imagine discovering a bar that perfectly balances two flavor notes because an AI helped fine-tune the formula behind the scenes.

Moreover, automation can ensure that flavor quality is protected during production. For example, the delicate flavors of high-quality cocoa can be muddled or lost if temperatures or mixing speeds go awry. Automated controls vigilantly keep these factors in check. If a conche runs too hot, it might strip some of the aromatic compounds that give fine chocolate its complexity; a smart conche won't let that happen, because its sensors and feedback loops adjust the energy input continuously.

Similarly, sensitive inclusions like freeze-dried raspberries or aromatic spices can have their flavors preserved better if the timing of their addition and the mixing intensity are carefully managed by machines rather than tossed in haphazardly. So in many respects, automation is a friend to flavor, guarding against the small mistakes that can ruin a batch and making it easier to repeat success.

However, there is an opposing perspective championed by artisan chocolatiers and devoted connoisseurs: that some of the best flavors in chocolate come from *imperfection* and *individual touch*, which risk being ironed out by industrial automation. Craft chocolate makers often differentiate their products by doing things a little differently each time – maybe adjusting a roast because they sense the beans from this farm are extra floral and they want to highlight that, or stopping the conche early to retain a certain earthy note that might be homogenized with longer processing.

These kinds of spontaneous, intuitive decisions are hard to replicate in a fully automated context, where the machinery is optimized to produce a consistent result. Indeed, mass-produced chocolate has historically been criticized for tasting uniform and "safe" compared to the bolder, more distinctive flavors found in some small-batch chocolates.

It's not the machines per se that cause this difference – it's often the process choices (like using a shorter roast for efficiency, or adding emulsifiers and vanilla to cover flavor shortcomings) that big manufacturers make to keep production efficient. Automation tends to encourage processes that favor efficiency and predictability, which can mean less room for the serendipity that sometimes leads to a memorable flavor.

Consider conching time: A large industrial producer might conche a batch of chocolate for 8 hours and find that sufficient for a smooth, mild flavor suited to a broad market palate. An artisan might conche a similar chocolate for 48 or 72 hours, believing that the extended slow refinement develops deeper flavors and a cleaner finish (and they might be right, though it's subjective). For the big factory, a 72-hour conche is too time-consuming to be economical, but for the artisan that is an acceptable cost for the outcome they want.

Automation in itself doesn't force a short conche – you could program a machine to conche as long as you like – but economics and output demands do. So one could argue that automation *enables* large volume production that might cut certain corners; meanwhile, artisanal methods purposely don't maximize throughput, focusing on flavor above all.

The result can be differences in taste that chocolate aficionados notice: perhaps the handcrafted bar has a more complex aftertaste or a unique texture due to stone grinding, whereas the mass-produced bar is ultra-smooth and consistent but a bit one-note in flavor.

That said, the gap between craft and automated flavor is not as wide as it once was. With today's sophisticated control over variables, large manufacturers can slow down or tweak processes when they want to create a premium product.

We're seeing a trend of big chocolate companies introducing small-batch or single-origin lines, made possible by their new flexible factories. They might take extra time with those batches, leveraging automation to do it efficiently at scale. In these cases, the machines are actually helping replicate some artisanal techniques on a bigger scale. For instance, a company could run a special conching cycle that mimics a traditional approach (maybe a lower temperature, longer time) using automated controls, to produce a limited-edition chocolate that has the kind of flavor depth usually only found from a small chocolatier.

Without modern equipment, doing that in a big factory would be impractical or inconsistent. So technology can also help preserve or recreate traditional flavor qualities in a controlled way.

From the perspective of the chocolate-eating public, what matters is that *delicious* chocolate keeps coming. And indeed, by most accounts, automation has not ruined chocolate's taste—in many cases it has elevated the baseline quality. Even mass-market chocolate today, made in huge automated facilities, is often better in texture and consistency than decades ago, because the machinery can achieve finer particle sizes and better tempering. Of course, personal preference plays a role.

Some chocolate lovers will always favor the rustic charm of a slightly grainy stone-ground chocolate made by a tiny workshop, over a perfectly refined corporate candy bar. But the exciting thing about the current chocolate landscape is that automation might give us the best of both worlds: more of the dependable classics we love, and new innovative chocolates that marry craftsmanship with science.

One area where automation undeniably shines is food safety and purity of flavor. Automated systems can eliminate human contact with the product, which is great for hygiene (fewer chances for contamination). They also operate in controlled environments, so the chocolate isn't picking up ambient moisture or odors from a busy kitchen.

This yields a very clean flavor expression of the ingredients. Artisans working in small kitchens have to be meticulous to avoid flavor cross-contamination or inconsistencies that can sneak in with more hands-on processing. In a sealed, optimized automated system, every step is like a tightly run ship, preserving the integrity of the chocolate's taste.

In summary, automation doesn't inherently make chocolate taste better or worse—it's all in how the technology is applied. When used thoughtfully, it can ensure a high standard of flavor quality and even help discover new taste frontiers (like precisely dialing in fermentation or roast profiles for novel flavor outcomes). But if used purely to maximize output with little regard for nuance, it can certainly lead to chocolate that, while technically proficient, lacks the character that makes certain chocolates special.

The encouraging news is that many chocolate makers, big and small, seem aware of this balance. The ethos emerging in the industry is "precision where it matters, and tradition where it counts." That means using automation to handle the parts of production that benefit from consistency and fine control, while still valuing the expert tasters, chocolatiers, and product developers who craft the recipes and make the nuanced decisions about what tastes good. That brings us to the people behind the machines—and the question of what happens to craftsmanship and artisanship in an automated age.

～

CRAFTSMANSHIP AND TRADITION in the Age of Machines

Chocolate isn't just another food commodity; it's a product with a rich history and a sense of artistry that has been passed down through generations. From the master chocolatiers of Europe to family-owned cocoa farms in Africa and Latin America, tradition is deeply woven into the story of chocolate. So how are these traditions faring as automation becomes more prevalent? The relationship between human craftsmanship and machine efficiency is evolving in interesting ways, often turning out to be more collaborative than one might expect.

First, it's worth dispelling a common fear: that robots will completely replace humans in chocolate making, rendering chocolatiers obsolete. In reality, what we're seeing is human-machine collaboration, where each brings their strengths. Machines excel at the repetitive, precision tasks (never getting tired or inconsistent), while humans excel at creative problem-solving, sensory evaluation, and injecting passion into the product.

The best modern chocolate factories recognize this and design their processes accordingly. A clear example is in quality assurance: even with all the sensors and automated quality checks, many chocolate makers still employ tasting panels and experienced chocolatiers to regularly sample the product and give feedback.

A machine can tell you if the chocolate's particle size is correct and if it was tempered properly, but only a human can fully judge the harmony of the flavor and the emotional satisfaction of eating it. So the craft isn't gone; it's augmented by data. Think of automation as giving chocolatiers superpowers – the ability to implement their vision more exactly – rather than replacing their role entirely.

In fact, automation is altering the roles of people in the chocolate industry, but not eliminating them. Workers who once stood on the line wrapping bars or stirring vats are now often operating computers, analyzing production data, or managing teams of machines.

Training and upskilling have become crucial. Companies that introduce robotics typically invest in teaching their staff how to maintain and program these systems. It's not unusual to find line workers being retrained as robot operators or technicians. Many have embraced the change, finding that their jobs have become less physically punishing and more intellectually engaging.

===

MAN VS. MACHINE: WHO DOES IT BETTER?

Not all tasks are created equal. Here is where robots win, and where they fail.

- **The Robot Wins At:**
  - Tempering: Maintaining a precise temperature curve (within 0.1°C) is hard for humans, easy for sensors.
  - Sorting: Scanning millions of beans for defects at high speed.
  - Enrobing: Creating a perfectly thin, uniform shell around a truffle.
- **The Human Wins At:**
  - Flavor Development: Adjusting a roast profile based on the smell of a specific batch.
  - Creativity: Inventing a new ganache flavor (e.g., Rosemary-Caramel).
  - Finishing: Hand-painting delicate details on a bonbon. Robots lack the "imperfect" artistic touch.

===

One chocolate factory technician described the shift like this: "I used to spend all day doing the same manual task over and over. Now I spend my day ensuring the machines are doing *their* tasks right, and figuring out how to solve issues when the data shows something's off. It's actually more interesting work." This points to a broader trend of redefining craftsmanship in a digital context: the craft is in mastering the technology that makes chocolate, as much as in the direct hand-making. The pride of the worker can still be there, just directed at achieving excellence through machines.

Many artisanal and high-end chocolate makers have found a comfortable balance between tradition and automation. They adopt selective automation that supports their craftsmanship without overshadowing it. For example, a small gourmet chocolatier might use a computerized tempering machine to ensure their chocolate has the perfect crystalline structure (and shine and snap) because that device can do in minutes what might take a person much longer to get just right by hand.

By automating tempering, they free up time to focus on the artistic aspects like developing new fillings, hand-painting bonbons, or perfecting decorations. Likewise, some bean-to-bar craft chocolate makers use small-scale automated grinders and mixers to refine their chocolate – these are essentially scaled-down versions of industrial equipment, tuned to an artisan scale.

They still control the parameters intimately, but they don't have to hand-grind nibs for hours (a task that doesn't particularly add romance or value if a machine can do it precisely). The mantra becomes "automate the boring or strenuous stuff, keep the soulful stuff human."

A great illustration of this balance is again Zotter Chocolate in Austria. Josef Zotter, the founder, is known as an innovative artisan chocolatier who also isn't afraid of technology. He incorporated robots into his production not primarily to cut costs or replace people, but to solve specific challenges and push the envelope of creativity. Space was limited in his factory, and using robots for molding allowed him to design a more compact, efficient production layout than traditional conveyor lines would allow.

This in turn enabled Zotter to make an astounding range of over 500 chocolate varieties – many more than a comparably sized operation could traditionally manage – because the robots can switch between tasks and recipes quickly. Zotter explicitly stated that his motivation was not to reduce his workforce; on the contrary, after installing the robots he hired more staff, repurposing workers into roles that work alongside the robots. The robots handle the pouring, cooling and other repetitive tasks "that they can do better than humans," as Zotter put it, but he still relies on skilled chocolatiers for developing recipes, doing finishing touches, and ensuring the human creativity remains at the heart of the business.

Automation for Innovation: By assigning repetitive tasks to robots, Zotter Chocolate can produce over 500 unique varieties in a compact, efficient space.

In Zotter's visitor center, they even turned the robots into an attraction that underscores this philosophy: the robots serve guests chocolates with showmanship, symbolizing that machines can enhance the experience rather than detract from it. Zotter's story is evidence that automation and tradition can coexist. A forward-thinking artisan can embrace technology and still uphold quality and creativity – using machines as just another set of tools, like an extension of their craft.

What about the venerable traditions of places like Switzerland or Belgium, where the image of the *maître chocolatier* (master chocolate chef) is central to the culture? Even there, change is happening subtly. Many Swiss and Belgian companies have ultra-modern factories under the hood, but they often keep certain traditional elements in play for heritage and marketing. For example, a famous Belgian praline company might use a high-speed automated line to produce the shells of their chocolates and fill them, but still employ humans to hand-garnish or inspect the top of each praline, preserving a final human touch.

In Switzerland, a brand like Lindt has enormous automated factories churning out chocolate bars and truffles, yet they cultivate the image of the Lindt Master Chocolatiers, a team of experts who design new chocolates and occasionally appear in ads stirring melted chocolate by hand. It's not just marketing fluff; those experts really are guiding the product development and ensuring the machines are doing things right. So one could say the tradition now lives both in symbolic gestures and in oversight roles – the guardians of quality are still there, even if they're not hand-producing every piece.

There is also a cultural aspect to consider. In some countries that are newer to chocolate manufacturing (or where industrialization of chocolate is a newer phenomenon), adopting automation doesn't carry the same sense of "loss of tradition" because the tradition is being built alongside the technology.

In places like India or China, where chocolate consumption has surged mainly in recent decades, the focus is on producing high quality at large scale to meet demand. There aren't centuries-old family chocolate shops on every corner as in Europe, so the introduction of automation is seen more as a leapfrogging into the modern food processing era rather than a threat to heritage. In these contexts, craftsmen are more likely to be food scientists or engineers who take pride in designing brilliant processes and machines that can make great chocolate efficiently for millions of people. The *craft* is different but it's still craft of a sort—an engineering craft.

One cannot discuss automation and workers without addressing the elephant in the room: jobs. The fear of job loss due to automation looms in any industry. The chocolate industry, with its mix of large factories and small artisan shops, shows a mixed picture. Large companies that automate extensively often streamline their workforce in repetitive task areas, potentially reducing the number of workers needed on a line.

However, those companies also tend to grow overall output, and thus sometimes end up employing more people in total, albeit in different roles (like maintenance, IT, and supervision). Small and medium producers might use automation to expand capacity without having to hire dozens of extra workers, which can actually keep them viable and competitive. In regions where manufacturing jobs are important, there's understandable concern whenever a new robot arrives on the scene.

Some chocolate factories have dealt with this by retraining staff for higher-skilled positions and assuring that no one loses their job outright from automation, but rather transitions into a new role. This requires commitment from management to value their people as much as the new machines. Not every company does this perfectly, but the ones that do often see smoother adoption of technology and even improved morale—workers appreciate not having to do the drudgery or back-breaking work, and they feel valued for their knowledge and experience which is now supplemented by automation, not steamrolled by it.

There's also the angle of how tradition itself adapts and evolves. The history of chocolate making is actually full of technological innovations that were once controversial. Go back to the 19th century: the invention of the cocoa press made it possible to separate cocoa butter, leading to cocoa powder and new types of chocolate; conching technology revolutionized chocolate texture; and pioneers like Milton Hershey built fully mechanized production lines in the early 1900s that brought chocolate to the masses.

Each of these leaps likely caused waves in the industry and among traditionalists of their time. Yet, each became part of the new tradition of chocolate. We may well look back at the current robotics and AI innovations as just the latest chapter in the ongoing story of chocolate technology – the era that made chocolate production smarter, more efficient, and opened up possibilities like personalized chocolates produced on-demand or 3D-printed chocolate sculptures at scale. What remains constant is the end goal: delighting people with delicious chocolate. The tools and methods may change, but the heart of the craft – combining science and artistry to transform cacao beans into something sublime – endures.

For small artisan chocolate makers, one tradition likely to persist is the personal connection and storytelling. They might adopt some automation, but they will still highlight the human aspect: who sourced the beans, who developed the recipe, how they innovate with flavors. These stories resonate with chocolate enthusiasts. In the Machine Age, ironically, authentic human stories and hands-on elements become even more precious as a differentiator.

We see many craft chocolatiers using a hybrid model: leveraging technology to ensure quality and safety, while emphasizing hand-finishing or manual selection steps that underscore an artisanal vibe. This way, they gain the benefits of modern tools without losing the charm that sets them apart from industrial chocolate.

THE FUTURE: Reimagining How Chocolate Is Made

As we stand at this juncture in the Chocolate Machine Age, it's clear that chocolate manufacturing will never quite be the same. The coming years promise even more integration of advanced technology.

We can expect AI systems that manage entire chocolate supply chains, from predicting the optimal time to buy cocoa beans to scheduling production runs based on real-time sales data from stores. We may see more robotic chefs—machines capable of more intricate "creative" tasks like decorating chocolates or even inventing new recipes by analyzing huge datasets of ingredient combinations and flavor chemistry.

One fascinating area on the horizon is the concept of on-demand chocolate manufacturing. Imagine walking into a store or cafe, selecting a few flavor preferences on a screen, and then watching as a robotic system actually makes a custom chocolate bar for you while you wait: roasting a particular batch of beans from inventory, grinding, mixing with your chosen inclusions (say, Himalayan salt and dried mango), tempering and molding it all within an hour. This might sound far-fetched, but startups and big companies alike are tinkering with modular micro-factories and advanced 3D printing of chocolate that could make such personalized confections a reality.

Automation and robotics are key to these concepts, because a human could hardly perform all those tasks so quickly and precisely on demand. If these ideas take off, buying chocolate could become an experience that blends retail and manufacturing in real time, giving chocolate lovers unprecedented customization.

From an economic and environmental standpoint, automation could help make chocolate production more sustainable. Smart systems are already reducing waste by improving yield (fewer botched batches, less scrap). They also can optimize energy use—machines can power down when not needed, or run at off-peak energy hours. There's research into using AI to perfect fermentation of cocoa at the farm level, which could improve bean quality and thus flavor while reducing spoilage.

We might see more origin-country production of chocolate boosted by compact automated factories that can be set up even in cocoa-growing regions. This could add value locally rather than shipping all beans overseas for processing, potentially a win for farmers and emerging economies. Automation, if accessible and scaled appropriately, might enable a small cooperative in Ghana or Ecuador to produce world-class chocolate bars right where the beans are grown, marrying traditional knowledge of the crop with modern manufacturing techniques.

Of course, with any rapid change, there are challenges. Small producers worry about affording new technology and not being left behind. Larger ones must ensure that increasing automation doesn't alienate consumers who crave authenticity. And the industry as a whole must carefully manage the transition of its workforce, keeping chocolate making as a source of good jobs even if the nature of those jobs changes.

There's also something to be said for maintaining a tactile, hands-on training for future chocolatiers: Even if the factories are robotic, the best chocolatiers will still benefit from knowing how to work with chocolate manually, to truly understand it. Many experts suggest that training programs in confectionery now include both old-school technique and new technology, to create well-rounded professionals for this new age.

In the end, what's most compelling about the Chocolate Machine Age is how it highlights the adaptability and innovation in an industry that is both very old and very new. Chocolate as a treat dates back thousands of years to ancient Mesoamerican cultures, but the way we make chocolate has constantly evolved, especially in the last couple of centuries.

Automation and robotics are just the latest tools we are using to continue that evolution. They are helping us make more chocolate, more safely, and often at a higher baseline of quality than ever before. They are enabling creativity by handling drudgery and precision, thus giving humans more bandwidth to dream up the next great chocolate sensation. And they are making it possible to bring chocolate to more people in more forms—whether it's a classic candy bar available cheaply and consistently everywhere, or a wild new flavor combo that only a data-crunching AI would have dared to suggest.

The latest tool in centuries of evolution: Robotics ensure a higher baseline of quality and safety, continuing the long history of adaptability in the chocolate industry.

For chocolate lovers, this should come as encouraging news. The factories reimagining how chocolate is made are, at their best, working to ensure that every bite of chocolate you enjoy is as perfect as it can be. They are also safeguarding the future of chocolate by making production more efficient and sustainable, which helps keep chocolate affordable and available even as global demand rises.

Yet, as we've explored, these advancements don't necessarily mean losing the heart and heritage of chocolate. If anything, many in the industry are more in touch with the origins and fine details of their product than ever—because to program a machine or train an AI to make great chocolate, you have to first *truly know* what great chocolate is.

The curtain is closing on our tour of the Chocolate Machine Age. We've seen robots dancing with pralines, data guiding flavor development, and people and machines working side by side to carry on a delicious tradition. It's a future where a 150-year-old chocolate company might use a digital twin to perfect a recipe, and a startup might use a tabletop factory to produce bean-to-bar chocolate in a grocery store.

It's a future where the ancient cacao bean meets high-tech treatment, and the result is something that can still feel magical to the person who finally unwraps and tastes it. After all, no matter how advanced our factories become, the true measure of progress in chocolate is simple: Does it make people smile when they taste it? With automation taking care of consistency and efficiency, and skilled humans ensuring soul and creativity, the answer will hopefully remain a resounding yes, one joyful bite at a time.

37

CHOCOLATE 2.0: THE RACE
TO GROW COCOA IN A LAB

I n a quiet California lab on an early morning, a researcher gently lifts the
lid of a petri dish, holding her breath. Inside, a delicate film of pale beige
cells clings to the agar surface. These are cocoa cells – the same cells that
would form a cacao bean on a tropical tree – but here they are growing in a
sterile dish, thousands of miles from any rainforest. Across the room, a stainless
steel bioreactor hums softly. There is no smell of damp earth or fermenting pulp
here; the air is sterile and cool. Inside the polished tank, billions of cacao cells
swirl in a warm broth of sugars and plant nutrients, slowly multiplying in a
stainless steel womb. To a casual observer, this antiseptic scene resembles a
medical lab more than a kitchen, yet to this team of scientists, it smells like the
future of chocolate.

LEADING the effort is a visionary biotech startup founder and her small
team of food technologists. Their mission sounds audacious: create real
chocolate without a single cacao pod. Instead of farming cocoa trees in
equatorial climates, they are brewing cocoa in beakers and bioreactors.

It's a high-tech approach to an ancient indulgence. If they succeed, it
could remake an industry. But as they race to perfect their lab-grown
cocoa, tension is building between innovation and tradition. Traditional

chocolate makers – from West African farmers to Swiss chocolatiers – are watching warily, many deeply skeptical that something as magical as chocolate can be born in a petri dish. Will consumers embrace a cacao that's cultured in steel tanks rather than grown on a tree?

Can this breakthrough ease the ethical and environmental strains that plague conventional cocoa farming? Those questions loom large as the lab team coaxes microscopic cocoa cells to bloom. The stakes are high: this is not just about making candy in a new way, it's about securing the future of chocolate itself.

THE BITTERSWEET REALITY of Cocoa

Why try to reinvent chocolate in a lab in the first place? The answer lies in the growing turmoil facing the world's cocoa supply. Globally, people consume more than seven million metric tons of chocolate per year, and our appetite only continues to grow. Yet cacao trees are finicky plants, vulnerable to drought, disease, and extreme weather. In West Africa – where roughly two-thirds of the world's cocoa is grown – unpredictable weather linked to climate change has already caused poor harvests and worries about future yields. Plant diseases like cacao swollen shoot virus and fungal blights periodically ravage farms, adding to the instability.

On top of that, the economics of cocoa are unsustainable for many communities. Côte d'Ivoire and Ghana produce the bulk of the world's cocoa, but most farmers there live on the brink of poverty. The price of cocoa beans has surged to historic highs (briefly reaching around $12,000 per ton in 2024) due to supply shortages, yet the farmers see little of that windfall. Low incomes have led to persistent problems like child labor on farms and a lack of investment in plantations.

Meanwhile, to meet ever-growing demand, farmers often clear patches of rainforest to plant more cocoa, fueling deforestation and soil depletion. A senior adviser to one major chocolate manufacturer has warned that "cacao is in danger" and that without major changes, a decade from now the chocolate industry's outlook could be bleak.

Big chocolate companies are alarmed enough to be making contingency plans. Some have resorted to "shrinkflation" – quietly reducing bar sizes or the cocoa content in their recipes – to stretch supplies. Others are reformulating products to use less cocoa or to substitute cocoa butter with cheaper vegetable oils. Confectionery giants have even started promoting more non-chocolate candies to hedge against cocoa shortages.

These measures underscore a hard truth: the traditional cocoa supply chain is under serious stress, and the world may not be able to produce enough chocolate in the future without new solutions. This is the urgent backdrop against which our California startup – and a handful of others – are pursuing high-tech chocolate. They see it as a necessary evolution, Chocolate 2.0 for a warming, resource-constrained world.

Brewing Chocolate Without Pods

In a nondescript industrial park in California, the lab-grown cocoa startup's facility looks more like a microbrewery than Willy Wonka's workshop. Shelves are lined with flasks and coiled tubes; climate-controlled incubators blink with digital readouts. This is where cocoa is being grown *in vitro*.

The process starts with something taken from a real cacao plant – often a few cells scraped from a cacao seed or a snippet of leaf tissue. These cells, which contain all the genetic instructions to create cocoa, are placed onto petri dishes filled with a gel rich in nutrients and plant hormones. Fed with the right mix of sugars, vitamins, and growth regulators, the cocoa cells awaken and begin to divide. What starts as a pinprick-sized sample soon multiplies into a pale beige mass of cells visible to the naked eye.

Once the cacao cell cultures are established on plates, the team transfers them into bioreactors for scaling up. Inside a bioreactor – essentially a sanitized steel tank equipped with sensors, pumps, and stirring paddles – the cells are coddled with optimal warmth and nourishment, mimicking the tropical conditions they thrive in but within a controlled environment.

Cellular Agriculture: Scientists are now brewing chocolate in
bioreactors, growing the cells of the bean without the tree.

OVER SEVERAL DAYS, the cells proliferate by the billions. Some
bioreactors are tuned to encourage cells to accumulate cocoa butter
(the natural fat that gives chocolate its melt-in-your-mouth richness);
other cultures might be optimized to produce flavor-rich polyphenols
and aromatic compounds. After about a week of growth, the yield is
ready to harvest. The scientists filter out and collect the cocoa cell
biomass – a wet, brown slurry that, at this stage, smells vaguely earthy
and sweet.

Turning that slurry into something recognizable as chocolate
requires the age-old steps of fermentation and roasting – only now
applied to cell-grown cocoa instead of farm-grown beans. The lab team
spreads the harvested cell mass out and ferments it with carefully
selected microbes, much as farmers ferment piles of cacao pulp and
seeds to develop flavor on the farm. This fermentation step generates
many of the precursor compounds that later transform into chocolate's
complex taste.

Next comes roasting: once dried, the cell-derived material is gently
roasted to refine its aroma and deepen the flavor. The result is a powder
that is, chemically speaking, real cocoa – it contains the same key
flavanols, fats, and flavor molecules found in conventional cocoa beans.
From here, it can be ground and conched with sugar, milk, and other
ingredients to make actual chocolate. In essence, they have grown a
cacao crop in stainless steel vats and ended up with cocoa powder and
cocoa butter, no plantation or cacao pods needed.

The startup's founder is intimately familiar with both the science
and the romance of chocolate. She spent years working in food technology (and even visiting cocoa farms) before launching this venture in

2020. On one trip to Ghana, she recalls local farmers anxiously talking about how droughts and floods were hurting their cacao trees.

```
===================================================
```

THE FUTURE RECIPE: FEEDING THE TANK

You don't need soil to grow cocoa. You need a "Growth Media." Here is what the scientists feed the cells.

- The Starter: 1 gram of Cacao Callus (Stem Cells).
- The Energy: Sucrose (Sugar) + Glucose.
- The Vitamins: Thiamine, Pyridoxine, Nicotinic Acid.
- The Minerals: Nitrogen, Phosphorus, Potassium (The same N-P-K found in fertilizer).
- The Hormones: Auxins and Cytokinins (To tell the cells to divide).

```
===================================================
```

Those conversations planted a seed of their own – an idea that cocoa might need a radically different growing method to survive. Back home in California, she teamed up with a veteran plant biologist and set to work in a borrowed corner of a university lab. Early experiments were small and unpredictable: a few petri dishes of cocoa cells that sometimes turned fuzzy with mold or refused to grow at all. But through trial and error they learned how to coax the fragile plant cells to thrive. They discovered which mix of nutrients made the cells produce more cocoa butter versus more antioxidants, and which strains of yeast during fermentation gave the best flavor. Bit by bit, they were learning how to brew chocolate.

After several years, the team produced their first small batch of lab-grown chocolate. It was a simple milk chocolate – an easier target than a dark chocolate, since milk and sugar can mask minor flavor differences. The bar looked and snapped like ordinary chocolate. When they tasted it, to their delight, it was remarkably close to the real thing.

Not *perfect* – a trained chocolatier might notice a slight difference in aroma or aftertaste – but undeniably chocolate. Encouraged, the startup began refining their process for a deeper, darker chocolate profile, tweaking fermentation cultures and roasting curves to tease out more nuanced cocoa flavors. Each iteration brings them closer to a product that could fool even seasoned taste buds.

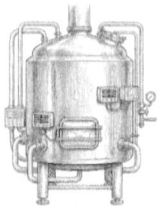

The Fermenter: In the future, chocolate may be brewed in vats like beer, using cell cultures instead of farm-grown beans.

Now their lab-grown cocoa is on the cusp of leaving the lab. The company has formed a partnership with a large Japanese confectionery brand that shares its vision and is helping fund the next stage of development. They are also seeking regulatory approval in the United States, since selling an entirely new kind of cocoa ingredient requires a green light from the Food and Drug Administration.

If all goes well, the startup hopes to debut its cocoa powder on the market soon – perhaps even within the next year or two. The founder imagines a day in the near future when chocolate lovers can buy a bar that proudly sports a label saying "Lab-Grown Cocoa" – and when most people won't be able to tell any difference in taste. Importantly, her goal isn't to replace the experience of artisanal, single-origin chocolate; rather, it's to provide a sustainable base for the mass-market chocolate that satisfies millions of sweet tooths every day.

As she often explains to skeptics, the average candy bar contains only a small percentage of actual cocoa – so if lab-grown cocoa can supply that portion without the baggage of deforestation or child labor, why not use it?

～

NEW CHOCOLATE PIONEERS **Around the Globe**

The California lab is not alone in this quest. In fact, a global wave of startups has emerged, all trying to reinvent chocolate in one way or another. They use different methods – from cultured cells to clever fermentation of novel ingredients – but their goal is the same: a more sustainable chocolate. Here are some of the notable players making headlines in the race for Chocolate 2.0:

- Planet A Foods (Germany) – A Munich-based startup (formerly called QOA) that ferments locally abundant crops like sunflower seeds and oats to create a cocoa-free chocolate alternative. Their product, branded *ChoViva*, mimics the taste and function of cocoa and is already being used by European manufacturers (including major brands like Lindt) in products such as cookies and candy bars. By using regional crops instead of tropical cacao, Planet A claims to cut the carbon footprint of chocolate by as much as 80%. The company recently raised significant investment to scale up production and is eyeing expansion into the U.K. and U.S. markets, signaling confidence that chocolate made from seeds and fermentation tanks can succeed beyond the lab.
- Voyage Foods (United States) – Based in California, Voyage Foods takes a molecular gastronomy approach to chocolate. The company analyzes the chemical makeup of cocoa and then sources the same key flavor compounds from other plants. The result is a chocolate bar made primarily from unexpected ingredients like upcycled grape seeds, sunflower oil, and sugar – but formulated to look, melt, and taste much like the chocolate we know. Voyage has already launched cocoa-free chocolate chips and baking wafers that are vegan and allergy-friendly, landing them in some grocery stores. The founder often points out that "chocolate doesn't grow on trees – it's the product of a process," meaning if you can replicate the process (roasting, fermenting, Maillard reactions) with different inputs, you can create chocolate

without cacao. Backed by tens of millions in funding and even a partnership with agribusiness giant Cargill, Voyage Foods aims to eventually make its way into mainstream retailers with affordable, familiar-looking chocolate bars made in a wholly new way.

- WNWN (United Kingdom) – Pronounced "win-win," this London-based startup (the name stands for "Waste Not, Want Not") is reimagining chocolate through the fermentation of unconventional ingredients. WNWN uses foods like carob (a naturally sweet pod from the Mediterranean), barley malt, and even surplus bread and brewery grains to brew a chocolate-like confection. By fermenting and roasting these ingredients with carefully crafted techniques, they develop flavor compounds that resemble those of cocoa. WNWN's chocolate alternative, simply called "Choc", contains no cacao or cocoa butter (they use shea butter as a substitute for the fat) yet manages to deliver a surprisingly chocolatey experience. The startup has released limited batches of its vegan chocolate bars online and supplied some high-end UK restaurants and bakeries with "Choc" for desserts. In early 2025, their product won innovation awards in the food industry, suggesting that even culinary experts see promise in a carob-and-barley chocolate stand-in.

- Foreverland (Italy) – An Italian food-tech venture, Foreverland focuses on an often-overlooked chocolate substitute: carob. Grown around the Mediterranean, carob has a naturally sweet, cocoa-adjacent flavor when dried and roasted. Foreverland developed an innovative fermentation process to amplify carob's chocolate-like notes and created a cocoa-free ingredient they call *Choruba*. They have opened a production facility in Puglia, Italy, capable of churning out over 500 tons of Choruba per year. This carob-based chocolate alternative has already found its way into traditional confections – for example, an Italian bakery used Choruba in a special edition panettone (normally a chocolate-studded holiday bread), and a confectioner debuted chocolate-coated almonds using Choruba instead of cocoa. Foreverland's success illustrates that even in a country famous for its chocolate hazelnut spreads, there's appetite for a high-tech twist on chocolate when it promises local sourcing and sustainability.

- Nukoko (United Kingdom) – Nukoko is a UK startup reinventing chocolate using the fava bean (broad bean). The team discovered that fava beans share certain proteins with cocoa beans, which, when fermented and roasted, can generate a similar flavor profile to chocolate. Using this insight, Nukoko ferments fava beans in a process that mirrors traditional cocoa fermentation, then roasts and grinds them into a fine powder. The result is a cocoa-free "chocolate" powder designed to substitute for cacao powder in making chocolate bars or drinks. The company's motto – "We love chocolate but the industry is unsustainable" – speaks to its mission. Having secured over a million dollars in funding, Nukoko is finalizing its fava bean chocolate recipe and expects to launch products by 2025. Their hope is that confectioners could one day blend Nukoko's powder with conventional cocoa to stretch supplies, or even create entirely cocoa-free chocolates that most consumers wouldn't distinguish from the real thing.

- Big Chocolate's Bets – Even the established chocolate industry players are dipping their toes into these new waters. For instance, Mondelēz International (the global giant behind brands like Cadbury) has invested in an Israeli startup called Celleste Bio, which is developing its own lab-cultured cocoa using plant cell technology. And in Switzerland, premium chocolatier Lindt & Sprüngli recently backed a startup named Food Brewer that grows cocoa cells in bioreactors. These moves signal that major companies want a stake in chocolate's high-tech future – or at least a front-row seat to monitor its progress. Meanwhile, other food-tech firms around the world (from Latin America to East Asia) are also exploring cacao-free chocolate formulations, often tailored to local crops. It truly is a worldwide race to invent the next chapter of chocolate, with the traditional bean-to-bar model facing competition from beaker-to-bar innovation.

Tradition Meets Tech: A Culture Clash

For many in the chocolate world, the idea of growing cocoa in test tubes is difficult to swallow. Chocolate isn't just a flavor or a commodity; it's a culture and a livelihood for millions of people. Artisanal chocolate makers often pride themselves on the distinct terroir that cacao beans carry from regions like Ghana, Madagascar, or Ecuador, and on the human touch involved in processing those beans into fine chocolate.

The notion that science can replicate all of that in a lab strikes some as implausible or even heretical. As one skeptical chocolate expert observed, we still only understand a fraction of what gives chocolate its flavor – potentially thousands of different aromatic compounds are at play – so how can a lab be sure to capture that full symphony?

Early experiments with cocoa alternatives have given some credence to the skeptics: in one well-publicized tasting, a veteran chocolatier tried a prototype cocoa-free chocolate and quipped that she had to brush her teeth five times to get the odd taste out of her mouth. Reactions like that underscore the challenge of convincing purists that *lab chocolate* can measure up.

Cocoa-producing countries are also watching this trend closely. In West Africa, where farming communities rely on cocoa for income, there is understandable concern that lab-grown chocolate could one day reduce demand for their crops. *"Lab-grown chocolate may be innovative, but it can't replace the heritage, livelihoods and soul behind real cocoa,"* said a Ghanaian chocolate company CEO, expressing a common sentiment in producer nations that the soul of chocolate is inseparable from the cacao tree and the hands that farm it.

If big candy companies in the future buy tanks of cocoa from California or Berlin instead of beans from Ghana, the economic ripple effects could be severe for thousands of villages and families. It's a scenario that evokes the broader question of food tech disruption: whose jobs and traditions are at stake when we reinvent a food from the ground up?

The proponents of Chocolate 2.0 are quick to respond that their goal is not to wipe out traditional cocoa farming or displace farmers. They argue that the demand for chocolate worldwide is growing so fast that even increasing conventional production may not be enough – and that alternative methods can fill the gap without encroaching on the domain of fine chocolate.

In their vision, the future might see a two-tier chocolate industry: the high-end market continues to cherish bean-to-bar chocolates made from real cacao (ideally with improved wages and conditions for farmers), while the bulk chocolate used in candy bars, baking chips, and snacks increasingly comes from sustainable high-tech sources. In other words, your single-origin dark chocolate bar from a small chocolatier would still come from a cacao farm and carry the story of that origin, whereas your mass-produced chocolate candy could quietly switch to lab-grown cocoa and be virtually indistinguishable in taste.

They point out that much of the chocolate consumed today – in candy bars or cookies – uses beans of fairly average quality and in low percentages, providing just enough cocoa flavor. "We're not taking away your premium Origin chocolate," one startup founder insists. "We're after the industrial chocolate used in Snickers and KitKats – the stuff most people eat by the handful." From that perspective, the lab-grown approach is positioned as a complement to tradition, not an enemy of it.

Even with those assurances, acceptance in the chocolate community will have to be earned over time. The new startups know they must prove that quality and flavor are not sacrificed, and that they respect the heritage of chocolate even as they innovate. Some have begun to collaborate with well-known chefs and chocolatiers for blind taste tests, aiming to demonstrate that their products can stand toe-to-toe with the real thing.

And tellingly, a few major chocolate companies are quietly backing these efforts rather than publicly fighting them, indicating that even traditional industry players see a potential place for lab-grown cocoa in the future landscape. Still, the rollout of lab-grown chocolate will likely be met with a mix of excitement and apprehension. Chocolate has a powerful emotional hold on people – it's tied to childhood memories, to holiday rituals, to notions of comfort and love.

Changing how it's made isn't just a technical tweak; it's asking people to reconsider something deeply familiar. The coming years will reveal how flexible those traditions can be, and whether technology and terroir can find a harmonious coexistence in the world of chocolate.

Tasting the Future: Will People Bite?

Even if the chocolate industry can be convinced, the ultimate test will be the reaction of everyday chocolate lovers. Will people be willing to eat chocolate that was born in a bioreactor instead of a rainforest? The answer likely depends on both taste and trust. For most consumers, taste is paramount – if a lab-grown chocolate bar doesn't delight the palate, it won't last long on store shelves.

Early indications, however, are promising. In blind taste tests, some cocoa-free or lab-cultured chocolates have fooled tasters or at least come surprisingly close. One food journalist who sampled a prototype of fermented sunflower-seed "chocolate" confessed she wouldn't have known it wasn't traditional milk chocolate if she hadn't been told. Especially when used in products like candy bars, cookies, or milk chocolate confections (where cocoa is only one component among many), these alternatives can blend in seamlessly.

Technically speaking, a product needs only around 10% cocoa content to be legally called "chocolate" in many countries – meaning a lab-grown cocoa powder could be used to meet that requirement in a candy bar, and most consumers might never notice any difference in their Snickers or M&Ms.

The bigger hurdle may be psychological. There is a natural emotional connection to chocolate's origins – people often imagine cacao pods ripening under tropical sun, farmers harvesting and fermenting them using age-old techniques, and the tactile, earthy process that eventually yields a chocolate bar.

The idea of chocolate being engineered in a lab could strike some as jarring or too synthetic, even if the end product is chemically identical to the traditional kind. Food technologists talk about "food tech neophobia," the instinctive distrust some folks have toward new food technologies (a phenomenon seen with things like GMO foods or lab-grown meat).

In surveys, many consumers express wariness about the concept of cultured meat or other lab-made edibles; and yet, a fair number also say they would at least *try* these products out of curiosity or for perceived ethical benefits. Lab-grown chocolate might follow a similar pattern: a niche of early adopters and eco-conscious consumers could be excited to taste it and champion it, while others might take a wait-and-see approach, sticking with what's familiar until lab chocolate proves itself.

It's worth noting that younger generations, having grown up amid rapid tech innovation in food (like plant-based milks and meat substitutes), may be more open-minded about a high-tech chocolate, especially if it's marketed as *better for the planet*.

Pricing will also influence consumer acceptance. In its early days, chocolate made in tanks and fermenters is likely to cost more than conventional chocolate. These are still experimental processes, not yet optimized for low-cost mass production. A $5 high-tech chocolate bar – no matter how virtuous its origin – might be a tough sell when a $1 classic milk chocolate bar sits right next to it.

However, the companies in this space are aiming to achieve cost parity (or even cost advantage) with traditional chocolate by scaling up and improving efficiency. Unlike farmed cocoa, which is subject to the whims of weather and global commodity markets, lab-grown cocoa could be produced year-round at a steady output. Proponents argue that once the technology matures, it could actually stabilize chocolate prices and ensure supply even in bad harvest years.

Some startups predict that within a few years of commercial production, they can get the cost of lab-grown cocoa down enough that using it becomes a financially attractive option for big manufacturers – especially as the price of traditional cocoa continues to be volatile. If that scenario plays out, a consumer might one day find that the *cheapest* chocolate chips in the baking aisle happen to be the ones made without any cacao at all.

How this new chocolate is presented to the public will also shape perceptions. Will companies market it loudly as a high-tech, climate-friendly alternative – *"Real chocolate taste with zero cacao"* – hoping to attract adventurous and ethical consumers? Or will they quietly blend it into products without drawing attention to the difference, to avoid scaring off the skeptics?

Early approaches might lean toward niche marketing: for instance, a premium chocolate bar that advertises *"sustainably cultured cocoa"* on its wrapper, targeting shoppers who are willing to pay a bit more for an environmentally friendly treat. On the other hand, if a big brand like Hershey's or Mars ever adopts lab-grown cocoa for a flagship product, they might not shout it from the rooftops at first; they might simply ensure the taste is the same and let consumers discover over time that their beloved candy bar got a sustainable upgrade.

Either way, the initial introduction of lab-grown chocolate into the market will be a delicate dance of framing and education. The first time a major supermarket sells a chocolate bar with lab-grown cocoa, it will likely garner headlines – some heralding a sustainability win, others questioning if it's "real chocolate" at all.

In the end, widespread consumer acceptance will hinge on a combination of factors: taste, price, trust, and values. If the new chocolate can check those boxes – tasting as good, costing about the same, and aligning with consumers' desire to do good – there's a strong chance that people will bite, and keep biting.

Ethical and Environmental Stakes

Beyond the excitement of new flavors and futuristic food tech, the rise of lab-grown and cacao-free chocolate carries significant ethical and environmental implications. On the positive side, these innovations could dramatically shrink chocolate's environmental footprint. Traditional cocoa farming is land- and resource-intensive – it often encroaches on tropical forests, contributes to biodiversity loss, and requires specific hot, humid climates. By contrast, producing cocoa in tanks or creating chocolate from locally grown alternative crops can be done almost anywhere, potentially taking pressure off equatorial rain-forest regions. One startup estimates that its method of making chocolate from fermented plant seeds can cut carbon emissions by up to 80% compared to conventional chocolate production. No tropical shipping or refrigeration is needed, and no new farmland has to be cleared; a chocolate factory of the future might look like a microbrewery on the outskirts of a city, sourcing inputs like sunflower seeds from nearby farms. Furthermore, lab cultivation means no pesticides or chemical fertilizers runoff into the environment. And consider water usage: cacao farming demands significant water (directly or via rain), whereas a controlled fermentation or cell culture process recycles water in a closed system. In a world anxious about climate change, a chocolate supply that isn't tethered to deforestation and monsoon rains has enormous appeal. The promise is of a *greener* chocolate that satisfies our sweet tooth with a fraction of the environmental cost.

===

TALE OF THE TAPE: FARM VS. BIOREACTOR

Why is Silicon Valley betting on the lab? Look at the stats.

- Traditional Farm
  - Time to First Harvest: 3–5 Years (Tree maturity).
  - Harvest Frequency: Twice a year (Seasonal).
  - Climate: Tropical Only (Equator).
- Lab Bioreactor
  - Time to First Harvest: 7 Days (Cell replication).
  - Harvest Frequency: Continuous (Year-round).
  - Climate: Anywhere (San Francisco, Berlin, Tokyo).

===

Ethically, the picture is more complex. In theory, chocolate divorced from the cacao bean means an end to some of the troubling aspects of the traditional supply chain – no more farmers trapped in poverty, no more stories of child labor on cocoa plantations, no volatile market swings that leave growers in the lurch. A bioreactor does not exploit anyone's labor.

However, sidelining the cacao bean also raises the question: what becomes of the millions of people for whom cacao farming is a primary livelihood? In Côte d'Ivoire, Ghana, Nigeria, Cameroon, Indonesia, Brazil, and elsewhere, countless families depend on income from cocoa. If in 10 or 20 years a significant share of the world's "chocolate" comes from fermentation vats and cell culture labs, demand for actual cocoa beans could stagnate or even fall. That could threaten jobs and economies in those regions, unless there are plans to help farmers transition or diversify. The very innovation that could make chocolate sustainable for the planet might make it unsustainable for the people who grow it. This dilemma weighs heavily on the minds of both critics and creators of lab-grown chocolate.

Many of the startups involved are quick to emphasize that they see their products as *complementing* traditional cocoa, not outright replacing it. Their often-stated hope is that by providing an alternative source of bulk chocolate, they can ease the pressure to expand cocoa farming into vulnerable ecosystems and improve overall sustainability, *while* giving the market room to pay traditional farmers more for producing less volume of higher-quality cocoa.

In a best-case scenario, lab-grown cocoa would handle the ever-increasing baseline demand (so chocolate prices don't skyrocket and lead to further deforestation), and cocoa farmers could focus on smaller, more sustainable yields – ideally with better compensation, especially if their beans are used in premium, origin-focused chocolates. Essentially, the world could produce *enough* chocolate without needing to double the number of cacao plantations, and consumers could enjoy chocolate that is both ethical and abundant.

Of course, achieving that ideal scenario will require conscious effort and global cooperation. It raises questions of fairness and responsibility: If wealthy tech-driven companies start making a profit from "growing" chocolate in labs, should they contribute to funds to support and retrain traditional farmers? Could cacao-farming communities share in the benefits of this new industry, perhaps by cultivating other crops (like seeds or legumes) that feed into the chocolate alternatives supply chain?

There are precedents in other industries – for example, energy companies investing in coal regions when shifting to renewables – that might guide chocolate's transition. Some experts argue that even with lab-grown chocolate on the horizon, we must continue to push for improvements in the conventional cocoa sector: paying farmers a living wage, enforcing bans on child labor and deforestation, and planting more resilient cocoa tree varieties. Technology alone won't magically solve issues of social justice.

What is clear is that the creators of Chocolate 2.0 are motivated by a desire to solve problems in the status quo, not to abandon the people behind our chocolate. They often speak about their respect for cocoa farmers and their hope that new methods can *"take the load off"* growers and the environment. If reducing reliance on unsustainably produced cocoa can prevent ecological damage and drive the industry to uplift farmers (for instance, by making fair trade the norm for all remaining cocoa bean production), then the net effect could indeed be positive.

But if the transition is mishandled, there is a risk of leaving traditional growers worse off. This balancing act – maximizing the environmental and ethical benefits while minimizing harm to existing livelihoods – will be one of the critical challenges as lab-grown chocolate moves from concept to reality. The world will be watching to see if we can truly create a chocolate that is *guilt-free* in every sense of the word.

A New Chapter for Chocolate

The story of lab-grown cocoa is still being written, and it may be years before we know just how transformative it will be. But already, the vision of *Chocolate 2.0* has given us a glimpse of how an ancient pleasure might adapt to modern challenges. In a way, it brings chocolate to a crossroads moment.

Here is a treat that humans have cherished for centuries – from its sacred status in Aztec rituals, to the European chocolatiers of the 19th century, to the global mass-market chocolate bars of today – now being pushed to evolve once more, this time in the labs of food-tech pioneers. The fact that major chocolate companies, tech investors, scientists, and environmentalists are all paying attention to this development suggests that it's more than a gimmick. It could very well mark the beginning of a new chapter in chocolate's long history.

That chapter will not be written without debate. Every disruptive innovation in food, from margarine to GMOs to plant-based meat, has sparked questions and resistance, and chocolate touches an even deeper emotional chord. We can expect lively discussions about what qualifies as "real" chocolate. There may be legal battles or labeling rules set by regulators:

Will a product made entirely without cacao be allowed to use the word "chocolate," or will new terminology like "cacao-free cocoa" or "cultured cocoa" emerge (much as "almond milk" had to navigate definitions of milk)? Traditionalists might lobby for protections, while innovators push for acceptance. And certainly there will be consumers who swear they can taste a difference and others who happily make the switch for reasons of cost or conscience. In short, the arrival of lab-grown chocolate will not be a simple binary event but a process – one that involves adapting our norms and expectations around this beloved food.

For the founder in that California lab – and indeed for all the entrepreneurs racing to reinvent chocolate – the motivation ultimately comes from a place of passion. They *love* chocolate, too, and that's exactly why they want to save it. They've seen the storm clouds gathering over the traditional cocoa industry and have decided that the best way to protect chocolate's future is to innovate now. In quieter moments, our startup founder reflects on the journey: from tinkering with cell cultures in petri dishes to producing the first cocoa powder that didn't come from a farm.

She thinks about the cocoa farmers she met who feared for their future, and hopes that in the long run, her work will mean those farmers' children and grandchildren can continue to enjoy a livelihood – perhaps growing specialty cacao, perhaps working in new high-tech chocolate facilities – but *not* having to witness the collapse of the crop that sustained their community.

She also thinks about chocolate lovers around the world, and how to ensure that in 20 or 50 years, people can still share chocolate at holidays and anniversaries without a pang of guilt. In her vision, technology is not the enemy of tradition but the tool that could allow chocolate to thrive without destroying its roots.

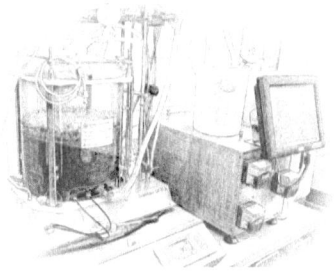

A pilot-scale bioreactor used to cultivate cocoa cells. This equipment represents a crucial step in the journey from "tinkering with cell cultures in petri dishes" to producing chocolate without a farm.

The race to grow cocoa in a lab is far from over – in fact, it's just heating up. There are technical hurdles yet to overcome, from scaling production to perfecting flavor profiles, and there are social hurdles like consumer education and regulatory approval. It will take time to see whether lab-grown or cocoa-free chocolates can truly deliver on all their promises at scale.

But whether or not these specific startups become the next big chocolate giants, they have already forced us to reimagine what chocolate could be. Perhaps the most likely outcome is not a total replacement of cacao farming, but a new equilibrium. Imagine a future where lush cacao forests are conserved and prized for the finest chocolates, while gleaming bioreactors and fermenters provide a steady supply of ethical cocoa for everyday treats. In such a future, technology and tradition would literally share the chocolate market – a blend of old and new that keeps our sweet indulgence both alive and sustainable.

One day in the not-too-distant future, you might unwrap a chocolate bar and not be able to tell whether its cocoa came from a pod or a petri dish. And maybe, you won't need to know – you'll simply savor it, confident that its creation didn't harm the planet or exploit anyone. That is the hope driving the Chocolate 2.0 movement. It's a bold vision where an ancient indulgence meets high-tech ambition in order to save itself.

As the founder and her team clean up their lab after another long day, this thought makes them smile: in striving to grow cocoa in a new way, they are not discarding what makes chocolate special. They are, in fact, working to ensure that the story of chocolate carries on for generations to come – a story where innovation and tradition are not enemies, but partners in creating a sweeter, more sustainable future.

38

CHOCOLATE IN SPACE: THE QUEST FOR COSMIC CONFECTIONERY

T wo hundred miles above the Earth, an astronaut floats in the cozy galley of the International Space Station, gently catching a drifting chocolate candy with a smile. Far above Earth, that small sweet bite is more than just a snack – it's a morsel of normalcy in an extraordinary environment. Chocolate, one of the most beloved treats on Earth, has steadily found its way into spacefarers' diets. Now, food scientists and engineers are pushing the envelope, transforming cacao into a cosmic confectionery suitable for zero-gravity kitchens, years-long missions, and even future colonies on Mars.

A Cosmic Craving: Why Chocolate Matters in Space

Chocolate might seem like a luxury in the harsh realm of space, but it has proven to be surprisingly important. From the earliest days of spaceflight, astronauts and cosmonauts have craved a taste of home, and chocolate often provided that familiar comfort.

Yuri Gagarin, the first human in space in 1961, famously squeezed sweet chocolate sauce from a tube as part of his pioneering meal – a far cry from a gourmet experience, but a significant morale boost during a tense mission. Ever since, mission planners have recognized that food is not just fuel; it's also psychological sustenance. A small dessert or piece of candy can offer a momentary escape from the stress and monotony of space travel.

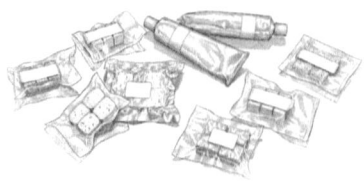

The first cosmic dessert: Early cosmonauts consumed chocolate
sauce from tubes to avoid crumbs in zero gravity.

Over the decades, space agencies gradually upgraded astronauts' menus from plain purees and bland cubes to more appetizing fare. By the Apollo era, crew members could enjoy cocoa beverages and even bite-sized chocolate pudding cubes – a modest but welcome improvement. During the Space Shuttle missions, NASA began including commercial candies – most famously candy-coated chocolates – as a regular treat.

These candy-coated chocolates became a Shuttle staple precisely because their hard shells—originally inspired by soldiers' rations in the Spanish Civil War—prevented the crumbs that are fatal to zero-gravity electronics. The trend continued on the International Space Station. Even today, astronauts mark celebrations or boost morale by sharing chocolate treats delivered in cargo shipments from Earth. In the isolation of orbit, such simple pleasures take on outsized importance.

THE FIRST TASTE: Chocolate's Journey to the Final Frontier

The relationship between chocolate and space exploration has always been intertwined with innovation. In the 1960s, keeping astronauts fed was a brand-new science. Early spacefarers had to endure peculiar foods packaged in squeezable tubes and foil pouches.

In those days, chocolate had to be delivered in unconventional forms – Soviet cosmonauts squeezed sweet chocolate paste from tubes, while Apollo astronauts nibbled on bite-sized chocolate cubes coated with gelatin to prevent crumbs. These solutions were primitive, but they opened the door for chocolate's place beyond Earth's atmosphere.

As technology progressed, so did the quality of cosmic cuisine. Skylab, America's first space station in the 1970s, even had a freezer and refrigerator, allowing crews to enjoy treats like real chocolate ice cream (a far cry from the chalky freeze-dried "astronaut ice cream" sold as a novelty on Earth).

For the first time, astronauts could have chocolate in a form recognizably close to what they had back home. Meanwhile, Soviet cosmonauts aboard space stations like Mir packed traditional chocolate bars for long missions – proof that across cultures, explorers couldn't resist a chocolate fix. By the late 20th century, Russian supply ships often ferried up care packages of chocolates from families, underscoring that even 200 miles above Earth, people celebrate birthdays and holidays with sweets.

==

A BRIEF HISTORY OF CHOCOLATE IN ORBIT

One small bite for man...

- **1961 (Vostok 1):** Yuri Gagarin eats Chocolate Sauce from a toothpaste-style tube. The first dessert in space.
- **1968 (Apollo 7):** NASA introduces Chocolate Pudding Cubes. They are coated in gelatin to prevent crumbs from floating into instruments.
- **1981 (Shuttle Era):** M&Ms become a staple (listed as "Candy Coated Chocolates" to avoid endorsement rules). Astronauts use them to demonstrate microgravity.
- **2019 (ISS):** The first Chocolate Chip Cookies are baked in the Zero-G Oven. They take 2 hours to bake and emerge as puffy spheres.

==

These early experiences demonstrated something crucial: providing favorite foods like chocolate wasn't just about indulgence, it was about keeping humans happy and sane in space. Tasty treats helped astronauts cope with cramped quarters and stressful work. They also spurred engineers to get creative with food preservation and packaging, laying groundwork for more ambitious culinary feats in orbit.

ZERO-G KITCHEN CHALLENGES

Creating and enjoying chocolate in space isn't as simple as it is on Earth. Microgravity turns even basic kitchen tasks into high-flying experiments. Consider the art of tempering chocolate – the precise melting and cooling process that gives a chocolate bar its glossy finish and satisfying snap. On Earth, tempering relies on gravity to help distribute and settle cocoa butter crystals. In zero-G, a melted blob of chocolate would just float, stubbornly refusing to take shape in a mold. Air bubbles that would normally rise out of liquid chocolate remain suspended like tiny planets in a molten brown galaxy, risking a chalky, irregular texture as the chocolate solidifies.

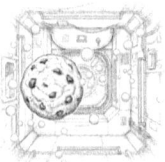

Baking in Orbit: Without gravity, hot air does not rise, making baking a cookie in space a complex engineering challenge.

Astronaut chefs have to contend with other quirks of microgravity too. Heat doesn't circulate the same way without gravity, making baking or melting a slow and uneven affair. In 2019, astronauts on the ISS attempted a bit of cosmic baking by making chocolate chip cookies in a special zero-G oven.

The result? The cookies took much longer to bake than on Earth and emerged puffier and oddly shaped – without gravity, the dough didn't flatten out. The chocolate chips inside melted, but stayed suspended within the dough rather than pooling at the bottom. It was a small victory for space cooking, proving that fresh-baked desserts are possible in orbit, but it also highlighted how different the physics of cooking can be in space.

Even simply eating chocolate requires forethought. Crumbs are a nemesis in spacecraft: a floating crumb can drift into vents or electronics and cause trouble. That's why many space chocolates are bite-sized or candy-coated. A bar of flaky, crumbly chocolate would be risky, but a mini candy or a solid piece of fudge can be popped wholly into one's mouth.

Similarly, astronauts often favor drinking their chocolate – hot cocoa mixes are a staple on the ISS menu, sipped through straws from sealed pouches. A warm cup of cocoa offers comfort and warmth without any stray droplets escaping, and it's easier to handle in microgravity than a crumbly brownie would be.

Engineering Chocolate for Spaceflight

To ensure astronauts can enjoy chocolate safely and reliably, food scientists are engineering cocoa-based treats specifically for space. At NASA's Johnson Space Center in Houston, the Space Food Systems Laboratory is where culinary dreams meet aerospace reality. Scientists like Dr. Grace Douglas – the lead scientist for NASA's advanced food technology research – are tasked with innovating foods that can last long, pack efficiently, and still delight the crew.

Chocolate presents a unique challenge: it's rich in energy and generally stable, but it can suffer in quality over time. The team in Houston experiments with formulations to create the ideal "space chocolate bar."

One major focus for these researchers is shelf life. A mission to Mars might last two to three years, and any chocolate on board must remain tasty and safe the whole time. Normally, chocolate can develop a white "bloom" on its surface when fat or sugar crystals migrate, especially under fluctuating temperatures.

While bloom isn't harmful, it makes the chocolate look unappetizing and gritty. To counter this, aerospace food engineers test different types of chocolate – from dark to milk to white – under controlled temperature cycles that mimic storage in space. Dark chocolate, with less milk content and more antioxidants, tends to have a longer shelf life and is less prone to flavor changes, so it's a prime candidate for deep-space voyages.

Researchers have also tweaked recipes, adding natural preservatives and adjusting the fat composition to improve stability. The goal is a chocolate bar that won't crumble, melt, or lose flavor even after years in storage.

Packaging is another vital piece of the puzzle. Every space chocolate treat is sealed in a special multi-layer pouch that keeps out oxygen and moisture – the arch-enemies of food freshness. For long missions, NASA is developing packaging that can also help block radiation or at least withstand its effects. Cosmic rays can slowly break down fats and vitamins in food over time.

Imagine opening a chocolate bar on Mars only to find it stale or tasteless due to radiation exposure – the disappointment would be enormous. To prevent that, packages might be lined with thin layers of aluminum or made of novel polymers that insulate against radiation. Some designs even involve vacuum-sealing the chocolate to eliminate all air, essentially putting the candy in suspended animation until it's needed.

Beyond preservation, scientists are also tweaking chocolate for nutrition. Traditional chocolate isn't exactly a vitamin powerhouse, but NASA sees an opportunity to make every bite count on a long mission. Space-developed chocolate bars might be fortified with extra nutrients like vitamin D (since astronauts get little sunlight) or calcium (to help mitigate bone loss in microgravity).

They are also looking at reducing the sugar content and using more of cocoa's natural flavonoids – compounds that could benefit cardiovascular health and mood. The trick is doing all this without ruining the taste or texture, because if astronauts don't enjoy eating it, all that effort is wasted. Through careful experimentation and taste-testing (often with astronauts as willing guinea pigs), the space food lab iterates on recipes until they strike the right balance between health and happiness.

SWEET PSYCHOLOGY: **How a Treat Boosts Astronaut Morale**

While nutrition and engineering are crucial, the psychological power of chocolate in space cannot be overstated. Living in a metal box orbiting Earth – or voyaging months away from Earth – takes a mental toll. In these extreme conditions, food often doubles as a source of comfort and emotional relief. A rich, sweet bite of chocolate can momentarily transport an astronaut away from recycled air and humming machines to the memory of a favorite dessert back home.

Space agencies have learned through experience that morale is a mission-critical factor. Astronaut journals and mission debriefs frequently mention how a favorite food lifted spirits during a tough week. A small dessert after a long day of work can become the highlight of an astronaut's day, a reward that makes the hardships more bearable.

Psychologists working with space crews make sure each astronaut has some personal "bonus" foods in their allotment – and these often include chocolate bars or candies. For instance, during his year-long mission aboard the ISS, astronaut Scott Kelly received surprise care packages containing M&Ms and other chocolates. Tearing open a bag of candy from home, after months in orbit, gave him a tangible reminder that people on Earth were thinking of him. In interviews, Kelly noted how those little taste-of-home moments boosted his mood and broke the monotony of freeze-dried meals.

Chocolate's mood-lifting qualities have a biochemical angle too. Cocoa contains theobromine and other compounds that can enhance mood and even provide a mild energy boost. There's also a social aspect: sharing treats fosters camaraderie among crew members who are living in close quarters.

While in orbit, astronauts from different countries often bond by exchanging goodies from their culture – an American astronaut might offer peanut butter chocolates while a Russian cosmonaut shares rich chocolate-covered wafers from Moscow. Trading candies and stories, the crew momentarily forgets about national flags on their sleeves and just enjoys a human moment. These simple social rituals become the glue that holds a team together during the isolation of spaceflight.

· · ·

THE LONG HAUL: Chocolate on the Journey to Mars

Looking ahead to Mars missions, the demands on food – chocolate included – become even more intense. A round trip to Mars, including travel and surface operations, could last well over two years. Unlike the ISS, there will be no supply ships arriving every few months with fresh goodies. Everything the crew might crave has to be packed at launch or produced en route. That means the "cosmic chocolate" for Mars must endure weightlessness, radiation, and the test of time without losing its appeal.

NASA has been simulating long-duration storage for various foods, chocolate among them. In laboratory tests, sample chocolate bars are kept in special chambers that mimic deep-space conditions. They cycle through temperature changes to simulate day-night cycles a spacecraft might experience and are even exposed to radiation similar to cosmic rays.

These tests have already influenced the design of space-worthy chocolate. Results showed that chocolates with certain creamy fillings or complex layers didn't hold up as well over many months; this led scientists to favor simpler, purer chocolate recipes for Mars – fewer mix-ins and components that could degrade or go stale.

One concept emerging from this research is a "Martian chocolate bar" that is essentially a vacuum-dried, ultra-condensed dark chocolate infused with extra nutrients. Vacuum-drying the chocolate (removing any residual water content) could help prevent ice crystals or microbial issues during long storage, and the high cacao content ensures a strong chocolate flavor even if some aroma is lost over time.

This prototype Martian bar might be a bit harder or less creamy than a freshly made truffle on Earth, but after many months in space it would still deliver that recognizable chocolate satisfaction. Astronauts could look forward to unwrapping one on the far side of the solar system and finding it tastes almost as if it were just bought from a store.

==

FUTURE FOOD: THE MARTIAN BAR SPECS
NASA's criteria for a chocolate bar that can survive a 3-year mission to Mars:

- **Shelf Life:** Must last 3–5 years without refrigeration.
- **Composition:** High cacao content (dark), low milk fat (to prevent rancidity).
- **Process:** Vacuum-dried to remove moisture that causes bloom or mold.
- **Packaging:** Multi-layer polymers to shield the fat molecules from cosmic radiation degradation.

==

ENGINEERS ARE ALSO TACKLING how to handle chocolate in different gravity environments. Mars has about one-third of Earth's gravity – enough to make things fall, but gently. Will a chocolate bar crumble or break differently under Martian gravity? Could a bar that is perfectly solid during weightless transit start shedding tiny crumbs when opened on Mars? These questions are driving innovative packaging solutions. One clever idea is a wrapper you can eat – an edible film around the chocolate, so once you peel off the outer protective foil, the bar is encased in a thin, rice-paper-like coating.

You can bite right through it along with the chocolate, and any flakes stay stuck to the edible wrap. Not only would this prevent mess in the habitat and spacecraft, it also means one less piece of trash to manage on a long mission. Such creative thinking shows how every detail, down to a candy wrapper, is being re-imagined for the next giant leap.

FARMING THE FUTURE: **Cacao in a Mars Colony**
The ultimate dream for cosmic confectionery is to go from "bean to bar" on another world. In a long-term Mars colony or a lunar base, relying on Earth to ship chocolate (or even just the raw cocoa beans)

would be expensive and impractical. So scientists and visionaries are pondering how future settlers might grow cacao and produce chocolate on site, closing the supply loop for sweets in space.

Growing a cacao tree on Mars or the Moon is a daunting proposition. Cacao is a finicky tropical plant: it thrives in humid, warm rainforests, nothing like the freezing desert of Mars or the airless grey of the Moon. However, inside a controlled environment like a pressurized greenhouse or bio-dome, it might be possible to create a mini tropical oasis.

Researchers in advanced hydroponics and space agriculture have already had success growing other plants on orbit – from lettuce and tomatoes on the ISS, to plans for dwarf fruit trees in future greenhouses. Many crops can adapt to LED lighting and carefully managed soil and climate. It's conceivable that, one day, horticulturists will cultivate dwarf cacao trees engineered to grow faster and shorter, producing pods even in the limited confines of a habitat. A "chocolate greenhouse" module on Mars might maintain balmy temperatures and misty humidity for the cacao, a little bubble of Earthly jungle amid the red Martian plains.

Red Planet Rainforest: Scientists envision pressurized greenhouses
on Mars to grow dwarf cacao trees for future colonists.

If Martian colonists manage to harvest cocoa pods, they'll face the complex process of turning them into chocolate. On Earth, after harvest, cocoa beans undergo fermentation in their sticky pulp for several days – a process reliant on a whole community of microbes and careful control of temperature. Martian chocolate-makers would likely carry a starter culture of Earth microbes to ferment cacao in sealed containers, kick-starting the chemical alchemy that develops chocolate's rich flavor.

Next comes drying and roasting the beans, steps that require energy but are straightforward with the right equipment. Grinding the roasted nibs into a smooth cocoa paste and pressing out cocoa butter would need robust machinery that's also compact enough to have been shipped to Mars. Finally, there's mixing, refining, and tempering the chocolate into bars – tasks that might need to be done in a shirtsleeve environment or an automated machine to avoid contamination and heat loss in the Martian air.

It's a huge effort for a treat, but the value of locally produced chocolate on a far-off world would be tremendous. Imagine the morale of a Mars crew, years into their mission, able to savor a chocolate bar made with cacao they grew under an alien sky. That taste of self-sufficiency and comfort would be as emotionally nourishing as it is physical.

Additionally, cacao might not be the only confectionery crop such pioneers attempt – future space farms could include sugar beets for sugar, peanuts or almonds for nutty add-ins, even a small dairy herd or soy culture for milk to make milk chocolate. Each of these introduces new challenges, but every success in cultivating them would mark a milestone in making life on other worlds feel a little more like home.

A GLOBAL EFFORT and a Galactic Dream

The push to create cosmic confectionery isn't just a NASA endeavor – it's an international and commercial pursuit as well. The European Space Agency (ESA) and other spacefaring nations have their own food research programs, often bringing cultural flavors to orbit. European astronauts, for example, have indulged in gourmet meal packs devised by famous chefs, including decadent desserts, for special occasions in space.

French astronaut Thomas Pesquet enjoyed a chocolate cake prepared by a Michelin-starred chef during one of his ISS missions – a treat that required advanced food-preservation techniques to remain delicious after launch. Such collaborations between chefs and scientists merge culinary art with aerospace engineering and highlight a shared understanding: no matter who you are or where you're from, good food in space makes a difference for morale.

Private companies, too, have joined the race. With the rise of space tourism and planned commercial space stations, businesses are envisioning menus that cater to customers in orbit. This includes iconic luxury foods – and what is more universally beloved than chocolate?

Some startups are developing compact ovens and even 3D food printers that work in microgravity, aiming to let future space hotel guests indulge in freshly baked chocolate chip cookies or custom-shaped confections, printed layer by layer from molten cocoa paste. The idea of enjoying a warm brownie or a designer bonbon while floating in a space hotel may sound far-fetched, but it's driving real engineering efforts today.

Meanwhile, famous confectionery manufacturers on Earth have also taken an interest in the final frontier. Mars, Inc., the maker of M&Ms (a brand that coincidentally shares its name with the Red Planet), has long provided their candies for astronaut care packages.

It isn't hard to imagine a day when they might sponsor the first candy shop on a space station or supply cocoa seedlings for a Mars greenhouse. Such scenarios sound whimsical, but they underscore a serious point: as space becomes accessible to more people, the demand for familiar comforts like chocolate will only grow.

The "race" to create the first cosmic confectionery is not a cutthroat competition at all – it's a collective effort to make life in space more livable and enjoyable. In truth, it's a race against the challenges of physics, distance, and isolation more than a race against one another.

Every breakthrough – whether it's a longer-lasting chocolate bar recipe, a successful batch of space-baked cookies, or a prototype for growing cacao in a habitat – is shared and celebrated by the global space community. Each sweet success brings us one step closer to a future where living and dining in space is just a little bit more like life on Earth.

One Giant Leap for Chocolate

In humanity's journey to the stars, it's often the small things that remind us why we venture forth. A simple bar of chocolate encapsulates the ingenuity, the resilience, and the very humanity of space exploration. It carries with it echoes of home and the promise of creativity unbound by gravity. The quest to create the first cosmic confectionery – to perfect chocolate that can be enjoyed in zero-G, endure the trek to Mars, or even be made on Mars – is about more than dessert. It's a symbol that wherever humans go, we carry our culture, our cravings, and our joy with us.

One day, when the first explorers bite into a silky-smooth chocolate bar handcrafted on another world, we'll know that we've not only extended our civilization across space, but also brought along the delights that make life worth living. That will indeed be one giant leap for chocolate – and a sweet victory for us all.

39

THE CRAFT REVOLUTION: FROM BASEMENTS TO THE WORLD'S MOST EXPENSIVE BAR

T*he basement of the Brooklyn brownstone wasn't built for food production; it was built for storage—for forgotten bicycles and boxes of winter coats. But at 2:00 AM on a humid Tuesday in July, it had become a laboratory of obsession. The air was thick, intoxicating, and suffocating—a dense cloud of roasting nuts, turning earth, and the sharp tang of acetic acid.*

Ben Rasmussen sat on a folding chair, staring at the spinning drum of a machine never designed for this. By daylight, Rasmussen was a software engineer, a man who dealt in the clean, bloodless logic of code. But here, in the subterranean dark, he was engaged in a chaotic, messy struggle with biology and physics.

The machine in front of him was a Spectra II, a countertop wet-grinder imported from India. In its intended life, it was designed to pulverize soaked lentils and rice into a fermented batter for *idli* and *dosa*. It was a regular, ordinary appliance, a staple of South Indian kitchens. Tonight, however, Rasmussen was pushing it to its mechanical breaking point. He was grinding cacao nibs.

The friction of the twin granite wheels against the granite base generated heat, slowly liquefying the fat inside the nibs. The mixture transformed. An hour ago, it had been a coarse, gravelly pile of crushed seeds, loud and clattering. Now, it was a thick, dark sludge, moving with the viscosity of volcanic mud. He reached out and adjusted the tension knob, tightening the spring that pressed the stones into the base. The motor whined in protest, a high-pitched keen that vibrated through the concrete floor.

Far removed from the clean logic of his software engineering day job, Rasmussen adjusts the tension on the Spectra II, engaging in a chaotic struggle with physics to force the wet-grinder to liquefy coarse cacao nibs.

It was a delicate, high-stakes dance. Tighten the stones too much, and the friction spikes, burning the chocolate or seizing the motor in a puff of ozone. Leave it too loose, and the particle size remains too large. The chocolate becomes gritty, a sandy failure of texture that no amount of complex flavor can forgive. The target was roughly 20 microns—the threshold of human tactile perception. Anything larger, and the tongue snags on the grit.

He picked up a hairdryer—a standard pharmacy-bought Conair, splattered with dark specks from previous batches—and pointed it at the spinning drum. He wasn't drying his hair; he was managing thermodynamics. He needed to keep the temperature high enough to encourage the volatile acids—the harsh, vinegary compounds left over from fermentation—to evaporate, but low enough to preserve the delicate floral esters that defined this specific bean.

This was not a factory. There were no cooling tunnels, no laser-guided tempering units, no white-coated food scientists monitoring pH levels with digital probes. There was only a man, a repurposed spice grinder, a hairdryer, and a bag of beans he bought off the internet from a guy in Oregon who swore they came from a single estate in the Sambirano Valley of Madagascar.

Rasmussen dipped a plastic spoon into the dark, swirling river. He tasted. It was intense—shockingly acidic, bursting with notes of raspberry and citrus that would be unrecognizable to someone raised on the flat, sugary profile of mass-market candy bars. It was rough, wild, and utterly distinct. This makeshift "chocolate lab"—complete with repurposed kitchen appliances, homemade contraptions of funnels and tubes, and burlap bags of exotic cacao beans stacked in the corner—was ground zero for a culinary insurrection.

Rasmussen was not alone in the dark. He was a soldier in a global army of tinkerers, obsessives, and flavor-seekers who were dismantling the industrial monopoly on chocolate, one micro-batch at a time. This is the story of the Craft Revolution, a movement that dragged chocolate out of the factory and into the kitchen, transforming it from a commodity into a canvas for high art.

The Fortress of Industry

To understand the magnitude of what the craft movement accomplished, one must first understand the world they rebelled against. For most of the 20th century, the barrier to entry for making chocolate was an impregnable wall of capital and steel.

Chocolate making was not like baking bread or brewing beer. It was heavy industry. To make chocolate, you didn't just need a kitchen; you needed a factory. You needed massive roasters capable of processing tons of beans an hour. You needed hydraulic presses to separate cocoa butter. You needed industrial winnowers to strip the shells. And most importantly, you needed the conche.

The barrier to entry was the conche. As detailed in Chapter 16, this massive granite beast remained the industry's gatekeeper. Industrial conches weighed tons, consumed massive amounts of power, and required capital investments that no home cook could justify. They were the reason chocolate making remained a fortress; you couldn't fit one in a garage, and you certainly couldn't afford one on a credit card.

The industry was a fortress guarded by a handful of giants—

Hershey, Mars, Cadbury, Nestlé, Barry Callebaut—who controlled the supply chain from the port to the vending machine. They bought cacao on the commodities market, a system designed to treat beans like coal or corn: a bulk product where consistency was the only virtue and volume was the only metric.

In this world, "chocolate making" was a binary proposition. You were either a multinational corporation, or you were a *chocolatier*.

A chocolatier is a culinary artisan, yes, but they do not make chocolate. They buy pre-made chocolate (couverture) from the big factories— huge blocks of calibrated, standardized industrial product—and melt it down. They might infuse it with cream to make a ganache, or dip strawberries in it, or mold it into shapes. But the fundamental character of the chocolate—the roast, the conche, the bean blend—was determined by a food scientist in a factory in Pennsylvania or Belgium, not by the chef.

The idea of being a *chocolate maker*—someone who actually processes the raw bean into the finished bar on a small scale—was as ludicrous as a home cook deciding to refine their own gasoline for their car. It was viewed as technically impossible and economically suicidal. But in the early 2000s, the fortress began to crack. The fissure didn't start in a boardroom; it started on the internet.

THE RISE of the Hardware Hackers

A loose confederation of geeks, foodies, engineers, and insomniacs began gathering on internet forums. Sites like "The Chocolate Alchemy," run by a chemist named John Nanci in Oregon, became the digital salons of the revolution. Nanci and his cohorts refused to accept that chocolate making was impossible for the little guy. They looked at the industrial process not as a monolith, but as a series of physics problems to be solved. They deconstructed the factory.

- Roasting: Instead of a continuous drum roaster, they used a standard kitchen oven or a rotisserie drum on a BBQ grill.
- Cracking: Instead of an industrial impact mill, they used a hand-cranked grain mill, or even a rolling pin.

- Winnowing: Instead of a vibrating aspiration table, they used a hairdryer and a bucket.

But the grinder—the machine that would replace the million-dollar conche—remained the elusive prize.

THE MELANGER EPIPHANY

The breakthrough came from an unlikely source: the kitchens of Southern India. The *melanger*, or wet grinder, is a staple appliance in Indian households. It consists of two heavy granite wheels rotating inside a stainless steel drum, crushing ingredients against a granite base. It is designed to run for hours without overheating, turning soaked rice and lentils into a silky batter.

To the early craft chocolate makers, the melanger was a revelation. It mimicked the mechanics of the 19th-century longitudinal conche but fit on a countertop. It combined two critical steps—refining (reducing particle size) and conching (aerating and developing flavor)—into one machine.

It wasn't perfect. The motors were underpowered for the heavy viscosity of cacao. The belts would snap. The plastic parts would crack under the strain of continuous 48-hour run times. But it worked. And it cost less than $500.

The sound of the granite wheels—a rhythmic, grinding *thrum-thrum-thrum*—became the heartbeat of the movement. In garages in Seattle, basements in Brooklyn, and spare rooms in London, the melangers began to spin.

THE SYLPH and the Shop-Vac

The next challenge was winnowing. After roasting and cracking the beans, you are left with a mixture of nibs (the meat of the bean) and husk (the papery shell). The husk is fibrous, bitter, and unpleasant. It must be removed.

Factories use complex systems of vibration and aspiration to separate the two. The underground solution was pure MacGyver engineering.

Inventors posted blueprints online for the "Sylph" winnower. It was a gravity-fed system built entirely from PVC pipes found at hardware stores. The concept was elegant in its simplicity: cracked beans were dropped through a vertical tube. A vacuum cleaner (a standard Shop-Vac) was attached to a side port, creating a precise amount of suction.

The "Sylph" winnower configuration: A DIY assembly of PVC fittings uses vacuum airflow to aspirate lighter husks away from the heavier falling nibs.

As the mixture fell, the heavy nibs had enough mass to fall straight down into a collection bucket. The lighter husks, caught in the airflow, were sucked sideways into the vacuum bag. It was loud. It was dusty. It required constant tuning of the vacuum pressure. But it achieved 99% purity. It allowed a home maker to process fifty pounds of beans in an afternoon, a feat that would have taken weeks by hand peeling.

The Agony of the Hand-Filled Mold

With the machinery solved, the makers turned their attention to the finer points of production. But scaling up from a hobby to a business presented brutal physical challenges. In Los Angeles, David and Corey Menkes launched their brand, LetterPress, from a tiny apartment using exactly these methods.

Their operation was a testament to the sheer force of will required in these early days. Lacking the budget for an automated dosing line—machines that cost tens of thousands of dollars and deposit precise amounts of chocolate into molds—David improvised. He manually injected tempered chocolate into hundreds of molds using a handheld syringe.

It was a painstaking labor of love. The syringe required significant hand pressure to force the viscous, tempered chocolate out. Doing it for five molds was fun; doing it for five hundred was a recipe for repetitive strain injury. But it allowed them to produce bars with zero air bubbles and perfect weight consistency, competing visually with the output of a factory line.

These pioneers were proving a point: You didn't need capital. You needed curiosity. They were driven not by profit margins or volume, but by a quest for flavor. They were chasing ghosts—the flavor notes that industrial processing, with its high roasts and heavy deodorization, had smoothed away. They were willing to burn out motors, clog vacuums, and cramp their hands to find them.

The Third Wave and the Cathedral of Cacao

If the basement was the engine room of the revolution, the retail shop was its cathedral.

Walk into *The Meadow* in Portland, Oregon, or *Cocoa Runners* in London, and the first thing you notice is the silence. These are not candy stores. There are no bins of gummy bears, no neon-colored lollipops, no frantic sugar-rush energy. The lighting is low and warm, designed to protect the cocoa butter from photo-oxidation. The air is climate-controlled to a crisp 65 degrees.

The Meadow: A quiet sanctuary for the geography of flavor.

Lining the walls, floor to ceiling, are shelves holding hundreds of chocolate bars. They are arranged not by brand, but by country of origin: a geography of flavor that spans from the volcanic soils of Vanuatu to the humid river deltas of Vietnam. Customers do not grab handfuls of product; they browse with heads cocked to the side, reading the back of a wrapper like a sommelier studying a vintage wine label.

This is the "Chocolate Library," a new retail concept that emerged in the late 2000s to service the output of the craft movement. Here, the shopkeeper is not a clerk but a monger—a guide trained to navigate the complex topography of terroir.

"I'm looking for something... earthy," a customer might whisper.

The monger nods, bypassing the fruity Madagascans and the floral Ecuadorians, reaching instead for a bar made with beans from the Polochic Valley in Guatemala. "Try this," they say. "It has a high-bass note. Leather, tobacco, and a finish like stout beer."

This interaction represents a seismic shift in consumer consciousness. For a century, chocolate was a commodity defined by consistency. A Hershey bar bought in 1950 tasted exactly like one bought in 1990. But the Craft Revolution introduced the concept of the "Third Wave," borrowing a philosophy that had already transformed coffee and beer.

THE THIRD WAVE Theory

To understand where chocolate is today, we must look at where it came from. Culinary historians divide the evolution of commodity foods into three distinct waves.

The First Wave was defined by access and affordability. In the 19th and early 20th centuries, Folgers put coffee on every kitchen table, Budweiser put beer in every fridge, and Hershey put chocolate in every pocket. The goal was caloric efficiency, safety, and price. Flavor was secondary to mass distribution; the product was a utility.

The Second Wave, arriving in the 1980s and 90s, brought pleasure and differentiation. This was the era of Starbucks, Samuel Adams, and Godiva. Consumers began paying a premium for a "better" experience—coffee became a latte, and chocolate became a truffle filled with liqueur. The defining characteristic was the perception of luxury, often signaled by European branding or higher sugar content. Yet, the supply chain remained opaque. A consumer might buy a luxury truffle, but they had no idea where the cacao came from. It was still a commodity, just dressed in gold foil.

The Third Wave is about transparency, terroir, and a reverence for the raw ingredient. It is the moment when the consumer stops buying the brand and starts buying the bean. In coffee, the Third Wave arrived when baristas began weighing grounds to the gram and discussing farm elevation. In chocolate, it arrived when makers stopped blending beans to hide defects and started highlighting them to show character.

In coffee, the Third Wave arrived when baristas began weighing grounds to the gram and talking about the elevation of the farm. In chocolate, it arrived when makers stopped blending beans to hide defects and started highlighting them to show character.

The craft chocolate movement is the Third Wave manifest in cocoa butter. It rejects the idea that chocolate should taste like "chocolate"—that singular, fudge-like flavor profile engineered by Dutching (alkalizing) the beans. Instead, it asserts that chocolate should taste like a fruit, a nut, a spice, or a flower, depending on its genetics and its soil.

This philosophical pivot required a complete overhaul of how chocolate was presented to the world. It couldn't look like candy anymore. It had to look like art.

THE SEMIOTICS of the Wrapper

If you pick up a mass-market chocolate bar, the wrapper is designed for velocity. It is made of thin, heat-sealed plastic (flow-wrap). The colors are bright primaries—red, blue, orange—screaming for attention in the impulse-buy zone of a checkout aisle. The text is minimal: the brand name is huge, the calorie count is mandated, and the ingredient list is hidden under a flap.

The craft revolution declared war on the flow-wrap.

The Mast Brothers, operating out of Brooklyn, arguably pioneered this aesthetic. Regardless of the later controversies surrounding their sourcing claims, Rick and Michael Mast fundamentally changed the visual language of chocolate in 2007. They wrapped their bars in heavy, textured butcher paper. The designs were not logos, but patterns: Florentine wallpapers, anchor motifs, and geometric tessellations.

The bars looked like they belonged in a museum gift shop or a high-end stationary store, not a bodega. They felt substantial in the hand. The friction of the paper, the weight of the foil inner-wrap, the tactile experience of unfolding the package—it all slowed the consumer down. It signaled that this was an object of value, justifying a price point of $10 or more.

Other makers escalated the arms race of design. Dick Taylor Craft Chocolate in Northern California utilized letterpress printing—an archaic technique where ink is pressed deep into the paper fibers—to create packaging with literal depth and texture. Their wrappers featured intricate nautical illustrations and boat-building diagrams, linking the craft of chocolate to the craft of woodworking.

Dandelion Chocolate in San Francisco took a different approach. Their packaging was wrapped in handmade paper sourced from India, created from recycled cotton scraps from the garment industry. The paper was thick, fibrous, and flecked with gold thread. Bound around it was a simple, elegant band listing the technical specs of the bar: harvest year, fermentation duration, and roast profile.

This wasn't just decoration; it was data visualization. The wrapper became a dossier.

- **Batch Number:** Signifying that this was a limited run, not an endless industrial stream.
- **Harvest Date:** Linking the flavor to a specific point in time, acknowledging the seasonality of agriculture.
- **Tasting Notes:** "Dried plum, toasted brioche, lemon zest."

This vocabulary primed the brain, teaching the consumer what to look for before the chocolate even touched their tongue.

By transforming the packaging, the craft movement transformed the act of eating. You don't rip open a letterpress wrapper while driving a car. You sit down. You unfold it. You inspect it. The packaging forced mindfulness.

THE CULT of Origin

As the aesthetic seduced the eye, the geography seduced the mind. The Craft Revolution turned chocolate lovers into amateur geographers.

Before the mid-2000s, "Single Origin" usually meant a country. A bar might be labeled "Ghana" or "Ecuador." But the craft movement zoomed in. A country is too big; a country has a thousand microclimates.

Makers began seeking out specific estates, valleys, and cooperatives, turning obscure geographical locations into legendary brand names.

- Chuao (Venezuela): The village of Chuao is perhaps the most famous appellation in the chocolate world. Accessible only by boat or a treacherous hike through the cloud forest, Chuao has been producing cacao for 400 years. The beans are dried on the patio of the village church. Craft makers fight for allocations of Chuao like knights fighting for a holy relic. The flavor is distinct—a bright, singing acidity of blueberries and tamarind—and owning a bar of "Real Chuao" became a badge of honor for the serious collector.

- Sambirano (Madagascar): The Akesson Estate in the Sambirano Valley became the gold standard for fruit-forward chocolate. Bertil Akesson, a Swedish diplomat's son who grew up on the plantation, realized that his beans possessed a startlingly high citric acid content. When crafted correctly, the chocolate tasted indistinguishable from raspberry jam. This origin became the "gateway drug" for the movement— the bar you gave to a skeptic to prove that chocolate could taste like fruit.
- Marañón (Peru): The rediscovery of the "Pure Nacional" white beans in the Marañón Canyon gave the craft movement its greatest romance. As explored in Chapter 26, this bean— thought extinct—became the holy grail for makers like Fruition Chocolate, who used its intense floral aromatics to win world championships.

This obsession with origin created a feedback loop. Makers would release "Micro-Batches"—perhaps only 500 bars made from three sacks of beans from a specific harvest. When they were gone, they were gone. This introduced the concept of FOMO (Fear Of Missing Out) to the candy aisle. Collectors began hoarding bars, creating a secondary market and a culture of vertical tastings—a practice explored in Chapter 15—where enthusiasts would compare the 2018 harvest of a specific farm against the 2019 harvest to see how the rainfall affected the flavor.

THE NEW GATEKEEPERS: **Awards and Critics**

With hundreds of new makers springing up from Tokyo to Toronto, the consumer needed a filter. The revolution birthed its own institutions of critique.

The International Chocolate Awards and the Academy of Chocolate became the Oscars of the industry. Judging panels composed of chefs, sommeliers, and food journalists would blind-taste thousands of bars, awarding Gold, Silver, and Bronze medals.

A sticker on a bar became a powerful sales tool. A Gold Medal from the International Chocolate Awards could sell out a maker's inventory overnight. It validated the obsession. It told the guy grinding beans in his garage that he wasn't crazy—he was world-class.

Critics emerged as tastemakers. Bloggers and writers like Georg Bernardini, author of *The Chocolate Tester*, began reviewing bars with the rigor of Robert Parker rating Bordeaux. Bernardini's book reviewed over 4,000 products, assigning them 0 to 6 cocoa pods. He was ruthless. He called out big brands for using vanillin to mask poor beans and praised obscure makers for their bravery in fermentation.

These gatekeepers codified the values of the movement. They penalized the use of lecithin (seen as a cheat for texture). They deducted points for over-roasting. They rewarded "length of finish" and "clarity of flavor." They created a canon of excellence that defined the Third Wave.

The Social Signaling of the $12 Bar

Ultimately, the retail revolution was sociological. Buying a $12 bar of chocolate became a social signal. It said something about who you were.

It aligned the consumer with the values of the "Slow Food" movement. It signaled a rejection of industrial exploitation (child labor, deforestation) in favor of ethical transparency. It showed sophistication—a palate capable of appreciating bitterness and acidity, traits often rejected by the mainstream sweet tooth.

The craft chocolate bar became the perfect affordable luxury. You might not be able to afford a Tesla or a trip to the Maldives, but you could afford the absolute best chocolate in the world. For the price of a cocktail, you could hold a product that represented the pinnacle of agricultural and culinary achievement.

In the specialized retail shops, surrounded by the hushed atmosphere and the smell of cocoa, customers found something more than a snack. They found a connection. They found a story that linked the volcanic soil of a distant jungle to the foil-wrapped square in their hand. The Craft Revolution didn't just change the chocolate; it changed the people who ate it.

The Heresy of Milk and the Savory Invasion

For the first decade of the Craft Revolution, the movement was defined by a rigid, almost Puritanical dogmatism: Dark Chocolate was the truth; everything else was a distraction.

The early makers were reacting against a century of industrial dilution. In their eyes, milk powder was the tool of the enemy—a cheap filler used by Hershey and Cadbury to lower the cost of goods and mask the flavor of sub-par beans. To add milk to a single-origin, micro-fermented bean from Peru felt like pouring Coca-Cola into a vintage Bordeaux. It was a sacrilege.

The "70% Club" became a badge of honor. Makers competed to produce the purest expression of the cacao, stripping away anything that might interfere with the acidity and the tannins. Retailers like *The Meadow* reported that serious customers would often refuse to even taste anything under 80%.

But by 2015, a fatigue had set in. The relentless acidity of pure two-ingredient chocolate—while intellectually stimulating—was exhausting to the palate. Makers began to secretly crave the comfort of creaminess. They began to ask a dangerous question: *What if we applied our obsessive standards of quality to the very ingredient we swore to destroy?*

Thus began the Era of Dark Milk, a sub-movement that would eventually outsell pure dark bars in many artisan shops and bridge the gap between the snob and the snacker.

The Dark Milk Definition

To understand why "Dark Milk" was revolutionary, one must look at the math of the candy aisle.

A standard industrial milk chocolate bar (think a Hershey's bar or a British Dairy Milk) typically contains between 10% and 25% cocoa solids. The rest—75% to 90%—is sugar, milk powder, and vanilla. It is essentially a sugar candy flavored with cocoa.

The craft makers flipped the ratio. They formulated recipes with 50%, 60%, or even 65% cocoa solids.

The result was a category-busting hybrid. A 60% Dark Milk bar possesses the intense, fruit-forward aromatic profile of a dark chocolate —the raspberry notes of Madagascar or the nuttiness of Venezuela—but the finish is softened by the fats and proteins of the milk. The milk acts as a flavor carrier, rounding off the sharpest edges of the acetic acid and extending the melt time on the tongue.

It was the "gateway drug" for the craft movement. Consumers who found 75% dark chocolate too bitter, but found mass-market milk chocolate too cloying, suddenly found their Goldilocks zone.

THE PROBLEM OF POWDER: **Hunting for "Dairy Terroir"**

Once makers decided to embrace milk, they ran into a logistical wall. Industrial chocolate giants do not use standard milk powder; they often use "milk crumb," a proprietary slurry of condensed milk, sugar, and cocoa liquor dried under a vacuum. This creates a caramelized, cooked-milk flavor (the signature taste of Cadbury) that is impossible to replicate in a small kitchen.

Craft makers had to source dried milk powder. But they quickly realized that, just like cacao, not all milk is created equal.

Most commercial milk powder is spray-dried at high temperatures, scorching the proteins and leaving a flat, cardboard-like taste. It is a commodity product designed for shelf stability, not flavor. The makers needed better dairy.

They began sourcing roller-dried whole milk powders from small dairies in the Alps, New Zealand, and Iceland. Roller-drying is a gentler process that preserves the creamy, grassy notes of the fresh milk.

Suddenly, the concept of "terroir" expanded from the bean to the cow.

- Icelandic Milk: Makers like *Omnom Chocolate* in Reykjavík utilized local Icelandic dairy, which is high in fat and low in sugar, imparting a distinct savory, almost salted-butter profile to the chocolate.

- Alpine Milk: Swiss and Austrian makers leaned into milk from cows grazed on high-altitude summer grasses, which carry terpene compounds from the wildflowers they eat, adding a subtle floral complexity to the bar.

THE MENAGERIE: Goat, Sheep, and Camel

If cow's milk was the standard, the spirit of the craft revolution demanded experimentation. If you could source single-origin beans, why not single-origin animals?

- Goat Milk Chocolate: This became the cult favorite of the movement. Goat milk lacks the carotene of cow's milk (making the chocolate a stark, ghostly white or pale brown) and contains short-chain fatty acids (capric, caprylic, and caproic acids) that give it a distinctive "goaty" tang. When paired with a bright, acidic cacao like Madagascar, the result tastes remarkably like a chocolate cheesecake. It is funky, sour, and incredibly rich.
- Sheep Milk Chocolate: Sheep milk is naturally higher in fat and protein than cow or goat milk. It produces a chocolate with an ultra-creamy, almost oily melt and a sweet, nutty finish.
- Vegan "Milks": The craft movement also pioneered the high-end vegan milk chocolate. Rejecting the waxy texture of cheap vegan treats, makers used oat milk (for its malty, cereal notes), coconut milk (for its tropical fat profile), and even almond flour to create creamy emulsions that rivaled dairy. This was not about dietary restriction; it was about flavor exploration.

∼

The Inclusion Revolution: The Chef's Pantry

As the "purity law" crumbled, the floodgates opened for inclusions.

In the industrial world, "inclusions" meant cheap fillers: peanuts, raisins, crisped rice. They were volume-bulkers designed to lower the cost of the bar. In the craft world, inclusions became a culinary technique. Chocolate makers began thinking like pastry chefs, using the chocolate bar as a plated dessert.

The leader of this "inclusionist" philosophy was likely Zotter in Austria, whose wild experiments (Fish and Coconut, Bacon and Banana) proved that chocolate could handle savory flavors. But in the Anglo-American craft scene, the trend moved toward refined, comforting, savory combinations.

The Sourdough Phenomenon

Perhaps the most emblematic bar of this era came from Pump Street Chocolate in Suffolk, England. Pump Street began as a bakery, famous for its slow-fermented sourdough bread. When they pivoted to making bean-to-bar chocolate, they had a problem: leftover bread.

They decided to combine the two. They took sourdough crumbs, toasted them in olive oil and sea salt until they were crisp, and folded them into a 66% dark chocolate from Ecuador.

The result—the Sourdough & Sea Salt bar—was a sensation. It hit every pleasure point in the brain: the snap of the chocolate, the crunch of the crumb, the acidity of the cacao, the sour tang of the yeast, and the salinity of the salt. It won every major award in the industry. It proved that texture was as important as flavor, and that "savory" elements could elevate chocolate rather than clash with it.

The Savory Pantry

This opened the door for ingredients previously banned from the candy aisle.

- Olive Oil: Instead of adding cocoa butter to smooth out a bar, makers began emulsifying high-quality extra virgin olive oil into the chocolate. This lowered the melting point, creating a ganache-like texture that dissolved instantly on the tongue, leaving a peppery, grassy finish that highlighted the herbal notes in certain cacaos.

- Pine and Spruce: In the Pacific Northwest, makers foraged for spruce tips and pine needles, infusing them into the cocoa butter. The result was a "forest floor" chocolate that tasted of resin and citrus, evoking the landscape where the bar was made.
- Black Truffle: Not the chocolate confection, but the fungus. Makers shaved dried Italian truffles into dark chocolate, creating a bar that smelled of earth and musk—a polarizing flavor that found a dedicated audience among wine lovers.

THE LOCAL-GLOBAL SYNTHESIS

This explosion of creativity solved one of the fundamental disconnects of the chocolate industry. Cacao is a tropical product; it cannot grow in Europe or North America. A maker in Brooklyn or Berlin can never truly claim their product is "local."

But by using inclusions—local sourdough, local milk, local sea salt, local herbs—craft makers grounded their global ingredient in their local soil. A bar made with Tanzanian beans and Oregon hazelnuts became a bridge between two worlds. It allowed the maker to put their own culinary fingerprint on the product, transforming a raw material from the equator into a cultural artifact of their home city.

The chocolate bar had ceased to be a simple sweet. It had become a complex, composed dish, requiring the sourcing skills of a coffee roaster, the technical precision of a chemical engineer, and the palate of a Michelin-starred chef.

THE VALLEY of Death and the Future of Flavor

The romance of the chocolate revolution usually ends at the spreadsheet.

In the basement of the Brooklyn brownstone, Ben Rasmussen eventually turns off the grinder. The silence that rushes back into the room is heavy. He looks at the bucket of finished chocolate. It represents three days of sleepless labor, $400 in bean costs, and electricity bills that spike every time the roast begins. He does the math. If he sells every bar for $10—a price that makes customers wince—he will make a profit of roughly $2.50 per hour.

This is the dirty secret of the Craft Revolution: almost nobody is making money.

For the first decade of the movement, the energy was sustained by pure passion. Makers were subsidized by day jobs in tech, law, or design. They were willing to lose money to chase flavor. But as the movement matured, the "hobby trap" began to snap shut. Makers faced a brutal choice: scale up or shut down.

THE MATH of the $12 Bar

To the average consumer, $12 for a chocolate bar feels like price gouging. They compare it to a $1.50 Snickers and assume the craft maker is pocketing a massive margin. The reality is the opposite.

The economics of craft chocolate are inverted compared to Big Chocolate.

- The Beans: A commodity maker pays roughly $2.50 per kilogram for bulk cacao. A craft maker pays between $8.00 and $15.00 per kilogram for specialty beans. They pay for the genetics, the fermentation labor, and the ethical premium.
- The Yield: Industrial factories achieve nearly 100% efficiency. Garage makers lose 30% of their product to winnowing loss (bits of nib stuck to the shell) and grinder residue.
- The Labor: Industrial lines produce 50,000 bars an hour. A craft maker hand-wrapping bars might manage 50 an hour.

When the costs are tallied—packaging, distribution, retailer margins (stores typically take 40-50%)—the maker is often left with pennies. The "luxury" price tag is not a markup; it is the bare minimum required to keep the lights on.

THE SCALE GAP: The Valley of Death

For the makers who survived the garage phase, the next step was the most dangerous. In manufacturing, there is a phenomenon known as the "Valley of Death." It is the gap between the home kitchen and the industrial factory.

A maker can produce 500 bars a month in a garage with $2,000 worth of equipment. But to make a living, they need to produce 10,000 bars a month. To do that, they need a dedicated facility, health department certifications, and industrial machinery.

The equipment simply didn't exist. There were no mid-sized chocolate machines. You could buy a 10lb melanger for $500, or a 5,000lb ball mill for $250,000. There was nothing in between.

This forced makers to become engineers again. They bought antique equipment from defunct factories in Europe—rusted winnowers from the 1920s, cast-iron roasters from the 1950s—and refurbished them. They became mechanics, spending as much time greasing gears as tasting chocolate.

Those who couldn't bridge the gap burned out. The physical toll of lifting 60kg jute sacks, the repetitive strain of hand-foiling thousands of bars, and the stress of cash flow led to a wave of closures in the late 2010s. The revolution lost many of its pioneers not to bankruptcy, but to exhaustion.

THE MAST BROTHERS EVENT: A Crisis of Faith

In 2015, the movement faced an existential crisis that had nothing to do with money and everything to do with trust. The Mast Brothers, the darlings of the Brooklyn scene known for their beards and beautiful butcher-paper packaging, were accused of fraud.

Food bloggers and industry insiders alleged that in their early days, the brothers hadn't been making chocolate from beans at all. The accusation was that they had been melting down industrial couverture (Val-rhona), repacking it, and selling it as "bean-to-bar."

The scandal shook the industry. It exposed the fragility of the "craft" claim. If a consumer paid $10 for a bar because they believed a bearded artisan roasted the beans, but it turned out to be melted industrial chocolate, the value proposition collapsed.

The fallout, however, was ultimately healthy. It forced the industry to define its terms. "Bean-to-Bar" could no longer be a vague marketing buzzword. Makers began practicing radical transparency. They posted videos of their roasters running. They published open logs of their bean purchases. They invited customers into the factories.

The scandal codified the definition of a Craft Chocolate Maker: someone who controls the entire process, from the raw bean to the finished bar. Anything else was just melting.

THE SURVIVORS: Scaling the Soul

Despite the hurdles, a few companies navigated the Valley of Death and emerged as the new standard-bearers.

- **Dandelion Chocolate** in San Francisco wrote the playbook for scaling. Instead of trying to compete with Hershey on grocery store shelves, they pivoted to the "Experience Economy." They built a factory that doubled as a café and theater. Customers could drink a hot chocolate while watching the beans being winnowed through a glass wall. They monetized the *process*, not just the product.
- **Taza Chocolate** in Massachusetts leaned into a specific niche: stone-ground, Mexican-style chocolate. By refusing to conche their chocolate (leaving it gritty and raw), they created a product that industrial machines couldn't replicate. They bypassed the need for expensive refining equipment and created a texture that became their trademark.

THESE SURVIVORS PROVED that you could scale without selling out. They showed that if you stayed true to the flavor, the customer would follow you up the price ladder.

THE FUTURE: **The Dilution or the distinct?**

As we look to the future, the Craft Revolution faces a new threat: success.

Big Chocolate has woken up. The multinationals are no longer ignoring the movement; they are buying it. Hershey acquired Scharffen Berger and Dagoba. Mondelez acquired Green & Black's.

With these acquisitions comes distribution, but also dilution. When a craft brand goes mass-market, the supply chain inevitably changes. You cannot source single-origin beans from a micro-lot in Belize to feed a supply chain that stocks every Target in America. The beans get blended. The roast gets standardized. The "funk" gets smoothed out.

We are seeing a bifurcation of the market.

- Mass-Craft: Brands that look artisanal but are produced at scale, offering "better" chocolate than the candy aisle, but lacking true terroir.
- Ultra-Craft: The die-hards. The makers producing 500 bars a batch, aging them in whiskey barrels, and charging $20.

The future of the revolution lies in the latter. It lies in the hyper-specialized, the local, and the weird. It lies with the makers who are experimenting with fermenting beans with wine yeast, or smoking nibs over peat, or aging chocolate like cheese.

THE FINAL BITE

In the end, the Craft Revolution was never really about chocolate. It was about agency. It was a rebellion against a food system that asked us to accept mediocrity in exchange for convenience. It was a declaration that flavor is worth fighting for, worth paying for, and worth waiting for.

Ben Rasmussen, rubbing his tired eyes in the Brooklyn basement, represents a fundamental human impulse: the desire to make something real. When he finally pours that chocolate into the mold, watching it settle into a glossy, dark mirror, he isn't just making candy. He connects the labor of a farmer in Madagascar to the pleasure of a neighbor in New York.

He spins the straw of the commodity market into the gold of experience. The next time you unwrap a craft chocolate bar, take a moment before you bite. Look at the sheen. Listen for the snap. Smell the fruit, the earth, the smoke. You are holding the result of a global conspiracy of obsessives who refused to compromise. You are holding a victory. Taste it. It's sweet, yes. But if you pay attention, you can taste the sweat, the risk, and the revolution.

EPILOGUE

The taste of chocolate can carry a person into the past. A single bite might resurrect a childhood afternoon – a grandmother in the kitchen slowly stirring a pot of cocoa, the walls redolent of cinnamon and memory. In that moment, the smallest square of chocolate becomes a key to the vault of time, unlocking laughter and long-forgotten feelings. On the tongue, it melts into recollection. Such is the quiet magic of chocolate: it holds the power to summon what is cherished and seemingly lost, blending the richness of cocoa with the poignancy of memory.

Chocolate's power to evoke memory is matched by its place in ritual. Across cultures and generations, it has marked celebrations and rites of passage, both grand and intimate. It is the sweet offering exchanged to honor love or friendship – pressed into the hands of a bride and groom as a symbol of good fortune, or given to a child at a festival to mark the turn of seasons.

It is part of solemn traditions, from the ancient Maya who drank cacao in sacred ceremonies to families today who hide foil-wrapped eggs in spring gardens or share rich desserts on winter holidays. Even in the quiet moments of an ordinary day, the ritual may persist: a square of dark chocolate at twilight, a familiar comfort that closes the day as reliably as the sunset. In these acts, chocolate becomes more than a mere treat; it becomes an expression of continuity and comfort, a small ceremony that links one day or one generation to the next.

In chocolate, there is also longing. When something or someone is absent, a simple confection can become a bridge across the gap. A traveler far from home unwraps a chocolate bar carried in her suitcase and finds that the taste transports her to familiar streets and beloved faces – a momentary remedy for homesickness.

Two lovers separated by distance might each bite into the same kind of chocolate, miles apart, and feel for an instant as if they share that sweetness together despite the separation. The craving for chocolate often hints at a deeper hunger: a longing for comfort, for the presence of loved ones, for the warmth of home or the innocence of childhood. In satisfying that craving, even briefly, chocolate gives shape to longing and offers gentle consolation.

Chocolate has always kindled human creativity. Its very malleability – flowing as liquid velvet or snapping into crisp solidity – invites endless invention. Over centuries, people have molded it into forms limited only by imagination. Artisans temper and torch it into glossy sculptures; confectioners whip it into mousses light as air or fudge dense as clay. In hands both young and old, chocolate becomes a medium of expression and play.

A child swirling chocolate syrup into milk is a tiny alchemist, experimenting with flavor and delight. A master chocolatier devising daring new truffle recipes – infusing ganache with chili heat or perfuming it with jasmine – is part of a long lineage of creators inspired by cacao's potential. Each new shape or flavor is a celebration of ingenuity, reflecting the human delight in creation for its own sake.

In kitchens and ateliers around the world, chocolate continually teaches the same lesson: from the simplest raw materials can emerge endless novelty, beauty, and joy. And yet, even as it inspires personal imagination, chocolate's story reaches beyond the individual. Each imaginative confection is part of a greater narrative, one that spans the globe.

That larger story of chocolate is one of connection across continents – in many ways, a story of globalization itself. Few things so common on supermarket shelves carry such a tapestry of journeys within them. The cacao in a single bar of chocolate might have been grown on a small farm in Ghana or Brazil, fermented and dried under tropical suns.

Those beans could travel by ship to factories an ocean away, where knowledge and techniques from various corners of the world transform them into a finished delight. Then the chocolate finds its way to distant markets, to be unwrapped in places far from the tree that bore the fruit.

Each step in this journey involves human hands and hopes – a farmer's careful tending, a worker's skill at the roaster, an engineer's precision with the conching machine, a designer's artistry in the wrapper, a family's anticipation of a shared treat. In a small square of chocolate, the world is condensed: the rain that fell in the equatorial forest, the labor and expertise of countless individuals, the interwoven trade that binds their destinies. It is a sweet emblem of how closely knit humanity has become.

And within that interconnection lies responsibility and awareness. The meaning of chocolate encompasses these global links – reminding those who enjoy it that even a simple pleasure is made possible by a vast, unseen network of people and nature working in concert.

Woven through all these themes is the thread of resilience. Chocolate exists only through perseverance – both of nature and of human effort. The cacao tree, delicate and particular about climate, can be fickle to cultivate. It withstands the threats of drought and blight through the careful stewardship of farmers who persist in coaxing its precious fruit from the earth. Likewise, chocolate has endured through the turbulence of history.

During times of scarcity and war, people learned to stretch a meager ration of cocoa, to substitute ingredients and innovate, just to keep the tradition alive. In World War II, a single square of chocolate in a soldier's kit could become a treasure – a small reminder of home and hope amid devastation. Even when peace returned and sweets were scarce, communities found ways to share tiny portions during holidays, ensuring that the thread of tradition was never broken.

The chocolate industry, too, has begun to adapt and address its own challenges – from the hardships of growers to the pressures of climate change – with a resolve to sustain this beloved treat for future generations. The resilience of chocolate is a reflection of human resilience: the determination to nurture what people love, to overcome obstacles, and to find sweetness even in bitter times.

Ultimately, chocolate is a celebration of simple joy. There is an unassuming pleasure in peeling the foil off a favorite chocolate bar and snapping off a piece. A smile often comes unbidden at the first taste – a childlike sense of wonder that never fully fades. That delight, as brief as it may be, is universal.

It crosses languages and borders, lighting up gatherings from bustling city cafés to remote village kitchens. A grandmother shares a cherished candy with her grandchild and sees her own joy reborn in the child's eyes. Friends pass around a box of chocolates, and in that wordless act of giving and receiving, happiness ripples outward.

These moments of sweetness remind people of life's capacity for delight. In savoring chocolate, in giving it, in craving it, there is an affirmation that joy can be found and shared. However complex the world may be, however troubled, the simple pleasure of chocolate remains a small beacon, shining with the promise that happiness is within reach.

As this journey through chocolate's world comes to a close, a final reflection emerges. The meaning of chocolate is not contained in any single tale or scientific finding, but in the union of all these threads – memory and ritual, longing and creativity, globalization and resilience, and the joy that crowns them. It is a symbol and a sustenance.

It represents both the commonplace and the extraordinary. A square of chocolate can be at once a mundane indulgence and a vessel of meaning – carrying the weight of history, the flavor of far-off lands, the emotion of personal moments. In its richness and complexity, chocolate's story offers a microcosm of humanity itself. It shows how something small can hold a universe of experience: the dreams of explorers and farmers, the innovations of artisans, the comforts of families, the hopes of children.

Perhaps this is chocolate's greatest gift to the world: it is a reminder that in the sweetness people crave lies a deeper hunger for connection, for wonder, for the eternal simplicities of life. In the end, the meaning of chocolate is the meaning one finds in it. It is the understanding that even amid life's bitter trials, there can be sweetness – a sweetness created by human hands, shared among friends, and carried forward through time.

Chocolate invites reflection on gratitude and desire, on what is cherished and why. And as long as people continue to delight in that familiar taste, unwrapping it with hopeful expectation, a small part of the human spirit remains ever curious, ever resilient, and ever ready to be enchanted by the possibilities of the next bite.

From the splitting of that first pod in the emerald hush of the Olmec jungle to the robotic arm pouring a praline in a futuristic factory, the journey of chocolate is complete. The ancient biotic process has met the modern engineered marvel, yet the result remains the same. With every wrapper opened, the story begins again.

APPENDIX

THE ART OF TASTING: A FIELD GUIDE FOR THE SENSES

Reading about chocolate is only half the journey. To truly understand the complexity of the bean—to detect the ghosts of the rainforest or the fingerprint of the fermentation—one must engage the senses.

Professional chocolate tasters do not simply eat; they evaluate. They slow down the biological process of consumption to catch the fleeting nuances that the brain normally ignores. Below is a guide to conducting your own sensory analysis, based on the protocols used by professional judges and sommeliers.

I. The Setup

- **The Environment:** Taste in a quiet room free of strong odors (no perfume, scented candles, or coffee brewing nearby). Use natural light if possible to judge color accurately.
- **The Temperature:** Ensure the chocolate is between 68–72°F (20–22°C). If it is too cold, the cocoa butter tightens, locking the aromatic molecules inside like a vault. If too warm, the texture becomes muddy.
- **The Palate:** Your mouth should be neutral. Room-

temperature water, a slice of cucumber, or a piece of tart green apple act as excellent palate cleansers.

===

THE STORAGE COMMANDMENTS: STOP RUINING YOUR STASH

Good chocolate is fragile. Follow these three rules to keep it alive.

- **THOU SHALT NOT REFRIGERATE**
  - Why: Fridges are humid. Moisture dissolves sugar, creating a rough, gritty surface ("Sugar Bloom").
  - The Fix: A dark cupboard or wine cooler (60-70°F) is perfect.
- **THOU SHALT SEAL TIGHTLY**
  - Why: Cocoa butter is a fat sponge. If you leave chocolate unwrapped near onions or leftovers, it will absorb those odors.
  - The Fix: Air-tight Tupperware or double-bagging.
- **THOU SHALT AVOID HEAT SHOCK**
  - Why: Rapid temp changes cause fat to migrate to the surface, creating gray streaks ("Fat Bloom").

===

II. The Ritual

1. **The Gaze (Visual Analysis)** Inspect the surface of the bar before breaking it.
   - **Sheen:** A perfectly tempered bar should possess a satin gloss, reflective like polished mahogany or obsidian. A dull or matte finish often suggests poor handling or age.
   - **Color:** Note the hue. Does it lean toward reddish-brick (often typical of Madagascar or Criollo beans)? A deep, almost black charcoal (heavy roasting)? Or a warm, earthy brown?

- **Defects:** Look for "bloom"—white streaks or dots. Sugar bloom (caused by moisture) feels gritty; fat bloom (caused by heat) feels greasy. While safe to eat, both compromise the texture.

2. **The Snap (Auditory Analysis)** Hold the piece near your ear and break it decisively.
   - **The Sound:** You are listening for a crisp, clean *snap*. This sound is the auditory signature of a stable crystal lattice. High-quality dark chocolate snaps sharply. Milk chocolate, due to the softer milk fats, will have a duller thud. If the bar bends or crumbles without snapping, it is likely untempered or stale.

3. **The Bouquet (Olfactory Analysis)** Flavor is 90% smell. To release the aroma, rub the surface of the chocolate gently with your thumb. The friction creates just enough heat to volatilize the oils. Cup your hand over the chocolate and inhale deeply.
   - **The Hunt:** Look past the generic smell of "chocolate." Dig deeper.
     - *Earth:* Mushroom, forest floor, leather, tobacco.
     - *Fruit:* Red berries, citrus, banana, dried fig, raisin.
     - *Roast:* Coffee, toast, caramel, smoke, nuts.
     - *Spice:* Vanilla, cinnamon, licorice, clove.

4. **The Melt (Tactile Analysis)** Place a small piece on your tongue and press it gently to the roof of your mouth. **Do not chew.** Chewing bypasses the most critical phase: the melt.
   - **The Texture:** Notice the viscosity. Is it waxy (indicating cheap vegetable fats)? Is it gritty (coarse grinding)? Or does it flow like silk? A masterfully conched chocolate should dissolve into a smooth, coating liquid with no roughness.

5. **The Flavor Arc (Gustatory Analysis)** Flavor is not static; it evolves in a trajectory known as the "Flavor Arc." Pay attention to how the taste changes over time.

6. **The Head Notes:** The first impact (0–5 seconds). This is often

acidic, bright, or fruity—the immediate greeting of the bean's acidity.

- **The Body Notes:** The middle sensation (5–20 seconds). As the cocoa butter fully melts, the deeper flavors emerge. Look for roasted nuts, spices, caramel, or coffee. This is the heart of the chocolate.
- **The Tail Notes:** The lingering finish (20+ seconds). After you have swallowed, breathe out through your nose. What remains? A great chocolate will leave a pleasant, complex ghost of flavor that lasts for minutes. A poor chocolate will vanish instantly or leave a bitter, metallic, or chemical aftertaste.

THE CURATOR'S GUIDE: A CHECKLIST FOR THE CURIOUS

Now that you know the history and the science, the final step is the experience. You cannot find the soul of chocolate in a candy aisle. You must hunt for it. Use this checklist to explore the spectrum of flavor described in this book.

1. **The "Gateway" Bar (Madagascar)**
   - **Profile:** Bright, acidic, red berry, citrus.
   - **Why:** This is often the first origin that shocks people who think dark chocolate is just "bitter." It tastes like fruit because the bean is full of fruit acids.
   - **Look For:** 70% Akesson's Estate or Sambirano Valley origins.
2. **The "Comfort" Bar (Ecuador)**
   - **Profile:** Floral, nutty, honey, jasmine.
   - **Why:** Ecuador's *Arriba Nacional* is the classic "fine flavor" profile—approachable, low bitterness, and incredibly aromatic.
   - **Look For:** "Arriba" or "Nacional" on the label.
3. **The "Intense" Bar (Ghana/West Africa)**
   - **Profile:** Deep cocoa, fudge, coconut, leather.

- **Why:** This is the baseline "chocolatey" flavor of your childhood, but elevated. High-quality craft chocolate from Ghana reveals a depth of fudge that industrial bars mask with sugar.
- **Look For:** Single-origin Ghana (rare in craft, but worth finding).

4. **The "Heirloom" Experience (Chuao or Porcelana)**
   - **Profile:** Complex, lingering, delicate, evolving.
   - **Why:** These are the "Grand Crus" mentioned in Chapter 26. They are the rarest beans on Earth.
   - **Look For:** The word "Chuao" (Venezuela) on the label. Verify the maker is reputable; fake Chuao abounds.

5. **The "Wild" Bar (Bolivia/Amazon)**
   - **Profile:** Wild herbs, resin, grapefruit, malt.
   - **Why:** Made from "Beniano" or wild-harvested cacao that grows on islands in the Amazon basin, uncultivated by humans. It tastes untamed.
   - **Look For:** "Wild Cacao" or "Bolivian" origin.

6. **The "Alt-Milk" Bar (Dark Milk)**
   - **Profile:** Creamy but bold, caramel, toffee.
   - **Why:** A new category of "Dark Milk" (50–60% cacao) bridges the gap. It has the snap of dark chocolate with the creaminess of milk, often with heavy caramel notes.
   - **Look For:** "Dark Milk" or percentages between 50% and 65%.

THE CHOCOLATE PILGRIM'S GUIDE: MUSEUMS AND ARCHIVES TO VISIT

A global atlas for the obsessed. From the jungles of the Amazon to the salons of Paris, these are the holy sites of cocoa.

1. **THE AMERICAS: The Cradle of Cacao**
   - **Ecuador**
     - **To'ak Chocolate (Quito):** The home of the world's most expensive chocolate.
       - The Draw: Taste the ancient "Nacional" variety, once thought extinct, aged in cognac and whisky casks.
       - Must Try: The vintage-dated dark chocolate bars presented in handcrafted Spanish elm boxes.
     - **Santa Ana-La Florida (Palanda):** The archaeological site where the oldest known cacao traces (3500 BCE) were discovered.
     - The Vibe: Sacred ground. This is where humanity first fell in love with the bean.
   - **Mexico**
     - **Oaxaca City:** The spiritual heart of Mexican chocolate culture.

- The Draw: Visit the markets where vendors grind roasted cacao on stone *metates* with cinnamon and sugar to make *tabletas.*
- Must Try: *Tejate* (a maize and cacao drink) and a bowl of *Mole Negro.*
- **Chocolatería San Ginés (Mexico City Branch):** While the original is in Spain, the Churro tradition lives here too.
- **United States**
  - **The Hershey Story (Hershey, PA):** The town built on milk chocolate.
    - The Draw: See the cancelled check for Milton Hershey's ticket on the Titanic and the "Chocolate Spa".
    - Must Try: The "drinking chocolate" flights at the museum.
  - **Dandelion Chocolate (San Francisco, CA):** The pioneer of the modern tech-meets-chocolate revolution.
    - The Draw: An open factory floor where you can watch the entire bean-to-bar process.
    - Must Try: A single-origin brownie flight.
  - **Taza Chocolate (Somerville, MA):** The stone-ground specialists.
    - The Draw: Watch them use traditional Mexican *molinos* (stone mills) to grind gritty, sparkling chocolate discs.
- **Peru**
  - **ChocoMuseo (Sacred Valley/Cusco):** Hands-on history.
    - The Draw: Workshops where you roast beans over an open fire and grind them on volcanic stone.
2. **EUROPE: The Old World Refiners**
   - **Spain**
     - **Monasterio de Piedra (Nuévalos):** The birthplace of European chocolate.

- The Draw: The Cistercian monastery where monks first added sugar to the Aztec recipe in 1534.
- **Chocolatería San Ginés (Madrid):** The late-night institution.
  - The Draw: Open since 1894, this is the place for *Chocolate con Churros*—thick, pudding-like dipping chocolate.
- **Casa Amatller (Barcelona):** The house that chocolate built.
  - The Draw: A modernist palace built by a chocolate tycoon, featuring stepped gables and dragon gargoyles.
- France
  - **Angelina (Paris):** The Belle Époque tea room.
    - The Draw: *L'Africain* hot chocolate—so thick you almost need a spoon. A favorite of Coco Chanel.
  - **Debauve & Gallais (Paris):** The royal pharmacy.
    - The Draw: Founded by Sulpice Debauve, the personal chocolatier to Marie Antoinette. They still sell the "Pistoles" (chocolate coins) originally designed to deliver medicine to the Queen.
- Switzerland
  - **Lindt Home of Chocolate (Kilchberg):** The futuristic temple.
    - The Draw: It features the world's largest chocolate fountain—nine meters tall with a giant whisk.
- Italy
  - **Turin (Piedmont):** The capital of hazelnut chocolate.
    - The Draw: The birthplace of *Gianduja* (Nutella's ancestor).
    - Must Try: A *Bicerin*—a layered glass of espresso, hot chocolate, and cold cream.
  - **Domori (None, Turin):** The guardian of the Criollo.
    - The Draw: The home of Gianluca Franzoni's crusade to save heirloom cacao varieties.

- United Kingdom
  - **Cadbury World (Bournville):** The Quaker Utopia.
    - The Draw: A model village built to save workers from city slums. Includes the Cadbury archive with Victorian sketchbooks.
  - **Rococo Chocolates (London):** The eccentric artisan.
    - The Draw: Chantal Coady's shop that sparked Britain's real chocolate revival.
- Belgium & Germany
  - **Choco-Story (Bruges):** The medieval experience.
    - The Draw: Located in a 15th-century wine tavern, featuring live praline-making demos.
  - **Imhoff Chocolate Museum (Cologne):** The glass ship.
    - The Draw: A tropical greenhouse inside the museum growing live cacao trees on the Rhine river.

I. ASIA: The New Frontier
- Japan
  - **Minimal (Tokyo):** The Zen of chocolate.
    - The Draw: A bean-to-bar shop that treats chocolate like sushi—minimalist, precise, and obsessed with texture.
    - Must Try: The coarse-ground bars that crunch like sugar cubes.
- Vietnam
  - **Marou Faiseurs de Chocolat (Ho Chi Minh City):** The single-origin pioneers.
    - The Draw: Often called the "Apple Store of Chocolate," they proved Vietnamese cacao could be world-class.

GLOSSARY OF CHOCOLATE: A COMPENDIUM OF TERMS, TOOLS, AND TERROIR

A

- **Amelonado:** An heirloom variety of Forastero cacao, melon-shaped and widely grown in West Africa. It provides the classic, robust "chocolatey" base flavor found in most mass-market bars.
- **Anandamide:** A lipid known as the "bliss molecule" (from the Sanskrit ananda, meaning joy). Found in trace amounts in chocolate, it binds to the same brain receptors as cannabis, potentially contributing to the "chocolate high."**Arriba Nacional:** A legendary floral variety of cacao native to Ecuador. Historically prized for its distinct aroma of orange blossom and jasmine, it was nearly wiped out by disease in the early 20th century but is making a resurgence.
- **Astringency:** A drying, puckering sensation in the mouth (similar to red wine or green tea), caused by tannins and polyphenols in the cacao. A subtle amount adds structure; too much indicates poor fermentation or under-ripe beans.

B

- **Baba:** The sweet, mucilaginous white pulp that surrounds fresh cacao beans inside the pod. It tastes nothing like chocolate—more like lychee, lemonade, or tropical fruit. It is crucial for fermentation.
- **Bean-to-Bar:** A movement where the maker controls every step of production, from sourcing the raw beans to wrapping the finished bar. This distinguishes "chocolate makers" from "chocolatiers" (who melt pre-made chocolate).
- **Bloom:** The bane of the chocolatier. A white, dusty film that appears on the surface of chocolate.
- **Fat Bloom:** Occurs when chocolate melts and re-crystallizes incorrectly, bringing cocoa butter to the surface. It looks greasy.
- **Sugar Bloom:** Occurs when moisture touches the chocolate, drawing sugar crystals to the surface. It feels gritty.
- **Brix:** A scale used to measure the sugar content of the cacao pulp. Farmers use a refractometer to check Brix levels to determine the perfect moment for harvest.
- **Butter (Cocoa Butter):** The natural vegetable fat of the cacao bean. It is ivory-colored, flavor-neutral (usually), and possesses a unique triglyceride structure that allows it to remain brittle at room temperature yet melt precisely at human body temperature.

C

- **Cacao Belt:** The narrow band of latitude roughly 20 degrees north and south of the Equator where the cacao tree can survive. It encompasses the humid tropical rainforests of West Africa, Latin America, and Southeast Asia.
- **Cacao vs. Cocoa:** Though often used interchangeably, **Cacao** typically refers to the living tree, the pod, and the raw bean. **Cocoa** refers to the processed product (powder or roasted beans) after the fat has been pressed out or heat applied.

- **CBE (Cocoa Butter Equivalent):** Vegetable fats (such as palm, shea, or illipe oil) chemically engineered to mimic the melting properties of cocoa butter. The use of CBEs was the central conflict of the European "Chocolate Wars" in the 1990s.
- **CCN-51:** A high-yield, disease-resistant hybrid cacao clone developed in Ecuador. While agronomic gold for farmers, it is controversial among flavor connoisseurs for its high acidity and lack of nuance compared to heirloom varieties.
- **Chocolatier:** A culinary artisan who crafts confections (truffles, bonbons) from pre-made chocolate. Distinct from a **Chocolate Maker**, who engineers the chocolate itself from the bean.
- **Conching:** The refining process invented by Rodolphe Lindt in 1879. Heavy rollers or paddles push, aerate, and smear liquid chocolate for hours (or days). This polishes the particles to microscopic smoothness and drives off volatile acids (like vinegar notes), creating a velvety texture.
- **Couverture:** Professional-grade chocolate containing a high percentage of cocoa butter (usually 32% or more). It is designed to melt easily and temper beautifully, making it the preferred medium for dipping and coating.
- **Criollo:** The "Prince of Cacao." The rarest and most fragile variety of *Theobroma cacao*, native to Central America. It lacks bitterness and offers complex notes of fruit, nuts, and spice, but is notoriously difficult to grow.

D

- **Direct Trade:** A sourcing model where chocolate makers buy directly from farmers or cooperatives, bypassing traditional commodities markets. It usually ensures a significantly higher price for the farmer than Fair Trade certification.
- **Dutching (Alkalization):** A process developed by Coenraad Van Houten in the 19th century. Cocoa solids are treated with an alkaline solution (like potassium carbonate) to neutralize

natural acidity. This darkens the color (think Oreo cookies) and creates a mellower, woodier flavor, though it strips away many health-boosting antioxidants.

E

- **Emulsifier:** An ingredient (usually lecithin) added to chocolate to reduce viscosity. It coats the sugar and cocoa particles, helping the chocolate flow smoothly during molding without adding extra cocoa butter.
- **Enrobing:** The process of coating a center (like ganache, caramel, or fruit) with a thin layer of tempered chocolate. This can be done by hand-dipping or by a machine called an enrober, which creates a "waterfall" of chocolate.

F

- **Fair Trade:** A certification system designed to ensure farmers receive a minimum price for their cocoa, protecting them from market crashes. It focuses on poverty alleviation and community development, though distinct from the relationship-focused **Direct Trade.**
- **Fermentation:** The crucial first step of flavor development. Beans are heaped in boxes or banana leaves, allowing natural yeasts and bacteria to digest the sugary pulp. This chemical process kills the bean and generates the precursors for chocolate flavor. Without fermentation, cacao has no chocolate taste.
- **Flavanols:** A specific type of polyphenol found abundantly in cacao. They are the compounds responsible for increasing blood flow to the brain and heart, making them the focus of most chocolate health studies.
- **Forastero:** The hardy, high-yield variety of cacao that makes up the bulk (approx. 80-90%) of the world's supply. It is robust and disease-resistant but generally lacks the nuanced flavor of Criollo.

G

- **Ganache:** A smooth emulsion of chocolate and liquid (usually heavy cream). Legend says it was named after a French insult (*"Ganache!"* meaning "Idiot!") shouted at an apprentice who accidentally spilled hot cream into a vat of precious chocolate.
- **Gianduja:** A blend of chocolate and hazelnut paste, invented in Turin, Italy, during the Napoleonic era to stretch limited cocoa supplies. It is the ancestor of modern spreads like Nutella.

H

- **Heirloom Cacao:** Varieties of cacao with distinct flavor profiles that have been passed down through generations, often specific to a micro-region. The Heirloom Cacao Preservation Fund certifies these trees to prevent them from being replaced by industrial hybrids.

I

- **Inclusions:** Any solid ingredient added to chocolate for texture or flavor, such as sea salt, cacao nibs, dried fruit, or nuts.

K

- **Kokumi:** A Japanese concept meaning "rich taste." In chocolate, it refers to the mouth-coating sensation of depth and roundness—often described as the "sixth taste"—that enhances sweetness and creaminess without adding sugar.

L

- **Lecithin:** A natural emulsifier (usually derived from soy or sunflower) added to chocolate to lower its viscosity. It helps the chocolate flow smoothly during manufacturing.
- **Liquor (Chocolate Liquor):** Not alcohol. This is the paste produced when cacao nibs are ground. It is 100% pure cocoa mass, roughly half cocoa solids and half cocoa butter.
- **Living Income Differential (LID):** A pricing mechanism introduced by Ghana and Côte d'Ivoire in 2019. It adds a fixed premium (approx. $400/ton) to the price of cocoa exports, directly targeting the alleviation of farmer poverty.

M

- **Maillard Reaction:** The chemical reaction between amino acids and reducing sugars that occurs during roasting. It is responsible for the browning of the bean and the development of roasted, nutty, and savory flavor notes—the same reaction that makes toast and seared steak delicious.
- **Melanger:** A stone-on-stone grinder used by craft chocolate makers to crush nibs and sugar into a microscopic paste.
- **Metate:** A sloping stone grinding slab used by the Aztecs and Maya (and modern artisan makers) to grind roasted cacao beans into paste by hand. It is the ancient ancestor of the melanger.
- **Microns:** The unit of measurement for particle size. To feel smooth on the human tongue, chocolate must be refined to below 30 microns. (A human hair is roughly 50-70 microns).
- **Midges:** Tiny flies (genus *Forcipomyia*) that are the primary pollinators of the cacao tree. Unlike bees, they thrive in damp, rotting vegetation on the rainforest floor. No midges, no chocolate.
- **Mole:** From the Nahuatl *mulli* (sauce). A savory Mexican sauce where chocolate plays a supporting role to chilies, nuts, and spices, proving that cacao is not just for dessert.

- **Molinillo:** The traditional wooden whisk, carved with intricate rings, used in Mexico to whip hot chocolate into a frothy foam—a texture prized since the time of the Aztecs.

N

- **Nib:** The heart of the cacao bean. Roasted, cracked, and winnowed of its shell, the nib is pure chocolate before it is ground. It is crunchy, bitter, and complex.

O

- **Origin (Single Origin):** Chocolate made from beans harvested from one specific region or country.
- **Estate (Single Estate):** Even more specific than single origin; chocolate made from beans grown on a single farm. This offers the purest expression of terroir.

P

- **Percentage (%):** The number on the wrapper indicating the total amount of cacao (cocoa solids + cocoa butter) in the bar. A 70% bar is 70% cacao and 30% sugar/other ingredients. Note: A higher percentage does not always mean "more bitter"—it depends on the bean variety and roast.
- **Phenylethylamine (PEA):** A neurochemical found in chocolate that stimulates the release of endorphins and dopamine. Often called the "love drug," it creates a mild sensation of excitement and pulse acceleration similar to falling in love.
- **Pod:** The fruit of the cacao tree (*Theobroma cacao*). Shaped like an elongated football, it grows directly from the trunk (cauliflory) and contains 20–50 seeds.
- **Polymorphs:** The six different crystal structures that cocoa butter can form. Only "Form V" (Beta) is desirable for stable, shiny chocolate.

- **Polyphenols:** Chemical compounds found in cacao (specifically flavanols) that act as antioxidants. They are responsible for the health benefits of dark chocolate but also contribute to bitterness and astringency.
- **Praline:** Context is everything. In Belgium, it is a filled chocolate bonbon. In France, it is a caramelized almond confection. In the American South, it is a pecan and sugar patty.

R

- **Refining:** The process of grinding sugar and cocoa particles down to a size undetectable by the tongue.
- **Roasting:** The heating process that develops the flavor precursors created during fermentation. A light roast preserves fruit and floral notes; a dark roast emphasizes nutty and chocolatey notes (but can burn off subtle flavors).
- **Ruby Chocolate:** Introduced in 2017, this is considered the fourth type of chocolate (after Dark, Milk, and White). Made from specific "ruby" cocoa beans, it has a natural pink color and a distinct berry-fruit flavor without added dyes or fruit flavorings.

S

- **Scavina 6 (SCA-6):** A famous variety of wild cacao collected in the Amazon in the 1930s. It lacks fine flavor but possesses a "super-gene" for disease resistance, making it the parent of many modern hybrids.
- **Snap:** The auditory signature of a perfect crystal lattice. If your chocolate bends, it is out of temper or too warm. If it breaks with a clean, sharp *snap*, the physics are perfect.
- **Stone Ground:** A rustic style of chocolate (famously from Mexico, e.g., Taza) where the particles are not refined to complete smoothness, leaving a gritty, sugary texture that explodes with flavor.

T

- **Tempering:** The process of heating and cooling chocolate to specific temperatures to encourage the formation of stable "Form V" cocoa butter crystals. Proper tempering gives chocolate its shine, snap, and heat resistance.
- **Terroir:** Borrowed from wine culture, this term describes the "taste of the place." The specific combination of soil, rain, and sunlight in a region that gives cacao its unique fingerprint— why a bean from Madagascar tastes like raspberries and a bean from Ecuador tastes like jasmine.
- **Theobroma:** The Latin genus name for the cacao tree, coined by Linnaeus. It translates to "Food of the Gods."
- **Theobromine:** The primary alkaloid in cacao. Unlike caffeine, which is a nervous system stimulant, theobromine dilates blood vessels and stimulates the heart. It is the chemical reason chocolate makes you feel energized yet relaxed.
- **Trinitario:** A natural hybrid of Criollo and Forastero varieties, originating in Trinidad in the 18th century. It combines the hardiness of Forastero with the fine flavor profile of Criollo.

U

- **Umami:** The "fifth taste" of savory deliciousness (glutamate). While associated with cheese or soy sauce, it exists subtly in fermented cacao, providing the savory bass note that balances the treble notes of fruit and acid in dark chocolate.

V

- **Viscosity:** The measure of how thick or thin melted chocolate is. A low-viscosity chocolate is thin and runny (good for molding shells); a high-viscosity chocolate is thick (good for holding inclusions like nuts).

- **Volatile Compounds:** The aromatic molecules in chocolate that evaporate at room temperature, traveling from the back of the throat to the nose to create flavor.

W

- **Winnowing:** The process of removing the papery outer shell (husk) from the roasted cacao bean to isolate the nib.
- **White Chocolate:** A confection made from cocoa butter, sugar, and milk powder, but lacking the non-fat cocoa solids. While purists often scoff, it *is* technically chocolate by legal and chemical standards because it is based on the fat of the cacao bean.
- **Witches' Broom:** A devastating fungal disease (Moniliophthora perniciosa) native to the Amazon. It causes cacao trees to produce chaotic, broom-like vegetative growths instead of fruit. It famously destroyed Ecuador's cocoa industry in the 1920s and remains a major threat today.

X

- **Xocolatl:** Often cited as the Aztec word for 'bitter water,' though recent scholarship suggests this term may be a colonial invention or a mistranslation of Cacahuatl ('cacao water')."

ABOUT THE AUTHOR

Josh Lee is an author, Silicon Valley executive, and father who operates at the convergence of technology, strategy, and craft. Educated in finance and psychology at Santa Clara University and Indiana University, he currently serves as a CFO, drawing on deep experience in venture capital and a background as a finance executive and COO for high-growth technology companies.

Driven by a philosophy of continuous growth, Josh founded Codebase Studio, a pioneering AI media lab that produces interactive games and acclaimed educational podcasts listened to in over 50 countries. He applies this same exacting precision to the culinary world as the creator of the Menlo Park Chocolate Company, a small-batch atelier dedicated to the modern interpretation of nostalgic flavors. He resides in Menlo Park with his two children, Tyler and Katie.

ACKNOWLEDGMENTS

I'd like to acknowledge my appreciation and express gratitude to the generations of farmers, harvesters, and fermenters who have made the story of chocolate possible, and to the community of historians, botanists, and scientists whose published research provided the roadmap and information for this book.

To my parents, thank you for always being there to unconditionally support and encourage me in all my interests and endeavors.

To my kids, Tyler and Katie, I learn from you every day. Your infinite love, enthusiasm, and kindness inspire me to be a better person and the best father I can be for you. Thank you for all of your great ideas and your feedback along the way.

Finally, to the reader: thank you for joining me on this journey. My hope is that you'll be inspired to dive deeper into stories that you found interesting and that every time you see a chocolate bar for sale, take a sip of hot chocolate, or bite into a truffle, you'll have a new sense of appreciation and wonder.

SELECTED BIBLIOGRAPHY

A Note on Sources

This book is a work of narrative non-fiction. While I have dispensed with footnotes to maintain the flow of the story, the facts contained herein are drawn from the deep well of academic research, historical archives, and industry reporting that has come before. The dialogue in historical scenes is reconstructed from diaries, letters, and court records of the era. For readers who wish to inspect the primary sources or deepen their understanding of specific eras, I recommend the following definitive texts.

Selected Bibliography

Global History and Anthropology

- Coe, Sophie D., and Michael D. Coe. *The True History of Chocolate*. Thames & Hudson, 3rd Edition, 2013. (Universally regarded as the definitive text on Mesoamerican chocolate history and linguistics).
- Mintz, Sidney W. *Sweetness and Power: The Place of Sugar in Modern History*. Viking, 1985. (The seminal work on how colonial commodities transformed the global economy).
- Grivetti, Louis E., and Howard-Yana Shapiro. *Chocolate: History, Culture, and Heritage*. Wiley, 2009. (A massive, 1000-page academic compilation tracing chocolate through art, medicine, and society).
- Presilla, Maricel E. *The New Taste of Chocolate: A Cultural and Natural History of Cacao with Recipes*. Ten Speed Press, 2009. (The bible for fine-flavor cacao and the history of Latin American varietals).
- Norton, Marcy. *Sacred Gifts, Profane Pleasures: A History of Tobacco and Chocolate in the Atlantic World*. Cornell University Press, 2008. (An excellent scholarly look at how chocolate crossed the Atlantic and seduced Europe).
- Clarence-Smith, William Gervase. *Cocoa and Chocolate, 1765–1914*. Routledge, 2000. (The economic history of the early global trade).

The Science of the Bean (Botany & Chemistry)

- McGee, Harold. *On Food and Cooking: The Science and Lore of the Kitchen*. Scribner, 2004. (The definitive reference for the chemistry of food, including the physics of tempering and emulsion).
- Beckett, Steve T. The Science of Chocolate. Royal Society of Chemistry, 2nd Edition, 2008. (The standard textbook for understanding the physics of crystallization and flow properties).

- Minifie, Bernard W. Chocolate, Cocoa, and Confectionery: Science and Technology. Aspen Publishers, 3rd Edition, 1999. (The industry reference guide for manufacturing processes).
- Wood, G.A.R., and R.A. Lass. *Cocoa.* Blackwell Science, 4th Edition, 2001. (The definitive guide on cacao agriculture, botany, and pathology).
- Schwan, Rosane F., and Graham H. Fleet. *Cocoa and Coffee Fermentations.* CRC Press, 2014. (For those interested in the microbiology of flavor development).

Economics, Politics, and Ethics

- Leissle, Kristy. *Cocoa.* Polity, 2018. (A brilliant modern analysis of the geopolitics of trade, branding, and the power dynamics between the Global North and South).
- Off, Carol. *Bitter Chocolate: The Dark Side of the World's Most Seductive Sweet.* The New Press, 2006. (Essential reading on the economics of West African cocoa and the history of labor exploitation).
- Ryan, Orla. Chocolate Nations: Living and Dying for Cocoa in West Africa. Zed Books, 2011. (An on-the-ground account of the industry in Ghana and Côte d'Ivoire).
- Sethi, Simran. *Bread, Wine, Chocolate: The Slow Loss of Foods We Love.* HarperOne, 2015. (A critical look at biodiversity loss and the homogenization of flavor).

The Business of Chocolate (Rivalries & Industry)

- Brenner, Joël Glenn. *The Emperors of Chocolate: Inside the Secret World of Hershey and Mars.* Random House, 1999. (The go-to narrative source for the corporate rivalries of the 20th century).
- Cadbury, Deborah. *Chocolate Wars: The 150-Year Rivalry Between the World's Greatest Chocolate Makers.* PublicAffairs, 2010. (A deep dive into the Quaker capitalists—Cadbury, Fry, and Rowntree—and the moral complexities of their empires).
- D'Antonio, Michael. Hershey: Milton S. Hershey's Extraordinary Life of Wealth, Empire, and Utopian Dreams. Simon & Schuster, 2006.

Culinary Art and Sensory Science

- Doutre-Roussel, Chloé. *The Chocolate Connoisseur: For Everyone with a Passion for Chocolate.* Piatkus, 2006. (The book that defined the modern chocolate tasting movement).
- Williams, Pam, and Jim Eber. *Raising the Bar: The Future of Fine Chocolate.* Wilmor Publishing, 2012. (A history of the modern craft chocolate revolution).

- Greweling, Peter P. *Chocolates and Confections: Formula, Theory, and Technique for the Artisan Confectioner.* Wiley, 2nd Edition, 2012. (The textbook used by the Culinary Institute of America; the gold standard for aspiring chocolatiers).
- Shepherd, Gordon M. *Neurogastronomy: How the Brain Creates Flavor.* Columbia University Press, 2011. (Provides the scientific basis for the "Sensory Science" chapters).
- Giller, Megan. *Bean-to-Bar Chocolate: America's Craft Chocolate Revolution.* Storey Publishing, 2017. (A guide to the modern craft movement and the makers redefining flavor).